THE JEWISH PEOPLE
AND
JESUS CHRIST

THE JEWISH PEOPLE
AND
JESUS CHRIST

THE RELATIONSHIP BETWEEN
CHURCH AND SYNAGOGUE

THIRD EDITION

Jakob Jocz

BAKER BOOK HOUSE
Grand Rapids, Michigan

First published 1949
Reissued 1979 by Baker Book House
under special arrangement with SPCK,
Holy Trinity Church, Marylebone Road,
London NW1 4DU, England

ISBN: 0-8010-5085-5

PHOTOLITHOPRINTED BY CUSHING - MALLOY, INC.
ANN ARBOR, MICHIGAN, UNITED STATES OF AMERICA
1979

To
Joan Alice and our children

NOTE

The writer desires to thank the present Dean of the theological faculty of Edinburgh University, Prof. Hugh Watt, for encouragement; the former Dean, Principal W. A. Curtis, and Prof. O. S. Rankin for kind advice; the Rev. E. H. Kennedy for reading the script; Mr. Charles Johnson, M.A., and the Rev. W. N. Carter for reading the proofs, the latter also for compiling the Indices; and last but not least his wife for her patient criticism and for typing the MS. The writer is also indebted to Dr. D. Daube for his kindness in writing the Preface and to the Rev. F. N. Davey and his staff of the S.P.C.K. for their valuable help in the production of the book.

Since the first edition of this book was published, Prof. H. J. Schoeps' great work, *Theologie und Geschichte des Judenchristentums*, Tübingen, 1949, has appeared. Dr. Schoeps' construction of primitive Hebrew Christianity is founded upon a critical study of the pseudo-Clementine literature. Though the author of the present work finds the learned Professor's main premises unacceptable, some suggestive remarks have been incorporated in this new edition. Dr. Schoeps' second volume, *Aus frühchristlicher Zeit*, Tübingen, 1950, has proved equally helpful. Otherwise this new edition is substantially unaltered. A glossary has been added.

Author's Note to Third Edition

This work first appeared in 1949. It was written in Great Britain during the difficult years of war when the Island was under constant threat of a German invasion. The rumours then circulating about the fate of European Jewry were so gruesome that one suspected them to be mere war propaganda. Alas, the facts turned out to be worse than were the rumours. A second, somewhat amended edition appeared in 1954. By this time I was acquainted with the work of Hans Joachim Schoeps: *Die Theologie und Geschichte des Judenchristentums* (1949) and *Aus frühchristlicher Zeit* (1950). My friend, H. L. Ellison, in his review of my book expressed regret that I had not had the opportunity to consult Schoeps's work on Hebrew Christianity. My views, he thought, would have been greatly modified had I read Schoeps. By 1954 I had read Schoeps carefully but he failed to change my position regarding primitive Hebrew Christianity. Subsequent discoveries have proved me right. The Dead Sea Scrolls have served to confirm my conviction that the messianic movement centering upon the person of Jesus represented a genuine but different form of Judaism from that of the Pharisees.

Jacob Z. Lauterbach in his *Rabbinic Essays* (1951) still held to the monolithic concept of Judaism. For him Pharisaic Judaism, i.e. *halakhic* Judaism, is identical with the prophetic, i.e. biblical Judaism. This view still prevails among Jewish scholars. My own position I found later confirmed by David Daube's statement that during the three centuries preceding the destruction of the Second Temple "different classes, schools and individuals held different views even on important questions. But those warring parties never considered one another as outside Judaism" (David Daube, *The New Testament and Rabbinic Judaism,* 1956, p. 92).

Before the destruction of the Temple in 70 A.D. Judaism was not of one piece. This is now supported by the discovery of the Qumran sect. There were, as there still are in our day, different modes of Judaism, all claiming authenticity.

It is of particular satisfaction to me that after the lapse of thirty years the results of my research are still standing up to scholarly testing. On the three main issues underlying my book no major changes are called for: 1. The reason for the conflict between Jesus and the Pharisees; 2. The impact of the prayer against heretics (*birkat ha-minim*); 3. The rapid spread of Hebrew Christianity among Jews following the fall of Jerusalem and the collapse of the Bar Cochba insurrection in 135 A.D. Additional discoveries of ancient documents have confirmed the prevalence of faith in Jesus as Messiah in certain Jewish circles. Hebrew Christians survived for many centuries not only as heretical sectarians but also as orthodox Christians in close relationship to the universal church (cf. Walter Bauer, *Orthodoxy and Heresy in Earliest Christianity*, 1971). J. L. Teicher has shown that a third century Hebrew document found in Duro-Europos is in fact a remnant of a Eucharistic prayer; and what was hitherto held to be a Gentile Church appears to be a Jewish Synagogue. A Eucharistic prayer, related in style to the *Didache*, found in an ancient Synagogue is a remarkable coincidence (cf. *Jewish Quarterly Review*, Oct., 1963).

The extent of the success of Jewish Christians in the Synagogue is the only possible reason for the introduction of the malediction of heretics (Christians) in the Hebrew Prayer Book. After political disaster the gospel message offered new hope and vision to a defeated people. No less a luminary in Israel than Simeon Ben Zoma, the contemporary of Rab Akiba and the pupil of Joshua ben Hananiah, was, according to Samson H. Levey, a Jewish Christian (cf. *Judaism*, 1972, pp. 455 ff.). Levey describes his discovery as "the best kept secret of the rabbinic tradition." This was done, Levey explains, in order "to keep the matter as quiet as they could, so as not to lend strength to the aggressive evangelism of the early Church and its zealous missionaries who were working among the Jewish people." By pronouncing Ben Zoma of unsound mind the rabbis hoped to remove the scandal. The stratagem of misrepresentation or silence was a much practiced method used by the ancient rabbis. Lauterbach writes: "It is quite possible that these earlier teachers knew more about the origin of Christianity than they cared to report or had occasion to express even to their contemporaries and disciples" (*Rabbinic Essays*, p. 475).

Since the publication of my book, Jesus and the Pharisees, the Law and Gospel, and related subjects have received continuous attention from Jewish and Christian writers. The literature is too extensive to be quoted here. More recently John Bowker has stressed the accuracy of the Marcan Gospel in regard to the Pharisees: Jesus's offence was the assumption of authority, which his opponents regarded as blasphemous (cf. *Jesus and the Pharisees,* 1971). Walther Schmidhal denies a rift between James and Paul on the question of the Law. He believes that the "Judaizers" were of a much later date (*Paul and James,* 1965). Paul was not against the Law; what he denied was that the Law was sufficient for justification before God.

Similarly, the *birkat ha-minim* has been widely discussed, especially by Jewish scholars. Some still deny the connection between the malediction of the heretics and early Jewish Christianity. Arthur I. Waskow applies the malediction to Jewish informers who betrayed revolutionaries to the Roman government. He rests his view on the term *malshinim* (slanderers), ignoring the fact that the term does not belong to the original text (cf. *Judaism,* 1971, p. 404). Similarly, Peter Schäfer holds that the malediction was intended against Rome and was not the cause of separation between Christians and Jews (cf. *Judaica,* Heft 2, June, and Heft 3, Sept., 1975). But his argument is not convincing.

Many and extraordinary events have taken place since this book was first published. Just to mention a few: the Holocaust of European Jewry; the changed attitude towards Jews on the part of the Church since Vatican II; the creation of the State of Israel; the emphasis upon dialogue instead of mission on the part of the churches in respect to Jews; the ever widening concept of ecumenicity; and, of course, the already mentioned discovery of the Dead Sea Scrolls. It was materially impossible to incorporate the impact of these events in the present volume. I have therefore decided to publish a second volume under the title: *The Jewish People and Jesus Christ After Auschwitz.* This will bring the convoluted story of Jews and Christians up-to-date. The two volumes, though independent, complement each other. The first volume provides the historic background for what became burning issues for the Christian Church after World War II, namely the fate and destiny of historic Israel and Christian guilt in respect to the Jewish people.

Writing as a Jewish Christian I stand between Church and Synagogue. In this unusual position I owe a debt to both. It has been my endeavour to treat a difficult subject in a scholarly manner, though I have not tried to hide my own convictions regarding Jesus Christ. The book was received with acclaim by most scholars and the reading public. To my knowledge the only negative review was by James Parkes, a fellow-clergyman and a member of my own Church. Writing for the *Jewish Chronicle* (London) he showed unreasonable prejudice against Jewish Christians. On the Jewish side, Chaim Lieberman of the New York Yiddish daily *Forward* (June 26, 1951) gave vent to as much malignment as he could master. His avowed intention was to mislead the public by inventing his own version of the book. His article under the heading "Miserable and Lonely Souls" had almost nothing in common with the original text he was supposed to review. But considering the scurrilous way he dealt with Sholem Asch I have no right to complain, though he did everything possible to be offensive. It is a rare thing for a Hebrew Christian to be treated courteously by a fellow Jew.

This present paperback edition is substantially unaltered except for some corrections in text, some additional footnotes, and a few entries in the bibliography.

I am grateful to Baker Book House for making the book available to a wider public.

J. Jocz
Toronto, 1979

CONTENTS

PREFACE

NO FAIR-MINDED person, Christian or Jewish, will be able to read this book without being deeply moved by the sincerity, humanity and fervour of its author, and without profiting by his profound analysis of, and his balanced judgements about, the problem he has set out to investigate. The majority of Jews hold that no educated Jew can become a Christian from conviction; the simple truth of Judaism seems to them so clearly superior to the irrational dogma of Christianity that no one in possession of the former could ever come genuinely to believe in the latter; the writer of this Preface has heard this opinion expressed by great, enlightened Jewish scholars. In the face of the present book, however, it is impossible to maintain this attitude. There is no falsehood here. If we of the Jewish faith desire a discussion based on facts and not on prejudice, we must acknowledge the phenomenon of Jews accepting baptism from pure motives. After all, little worldly gain could be expected by a Jew who joined the Christian community in the first hundred years of its existence.

It is precisely the author's thesis that the genuine convert from Judaism, ostracized by the Jews as a traitor to his people, and a stranger among gentile Christians because they, too, are nationalists, re-enacts the drama of primitive Christian discipleship. "Faith ceases to be intellectual acquiescence and becomes once more a hazardous venture. Abraham's experience is the experience of every true Jewish Christian. . . . By the sacrifice of national loyalty for the sake of a higher good, the Hebrew Christian demonstrates before the Church and the Synagogue that the flesh profiteth nothing; it is the Spirit which giveth life."

It is usual for a Jew who contributes to a Christian work, or for a Christian who contributes to a Jewish, to emphasize that he does not subscribe to everything said by his friend. The present writer confesses that he has found few points of real importance in the book before him which appear to him to need modification. He certainly agrees that the conflict between Synagogue and Church always was and still is about the question of the divinity of Jesus, not about any minor issues. Even the authority of the

Law is a secondary matter, our view of which must depend on our answer to the main challenge; this is also the conclusion of W. D. Davies's recent study *Paul and Rabbinic Judaism*. Certain developments about to take place may, indeed, produce considerable changes in the prevalent setting of conversions of Jews to Christianity. In a Jewish State, there will be no such conversions for the sake of material advancement. On the other hand, should the existence of such a State render less desperate Jewish anxiety for national self-preservation, hostility to converts on the part of the unconverted might well diminish. But it is too early to be over-confident.

Synagogue and Church must go on questioning one another— and they must learn to help one another. Amidst a civilization which has largely lost its bearings, they both call men to return to God. Their position in the world is rapidly becoming the same; for the Church's staff is breaking. If, in this new situation, they find one another, they will also find themselves. Dr. Jocz's treatise, by showing where we stand, also shows where we should strive to go. Thus it is itself a big step along the road leading towards a strengthening of both Judaism and Christianity and at the same time a deeper mutual understanding between the two faiths—the " two young roes that are twins which feed among the lilies ".

DAVID DAUBE

HEBREW TRANSLITERATIONS

The transliteration of Hebrew presents a real difficulty. Some of the systems adopted, especially by the Germans, are complicated to the point of being unreadable. To avoid mystifying the reader unfamiliar with Hebrew we have kept to the more popular system adopted by Jewish writers. Following the example of C. G. Montefiore and H. Loewe (cp. *Rabbinic Anthology*, p. CVII) we have not always indicated the presence of the Dagesh forte, the sheva, etc.

ע	is indicated by		'
ח	,,	,,	ḥ
ק	,,	,,	ḳ
ט	,,	,,	ṭ
ס and שׂ	,,	,,	s
צ	,,	,,	ẓ
שׁ	,,	,,	sh

The most familiar Hebrew words and phrases have been left untranslated.

CHAPTER I

INTRODUCTORY REMARKS

SOME YEARS ago Dr. Chaim Zhitlowsky, the father of Jewish socialism and the foremost exponent of the Yiddish culture movement, published an article in his journal *Das Neue Leben* in which he called upon the Jewish people to "revise the Dreyfus case, by which our innocent brother of Nazareth is daily condemned and crucified".[1] Behind these words of a great Jew lies the strange and complicated history of the Jewish attitude to Jesus of Nazareth.

Gösta Lindeskog makes reference to the picture drawn by Joseph Norden in an article *Jesus von Nazareth in der Beurteilung der Juden einst und jetzt*, which may well serve as a symbol of all the prejudice and antipathy the Jew has kept in his heart for many centuries towards Israel's greatest son. An old, weary Jew, on the highroad approaching the town, on the eve of the Sabbath, full of anticipation of family bliss, suddenly notices a crucifix. His features change, his face becomes tense with pain and anger, his lips murmur: "ימח שמו וזכרו—May his name and his memory be blotted out."[2] The name of Jesus and the symbol of his suffering evoke bitter memories in the Jewish mind. Jesus of Nazareth is still held responsible by many Jews for much that they have suffered for centuries at the hands of Christians. Norden explains: "Thus was all the hatred of the tortured against their torturers poured upon the head of him whom the Church worships as her Saviour".[3] But the fact that Jesus became a complete stranger to the Jewish people is not merely explained by the behaviour of the Christian Church. To put the entire blame upon Christianity is to ignore important historical evidence.

It must not be forgotten that the decision concerning Jesus of Nazareth was taken at a time when Gentile Christianity was scarcely of any consequence to the Synagogue. The parting of the roads between the Messianic movement and Judaism began upon Jewish soil as a result of a religious controversy between Jews and Jews. This does not diminish the guilt of Christendom.

1

The Church was, and still is, an important factor in the Jewish attitude to Jesus Christ, but not the only one. There are further internal factors which determined the relation between Jesus and the Jews.

It is the purpose of this work to investigate the deeper reasons that have led, first to the separation of the Jews from Jesus Christ, and later to their complete estrangement.

How did it happen that Jesus the Jew, passionately concerned with the welfare of his people, was for centuries looked upon as a bitter enemy, whose name was not to be mentioned and whose teaching was to be despised? There is still a further question, of equal if not of greater interest: how did an essentially Jewish movement detach itself completely from its original background to flourish as a non-Jewish religion?

There are two standard answers to the last question, emanating from two different schools of thought:

(1) Traditional Christianity held for centuries that the Jews as a people rejected and the Gentiles accepted Jesus Christ. The crowd which on Good Friday shouted "Crucify, crucify him" expressed the will of the entire Jewish nation, with the exception of a small minority. Thus, the Jewish people having rejected their true Messiah, Israel's spiritual heritage passed on to the Gentile world.

(2) A more modern answer is connected with the person of Paul the Apostle. Between Jesus of Nazareth and the Gentile Church stands the man of Tarsus. The gospel which Jesus preached and the gospel which Paul preached were two different gospels. While Jesus was and remained a Jew, Paul, under the influence of Hellenistic ideas, deviated from the path of pure monotheism. Thus it happened that while Jesus himself was pointing to God, Paul, the Hellenistic Jew, was pointing to the glorified Christ. In reality, therefore, historical Christianity has only slight connexions with Jewish Palestine: its sources are to be sought in the philosophico-metaphysical ideas of the heathen world.

Both answers, however, are inadequate for the following reasons.

1. JESUS AND THE JEWISH PEOPLE

Jesus of Nazareth was born into a Jewish family.[4] He was brought up in the faith and traditions of the Jewish people. His teachers were Jews, his primer was the Hebrew Bible. He shared in the life of the common people and dressed in the customary dress of the pious Jew.[5] His disciples were Jewish men and it was primarily to his own people that he knew himself called to preach. The first Church in Jerusalem was a Jewish Church. They were Jewish men and women who first proclaimed Jesus the Messiah. Early Christian records bear evidence to the fact that, at least for a time, Jesus was a popular and much favoured preacher. Wherever he went, throngs followed the Master and hung upon his lips. His struggle against the Pharisees seems to have met with approval amongst the common people. The behaviour of the crowd before Pilate was by no means *vox populi* in any sense. The Gospels make it clear that the crowd demanding the death of Jesus was the *priests'* crowd. There is a passage peculiar to Luke which may well portray the sentiment of many Jews. We read that Jesus on his way to Golgotha was followed by "a great multitude of the people and of women who bewailed and lamented him".[6] There is no need to assume that the crowd consisted of enemies only and of the usual rabble led by curiosity and boredom. Many will have been guided by deep-felt devotion to the great Master of Nazareth. From Acts it would appear that after the Crucifixion Palestine was experiencing something of a Messianic mass-movement. Judging by the reaction of the Synagogue some fifty or sixty years later, this movement was only subdued after a long and bitter struggle.[7] How, then, can we maintain, in face of these facts, that the Jews as a people have rejected Jesus Christ? Are we to regard the crowd before Pilate as more representative than the thousands of believers who joined the Church?

There is still a further point to be considered. The Christian Church began as a movement of individuals and remained such for some centuries. It was only at the price of an unfortunate compromise that Christianity assumed a national form. To say that the Jews have rejected Jesus is to give to the Messianic movement a connotation which was contrary to its character. The idea of the remnant and the consciousness of election form the psychological background of the early Church. It was the individualistic character of the Messianic movement which contributed to the alienation of the followers of Jesus from the leaders of Judaism. While the Synagogue thought, and still thinks, to a large extent in collective terms, Christianity is essentially dependent upon the personal decision of the individual. To deny this is to deny its very nature. Outward conformity belies the meaning of the Christian message: "Not every one that saith unto me, Lord, Lord, shall enter into the Kingdom of heaven, but he that doeth the will of my Father which is in heaven" (Matt. 7. 21). Events have abundantly revealed the baselessness of the affirmation that the Jews have rejected and the Gentiles accepted Jesus Christ. This is a view which demands correction. It is thus the second aim of this work to establish the fact of an always present Jewish element within the Christian Church. All through the centuries there was a steady flow of Jewish converts to Christianity. We shall have occasion to show that in the second century there was an indigenous Jewish Church closely related to orthodox Christianity. This fact is of signal importance to the Church historian, for it links the Gentile Church with Palestine and the Hebrew Christian tradition. Scholars have hitherto worked on the assumption of a complete breach between Jewish and Gentile Christianity. Their attention was focused upon Ebionism as the Jewish form of Christianity, overlooking the fact that there was in existence another branch holding similar views to those of the Gentile Church.

In our own days there has been a rebirth of the Hebrew Christian tradition, which remains almost unnoticed by modern writers. But the growing number of Jewish Christians belies the assertion that Christianity is a Gentile prerogative. It would be impossible to prove that the Jews have rejected and the Gentiles accepted Jesus Christ. The truth is that *some* Jews and *some* Gentiles have accepted him as their Master and Lord, while many Jews and many Gentiles have remained either indifferent or hostile to the claims which he makes upon men.

2. PAUL AND THE HEBREW CHURCH

The school which makes Paul responsible for the distinctly Christian theology of the Church offers only an apparent solution of the genesis of Christianity. It is now increasingly recognized that Paul's missionary activity would have been impossible without the authority and support of at least a section of the Church in Jerusalem. It must never be forgotten that at the time of Paul's conversion there was already in existence a Church enduring persecution. Paul entered the Church as a learner and a disciple. Ananias, who visited Paul in Damascus, was a Jew, and so probably were the other disciples with whom he stayed after his conversion (Acts 9. 10 ff). Significantly enough, the belief that Jesus was the Son of God, a fact which dominated Paul's entire theology, was already preached by him in Damascus. The notion that Paul's views are derived from Antioch and not Jerusalem makes a division between these two Christian centres at such an early date historically unwarranted. There is, however, another factor which deserves all possible attention.

The fact of the Crucifixion of Jesus and the early persecution of the Christian Church is not an accidental but a constituent element in the Messianic movement. The reasons which led to the death of Jesus are still a puzzle to the careful observer. Objectively speaking, there is nothing in the teaching of Jesus to explain the enmity on the part of the Jewish leaders.[8] It is for this reason that scholars have tried to give Jesus' activity a political significance. Admittedly only on political grounds is the condemnation of Jesus explicable. But against such a view stands the Christian primitive tradition bearing evidence to the aloofness of Jesus Christ from political issues. Some scholars have therefore called in question the veracity of the early tradition, explaining it by a pro-Roman tendency. But the whole character of the Christian movement makes such an explanation doubtful. In our view, the controversy between Jesus and his opponents was essentially of a religious nature and centred round his personal claims. The offence which he constituted to Judaism lay in the unique authority which he assumed. If this be the case, then the death of Jesus, the persecution of the disciples, and the preaching of Paul become logically connected. There is an intimate relation between the Crucified Messiah of the Hebrew Church and the glorified Christ of Pauline theology. If Jesus, after his Crucifixion, was still regarded by his followers as the true Messiah, then he could have been preached only as the ascended and glorified Christ. Faith in the Resurrection of the Messiah was no Pauline invention; it was a firmly held belief in the Jewish Church. Thus only is the Pauline Christ linked up with the historic Jesus, and this via the Church in Jerusalem. Paul's merit was to have given some coherence to a faith which was not latent but actually present amongst the Jewish believers. The interposition of Paul between Jesus (viz. the Jewish disciples) and the Gentile Church does not therefore yield a satisfactory answer.

The third aim of this work is thus to show how an essentially Jewish movement became entirely detached from its original background and assumed a non-Jewish character.

3. THE NATIONAL ELEMENT

It appears to us that an important element in the relation between Jesus and the Jews has been strangely overlooked.

Most scholars are agreed that the struggle between Jesus and his opponents was of a religious nature. This is certainly true of the Synagogue and the early Church. The controversy between Judaism and Hebrew Christianity was naturally a *religious* controversy. After a protracted and bitter struggle it ended in the triumph of the Synagogue. But the success of the Synagogue is closely connected with the political situation of Jewry. The reason why this fact has been overlooked springs from the unfortunate assumption that the Christian movement was from the beginning mainly associated with the Gentile world and that Judaism remained relatively unaffected by it. It is our aim to show that such was not the case. The Messianic movement scored considerable success amongst the Jewish people, notably in the period between the destruction of Jerusalem and the Bar Cochba rising, and affected Judaism considerably. It was only after the Bar Cochba incident, when national survival became the sole consideration, that the initial success of Christianity abated.

The struggle between the Church and the Synagogue came at a critical period in Jewish history. It is therefore natural that a religious controversy should at such a time become a national issue. The decision was hastened by the calamities which befell the nation. To maintain old established customs, to cling to the past, to turn away from everything which might endanger national survival became imperative for the continuance of Jewish life. For this purpose, new barriers were erected, which were to segregate Israel from the world.[9]

The destruction of the Temple assigned a new task to the Synagogue. It now became the centre of all spiritual and cultural life. This brought about the decline not only of Sadducean influence but also of every other form of religious opposition. While before the Destruction one could be a good Jew without being a Pharisee, now Pharisaism and Judaism became synonyms. To this must be added the fact that the rapid growth of the

Gentile Church constituted a new danger to the Jewish nation. There is an undeniable denationalizing tendency associated with the Christian message. The breaking down of the barrier between Jew and Gentile spelt nothing but danger to a scattered people. From henceforth resistance to the Church became a national duty. Christianity ceased to be a sect within Judaism and became a dangerous rival threatening to disrupt Jewish life.

The importance of the national element in the Jewish-Christian relation can be gauged from the attitude to the Jewish convert even in modern times.

4. THE JEWISH-CHRISTIAN CONTROVERSY AND JESUS CHRIST

Both Church and Synagogue have always looked upon Jesus as the Founder of Christianity. Traditional Judaism opposed Christianity because it opposed Jesus, and, vice versa, it opposed Jesus because it opposed Christianity. The religious associations connected with his name kept Jesus in age-long obscurity from his own people. Owing to certain trends in the modern study of primitive Christianity, however, it became possible to dissociate the Master of Nazareth from the subsequent Church. This prepared the way for a re-examination of the Jewish attitude to Jesus Christ. Since the appearance of the first Jewish monograph by Joseph Salvador (1796–1873), *Jésus-Christ et sa doctrine* (1839),[10] books written by Jewish authors on this subject have greatly multiplied. It is now possible to speak of a distinctly Jewish *Leben-Jesu-Forschung*. The Jewish effort is directed to reclaiming Jesus the Jew from the Gentile Church and to reinstating him to a place of honour in Jewish history. This process of reclamation has continued for over a century and has been greatly accelerated in recent years.

It must, however, be remembered that Jewish interest in Jesus has little spiritual and no religious significance. The whole emphasis is upon the historical Jesus. Jewish attention is concentrated not so much upon the person as upon the teaching of Jesus and its relation to Judaism. Every effort is made to keep separate the prophet of Nazareth from the Second Person of the Trinity. Thus, the discussion is shifted from the religious to a purely historical plane. The Jewish age-old controversy with the Church that hitherto centred round the significance of Jesus is thus brought to an abrupt end. The Christ of the Church, who owes his existence to Greek philosophy and Jewish apocalyptic speculations, has nothing in common with the great Nazarene. The discussion concerning Christian doctrine and the discussion concerning Jesus of Nazareth are two distinct themes. But the nature of the Gospel and the claims which are associated with the person of Jesus inevitably force the discussion from the secular to the religious. Inasmuch as the significance of Jesus is not limited to a certain period of time and his spiritual challenge extends to all ages, it is not easy to avoid entering upon a theological controversy, especially as the life and teaching of Jesus are so closely related to religion. Furthermore, the complete separation between Jesus and the Church makes the fact of Christianity inexplicable. We have already had occasion to notice that Christianity is closely connected with the Church in Jerusalem and the Jewish disciples. Its foundation and its history are anchored in the person of Jesus Christ. Jewish scholars have therefore been unable to discuss Jesus of Nazareth without involving themselves in a theological dispute. This is specially the case with orthodox Jewish writers. Here it is admitted that Jesus and Christianity are closely related by ties of history and tradition and that to accept the one is to accept the other. Gösta Lindeskog has shown that the attempt of Jewish scholars to place Jesus within the boundaries of formative Judaism has proved unsuccessful.[11] Jesus of Nazareth still stands outside the course of reconstructed history. He is still the great puzzle, the enigma, requiring a solution. But even liberal Judaism has been unable to assign to Jesus a satisfactory position without jeopardizing its fundamental principles. Dr. C. E. Raven's opinion that the position of some liberal Jews approaches in certain respects the position of some Christians regarding the person of Jesus, must be taken with utmost caution.[12] For even the most liberal Christians will have to admit the *unique* significance of Jesus if they are to maintain their right to historic Christianity. But liberal Judaism can admit no such *uniqueness* to any historical person without affecting the whole structure of Jewish thought.

It is the fourth purpose of this work to give a survey of the discussion in Jewish quarters concerning Jesus of Nazareth. The subject has been ably discussed by Gösta Lindeskog, and the present writer had to guard himself against the temptation of trespassing upon well-covered ground. This work is, in one sense, a continuation of the work done by Lindeskog, in that it brings back the discussion from the purely historical to the religious plane. In the last resort the question concerning Jesus is a religious question. Jewish reclamation of the "historical" Jesus is of no real consequence to the Church or the Synagogue. The discussion between Judaism and Christianity transcends historical interest and is essentially a discussion of faith.

5. THE JUXTAPOSITION OF CHURCH AND SYNAGOGUE

The ultimate purpose of this work is to provide the reasons which make Jesus in the Christian interpretation impossible to Judaism. Such a task demands a clear recognition of the essential differences between Judaism and Christianity. These differences lie in the sphere of philosophical and theological thinking; but inasmuch as human thought is the expression of an attitude to life, theological or philosophical differences lead back from the realm of abstract thinking to the concrete fact of existence. Thus, the differences between Church and Synagogue are not mere thought-differences but real differences between men and men. They reveal a difference of attitude to the complex phenomena of life. Jewish-Christian relationship is conditioned by more than the historical, national, and religious factors, though these are of vital importance. The fact that Jews are not Christians cannot be merely relegated to the caprice of history. The reason why Christianity won the hearts of millions, while Judaism did not, is not adequately explained by the adaptability of the former, as Klausner suggests, or by the political preoccupation of the latter at the crucial moment, as Ziegler would have it.[13] Judaism is, above all, a characteristic religious attitude, independent of history and tradition. This attitude, though historically bound up with the Synagogue, is not confined to a particular race or creed, but underlies all religious endeavour. Deeply imbedded within the human soul is the inexorable will of man to work out his own salvation and to remain the master of his fate. This will to self-assertion is as much a fundamental fact in the Christian as in the Jew. It is here that the often repeated assertion that Christianity runs against the grain of human nature comes into evidence. The Christian attitude is essentially the attitude of surrender. Christianity begins with man in crisis; Judaism begins with the

assertion of human strength. The real difference between
Judaism and Christianity lies in the difference of attitude to God
on the part of the individual believer. Seen from this angle, the
Church indeed is invisible. The traditional division between
Judaism and Christianity has only the outward form in view, but
not their inner nature. In terms of spiritual life, such a division
is inaccurate. A Gentile can be a Jew by his inward attitude,
though by reason of tradition he is a member of the Christian
Church. On the other hand, a Jew can be a Christian without
knowing it, though his religious connections tie him to Judaism.[14]
Thus, the traditional boundaries dividing the two faiths become
fluid and their juxtaposition, in the customary sense, impossible.
From the subjective point of view, the difference between Judaism
and Christianity becomes a difference of emphasis, tendency, or
direction rather than of clear-cut dogma. This has led some
writers to the conviction that the antagonism between Judaism
and Christianity rests upon a misunderstanding; that by reason
of their historical kinship, the two faiths, though expressing
themselves in somewhat different language, mean the same thing;
they strive towards the same end and are moved by the same
spirit. In our concluding chapter we have therefore placed
the most characteristic tendencies in Jewish thought *vis-à-vis*
the basic principles in Christian theology in order to bring out
the deep difference between the two faiths. The result of such
a juxtaposition reveals that the fundamental difference is
derived from their respective teaching regarding man; and
because they differ on this vital point, they of necessity differ on
every other point.

Both Judaism and Christianity are the result of a major
controversy which took place during the first century and the
first half of the second. This controversy was of a theological
nature and centred round the significance of Jesus of Nazareth.
Our study has led us to the conviction that the general view,
which holds that Judaism remained unaffected by the Christian
episode, is untenable. Judaism had been deeply affected by the
rise of Christianity and was pushed in the opposite direction.
The opposition between the two creeds is thus an integral part
of their separate existence. Only in opposition to each other
do they learn the truth about themselves.

6. THE PROBLEM OF SUBJECTIVITY

Every writer on a religio-historical subject strives to eliminate the personal element and to present as much as possible an objective, *i.e.* "scientific", point of view. But the nature of our study has made such an approach impossible. For underlying this work is the assumption that a discussion concerning Jesus of Nazareth inevitably becomes a religious discussion. A religious discussion, however, in any real sense is only possible by taking sides. Buber and Schoeps have rightly stressed that a Jew can view Christianity and a Christian Judaism only from the outside. The recognition of this fact makes a purely academic approach difficult, if not impossible. We have thus tried to see and understand the Jewish point of view. But to carry on the discussion, we have been forced to take sides and we have made our stand upon positive Christianity. This work thus ends on a subjective note. To the Christian, the Jewish refusal to see in Jesus of Nazareth the promised Messiah is *unbelief*—not Jewish unbelief, but human unbelief. For the Jew in retaining his attitude of negation to the Son of Man becomes part and parcel of an unbelieving world. The Synagogue's no is the human no to the Son of God, who still knocks at the door of the heart of humanity.

CHAPTER II

JESUS CHRIST AND THE SYNAGOGUE

IT IS not possible to investigate the attitude of the Jewish
people towards Jesus Christ without taking into full account
one of the most potent factors in Jewish life, the Synagogue.
The Synagogue has for centuries moulded Jewish thought and
fashioned the opinions of the individual Jew.

1. JUDAISM AND CHRISTIANITY

Modern Jewish scholars have repeatedly maintained that
Judaism has no dogmas [1] and that, unlike Christianity, its stress
is not upon orthodoxy, for which it has not even a "proper
Hebrew equivalent",[2] but rather upon "orthopraxy". This is
true with some modifications. Judaism is certainly not a
"dogmatic religion". "It possesses no organ having authority
to regulate or control faith. We may even maintain that it does
not permit of orthodoxy in the strict sense and leaves room for
the widest freedom of thought".[3] But it nevertheless has very
definite dogmas, which are absolutely essential to Judaism.[4]
This is borne out by the fact of the Synagogue's reaction to heresy.
The Talmud knows of four main kinds of heresies, one of which is
undoubtedly Hebrew Christianity.[5] The attitude of the Synagogue to Gentile Christianity varied with the circumstances
under which Jews lived in Christian countries. The question
sometimes discussed by the Rabbis was whether Christianity was
to be classed with 'Abodah Zarah (idolatry) and the Christians
regarded as 'Obde kokabim u-mazzalot (Cultores stellarum et plane-
tarum).[6] This question has actually remained undecided and
is still so for the orthodox Jew. Judah ha-Levi (1085–1142)
regards Christians and Mohammedans as proselytes who have
not accepted the Law in its entirety, and who still hold to idolatrous practices.[7] Maimonides (1135–1204) holds a similar view.[8]
It is the traditional view of the Synagogue "that Christianity's
function is to be a sort of half-way house between heathenism and
Judaism".[9] The orthodox position, at present, seems to be that

12

though "for purposes of social conduct, our contemporary Gentile friends cannot, of course, be compared with the idolaters, nevertheless, it must remain our bounden duty to eschew contact with them in religion and in matters having a religious basis, *e.g.* marriage".[10] It is characteristic that in the language of the Talmud and the Rabbis, the words "idolater" and "non-Jew" are synonyms. *Cultus alienus* and *cultus idolorum* ('*abodah zarah* and '*abodat elilim*) are the usual terms applied to the religious practices of the *goyim*. "They signify always and everywhere idols and idolatry, *i.e.* every non-Jewish cult."[11]

Christianity would naturally fall under the category of non-Jewish religions. But both Islam and Christianity were recognized as serving a special purpose as having closer relation with Judaism. Both were, nevertheless, severely criticized for falling below the standards of the Synagogue.[12] Christianity was chiefly censured for its Trinitarian doctrine and for some idolatrous practices.[13] It must be admitted that some Jewish criticism was justified. Referring to R. Isaac's criticism of the worship of images in the Christian Church, Lukyn Williams remarks: "In this last I confess that R. Isaac is right, right also in pointing out that although Christians may argue that images are made by them only for the honour of the saints, male and female, and not for prayer, yet even though this were said with truth of images made in metal, wood, and stone, Christians cannot deny that they worship idols of bread, and pray to them, and say of each of them that it is God."[14] We must therefore understand the scruples the Jews had with regard to Christianity. L. Rabinowitz has shown how circumstances and the ordinary necessities of life have had a modifying influence upon the stricter views as laid down in the Talmud with regard to the non-Jewish world.[15] The leading Jewish theologians of the Middle Ages have thus decided that strict monotheism is only an obligation upon the Jewish people, while the Christians as the "Sons of Noah" were under no such obligation. *Shittuf, i.e.* the combining of the name of God with something else,[16] was not idolatry in the case of Christianity. R. Gershom of Mainz (d. 1040), Rashi (1040–1105), Isaac ben Sheshet (d. 1408), Joseph Caro (1488–1575), and many others have held that the Christians are proselytes of the gate (*gere ha-sha'ar*) and not idolators.[17]

But the Synagogue's attitude to early Hebrew Christianity was not determined by the same factors. To begin with, the notion of idolatry could not have arisen. The Jewish Church in Palestine was as far removed from idolatry as the Rabbis were. Yet the Synagogue's attitude to the Messianic movement was not accidental. It saw in Christianity a grave departure from the Rabbinic point of view. Thus, the answer of the Synagogue was the only possible answer it could afford to give, a determined and absolute no.

Most Jewish scholars and some Gentile scholars connect the hostility of the Synagogue towards the Christian movement with the name of Paul. They maintain that prior to the formulation of Paul's antinomian theology, there was no real antagonism.[18] Both Jesus and Hebrew Christianity were firmly planted upon Jewish soil, and their Messianic faith gave no real cause for hostility. Antagonism developed later during the process of transformation from Hebrew Christianity to Gentile Christianity. But even then, Jewish animosity was provoked by the ever-growing anti-Jewish trend within the Church. In support of this view, it is pointed out that there is manifestly less enmity amongst the *Tannaim* towards Jesus than amongst the *Amoraim*.[19]

But the whole background of the New Testament points to an early hostility between the new Messianic movement and the Synagogue. Upon investigation, the tension leads back to the earliest days and centres round the person of Jesus himself. Prof. W. D. Niven rightly stresses the point "that the Apostles are preaching Jesus, whom the Council had condemned".[20] This fact must not be overlooked in an attempt to understand early Jewish-Christian relations. To find the reasons which led to an open condemnation of Jesus is the problem which Church historians have repeatedly to face.

On the Jewish side, it is often emphatically denied that there was any legal procedure against Jesus, as all the evidence points against it. Rabbi I. M. Wise makes much of the fact that the Jews at that time were not at liberty to execute capital punishment.[21] Jesus was never brought before the court of the Sanhedrin, "the only body competent, under Jewish law, to try a charge involving the death penalty. Almost every rule of that law was, indeed, trampled on in the case of Jesus of Nazareth". [22] But both Montefiore and Klausner admit the possibility of a trial, though "that there was any meeting of the full Sanhedrin is most doubtful".[23]

Jewish scholars are almost unanimous in their plea that the

Gospels contain a definite anti-Jewish bias and that their evidence therefore does not reflect true history. The object of the Gospels is "to whitewash Pilate, and to throw the responsibility of the crucifixion upon the Jews".[24] But however the case may be, it cannot easily be denied that Jesus met with strong opposition. Who were Jesus' enemies, and why?

2. JESUS AND THE TWO MAIN PARTIES

The importance of the political background in the struggle between Jesus and his opponents is an element which deserves due notice. Jewish scholars have paid much attention to this aspect as it appears to provide a clue for the solution of the problem of the reason for the condemnation and death of Jesus. Some hints of the political significance of the struggle between Jesus and his opponents are contained in the Gospels. But Jewish emphasis upon the political implications of Jesus' activity is due to a desire to exonerate the Pharisaic party. The prevailing view amongst Jewish scholars is that there were no basic points of difference between Jesus and the Pharisees; on the contrary, they had much in common. The Pharisees, therefore, could not have been involved in the plot against Jesus. This led to two conclusions, first, that the Gospels misrepresent the case, and, secondly, that Jesus' enemies are to be sought outside the Pharisaic party.

(a) The Sadducees

It was therefore held that the most obvious enemies of Jesus were the Sadducees. They were the only people whose interest it was to maintain the political *status quo*. They must have objected to Jesus not only on doctrinal grounds but also for the political implications of his Messianic claims, and for his interference with the established institutions. Their first concern was not to provoke the Roman masters, in case they "come and take away both our place and our nation".[25] This does not mean, of course, that the Sadducees were friends of Rome by choice. But they were realists, they understood the utter impossibility of freeing themselves from Roman supremacy and as their own position was safeguarded, they readily accepted foreign domination.[26] Klausner calls them "practical politicians" who had reasons to oppose "any change which might disturb their peace and their enjoyment of the pleasures of this life".[27]   To the Sadducees, Jesus was nothing more than another political rebel who must be dealt with quickly before it was too late.   Thus, Jewish scholars are almost unanimous in putting the blame for the condemnation of Jesus upon the shoulders of the priestly party, "who were Israel's despots and the tools of Roman masters".[28]   C. G. Montefiore, who usually exercises restrained judgement, inclines to that view, but he cautiously admits the possibility that the Sadducean priesthood may have had the support of some of the leading Rabbis, and who, together with the Sadducees and the Romans, may be held responsible for the death of Jesus.[29]

An unusual view is presented by Rudolf Leszynsky, who is the only Jewish writer to champion the cause of the Sadducees.[30] Leszynsky is able to find important points of agreement between Jesus and the Sadducees.   He contends that Christianity, in fact, was at one time much nearer to Sadduceeism than is usually held possible.[31]   Thus, Jesus' attitude to the ritual washing of hands (pp. 43, 207); his attitude to the obligation of paying the Shekel (p. 69); his views concerning the Davidic descent of the Messiah (p. 297); but above all, his interpretation of the Law of Moses, was essentially Sadducean (p. 284).   Leszynsky attaches importance to the fact that Jesus never spoke against the sacrifices. This leads him to the conclusion: "It was therefore not the Law of Moses which Jesus refused (ablehnen) but the laws of the Pharisees."[32]   The fact that the Christian Church has fixed Easter day to fall on a Sunday and has thus decided in the controversy between Sadduceeism and Pharisaism regarding the interpretation of "*mimaḥarat-ha-shabbat*" ("the morrow after the Sabbath")[33] in favour of the Sadducees is, to Leszynsky, another link in his chain of evidence.[34]

This does not mean that Leszynsky claims for Jesus absolute agreement with Sadduceeism.   He does not.   We are told that in several important points Jesus differed from the Sadducees. In his faith in the Resurrection and in his attitude to the *Lex talionis* Jesus approached the Pharisaic view.[35]   Otherwise Jesus was on the side of the Sadducees.   His whole effort was directed against Pharisaism: "The Pharisees were from the beginning the main opponents of the new doctrine (Lehre).   Against them Jesus directed his attacks."[36]   Though the Sadducees had little sympathy with him, the real enemies against whom he fought throughout his life were the Pharisees. Leszynsky suggests that the reasons why these facts were hitherto overlooked, lie in the difficulties of investigating the history of Sadduceeism. "While we are able to follow the development of Pharisaism step by step, the history of Sadduceeism lies for us pretty well in darkness." [37]

Leszynsky's efforts have not been received favourably by Jewish scholars. His views are regarded as extravagant and ill-founded. Abrahams dismisses him with an exclamation mark,[38] and Klausner with a few sentences.[39] Admittedly, Leszynsky's evidence is slender and his conclusions lack convincing power. But the importance of his work lies not so much in his assertions as in the fact that it is possible to make out a reasonable case for the Sadducees. This ought to caution those who make unqualified affirmations about the sole importance of Pharisaism and its influence upon Jesus.

Chwolson's views regarding the Sadducean attitude to Jesus may be taken as the accepted opinion of Jewish scholars up to this day.

Chwolson is convinced that the Sadducees are solely responsible for the death of Jesus.[40] From the case of James (Jos., *Antiq.* xx, 9, 1), he deduces "that the Sadducees were the persecutors and the Pharisees were still the defenders of the persecuted Christians in the year 62".[41] He points to the fact that at the time of Jesus, the Pharisees were only aspiring to power; they were in the minority in the Sanhedrin and decisively overruled by the Sadducean majority. They had no cause for condemning Jesus, who faithfully observed the commandments, and who never opposed Pharisaism as such, but only certain private opinions of individual Pharisees. Chwolson ends his remarkable essay with the following words: "Neither the Jewish people nor the Pharisees are guilty of the death of Christ, but the avaricious, aristocratic priests, the cowardly instruments of Rome (Römlinge) who, in fear for their rich revenues, trembled before the Roman authorities and who suspected Christ to be a political agitator, a new Judas Galiläus—these and none other were the hangmen of Jesus Christ." [42]

(b) The Pharisees

We owe a real debt to Jewish scholarship for correcting many long-established views about Pharisaism. Jewish scholars have vigorously protested against the indiscriminate condemnation of the Pharisaic party by Christian writers.[43]   Their main line of defence is (a) that the Gospels exaggerate Jesus' opposition to the Pharisees, and that far from holding diverse views, they had much in common ; and (b) that Jesus' attack was directed against the *bad* Pharisees only, a feature which we also meet in the Talmud.

(i) THE SYNOPTIC ACCOUNT OF THE PHARISEES

Dr. James Parkes, who is strongly influenced by the Jewish point of view, is driven to the conclusion that all the anti-Pharisaic passages in the Gospels, "come from a Judeo-Christian source, from Christians very conscious of their membership in Israel, of their obedience to Torah, but in violent conflict with the Pharisees over the orthodoxy of their position".[44]   But Dr. Parkes offers this only as a "probable explanation".   It is, however, clear to him that the Gospels were written "on a background of the steady intensification of the conflict between Gentile Christians and the Jews" and that none of the authors was personally acquainted with Palestinian Pharisees or Rabbinic Judaism.   "They were not themselves aware of how much of the teaching of Jesus which they recorded was Pharisaic." [45] Such is also the Jewish view.

H. Loewe, referring to Matt. 23, says : "It seems to me most natural to regard the chapter as intentionally altered by later hands.   The objection to it is not the denunciations, but the fact that the denunciations are wholesale." [46]   Klausner accepts in part D. Chwolson's suggestion "that much of the opposition shown in the Gospels to Pharisaism and Judaism generally was directed against the Sadducees".[47]   But the real explanation for Klausner is contained in A. Büchler's view that the Gospel writers have confused, out of ignorance, the terms Scribes and Pharisees, and used them as if they were synonyms, ignorant of the fact that "the chiefs of the priests and the Scribes and the elders" of whom we read in the Gospels "were almost entirely Sadducees".   Such a mistake could have arisen only at a time when "the Sadducees had lost power and importance" as actually happened in the period when the Gospels were written.[48]   A similar view is put forth by Montefiore, who explains that : "Matthew often unites the Pharisees and the Sadducees.   He probably had only a vague, unhistorical idea who the Pharisees and Sadducees were.   All he knew, or cared to know, was that they were opponents of his hero." [49] Such a theory implies three assumptions: a late composition of the Gospels in a non-Jewish milieu; complete ignorance concerning Jewish life, especially in the case of the author of Matthew (!); and the immediate disappearance of the Sadducean party after the destruction of Jerusalem. Indeed, Jewish scholars have tended to accept a very late date for the Gospels.[50] Klausner's moderate view is that Mark was composed between 66–68, Matthew "after the Destruction and near the end of the century", and Luke "at the beginning of the second century".[51] Almost all Jewish writers stress anti-Jewish tendencies in the Gospels, and ignorance concerning things Jewish. It is also generally assumed by Jewish as well as Christian scholars that Sadduceeism ceased to exert any influence with the destruction of the Temple. But it must be admitted that our knowledge of Sadducean history is entirely based on Pharisaic evidence, and that it remains an unexplored field. Jewish scholars, partly through apologetic motives, have devoted much time to the study of Pharisaism. Sadduceeism, as Leszynsky has pointed out, is still a mystery to us. S. Schechter in his introduction to the *Documents of Jewish Sectaries* appends the following note to his remark concerning the unsatisfactory state of knowledge regarding the history of Sadduceeism: "It need hardly be pointed out that there are both in the *Hagada* and in the *Halacha* of our sect (*i.e.* the Zadokites) features which strikingly recall the famous hypothesis of Geiger regarding the Sadducees and the Old *Halacha*. But this hypothesis is still so undeveloped in its details, that it seems better to leave the subject in abeyance. It is a further and larger question whether we have to deal with a sort of counter-tradition or with an interpretation claiming to go back to primitive Judaism." [52] Leszynsky, who seems to owe much to the hints contained in Schechter's study, affirms the connection between the ancient Sadducees and the Karaite movement. He even suggests that Sadducean traditions have survived amongst the Abyssinian Falashas and the Samaritans! [53] However the case may be, the assumption that the Sadducees disappeared immediately after the destruction of the Temple is nothing more than a generally accepted hypothesis, founded on the usual *argumentum ex silentio*. As to the exact dates of compilation of the various Gospels in their present form, the question is open to argument and we are entirely left to conjecture. To assume complete ignorance concerning the difference between

Pharisaism and Sadduceeism on the part of the Evangelists, is to ignore obvious facts.   For it cannot be easily denied that the Gospels presuppose a very thorough knowledge of Jewish traditions and *local* circumstances.   Israel Abrahams claims such knowledge even for John.[54]

(ii) JESUS AND THE BAD PHARISEES

The other alternative is to assume that the criticism of the Gospels directed against the Pharisees, much of which undoubtedly goes back to Jesus, has only the *bad* representatives of that party in view.   Most Jewish scholars take this view.   Moriz Friedländer is an exception.[55]   Klausner explains Jesus' attitude in the sense that his criticism was actually not an attack, but a defence of Pharisaism against cant and hypocrisy.[56]   Israel Abrahams warns against the danger of confusing a system with its abuses.[57]   Montefiore readily accepts the possibility that there could have been living examples of a perversion of the Pharisaic religion, but to apply Luke's parable of the Pharisee to all members is a "*ludicrous* caricature of the average Pharisee, a *monstrous* caricature of the Pharisaic ideal".[58]   H. Loewe refuses to accept Prof. Burkitt's suggestion that the discrepancy between the Gospel account and the Rabbinic picture of the Pharisees may have been caused by the transformation which took place in their ranks after the national disaster of A.D. 70.   Loewe rather favours the opinion that Jesus' attacks were directed against some sectaries who stood midway between Pharisaic and Sadducean tradition, trying to reconcile their divergence, and thus giving the impression of being Pharisees.   Loewe is convinced that "against *the* Pharisees, as the term is commonly understood, they could not have been directed".[59]   On the contrary, Jewish scholars have repeatedly affirmed that Jesus stood firmly upon Pharisaic ground.   All the noble and commendable features of his teaching have their origin in the Pharisaic ideal.   It is commonplace amongst Jewish writers to present Pharisaism in Lindeskog's words, "as the most noble production (*Erzeugnis*) of the Jewish people", the deepest and most perfect expression of Judaism.[60]   However, Jewish scholars admit the existence of friction between Jesus and the religious leaders of his time.[61] For it is not possible to overlook the unanimous witness of the Gospels to such a struggle.   But only reluctantly do they admit the participation of the Pharisaic party in the contest.   The reason for this is in the eagerly made assertion that there is absolute unity of purpose between the Pharisees and Jesus.[62]

From the Synoptic account, it would appear that the Pharisees, in so far as they enjoyed greater popularity as the leaders of religious life, play also a more prominent part as the antagonists of Jesus. Herford's presentation of Pharisaism and its attitude to the Christian movement shows a definite bias.[63] A. T. Robertson has conclusively shown the prominence given in the Synoptic Gospels to the tension between Jesus and the Pharisees.[64] Even Parkes admits that "every source deals with points of conflict between Jesus and the Pharisees, the leaders of Rabbinic Judaism".[65] Parkes, however, dissolves the conflict by accepting the theory that Jesus' attack was directed against the *bad* Pharisees; against those who "failed to live up to the truth they already possessed".[66] This emphasis upon Jesus' agreement with the good Pharisees and his castigation of the bad is by no means a Jewish invention. This has been, and still is, an often repeated view on the part of Christian writers, but it avoids the main problem.[67]

The Synoptic tradition does not merely present Jesus as a moral teacher castigating the sins and shortcomings of religious devotees; he stands out, rather, as a royal figure making supreme claims. It is difficult to escape the impression that the clash between Jesus and the Pharisees is of a fundamental nature. The issues involved are greater than mere petty failings. The actual cause of the friction cuts right across the very essence of religious life. The clash between Jesus and the Pharisees is ultimately the clash of two vital principles in constant opposition to each other: the categorical imperative of eternity, and the ever compromising principle of time. There may be more than would appear in the Jewish contention that the demands which Jesus made are irreconcilable with the experience of life.[68] The theory which attributes the anti-Pharisaic passages to later accretions completely ignores the basic nature of the conflict.

(c) *The Law* [69]

Jewish scholars have naturally paid much attention to Jesus' attitude to the Law. Both Montefiore and Klausner have discussed the subject carefully. In Montefiore's view, Jesus, driven by his prophetic temperament, "was compelled to take

up a certain attitude towards the Mosaic Law itself, and this
attitude was novel and even revolutionary".[70]   Klausner, too,
after considering the various instances in the Gospels bearing on
the subject says: "Thus, Jesus would abrogate not only fasting
and decry the value of washing of hands in the 'tradition of the
elders', or in current traditional teaching, but would even permit
(though he does this warily and only by hints) the foods forbidden
in the Law of Moses." [71]   It is held that this strange laxity
towards the Law ultimately completed the breach between him
and the Pharisees.   But in spite of this, Klausner claims for Jesus
absolute and faithful adherence to Judaism.   "Jesus was a Jew
and a Jew he remained till his last breath" [72]—a Jew, of course, in
the religious sense.   Lindeskog has already pointed out the inconsistency.[73]   Israel Abrahams avoids the difficulty by assuming
that the controversy about the Law revealed only a difference of
interpretation and in the case of the most vital point of the dispute, the Sabbath, the controversy was only of a *local* character.[74]
Jesus thus still stands within the Jewish tradition.   His attitude
to the Law simply represents a different point of view.   While to
the Pharisees "all labour not pressing and postponable was
forbidden", to Jesus "no act of mercy, whether the need pressed
or not, was to be intermitted because of the Sabbath".[75]   Jewish
scholars, however, are aware that there is an air about Jesus which
is very different from the submissive acceptance of the Law we
meet in Pharisaism.   Klausner brings this point out very clearly.
He even attributes Paul's revolutionary attitude to the Law to
the fact that the Founder of Christianity gave the precedent.
This is an important admission, which throws new light upon the
discussion on the relation between Jesus and Paul.   To quote
Klausner himself: "Had not Jesus' teaching contained a kernel
of opposition to Judaism, Paul could never *in the name of Jesus*
have set aside the ceremonial laws, and broken through the barriers of national Judaism." [76]   But this "kernel of opposition"
is to Klausner nothing more than an implicit tendency, an over-
emphasis of characteristic Jewish teaching; it is, in fact, nothing
more than "exaggerated Judaism".[77]   Travers Herford, who
usually represents the Jewish point of view, holds, that Jesus "was
really rejected, so far at all events as the Pharisees were concerned,
because he undermined the authority of the Torah and endangered the religion founded upon it".[78]   But it is here that we
meet with a strange contradiction.   Jewish scholars generally

deny that Jesus was consciously opposed to the Law.[79]   Klausner inconsistently holds that Jesus did not even attack the ceremonial laws, but that he laid little stress on them.[80]

This basic dilemma is not easily solved.   Both views, though contradictory, seem to contain a kernel of truth.   In view of the evidence we have, it cannot be easily maintained that Jesus impeached the authority of the Law, consciously or unconsciously. Prof. Branscomb's opinion, that Jesus arbitrarily, as it seems, selected a few basic commandments of a positive religious and ethical character "and disregarded the other precepts whenever they came in conflict with these primary commandments in any way",[81] is unacceptable, unless his action was supported by an authority exceeding that of the Law.   Prof. Branscomb probably implies this, though he brings it down to a specific "understanding of the divine Revelation" on the part of Jesus himself, and to his conscious opposition to the "Pharisaic interpretation of the Torah given by God".[82]   Prof. Branscomb's statement to the effect that Jesus "dealt with the written law as freely as he did with the oral", and his stress upon "the basic moral principles of the Torah",[83] are inclined to impute modern liberal ideas to the mind of Jesus.   Neither is it possible to subscribe to the view that Jesus' intention was wholesale repudiation of the Pharisaic understanding of the Law, as Branscomb suggests,[84] since the Gospels record instances where the contrary is asserted.   Prof. T. W. Manson's views are more convincing.   Jesus neither rejected the Law nor did he lightly disregard any of its commands and prohibitions.   If he breaks them, he does so consciously in "the interests of something greater than the Law and the Temple. That something is the Kingdom of God". [85]   But even Prof. Manson's view is defective.   It does not draw the last conclusion; it avoids the problem of ἐξουσία which inevitably comes to the front and which was actually the point under discussion between Jesus and the Jewish authorities.[86]   Manson presents Jesus "as the Servant *par excellence* of the Kingdom of God",[87] who is ready to sweep away all obstacles hampering its approach.   Jesus, however, was not only the *Servant* of the Kingdom, he knew himself also to be the *King*.   This aspect of Jesus' Messianic consciousness is an essential element underlying his action.[88]

Montefiore denies that Jesus claimed the right as Messiah to dispense men from the obligation of the Law.   He holds with Menzies, however, that when necessity arose to defend a higher principle, Jesus did not hesitate to break the Mosaic precepts. But that the Son of Man is lord also of the Sabbath, applying ὁ υἱὸς τοῦ ἀνθρώπου to his own person, Montefiore rejects as improbable.[89]   At the same time, he favours the view that Jesus held himself to be the Messiah, though he "does not appear to claim authority over the commands of the Law in virtue of his Messiahship". By what right then, we would ask, does Jesus set at naught Mosaic commandments, which both he and his opponents believed to have been ordained by God himself? Montefiore's assertion has no support in the Gospels, which unequivocally create a contrary impression, especially Mark 2. 28. The question round which the whole issue revolves is not whether Jesus' conception of the Messiah was in accordance with Jewish views, apocalyptic or otherwise; but whether Jesus assigned such extraordinary authority to the Messianic office as to set the Messiah above the Law.   It cannot easily be denied that the intention of the Gospels is to propagate such an impression.   The question whether such an attitude is true to the historical picture of Jesus is open to discussion.   In our view, the Gospels record actual fact.   Jesus did not hesitate to brush aside certain Rabbinic injunctions.   But this could have been relegated to a mere difference in exegetical method, as Abrahams suggests.   He actually did more.   To use Prof. Branscomb's words, he "dealt with the written law as freely as he did with the oral".   But this not in defence of some dogmatic principle or moral ideal.   The authority for such unexemplified behaviour must be sought somewhere else, namely in his *Messianic consciousness*.

Jesus' attitude to the Law was determined neither by humanistic motives nor moralistic scruples.   Not even the cause of the Kingdom of God would justify his action, had it not been for the fact that he identified the Kingdom with his own person.[90] The claim to highest authority is not inconsistent with the Suffering Servant, as Montefiore appears to admit.[91]   It is as the Servant of God, the King Messiah, that Jesus claimed the authority which he knew to be delegated to him by God.   In view of his humble, submissive acceptance of the will of God, Constantin Brunner's theory that Jesus, claiming the highest authority, approached an atheistic point of view, falls extremely flat.[92]

Jesus never questioned the authority of the Law.   He accepted it as divinely appointed.   God had given it, and only God could

annul it.   Its duration was determined by the approach of the
Messianic Age.   Only the Messiah, as the Messenger of God,
stood above the authority of the Law.   Such an attitude was
neither rebellion nor presumption; it was dictated by an unique
self-consciousness.[93]

The Messianic Age, however, was not to terminate the Law,
nor to supersede it.   The purpose of its coming was the fulfilling of the same.   Mt. 5. 17—[οὐκ ἦλθον καταλῦσαι ἀλλὰ
πληρῶσαι (τὸν νόμον)]—throws important light upon the Christian
attitude towards the Law, and may well reflect Jesus' own position.   Admittedly this much discussed passage is full of difficulties.
To start with, it has no parallel in the Synoptic tradition; it
is peculiar to Matthew only.   It belongs to the passages with a
definite " Judaistic tendency".[94]   It has been questioned whether
the passage can be safely attributed to Jesus himself, and opinions
are naturally divided.[95]   Once we have accepted the passage
as genuine, there is still the exegetical difficulty of determining the
meaning of " πληρῶσαι."

Streeter regards Mt. 5. 17–20 as reflecting the attitude of
the Jewish Christians who grouped themselves round the person
of James.   Referring to this and other "Judaistic passages"
in Matthew, Streeter remarks: "It is difficult not to suspect the
influence of the desire of the followers of James to find a justification for their disapprobation of the attitude of Paul by inventing
sayings of Christ, or misquoting sayings which, even if authentic,
must originally have been spoken in view of entirely different
circumstances." [96]   On these grounds Streeter seems to deny
authenticity to the whole paragraph.   But his argument is not
conclusive: (1) the fact that *v.* 17 was not in Q does not therefore
qualify it as unauthentic.   (2) *v.* 18 has a parallel in Lk. 16. 17,
and is therefore derived from a common source.   (3) Matthew's
attitude to the Law is not as "Judaistic" as some would make out.
This is testified by the presence of Mt. 11. 13, of which Streeter
admits that "whatever its original meaning, certainly lends itself
to the view that the Old Law was in a sense suspended by the
Gospel".[97]   (4) The whole passage is in complete agreement
with Jesus' attitude to the religious past of Israel.   We therefore
accept *v.* 17 as authentic.

The further question concerns the meaning of πληροῦν.
Montefiore, who discusses the passage at some length, cautiously
says: "It seems to say that the standpoint of Jesus is not that he

desired to abolish the Law, but to deepen it, and in that sense to fulfil or complete it. The righteousness of the Law, so far as the mere letter goes, is inadequate for the disciples or for the Christian." [98] The intention of the Sermon on the Mount was to give to the Commandments larger scope and greater depth. Montefiore, therefore, speaks of Jesus as "the new legislator". But this may prove a misapplied term. The passage in question gives no warrant for such an appellation.

The question is, what was the original word which Jesus used for πληροῦν? Strack-Billerbeck say: "For πληροῦν Jesus would have said *kayyem* the opposite of which formed the above conjectured *baṭel* for καταλύειν . . ." [99] *Ḳayyem* is the most obvious word to suggest: it was and still is in universal usage, and always associated with the fulfilment of the *miẓwot*. But if this be the case, then the attitude of Jesus towards the Law is that of humble submission.[100] Such a view may suggest an inconsistency on the part of Jesus, and Montefiore is quick to recognize this. He thinks that it is not possible to arrive at a certain conclusion "as to Jesus' theoretic attitude towards the Law, because he probably had not faced the question himself".[101] In our view, however, there is no actual inconsistency involved. If we accept the passage as it stands, then the clue to the puzzle is contained in the words: ἕως ἂν πάντα γένηται, to which Montefiore remarks "it is a strange expression as applied to the Law".[102]

There is an inner connexion between ἕως ἂν πάντα γένηται and the words of Mt. 11.13: πάντες γὰρ οἱ προφῆται καὶ ὁ νόμος ἕως 'Ιωάννου ἐπροφήτευσαν. If we accept Lk. 16. 16 as the more original, at any rate the more lucid, text,[103] then the connexion becomes even more apparent.[104]

The Law and the Prophets form the background of Jesus' activity.[105] His appearance, which marks the approach of the new age, does not annul or abrogate the Law; it *fulfils* it. All that the Law and the prophets were standing for, hinting at, is now being realized, fulfilled, and accomplished. Thus, the King Messiah has not come to annul (*baṭel*) the Law; on the contrary. The Law stands (*ḳayyem*) in all its sanctity, in all its significance, but only: ἕως ἂν πάντα γένηται.[106] In the days of the Messiah, however, the Law will be written *within* the hearts of God's people. This is the mark of the New Covenant (Jer. 31. 31 ff.). To Jesus his Messianic activity was the commencement of the new era: his coming breaks history in two parts. The Law and the

Prophets on one side; the Gospel of the Kingdom on the other side (Lk. 16. 16). But in a deeper sense, the Law and the Prophets and the Gospel of the Kingdom are *one*. They stand to each other as promise to fulfilment.

We would therefore repudiate the view that Jesus sought to abolish the Law. It is even doubtful whether he opposed the Pharisaic interpretation of it, as is sometimes asserted. Mt. 23 appears to be not a condemnation of Pharisaic exegesis but rather of Pharisaic deeds.[107] Oesterley's suggestion that Jesus accepted the Law in principle " but modified and expanded it where necessary", even to the extent of abrogating it altogether in the name of a "higher morality and a more spiritual religion",[108] we categorically repudiate. Such a view is only possible on the assumption that to Jesus the Law was not divinely instituted. But such an assumption has no foundation. On the contrary, there is every reason to assume that Jesus regarded the Law as God-given. But, to quote Montefiore again: "If you believe that the Law was divine, you believed that it was all divine, and not only a few sentences here and there; you took the Law at its own valuation." [109] Montefiore's complaint that "some commentators do not seem to understand what divineness of the Law means" is well justified.[110]

It appears to us that the whole problem concerning the Law must be placed against a wider issue. We would deny that the central point in the controversy between Jesus and his opponents was concerning the permanency of the Law. This was only a side-issue, by way of implication. It became a burning problem at a somewhat later stage between the Church and the Synagogue. But the main point at issue between Jesus and the authorities was on a different plane. Here we concur with Prof. Schoeps' view.[110a] It centred round the person of Jesus himself. Before we enter upon this vital question, there is still one point to be considered.

(d) The teaching of Jesus

Jewish scholars have emphatically affirmed the utter Jewishness of Jesus. They have, with great patience, collected abundant material to prove the close connexion between Jesus and Judaism. This led to the conclusion that the subject-matter of Jesus' teaching contained nothing new for the Synagogue.[111] Abraham Geiger, in his essay *Das Judentum und seine Geschichte* had already pointed to this fact. To Geiger, Jesus was a Pharisee "with Galilean colouring, a man who shared in the hope of his age and who believed that hope fulfilled in his person. In no way did he utter a new thought and he also never broke the national barriers".[112]   Almost all Jewish writers of more recent date hold a similar view.   An extreme example is Paul Goodman. Mr. Goodman tells us that: "It can be safely asserted, without any attempt to depreciate his greatness, that there was no utterance, however striking or characteristic, emanating from Jesus (with the sole exception of the idea of non-resistance) which cannot be traced often in identical words to the teachings of the Jewish schools." [113]   Even Montefiore, who is characteristically cautious in his judgments, finds it difficult to detect new elements in the teaching of Jesus unknown to the Judaism of his time: "If we ask wherein his hearers found the teaching of Jesus new, inspired, prophetic . . . it is not quite easy to reply." [114]   This statement is the more important when we remember that of all Jewish writers, Montefiore shows the most earnest desire to appreciate the significance of Jesus.   He warns against the Jewish tendency of depreciating his originality, and contends that the teaching of Jesus must be taken as a whole, and thus it will prove to be more than a mere dissected list of injunctions.[115]   He admits that in comparing Talmud and Gospels "the originality is almost always on the side of the Gospels".[116]   But, for all that, there is no *actual* difference between Jesus and the Rabbis.   Montefiore thus concludes: "My verdict would be that Jesus unites himself with the *very* best Rabbinic teaching of his own and of later times. It is, perhaps, only in trenchantness and eager insistency that he goes beyond it.   There is a fire, a passion, an intensity, a broad and deep positiveness about these verses (Lk. 6. 27 ff.) which is new." [117]   It is thus not the subject-matter of his doctrine but the spirit of Jesus which distinguishes him from the Rabbis: it is heroic, ethical, compelling to action.   But it also contains "a remarkable blend" of "the higher selfishness and the highest unselfishness"; it shows signs of a double ethic.[118] The originality of Jesus is thus to be sought in his attitude and bearing rather than in novelty of doctrine.   "It was in these more undefinable and subtler ways that the teaching, like the bearing, of Jesus was new, inspired, prophetic, rather than in any novelty of doctrine in any one definite particular." [119]   To Montefiore, therefore, the significance of the New Testament lies in that it corrects and supplements "sometimes more fully, sometimes more brilliantly, sometimes with fresh illumination and from a novel point of view" what was already in the possession of Rabbinic Judaism. "But it does not, for the most part, contain what we, from our liberal Jewish point of view, can regard as *completely new* doctrine which is also *true* doctrine." [120]

Orthodox Jewish writers are even more emphatic in asserting Jesus' dependence upon Judaism. Loewe, who at first admitted an element of novelty in Jesus' conception of faith, on second thoughts retracted. He holds that the conception of faith we meet in the Gospels is a regression to a more primitive stage in Israel's development. It is a faith based upon miracles and upheld by the desire for direct answer to prayer. The Rabbis were less primitive in their views. In this respect, they stood above Jesus.[121]

It is, however, admitted that there existed points of difference between Jesus and the Pharisees, though I. M. Wise and Ziegler deny such a possibility. They both protest against the idea that "the noble ethical teachings of Jesus could have been the cause of his fall".[122] It is Ziegler's conviction that neither Pharisees nor Sadducees could have possibly objected to the teaching of Jesus: "The ideals of Jesus were public property (Gemeingut) of Jewish thought-life (Gedankenleben) originating from the old Prophets. . . . He who admires the Sermon on the Mount, admires Judaism, admires Jewish ethics." [123] It is for this reason that Ziegler holds the Herodians solely responsible for the death of Jesus.[124]

Klausner enumerates several points which mark the difference between Jesus and the Pharisees. (1) While to Jesus the near approach of the Kingdom was the main burden of his message, to the Scribes and Pharisees it was only of secondary importance. (2) While the Scribes and Pharisees laid equal stress upon the ceremonial and moral laws, Jesus singled out the moral laws as of greater importance. (3) Whereas for the Scribes and Pharisees the exposition of Scripture was of basic importance, "Jesus relied but slightly on Scripture, wrapping up his teaching altogether in parable form". (4) While to the Pharisees the teaching was of primary importance and miracles only secondary, to Jesus "teaching and miracles possessed equal importance".[125]

On examination it soon becomes evident that none of Klausner's points explains fully the breach between Jesus and the religious authorities. On his own evidence, three points reveal only a difference of emphasis. Point (2), the most likely to cause friction, is also eliminated by Klausner's assertion that Jesus did not try to abolish the ceremonial laws. For all that, Klausner is aware of an important division between Jesus and the Pharisees. It is here that the weakest point of his contention appears. We are told that "the Pharisees objected to Jesus' behaviour—his disparagement of many ceremonial laws, his contempt of the words of the 'sages' and his consorting with publicans and ignorant folk and doubtful women. They [*i.e.* the Pharisees] considered his miracles sorcery and his Messianic claims effrontery". "Yet with all that", Klausner continues, "*he was one of themselves*: his convinced belief in the Day of Judgement, and the resurrection of the dead, the Messianic age and the kingdom of heaven, was a distinctly Pharisaic belief; he taught nothing which, by the rules of the Pharisees, rendered him criminally guilty." [126]

Klausner thus reveals an indecisive position in which Jesus and the Pharisees appear friends and enemies at the same time: they have much in common, but they also greatly differ. Psychologically impossible is his suggestion that the Pharisees whom he himself calls the enemies of Jesus, withdrew at the critical moment, leaving his trial in the hands of the irritated Sadducees. Such a supposition is necessitated by the determination to exonerate the Pharisees at all costs.

There can be little doubt that Jewish criticism has had a salutary effect upon the natural tendency to reduce the importance of Jesus to the originality of his teaching. In this way Jewish scholars have helped considerably to rectify an old established notion. It is still held in certain quarters that the significance of Jesus lay in the new values which he taught. Dr. G. Hollmann thus tells us that Jesus brought about "a complete change of value in the decisive, fundamental factors" of Judaism. He explains that before the time of Jesus, Judaism "oscillated dubiously between two extremes. There was no certainty of salvation".[127] Jewish writers have vigorously protested against such affirmations. In view of this situation, it is no longer possible to insist upon the absolute novelty of the teaching of Jesus.

This brings us to the question of the nature of Jesus' mission. It is sometimes held that his aim was the reformation of Judaism.

According to this view, Jesus was essentially a moral reformer. He never intended to replace Judaism or to break away from it. His aim was "reform and not abolition".[128] His quarrel with Pharisaism was not because of its refusal to accept his doctrine but because the Pharisees "failed to live up to the truth they already possessed".[129] Dr. Parkes finds proof for his assertions in the following facts: Jesus accepted the Torah as Divine revelation; he visited the synagogues and preached in them; his teaching in so far as it was connected with the past "was Pharisaic in character"; Jesus and the Pharisees shared the same ideals; and, finally, Jesus never rejected Judaism nor the Jews. On these grounds Dr. Parkes sees reason to maintain that Jesus, like the other prophets, stood in the main stream of Judaism, and that he never intended "either to supersede or to reject the religion of Israel".[130] This, however, opens once again the question as to the reason for the conflict between Jesus and the Synagogue. Dr. Parkes explains it by the attested rule that "the prophet is not accepted by the regular authorities of established religious institutions, and that reform in religion comes slowly".[131]

Some of Dr. Parkes' conclusions deserve full acknowledgement, especially his insistence upon the continuity of Jewish tradition in the New Testament. But though Parkes tries to guard himself against the charge "that the whole mission of Jesus was simply to reform certain abuses in Pharisaism", he has not succeeded in preventing such a conclusion.

Against Dr. Parkes' assertion that "nothing in the teaching of Jesus made necessary the separation between Judaism and Christianity",[132] we would place Klausner's maxim: *ex nihilo nihil fit*. We agree, however, that the main cause of friction was not connected with his teaching, which was basically Old Testament doctrine.

Dr. Parkes has failed to include in his considerations some important facts: (1) Jesus, by assuming the rôle of Messiah (a fact Dr. Parkes does not deny) set himself above the position of a prophet; (2) Jesus, as Messiah, knew himself to be inaugurating the Messianic age; his intentions must have therefore been different from that of a reformer. (3) Pharisaism is not the only offshoot of Old Testament religion. This is a fallacy which has obscured the vision of many writers. The question, therefore, whether Jesus intended to separate himself from Judaism is fallacious.   It presupposes that Rabbinic Judaism in New Testament times was the sole heir of Old Testament tradition.   Jewish writers have vigorously asserted that Pharisaism is the only legitimate offspring of the prophetic tradition and the direct heir of the Hebrew Bible.   It has retained its original purity and "has no Greek strand" like Christianity.[133]   L. I. Finkelstein goes so far as to assert that half the world derives its faith from the Pharisaic tradition.[134]   The final argument for the truth of Pharisaism is usually seen in the fact of its survival.   But it may be questioned whether Rabbinic Judaism continued in a straight line the Hebrew tradition.   In the New Testament period, representing the last stages of the formative process of Judaism, there still existed a parallel tradition closely related to the Prophets of the Old Testament.   Prof. Burkitt maintains with good reason that Christianity and Judaism are both two daughters of what he calls "Old-Judaism".[135]   Christianity has as much a claim upon heirship as Judaism has, unless spiritual rights are narrowed down to physical descent.   Whether Jesus belonged to Judaism of the strictly Rabbinic type may be doubted.   But that the Pharisees and Jesus had much in common is now a well established fact.   It is not here that we can find the reason for the cleavage which finally led to the Crucifixion.

An interesting attempt to solve the puzzle was recently made by Vladimir G. Simkhovitch.   He views the struggle between Jesus and the Jewish authorities from the angle of the political situation.   To Simkhovitch "the great and fundamental cleavage was constituted by Christ's non-resistance to Rome".   But because this could not be used as an accusation against him, other charges had to be invented.[136]   This explains why Pilate tried to save Jesus.   Simkhovitch takes up the traditional line that Jesus aimed at a religious revival.   This, however, clashed with the prevailing political sentiment and also constituted an offence to organized religion.[137]   Prof. Simkhovitch, however, does not mean to imply that Jesus remained indifferent to the political situation.   He resented Roman aggression and the humiliating position of his people.   But using deep spiritual insight, Jesus understood that "the balm for that burning humiliation was humility.   For humility cannot be humiliated. . . .   Thus he asked his people to learn from him".[138]   Contrary to the general Jewish expectation, Jesus understood the Kingdom of Heaven as an inward change.   "The great trouble was that Christ was teaching an insight, preaching ideas, while the people could only understand things." [139] For Prof. Simkhovitch, Jesus' teaching reveals an "overwhelming intellectual system" of unusual grandeur, which only modern man can grasp in all its significance.[140] To men of his own days, Jesus' views presented an offence which inevitably led up to his Crucifixion.

No doubt Prof. Simkhovitch has given expression to some profound truths, especially in his concluding paragraphs. Mere misunderstanding, however, does not fully explain the violence of the conflict. We know that Sadducean sentiment was, within limits, pro-Roman. The Pharisaic party, or a section of it, was steering clear of political conspiracy. Though it must be admitted that the passivity of the Pharisees in the great struggle has been over-emphasized.[141] Israel Abrahams rightly holds that there were definite limits for Pharisaic conformity to Roman demands.[142] This is borne out by the picture Josephus draws of the Pharisees [143] and also by the connection between the Pharisaic party and the Zealots.[144] But the answer to Prof. Simkhovitch is contained in the fact that the Gospels unanimously present a definite religious conflict with almost no political implications. It is for this reason that Klausner bitterly resents the "other-worldliness" of Jesus.[145]

In this connexion Louis Finkelstein's theory may be mentioned. Dr. Finkelstein views Judæan history from the angle of a social struggle between the "plebeian" and "patrician" elements of Jewish society. He regards Christianity as a country movement directed against the urban population, whom the peasants viewed with suspicion, confusing "the social grace of the trader with dissembling and hypocrisy".[146] H. Loewe accepts Finkelstein's theory as the most satisfactory for explaining certain religious and social problems connected with the rise of Christianity.[147] It is certainly striking that Jesus' greatest success and best support were associated with the provinces, especially Galilee, and that his closest followers were countryfolk and not townspeople. But the natural antipathies between town and country would have little influence upon the struggle between Jesus and the Pharisees, who were, according to Finkelstein, predominantly townspeople. Class-consciousness does not appear to have been a decisive factor in the early Christian movement.

Prof. James Moffatt has drawn attention to the novelty which the ministry of teaching as practised by Jesus must have presented to the Jews, as this was not usually associated with the Messianic function.[148]   It is obvious, however, that the practice could have constituted no offence, as the democracy of the Synagogue admitted free expression of views, provided these views were in agreement with the great principles of Judaism.   It is generally held, as we have already seen, that Jesus' teaching was not opposed to Judaism.

We are thus driven to the conclusion that Jesus' teaching in itself could have been no sufficient reason for the deep cleavage between him and the authorities.   Prof. W. Manson has shown that though parallels to the teaching of Jesus may be found in Rabbinic literature and among the heathen moralists, nowhere can be found "the same rigour either in the formulation or in the application".[149]   But if we understand Prof. Manson aright, it is not the subject-matter forming the substance of Jesus' teaching which marks him as the Messiah, but rather the *realism* "with which the sovereignty or kingdom of God is brought home to men".   It is thus that men confronting Jesus found themselves in a crisis, facing the supreme demand of the Kingdom which Jesus represented in his own person.   Prof. Manson, therefore, insists that the ethic of Jesus is the ethic of the Kingdom.[150] The Sermon on the Mount is neither a moral code nor the expression of an utopian *Weltanschauung*, but rather an "existential summons to our spirit, by which we are called primarily not to thought but to action; and to action *vis-à-vis* with God".[151]

The ultimate reason for the friction between Jesus and the authorities, therefore, is not to be sought in a divergence of views on matters of doctrine.   The background of the struggle is the claim to unique authority underlying the words and actions of Jesus Christ.   It is a mistake to define the significance of Jesus in terms of abstract truth.   "His coming", says Principal Curtis, "was not simply to give to mankind by his actions and character an example, and by his words a teaching or a rule of guidance, but through both media a Spirit.   The life he lived, the things he said, combine to embody the Truth he was. . . ."[152]

(e) *The claims of Jesus*

Most scholars are agreed that Jesus made extraordinary claims. Jewish scholars readily accept the view that Jesus made the claim to Messiahship.   The crucial question is whether the exaggerated claims connected with that office were made by Jesus himself or by later generations; in other words: what meaning did *Jesus* attach to the function and person of the Messiah?

It may be said at the outset of our inquiry that an unbiased answer is almost impossible. An attempt to give an objective answer deduced from a critical study of New Testament sources must fail, for these sources, however critically examined, are in themselves biased. Whatever importance we assign to Q, it is nothing else than a *Christian* document.[153] There is no other evidence outside the Christian tradition which could throw light upon our problem. It must be remembered that the various answers offered by scholars are merely a reflection of their own convictions. For it is at this critical point that we are left to our own intuition. In this connexion it may be interesting to note Albert Schweitzer's remark: "There can be no more personal historical enterprise than the writing of a Life-of-Jesus."[154] There is great truth in E. Hermann's statement that the character of every individual mind that approaches the person of Jesus leaves an infallible stamp upon the great Portrait: "Renan's Jesus reveals Renan more than Jesus. Hausrath's Jesus is the wise and benignant rabbi, emitting brilliant aphorisms which strike home even to the *blasé* mind of the nineteenth century; and there we have Hausrath's own somewhat amateurish and shallow mind. For Matthew Arnold, Christ is sweetness and light. . . . Caird's Jesus is a poetical Hegelian; Seeley's, a moralist touched with emotion."[155]

It is thus natural that Jewish scholars should offer an answer from their own point of view. It is characteristic of Jewish historical realism that most scholars affirm Jesus' claim to Messiahship: "The peculiarity of Jewish research shows itself in that almost without exception Jesus is looked upon as the pretender to Messiahship. Without this Messianic consciousness of Jesus, his history and its consequences would according to the Jewish view remain a puzzle."[156] The best Jewish scholars, like Montefiore and Klausner, have firmly held to this view.[157] But they differ considerably as to the nature of the claims which Jesus made in connection with his Messianic mission. Montefiore asks: "Did he call himself Son of Man, and what did he mean by the appellation? Did he regard himself as the Son of God in some unique special sense which could be applied to none other than himself? Had God entrusted him with powers such as he had entrusted to none after him again? And had he these powers given him because he was not only human, but divine?"[158] It is clear to Montefiore that Jesus made extensive claims: "Jesus as the Messiah *in posse* felt that he possessed greater power, and claimed a more personal allegiance, than any prophet before him."[159]   He also attached a unique significance to his own person: he believed he stood in an important personal relation to the Kingdom of God.[160]   "A deduction of this kind from the Synoptic records does not appear to be unwarranted." But granted all this, Montefiore holds that the claims recorded in the New Testament were not Jesus' claims, but were made on his behalf: "Yet so far as we can judge, his estimate of his own power, and of his relation to God, was gradually intensified by the sources and the editors."[161]

Montefiore, in admitting that Jesus made unique claims, goes further than most Jewish scholars.   Klausner refuses to believe that Jesus could have made any extraordinary claims, apart from the claim to Messiahship.   Evidence for this Klausner finds in Jesus' use of the phrase *ben-adam*, which occurs, according to him, not in its technical sense, but instead of the pronoun "I"; its meaning being simply "man", "without any qualification or specific intention".[162]   A similar view is taken by Herbert Loewe: "I do not believe that Jesus called himself 'son of God' in a sense different from 'children are ye to the Lord your God' (Deut. 14. 1), that he rejected the Law, or that he did or said anything that a good Jew in that environment and in that age would have abhorred.   For example, I do not believe that he claimed a mystic or supernatural power to forgive sins, in spite of Mk. 2. 10–12."[163]   That such opinion is utterly subjective and devoid of historic support can be seen from the striking plea made by Montefiore.   Admitting that Jesus "may have regarded obedience to his commands as equivalent to the doing of God's will", he is determined that "Jewish admirers will cling to the hope that he did not believe that he was a better, wiser man, with a fuller knowledge of God, than anybody who had ever lived".[164] This is indeed a fine example of *wishful* thinking.   What if the *historic* Jesus did not fulfil modern Jewish hopes?

Dr. J. K. Mozley in his book *The Heart of the Gospel* has a striking paragraph which deserves quoting in full: "Is the Son of Man who forgives sins, who overrides the Law of the Sabbath, who gives his life a ransom for many, who shall come to judge in glory, and sit upon his Throne, so much less than the message which he brings that really he is quite outside it?" And he continues: "Of course it is tremendous—far more so than we often realize—that Jesus should have spoken in this way, and I think I can understand how scholars like Bousset are drawn to reject such sayings as reflecting the mind of the later Church read back into the words of Jesus. But to understand is not to justify." [165] However biased Dr. Mozley's opinion may appear to the critical mind of a modern scholar, it has the merit of possessing the whole weight of the New Testament evidence on its side. Jewish writers have sometimes made ingenious efforts to shift at least some of that evidence in support of their own theory. Thus H. P. Chajes has tried to make out that "ἐξουσία" in Mt. 7. 29, goes back to misreading the Hebrew *bemashal* to mean *kemoshel*, which is to say that, instead of "he taught as one having authority", the original text must have read, "he taught in parable".[166] Another example is S. Schechter's suggestion that ἠκούσατε . . . Ἐγὼ δὲ λέγω ὑμῖν is a translation of the Rabbinic formula *shome'a ani . . . talmud lomer* where *shome'a ani* means "I might hear" or "one might hear", that is to say "one might be mistaken in pressing the literal sense of the verses in question too closely": therefore *talmud lomer* "there is a teaching to say that the words must not be taken in such a sense".[167] This would explain, in Schechter's view, how Jesus could have declared in the same breath his attachment to the Torah and have quoted passages to show its inferiority. "The formula being a strictly Rabbinic idiom" was rendered inaccurately by a Greek translator. But if Schechter were right, the whole *pointe* of Mt. 5. 21 ff. would have lost much of its power and the impression upon the crowd (Mt. 7. 29) could not have been so profound. Montefiore rightly observes that such an explanation "is unsuitable for the last two, and rather awkward though not impossible for the middle two examples".[168] The fact remains that according to the Gospels, Jesus claimed extraordinary privileges and exceptional authority. This is the impression conveyed on almost every page. Montefiore, with his usual scholarly honesty, admits that the Synoptic records warrant the deduction that: "Jesus was not mere herald or prophet of the Kingdom, such as John. He was more than a prophet. . . ." [169] It is the "more" which conceals the mystery, but also gives a clue to the riddle why Jesus met with opposition and a cruel death.

The Roman Catholic writer André Charue, like A. T. Robertson, strongly opposes the view prevalent amongst modern scholars that the Gospels represent a false picture of Pharisaism.   Charue, like most orthodox writers, agrees that there were saints amongst the Pharisees, but on the whole the portrait in the Gospels faithfully reflects the truth about the Pharisaic character.   Charue appeals to Josephus and quotes the authority of P. de Grandmaison.[170]   On the other hand, there is the whole weight of modern scholarship in defence of a misrepresented and a misunderstood religion.   Chwolson's plea has ever since been the plea of many Gentile and most Jewish scholars: "The Pharisees had no cause for the persecution of Jesus as on the whole his and their teaching stood not in opposition but in full harmony to each other." [171]   Orthodox Christian writers fall back upon the authority of the New Testament.   Jewish writers appeal to Rabbinic literature.   To find a solution many explanations have been proposed, none satisfactory.   The reason for this failure lies in the desire to fit Jesus into a preconceived theory: to modernize him and to present him as an acceptable figure to men of his age.   Thus the possibility that Jesus made unusual claims for himself is from the start ruled out as improbable.

After careful examination, we are driven to the conclusion that the opposition which Jesus met was not specifically actuated by political motives on the part of the Sadducees.   It was also not called forth by any provocative teaching or behaviour on the part of Jesus in opposition to the Pharisees.   Even in the case of the Law, Jesus was no mere revolutionary.   There is much truth in J. Gresham Machen's statement to the effect that "there is definite reason to suppose that he (Jesus) observed the ceremonial Law as it is contained in the Old Testament, and definite utterances of his in support of the authority of the Law have been preserved in the Gospels".[172]   Chwolson rightly argues that the claim to Messiahship could have never constituted a capital offence in the eyes of the Pharisees.   Jesus could not have been classed as a *massit um-maddiah* nor as a *nabi ha-sheker*, as there is no trace of his inducing the people to idolatry.[173]   We must also recognize the justice of the plea of Jewish apologists that it is wrong to form a picture of Pharisaism solely on the Gospel evidence.   The fact is that Jesus does not attack the Pharisees *qua* Pharisees.   It is not that because they were Pharisees he was opposed to them.   There was nothing wrong in being a

Pharisee; on the contrary, the Pharisaic ideals were close to the heart and mind of Jesus.

H. Loewe finds it somewhat amusing that the Barthian "assault" upon the Pharisees is on the ground that they were good men.[174] But strange as such a view may seem to a Jewish Rabbi, there is more psychological and religious truth in Barth's perception of the case than would appear on the surface.[175]

Jesus does not criticize Pharisaism as an outsider. He stands right in the midst of Pharisaic life. His first concern was with the pious. The Pharisaic effort was the most heroic effort man could make. But such heroism involved great spiritual danger. It made for self-reliance and self-sufficiency: the publicans and the harlots entered the Kingdom before the just and the Pharisees.[176] The first shall be last and the last first is the recurring note of the Gospels. The elder son in the parable who was offended by the reception of his prodigal brother exhibits all the psychological reactions of the sincere and the pious. This has been re-enacted throughout the whole history of religious life in Church and Synagogue alike. Such is human nature. It is not a case of how good or how bad the Pharisees were: before the absolute demands of God, no human being holds his own. This is the burden of Paul's message. The danger is with the religious man who inevitably takes up the position of spiritual self-assertiveness. But Jesus said: Blessed are the humble in spirit, for theirs is the Kingdom of Heaven.[177] He knew himself sent not to the strong who need no physician, but to them that are sick: "I came not to call the righteous, but sinners." Montefiore is right, there is biting irony in these words.[178] The tragedy of the religious man is that he *knows* about his righteousness. Montefiore's constant contention is that there were pious, sincere, and righteous Pharisees. Indeed, judged by human standards, the Pharisees were the most noble section of Jewish society; but judged by the eternal standards of God, all men are under sin, there is none righteous, all are unprofitable, there is none that doeth good.[179] This levelling of all human prerogatives and the revaluation of all standards was the first cause of offence to the pious Pharisee.

The second cause of offence was Jesus' supreme claim. There can be no doubt that Jesus not only claimed to be the Messiah, which could have been no real offence to an Israelite, but that together with that claim he made demands and assumed an authority which were nothing short of blasphemy.[179a]   Those who came in immediate contact with the Master of Nazareth had to face the alternative: of either becoming disciples or opponents. The challenge which Jesus presented, pressed for decision.[180] It is only natural and psychologically explicable that the pious, those deeply concerned about God and his Law, should lead the opposition.   It could not have been otherwise.[181]   There is some truth in Montefiore's statement that both Pharisees and Jesus were right.   For the Pharisees to leave Jesus unchallenged would have been equal to complicity in the greatest offence— blasphemy.[182]   For Jesus to limit his message to the publicans and sinners would have been an offence against his Messianic consciousness.   As the Messiah, his first claim was upon the pious in Israel.   His first concern was with those who lived and hoped for the Kingdom of God.   Thus two loyalties have clashed, two rights have resulted in a bitter struggle.   The lesser right won, as it always wins.   But the defeat of Jesus was paradoxically a manifestation of his *greater* right.   Vladimir Simkhovitch well said: In the conflict between moment and eternity, the moment wins; [183] to this we would like to add: but eternity *ultimately* conquers.

Only seldom do Jewish scholars view the conflict between Jesus and the religious authorities as connected with the extraordinary claims he made.   The general tendency is to explain the struggle as a controversy centring round the validity, permanency, and holiness of the Law.[184]   This preoccupation with the Law is only natural, but has obscured the main issue.   In this, Pauline teaching and persistent Jewish reaction against it have been projected upon the person of Jesus.   But the real conflict between Jesus and the authorities, Sadducean or Pharisaic, as the case may be, was not of an academic nature.   It was personal. The offence laid to the charge of Jesus was his claim—as already said, not the claim to Messiahship, which in itself was no offence, but the claim to unique authority.   Such claim the pious Jew could only repudiate.   That this was so is sufficiently borne out by the Synoptic evidence.   It appears to us that the Johannine Gospel betrays an apologetic interest in laying stress on the claim to supreme authority on the part of Jesus.   The whole controversy with the Jews seems to turn round the question of ἐξουσία.   It thus adds another genuine feature in its presentation of certain historical facts.   It is of psychological importance

that this claim to supreme authority constituted an offence not
only to the leaders of Judaism but to many others throughout the
ages.   For it is at this point that the last decision is made concerning the Man of Nazareth.

Jesus' claims were extensive and unusual, they revolved round
the significance and the authority of the Messiah.   There
is a certain truth in Dr. Lee Woolf's contention that Jesus' interpretation of Messiahship exceeded those of popular expectancy.[185]   But Dr. Woolf is hardly justified on this account in
detaching the authority of Jesus from his Messianic office.   He
does it on the grounds that Jesus refused to be the Messiah in
the traditional sense.   But, we would ask, how does Dr. Lee
Woolf know that?   His only evidence lies embedded in the
Gospel accounts, but is it not so that, in spite of all the secrecy
surrounding Jesus' Messiahship, our records are intent on con-
veying the impression that he *was the Messiah*?   To detach the
authority of Jesus from his Messianic office and to transfer it to
his own self-consciousness seems to us unwarranted.   It is a
suggestion which may have far-reaching consequences if thought
out to the end.   Dr. Woolf says that Jesus became the Messiah
not by virtue of an external "call" but through an inner experience.   This may be so; in the last resort it is futile to attempt
an explanation as to the nature of "experience" the Messiah
may undergo.   When, however, Dr. Lee Woolf maintains that
the Messiahship of Jesus was "born of his own soul, through his
own communion with God", and that consequently Jesus'
ministry was not a "conferred rôle" but a self-assumed vocation,
he lays himself open to grave objections.   Such a presentation of
the case puts Jesus under the suspicion of arbitrariness and subjectivity.[186]   It actually defeats Dr. Woolf's own ends, for the
Church has always held that Jesus, by virtue of his Sonship, was
the Messiah, and not because he thought himself to be the Messiah
did he become the Son of God (Adoptionism).[187]   We would,
therefore, maintain that Jesus derived his claim to supreme
authority from his office.   It was this that turned the controversy into a personal issue.   A compromise became impossible:
either he was right in his claim, then the only answer was submission; or he was wrong, then he committed blasphemy.

It is important that at an early stage of Christian history
Jesus came to be called "Lord" by his disciples.   This has been
vigorously denied, notably by Bousset, who contends that the

title "Lord" is of Gentile origin and was never used by the primitive Church in Jerusalem.[188]   To this may be added Dalman's evidence which would go to prove that on Palestinian soil the title "Lord" was nothing more than "a term of deferential homage".[189]   Κύριος would therefore, in most cases of Synoptic tradition, lead back to the Aramaic form of *mari* or *marana*.   But Machen has shown with considerable force that at least in a few instances, the Synoptic Gospels imply by the use of the word more than mere reverence.[190]   From Acts, but especially from the Pauline Epistles, it is clear that the Lordship of Jesus was an early and universally accepted doctrine of the Church. Moreover, the use of the Aramaic phrase "Maranatha" by Paul points to the Hebrew Christian community in Palestine, thus discrediting the theory which associates the term only with Gentile Christianity.[191]   Such an appellation reveals the extraordinary authority exercised by Jesus.   In that the early Church called Jesus "Lord", it acknowledged his claims and submitted to them.   It was this that characterized the *believers* and singled them out from among the other Jews.

(f) The continuation of the struggle

The opposition which Jesus met, and which finally led to the Cross, did not cease after his death.   It passed on as a legacy from the Master to the disciples.   It could not have been otherwise: the Synagogue rejected Jesus, and, because it rejected Jesus, it consequently had to reject the movement which was associated with his name.   The stronger Christian influence grew upon Jewish society, the stronger grew also the opposition of Judaism towards the Church.

The Messianic movement which centred round the person of Jesus was later continued by his disciples, spreading with remarkable rapidity upon Jewish soil.   It soon reached the Jewish Diaspora, and found ready acceptance among the semi-Hellenized communities abroad.   The fact that Hellenistic Judaism showed more response to Christianity than Palestinian Judaism would refute the theory proposed by Montefiore and accepted by Parkes, that "the Judaism which Paul opposed to his Christianity was *not* Rabbinic Judaism"; but the Judaism which Paul knew, *i.e.* that of the Diaspora.[192]

There is reason to suppose that the national disaster of A.D. 70 increased the influence of the Christians.   The frustration which followed the fall of Jerusalem and the destruction of the Temple gave the Hebrew Christians a new impulse and provided them with a new weapon: the calamity was interpreted as God's punishment for the rejection of the Messiah. Such reasoning must have made a deep impression upon the perturbed minds of many Jews.[193] It is possible that a trace of it is still preserved in a strange passage of the Talmud which explains the destruction of the second Temple *mipne sinat ḥinnam* (because of undeserved hatred).[194] R. Johanan ben Tortha, who lived about A.D. 110, must have in some way received this tradition from Hebrew Christian sources. The phrase which goes back to Ps. 35. 19 strikingly reminds one of Jn. 15. 25: Ὅτι ἐμίσησάν με δωρεάν, which Delitzsch translates *sinat ḥinnam seneuni*.[195] Hebrew Christian influence upon Jewish society increased to such an extent as to cause apprehension amongst the Rabbis. This is evident from the countermeasures taken: active persecution, alterations in the liturgy, introduction of the *Birkat ha-minim*, and calumniation of the person of Jesus.

(i) PERSECUTION

Rabbi Ignaz Ziegler, who attributes to Paul alone the creation of Christianity, admits that persecution began with the appearance of the Pauline party. Saul accomplished what the other Apostles would have never even attempted—the removal of the Law. "This caused the breach" between Judaism and the Antinomian movement led by Paul, his friends, and his successors.[196] The Jews have taken up the challenge and have fought the new heresy with all available means. Ziegler adds: "I would have been ashamed of my ancestors even to this day had they in thoughtless cowardice failed to make use of every means in the fight against their enemy."[197] This frank admission needs only one correction: persecution did not begin with the appearance of Paul: it began with Jesus. But, no doubt, Paul's attitude to the Law and the Gentile world must have provided a new stimulus.

Evidence of definite hostility towards Jesus and his disciples is to be found in the whole New Testament literature. The impression the Gospels try to convey is that the Messianic movement initiated by Jesus was bitterly opposed by an important section of the Jewish community. That opposition developed into violent hatred, causing the death of the Master and endangering the lives of his disciples. When Paul entered the Church, he entered as a former *persecutor*. How this fact could have escaped the attention of Dr. Ziegler is not easy to explain.[198] Israel Abrahams, who discusses the question of Jewish persecution directed against Christianity more fully, shows with good reason that it was mainly a measure of self-defence and that it was directed against Hebrew Christianity only. As to Gentile Christianity, the Synagogue was not vitally concerned with it, at any rate, not "until the organized Church had become imperial and was in a position and displayed the will to persecute the Synagogue". Until then, "Christianity as such was not the object of much attention, still less of attack." [199] Abrahams admits, however, a certain measure of persecution, but thinks that "the protagonists of a new movement, and their heirs and historians in later ages, are always inclined to mistake opposition for persecution". His main point of emphasis is upon Jewish lack of interest in Gentile Christianity. He therefore contests Harnack's affirmation that the Jews were the main source of anti-Christian activity and the instigators of persecution.[200] However the case may be with regard to Gentile Christianity, and after careful examination of the arguments on both sides, Harnack's opinion seems psychologically more justifiable and, though some of his remarks are based on conjecture, there can be no doubt about the Synagogue's attitude to Hebrew Christianity. If Abrahams questions the historicity of some of the New Testament passages recording persecution on the part of the Jews, there is ample evidence from Rabbinic literature to establish the case. To use Abrahams' own words: "The Jewish sources have a good deal to say about Christians, but almost invariably it is *Jewish Christians* that are the object of castigation."

The attitude of Judaism towards Hebrew Christianity must be viewed from the angle of national emergency. Prior to A.D. 70 the Messianic movement was looked upon as another kind of heresy; but after that date, and especially after the Bar Cochba incident, a new element came into play. The Jewish people, deprived of its national life, could not afford to its members freedom of conviction without endangering its national existence. To preserve a small religious minority surrounded on every side by hostile nations was a task which only the ingenuity of the Synagogue could accomplish. Christianity, with its universalistic outlook and supra-national tendency, constituted a menace to the integrity of Jewish life. Hebrew Christianity was a breach in the walls of nationalism, opening wide the doors to assimilation. Opposition, therefore, towards Jewish Christianity tended to grow in violence in proportion to the worsening of the Jewish national position. In the end it became relentless and uncompromising. The weapons the Synagogue used were social ostracism, religious excommunication, and every other form of suppression.[201]

All that the Talmud has to say about the Jewish attitude to the *minim* primarily relates to Hebrew Christians.[202] The rules laid down aim at a complete separation from those in any way suspect of that heresy. These rules are severe, almost ruthless, but have probably never found full application in actual life.[203] Thus, a *min* was to be treated worse than a heathen. Nobody was to sell to him; nobody was to buy from him. No business transactions were made with him. His son was not to be taught a profession. Medical treatment was not to be accepted from him. He was to be regarded as a renegade and traitor, who is not helped in need and whose life may be exposed to danger.[204]

The books of the *minim* were not to be rescued from fire, though the name of God is to be found in them; but R. Jose the Galilean (*circa* A.D. 110) suggests that if the burning of the *gilionim* takes place on a week-day, the name of God may be cut out.[205] Meat slaughtered by a *min* was to be regarded as if purposed for idol sacrifice; his bread like that of a Samaritan;[206] his wine as if destined for idols; his fruit as untithed; his books as books of sorcerers; and his children as bastards.[207]

(ii) LITURGICAL ALTERATIONS

R. Travers Herford, in a short essay on the separation of Christianity from Judaism, says: "Judaism was hardly at all affected by the rise and separation of Christianity, except while the process was going on."[208] This process Herford puts as covering a period of about fifty years: "It began with the ministry of Jesus and it ended when the declaration against the *minim* (Jewish Christians) was officially made by the assembly of Rabbis at Jabneh, in the year 80 or thereabouts."[209] But actually, the process of separation covered a much longer period and its influence upon Judaism was considerable. In fact, the whole stress of the Synagogue since that time was upon those features of Judaism which emphasized its difference from the new faith. It is true that the Synagogue's opposition was directed not only against Christianity but also against gnostic and other heresies. Moore makes it abundantly clear that Judaism was not only opposed to the Christian weakening of the Unity of God, but to every kind of dualism which was "in the atmosphere of philosophical and religious thought".[210]   But the Synagogue's chief antagonists were the Hebrew Christians; we owe the emphasis of this fact to Herford's thorough labours in his valuable book on Christianity in Talmud and Midrash.   Herford rightly says that the Hebrew Christians "were the class of heretics most likely to be affected by regulations concerning the liturgy to be used in worship.   No doubt other heretics would be detected if any such were present; but the Jewish Christians were the most important".[211]   The above quotation refers to *Mishnah Megillah* iv. 8 and similar passages, where it is laid down how to detect the presence of a *min*.   The Hebrew Christians naturally visited the Synagogues, participated in the services, took part in the discussions, and based their arguments upon Scripture.   Thus we hear of a certain *min* who used to plague R. Joshua b. Levi with questions about the interpretation of Scriptural texts.[212]   Indeed, the controversy between Judaism and Christianity was, to a large extent, of an exegetical nature.   Characteristic is the case of R. Simlai, an eminent Haggadist who lived in Palestine and Galilee, and who engaged in many controversies with Jewish Christians.[213]   Prominent amongst the christological proof-texts were the passages which indicated a plurality in the Godhead: the word *Elohim* in Gen. 1, and Deut. 4. 32—the recurring question put to the Rabbis was, how many divine personalities were responsible for the creation of the world?   Who assisted God in the creation of man (Gen. 1. 26)?   What is the meaning of the threefold name of God in Jos. 22. 22; Ps. 50. 1?   What is the meaning of *Elohim kedoshim* in Jos. 24. 19?   What is the meaning of *Elohim kerobim* in Deut. 4. 7? etc.[214]   Other questions under constant discussion were as to the time of the coming of the Messiah, and the Resurrection from the dead.[215]

An amusing story is attached to the name of R. Safra.   R. Abbahu (*circa* A.D. 300) recommended him to the *minim* as a great scholar.   R. Safra was therefore exempt from paying taxes for thirteen years.[216]   One day the *minim* on meeting the Rabbi said to him: "It is written, 'You only have I known from all the families of the earth, therefore I will visit upon you all your iniquities' (Am. 3. 2).   If one is angry does one vent it on one's friend?" The Rabbi could not answer; so they wound a scarf round his neck and began to torture him. When Abbahu came, he asked why they were thus treating him, to which they replied: "Have you not told us that he is a great man? He cannot explain to us the meaning of this verse!" R. Abbahu explained: "I may have told you (that he was learned) in Tannaitic teaching; did I tell you (he was learned) in Scripture?" The *minim* then inquired how he himself knew the answer to their question. Abbahu replied: "We who are frequently with you, set ourselves to the task of studying it (*i.e.* Scriptures) thoroughly, but others do not study it as carefully." [217] Herford places the incident in the beginning of the fourth century. R. Abbahu, was the disciple of R. Jochanan and lived in Cæsarea. R. Safra was a Babylonian. Herford does not think there is sufficient ground for dismissing the story as a fiction. He is also convinced that the *minim* here are Hebrew Christians. However the case may be, the frank admission of R. Abbahu that the *minim* forced the Rabbis to a more thorough study of Scripture, throws much light upon Jewish reaction to Christianity. This took the form of eliminating passages from the Synagogue worship which might give support to the *minim* for their interpretation; of *reinterpreting* texts with a Messianic tradition; and of placing special emphasis upon the absolute humanity of the expected Messiah and the absolute unity of God. But the contact with Christianity was not without influence upon the Rabbis themselves. R. Abbahu, who seems to have acquired expert knowledge how to answer the many questions of the *minim*, and who plays so prominent a part in Jewish-Christian controversies, himself shows traces of Christian influence.[218]

Joël mentions some immediate effects upon Judaism as a result of the Jewish-Christian controversy:

(1) The omission of the Decalogue in the daily Services (*Ber*. 12a).

(2) The injunction to recite Num. 15. 37–41, morning *and evening* (*Ber*. 12b).

(3) The prohibition of the use of the LXX.[219]

(1) *Mishnah Tamid* (v. 1) records that the Ten Commandments, together with the Shema and several other passages of Scripture were daily recited in the Temple. This was also the custom in the Synagogue worship.[220] "But the custom was discontinued

in the Synagogues outside Jerusalem 'because of the cavilling of
the heretics, for they might say: These only were given to Moses
on Sinai' (*Ber.* 12a)."[221]   Thus the Decalogue was omitted
in order not to create the impression that it is singled out as of
greater importance than any of the other Commandments contained in the Torah.   But the whole case is wrapped up in
mystery and lacks an adequate explanation.   Finkelstein refers
to it as "the curious excision of the Decalogue".[222]   The crucial
question, of course, is, who were the *minim* who forced the
Synagogue to make so drastic a change?   They could not have
been Gentile Christians, for controversies with such would hardly
affect the Synagogue's liturgy.   They must have been Jews;
either Jewish Christians or other heretics.   In view of the fact
that the validity of the Law was the main issue between the
Church and the Synagogue, the heretics were obviously Hebrew
Christians.   This view is supported by the early date of the
change.   Finkelstein puts it as early as the middle of the first
century.   Oesterley and Box say that though it is impossible to
determine the exact date when the exclusion of the Decalogue
from the Liturgy was effected, "in all probability it was during
the first century A.D.".[223]   A. L. Knox suggests two reasons why
the Decalogue was withdrawn from public service: "in the first
instance the withdrawal took place in the synagogues of the
Dispersion as a precaution against blasphemous parodies",
by Gentile opponents.   The second reason being the "cavillings
of the heretics", as the Talmud explains.   Knox adds: "The
heretics here are, no doubt Christians."   But the writer seems to
imply that the excision of the Decalogue from the liturgy in the
Synagogues of the Diaspora was not directly effected by the
"cavillings of the heretics", but occurred at an earlier date "in
order to avoid the danger of blasphemy by Gentile opponents".[224]
Such a step, according to Knox, was prompted by the feeling of
special reverence towards the Decalogue in some Jewish circles.
It is, however, difficult to see how the danger of blasphemy
from outside could affect public worship *within* the Synagogue.
The fact that there existed an ancient Christian, though unorthodox, opinion, that the Decalogue was the original Law, and
that the rest of the Law was given as a punishment for the sin
of the Golden Calf,[225] together with the other fact that the Rabbis
stressed the validity of the *whole* law, even trying to prove by way
of *gematria* that the Decalogue "implied the whole Torah *plus*

the Rabbinic commands",[226] favours the argument that the decision was taken with the view of refuting Christians. Knox
cautiously accepts such a probability. It is, therefore, reasonable
to say that the excision of the Decalogue from Synagogue worship
was *primarily* dictated by apologetic reasons in the controversy
with Hebrew Christianity.[227] The later argument of the Gentile
Christians regarding the Decalogue was merely a clumsy elabora-
tion of an earlier view. The Decalogue played an important
part in early Christian thought. It is frequently referred to in
the Gospels. It is summarized by Paul in the law of love
(Rom. 13. 8ff.), it forms the background of the Didache. It is
only natural that later Christians, following Paul's example,
should see in the Decalogue the essence of the whole Law. The
section of Hebrew Christianity which refused to adhere to the
ceremonial law must have laid special emphasis upon the permanent validity of the Ten Commandments *only*. The fact that
there were Jewish Christians in greater numbers who took a
Pauline view of the Law is of far-reaching consequence.

(2) The second point mentioned by Joël is of less importance.
It concerns the last section of the *Shema* (Num. 15. 37-41).[228]
There seems to have been some difference of opinion whether it
was obligatory to recite this section in the evening as well as
in the morning. The *Mishnah* definitely enjoins that it be recited
in the evening also.[229] The case seems to have some connexion
with the controversy against the *minim*. This is also Joël's
opinion. In his view, the decision to recite Num. 15. 37-41,
morning *and* evening was taken, "in order that twice every day
one could submit to the yoke of the Law". Joël adds: "at all
events, the fathers (*die Alten*) saw in it an anti-Minean tendency",
and he points to *Berakot* 12b.[230] If Joël's be the correct explanation, this is another case where the dispute centres round the
validity of the *whole* Law.[231]

In this connection it may be mentioned that another ancient
custom underwent alteration because of the *minim*. It used to
be the practice to recite the Benediction: "Blessed be His name,
whose glorious Kingdom is for ever and ever", which follows
immediately after "Hear, O Israel, etc.", in a low voice. But
because of the *minim* this custom was abandoned. R. Abbahu
explains that in Nehardea (Babylonia), *i.e.* where there are no
minim, this doxology is still said in a whisper.[232] The reason for
this alteration is obvious: the suspicion arose that the *minim*

might take advantage of the occasion and insert a heretical prayer, or in the case of Christians, the name of Jesus the Messiah.[233]

(3) The main reason for the hostile attitude to the LXX lies in the fact that it provided the Christians with specific christo-logical arguments, and the many gnostic sects with a vast field for speculation. Together with the denunciation of the Greek text went an aversion to the Greek language. There is a pro-hibition to teach the Jewish youth Greek recorded in the *Mishnah* which dates back to *circa* A.D. 116.[234] Joël thinks of four further reasons which led the Rabbis to prohibit the Greek language and the Septuagint: (*a*) The LXX contained not only mistransla-tions (*Missverständnisse*) but also a number of spurious texts. This Joël bases upon Justin Martyr's accusation that the Jews have left out certain passages from Scripture.[235] (*b*) The importance the Gnostic sects attached to Old Testament exegesis, basing their arguments upon the Greek version. (*c*) The fact that the Gnostic sects began to betray signs of hostility towards the Jews (*Judenthum*), may have been a further consideration. (*d*) The political effect which Greek understanding (*Auffassung*) of the Old Testament had upon Jewish life, may have also come into play.[236] But to our mind, the main reason for the prohibition to use the LXX, is closely connected with the Jewish-Christian controversy. To provide a more reliable translation which would eliminate the LXX from general use was attempted by the Greek proselyte, Aquila (middle second century),[237] a convert from Christianity to Judaism. His aim was to give a literal translation closely related to the masoretic text. But though upheld by the Synagogue, it was not a success. Joseph Reider describes it as something of a monstrosity, "its Greek vocabulary and gram-matical forms being often uncouth and barbaric".[238] Its signi-ficance lies in that it provided a separate Greek version authorized by the Synagogue, while "the Septuagint became the official Bible of the Christian Church".[239] The Jewish attitude to the Apocrypha was also conditioned by the dispute between the Church and the Synagogue. Ephraim Levine observes that Akiba's objection to this literature "was directed against Jewish Christians, who drew many of their arguments from that source".[240] To this ought to be added the fact that there is some connexion between the fixation of the Canon at Jabneh and the Jewish-Christian controversy.

Fr. Buhl has shown with good reason that the Canon was already in existence prior to the Destruction of the Temple, and that even the Hagiographical part of the Old Testament was firmly determined before the first century.[241] The discussion at Jabneh, therefore, was not concerned with the fixation of the Canon, but with the revision of it. There appear to have been objections to some of the canonically sanctioned books. The Rabbis reaffirmed the canonicity of these books. Buhl sees a connection between the decisions at Jabneh and "the conflict with the powerfully advancing Christianity".[242] Loewe seems to hold a similar view. He remarks: "When Christianity had definitely parted from Judaism, the provision of a canon became imperative." [243] It appears to us, however, that the incident at Jabneh still belongs to the process of separation itself. The reaffirmation of the already existing canon and the removal of objections to some of its books was probably designed to separate the Old Testament from the Hebrew Christian literature and to provide an answer to the Christian contention that not all the books of the Canon enjoy equal authority.

In a curious passage in *Pes. R.* 14b we get a glimpse of the Jewish reaction to the Gentile (?) Christian claim which was made possible by the possession of a Greek Bible: God foresaw that the Gentile would one day translate the Torah and read it in Greek and say: "They (*i.e.* the Jews) are not (the true) Israel." God said to Moses: "The nations will say, we are (the true) Israel, we are the sons of God; and Israel will say, 'We are the sons of God'." So God said to the Gentiles: "Why do you claim to be my sons? I know only him who has my mystery in his possession, he is my son." Then the Gentiles ask, "What is thy mystery?" God answers: "It is the *Mishnah*" (*i.e.* the Oral Law).[244] The meaning of the passage is two-fold: it denies the Christian claim to have superseded Israel, and it claims on behalf of the Synagogue the key to the *right* interpretation of Scripture.[245]

(iii) THE BIRKAT HA-MINIM

The *Shemoneh Esreh*, which is the *Tephillah* par excellence and "the central feature of the three daily prayers",[246] contains a strange "blessing", the much discussed *Birkat ha-minim*. It is associated with the names of Gamaliel (*circa* A.D. 100) and Samuel the Small (died *circa* A.D. 125). The classical Talmudic passage recording the introduction of the "benediction" reads:

Our Rabbis have taught: Simeon the cotton-dealer (Dalman transl. *Flachsschäler*) arranged the eighteen benedictions in order in the presence of Rabban Gamaliel at Jabneh. Rabban Gamaliel asked the sages: "Is there anyone who knows how to word the benediction relating to the *minim?*" Samuel the Small stood up and worded it.[247] The *Shemoneh Esreh*, which according to tradition, was drawn up by the Men of the Great Synagogue,[248] has thus acquired an *extra* "benediction", though it still retained the former name of "Eighteen" (benedictions). Immediately preceding the passage quoted above the question is being asked: "As to those eighteen benedictior ;—there are nineteen! R. Levi said: The benediction relating to the *minim* was subsequently instituted at Jabneh. Corresponding to what was it instituted? R. Levi said: According to R. Hillel, the son of R. Samuel b. Nachmani, it corresponds to 'The God (*El*) of Glory thundereth' (cp. Ps. 29. 3); according to Rab Joseph, it corresponds to 'One' in the *Shema*; according to R. Tanchum in the name of R. Joshua b. Levi, it corresponds to the small vertebra in the spinal column." It is obvious from this passage that the Rabbis have tried to find some justification for the introduction of a curse into the otherwise lofty prayers of the *Shemoneh Esreh*. Jewish scholars have for a long time maintained that the *Birkat ha-minim* was mainly directed against heresy as such, and only indirectly against Hebrew Christianity.[249] Even Israel Abrahams in his notes to *Singer's Prayer Book* says that the benediction "was directed against Antinomians—those who rejected or neglected the Law—and also against sectarians (*minim*) within the Synagogue. The statement which originated with Justin Martyr that the paragraph is an imprecation against Christians in general has no foundation whatsoever".[250] This is correct in so far as it applies to Gentile Christianity. It can hardly be expected of the Synagogue to be so concerned with Gentile Christians as to denounce them publicly in its liturgy. The course of the Gentile Church only indirectly affected Jewish religious life. From this quarter, the danger to the Synagogue was remote. But the case with Hebrew Christianity was different. The Jewish believers in Jesus of Nazareth were the real and immediate danger to the Synagogue. There can be little doubt who are meant by the *minim*. There was no other sect or heresy which could compare in importance with Hebrew Christianity.

The Hebrew Christians were steeped in the traditions of

Judaism, many of them were loyal to the "traditions of the elders".251 They were spiritually alive, abounding in religious zeal. They were aggressive, and, above all, they were the enthusiastic bearers of the greatest Jewish heritage—the Messianic hope. They were dangerous because they had the advantage of attacking Judaism from *within*. It therefore became imperative for the Synagogue to isolate them. For that purpose the *Birkat ha-minim* was composed. Loewe rightly calls it a "test passage"; 252 its intention being to "separate the sheep from goats, and compel the *minim* to declare themselves".253 It naturally had the effect of widening the breach between the Jesus-believing and the non-believing Jews in that it made it impossible for the believers to worship in the synagogues.

The present text of the 12th benediction which begins with the word *we-lamalshinim* reads: "And for slanderers let there be no hope, and let all wickedness perish as in a moment; let all thine enemies be speedily cut off, and the dominion of arrogance do thou uproot and crush, cast down and humble speedily in our days. Blessed art thou, O Lord, who breakest the enemies and humblest the arrogant." 254 But in this form the prayer is a "comparatively late substitution".255 The *Birkat ha-minim* has undergone alterations, made by the Jews for fear of censorship, and by the medieval censors for fear of blasphemy.256 That the original text of the *Birkat ha-minim* must have made mention of the Christians was anticipated by the learned Prof. Samuel Krauss. Dr. Krauss rightly concluded from the repeated complaints by the Church Fathers that the Jews curse the Christians in their synagogues three times daily, that this must have constituted an integral part of the Daily Prayers.257 This assumption was borne out by an old text found in a Cairo *Genizah* by Dr. S. Schechter. That text reads: "For the renegades (*lameshummadim*) let there be no hope, and may the arrogant kingdom (=Rome?) soon be rooted out in our days, and the Nazarenes (*we-ha-nozrim*) and the *minim* perish as in a moment and be blotted out from the book of life and with the righteous may they not be inscribed. Blessed art thou, O Lord, who humblest the arrogant." 258 It is difficult to assess the age of the Genizah fragment, but it is not the only instance where the *nozrim* are explicitly mentioned in the *Birkat ha-minim*.

Strack, referring to Schechter's text, remarks: "Also the Siddur of the Gaon Rab Amram completed at the beginning of the year 1426, Codex Bodl. 1095, mentions in this *berakha* the Christians. . . . Also the *Maḥzor*—Codex de Rossi Nr. 159 of Parma—explains (*sagt*) on page 2 that the *berakha* is directed against the disciples of Jesus of Nazareth, talmidê *Ješu ha-noçrî*."[259] He also points out that Rashi, in one MS. to *Berakot*, expressly says that the 12th benediction has the Christians in mind. But the question what was the original form of the *Birkat ha-minim* is a difficult one. Many scholars, like Derenbourgh, Hamburger, M. Friedländer, Bousset and Hirsch favour the view that the *Birkat ha-minim* has been added to some similar prayer already in existence. In support of this theory an old *baraita* is brought forward, where, strangely enough, *minim* and *perushin* occur together.[260] Levy translates in this case the word *perushin* by "*Dissidenten*", apostates. But Schwaab rightly holds that this is untenable[261]. It rather looks as if *perushin* is a scribe's mistake. *Pal. Ber.* 2. 4 contains the phrase *minim we-shel resh'aim*, and 4. 3 reads: *minim shel posh'im*; *perushin*, therefore, may easily be a mistake for either of these.[261a] But there are other considerations which favour the view that the *Birkat ha-minim* was an entirely new addition.

(1) The *Talmud Jerushalmi* says explicitly that before the introduction of the prayer against the *minim*, there were only seventeen benedictions. This led Schwaab to the view that the number Eighteen was fixed at the time of Gamaliel II. Though the number of the petitions was fluid, prior to the destruction of the Temple, there were already in existence 17 benedictions in the *Amidah*. After A.D. 70, the benediction *Abodah* was augmented by the words: *we-ha-sheb ha-'abodah lidebir beteka* and later the *Birkat ha-minim* was added.[262] But there still remains the fact that the *Babylonian Talmud* actually counts 19 benedictions.[263] In order to account for this, Schwaab, following the Midrash, explains the process: "first 17 benedictions, then by addition of the 12th petition 18, and lastly 19 as a result of adding the 15th benediction".[264] The 15th benediction having arisen out of the 14th, which was divided in two parts. But a glance at the text suffices to contradict this view. The process seems to have taken place in the opposite direction: not that the *Babylonian Talmud* has divided the 14th petition into two, thus creating 19, but that the *Jerushalmi* has contracted petitions 14 and 15 into one, thus retaining the original number "Eighteen". Strack-Billerbeck show that the number *Shemoneh Esreh* was known

at least before Gamaliel's retirement from the presidency at
Jabneh.[265] It is fairly safe to assume that it was known before
his time; otherwise it would be difficult to account for the fact
that the Babylonian Talmud uses the name *Shemoneh Esreh* for
the *Amidah*.[266]

(2) Samuel the Small, the composer of the *Birkat ha-minim*, a
year after he had composed the prayer, was leading the service
at the synagogue. When he came to reciting the *Birkat ha-
minim*, he could not remember it. He tried to recall the prayer
"*shetayim we-shalosh sha'ot*",[267] but he was not dismissed. The
question is asked, why did they not dismiss him? The rule laid
down by Rab Jehudah (died 299) on the authority of Rab (*i.e*
Abba Arika, 167–247) was that if the precentor errs in any of
the benedictions they do not dismiss him, but if he errs in the
Birkat ha-minim, they dismiss him, because there is the possibility
of his being a heretic. But in the case of Samuel the Small it is
different, because he himself composed it. But could not he
have changed his mind? To this, Abaje (died 338/9) replied
that there is a traditional saying: A good person does not
become bad.[268] From this story, one conclusion is certain: the
Birkat ha-minim was introduced as something new and even its
composer found it difficult to get used to it.

(3) The next question is as to the exact time of the composition of the *Birkat ha-minim*.

Joël attempts to prove that the prayer was introduced at the
time of Trajan, as a reaction against the Christian interference
with the rebuilding of the Temple.[269] This is a conjecture which
is devoid of any historical evidence,[270] but it shows that even a
conservative Jewish writer like Joël puts the *Birkat ha-minim* at
an early date. Chwolson does not think that it could have taken
place before A.D. 100, as, prior to that time, the leaders of Judaism
were preoccupied with important political questions; but it
could not have been composed after A.D. 120, as Samuel must
have composed it a few years before his death, which occurred
in A.D. 125.[271] At present, most scholars are agreed that the
introduction of the *Birkat ha-minim* took place some time before
the end of the first century.[272] The exact time is naturally
impossible to fix, but taking into consideration the inner circumstances, we may surmise that the inclusion of so violent a
curse into the *Amidah* points to a time when the Synagogue was
witnessing a new surge of Hebrew Christianity in the form of a

revival of Messianism. This must have taken place not many years after the destruction of Jerusalem. The frustration which followed that greatest national disaster prepared the ground for Christian propaganda. Since it is possible that Gamaliel II took over the presidency at Jabneh before the death of his predecessor, R. Jochanan ben Zakkai,[273] it is safe to assume that the *Birkat ha-Minim* was introduced about the year A.D. 90, or even earlier.

(4) The second question which presents itself is, against whom is the prayer directed? There are two opinions on this point: (a) The *Birkat ha-minim* had in view *all* heretics *including* Christians. This is the view of most Jewish scholars. (b) The *Birkat ha-minim* was *chiefly* directed against Christians, but naturally included other heretics. An adequate answer to the problem depends on what meaning we assign to the word *minim*, and whether we assume that the word *nozrim* originally belonged to the wording of the prayer. It must be admitted that these are difficult questions, and that a final decision is impossible. But there are some considerations in favour of the second view.

Schürer explains that the word *nozrim* in the *Birkat ha-minim* is "the more narrow conception, *minim* the wider one (=heretics, apostates in general)".[274] Schwaab, too, tries to answer whether *nozrim* and *minim* were the original words, and whether they stand in some relationship to each other. He asks: " Stood then this word (*i.e. nozrim*) from the beginning next to the term *minim* as its 'more narrow conception'?" [275] And though he differs from Hoennicke as to the reason why the word *nozrim* was inserted at a later date, he agrees with him that it was not originally in the text. Schwaab finds the answer to the puzzle in Schlatter's statement that the complete Hebraization of the liturgy in the Greek Synagogue was in the fourth century by no means an established fact: "*Minim* required translation and the nearest rendering was that of Ναζωραῖοι as is confirmed by Epiphanius and Jerome."[276] Schwaab, accepting Schlatter's opinion, adds: "Thus would *nozrim* appear to be a more popular pleonastic addition."[277] According to this theory, the Hebrew word *minim* was translated into Greek for liturgical use by Ναζωραῖοι which, in course of time, became a literal re-translation next to *minim*, and slowly both words came in use. There seems to be some reason in Hoennicke's argument that Krauss has attached too much importance to the evidence of the Church Fathers in trying to prove that in the original prayer the word *ha-nozrim* was already present.   In the case of Justin, it cannot be shown that he is actually referring to the 18 benedictions, and in the case of Epiphanius, it must be borne in mind that his evidence refers to the prayer the Jews had in use in his own time.   Hoennicke, therefore, concludes: "The original reading (*Textform*) will have been והמינים כרגע יאבדו; later was added the word הנצרים".[278]   This is important; whatever view we accept in explaining the presence of the word *nozrim*, there is reason to surmise that it was not originally in the text.   It was added at a time when the word *minim* assumed a wider meaning including all heresies, and when the bitterness against Christianity assumed such depth as to require special mention.   Justin's testimony, on the other hand, cannot easily be brushed aside.   We would, therefore, assume that Justin knew that the *Birkat ha-minim* had primarily Christians in view.   This he could have easily learned from Hebrew Christians or from sources related to them.

We therefore feel justified in drawing the following conclusions:

(1) The *Birkat ha-minim* had no precedent in the Synagogue; it was a new creation, entirely dictated by internal necessity.

(2) It was composed at an early date, not many years after the destruction of Jerusalem.

(3) It did not contain the word *nozrim*, but it did contain the word *minim*.

(4) It was primarily directed against Hebrew Christians. In this we go a step further than Schwaab, who says that the 12th benediction was directed "at least also—against the Christians".[279]

It is only natural to assume that the introduction of the *Birkat ha-minim* resulted, not only in widening the breach between Hebrew Christians and orthodox Jews, but also in further prejudicing the Jews against Jesus of Nazareth.[280]

(iv) CALUMNIATION OF THE PERSON OF JESUS

Both the Talmud and the vast Midrashic literature contain some references to the person of Jesus.   Scholars are agreed that these references are mostly, with a few exceptions,[281] legendary and devoid of all historical authenticity.   In the words of Klausner: "They partake rather of the nature of vituperation and polemic against the founder of a hated party, than objective accounts of historical value".[282]   This is also Laible's view. After carefully examining all the data, Laible says: "Two points are continually presented to us in a striking way: (1) The extraordinary paucity and scantiness of those accounts; (2) their fabulous character".[283]   This is a curious and disappointing fact.   We should have expected historically well authenticated evidence from Jewish sources respecting the person of Jesus of Nazareth.   But this is not so.   Klausner gives two reasons for this: (1) the Talmud authorities rarely allude to events which took place in the period of the Second Temple; (2) the contemporaries of Jesus hardly noticed his appearance in the turbulent days of the Herods and the Roman Procurators.   By the time Christianity, however, became an important sect, a generation grew up which had no knowledge of the facts.[284] This probably explains the case, though it is difficult to see how the Rabbis have completely overlooked the historical facts connected with the life of Jesus or remained ignorant of them. Klausner's second point suggests that the life of Jesus did not create the stir and its effects were not as momentous as we are led to suppose on New Testament evidence.   But there may still be another explanation.   The Talmud seems to adopt two methods in dealing with opponents.   The one method is to ridicule, the other is to ignore the adversary altogether.   It adopted the first in its presentation of the life of Jesus, and the second in its attitude to John the Baptist.   It is a curious fact that the whole Rabbinic literature does not contain a trace of the existence of John.   But John's activity was important enough to be noticed by Josephus.[285]   The same, however, can be said about other important events in Jewish history which find no mention in the Talmud.   Klausner rightly draws attention to the fact that, had it not been for 1 and 2 Maccabees and the writings of Josephus, the Talmud would not have conveyed to posterity even the name of Judas Maccabæus!   But whatever the reason may be, the Talmud makes some statements about the person of Jesus, though admittedly under the strain of heated controversy.   Later references contained in the Rabbinic literature were called forth by way of reaction against Christian oppression, "a highly treasured, private form of vengeance in return for the attitude of the Christians towards the Jews." [286]

1. *Talmudic statements about Jesus.*—Neither the historical value, nor the authenticity of references or hints regarding Jesus contained in the Talmud is decisive for our investigation. All we are concerned with is to collect the features which formed the portrait for those Jews who sought information about the Man of Nazareth from the pages of Rabbinic literature.

There is extant at least one *Mishnaic* reference to Jesus; it is generally held to be the oldest mention of our Lord. R. Simeon b. Azzai said: "I found a family register in Jerusalem, and in it was written, 'Such a one is a bastard through (a transgression of the law of) thy neighbour's wife', confirming the words of R. Joshua." [287] There are also several *baraitot* and a number of *Midrashic* allusions either to Jesus himself or disciples of Jesus. Only occasionally does the actual name of Jesus occur, in the form of *Yeshu, Yeshu ha-nozri* (or, *nozri*) or *Yeshu ben Panteri* (also *Pantera, Pandera*).[288] More often he is referred to as *ish ploni* ("the anonymous one") or *oto ha-ish* ("that man"); this is chiefly due to medieval censorship.[289] Later Jewish authorities seem to have confused the person of Jesus with a certain Ben Stada, and have thus added another synonym to the collection.[290]

The contents of the passages referring or alluding to Jesus in the Talmudic and Midrashic literature have been carefully examined by many authorities. After the work done by scholars like Laible, Strack, Herford, and more recently, Klausner, there is no need for a detailed discussion. It may suffice to quote the summary of the story as given by Herford: "Jesus, called *ha-Notzri, B. Stada,* or *Pandira*, was born out of wedlock (*M. Jeb.* IV, 13, cp. *Bab. Shab.* 104b). His mother was called Miriam, and was a dresser of women's hair (*Bab. Shab. ibid.* where "*Miriam megaddelah nashaia*" is a play on "*Miriam Magdalaah*", *i.e.* Mary Magdelene).[291] Her husband was Pappus b. Judah,[292] and her paramour Pandira.[293] She is said to have been the descendant of princes and rulers, and to have played the harlot with a carpenter (*Bab. Sanh.* 106a). Jesus had been in Egypt, and had brought magic thence. He was a magician, and deceived and led astray Israel.[294] He sinned and caused the multitude to sin. (*Bab. Sanh.* 107b). He mocked at the words of the wise, and was excommunicated (*ibid.*). He was tainted with heresy (*ibid.* 103a).[295] He called himself God, also the Son of Man, and said that he would go up to heaven (*Jer. Taan.* 65a; Jesus is not mentioned by name, but there is no doubt that He is meant).

He made himself live by the name of God (*Bab. Sanh.* 106a; also anonymous). He was tried in Lydda (Lud) as a deceiver and as a teacher of apostasy (*Tos. Sanh.* X. 11; *Jerus. Sanh.* 25c, d). Witnesses were concealed so as to hear his statements, and a lamp was lighted over him that his face might be seen (*ibid.*). He was executed in Lydda, on the eve of Passover, which was also the eve of Sabbath; he was stoned and hung, or crucified (*ibid.* and *Tos. Sanh.* IX, 7). A herald proclaimed, during forty days, that he was to be stoned, and invited evidence in his favour; but none was given (*Bab. Sanh.* 43a). He (under the name of Balaam) [296] was put to death by Pinhas the Robber (Pontius Pilatus), and at the time was thirty-three years old (*Bab. Sanh.* 106b). He was punished in Gehenna by means of boiling filth (*Bab. Gitt.* 56b, 57a). He was 'near to the Kingdom' (*Bab. Sanh.* 43a). He had five disciples (*ibid.*).[297] Under the name of Balaam, he was excluded from the world to come (*M. Sanh.* X, 2)." Two things are obvious from this account: (1) The Rabbis "deliberately attempted to contradict events recorded in the Gospels." [298] (2) An effort is made to present Jesus in an unfavourable light. In the words of Hennecke: "On the whole one is forced to admit that in the Talmud Jesus is nothing else than the reflexion of the Jewish—or Gentile—Christian portrait of Christ, *but naturally distorted by Jewish aversion.*" [299]

2. *The Tol'dot Yeshu.*[300]—Besides the sparse and inadequate Talmudic references to Jesus, there is in existence an old Jewish source which offers a more elaborate and rather fantastic account of his life. It has been the object of much discussion since the Middle Ages. More recent investigation of the *Tol'dot Yeshu* was in respect of their origin and age. The most valuable work was done by the learned Samuel Krauss, who carefully selected and classified the MSS, and minutely and critically examined their contents.[301] A more recent study of the *Tol'dot Yeshu*, with the object of establishing a connection between the Jewish source and the Gospel according to the Hebrews, was made by Mr. Hugh J. Schonfield, himself a Hebrew Christian.[302]

This strange parody of the Life of Jesus shares some features with the traditional account in the Talmud, but is more elaborate and less restrained. Its readers were the more ignorant people in Jewry.[303]

The *Tol'dot* differ in two important points from the Talmudic account: (1) They purport to *replace* the Gospel story, thus offering a coherent account of the Life of Jesus of their own making; (2) their intention is not only to replace the Gospels, but also the Acts of the Apostles, offering instead "eine entsprechende jüdische Darstellung".[304] Dr. Krauss does not regard the Talmud as the main source of the *Tol'dot Yeshu*. He says: "Already the fact that the *Toldot-Recensions* speak of Jesus as *ben Pandera*, and not as *ben Stada*, thus belonging to the same legend-cycle (Sagenkreis) which was also known to Celsus, proves that the *Toldot*-writer draws his material not from the Talmud but from living Jewish tradition; one part of this tradition entered the Talmud, the other part was fixed in the *Toldot*. . . ."[305] Krauss regards the canonical and apocryphal Gospels as the background of this Jewish tradition, but its immediate and most important source was "the Hebrew historical work *Yosippon*, which recorded also about Jesus and the beginning of Christianity".[306] On the other hand, Schonfield, after comparing the *Tol'dot* with the canonical and extra-canonical Gospels, arrived at the conclusion that the author must have had another source before him. Schonfield identifies that other source with the lost Gospel according to the Hebrews. He even thinks that a reconstruction of the lost Gospel is possible by following closely the order of the *Tol'dot* account. In Mr. Schonfield's view the author of the *Tol'dot* wrote his "counter-Gospel" by copying the form and arrangement of the Gospel according to the Hebrews, but perverting its contents. Schonfield then concludes: "The *Tol'dot Jeshu* will be found on serious examination to supply a most important witness to the structure of the lost *Gospel according to the Hebrews*."[307] It seems that Mr. Schonfield's main argument is based on the fact that the *Tol'dot* has appended the story of the Acts of the Apostles, or rather a perversion of it, while Prof. Benjamin Bacon has suggested that the Ebionite Gospel must have had a similarly appended story in which Peter, and not Paul, was the chief hero. Epiphanius actually mentions such Acts of the Apostles according to the Ebionite version.[308] Schonfield goes a step further and declares that the *Ascents of James* in the *Clementine Recognitions* are "an expanded form of a section of the Hebrew Acts" which concluded the *Gospel according to the Hebrews*.[309] From this Schonfield adduces: (1) That many Jews adhered to the doctrine of Jesus; (2) that serious disorders resulted from the Nazarene preaching; (3) that the Nazarenes accused the chief priests of slaying the Lord's anointed; (4) that the Nazarenes did not leave the Jewish community; (5) that strife and discord developed between the opposing parties. But Schonfield's patristic evidence is very meagre and his conclusions forced. There is no need to rely upon so dubious a source as the *Ascents of James* to prove the above-mentioned points. Every point is amply borne out by the first chapters of Acts. A very weak link in Schonfield's argument is the assertion that the compiler of the *Tol'dot* has utilized the appropriate points in his narrative, taking care not to do too much violence to his source.[310] This seems to contradict the whole thesis that the author of *Tol'dot* was bent upon presenting "a satirical Gospel" in spirit truly related to Celsus' *The Discourse* and Lucian of Samosata's *De Morte Peregrini*. It is difficult to see why historical fact should have had a restraining effect upon the author's imagination.

As to the time of the *Tol'dot*, there is great difference of opinion, but Krauss' reasoning seems to compare favourably with other views. He says: "It is probable that the *Toldot* originated in the fifth century. The book records incidents which extend into the fifth century; it speaks, in addition to Jesus, of Peter and Paul, of Simon Magus, of the migration to Pella, of the bishops Kleophas and James; it contains material (Tatsachen) which points to pseudo-Hegesippus, it tells of the finding of the Cross, it knows of Nestorius, but nothing beyond it, not even of the removal of the Cross by the Persians in 614, a fact which would have been very welcome to the Jewish author, had he known of it." [311] Krauss also points to the list of Christian festivals referred to in the *Tol'dot*, and especially to Christmas (natalis). Schonfield thinks that the original form (the *Ur-Tol'dot*) is probably earlier than the fifth century.[312] Klausner rejects the view that the present *Tol'dot* goes back to the fifth century. But he admits the possibility "that some book entitled *Tol'dot Yeshu*—though more or less different in content and altogether different in form and Hebrew style—was in the hands of the Jews as early as the fifth century, and that it was the same book which tell into the hands of Agobard, Bishop of Lyons (who refers to it in his book, *De judaicis superstitionibus*, which he composed in conjunction with others about the year 830), and into the hands of Hrabanus Maurus, who became Archbishop of Mainz in 847, and, in his book, *Contra Judæos*, referred to Jewish legends about Jesus which correspond to much of the contents of the

surviving *Tol'dot Yeshu*." [313]   But Klausner affirms that the
present Hebrew *Tol'dot*, "even in its earliest form, is not earlier
than the present *Yosippon*, *i.e.* it was not composed before the
tenth century." [314]   But this statement refers only to MSS which
have come down to us.   The tradition itself is very old and goes
back to a time when "the propaganda of the Nazarenes among
their non-Christian brethren, and the circulation of their
Gospel" [315] was counteracted with the story of the *Tol'dot*.
Krauss rightly relegates the *Tol'dot* to the class of apologetic and
polemical writings.   Schonfield's suggestion that it originated at
Tiberias may point to an even earlier date than the fourth
century.

A brief summary of the contents of the *Tol'dot* can be found
in Klausner's book. [316]   The main gist of the story is the assertion
that Jesus was an illegitimate child, that he performed miracles
by means of sorcery which he learned from the Egyptians; that
he acquired the power of performing miracles by stealing the
Ineffable Name from the Temple and sewing it underneath his
skin; that he was arrested on the eve of Passover; that he was
hanged on a cabbage stem (the reason given is that Jesus had
previously adjured all trees by the Ineffable Name not to receive
his body, but he failed to adjure the cabbage stem, which does
not count as a tree!); that his body was removed on the eve
of the Sabbath and interred; that the gardener removed his
body and cast it into a cesspool.

Such is the story which Krauss affirms "was intended seriously
as a history of Jesus", to Herford's great surprise. [317]   To indicate
the influence of the *Tol'dot* upon the Jewish people, we will
quote an interesting passage from Klausner: "This book is not
now common, though at one time it had a wide circulation . . .
in Hebrew and Yiddish among the simpler minded Jews, and
even more educated Jews used to study the book during the
nights of *Natal* (Christmas). . . . Yet the book may still be
found in MS, and in print among many educated Jews.   Our
mothers knew its contents by hearsay—of course with all manner
of corruptions, changes, omissions, and imaginative additions—
and handed them on to their children." [318]   In the Middle
Ages and even up to our own days the *Tol'dot Yeshu* served as a
popular handbook and was almost the only source left to the
Jewish people from which to draw their knowledge concerning
Jesus Christ.   It used to be read with great relish, especially on

Christmas Eve, and even now Jewish schoolboys in countries like Poland are given the evening free to enjoy the story on the night of *Niṭ'l*.[319]

(v) THE LINGERING PAST

The scanty references in *Talmud* and *Midrash* and the derisive account offered by the *Tol'dot Yeshu* were the two main sources upon which the children of Israel drew concerning Jesus, his life, his labours, his teaching, and his end.   The characteristic feature of both these sources is best described by the *Jewish Encyclopaedia* when it says: "It is the tendency of all these sources to belittle Jesus by ascribing to him illegitimate birth, magic, and a shameful death." [320]   To quote once again the authority of S. Krauss: "Jesus' illegitimate birth was always a firmly held dogma in Judaism, which found clear expression in its ancient and modern literature, passed over to the heathen of antiquity and lives to-day in the consciousness of every simple-minded Jew, who only knows as much on this subject as he has learned from his parents." [321]   The purpose of these disfigured and fantastic statements was to repel the Jew from the person of Jesus and to keep him immune from Christian influence.   No doubt, in the past the effort was crowned with success.

Generations of Jews have lived and passed into oblivion, and though surrounded by Christianity on every side, have never actually faced the truth about Jesus.   Equally little have they known about Christianity itself.   To the son of Israel, his Christian neighbour remained a Gentile who believed in three gods, worshipped the Cross and hated the Jews.   A large measure of the guilt for this state of affairs falls upon the Church itself; an equally large measure falls upon the spiritual leaders of Judaism.[322]

Conservative Judaism still refuses even to discuss the case of Jesus.   Appeals made by enlightened Jews to reconsider the Jewish attitude towards Jesus of Nazareth immediately raise in these quarters an outcry of indignation.   In this respect, nothing has changed.   Even critical studies of the life of Jesus made by Jews seem to be, in the eyes of conservative Judaism, an unpardonable sin.   Thus Prof. J. Klausner's book, which is anything but favourable to Christianity, has raised a storm of protest; [323] "*Jesus must never again even cross our minds*" is the rule of the orthodox camp.[324]   Yet even more astounding is the fact that this persistent and uncritical, almost wholesale, rejection of Jesus is by no means characteristic of the Orthodox group alone. The attitude of supreme negation is the general rule for Jewry at large. Thus Aḥad Ha-'Am (Asher Ginzberg), rationalist and progressive, looked upon as the father of "Spiritual Zionism", is filled with indignation at the appearance of Montefiore's *Synoptic Gospels*.[325] Here, as nowhere else, do we meet with the lingering memory of Jewish suffering which, in the Jewish consciousness, is closely associated with the name of Jesus.[326] This is the burden of the *Christian* guilt.

CHAPTER III

THE CHURCH AND THE JEWS

THE SECOND potent factor in the process of alienation between Jesus and the Jewish people was the Church. This is the darkest spot in the history of Christianity. The Christian record of Jewish wrongs and suffering is the most incriminating testimony against the Church. This explains why, to the Jew, Christianity became a synonym for Jew-hatred. It is commonplace for the Jew to associate the name of Jesus with the Ghetto, the Badge, and the Inquisition. To Jews of Eastern Europe the Cross to this day is the symbol of persecution. And how could it be otherwise?

Dr. James Parkes has studiously traced back the evil which is usually called anti-Semitism to Christian exegesis and theology. He has shown in his valuable work on the origins of anti-Semitism the extent to which the Church is to be held responsible for the suffering of the Jews throughout the ages.[1] Much has been written on the subject, especially by Jewish writers. Every detail has been thoroughly investigated by Jewish and Christian historians. All that remains for us to do is to give a general outline.

1. THE ASCENDENCY OF THE CHURCH

We have already seen the extent of reaction on the part of the Synagogue to the Christian heresy. But the Synagogue's struggle against *Hebrew* Christianity was entirely an *internal* affair. It was a controversy between Jews as to the significance and meaning of certain events which had taken place in their own midst. The dispute was of a religious nature and, as is always the case, it grew in violence until it came to a split. The minority, which in this case were the "Christians", was defeated. This involved suffering and persecution. Jews were persecuting Jews. Such internal strife is no isolated case in history. But soon a new element came into play. The Messianic movement broke its national ties and confronted the Gentile world. Jewish missionaries began to preach the Jewish Messiah to the heathen and met with remarkable success.[2]

The starting-points for the Christian evangelists were the Synagogues of the Diaspora, which attracted considerable numbers of Gentiles. The σεβόμενοι and φοβούμενοι in Acts, however we interpret their status in the eyes of Judaism, were naturally the first of the Gentile world to respond to the Gospel message.[3] The reason Harnack gives for assigning the name χριστιανοί exclusively to Gentile Christians has convincing force.[4] The heathen populace at Antioch coined the name to designate the Gentile believers.[5] Acts 11. 26, therefore, marks a new stage of development, where the Christian community shows already a preponderance of Gentile members. But this may have been an isolated case. At first, the proselytes who were won for the Gospel remained in the Synagogue or attached themselves to small Hebrew Christian groups within the Synagogue. But soon new converts were added who had no previous attachment to Judaism. The question whether these newly won heathen were first to be received in the Synagogue or might become Χριστιανοί without the mediacy of Judaism was bound to become a burning issue. On this point opinions were divided, and it came to a split between the "liberal" party headed by Paul and the "Judaizers", whom Paul calls the "false brethren".[6] The rôle which the leaders at Jerusalem played in the dispute is not clear. The name of James is usually associated with the Judaizing party, but with what justification it is difficult to decide. A general agreement will probably never be reached in this matter. But one thing is fairly certain, Paul was by no means the only champion of "antinomianism", as is sometimes maintained. He was backed by a considerable body of men, and not all of them came from the Diaspora or were tainted with Hellenism. This is borne out by the behaviour of Peter at Antioch. Machen, who has discussed the relationship between Peter and Paul at great length, significantly says: "The very existence of the Church would have been impossible if there had been a permanent breach between the leader in the Gentile mission and the leader among the original disciples of Jesus." [7] The existence of a strong antinomian party within Hebrew Christianity is well authenticated from Jewish sources, as we have seen in the preceding chapter.[8]

It is at this point that the Apostolic Decree of Acts 15 becomes of vital importance. This highly controversial subject has been keenly discussed for over a century without any conclusive

results. The main difficulty is the interpretation of vv. 28 and 29.
The question whether the Decree aimed at purely ethical
standards or also involved a certain adherence to ceremonial
law, is not easy to decide. Prof. A. S. Peake calls it "one of the
most tangled problems in the history of the early Church".[9] The
great problem is the decision regarding the text, as there are
considerable differences involved. The generally accepted text
has three food prohibitions and one ethical prohibition. But
early and important MSS omit "things strangled." This would
leave two food prohibitions and one ethical prohibition. "But
the removal of 'things strangled' makes it possible to take all
three as ethical, that is, as prohibitions of idolatry, murder and
impurity." [10]

Strangely   enough,   most   authorities   which   omit   "things
strangled" (πνικτόν) add the "Golden rule" in its negative
form.[11] First Hilgenfeld [12] and later Gotthold Resch [13] have
accepted the Western reading as the original, i.e. the version
which omits the clause "things strangled" and adds the "Golden
rule" in the negative form. Harnack previously fought for the
Eastern, i.e. the common text,[14] but has later accepted Resch's
view with the exception of the Golden rule, which he regards as
a later addition.[15] Harnack's change of opinion is important;
only grave considerations have caused him to accept the other
view.[16] This is now the generally accepted view. Kirsopp
Lake says: "The 'three-clause' Western text of the Decrees
seems to be right." [17] But Kirsopp Lake finds it more difficult
than Harnack to interpret the "three clauses" in a strictly
ethical sense, as the "summary of an ethical catechism", to use
Harnack's phrase. And it seems to us that this balanced opinion
is nearer the truth. Lake says: "πορνεία, whether it means
'fornication' or marriage within prohibited degrees, has no
place in a food-law, and αἷμα, though it might have meant
murder, is not likely to have done so. . . . Therefore the theory
of a 'food-law' seems to be blocked by one word and that of a
'moral law' by the other." [18] The Decree, in our opinion,
actually represents both the elementary moral and 'food-laws'
required from the Gentile if social intercourse with a Jew was to
become possible. The division between the strictly moral and
the "ceremonial" in our modern sense was entirely unknown to
the Jews. In view of the fact that both Weiss and Harnack are
inclined to regard Acts 15. 23–29 not as the original letter, but

only a "Compilation" made by the hand of Luke from an older document (Urkunde),[19] it is not unreasonable to assume that Luke's decree is an abridged form of a slightly longer statement. To this we would add the fact that most scholars are agreed that the Decree has affinities with the Rabbinic rules concerning Gentile "God-fearers". Prof. Lake says: "there is sufficient resemblance between the Apostolic decrees and the Noachian rules to make it probable that both represent the regulations which controlled the intercourse of Jews and God-fearers in the middle of the first century." [20] The rules concerning the "Sons of Noah" were the minimum the Rabbis required from the Gentiles who lived in their midst if any social intercourse was to become possible. These seven *mizwot bene-Noaḥ* consisted of submission to the authorities, the rejection of idolatry, and the prohibition of blasphemy, incest, shedding of blood, robbery, and the cutting of a limb from a living animal.[21] These Noachian Commandments have played considerable importance in Jewish jurisprudence, though their actual application was only seldom in use for lack of opportunity. It is possible that these were the rules to which the *Gere-toshab* had to submit; those Gentiles who were only semi-proselytes.[22] Maimonides declares: "Whosoever receives the seven commandments, and is careful to observe them, he is one of the pious of the nations of the world, and has a share in the World to come." [23] There is therefore every reason to suppose that these or some similar commandments [24] were to form the basis for the intercourse between the Gentile Christians and the Church at Jerusalem. But the acceptance of the Noachian rules in itself did not put the Gentile on an equal footing with the born Jew. To become a full member of the Commonwealth of Israel, complete conformity with the requirements of the Law was expected. The Apostolic Decree has therefore left the Gentile position undefined, so much so that Peter himself was uncertain to what length it was permissible to go.[25] Paul's silence about the Decree may be due not so much to his refusal to accept the verdict, as Prof. Lake suggests, but rather to a desire to avoid a controversial issue; there must have been considerable division of opinion as to the interpretation of the Decree. The Judaizers interpreted it one way, the circle of which Paul was representative another way. The clash between the two parties centred round this problem, as the Epistles of Paul testify. A solution was never reached, a compromise was

impossible.[26]   In the course of time, however, the Pauline view
prevailed.   Such a triumph was only possible thanks to the
leniency, if not active co-operation of the Church at Jerusalem.
This is a point too often overlooked.

The reaction of the Synagogue to the antinomian tendency in
their midst was naturally violent.   The position was aggravated
by the fact that many semi-proselytes to Judaism embraced the
new faith, which offered them equality without the requirement
to undergo the painful ceremony of circumcision and without
submission to the ceremonial part of the Law.[27]

Jewish scholars, as we have seen, have strongly opposed the
generally accepted view that the Synagogue was guilty of persecution.   Abrahams categorically repudiates Harnack's statement
that the Jews were the first and the greatest enemies of Christianity.[28]   Making allowance for Jewish protestations, we would
still hold that the Synagogue was responsible for a good deal of
persecution not only of Hebrew Christians but also of the Gentile
Church.[29]   The reason for such behaviour lies not only in the
fact that in the eyes of Judaism Christianity was a *heresy*, but that
it was also a *rival* religion which soon proved a dangerous com-
petitor in the mission-field.   This psychological factor is of considerable importance.

Jewish writers have sometimes alleged that the Church was at
pains to explain to the Roman authorities the essential difference
between Judaism and Christianity.   This was done in order to
escape "the penalties attached to the observance of the Jewish
religion" [30] after the Destruction of the Temple and especially
after the Bar Cochba incident.   Mr. Ephraim Levine suggests
the possibility that Christians who opposed the Bar Cochba
insurrection gained special favour with the authorities and were
thus not hindered in setting up a bishopric in Aelia Capitolina,
the pagan city built on the ruins of Jerusalem.[31]   But none of
these views can be supported by reliable evidence.   On the other
hand there is the witness of the New Testament and the Church
Fathers.   Even allowing for the measure of exaggeration suggested by J. Weiss,[32] the Synagogue still appears in violent
opposition to Christianity.   Trypho himself was not indifferent
to the fact that Justin was a Christian; to him Christianity was
tantamount to forsaking God and reposing confidence in man.[33]

Jewish scholars who emphasize the Synagogue's lack of interest
in Gentile Christianity, overlook the fact that the Church con-

stituted a continual challenge to Judaism. Justin's Dialogue is
a classical example. The Synagogue could not possibly remain
indifferent to the Christian appropriation of all Jewish hopes, the
national hope included.[34] The Church disinherited the Synagogue and usurped all its privileges. The Synagogue naturally
refused to accept such a situation. A clash was inevitable where
Synagogue and Church had to live side by side. Justin remarks
that Jews don't hesitate to put Christians to death, when they
have the power to do so (ch. 95). But by A.D. 160 (*i.e.* the time
the *Dialogue* was written), the actual division has taken place, and
the controversy has lost much of its heat. Harnack rightly
observes: "The dialogue with Trypho is in reality the victor's
monologue. It is not the opponent who speaks, but Justin who
lets him speak." [35] Christianity is already in the ascendency,
the Gentile Church has won the field.

Hebrew Christian connexion with Jerusalem was broken prior
to A.D. 70 when the community migrated from Jerusalem to
Pella.[36] The second crisis which deepened the disruption between
the Jewish followers of Jesus and their brethren was caused by
the difficult situation which arose during the Bar Cochba insurrection. Bar Cochba made claim to Messiahship and was upheld
by the most prominent Rabbi of the day, Akiba.[37] For Hebrew
Christians to lend a hand in the struggle virtually meant a denial
of the Messiahship of Jesus, as there could not be two Messiahs
to command their loyalty. Hebrew Christians therefore refused
to join the insurrection and were bitterly persecuted.[38] This
marks the end of Jewish-Christian relationship. When, after the
insurrection, the broken tradition was re-established by setting
up a bishop in Jerusalem, now a pagan city called after a pagan
god, the new bishop was a Gentile and a stranger to the old life
of the Hebrew Church.[39] From now onwards, Hebrew Christianity is pushed into the background. It is Gentile Christianity
which occupies the forefront of history.

2. THE VICTORY OF THE CHURCH AND ITS
EFFECT UPON JEWISH LIFE

The Gentile Church, together with the primitive tradition, has
taken over the struggle between the Jewish-Christian minority
and orthodox Judaism, as a legacy from the early Church. But
here an important change took place: (1) The champions of the
new faith were now strangers and by nature deeply prejudiced

towards the Jewish people. (2) While the controversy between the "Judaizers" and Pauline Christianity was an *internal* controversy between Jews, against the new background of the Gentile Church it assumed an altogether different proportion. The original struggle of the *Judaic* Church against *Judaistic* [40] tendency assumed in the Gentile Church the aspect of direct opposition to the Jews. Thus, two elements have combined, the racial and the religious, to form a barrier dividing Gentile Christianity from the Jewish people. Both Church and Synagogue have developed under the sign of opposition to each other, and as is usual in human relationships, the weaker antagonist was destined to carry the burden of responsibility.

(a) Spiritual disinheritance

The Apostle Paul introduced a new conception regarding the meaning of Israel. While hitherto "Israel" was a purely national conception, Paul widened it to include all those who by faith in Christ Jesus entered the spiritual tradition of the Jews. Thus, those who were formerly "alienated from the commonwealth of Israel" (Eph. 2. 12) became through faith sons of Abraham (Gal. 3. 7). For in Christ Jesus, the Gentiles become united with the seed of Abraham, and therefore, "heirs according to promise" (Gal. 3. 29). But Paul goes actually further than this. He distinguishes between Israel κατὰ σάρκα (1 Cor. 10. 18) and the Israel of God (Gal. 6. 16). "For he is not a Jew, who is one outwardly . . . but he is a Jew who is one inwardly" (Rom. 2. 28, 29); therefore: "they are not all Israel, who are of Israel" (Rom. 9. 6); for "it is not the children of the flesh that are the children of God"(Rom. 9. 8). Yet with all that Paul holds on tenaciously to the election and prerogatives of the Israel κατὰ σάρκα (cp. Rom. 9. 4, 5). He refuses to believe that God hath cast off his people (Rom. 11. 1f.) and he expresses his hope in the day when all Israel shall be saved (11. 26): "For the gifts and the calling of God are *irrevocable*" (ἀμεταμέλητα v. 29). It has been said "that St. Paul is not always consistent with himself" [41] and that "he shies away from the logical conclusions of his own arguments".[42] But it must be borne in mind that Paul is a stranger to the modern secularized conception of nationality. To him, a Jew who detaches himself from his religious background forfeits all privileges. Israel for the Apostle is not racially or nationally but *religiously* defined. Rom. 9–11 is not concerned with nationhood, but the Church. It does not constitute a political discourse, but an interpretation of the history of grace, *i.e.* God's sovereign dealing with man. Conclusions as to the future of the Jewish people in the secular sense are therefore misapplied. But however we interpret these chapters, Prof. Goudge rightly observes that the Apostle discloses here a "passionate love for his nation".

But with the transformation of the background there soon came into existence a different attitude towards the Jews. The Jewish people, to the Apostle of the Gentiles still the elect people of God, gradually becomes in the eyes of the Gentile Church a God-forsaken people divested of all merits. The Church appropriates not only the spiritual heritage of Israel, but even the national history of the Jews, their patriarchs, saints, and prophets. In time, the whole spiritual and national background of Judaism was torn away from the Synagogue and claimed as the sole property of the Church. Even the heroes of the Maccabæan wars were included in the Christian legacy.[43] Eusebius makes a clear distinction between the Hebrews, God's chosen people, the most ancient people in the world, and the Jews, a reprobate people which rejected the prophets and crucified Jesus.[44]

The process of appropriation began early in Christian history. Justin Martyr makes already full claim to the Hebrew Scriptures. He says to Trypho that the Jewish Scriptures belong to the Christians: "For we believe them; but you, though you read them, do not catch the spirit that is in them." [45] This was a natural claim, for the Church knew herself to be in possession of the Holy Spirit, the only competent interpreter of the Scriptures. But with Justin, the affinity between Church and Synagogue is still clearly realized. The whole discussion with Trypho makes this apparent. Here the Christian appeals to the better judgment of the Jew; the appeal is based upon Scripture: What David sang and Isaiah preached, and Zachariah proclaimed and Moses wrote is familiar to both Trypho the Jew and Justin the Christian.[46] The difference between them is a difference of interpretation. A dialogue is therefore still a possibility. There is still close proximity between the Church and the Synagogue and the middle link between the two is Hebrew Christianity.[47] But Hebrew Christianity, that vital bridge between the two parties, gradually faded away from history. With the weakening of Hebrew-Christian influence the breach between Judaism and

the Church became complete.[48] Jerome (340–420) already goes
as far as to maintain that God gave the Jews the Law with the
deliberate intention of deceiving them and leading them to
destruction.[49] To him, the Jewish place of worship is nothing
else but the "Synagogue of Satan"; Ambrose calls it the Temple
of Impiety. Dr. Parkes points out that Constantine in the first
law dealing with the Synagogue refers to it by a term which, in
Roman slang, meant a brothel.[50] When we come to Chrysostom
(347?–407), we find the process of alienation completed and
hostility the guiding rule in Christian-Jewish relationships.
Chrysostom's denunciations of Judaism, of which he knew little,
can scarcely be surpassed.[51] Lukyn Williams, whose balanced
judgement may be relied upon, comments on Chrysostom's
attitude to the Jews: "There is no sign that he felt the slightest
sympathy with them, much less a burning love for the people
of whom his Saviour came in the flesh, or, indeed, that he
regarded them in any other way than as having been rightly and
permanently punished for their treatment of Christ, and as being
emissaries of Satan in their temptation of Christians." [52] Apart
from the notorious eight *Homiliæ adversus Iudaeos*, there are many
disparaging references to the Jews scattered throughout his many
works.[53] They all breathe the same spirit, that of contempt and
utter rejection, with the exception of his treatise *Contra Iudaeos et
Gentiles, quod Christus sit deus*, which Chrysostom must have
written at a much earlier period.[54] It must, however, be borne
in mind that Chrysostom is *primarily* a religious opponent. His
first concern was the purity of the Christian faith, which he
thought jeopardized through too great familiarity between Jews
and Christians.[55]

It was these religious considerations which aggravated Jewish-
Christian relationship and made friendship impossible. The
Church viewed with misgiving Christians who entertained too
friendly relations with Jews. The fear of "Judaizing" and
proselytism on the part of the Synagogue was ever present in the
mind of Christian leaders.[56] The whole situation must be viewed
from the aspect of *religious rivalry*. Most of the Papal bulls and
the many decrees of Church Councils concerning the Jewish
people were *protective* measures. Their aim was to hinder the
Jews from exercising religious influence upon Christians. This
legitimate aim was ensured by methods, not only sub-Christian,
but inhuman. In this respect the Jews fared no worse than other

heretics. Religious intolerance is a general human failing. The Church felt no compunction in putting obstacles to the free exercise of the Jewish religion, but was full of holy indignation at any sign of proselytism on the part of the Synagogue. At the same time, the Church was using every conceivable device to force the Jews to conversion. The right of the strong and the right of the weak are two different rights.[57]

The picture which the Church drew, for the benefit of the faithful, of the Jew and Judaism, was detached from experience; it was a distorted picture with little reference to actual fact. Dr. Parkes hardly exaggerates when he describes the impression gained from the pages of early Christian literature of the Jew as a "monster, a theological abstraction, of superhuman cunning and malice and more than superhuman blindness".[58] The extent of Jewish unworthiness in the eyes of Christianity is well illustrated by the case of Anacletus II, the "Jewish Pope." [59] On his accession to the see in 1130, Christendom split into two parties. On the side of Cardinal Pierleoni were "the majority of the cardinals with the Bishop of Porto, the Dean of the Sacred College", and the Roman clergy and dignitaries, and almost the whole population of Rome.[60] In the rival camp supporting the anti-pope, Innocent II[61], was his chief champion, St. Bernard of Clairvaux, the emperor Lothair III, and "the entire European royalty of the time, the Councils of Rheims and Pisa, and the majority of the Roman Catholic clergy".[62] The main cause of the schism, at any rate the centre of attack by the opposing party, was concentrated upon the Jewish descent of Pierleoni.[63] For his great-grandfather was a Jew called Baruch, who after baptism assumed the name of Benedictus Christianus and married a lady of an old Roman aristocratic family. Anacletus himself was at first a monk at Cluny, who later attained to the dignity of Cardinal. He was accused of a Jewish physiognomy, of using bribery to effect his election, of Jewish perfidy, and even of the crime of having a deformed brother who looked more like a Jew than a Christian.[64] The temper of the Church was expressed in the words of St. Bernard in a letter to the Emperor: "Ut enim constat, Judaicam sobolem sedem Petri in Christi occupasse injuriam: sic . . ." [65] To that extent had the Church forgotten its connections.

The process of spiritual expropriation was completed at an early stage of Church history. An interesting example is the attitude of Archbishop Gregentius concerning the Scriptures and the Promises given to Israel. In his discussion with the Jew Herban in c. A.D. 480 the Christian prelate finds it quite natural to adduce proof from the Scriptures that Israel had forfeited his rights.[66] Such a deduction was easy in the light of the Pauline Epistles, but it is doubtful whether it actually represents the Pauline view. For the inclusion of the Gentiles in the common-wealth of Israel is one thing, but the inclusion of the Gentiles at the expense of the Jews is another. In this respect the Gentile Church was nearer to the view of Marcion than that of Paul.

(b) Legal discrimination

It would exceed the scope of this work to trace the various stages of the process which changed the legal position of Judaism from a *religio licita* under Roman rule to the inferior position it occupied under the rule of the Church. Dr. James Parkes has carefully examined the subject and we shall mostly draw upon his work.

We have already noted the fact that many of the decrees which the Church has promulgated against Judaism were dictated by necessity.[67] The two rival faiths called to exist side by side were forced to take protective measures in order to guard their followers from harmful influence. In this respect, both Church and Synagogue acted on the same principle, though their methods were of necessity different. The Synagogue lacking legislative power resorted to moral coercion in enforcing the strictest rules of separation from Christian influence. The Church enjoying enormous political power endeavoured to protect its faithful by legally restricting Jewish rights. The fact that the Jews were not only religious opponents but ethnically strangers facilitated the process.[68]

It may be argued that the Church cannot be held immediately responsible for laws enacted by the secular powers or for the many acts of violence committed by infuriated mobs. Admittedly, the Church has often exerted a restraining influence upon over-zealous authorities and repeatedly denounced mob-violence. A characteristic case is the action taken by Gregory the Great at the complaint of the Jews in Rome. Bishop Victor of Palermo had, without cause or provocation, confiscated some of the synagogues and thus deprived the Jews of their places of worship. This was an act of violence and against the law which provided that new synagogues were not to be built, but that old ones were not to be confiscated without reasonable cause. Gregory at once investigated the case and finding the Jews innocent, ordered that due amendment be made. His pronouncement is significant of the official attitude of the Church: "If the Jew may not exceed the law, he ought to be allowed peaceably to enjoy what the law permits." [69] The Church was deeply concerned that the disabilities imposed upon the Jews be applied without slackening. We hear of constant threats and admonishments addressed to kings and prelates, occasioned by their failure to apply the oppressive laws in all their rigidity. Gregory VII (Hildebrand, 1073-1085) rebuked Alfonso the King of Castile for employing Jews in high offices of state; he admonished the Spanish bishops to desist from too friendly relations with Jews. Similarly, Innocent III (1198-1216), who strongly disapproved of acts of violence and rebuked the Crusaders for their despicable practices upon the Jews of France, was anxious that none of the restrictive laws be infringed. Philip of France, who according to the Pope's view was too lenient with the Jews, met with severe criticism. The Count of Nevers was told in a letter dated 1208, that: "The Jews must wander about the earth like the fratricide Cain, they are fugitives and vagabonds and are to be covered with insults." [70] Against the few humane Popes, like Alexander III (1159-1181), Innocent IV (1243-1254), Gregory X (1271-1276), and Paul III (1534-1540), who attempted to shield the Jews from acts of violence, there is the long list of Roman pontiffs who pursued an opposite course. Many of them regarded the Jews with contempt, some were indifferent, others were guilty of active persecution even to the extent of allowing acts of violence. In Rome itself "the fate of the Jews hung upon the personal character of the Popes, who sometimes bravely and humanely protected them; sometimes threw over them a shield from the selfish advantage they might reap from their presence; sometimes drove against them with fagot and sword as bitter persecutors." [71] Thus, John XXII (1316-1344) is held to have been personally responsible for the massacres of Jews. He ordered their expulsion from the provinces outside Rome and only revoked the edict against the sum of 20,000 golden ducats.[72] Eugenius IV (1431-1447) re-enacted a decree dating from 1412, which forbade every form of intercourse between Jews and Christians.[73] Paul IV (1554-1557) excelled his predecessors in

harshness and intolerance towards the Jews. He ordered synagogues to be destroyed, the practice of Judaism to be severely
restricted, the enforcement of a distinctive headgear for Jewish
men and women, and every form of intercourse with Christians
to be avoided. Jews were precluded from belonging to guilds,
forbidden to own property; even the number of annual marriages
was strictly limited by law.

The legal position of the Jews is closely connected with the
relation between Church and State in Christendom. Fishberg
observes that "in countries where the Church has been part and
parcel of the machinery of the State the fate of the Jews had been
more or less deplorable, while wherever the Church has been
divorced from the State, the Jews have enjoyed some degree of
civic and political liberty." [74]   This may seem a biased view,
but Dr. Parkes' opinion is to the same effect. Speaking on the
influence of the Church upon anti-Jewish legislation in Spain,
Parkes remarks: "Those kings who were not elected by the
favour of the clerical party, either passed no laws against the
Jews at all or reversed and ignored those of their more pious
predecessors." [75]

The first steps towards legal discrimination were made by
Constantine the Great. This mainly affected the Jews in three
points: their treatment of Jewish converts to Christianity, their
treatment of non-Jewish slaves, and their proper share in the
duties of the decurionate from which they were hitherto exempt.
It is mainly in the second of these points that the legal rights of
Judaism were infringed. Jews were prohibited from circumcising
their slaves and conversion to Judaism came to be regarded as
an offence.[76]   Constantius went one step further and imposed
additional restrictions upon the Jewish possession of slaves: no
Jew was to be in possession of a Christian slave. The contravention of this law became a criminal offence punishable with the
confiscation of all property. Furthermore, it was decreed that
the circumcision of a slave was an offence deserving capital
punishment. Under Gratian, the burden of the decurionate was
extended to include Jewish Rabbis, while the Christian clerics
were naturally exempted. "This is the first real infringement
of the rights of Judaism as a lawful religion, for it placed it on a
definitely inferior plane to orthodox Christianity", writes Dr.
Parkes.[77]   Theodosius I went still further. He enacted that
marriage concluded between Jew and Christian was equal to

adultery; Jews were only to marry amongst themselves, and this according to the *Christian* tables of affinity. Dr. Parkes expresses the opinion that the law prohibiting the building of new synagogues, a law very burdensome to Judaism, the infringement of which was one of the causes which led to the deposition of the last patriarch, Gamaliel, in 415, belongs to this period.[78] The prohibition to build new synagogues became a general rule in Christian legislation. Its purpose was to reduce Jewish influence upon the Gentile population. But at this stage Jewish freedom was still only limited. The Jews still enjoyed internal liberty to live in accordance with their own custom. Yet such a peculiar position could not last long. As Parkes well remarks: "Inferiority and equality cannot be permanently combined. The equilibrium is bound to change in one direction or the other." [79] The defenceless position of Jewry decided the direction of the change. The Jewish minority had no means in its power to arrest the process. New legislation further curtailing Jewish rights followed in continuous succession until, in the Middle Ages, we find the Jew the personal property of the reigning prince.

The transition from antiquity to the Middle Ages is marked by a steady decline of the Jewish legal position in Christendom. But the process itself took many centuries and went through various intermediate stages, until finally the Jews sank from the status as *cives Romani* to that of *servi camerae*. This process progressed at a varying speed in different parts of Christendom. The *Apocriticus* of Macarius Magnes, a book which was certainly not later than A.D. 410, but probably much earlier,[80] shows strange embarrassment in answering the question of a heathen critic,[81] how St. Paul could have laid claim to being both a Jew and a Roman. The only answer Macarius can think of is by making a pun on the word ῥώμη. He attempts three explanations: (1) Paul was driven by the Jews into the hands of the Romans, and so he could say he was not a Jew but a Roman. (2) He was right in calling himself a Roman, for by the might (ῥώμη) of the spirit he was to teach the Roman nation. (3) When he calls himself a Jew, he honours his countrymen; when he calls himself a Roman he proclaims his nobility.[82] Crafer, in a footnote, remarks: "Macarius does not seem to have grasped that a Jew could be a Roman citizen." But this is not the case. Elsewhere Macarius explicitly says that there was a time when

Jews *were* Roman subjects.[83]   In view of the fact that Caracalla
conferred Roman citizenship on all free-born subjects of the
Empire in A.D. 212, the discussion must have taken place long
afterwards, at a time when the legal position of the Jews had
already changed considerably.   At the beginning of the fifth
century it was therefore an already established fact that to be a Jew
was to belong to an inferior race.   For, once a precedent was set,
as in the case of Constantine, the logic of events proceeded with
mathematical precision until legal discrimination ended in legal
nonentity.[84]

Gratian deprived converts to Judaism of all testamentary
rights.   Honorius removed the Jews from all political influence
and from military service.   Valentian III enacted a law forbidding parents and grandparents of Jewish converts to disinherit
them after their baptism.   Theodosius II went so far as to impose
upon his Jewish subjects the observance of Christian feasts and
fasts.   His successors enforced his laws not only in the Byzantine
Empire, but also in Babylonia, where Mar Zutra II (*c.* 496–520),
the Prince of the Captivity, managed to maintain for some seven
years a measure of independence against the Persian king
Qubad I.[85]   Such interference will have contributed to the
decline of intellectual life in the hitherto flourishing Talmudic
academies of Sura and Pumbeditha.

It is difficult to say to what extent Jewish behaviour was
responsible for some of the edicts against them.   There are
naturally instances on record where the provocative behaviour
of some Jews called forth restrictive enactments.   Purim, the
festival commemorating Esther's triumph over Haman, sometimes gave occasion for grave offences.[86]   Theodosius introduced
a law, 29th May, 408, prohibiting the burning of Haman's
effigy, which apparently in some cases led to the mockery of the
Cross.[87]   Such misbehaviour was probably prompted by the
desire to retaliate for the humiliation they suffered.   But whenever an opportunity for revenge occurred, the Jews were not
slow to seize it.   A typical instance is the case in Alexandria,
which ultimately led to their expulsion under Cyril in 415.   It
is, however, doubtful to what extent the Jews are to be held
responsible for the massacre.   It is significant that Orestes, the
governor of the city, the authority immediately responsible for
law and order, sided with them and refused to be reconciled to
Cyril for this act of violence.[88]

Gradually the restrictive measures against the Jews in Spain and France reached a severity far exceeding the enactments of Justinian I (527–565) and Heraclius (610–641) in the East. While the Jewish community soon recovered under Omar (c. 581–644), after his victories against the Persians, the Spanish Jews under Egica (687–702) continued to meet with new restrictions. They were forbidden to own land and houses, to trade with North Africa, to transact business with Christians. In the end, on the pretext that the Jews were plotting with the Moors, the whole population was virtually sentenced to slavery and their children of seven years and upwards were handed over to Christians to be brought up in their faith.[89] Fortunately, this state of affairs came to an abrupt end when Egica's second successor, Roderic (711–713), the last Visigothic king in Spain, was defeated and killed by the Mohammedans in the autumn of 713. It is of no mean significance that during the occupation of Spain by the Saracens the Jews enjoyed a period of peace and security, with the exception of the persecution started by the Caliph of Damascus, Omar II, in 720.

A strange consequence of the legal discrimination which the Jews had to endure was the necessity of taking them under the special protection of the selfsame authorities which brought about such a situation. The legal enactments aimed at severely restricting Jewish freedom, but they did not sanction violence. The margin, however, between law and lawlessness became so narrow that mob-violence prompted by greed was the inevitable result. Measures, therefore, had to be taken, to protect the Jews against injury. The first instance of such protection is connected with the name of Louis the Pious. We learn thus that in 825 the king granted special letters with the purpose "to protect the Jews from arbitrary acts of violence, to allow them to carry on their trade undisturbed".[90] The fact that the Jews had already reached a state in which special protection of the crown became necessary reveals the precariousness of their position. It foreshadows the future development which will ultimately make them the private property of the ruling prince. An analogous case is in the gradual development of the ghetto. The Bishop of Speyer, Rüdiger, in order to protect the Jews against the mob, conceived the idea in c. 1084 of confining them to a special quarter of the town. Gradually, what was at first a measure of protection became a place of involuntary confinement enforced by law. In Spain, in 1412, every city was enjoined to establish special quarters for Moors and Jews surrounded by a wall with one single gate.[91]   In the end, the Council of Basle in 1434 decreed that the ghetto be universally applied in Christendom.[92]

In 920 we hear of Louis of Provence confirming to the Archbishop of Arles not only the possession of the city but also of its *Jews*.[93]   In 1103 the Emperor, Henry IV, was forced to include the Jews, for their own safety, in the *pax generalis*, thus singling them out from the rest of the population and putting them on a level with the women and clergy.[94]   The Jew was now not only under the special protection of the prince, but to all intents and purposes the personal property of his host.   All he had, his life included, was no longer his own.   His disabilities were innumerable : "He had to obtain royal permission to settle in any city or town, from which he could not remove without similar leave; his property was continually liable to be taxed or tallaged; at his death the King claimed the whole, and secured a large share of his possessions."[95]   Like other serfs, he was obliged to do work for his master, but while the Christian was privileged to till the soil, the Jew was pressed into the business of usury.   With some variations, such was the Jewish position in Christendom till the French Revolution.

It is vain to argue that Jewish disabilities were chiefly imposed by the secular powers and that the Church exercised a mitigating influence.   The fact is that the moving spirit behind the secular arm was the Christian Church, which relentlessly pressed for discrimination.   This is clearly seen by the many edicts of the various Councils affecting Jewish life.   It must also be remembered that the distinction between ecclesiastical and secular spheres is a comparatively modern division.   The close relation between Church and State which pervaded Christendom makes a distinction of that kind inadmissible.   On the contrary, there was a great measure of unity of purpose between Church and State concerning the Jewish people.   Church and State worked hand in hand in the policy of keeping the Jew at bay.   Frequently, the Church interfered in the life of the State, to the State's disadvantage,[96] by demanding the elimination of Jewish influence in the political and social spheres.   It is therefore not surprising that for almost every law passed by the secular authorities there can be found parallels in the canons of the Church.

The first canons were chiefly concerned with creating a barrier between Jews and Christians with the purpose of eliminating Jewish influence upon the latter. Such influence was very considerable at first. In later centuries, when Jewish-Christian relationship became more strained, the various Church Councils entered upon the path of direct anti-Jewish legislation. Outstanding examples are the canons passed by a succession of Councils at Toledo in the seventh century.[97] These Toledo enactments were the main source of incitement "in the persecuting policy of the later Visigothic kings".[98] The nature of that policy we have already described. It was thus the Church which not only encouraged but often compelled the State to bar the Jew from citizenship and from the enjoyment of the ordinary human rights.

(c) Forced baptisms and other means of coercion

The most outrageous crime committed, not only against the Jews but also against the Church itself, was the many instances of forced baptism. It must be said, however, to the honour of the Church, that officially it never approved of such action. But in spite of official disapproval, forced baptisms were a widely practised evil in which not only fanatical mobs and ignorant clergy, but often high ecclesiastical dignitaries indulged. Even the bulls issued by the papal see were unable to stop the evil.[99] The oldest bull of this kind which has been preserved is that by Alexander II (1159–81). In it the Pope announces his intention to follow his predecessors, Calixtus II (1119–24) and Eugene III (1145–53) in their charitable treatment of the Jews.[100] But already Gregory IV (827–44) asked that Jews should not be baptized by force, though he thought that once baptized they ought to remain Christians. It was this inconsistency which made such a situation possible. On the one hand, the Popes, frequently under pain of excommunication, prohibited violence against the Jew; on the other hand, they often held the impossible position that once baptism had taken place, though against the will of the baptized, that person was a Christian. Such an attitude towards baptism has a long history behind it, and was primarily dictated by doctrinal considerations. Once the *opus operatum* view predominated even to the exclusion of the proviso of *non ponere obicem*, the Church had consistently to demand of those baptized against their will that they *remain* Christians: thus, those who were guilty of such violence knew they were performing a pious deed. This is probably one of the reasons why forced baptisms, in spite of frequent protests, were a constant feature of medieval life. Another reason was the fact that even the highest dignitaries of the Church were often guilty of using compulsion.

A mild form of compulsion was the practice of conversional sermons. It seems to have been a generally accepted practice to send preachers on the Sabbath day to the synagogues in order to instruct the Jews in the tenets of the Christian faith. This often led to scenes of violence, especially when, together with the appointed preachers, a Christian mob entered the synagogue to support them.[101] In other instances, Jews were compelled to attend sermons in church on special occasions. James I of Aragon (1213–76), who tried to protect the Jews of Lerida from the interference of the Inquisition, granted to them as a special privilege the right of non-attendance when these sermons were delivered outside the Jewish quarters. But he seems to have been either unwilling or unable to relieve them of the obligation of listening to the friars in their own synagogues. The only stipulation he made was that those friars be accompanied by not *more* than ten Christians of good repute.[102] Since the establishment of the Inquisition, the Dominicans enjoyed the privilege of entering Jewish synagogues with the view of preaching to the worshippers.

The compulsory hearing of sermons by Jews in Christian churches was already practised in the thirteenth century. Two centuries later it became a general custom, especially in Italy. Abrahams records the comic situation that the ears of Jews used to be examined on entering the churches "for they were suspected of stopping them with cotton". Overseers were appointed to ensure that the Jews remained awake during the two-hours' sermon delivered to them. The conversion of at least one Jew was a necessary part of the function in some instances.[103] The bull of Benedict XIII of 1415 decreed that three public sermons were to be preached to the Jews annually and that all above twelve years of age "shall be compelled to attend to hear these sermons".[104] But there was already in existence a bull of Nicholas III issued in 1278 in which the Dominican and Franciscan Orders were instructed to gather the Jews as often as suitable and to read to them a lesson with the object of winning them for the faith.[105]

Another form of compulsion of much greater severity was the repeated choice put to the Jews to accept either baptism or expulsion. Here, again, the official policy of the Church was towards leniency. But in most cases the secular powers acted either under Church influence or in order to please the ecclesiastical party. This is particularly the case with the Visigothic rulers of Spain after the Conversion of Recared from Arianism to Catholicism in 586. Thus Sisebut in Visigothic Spain decreed that all Jews within his Kingdom were either to leave the country or to accept baptism. Similar decrees were enacted by his successors.[106] Dr. Parkes records an interesting case where the alternative of baptism or expulsion is actually propagated by the Pope himself. The Archbishop of Mainz asked Leo VII (936–939) for advice as to how to deal with the Jewish population within his jurisdiction. The Pope's reply was that the religion of the Holy Trinity and the Mystery of the Incarnation be preached to them "with the utmost wisdom and prudence". But should this effort to win them fail, the Archbishop is at liberty to expel them, "since we ought not to dwell with the enemies of God". [107]

Apart from direct interference in Jewish life many indirect methods were used to induce the Jews to conversion. In this category will fall the prohibition of building *new* synagogues. Such a law was first introduced in the fifth century, or perhaps even earlier.[108] One of the many restrictions imposed upon the Jews by Theodosius II was that new houses of worship were not to be erected. But at the same time the emperor made it plain that the pulling down and the confiscation of already existing synagogues was not lawful. In later years, Theodosius assumed a harsher tone. In the third *Novella* (A.D. 439) he declared: "Whoever builds a synagogue shall know that he has laboured for the Catholic Church . . . whoever repairs a synagogue shall be fined fifty pounds: whoever corrupts the faith of a Christian shall be put to death." [109] The law regarding new synagogues was included in the Barbarian recension of the Theodosian Code and is contained in the Breviary of Alaric, thus being transmitted to the West. This law was repeated in other legislations and was jealously guarded by the Church. One of the offences which fell under the punishment of the Inquisition was the building of new synagogues, an act forbidden by secular as well as canonlaw.

Historical records tell not only of the prohibition of building new synagogues or the repairing of old ones, but also of the barbarous practice of destroying and confiscating Jewish houses of worship. Thus Justinian, in his *Novella* 37 to Salomon, the Governor of Africa, ordered all synagogues to be confiscated and handed over to the Catholic Church.[110] It is recorded of the Bishop of Dertona in Northern Italy, that he, together with his flock, destroyed a synagogue and built a church on its site. The bishop's name was Innocentius![111] John of Ephesus boasts that during his mission to Asia he had turned no less than seven synagogues into churches.[112] There were other forms of subtle compulsion serving the same end. Thus Paul III established an institution for Jewish converts; the support of the inmates was laid to the charge of the Jewish community in Rome. Under Gregory XIII the Jews were made to pay the monks who sermonized them against their will! The most effective pressure, however, was that of economic coercion. Jews were frequently offered wealth and honour in exchange for their religion. To return once again to the strange incident in Minorca: Reuben the Jewish convert says naïvely enough to Theodorus, a prominent Jew: If you wish to live securely, "in honours and riches, believe, like me, in Christ".[113] This is not the voice of Reuben the convert, but of an impatient, intolerant Church sanctioning any method in order to attain her end. But the most repulsive form of coercion was the Church's attitude towards those who had been baptized against their will or, in the case of minors, against the will of their parents.

In an effort to break Jewish resistance there have been many instances when fanatical mobs imposed baptism upon defenceless Jews, notably at the time of the First Crusade. In contravention of canon-law and with the disapproval of the official Church there were also cases when local churches and councils made themselves guilty of using force in inducing the Jews to accept Christianity. Thus at a council held in Paris in 614, it was decided that any Jew found holding official position prohibited by law was to be taken by the bishop and immediately baptized together with his whole household. The VIth Council of Toledo decreed that only Catholics could reside in the Kingdom. Jews were thus given the choice between baptism or expulsion. We learn of Sulpicius, the Bishop of Bourges, that he is to be held responsible for a number of forced baptisms taking place between

620 and 644.[114]   The Bishop of Trier, Everard, four hundred years later, put before the Jews baptism or expulsion,[115] thus sustaining the spirit of intolerance which has persistently continued till modern times.

The Church officially condemned such practices. Alexander II (1061–73) reprimanded Landulph VI, Prince of Benevento in 1065 for forcing Jews into baptism. But notably Calixtus II (1119–1124) in his bull *Sicut Judaeis non* (*c*. 1120) explicitly forbade the practice of compulsory baptism on the grounds that it encouraged hypocrisy. The question, however, arose, what was to become of those who had been baptized? Were they to be allowed to return to Judaism?

Such a problem arose after Sisebut's death. The king had ordered all Jews who had remained in his dominion after the expulsion to be forcibly baptized. The IVth Council of Toledo, presided over by Isidore of Seville, strongly condemned Sisebut's action, but it nevertheless declared these baptisms valid. This was due to the peculiar view regarding the efficacy of the sacraments, as already indicated. The same council devoted much of its time to meting out punishment to those Jews who after having been forcibly baptized relapsed into Judaism, under the mild rule of Swinthila. The VIth Council of Toledo upheld the view. In a letter addressed to the Pope Honorius, the Council expressed its surprise at the Pope's leniency in allowing baptized Jews to return to their former faith. It assured the Pope that such a thing could never have happened in Spain.[116] Gradually it became the general rule in the Church that once a Jew was baptized, he was under obligation to remain a Christian. Urban II strongly disapproved of the Emperor Henry IV's decision to allow the Jews who had been forcibly baptized during the disturbances of 1096 to return to Judaism.[117] Similarly, Hugues Aubriot, the Prévôt of Paris, was severely reprimanded in 1380 and made to do penance for allowing Jews to reclaim their children who had been forcibly baptized. Louis VII was even persuaded by the Church to compel Jews thus baptized to remain *faithful* Christians "under pain of banishment, death, or mutilation".[118]   Men like Vincent of Beauvais and John Duns Scotus "vehemently defended the practice of enforced baptism".[119]

Such practice was only gradually evolved. The Church fathers were champions of tolerance. Tertullian laid down the

rule that the natural law authorized man to follow only the voice
of conscience in the practice of religion, since its acceptance was
a matter of free-will and not of compulsion.[120]   Origen points
to the difference between the law of Moses and that of Christ:
Christians were no more at liberty to kill their enemies and to
burn or to stone violators of the law.[121]   A fine plea for tolerance
is made by Lactantius.   He lived at a time of bitter persecution.
In 308 he wrote his *Divinae Institutiones*, where he pleads for
tolerance, as "there is no occasion for violence and injury, for
religion cannot be imposed by force: the matter must be carried
on by words rather than blows, that the will may be affected".[122]
But in the struggle against the Donatists, at a time when the
Church could already count on the support of the State, the tone
towards those whom she regarded to be in error gradually
changed.   Even Augustine, who displayed so much restraint and
tolerance towards the Manichæans, who after their expulsion
from Rome and Milan sought refuge in Africa, seemed to have
changed his views in later life.   Writing against the Donatists,
Augustine admits the right of the State to use force, for it may
sometimes prove wholesome to the erring and give protection
to the faithful.   Aquinas quotes Augustine's well-known sentence:
"It was once my opinion that none should be compelled to union
with Christ, that we should deal in words and fight in arguments.
However, this opinion of mine is undone." [123]

The first Catholic bishop to justify the co-operation of the
State in questions of religion was Optimus of Mileve.   He even
asserted the right of the State to inflict the penalty of death on
heretics, appealing to the authority of the Old Testament.[124]
But such was not the common view.   Chrysostom, for instance,
thought that "to consign a heretic to death is to commit an
offence beyond atonement".   The Second Council of Nicaea of
787 refused to administer baptism to the children of Jewish
Christians who were insincere in their faith.[125]   St. Bernard of
Clairvaux still held that the only way of dealing with heretics was
by argument, since *fides suadenda non imponenda*.[126]   But gradually
the harsher view prevailed.   In the end heresy was associated
with *crimen laesae maiestatis*.   The position of the Roman Church
has been defined theologically by Thomas Aquinas.   In his
Summa Theologica, Part II, Q 10. 8, he quotes Chrysostom:
"unbelievers ought not to be compelled to the faith"; he also
quotes the Decretals (*Can. De Judaeis*): "The holy Synod pre-

scribes with regard to the Jews that for the future none are to be compelled to believe"; also Augustine's earlier view: "... it is possible for a man to do other things against his will, but he cannot believe unless he is willing". Aquinas therefore concludes: "Among unbelievers there are some who have never received the faith, such as the heathen and the Jews: and these are by no means to be compelled to the faith, in order that they may believe, because to believe depends on the will: nevertheless they should be compelled by the faithful, if it be possible to do so, so that they do not hinder the faith, by their blasphemies, or by their evil persuasions, or even by their open persecutions. ... On the other hand, there are unbelievers who at some time have accepted the faith and professed it, such as heretics and all apostates: such should be submitted even to bodily compulsion, that they may fulfil what they have promised, and hold what they, at one time, received. ... Those Jews who have in no way received the faith ought by no means to be compelled to the faith: if, however, they have received it they ought to be compelled to keep it."

It is obvious, then, that Aquinas is emphatic as to the attitude to the "lapsed" and ambiguous with regard to unbelievers. Such has been the Church's position throughout. L. I. Newman rightly says: "Conversions by force were officially condemned by the medieval Church, but in a fashion which left room for other missionary methods, the result of which was almost equally distasteful."[127]

The fate of the Jews who had been forcibly baptized was more than tragic. At times of popular uprisings, Jews had often out of fear accepted baptism and allowed their children to be baptized. When persecution abated, however, they returned to their former faith. Newman records an instance of such lapsed Jews being imprisoned and excommunicated. After they had been kept for a year without recanting their error, the Inquisitors inquired of the Pope, Nicholas II, as to the further steps to be taken. The Pope's answer was that they were to be treated as heretics, *i.e.* burned for continuous obstinacy.[128] It was a rule in the Church that children under seven years of age were not to be baptized without the consent of their parents, but once baptism had taken place they had to remain Christian, living in separation from their unbaptized parents. The Church however took the view that children past the age of seven were sufficiently grown up to choose for themselves and could be baptized even against the will of their parents.[129]

It was with heretics and "lapsed" Christians that the Inquisition was called upon to deal. To elicit the truth from its victims, it received the sanction from Pope Innocent IV (May, 1252) to apply torture. This was later confirmed by other Popes.[130]

Henry Charles Lea, who has made the most detailed and scholarly study of the Inquisition,[131] "exonerates the papacy and the Church generally from any large measure of responsibility for the constitution or practice or methods of the Inquisition". [132] It is enough to read Adler's book, where a brief summary of Dr. Lea's work is contained, to gain the conviction that the Church must take a large share of the blame. Adler rightly remarks that: "Persecution was not uncongenial either to Pope or King, and, if nôt always welcomed for its own sake, was rejected by neither when it could advance some high political purpose." [133] The Holy Office,[134] which put on its banner the words *Misericordia et justitia*,[135] became the most unholy institution of blackmail and robbery. The saddest part of the story of the Inquisition is the important part played by bribery in its procedure, deciding about the life and death of its victims.[136] The Church ingeniously left to the secular powers the task of carrying out the sentences passed by the Inquisition.[137] There was much jealousy between Pope and King only regarding the spoil [138]; otherwise there was complete unity of purpose.

To the Jews the activities of the Inquisition were a source of untold suffering, though as such they could have hardly come under the category of Christian heretics. In fact, Pope Martin V explicitly forbade the Inquisitors to inquire into matters concerning the Jews. But an institution which was set up to deal with blasphemy and witchcraft and since 1257 with usury could not have passed by the Jews, who, in the eyes of Christianity, were guilty of the three crimes combined.[139] But in addition to these three cardinal crimes which fell by law under the authority of the Holy Office, medieval ingenuity invented a number of other offences which exposed the Jews to the inquiries of *La Suprema*, as the supreme council of the Inquisition was called. Philip the Fair extended the authority of the Inquisition to deal with Jews who were found guilty of inducing Christians to heresy; of handling the Host; of blaspheming against the Sacraments; of circumcising Christians; of sheltering heretics;

of building synagogues, or singing too loudly in them; of possessing copies of the Talmud, or deluding Christians.[140] It was fortunate for the Jews that the King soon afterwards renewed his quarrel with the Pope, and thus restricted the privileges of the Inquisition. At times the chicanery of the Inquisition went so far as to use force to induce Jews to accept baptism in order to be able to accuse them afterwards of heresy.[141] Proof that at least in some instances the Church's concern was not *only* the purity of the Catholic faith can be seen from the readiness it showed in accepting the offer by Solomon ben Abraham of Montpellier and his supporters to proceed against the Maimonists in the same manner as against Christian heretics. The Dominicans and Franciscans were only too glad to lend a hand in purging Judaism from heresy, with the result that all Maimonist books were confiscated and publicly burned in December, 1233. Thus was set a precedent for the future burning of Hebrew books.[142] But it was not until the fifteenth century in Spain, under Ferdinand and Isabella, the "Catholic" monarchs,[143] that the Inquisition reached the height of its activities. Its main victims were the *Marranos*, a disparaging name for Jewish Christians suspected of heresy.[144]

The true organizer of the Spanish Inquisition was Frey Tómas de Torquemada (1420–1498), whom Sabatini describes as "the arch-enemy of the Jews".[145] He was appointed inquisitor-general of Castile and Aragon in 1483 or earlier,[146] by Pope Sixtus IV. During the fifteen years of Torquemada's activity as leader of the Holy Office, thousands of heretics were sent to the stake and tens of thousands suffered lesser penalties.[147]

It is strange to hear a modern Roman Catholic writer explain that "the much maligned *autos-da-fé* were in reality but a religious ceremony (*actus fidei*)". The same writer tells us that: "The Church established by Christ, as a perfect society, is empowered to make laws and inflict penalties for their violation. Heresy not only violates her law, but strikes at her very life, unity, and belief; and from the beginning the heretic had incurred all the penalties of ecclesiastical courts."[148] Such an attitude glaringly reveals the gulf which divides a Christian scholar from the forbearing spirit of his Master.[149] But in the case of the Jews or the *New Christians*, as the *Conversos* were called, Blötzer's explanation can hardly apply. Who was responsible for creating a situation by which thousands of Jews were condemned to the humiliation of outwardly feigning Christianity and inwardly clinging to the faith of their fathers? Was it not that the terrible massacres of 1391, which enveloped the whole of Spain, created a new class of "Christian", consisting of Jews who accepted baptism as the only alternative to death and destruction? It is not surprising that the Church looked with suspicion upon those *Conversos* whom she had gained in so unworthy a manner. The grim irony lies in the fact that these converts, in whom "panic destroyed the unyielding fortitude so often manifested by the Jews under trouble", [150] were held responsible for a situation which they had neither created nor could they help.

In order to rid the Church of a dangerous and undesirable element which she acquired by her own intolerance, the Inquisition resorted to the rack and the stake. At the height of its activity it was enough to have the smallest admixture of Jewish blood to make a man a suspect. "Much of the time of the Inquisition was taken up also in examining *limpieza*, or purity of blood from any Jew or Moslem admixture, of which it would grant certificates, which were requisite before taking up any public office." [151] Spies were sent about the country and denunciations were made on the slightest pretext. But here, as nowhere else, the tenacity of the Jew has been tried and proved. Though whole congregations under the heavy blows of persecution accepted Christianity, love for the faith of their fathers and abhorrence of a religion which employed such barbarism only stiffened their inner resistance. Nothing could erase from their embittered hearts their love for Judaism. They remained Jews. Many *Marranos* were burned at the stake, many fled for their lives abroad, some survived for centuries upon their native soil. As recently as 1920 a number of Marranos in Northern Portugal openly professed Judaism and under the leadership of Captain Arthur Carlos de Barros Basto established a synagogue of their own. [152]

3. JEWISH REACTION

It is no exaggeration to say that the empirical Church, *i.e.* the Church of history, has shown herself the greatest enemy of the Jewish people. The Church has, therefore, been the first and foremost stumbling-block in the Jewish appreciation of Jesus. In the words of Canon Danby, no mean authority on the subject: "The Church, by its deliberate choice and conduct, has made itself one gigantic and seemingly impenetrable obstacle between them and the figure of our blessed Lord." [153]

The memory of terrible wrongs suffered at the hands of Christians has deeply entered the Jewish consciousness. It could not have been otherwise. Crimes perpetrated in the name of one religion against another religion make the victims into martyrs, and martyrs are not easily forgotten. The experience of the past still lives on in the Jewish tradition and has become an integral part of Judaism. An instance is the introduction to the prayer *u-netanneh tokef* in the Musaph Service of New Year, still retained in some old editions of the Jewish Prayer Book, according to the German and Polish rite. Legend has it that Rabbi Amnon of Mayence, a learned and wealthy Jew, was repeatedly pressed by the Archbishop to accept Christianity. In a moment of weakness he promised to consider the matter in the space of three days. But on leaving the palace he repented of his promise and at the end of the three days refused to follow the summons of the Archbishop. For this he had his members amputated and placed next to him in a coffin. After his mutilation, at his own request he was carried to the synagogue. It was New Year's Day, and the reader was just about to begin the *kedushah* when the Rabbi interposed and began to recite . . . *u-netanneh tokef kedushat ha-yom* . . . (we will express the mighty holiness of this day).[154] The fact that Amnon of Mayence is only a "legendary martyr" and that "the poem itself is much older than the period of the Crusades" [155] has left the main impression unimpaired: Amnon the Rabbi dies at the hands of the Archbishop, paying the price for his constancy to the God of Israel. That such a price was exacted and exacted frequently has for ever embittered Jewish-Christian relationship. Characteristically enough, the great Hebrew poet, Judah Halevi (*c*. 1085–1142), lets his hero say to Al Khazari: "I only seek freedom from service of those numerous people whose favour I do not care for, and shall never obtain, though I worked for it all my life." [156] This was the mood of a Jew in the twelfth century. The coming centuries were to add still heavier burdens upon the children of Israel.

The most eloquent witness of what the Jews thought about Christianity comes from a letter addressed to German Jewry by Isaac Zarphati, a fugitive from Christian Europe to Mohammedan Turkey: "I have been informed of the calumnies, more bitter

than death, which have befallen our brethren in Germany; of
the tyrannical laws, the compulsory baptisms, and the banish-
ments which daily take place.   And if they flee from one place,
greater misfortunes befall them in another.   I hear an impudent
nation raising up its impudent voice against the faithful, and see
its hand swinging over them.   There are woes within and woes
without;   daily edicts and taskmasters to extort money.   The
spiritual guides and the monks, the false priests, rise up against
the unhappy people, and say 'We shall persecute them to
destruction, the name of Israel shall no longer be remembered'.
They imagine that their religion is in danger because the Jews in
Jerusalem, peradventure, purchase the Church of the Sepulchre.
For this reason, they have issued a decree that every Jew who is
found on a Christian ship sailing for the East is to be cast into the
sea.   How are the holy German communities treated!   How are
their energies weakened!   The Christians not only drive them
from place to place, but lurk after their lives, brandish over them
the sharpened sword, cast them into the flaming fire, into surging
waters, or into stinking swamps.   My brethren and teachers,
friends and acquaintances, I, Isaac Zarphati, who came from
France, was born in Germany, and there sat at the feet of masters,
proclaim to you that Turkey is a land in which nothing is wanted.
'If you are willing it shall be well with you'.   You shall go safely
from Turkey to the Holy Land.   Is it not better to live among
Mohammedans than among Christians?   Here we are allowed
to dress in the finest material, here everyone sits under his own
fig-trees and vines, while in Christian countries you are not permitted even to dress your children in red or blue without exposing
them to be beaten red or blue.   Hence you are obliged to walk
about like beggars and in rags!   All your days are gloomy, even
your Sabbaths and festivals; strangers enjoy your possessions,
and what use are treasures to a wealthy Jew?   He keeps them
only to his misfortune, and they are all lost in one day." [157]

But it must not be inferred that the present attitude towards
Christianity is simply determined by past history, thus showing
an irreconcilable spirit on the part of the Jews.   Jewish experience
is not only coloured by past events handed down by tradition.
Every generation has added its own bitter knowledge to the
common stock.   And this is as much true of the twentieth century
as of the twelfth.   It was not only a medieval bishop who, on
obtaining an additional few cities to his jurisdiction and finding

some Jewish inhabitants there, decided to solve the "Jewish problem" by burning the Jews.[158] The president of the Holy Synod in Czarist Russia, in our own modern days, followed the path of hallowed tradition when he suggested that the solution to the Jewish problem lay in the emigration of one third, the "conversion" of another third, and the massacre of the rest.[159] More recently, in 1938, when the Patriarch of the Church in Roumania, Miron Cristea, became Prime Minister, he solemnly declared himself in favour of anti-Semitism. In the long list of inveterate Jew-baiters is a strange collection of Christian names from fanatics like Peter the Hermit, Peter of Cluny, to men like Stephen Langton, Innocent III, and Martin Luther.[160] A new note was struck by the late Pope Pius XI in a famous broadcast in September 1938. Commenting on the Canon of the Mass *sacrificium Patriarchae nostri Abraham*, the Pope said: "Notice that Abraham is called our Patriarch, our ancestor. Anti-Semitism is incompatible with the thought and sublime reality expressed in this text. It is a movement in which we Christians can have no part whatsoever. . . . Anti-Semitism is unacceptable. Spiritually we are Semites." [161] These unequivocal words, uttered at a time when anti-Semitism in Germany had reached its height, have made a deep impression upon the Jewish people. But it is rightly felt that such pronouncements have come too late. It is understandable that at a time when racial philosophy had begun to threaten the very life of the Christian Church, official Christendom should dissociate itself from the taint of anti-Semitism. It is, however, doubtful whether the Church is able at this juncture to ward off the evil. There are still countries in Europe where anti-Semitism and Catholicism are almost synonyms. A popular way of demonstrating one's love for the Church is to hate the Jews.[162]

It is therefore not surprising that in the Jewish consciousness Christianity is associated with terrible wrongs and bitter suffering. It is a fact that to many Jews the Cross meant to be the sign of love has become a sign of hatred. It is only natural that Jewish aversion to Christianity should take the form of suspicion and antipathy to Jesus Christ. If it is true that "in the sinister shadow of the Cross, the Church has forgotten not only the words 'Father, forgive them, for they know not what they do', but the vast extent of her indebtedness to the Jews", [163] it is equally true that the Jews have forgotten to distinguish between historic Christianity and Jesus Christ. But the Jewish mistake is easier to explain. A. Fürst rightly says about the Jewish attitude to Jesus: "That the Jewish heart so susceptible to love could shut itself with such stoic persistence against the self-sacrificing love of the Just One from its own midst, is a psychological puzzle which can only be explained by Israel's long history of suffering among Gentile Christians." [164] He aptly remarks that to Treitschke's famous phrase "The Jews are our misfortune" the Jewish people has greater right to retort: The Christians have been for nearly two thousand years our misfortune. [165]

Nobody can seriously deny that there was tension between the Church and the Synagogue from the earliest days. Such tension is almost inevitable considering the uncompromising claim of both. The existence of Church and Synagogue side by side make a compromise impossible if both are to remain what they are. Any *rapprochement* on a religious basis can only prove detrimental to both parties. The nature of Judaism and Christianity is such that they exclude each other. Any attempt to create a "bridge theology", however well intended, will prove futile. Church and Synagogue can only exist in eternal challenge to each other. Martin Buber has grasped this significant fact. [166] Lev Gillet has not. [167] It is vain to seek an understanding between Christianity and Judaism on the basis derived from the common Bible. Church and Synagogue have actually two different Bibles [168] and a different approach to the Old Testament. While to the Jew the Old Testament points to Moses, to the Christian it points to Jesus Christ. [169] The dividing line between them is the Cross. This St. Paul and the Old Church knew better than our modern theologians. Yet the struggle between the two rival faiths is of a purely *spiritual* nature; the Church's claim to represent the New Israel, the Israel of God in the spiritual sense, should have been a stimulus to herself and a challenge to the Synagogue, for this is a holy rivalry. Alas, the Church exchanged the Sword of the Spirit for the sword of steel. In an attempt to defend her faith she betrayed it. The struggle which began on a spiritual plane ended in an earthly fight for privilege, honour, and gain. Here we have found the second answer to our question: How did it happen that Jesus of Nazareth became a stranger to his own people?

Between Jesus and the Jews stands the *Christian* Church.

CHAPTER IV

CONTEMPORARY JUDAISM AND JESUS CHRIST

FROM THE middle of the second century A.D. until the time of their emancipation, *i.e.* from the time when the process of separation between Judaism and Hebrew-Christianity was completed till the time when they re-emerged from the medieval ghettos, there was no Jesus-problem to the Jews. For many generations, Jesus' name was not mentioned amongst them, unless in derision. His life was not seriously considered, as is evident from the *Tol'dot Yeshu*. His claims were made the subject of ridicule. Somehow the Jews managed to shut themselves up in their own dreamy world and to ignore the Man who changed the course of history before their eyes. There were, of course, great Jews who fully realized the significance of Jesus for the Gentile world, like the great commentator Rabbi Sh'lomo Yizḥaki [1] or the great religious philosopher Moses ben Maimon,[2] but these were exceptions.

The ever-growing difficulties of Jewish life in the Middle Ages —the repeated expulsions, the destruction of schools of learning, the severe censorship of literature, the burning of Hebrew books— ultimately caused an intellectual decline. Thus the Jews, who had played so prominent a part in philosophy and science and who had made such vital contributions to the revival of learning in Europe[3]—thus paving the way for that mighty spiritual awakening which goes under the name of the Reformation [4]—became themselves intellectual paupers. It is no exaggeration to say that after the fifteenth century, the end of which was marked by the tragic expulsion from Spain, Jewish importance in the sphere of learning rapidly declined until it sank into insignificance. Laurie Magnus describes this period of decline: "Socially, and morally too, to some extent, it is a story of degraded conditions; linguistically, it was an age of jargon; and intellectually, the influence of Jews on literature and thought was either merely occasional or chiefly revived from earlier times." [5] Such was the inevitable result of the stress under which Jewish life was lived.

An eloquent example of the difficulties the Jews had to face is furnished by the vicissitudes of the Talmud in Christian Europe.[6]

Already Justinian tried to force upon the Jews by an imperial decree the Greek translation of the Old Testament, and the abandonment of δευτέρωσις (*Mishnah*). In later centuries, after the establishment of the Inquisition, the Talmud was singled out for special attack. A famous instance of wholesale destruction occurred in Paris in 1242, when twenty-four cartloads of copies were publicly burned. Later, by a papal bull of 1554, severe censorship of the Talmud and other Jewish literature was introduced. In 1559 the Talmud was included in the first *Index Expurgatorius*.[7] Pope Pius IV decreed in 1565 that the Talmud be deprived of its very name. But all efforts to suppress it proved altogether unsuccessful. Renewed attacks upon the Talmud were made by Gregory XIII. In 1593 Clement VIII again interdicted the possession of copies of the Talmud. The beginning of the sixteenth century saw the great controversy between John (Joseph) Pfefferkorn, a baptized Jew in the service of the Dominicans, and the great and noble scholar John Reuchlin (1455–1522). The violent controversy lasted over ten years and ended with the actual triumph of Reuchlin, though he himself was condemned by the Pope. But, as Canon Danby says, the condemnation was only "on principle", for the decree against Hebrew literature was not renewed.[8] For the first time in history the Talmud was printed, together with other Jewish books, by a Christian printer, Daniel Bomberg of Antwerp. This was the immediate result of Reuchlin's victory. But many years had still to elapse before the Jews were given the freedom to read and write as they pleased. Meanwhile, not only the possession of the Talmud but in some instances the possession of any Jewish literature was regarded by the authorities as a criminal offence. The Jewish struggle against the severe censorship exercised by the Church and the many prohibitions against Jewish writings was carried on with courage and self-denial.[9] But it was certainly no inducement to the furtherance of learning. Small wonder that under such circumstances intellectual life became stagnant. The ghetto became not only the symbol of physical enslavement but also of intellectual decline. In the end the Jews grew accustomed to ghetto conditions, and as a psychological reaction deliberately refused to show any interest in what was happening in the outside world. As a Jewish writer put it: "The answer to the *outward Ghetto* was the willed, conscious inward Ghetto." [10]   Thus the Jew, confined to the narrow walls of his own home, concentrated all his intellectual faculties upon the study of the Talmud and upon mystical speculations. There was neither the freedom nor the will to gain an independent view regarding Jesus. For critical study and open expression of thought conditions were unpropitious. The Jews only entered into public discussion with the Church under duress, as the weaker partners labouring under severe handicaps. The extent of the Jewish disadvantage can be seen from the two most famous public discussions of that kind. The first took place between Pablo Christiani, a Jewish convert, and the famous R. Moses ben Nachman (1194–1270) at Barcelona in 1263, lasting four days.[11] The second was the one between Geronimo de Santa-Fé (the former Jewish physician Joshua ben Joseph ha-Lorki) and a body of representative Jews led by the physician and poet Don Vidal Ben-Benveniste Ibn Labi (Ferrer) of Saragossa. It took place at Tortosa in the Kingdom of Aragon and extended over a year and nine months (February 1413–November 1414) covering 68 (or 69) sessions in all.[12]

The public dispute between Pablo Christiani and R. Moses ben Nachman was turned into a state occasion and was held in the presence of the King of Aragon, Jayme I. In spite of the fact that the Rabbi was assured by the king of no evil consequences and was granted freedom of speech, the Dominicans procured the public burning of his pamphlet which gave an account of the discussion and a sentence condemning him to exile for two years.[13] The disputation at Tortosa, which is unique in Jewish history both for the length of time it covered and for the interest it aroused, ended with even more disastrous consequences. For it resulted in a bull (1415) forbidding the study of the Talmud and other forms of degradation.[14]

A unique case is that of the Karaite Isaac b. Abraham of Troki (1533–1594), the author of *Chizzuk Emunah*.[15] His freedom in expressing his views was due to the peculiar circumstances of Polish life at that time, permitting great liberty of speech and lively exchange of thought [16]—a striking exception to the conditions in Europe at that period.

1. EMANCIPATION AND ITS EFFECTS UPON JEWISH LIFE

Neither the Renaissance nor the great Reformation Movement following in its wake made any impression upon Jewish life. The great change came with the Age of Enlightenment.

The first condition for the re-entering of the Jewish people into European society was the removal of political and civil disabilities. Such a condition was created at the end of the eighteenth century. The process of emancipation was naturally a slow one, and the new problems it created are still acutely felt by both Jews and Gentiles. The process itself is still in progress and its ultimate success entirely depends upon the triumph of the great liberal ideals of the eighteenth century which initiated it.

The "natural rights" which Locke and Rousseau claimed for the individual have laid the philosophical foundations for our modern age, and have thus paved the way for Jewish emancipation. This became possible when the old medieval rule of *cuius regio eius religio* became obsolete. The famous sentence "In my state everyone may be saved after his own fashion" [17] marks the spirit of the new age.

The eighteenth century saw the beginning of a new epoch in world history. It was also one of the most pregnant periods in the history of the Jewish people. On July 4th, 1776, the Declaration of American Independence was published, thus adumbrating the French Revolution. It was soon followed by the famous Declaration of the Rights of Man, issued by the Constituent Assembly of France in August, 1789.[18] But Jewish emancipation was not won without a struggle. Characteristically enough, the extension of the Rights of Man to the Jewish population of France met with considerable resistance within the Assembly.[19] It was not till one day before the closing of the Assembly that better judgment prevailed. September 27th, 1791, brought political freedom for French Jewry, "although some minor political and civil disabilities were yet enforced for years thereafter".[20] This was the first instance of Jews in Europe becoming *citoyens actifs*, and thus enjoying equality of rights. The French example was soon imitated by other European states. Thus the King of Prussia, Frederick William III, under the guidance of his liberal-minded prime minister Hardenberg, issued his famous edict of toleration, March 1812, which raised the Jews to Prussian citizenship and opened their way to greater opportunities.

The process of Jewish emancipation in the West of Europe lasted throughout the nineteenth century, and though it has known many setbacks, its course remained unarrested. The conservative reactionary forces made a last attempt to stay the tide of progress and many political battles were fought, but the spirit of the New Age prevailed. Even in England, where first attempts at emancipating the Jews were made earlier than anywhere else in Europe, the actual removal of disabilities did not pass without a prolonged struggle. Already, John Toland (1670–1722), in an essay entitled "Reasons for naturalizing the Jews in Great Britain and Ireland" (1714), was demanding equality of rights for the Jewish population. In 1753, Pelham (1696–1754) tried to introduce a bill which would make it possible for the Jews to apply to Parliament for naturalization. Curiously enough, this bill passed without much opposition in the Upper House, but was defeated in the Commons. All the cities of England sent in their protests. A hundred years later it was the House of Lords which raised most objections, as can be seen from the fierce struggle over the well-known Oath Bill. It was not until 1858 that the effort at emancipation was crowned with success. But in some European countries the process was carried over to the twentieth century. In Russia full political equality came to the Jews with the Revolution of 1917.

The entry of the Jews into European life instantaneously met with a wave of reaction. European society was spiritually unprepared to accept the Jews as equal partners, and the old stored-up prejudice created a new phenomenon which passes under the inaccurate name of anti-Semitism. It is a characteristic product of our modern, secularized age. In that it is moved not by religious but by purely racial and economic considerations, it differs vastly from the older form of Jew-hatred.[21]

The home of modern or "scientific" anti-Semitism was Germany, and its most prominent prophet was Houston Stewart Chamberlain, an Englishman, who gave the finishing touches to its pseudo-scientific dress. There may be some psychological reasons for German prejudice against the Jewish people, but anti-Semitism itself is so irrational that an adequate explanation is impossible apart from the fact that xenophobia, "the instinctive hatred of the human being for the stranger",[22] is deeply ingrained in human nature. There is the fact that, according to ancient Germanic custom, the resident stranger was outside the protection of the law, unless by some agreement taken under the patronage of an important member of the tribe.[23]   National Socialist Germany, therefore, reversed the process of progress and returned to ancient Germanic custom when publishing the Nüremberg decrees of 1935.

In the early days the anti-Semitic surge, which rallied the most conservative elements in Europe, had definite associations with the Church. This was specially true of countries like Germany, Russia, and France. Behind it was the vain effort to stem the tide of rationalism and to preserve the old way of life.[24] Thus the name of Christianity was used as a weapon against the liberal spirit of the time, of which the emancipation of the Jews was one of its manifestations. But gradually, as the Church lost ground in the West, its propaganda value decreased. Anti-Semitism freed itself from all religious pretence and became, by the genius of German politicians, an independent science on a purely racial basis. The complete break between anti-Semitism and Christianity is of the greatest consequence in that it bears directly upon the Jewish approach to Jesus.

The moment the Jews found themselves outside the ghetto walls their first and immediate problem was that of *adjustment*. They had not only to find themselves a place in modern society, but also an *inner* attitude towards its prevailing trends.[25]   The corollary to external emancipation was the initiation of the process of *internal* emancipation with its revolutionary effects upon the Jewish mind.

(a) *The Haskalah* [26]

The Jews left the religious atmosphere of the ghetto to enter a society of growing rationalism and secularization. Their first impulse was, therefore, "to acquire western culture and to become like their neighbours in language, dress, and habits". [27] There was the feeling "that only lack of Western civilization hindered the Jews from achieving full legal equality with the other peoples". [28]   The work of Moses Mendelssohn (1729–1786) served as the opening phase of the long process of adjustment. His translation of the Bible in modern German [29] first brought the Jews in contact with a language which served as a medium of European culture. By the device of printing the new translation in Hebrew letters, it became possible to be read and understood by almost every Jew in Europe.

The desire to avail themselves of hitherto unknown spheres of learning gave birth to an educational movement known as the *Haskalah*. The *Maskilim* made it their objective to spread the knowledge of European culture amongst their brethren. They were prompted by the desire thus to hasten the inner process of cultural development. Their aim was "to secularize and Europeanize" Jewry. Their greatest achievements were attained in Eastern Europe, especially amongst Russian Jews, upon whom they left an indelible mark. It has been pointed out that the *Haskalah* is to be held responsible for the spiritual crisis into which the Jews were plunged immediately on coming in contact with Western civilization. For the *Haskalah*, by exerting a denationalizing influence upon Judaism and by secularizing Jewish life, called in question the separate existence of Jewry. The two basic principles of medieval Judaism, "the Messianic hope and the dismissal of the outer world", have been undermined by the surrender to European civilization.[30] But actually such a crisis became inevitable by the abruptness of the change from medievalism to modernism. What was achieved in Europe by a slow process of development covering several centuries, was appropriated by Jewry within the space of fifty years. The rapidity of absorption is exemplified by the intellectual transformation of the pioneer of Jewish enlightenment, Moses Mendelssohn.[31]

(b) Apostasy [32]

The urge for the appropriation of Western culture created a unique situation in Jewish history. What neither the sword nor the stake were able to achieve in the days of persecution, was unintentionally accomplished by the Liberalism of the eighteenth century. Jewish emancipation in the West was attended by an alarming drift towards Christianity. This phenomenon had already become evident at the initial stages of the emancipatory movement. Most of Mendelssohn's own children accepted baptism; later, not a single member of his descendants remained faithful to Judaism.[33]

We are told that of the 3,610 Jews who lived in Berlin in 1819, "only 1,236 became Christians within the next four years".[34]

Israel Cohen attributes the wave of apostasy to social pressure. He explains that "the secessions in Prussia were encouraged by the State, and welcomed by the King. Not only were the Jews excluded from all public positions, denied all civil and political rights, and subjected to special humiliations, but even when they attempted to reform the Synagogue service in the hope of stemming the tide of apostasy, they were hindered by the Government, which forbade the use in the Synagogue of the German language and the wearing of the *talar* (minister's gown)." [35]   However, while admitting a certain form of coercion, we hold that it does not explain the tide of apostasy itself.[36]   Jews have lived under similar and worse pressure for many centuries, staking their wealth and their lives for the faith of their fathers.   They have resisted greater temptations than the bonus of ten ducats offered by Frederick William III to every Jew at his baptism; or the wedding present offered by Frederick William IV to every baptized Jewess at her wedding.[37]   There can be little doubt that in the majority of cases the motives which led to baptism were anything but religious;   though it seems to us that the generalizations of which Mr. Cohen is guilty do injustice to a certain number of *converted* Jews.[38]   But the deeper reason for the drift from the Synagogue is to be sought in the prevailing spirit of the age. The fact was that the philosophical humanism of the eighteenth century had broken into the Jewish position with devastating effect.   This coincided with a surge of Liberalism in Christian theology which glossed over the points of doctrine appearing most offensive to the Jewish mind.   Christianity was reduced to a system of lofty ideals to which every educated person could subscribe.   There was more than mere opportunism on the part of many Jews who sought baptism.   It must be borne in mind that the second half of the eighteenth century was a time of great philosophical and ideological renaissance.   It saw the rise of humanism in Germany, of Deism in England, of materialism in France.   Most of these ideologies had the ethical standards of Christianity as their background.   Christianity, therefore, in the mind of the Jew, striving after emancipation, became the symbol of Western culture.   Baptism came to be looked upon as a necessary ceremony attending the entrance of the Jew into the civilized world.   There is ample evidence to show that both the Church and the Jews understood it in this way.

De le Roi quotes some interesting incidents which show up the laxity of the Church of those days. For example, Chr. Wm. Krause is supposed to have declared with conviction, in his sermon at the baptism of Ferd. W. Fliess (1783), that by this act, he is now receiving the "convert" into the religion of reason, taking him away from the God of the Old Testament. Fliess was assured by the pastor that from henceforth nobody would interfere with his religious convictions, his religious views being his own private concern. Even more striking was the sermon delivered at the baptism of Esther Moses (1795), in which the preacher, Pastor C. Fr. Zastrau of Breslau, ridiculed the missionary attempts of the Church.[39] What wonder that a man like Heinrich Heine (1797–1856) regarded his baptism as the entrance ticket to European culture?

On the Jewish side the Liberalism which did not hesitate to resolve the Christian faith into a vague and sentimental humanism, was hailed with enthusiasm and gratitude. Jewish scholars who have written on the subject usually miss the fact that it was not to orthodox Christianity but to German liberal theology of the eighteenth century that those "converts" subscribed.[40] An interesting case is that of David Friedländer (1750–1834), an intimate friend and collaborator of Moses Mendelssohn. Friedländer addressed an open letter: *Sendschreiben an den Oberconsistorialrath Teller zu Berlin von einigen Hausvätern jüdischer Religion*,[41] in which he suggests the union between Judaism and Christianity based on a mutual reform of doctrine. Friedländer offered to accept Christianity on condition that the interpretation of certain Christian dogmas be left to his own private judgment. Teller's answer is even more remarkable. De le Roi well observes that it reveals "the whole wretchedness of the rationalism of those days". In it Teller boldly declares that there is no need for the Jewish *Hausväter* to trouble themselves with the formal adherence to Christianity, as they are already the bearers of the spirit of Christ.[42] Though Friedländer himself later changed his views and has even written against the missionary activities of the Church, he was as incapable of preventing his family from being baptized as was his friend Mendelssohn. The drift towards the Church lasted throughout the nineteenth century.

(c) Reform

The Reform movement grew out of the need to adjust Judaism to the new conditions of life. Philipson admits that the first reformers were guided "not by the thought of Jewish development, but by the artificial motive of making the external expression of their faith respond to an æsthetic longing". [43] But it was not merely "æsthetic longing" which pressed for the reform of Judaism. In the Reform movement, the Jewish instinct for self-preservation asserted itself once more. Reform of the liturgy and ceremonial practice was the only answer to the breach which had been made in the age-old institutions of the Synagogue. To prevent the drift from Judaism, reform became an imperative demand. [44] It was an effort to save the sinking ship from utter destruction. The Reform movement bears evidence that the drift towards Christianity was more than the result of social pressure or the desire for gain, as Mr. Cohen makes out. [45] Philipson rightly points to the difficult position in which enlightenment had placed Jewish youth. The discrepancy between the spirit of the time and the demands of Judaism pressed for a compromise. Such a compromise could only be made possible by the re-thinking of Judaism and the re-defining of its essence. The first question which arose out of the discussion was the problem of authority. The conservative group naturally appealed to tradition; the progressive group held, in common with the spirit of the age, that reason was the final court of appeal. In this it could claim men like Maimonides and Mendelssohn as partisans. The basic principle of the reformers was that Judaism is not a static, but a growing religion, ever adaptable to the changing conditions of life. [46]

In liberal Judaism, especially as it developed in Great Britain and America, the Reform movement reached its final stage. It is distinguished by a marked rationalism, an over-emphasis of the ethical elements in religion, and a non-national outlook. The first philosopher of liberal Judaism was Solomon Formstecher (1808–89). [47] Simon Radowicz describes the movement as a tendency to "continuing more the prophetic than the rabbinical heritage, standing for limitation, reforming or abolishing the 'practical ritual laws', aiming at 'purifying' Judaism in the direction of the highest concept of monotheism, emphasizing the ethical character of Judaism and the universalism of the Jewish ethics, often interpreting the supernatural revelation not in the verbal traditional way or considering it not essential and central, and putting instead the general religio-ethical content of Judaism as its leading idea".[48]   Liberal Judaism repudiates all nationalistic traits in the Synagogue and regards the dispersion as an essential prerequisite of Jewish life.   It aims at "separatism in religion with assimilation in all the other elements of the national life, political, social and cultural". [49]

(d) The science of Judaism [50]

The necessity for justifying the existence of Judaism before the modern world gave birth to a new science: Die Wissenschaft des Judentums.   The recognized founder of this new branch of learning is the great scholar Leopold Zunz (1794–1886).   Next to him deserves to be placed Abraham Geiger (1810–1874). Lindeskog rightly describes his importance in these words: "He is the creator of *Jewish theology* in the modern sense of the word." [51] It is only natural that the Reform movement and the science of Judaism, two concomitant phenomena, should be closely related. They both served the same end and they sprang from the same need, namely the adaptation of Judaism to modern life.   The Reform movement stood in need of a scientific approach to the theological, philosophical, and historical problems which Judaism presented.   This need was met by Jewish scholars who strove to obtain a historical and connected picture of the development of Judaism.   The result was a philosophical and theological re-definition of Judaism in keeping with the spirit of the modern age.

(e) Assimilation and nationalism

Next to the question as to the seat of authority in Judaism, arose the correlated problem as to the meaning and purpose of a separate Jewish existence.   The broadening of the Jewish out-look in matters of religion went hand in hand with a tendency towards denationalization of Jewish life.   The Reform move-ment, with its emphasis upon abstract ethical values, was rapidly drifting towards national effacement, until in the end, "all recollections of national glory were stricken from the memorial tablets of the people, all striving for national redemption was denied.   They reduced themselves to the rank of a religious con-fession and repudiated the peculiar character and content of that religion—all this for the sake of winning the confidence of the European world, of showing themselves worthy of emancipation",

complains a Zionist writer.[52]   Geiger already contended that the
Jews are a religious community and not a nation in the usual
sense of the word.   This became a fundamental principle in
liberal Judaism.   The reformers argued that they were "Germans
of the Mosaic persuasion" and that their distinctiveness in the
past rested upon a misunderstanding of the essence of Judaism.[53]

The reformers' effort to detach Judaism from its racial background and to give it a universalistic dress, led to the unconditional "affirmation of the lands of their exile".   Such an
attitude was equal to national self-effacement.   But once again,
the Jewish will for existence asserted itself.   The *Haskalah* movement, which aimed at breaking the barriers dividing the Jews
from European life, became itself a means of awakening the
national consciousness.   By bringing about a revival of the
Hebrew language, it gave rise to a modern Hebrew literature,
thus preparing the way for the national renaissance.[54]

The contact with Western thought released destructive forces
within the Jewish community: "The sudden break with the
basis of Jewish life in the Galuth, without original values to
replace them, was bound to endanger the very existence of the
people." [55]   It led, on the one hand, to the violent desire of
breaking with the past and submerging among the nations; on
the other hand, there set in a sense of disillusionment and frustration.   This is specially true of Russian Jewry, which made noble
but vain efforts at emancipation.   Spiegel gives an accurate
picture of the spiritual struggle in those early days.   He quotes
the words of Moses Leib Lilienbaum (1843–1910), an outstanding
writer: "My heart is empty, I am barren as an ice-waste, like
an oak hewn down." [56]   This mood of frustration is best exemplified in the person of the most prominent Jewish writer of that
time.   J. L. Gordon (1831–1892) has been called "the leading
poet of the Haskalah period".[57]   Spiegel says of him: "He
believed himself to be the last of the singers of Zion and the
Jews, not a people nor a religious fellowship, but a hopeless,
aimless flock." [58]

The lapse from orthodox faith into nihilism, the prevailing
mood of the Russian intelligentsia in those days, the quick
disillusionment with European culture which set in early under
the stress of life under the Czar, co-operated in creating a vacuum
in the hearts and minds of many.   The reaction expressed itself
in a renewed affirmation of the cultural values of Jewish life.

There is an interesting connexion between the revival of European nationalism and political Zionism whose origin leads back to the *Maskilim* of Russian Jewry.[59] The rapid growth of the national consciousness in the Gentile world strangely contrasted with the spirit of national-abnegation amongst Western Jews. The appeal to national egotism proved stronger than the vague idealism offered by the assimilationists. Jewish national renaissance came at a time of spiritual stress and filled a gap created by the inroads of rationalism upon Jewish life. This was accelerated by the growing tide of anti-Semitism which swept across Central and Eastern Europe. It created new values for the Jewish youth and renewed the hope in a distinct Jewish future.

But an exaggerated emphasis upon nationhood is not an indication of strength, but of weakness. Behind the nationalist effort is a gnawing sense of defeat. The falling back upon one's own resources is a means to disguise the *rejection* meted out by the world outside. Nationalism is frequently an act of despair. Underneath the self-assertiveness of political Zionism is a yearning for the values of Judaism irretrievably lost. There is a subtle difference between ancient and modern Jewish nationalism: in the past, nationalism sprang from the *religious* consciousness; at present, the religious consciousness springs from *nationalism*. In other words: in the past, the Jew knew himself primarily a member of the Synagogue, and therefore a member of his people; at present, he knows himself a member of his people, and therefore feels some obligation to be *still* a member of the Synagogue. This difference indicates the extent of secularization of Jewish life.

(f) Conclusion

In summing up our investigation, we gain the following picture: Emancipation brought the Jewish people in immediate contact with European culture. The attempt to adjust Jewish life to the new conditions has profoundly endangered the former structure of Judaism. It led on the one hand to apostasy and assimilation, and on the other hand to secularization and nationalism. The Reform movement which grew out of the desire to find a *positive* answer to the new problems which Judaism had to face gave the impulse to the scientific study of Judaism and to a new theological orientation. It divided Judaism into two separate camps: orthodox and Reform (Liberal) Judaism, thus creating a schism, which broke the unity of Jewish life.[60]

The entry into European civilization demanded an attitude towards Christianity and thus brought to the forefront the problem of the Jewish attitude to Jesus.

2. CONTEMPORARY JUDAISM AND JESUS CHRIST

The discussion concerning the Jewish attitude to Jesus began in the early days of the emancipatory movement. It has now lasted for over a century and is still in progress. The subject is not of a purely academic nature. The moral and spiritual power of Christianity constitutes an ever present challenge. The decline of Judaism and the constant threat of Christian missions have added to the urgency of the problem. The rationalism of our age has created a vacuum in Jewish life which made Jews singularly susceptible to the Gospel story. Eminent Jews have, therefore, found it imperative to speak out freely in order to warn those who are not able to form an opinion of their own.

Apart from the practical side of the problem, there is also a definite historical interest. A closer study of Judaism has made it necessary to place the Christian "incident" in its proper perspective. By right, it belongs to Jewish history. The sources of the Christian Church have sprung upon Jewish soil. Its Founder, it is held, is an important product of the religio-historical process of Judaism. Who was Jesus? What did he teach? What is his significance for Judaism and the Jewish people? These are questions which legitimately belong to the realm of historical research.

Above all, the controversy concerning the person of Jesus is part, and an important part, of the "*Zwiegespräch*" (dialogue) between Judaism and Christianity.[61] It is a theological necessity for both, the Church and Synagogue, to continue the discussion till the end of time. It was to their mutual loss that such a dialogue became impossible. For centuries, the controversy lapsed into a monologue carried on by the Church, which lacked the grace and the patience to listen to the voice of her one and adequate opponent—the Synagogue. It was left to our modern age to create the conditions under which the resumption of the dialogue became again possible. To-day, the Jew may say openly and freely what he thinks of Jesus of Nazareth, without exposing himself to danger. Freedom of speech has become an integral part of modern life. The following is the result of the controversy carried so far.

For a closer analysis of the views regarding the person of Jesus expressed by a multitude of prominent leaders in Judaism, we select, for the sake of brevity, a few outstanding names. To give a balanced picture, we deem it necessary to choose from both camps, the orthodox and the liberal alike. Though both schools of thought differ widely on many important subjects, they show a striking similarity in their approach to Jesus of Nazareth; not so much in what they say about him, as in the way they circumscribe his person and limit his significance. Characteristic of both is the over-emphasis of the "Jewishness" of Jesus. But while for the orthodox group the Jewishness of Jesus is only a questionable quality, *i.e.* Jesus is only a Jew at his *best*, the liberal group is inclined to apply a text-critical method which presents him always as a Jew, and always at his best. It is a feature of Jewish criticism, with but few exceptions, to treat the Synoptic text recklessly. The text is always adapted to the preconceived portrait of Jesus; but this is not *only* a Jewish failing. Wherein the orthodox and the liberal school of thought differ fundamentally is in relating Jesus to Christianity. While for the orthodox, Jesus is the Founder of Christianity and inseparable from the Church, the liberals differentiate between Jesus and historic Christianity, assigning its foundation chiefly to Paul.

(a) Orthodox Judaism: Rejection [62]

Orthodox Judaism is naturally marked by the faithful adherence to *tradition*. This alone already predetermines the nature of the approach. The Synagogue's attitude towards Jesus in the past is an important factor in the discussion. There is a section amongst orthodox Jews which even avoids mentioning the name of Jesus. Characteristically, the Chief Rabbi, the late Dr. J. H. Hertz, invariably referred to him as the Founder of Christianity, without mentioning his name.[63] The attitude of this group is that of absolute negation. Such Jews look with misgiving upon all those of their co-religionists who engage in the study of the life and work of Jesus. Any sign of positive criticism is decried as a betrayal of Judaism. Guarded appreciation, such as Dr. Klausner's critical and, from the Christian point of view, negative book on Jesus, is enough to cause a storm of indignation amongst them. Judah David Eisenstein, the editor of the *Hebrew Encyclopaedia*, explained that Jews who speak appreciatively of Jesus do so only to flatter the Christians. These are his words: "Some

Reform Rabbis, eager to flatter Christians, are wont to praise
Jesus of Nazareth as a Prophet, and they commend His moral
Law. But these do us more harm than even Christian missionaries. . . . And still more are we injured by these Jewish
writers who come out from their holes and begin to paint things
falsely, and break out in praise of Jesus of Nazareth, as, for
example, Dr. Joseph Klausner does in his book *Jesus of Nazareth
and His Law*. He was the first among Jewish writers to compose
a whole book in vindication of Christianity and to describe the
life of Jesus and his 'Law', and to establish him as a teacher of
morals above all others. Ephraim Deinard in his book *The
Sword of the Lord and of Israel*", the writer continues, "says that
Klausner has given a scientific trend to his book that none may
suspect death in it: 'For his book is deadly poison to young
Jews, and a sharp sword in the hands of our adversaries'." [64]
Those who know Klausner's book will appreciate the exaggeration.[65]

A source of irritation to the conservative-orthodox group is
the frequent homage paid by liberal Rabbis to the person of
Jesus Christ. Dr. J. H. Hertz joins issue with those who by
their "attitude of indiscriminate adulation of the Founder of
Christianity, whose whole life was one of enmity and warfare
against the foundations of our Faith as well as of amazing vilifica-
tions of the Rabbis", cause great damage to Judaism. For in so
doing, "we not only condemn the attitude of our forefathers
towards him, but to all intents and purposes accuse them of
judicial murder". [66]

Such unconditional surrender to tradition, however, is quickly
vanishing. The most common attitude to Jesus even amongst
scholars of the orthodox school is that of guarded appreciation.

Paul Goodman's views are perhaps the most typical of the
whole orthodox group. Martin Buber, on the other hand, who
is a keen and independent thinker, is interesting for his peculiar
moral approach.

Goodman speaks of the charm of Christ's personality, and
frankly admits that countless human hearts have been inspired,
through faith in Jesus, with the spirit of love and self-sacrifice.[67]
The writer is aware "of the most extraordinary paradox of
history" which is that though "the roots of the life and thought
of Jesus lie entirely in Jewish soil", yet the Jews, "the kinsmen
of Jesus, have to this day remained the most consciously deter-

mined opponents of his supremacy". Goodman then puts the question: What is the Jewish argument against the claim of Jesus? The answer is: "It is the Jewish view that Jesus added no important original element to the religious and moral assets which had been accumulated by the Jewish prophets and sages, and that he has certainly been the more or less direct cause of lowering the pure and lofty ideas about God and man current in Judaism." The grounds for the refusal are to-day the same as of old: "For a good work we stone thee not, but for blasphemy, and because that thou, being a man, makest thyself God." [68] The Jews, the writer goes on to explain, "the standard-bearers of the highest form of ethical monotheism", cannot believe in the Christian doctrine of the Incarnation. Such a doctrine is offensive to the "inner springs of the noblest Jewish suscepti- bilities". Goodman dwells often on the subject of Jesus' depend- ence upon basic Jewish teaching, a feature common to all Jewish writers. He complains about the misrepresentation of the Pharisees on the part of the New Testament and Christian theologians. He regards the Essenes, *hasidim* (?), as forming the link between Pharisaism and the Nazarenes ("primitive Christians").[69] The "modernist" approach of Paul Goodman is marked by the fact that he makes an important distinction between the *real* Jesus and the Christ of the Gospels: "The four Gospels are not biographies of Jesus by men who knew him and were eye-witnesses of what they recorded." [70] He stresses the spuriousness of the Synoptic account and points to the impos- sibility of using it as warranted historical evidence; he thinks it ridiculous to make the Synoptic tradition the basis for dogmatic conclusions. His plea is that "it is conceded by those who have utilized the accumulated results of New Testament criticism that there is no acceptable basis for the Christian dogma of the Incarnation, and that the Christian idea of a Logos and of a Trinitarian Deity can be easily traced to pre-Christian Jewish and heathen philosophical conceptions which were grafted on to the monotheism of the Jews." [71] So much for Christian doctrine. Nevertheless, Jesus himself was a true "Jewish monotheist".[72] Here the author quotes not only Gospel sayings, but also utter- ances by St. Paul, to prove that Jesus never regarded himself, nor did others regard him, to be equal with God.

In the sphere of ethics, Jesus stands on Jewish ground.[73] This is an axiom for the author. With the exception of the idea of non-resistance, there is nothing in the teaching of Jesus which cannot be traced back to the influence of Jewish thought: "Competent Christian theologians have acknowledged the equality of Jewish ethics with the loftiest thoughts enunciated by Jesus." [74] But there is a serious flaw in Jesus' ethical teaching in that it oversteps "the righteousness of the Scribes and the Pharisees", thus turning the practical teaching of Judaism into "a set of fantastic rules followed by a very few, while it is consciously disregarded as utterly impracticable by the overwhelming mass of even the most earnest believers." [75] This accounts for the fact that Christians have so miserably failed to walk in their Master's steps. Contrasted with the heroic demands of Jesus "it is the distinction of the Mosaic rule of life that it requires no impossible, superhuman effort, no seclusion or morbid saintliness, to carry out our duty to God and man". It is therefore Mr. Goodman's conviction that from the Jewish point of view Jesus cannot be recognized as a teacher "who effected a revolution in the ethical domain of Israel".[76] Christianity, he holds, owes its success in the world not so much to what is "characteristically Christian, such as its teachings on poverty and non-resistance, as to the healthy and vigorous ethical principles derived from Judaism".[77]

Paul Goodman rightly sees the main issue between Judaism and Christianity to centre round the question: "Was Jesus God or man?" It is because he realizes that the person of Jesus "is indissolubly bound up with the Christian dogma of the Trinity" that he is driven to the conclusion: "The most rational attitude of the Jews towards Jesus is a purely negative one", as "there can be no place for Jesus in the religion of Israel." The significance of Jesus for the Jew lies in his world-historical importance, "as a Jewish figure, who has shed a light over vast masses of his fellow men".[78]

The views of Gerald Friedlander are very much the same. He too reiterates Jesus' dependence on the religious and ethical values of Judaism, derived from the prophets and the psalmists. He crosses swords with Mr. C. G. Montefiore for calling Jesus the "last of the prophets"; he finds it difficult to understand how Montefiore could consider him to be the greatest of them.[79] He attacks Montefiore for suppressing some of the evidence elaborated by Gentile and Jewish scholars which throws doubt upon the historicity of the person of Jesus, though Friedlander himself is not prepared "to go quite as far as Drews and Robertson in denying the possibility of the existence of Jesus".[80]   But he emphatically asserts the impossibility of relying upon the scanty records we possess: "We cannot obtain from the Gospels, the only available sources at our disposal, the necessary data for a critical and historical life of Jesus." [81]

Friedlander asks: Was Jesus a prophet?   He accuses Montefiore of "unbalanced judgment" for answering this question in the affirmative.   For himself, he asks: If Jesus be considered a prophet, "did he reveal an aspect of the Deity previously unknown or forgotten in his day"?   The answer is: to the Gentiles he may have been a prophet, for he taught them things they did not know before, but: "The Jews of the days of Jesus had nothing to learn from his message." [82]   Friedlander stresses the fact that "the Jews have refused steadfastly to see in the hero of the Gospels either a God, or an inspired prophet, or a qualified lawgiver, or a teacher in Israel with a new message for his people". [83]   There was nothing new or original in all that Jesus taught: "The Beatitudes have undoubtedly a lofty tone, but let us not forget that all that they teach can be found in Isaiah and the Psalms.   Israel finds nothing new here." [84]   Even the originality which Montefiore ascribes to Jesus in combining Lev. 19. 18 with Deut. 6. 4f., Friedlander flatly denies: "The Jew, the Pharisee, who wrote the Testaments of the Twelve Patriarchs had already said before Jesus: I loved the Lord, likewise also every man with all my heart." [85]   There is nothing in the Sermon on the Mount of special value to a Jew: four-fifths of it is exclusively Jewish,[86] the rest is of doubtful quality; [87] in other words: "the good is not new, the new is not good." [88]   With all that, Jesus may be counted among the teachers of humanity, though he was "less inspired than the prophets of the Old Testament".[89]   His significance is confined to the Gentile world; the same can be said of Mohammed.

Friedlander's greatest objection to Jesus is the authority he assumed and the claims he made: "No Jew could possibly admit these claims, which involve: (1) his right to abrogate the Divine Law; (2) his power to forgive sins; (3) the efficacy of his vicarious atonement; and (4) his ability to reveal God, the Father of man, to whomsoever he will." [90]

Thus Jesus, the apocalyptic dreamer and the eschatological preacher, whose message is "of little practical value to everyday

life",[91] is of no real consequence to the Jewish people. He belongs
entirely to the Gentile world.

Prof. Martin Buber, though in a sense representing orthodox
Judaism, occupies a position entirely his own. His great powers
of discernment and his depth of thought give him a characteristic
approach to the Jesus-problem which is consistently in line with
his religio-philosophical conception of Judaism.

Buber, who combines fervent Zionism with religious socialism,
regards as the most precious heritage of classical Judaism the
tendency towards actualization (die Tendenz der Verwirklichung) [92] : that is to say, it is a characteristic feature of Judaism
to translate the will of God in human action. Buber explains:
"God can only incidentally be seen in material things but he is
to be actualized amongst them." [93] The realization of the will
of God can only take place within society (Gemeinschaft), and
true society is where the divine is actualized among men.[94]
Judaism thus has only one aim, it tries to attain to the Truth
of Action. This is one of its fundamental principles.[95] Buber
finds it significant that the first word of Jesus' message, as presented by the Synoptic and the Johannine tradition, was the key-
word of the Prophets: *Shubu* (Return). "The impetus of Jesus'
message is the old Jewish demand for unconditional decision which
transforms man and lifts him into the Kingdom of God. And
this still remains the impetus of Christianity." [96]

Buber, therefore, views Jesus' activity in its prophetic setting
and calls him the "central Jew" in whom the Jewish will for
actualization found its deepest expression. When Jesus taught
that if two shall agree upon earth as touching anything, it shall
be done unto them; when he taught that no man who puts his
hand to the plough and looks back is fit for the Kingdom of
God; he was giving expression to the greatest truth of Judaism.
For the Kingdom of God to Jesus is "no vague heavenly bliss;
it is also no spiritual or devotional (kultische) union, no church;
it is the perfect communion (Zusammenleben) of men; it is the
true koinonia which thus becomes God's immediate rule, his
basileia". [97] Jesus' emphasis upon positive action, his insistence
upon the *doing* of the will of God, his conception of the Kingdom
as "the future fellowship (Gemeinschaft) in which all who
hunger and thirst after righteousness will be filled; the realization
of which does not solely depend on divine grace, but on its
co-operation with the human will as the result of the mysterious

union of both", distinguishes the Master of Nazareth not only from Essene teaching [98] but also from Pauline thought.[99]

"Gemeinschaft" is an important word in Buber's religious philosophy. To him, the purpose of Jesus was to make this ideal human relationship possible: "Jesus, who pointed from a spiritualized form of a late Theocracy towards the original certainty of God's kingship and its fulfilment, proclaims the (koinonia) by renewing and transforming the conception of the servant of God. His message however has not reached the Gentiles in its original form but in a duplication (Verzweiung) alien to the Gospel of Jesus." [100]   Herein lies the tragedy of the Christian Church: it lacks that essential Jewish dynamic element (Element der Aktivität) which presses towards unity and actualization.[101]   The Church, therefore, though in the teaching of Jesus it received Jewish teaching, missed its most vital element: "the tendency towards actualization has not entered the spiritual foundations of Gentile life." [102]   But for this the Teacher is not to be blamed.   In his *Three talks on Judaism* Buber deplores the fact that the most important paragraph of the spiritual history of the Jewish people, the appearance of Christianity, should have been obliterated from their records, through no fault of their own. It was due to circumstances which created the *galut* psychology, with its superstitious fear of the Nazarean movement; "we must place it back where it belongs: within the spiritual history of Judaism".[103]   It is obvious then that Buber claims Jesus for Judaism but not the Pauline Christ, and not the second person of the Trinity, but Jesus the Jew, one of the Synagogue's greatest representatives: [104]   "Jesus desired to create of Judaism the Temple of true fellowship (Gemeinschaft) before the mere sight of which would fall the walls of the state built upon force (Gewaltstaat)." [105]   That he failed does not detract from his importance. In a strictly limited sense, Jesus may even make a legitimate claim to Messiahship, without offending Judaism,[106] for it expects salvation from man, "because it is for man to establish God's power upon earth".   But as long as the Kingdom of God is not yet realized, Israel will never accept any man as the Messiah.[107]

Buber is distinguished from most orthodox writers by a sharp emphasis upon the difference between Jesus and Christianity, and by giving to Jesus a *positive* meaning *within* the history of Judaism.   He thus approaches the liberal attitude, standing, as it were, midway between the two groups.

(b) *Liberal Judaism: Appreciation*

The discussion concerning the Jewish attitude to Jesus became necessary the moment the Jews entered Western civilization; it is thus closely connected with the Reform movement. It was liberal Judaism, with its tendency to break the fetters of tradition and to assimilate surrounding culture, which initiated the controversy. The orthodox group was forced into it by way of reaction. The conditions for the resumption of the discussion were singularly propitious. Not only had the old prejudice against the Founder of the Church been broken down, thanks to a better understanding of history, but also improved relationship with Christianity had greatly helped towards a more sympathetic approach to the subject. The modern Jews were, therefore, prepared to face the problem independently and to form their own opinions. They entered the discussion at a moment when the field for critical investigation was already well prepared. So much so that Jewish scholarship has not been able to contribute anything original to the general discussion concerning Jesus of Nazareth. It had to be content with repeating, modifying, or correcting the views of Gentile scholars. Its main merit, however, lies in the field of Rabbinical studies, which helped towards a better understanding of the background against which Christianity was born.[108]

But we are here not concerned with the strictly scientific study of the origins of Christianity. Behind the liberal approach to the person of Jesus were deeper motives than academic interest. These motives are closely connected with the two main principles guiding the Reform movement—*inward* and *outward* readjustment.

Inward readjustment was necessitated by the evergrowing tide of rationalism, and by the profound upheaval caused through the collapse of the old structure of Jewish life. It led towards a re-examination of the foundations of Judaism, and a redefinition of its lasting values. The result was the rejection of Rabbinism in favour of *prophetic* Judaism. Interest in the prophetic conception of religion brought Jesus to the forefront.

Again, outward readjustment demanded a *positive* attitude to Western culture. It was soon recognized that an integral element of that culture was essentially Jewish. Jesus thus formed the link between the Gentile world and the Jewish people. It was recognized that Judaism and Christianity have much in common.

Behind the outward form of both, accretions which in the past have obscured their real essence, is the manifestation of the eternal Truth.[109] The eclectic tendency in liberal Judaism and its peculiar emphasis upon ethics has also helped to fix the attention upon the Master of Nazareth.

Still another important motive may be added; it is of a psychological nature. There is an undeniable need for the human mind to classify and co-ordinate. Jesus, the Great Enigma, created a feeling of discomfiture and presented a constant challenge. He had to be fitted into the long chain of religious evolution. A place had to be found for him, and honour demanded that such a place be within the precincts of Judaism. Hence the constant emphasis upon the *Jewishness* of Jesus.[110]

A detailed survey in the nature of an anthology of the views expressed by liberal Jews concerning Jesus is unnecessary. There is a strange affinity of outlook not only within liberal Judaism but within Judaism at large. In essence, both liberal and orthodox Jews are in agreement concerning Jesus of Nazareth. The difference is mainly of perspective and emphasis. By choosing, therefore, a few outstanding names within liberal Judaism, we receive a pretty accurate picture of the general outlook of that group.

The most outstanding figure in liberal Judaism is undoubtedly C. G. Montefiore (1858–1938). He has contributed more than any other Jewish scholar towards a dispassionate and critical study of the person of Jesus Christ. He may also claim the credit for being the first Jew to write a modern commentary on the Synoptic Gospels.[111]

Montefiore approaches the person of Jesus with great reverence. As far as it is consistent with his liberal views, he is prepared to go to any length in acknowledging the genius and the greatness of the Master of Nazareth.[112] He says of himself: "I believe that I hold a higher view of the greatness and originality of the teaching of Jesus than is common among liberal Jewish writers." [113] Lindeskog, who has studiously examined the author's many contributions to the subject, says with justifiable appreciation that Montefiore, like no other Jewish writer, was quick to grasp the quintessence of Jesus' teaching.[114] He also attaches special importance to Montefiore's contention that the teaching of Jesus must not be viewed piecemeal, bit by bit, but as an organic whole.[115] Lindeskog favourably contrasts this approach which he calls *Totalitätsbetrachtung* with the former method which aimed at finding analogies (*Parallelismus*), and he thinks that it will constitute a new departure for future discussion.[116]

Montefiore's Jowett Lectures for 1910, *Some Elements of the Religious Teaching of Jesus according to the Synoptic Gospels*, present in outline the author's views on the subject. His later contributions show but little deviation from his main line of approach.[117]

Montefiore readily concedes to Jesus the right to be called a prophet. He says: "The inwardness of Jesus, the intense spirituality of his teaching . . . show his connection and kinship with the Prophets. He takes up and renews their message." [118] Though he refuses to see in Jesus *the* prophet, he acknowledges him to be "*one* of the greatest and most original of our Jewish prophets and teachers"; he adds, however: "but I should hesitate to say that he was *more* original than any one of them." [119] To Montefiore, Jesus is essentially a reformer: he raised his voice in condemnation of self-righteousness and formalism and he was a seeker of souls. Jesus' main sphere of activity was amongst the afflicted and the unhappy. Though the Rabbis, too, attached great value to repentance and were always willing to welcome a penitent sinner, yet the redeeming activity "as practised with the methods and the intensity of Jesus" was "something new in the religious history of Israel". [120]   By introducing the idea of redemption, Jesus brought a new conception into the religious life of his time. But, otherwise, there was nothing new in the teaching of Jesus, which was neither anti-Rabbinic, nor anti-Jewish. All that Jesus did was to give to the old familiar doctrines "a high degree of purity, warmth and concentration". [121]   In one point Jesus differs from the prophets; against their impersonal function stands his personal authority, which goes far beyond that of a prophet: "None of them ask for renunciation or sacrifice for my sake." But Montefiore explains that this claim to authority was due to the fact that Jesus believed himself to be the Messiah.[122]   His Messianic consciousness prompted Jesus to connect the imminent Kingdom with his own person. But Montefiore is willing to overlook such a natural mistake and even thinks that such a view was not entirely unworthy of the Master.[123]

On the other hand, Montefiore is able to find weak points in the character of Jesus. Thus Jesus, "like every other great teacher, was not always consistent. Nor was he always at his highest level." [124]   Sometimes he appears tender and loving, teaching to forgive our enemies; at other times, he appears violent, impatiently denouncing the sinner, especially if he happens to be his opponent.[125]   There are two sides in the character of Jesus, "one stern and one tender, one forgiving and one severe".[126]   There is also a "double current in the teaching of Jesus". First, the particularistic Jewish tendency in the "anti-Gentile" utterances; secondly, there is the "universalistic" tendency to embrace all nations.[127]

Naturally, Montefiore's great difficulty is in deciding the authenticity of the Synoptic tradition. The last chapter deals with this problem exclusively. Though the author assures us of his sincere intention to approach the problem unbiassed and without prejudice, as a "modern and an unorthodox Jew", his judgments are often sweeping and sometimes ill-founded.[128] Passages in the Synoptic tradition which do not comply with his preconceived view of the "historic Jesus" are declared unauthentic or spurious.[129]   Not only are utterances of slight verbal difference in the Synoptic account attributed to later editors, but in a few instances some of the most noble words are put to their credit. Thus, the words uttered from the Cross, "Father, forgive them", are, according to Montefiore, "almost certainly not authentic".[130]   He solicits our gratitude to "an editor who could rise to such a noble height". Again, the words "Come unto me, all ye that are weary and heavy laden and I will give you rest", words which have brought, as Montefiore says, healing, strength, and courage to many sorrowing and suffering souls, were probably never uttered by the historic Jesus.[131]

But with all that, Jesus is a *real* person and occupies a central place in the history of religion. Not Paul but Jesus, against Wellhausen's view, was the great pathologist of Judaism: "Jesus put his finger upon real and sore places: upon actual dangers, limitations, shortcomings. But the author of the Epistle to the Romans fights, for the most part, in the air." [132]   Montefiore identifies three evils which Jesus attacked: (1) The putting of ritual in place of morality; (2) self-righteousness or pride; (3) ill-directed intellectualism. Herein Jesus fundamentally differs from Paul. While the Master of Nazareth was involved in practical issues of every-day life, Paul's chief concern was of a purely theological nature.[133]   But the main significance of

Jesus lies in his *person* and character. Thus Jesus, "by his teaching, and by certain qualities in his personality", broke down the barriers of law and nationality and made a diffusion of Judaism possible. He has accomplished what on a small scale has repeatedly been tried, but without much success, namely the breaking down of the barriers of race and nationality in order to bring the essential elements of Judaism to the Gentile world.[134]   In this Montefiore significantly differs from most Jewish scholars, who assign the missionary success entirely to the influence of Paul.[135] In several other respects, Montefiore's position is unique, particularly in his insistence upon the *originality* of Jesus.   We have already seen that Montefiore, like most Jewish scholars, stresses the dependence of Jesus upon his Jewish environment.   But while others are content with stating the fact and hunting for evidence, Montefiore has an open eye for the powerful personality of the Master.   "The originality of Jesus", Montefiore agrees with Wellhausen, "lies in this, that he felt and picked out what was true and eternal amid the chaos and the rubbish, and that he enunciated and emphasized it with the greatest possible insistence and stress."   Though much of the teaching of Jesus can be found in one form or another in Rabbinic literature, there is a definite difference of atmosphere.   "Here (*i.e.* in the Synoptics) we have religion and morality joined together with a white heat of intensity.   The teaching often glows with light and fire. Nothing is to interfere with the pursuit of the highest moral and religious ideal, nothing is to come before it." [136]   Already the fact of "bringing together so many excellent ethical and religious doctrines within the compass of a single volume constitutes an originality in itself". [137]

Montefiore has clearly stated his position with regard to the teaching of Jesus. But his appreciation of the person of Jesus in no place pierces the closed circle of his liberal outlook. He thus divides the Synoptic material in three parts, rejecting what he regards as inconsistent with his views and accepting what in his opinion is of lasting value. First, there are items in the teaching of Jesus (like retribution, merit, love for one's enemies, etc.) which seem both "original and striking", and which "deserve the fullest and most careful consideration". Secondly, there are elements in the teaching of Jesus respecting repentance, forgiveness, humility, etc., which are "essentially Jewish" and, though not original, present "Jewish doctrine in sayings and parables

of great power, beauty and impressiveness". Thirdly, there are
certain elements in the teaching of Jesus which are erroneous
and due to the "limited outlook of his time", such as the teaching
about the "strait gate", the "two ways", about Gehenna and
its fire, etc.: these are categorically to be rejected. There are
still some other elements of lesser importance and doubtful value,
like Jesus' teaching about prayer, riches, non-resistance, etc.
These are of an indifferent nature. The liberal Jew has the inner
freedom to approach the New Testament without prejudice,
selecting what is good and noble and rejecting what is inferior
and outgrown.[138]

But there still remains to be noted one other feature of Montefiore's criticism, which singles him out from among Jewish
scholars. It is the general line of Jewish criticism to point out
the impracticability of the ethics of Jesus, designed for angels and
not for human beings.[139] Montefiore challenges such a view.
He says: "A morality, devised for 'human beings and not for
angels', which takes account of human limitations and weaknesses, seems to be a morality which least of all enables men to
overcome their weaknesses and to transcend their limitations.
Ideals which can be fulfilled are not ideals at all. A great poet
has declared that 'a man's reach should exceed his grasp'."[140]
The positive values of the Gospel teaching are such that it can
be doubted whether the liberal Jew can ignore them with safety.
"The prophet of inwardness", as Montefiore calls Jesus, has still
a message for mankind and can serve as an example of the good
life. In fact, he cannot conceive a time when Jesus "will no
longer be a star of the first magnitude in the spiritual heavens,
when he will no longer be regarded as one of the greatest religious
heroes and teachers whom the world has seen".[141] But with all
that, to liberal Jews, Jesus can neither be "the one and only
Master", "the adored exemplar of all perfection", or "the One
Consummate Teacher". Neither can the New Testament be
anything else but "secondary and supplemental". Liberal
Judaism draws its life-blood from the Old Testament Scriptures,
where all its essentials are already present: "The bulk of our
religion and the bulk of our morality seem due neither to Jesus
nor to Paul, neither to Plato nor to Epictetus, but to the sacred
Scripture of the Jews."[142] In Jesus, Montefiore admires a great
man "aflame with love of God and love of man"; "a large-
hearted man, who gazed into the deepest nature of righteous-

ness"; "a man who loved and was beloved"; "a hater of shams and hypocrisy"; "a man of great tenderness, of deep compassion"; a strong and fearless man; "a lover of children, and a lover of nature"; a man who lived and died in the service of others and "in intimate communion with God". [143]   Such a man deserves our admiration and our homage. So far Montefiore goes. He can afford to do so without endangering his position. Between him and Christianity, not only in its orthodox but even in its Unitarian form, is still a margin of safety. His appreciation of the person of Jesus in no place even touches the periphery of religion. His advances, as he rightly says, are "only supposed advances".[144]   Further he cannot go. One step more would mean to lift Jesus from the contingency of history and to assign to him a place which in the Jewish mind can only be assigned to God. "The Jew cannot find God in man", he cannot call *any* man his Master. "The Master of the modern Jew—is, and can only be, God." [145]

Next to Montefiore in importance and influence stands Kaufmann Kohler (1843–1926). H. G. Enelow says of him that he was "universally regarded as the foremost exponent of Reform Judaism". [146]   Kohler's views are similar to those of Montefiore, with the exception that he lacks the sense of proportion so characteristic of the latter. His judgments are less cautious and his pronouncements are more dogmatic. His appreciation of the person of Jesus is characterized by a free use of superlatives and his style is more that of a rhetorician than that of a scholar.

Kohler's approach to the Synoptic story is naturally highly critical. He views the biographical data with great scepticism and detects legend and exaggeration at every step. Sometimes his inventiveness reaches unusual heights of ingenuity. Thus, he remarks about Mark's account of the temptation in the wilderness: "Mark relates that he (*i.e.* Jesus) was carried up to the upper sphere of the world, where he was with the Ḥayyot, that is, the holy beasts that carry God's throne-chariot—the translator erroneously took the word to mean wild beasts—and where the angels ministered unto him." [147]   But behind all the legends and miracles which tend to obscure the person of Jesus stands the Man of Nazareth full of power and charm, a man of a greater personality than even Hillel. "Indeed we do him little justice when, in comparing him with Hillel, the great and meek teacher, we fail to give him credit for the simplicity and incomparable humanity in which the man of the people eclipsed the Pharisean schoolmen." [148]

Kohler is convinced that both John the Baptist and Jesus belonged to the Essene sect, but the former must have exercised a far greater influence upon his contemporaries, judging from Josephus.[149]   Kohler deduces the Essenic connexions from the fact that Joseph of Arimathea—*Ramathaim*—"was anxious to provide a singularly honorable burial for Jesus". [150]   The probability that Joseph was an Essene he rests upon the dubious witness of Abot de-Rabbi Nathan, according to which there was a colony of Chasidim and Essenes in Bet Rama, which Kohler identifies with Arimathea.[151]   But he holds that there was an important difference between Jesus and the Essenes, in that Jesus represented no particular group, or school of thought; he was a man of the people.   Unlike John the Baptist, Jesus was specially drawn to the outcasts of mankind.   Being filled with true greatness, he sat down with publicans and sinners and communed with those whom the Essenes would have regarded as already condemned.[152]

Kohler protests against the common view which makes Jesus the Founder of Christianity.   Nothing was further from Jesus' mind, who was and remained "a perfect Jew", and who "shared the belief of his co-religionists in God as Father".[153]

We are told with great emphasis that the significance of Jesus lies in bringing the Essene ideal of love and fellowship to supreme perfection.   Jesus, therefore, ought not to be compared either with Hillel the Elder or with Philo of Alexandria.   He is a unique phenomenon in the history of religion.

The teaching of Jesus about purity of heart and thought, his condemnation of all superficial and ritualistic practices reveal him a prophet and fearless reformer.   But, strictly speaking, he is neither.   He is not a prophet in the accepted sense, because his emphasis upon his own "I" disqualifies him from being ranked with the Prophets of Israel.   Those Jewish scholars who try to place Jesus with the Prophets overlook this important fact.   Nevertheless, Kohler assures us, though Jesus claimed to be the Son of God in a unique sense, he was far from "ascribing to himself a divine character". [154]

Jesus was also no social reformer, nor was he a "universalist".[155] He cherished apocalyptic dreams and favoured asceticism.   His aim was to establish a worldly kingdom over against the Kingdom

of Satan, which was Rome. His outstanding quality was his
great sympathy with the outcast and despised. This "made him
a redeemer of men and an uplifter of womanhood without
parallel in history".[156]   Kohler can rise to great rhetorical heights
in his appreciation of Jesus, as his speech before the Religious
Congress of 1893 clearly shows. One passage deserves special
mention: "It cannot and ought not to be denied", he says,
"that the ideal of a human life held up by the Church is of match-
less grandeur; behind all the dogmatic and mystic cobwebs of
theology there is the fascinating model of human kindness and
love; a sweeter and loftier one than this was never presented to
the veneration of man. All the traits of the Greek sage and the
Jewish saints are harmoniously blended in the man of Golgotha.
No ethical system or religious catechism, however broad and
pure, could equal the efficiency of this great personality, standing,
unlike any other, midway between heaven and earth, equally
near to God and to man. . . . Jesus, the helper of the poor, the
friend of the sinner, the brother of every fellow-sufferer, the
comforter of every sorrow-laden, the healer of the sick, the
uplifter of the fallen, the lover of man, the redeemer of woman,
won the heart of mankind by storm. . . . Jesus, the meekest of
men, the most despised of the despised race of the Jews, mounted
the world's throne to be the earth's Great King."   Kohler
explains that Jesus' victory is, in fact, the victory of the Jewish
truth: it is the vindication "of the humanity and philanthropy
taught and practised in the Synagogue".

In one important point Kohler differs from Montefiore, i.e. in
the estimation of the *practical* value of Jesus' teaching. Already
in 1893 Kohler expressed the view that "while Judaism fails to
offer a perfect human model of individual greatness, it presents
a far safer basis of social ethics than the Church does. The
Decalogue is a better foundation to build on than the Sermon on
the Mount. Society cannot be reared on mere love, an element
which is altogether too pliable and yielding. Justice and law
are the pillars of God's throne." In his last book Kohler again
touches upon the same subject. He points out that Jesus, "an
idealist of the highest type", cared nothing for the requirements
of civilization, such as industry, science, and art. This naturally
diminishes his importance for everyday life.[157] Nevertheless, to
Kohler, Jesus remains the great Martyr in the cause of righteousness, love, and brotherhood.

To complete the picture, we will now turn to another prominent liberal Jew, Israel Abrahams, the late reader of Rabbinics in Cambridge (1858–1925).

Like Kaufmann Kohler, Abrahams was originally an orthodox Jew, who afterwards became a leading figure in the liberal movement. His *Studies in Pharisaism and the Gospels*,[158] intended by the author as an Appendix of notes to Montefiore's *Commentary on the Synoptic Gospels*, contain most of his views on our subject.

Abrahams holds that one of the problems in connexion with the study of the Synoptic Gospels is how to keep the balance between the teaching of Jesus on the one hand and the teaching of Judaism on the other. This remark in itself reveals the author's main purpose. His intention is to maintain the balance. For this reason he is forced into the much-trodden path of Jewish criticism: he is out to show Jesus' dependence upon Judaism. But there is still another purpose Abrahams has in mind. He wants to help Christian readers to understand the two sides of the teaching of Jesus, namely, his "prophetic-apocalyptic visions of the Kingdom, and his prophetic-priestly concern in the moral and even ritual life of his day, in which he wished to see the Law maintained in so far as it could be applied to existing circumstances". These two contradictory dispositions represent a real difficulty to the Christian, but "the Jew sees nothing inconsistent in these two aspects". [159] The issue of the discussion largely depends upon our picture of Pharisaism at that time. The author, therefore, wants to remove certain misconceptions and replace the negative picture painted by Christian theologians by a more positive one deduced from the evidence of Jewish sources.

Abrahams begins by pointing out that Jesus was given all freedom to teach in the synagogues; the only difference between him and other teachers was that he was entirely independent of any particular Rabbinical school. Jesus never appealed to any mediate authority in support of his doctrine. Abrahams coins a peculiar phrase to describe the nature of Jesus' teaching; he was an "original eclectic".[160] This explains why it is so difficult to place Jesus in any particular school. He had something of each, he was a mixture of them all. He thus created the impression of being his own authority. In this he differed from his contemporaries, whose custom it was to quote the authority upon which they based their views. Again, Abrahams bids us remember that in many cases the controversy between Jesus and his opponents was only of a local character and of no particular significance. But in one important point Jesus differed fundamentally from all Pharisees, *i.e.* in his attitude to the Sabbath. "He asserted a general right to abrogate the Sabbath law for man's ordinary convenience, while the Rabbis limited the licence to cases of danger of life." [161] In fact, Jesus went so far as to assert that no act of mercy should be postponed, whether it interfered with the Sabbath or not.

Another fundamental difference between Jesus and the Pharisees appears to lie in their teaching with regard to the human access to God. While Pharisaism on the whole, though not throughout, maintained the universality of access, Jesus, as represented by the Synoptic Gospels, often disputed it. "The contrast of sheep and goats, of wheat and tares . . . the declaration that those who refuse to receive Jesus or his apostles are in a worse case than the men of Sodom and Gomorrah, the invariable intolerance and lack of sympathy when addressing opponents . . . make it hard to accept current judgment as to the universality of all the Gospel teaching in reference to the divine forgiveness." Abrahams admires in Jesus the strong, unique sense of his own relationship and unbroken intercourse with God. But he adds: "This sense of nearness is weakened for all other men when the intercourse with God is broken by the intrusion between them and God of the person of Jesus." [162] Against this, Abrahams points to "the inherent universalism of Rabbinism", which shows itself in the *Alenu* prayer of the Jewish liturgy, in the saying that the righteous of all nations have a share in the world to come, and in the view that the Gentiles find repentance easier than even Israel does. [163]

Abrahams contrasts the rigorous demands as found in the Gospels with the lenient and broad-minded views of the Rabbis, who promise forgiveness to everyone who repents and who strive to make repentance easy. His sympathy is naturally with the Rabbis, who are radically opposed to the Pauline theory of grace: "The world is judged by Grace (*batob*), yet all is according to the amount of work"—"This antinomy is the ultimate doctrine of Pharisaism." [164]

Abrahams does not regard Jesus as the originator of the method of teaching by parables; at the same time he admits that some of Jesus' parables point to a "strong personality". Jesus was not outside the Jewish camp and he could count upon the sympathy of the best representatives of Judaism. His criticism of the bad Pharisees, his zeal for the purity of the Temple, his fight against empty ritualism could only meet with their approval. Jesus often stood upon Pharisaic ground as represented by its best exponents. On the question of forgiving one's enemies, of love to man, of devotion to God, there could be no difference between him and the Rabbis. Again, in his attitude to divorce, Jesus "appears to have been a Shammaite"; in many other points he shared the views and methods of other leading personalities of his own or earlier times. Abrahams compares Eccl. 28. 3–5 with Mt. 6. 12, 14f, and draws the conclusion that "this teaching of Jesus, son of Sirach, is absolutely identical with that of Jesus of Nazareth". [165] Abrahams traces a straight line of development running through Proverbs, Sirach, the Twelve Patriarchs, and the Synoptists. Jesus thus belongs to the spiritual history of Israel. He stands within the boundaries of the Synagogue: "When Jesus overturned the money-changers and ejected the sellers of doves from the Temple, he did a service to Judaism." The reason that this is not understood by Christian writers lies in their misconception of Pharisaism, which is being judged by its misuses and not by its merits. Abrahams bids us remember that the money-changers and dove-sellers were not the only people who visited the Temple. Pharisaism, like Christianity, ought to be judged by its saints and not by its sinners, by the great characters it produced and not by the false servants who misrepresented it.[166]

Abrahams, though not prepared to overlook the alleged weak points in the Synoptic teaching, fully appreciates the traits of originality and the lofty idealism of Jesus of Nazareth. On the whole he adds little to the discussion.

In summing up the controversy, it becomes clear that there is a surprising affinity between orthodox and liberal Judaism in their attitude to Jesus Christ: they both tend, with slight variations, to the same conclusions. What Buber says about Jesus is in essence the same as Kohler says about him. Judaism rejects, and rejects categorically, the specific Christology of the Church which removes the Man of Nazareth from his natural environment and from the causality of history. While there is a growing conviction amongst Jews that there ought to be assigned a place of prominence to Jesus in their spiritual history, all are agreed that "there can be no place for Jesus in the religion of Israel".[167]

In this Paul Goodman, an orthodox Jew, and Claude Montefiore, a liberal, stand united.[168]

3. THE JEWISH LEBEN-JESU-FORSCHUNG

The first Jewish monograph dealing with the life and teaching of Jesus was written by Joseph Salvador in 1838.[169] Since that time Jewish investigation has grown to considerable proportions.[170] Though Jewish scholars have added but little originality to the general discussion and have sometimes tended to rely upon the work of others, they show features in this field of study which make it possible to speak of a specific Jewish *Leben-Jesu-Forschung*.[171] The motives which have led Jewish scholars to such enterprise are varied. In some instances it is purely historical and scientific interest, as is the case with Robert Eisler; [172] in other cases it is the need for a definition as to the nature and character of Jesus' teaching and his attitude to Judaism and the Jews. Correlated to this is the urgent need for a clear statement concerning the Jewish attitude to Christianity, on the one hand, and to Jesus of Nazareth on the other.

The variety of views concerning Jesus and the mass of material which has accumulated have been sifted and co-ordinated in a masterly fashion by Gösta Lindeskog. For our purpose, we have to exclude work of a *purely* scientific nature and devote our attention to those scholars whose views are representative of the opinions of Jewry, and whose underlying motive betrays personal and spiritual interest. But, even so, we can pay attention only to a few outstanding names.

(a) *Jesus and Christianity*

The first feature of the Jewish approach to the *historical* Jesus is characterized by an effort to detach him from the dogmatic conception of the Church. Jewish scholars are not interested in the *Christ* of Christianity but in *Jesus* the Jew. Most of them assume that Jesus of Nazareth had no direct influence upon the creation of the Christian Church. Kaufmann Kohler ascribes the existence of Christianity neither to the life nor the teaching of Jesus, but to "his followers' vision of his resurrection".[173] Others make him only indirectly responsible for Christianity, indicating that its creation would have never met with the Master's approval.[174] Jesus stood firmly upon Jewish soil: "Not only did Jesus accept the fundamental religious ideas of his people, but he shared their superstitions, their mistakes, and their ignorances." Jesus firmly held to the particularism of the Jewish people.[175] Nothing was therefore further from his mind than to break with Judaism and to establish another religion.[176] All he wanted was "to reform and to purify the religion of his fellow-Hebrews".[177] It was only "after his death" that "his disagreements with contemporary Judaism were magnified in the interests of Gentile propaganda". [178] This is a commonly held view. It is pointed out that Judaism in its purity was not able to gain adherence amongst the heathen; thus it had to be modified, it had to assume a new name and new forms.[179] The teaching of Jesus has not reached the Gentile world in its purity, but in an adulterated form deviating strongly from his original message.[180] The rôle of mediation fell to Paul, the Apostle to the Gentiles.[181]

(b) Jesus and Paul

Paul is assigned a singular position by Jewish scholars. On the one hand he is spoken of with admiration; Enelow calls him "an intellectual giant"; [182] on the other hand, he is looked upon as the greatest enemy of Judaism.[183] But all are agreed that without him Christianity would have never come into existence, at any rate not in its present form. Graetz says: "Christianity might have died a noiseless death if Saul of Tarsus had not appeared, giving it new life and vigour." [184] Paul is therefore looked upon as "the real founder of the Christian Church".[185] Kohler goes so far as to place Paul entirely outside Rabbinic tradition. He thinks that only Christian writers who are unfamiliar with Rabbinic theology can find traces of Rabbinic thought in Paul's writings.[186] He denies that Paul could have ever sat at the feet of Gamaliel.[187] Kohler warns against stressing Paul's phrase "a Hebrew of the Hebrews" too much. He is even inclined to doubt the veracity of his being of the tribe of Benjamin, on the grounds that "we find nowhere that genealogical lists were kept in those days".[188] He holds, with other Jewish and Gentile scholars, that Paul owes his strange ideas to his Hellenistic upbringing. Paul was imbued with Philonic conceptions, but was probably more familiar with the Apocryphal Book of Wisdom and other apocalyptic writings than with Greek literature. Though it is difficult to measure the extent of pagan influence upon Paul, the author is certain that his "monotheism was not as sublime and absolute as that of the prophets".[189]

I. M. Wise goes so far as to claim that the whole story of the Crucifixion was a mere invention by Paul, "who made use of everything useful".[190]   It was Paul's influence which transformed the heroic death of Jesus into a vicarious sacrifice, with the result that "Jesus, the proclaimed Messiah, was turned into a son of David for Jews, and a son of God for Gentiles".[191]   With few exceptions, Jewish writers make Paul solely responsible for the creation of the Christian Church.   They point to the gap separating Jesus from Paul, representing two worlds which do not meet.   Paul "superimposed", says Reinach, upon the mild ethics of primitive Christianity "the harsh doctrine of original sin, redemption and grace, which gave birth to eighteen centuries of arid disputation and still weighs like a nightmare on humanity".[192]

Prof. Klausner, in his book *From Jesus to Paul*, has tried to place the Apostle of the Gentiles in the context of the religious struggle of his age.   This important study of the teaching and life of Paul sums up the most authoritative Jewish view on the problem of the relationship between Jesus and Paul.

Klausner says of the Apostle that he "consciously opposed paganism and brought over the pagans to Judaism in the new Christian form which he had created; but he was *unconsciously* influenced by paganism and took over from it most of its sacred practices (sacraments) in so far as he could find for them a precedent in Judaism, or he unintentionally coloured Jewish customs with a pagan-mystery colour."[193]   But with all that, Klausner, contrary to the opinions already quoted, recognizes Paul's important connexions with Judaism.   He does not think there is any warrant to doubt Paul's repeated assertions that, prior to his conversion, he was a strict and faithful Jew, of the Pharisaic sect.[194]   There is also no reason to deny Paul's claim to have been a pupil of Gamaliel; in fact, Klausner finds evidence in the Talmud in support of this claim.[195]   Klausner, thus, significantly concludes: "There is almost no doubt in my mind that 'that pupil'[196] means Paul, 'who sat at the feet of Gamaliel'."   But in spite of this, Paul was not a *Jew* in the proper sense: "His soul was torn between Palestinian Pharisaism, the teachings of which he learned particularly in Jerusalem (although he was a 'Pharisee, a son of a Pharisee' and thus a Pharisee by family descent), and Jewish Hellenism—and in a certain measure also pagan Hellenism, in the midst of which he was born and educated

in his childhood in pagan and half-Hellenistic Tarsus." The
result of this strange mixture of influences was that Paul "was
not completely at home either in his first religion or in his second,
after his conversion". The difference between Paul and Jesus
was the difference of environment; Jesus a Palestinian Jew,
Paul a Hellenistic Jew. Paul's inherited Hellenism explains his
tendency towards denationalization and division of soul.[197] Such
difference was of far-reaching consequence. But Klausner
departs from the generally accepted line of Jewish argument; he
says of himself: "Intensive research over many years has brought
the writer of the present book to a deep conviction that there is
nothing in the teaching of Paul—not even the most mystical
elements in it—that did not come to him from authentic Judaism.
For all the theories and hypotheses that Paul drew his opinions
directly from Greek philosophical literature or the mystery religions
of his time have no sufficient foundation. But it *is* a fact that
most of the elements in his teaching which came from Judaism
received unconsciously at his hands a *non-Jewish colouring* from
the influence of the Hellenistic Jewish and pagan atmosphere
with which Paul of Tarsus was surrounded during nearly all his
life, except for the few years which he spent in Jerusalem." [198]
This important acknowledgment of the Jewishness of Paul, by
as great and esteemed a scholar as Joseph Klausner, marks a new
departure in the study of Pauline theology not only in respect to
Jewish scholarship, but to scholarship in general.

Klausner, in a chapter, "Jesus and Paul", makes it clear that
Paul's function in the development of Christianity was decisive.
He thinks it is permissible to say, "of course with certain reservations, that it was not Jesus who created (or more correctly,
founded) Christianity, but Paul. Jesus is the source and root of
Christianity, its religious ideal", but Paul is its actual founder.[199]
It was he who gave Christianity its sacraments, its mysticism, its
organization, and its peculiar colouring. There is also another
point of great importance: in spite of all the tension between
him and the religious authorities, Jesus remained faithful to
Judaism: "He did not intend to found a new religion or a new
Church, he only strove to bring about among his people Israel
the Kingdom of Heaven, and to do this as a Messiah preaching
the repentance and good works which would result in the politico-
spiritual redemption of his people, and through them, of all
mankind." [200] But the case with Paul was different. Paul "was

prepared to found a new Church consciously and intentionally". [201]   The Nazarenes would have remained a *religious sect*
within Judaism and would have probably been reunited to the
Synagogue after a time, but for Paul.   Klausner therefore concludes: "Thus it can be said with finality: *without Jesus, no Paul
and no Nazarenes*; [202] but *without Paul, no world Christianity*.   And
in this sense, Jesus was not the founder of Christianity as it was
spread among the Gentiles, but Paul 'the apostle of the Gentiles',
in spite of the fact that Paul based himself on Jesus, and in
spite of all that Paul received from the primitive church in
Jerusalem." [203]

(c) *Jesus the Jew*

L. Neufeld admirably expressed the main tendency of Jewish
criticism concerning Jesus when he said: "Modern Judaism, at
least the intellectual élite of Judaism, sees in Jesus no more the
apostate and heretic as did the Rabbis of former centuries, but
the greatest man the Jewish people has produced." [204]   It has been
pointed out that the *Jewishness* of Jesus is common to most modern
Jewish writers.   In fact, the extent of his dependence upon Jewish
heritage is often over-emphasized to the exclusion of any signs
of originality on the part of Jesus.   Jesus is in everything and
always a Jew.[205]

The emphasis upon the Jewishness of Jesus is a natural reaction
against the Christian tendency to underrate Judaism; but also
against the traditional method of the Synagogue to under-
estimate the importance of Jesus.   Thus, even orthodox writers
have been emphatic to stress this point.   We have seen how Paul
Goodman, an orthodox Jew, has stressed that "the roots of the
life and thought of Jesus lie entirely in Jewish soil".   To prove
this, Jewish scholars have devoted much time to a detailed
examination of the teaching of Jesus.   They have carefully
scrutinized the Gospel narratives with a view to finding parallel
teaching in Rabbinic literature.   Their main purpose was to
show not only that Jesus taught in conformity with Jewish
tradition, but that all his life he remained faithful to the tenets
of Judaism.   Even Moriz Friedländer, so often in opposition to
Jewish opinion, says of Jesus: "Not even a reformer (Neuerer)
does he want to be, he only desires to continue the work of Moses
and the Prophets; he belongs to them and does not want the continuity with them disrupted." [206]   All that Jesus did was to give

"new expression of what the religious leaders of Israel and particularly the Prophets had sought to teach". [207]   He was a Jew, faithful to the Law even to the traditional dress: "He wore on his garments the fringes ordered by the Law and belonged so thoroughly to Judaism that he shared the narrow views held by the Judeans of that period, and thoroughly despised the heathen world." [208]   The prevailing view among Jewish scholars is that Jesus in most things followed the Pharisaic mode of life, and sometimes showed himself a disciple of Hillel.[209]   Though Klausner points to some important differences between them, yet none is of a fundamental nature.[210]   Cecil Roth well summarizes the Jewish view of the historical Jesus in the following words: "In his wanderings throughout the country, he had urged the people to amend their manner of life. He taught the Fatherhood of God and human brotherhood, the infinite capacity of true repentance to secure forgiveness of sin, the possibility of holiness even for the humblest and most unlearned, the certainty of life everlasting for those whose faith was complete and unquestioning, the equality of powerful and lowly before the Divine throne. His doctrines were not perhaps conspicuously original. He copied and elaborated the teaching of contemporary Rabbis, as he had heard them repeated from earliest youth in the synagogue of his native place. He presented them, however, in a new fashion untrammelled by the shackles of ceremonial law, and enlivened by continuous parables of haunting beauty. It was in the spirit of the ancient prophets of Israel that he inveighed against the exploitation of the poor by the rich, and at the strangle-hold which formalism seemed in his eyes to be establishing on religion." [211]

The prophetic strain in Jesus is an important point in the Jewish conception. Moriz Friedländer says in this connexion that Jesus "felt himself called to be another Isaiah, a deliverer from spiritual darkness to his people. He wished to give sight to the blind, to free the enslaved, to raise the poor and destitute." [212] In this, his prophetic activity, Jesus, like the Prophets of old, met with opposition; his was the fate "that every serious reformer encounters from the ranks of organized religion".[213]   "The idealist must be ready to pay the price of his ideals." [214]

Enelow calls Jesus "the arch-idealist".[215]   This feature in Jesus' character finds a recurring note in Jewish criticism. Sometimes it is made out that it constitutes a weakness which made him exaggerate the ethics of Judaism (Klausner), but in most cases it is looked upon as a sign of perfection. Thus, Danziger speaks of Jesus as "full of human charm and sweetness . . . whose sublime principles might have united all men, Jew and Gentile alike, under the banner of his Messiahship, had it not been for the errors and crimes of those who mistook his word and work and mission, and even in his name were guilty of deeds at which humanity revolts". [216] The ideals which Jesus taught and practised are not something new and strange to ethical conceptions of Judaism. They are *Jewish* ideals. The whole controversy concerning the originality of Jesus turns round this point.

Moriz Friedländer has gone furthest in acknowledging the originality and genius of Jesus.[217] But he occupies an isolated position amongst Jewish scholars. Some think that Jesus held no original views whatsoever; others, that his originality lay not in *what* he taught, but *how* he taught. Rabbi I. M. Wise, who speaks for the first group, challenges orthodox Christianity "to produce from the Gospels any sound, humane, and universal doctrine not contained in our 'Judaism'".[218] He claims that "nobody has ever been able to discover anything new and original in the Gospels".[219] But this is an extreme view. The general trend among Jewish scholars is to acknowledge a certain degree of independence on the part of Jesus. His significance, it is held, lay not in the novelty of the doctrine he taught, but in the peculiar emphasis upon certain truths already familiar to the Jewish people. Enelow, who speaks for the latter group, points out that the whole controversy rests upon a misunderstanding of the meaning of originality. He accepts Hazlitt's definition, to the effect that originality does not consist in showing what has never been, but in pointing out what is before our eyes. Applying this to Jesus, Enelow says: "He gave a fresh interpretation of the laws governing the spiritual life, a fresh message concerning the meaning and purpose of religion, a new illumination of the sense and the object of the old law and of the old prophetic utterances. Here lay his genius and originality." [220] We have seen how Montefiore contended against the pedantry of some scholars whose main objective consists in finding parallels between Jesus and the Rabbis. The originality of Jesus, according to Montefiore, lay in his "trenchantness", his "eager insistency", in the fire, passion, and intensity which characterize some of his sayings.[221] It seems to us, however, that Enelow goes beyond

Montefiore when he says "supreme personality is his greatest originality".[222]   But neither as a teacher nor as an original thinker does Jesus stand outside the circle of Jewish life: as Klausner puts it, "Jesus is the most Jewish of Jews, more Jewish than Simeon ben Shetach, more even than Hillel". [223]   The Jewish people has a right to claim the Man of Nazareth as its own.   Not only does Jesus belong to Judaism, but the whole Christian movement, "as long as its followers belonged to the Jewish people", is a part of Jewish history.[224]   Whatever ways primitive Christianity chose to pursue, there can be no doubt about Jesus: to quote Klausner once more, "Jesus himself did not deliver a single word with the intent to found a new religion or a new religious community". [225]   Christianity was the work of Paul, but Jesus was, and remained, a Jew, not only in the national but also in the religious sense.

(d) The nature of Jesus' activity

We have already made mention that some Jewish scholars connect Jesus with the Essenes in one way or another.   Foremost amongst those who hold this view is Graetz.   He says: "Although it cannot be proved that Jesus was admitted into the order of the Essenes, much of his life and work can only be explained by the supposition that he had adopted their fundamental principles." [226]   This view in a modified form Klausner accepts: "In a certain measure, Jesus had points of resemblance with Essenism." [227]   But there are also important differences between Jesus and John on the one hand and the Essenes on the other hand.[228]   Some, therefore, deny any connexion between Jesus and the Essenes.[229]   The problem which Jewish scholars had to face was as to the nature of his activity.   What did Jesus aim at?   Or, as Lindeskog phrased it: "Who did Jesus want to be?" [230]

Most Jewish scholars are agreed that Jesus thought himself the promised Messiah.   Upon this assumption was built up Salvador's view concerning the nature of Jesus' activity.[231]   Geiger, Graetz, Montefiore, and Klausner [232] are all agreed on this point.   The main question is, what is to be associated with this title.   Jewish scholars are convinced that whatever else Messiahship implied, it could not have meant what Paul makes it out to be.   To quote Herford, who though a Gentile closely approximates to the Jewish view: "The Jewish Messiah portrayed in the earlier Gospels, the purely human being . . . was replaced in the mind of Paul by an ideal figure scarcely to be called human, though Paul would have shrunk from calling it divine." [233]   This view would meet with Prof. Klausner's full approval. According to Klausner, Paul, though a typical Jewish Rabbi and a Pharisee, unconsciously yielded to foreign influence and thus presented the historical Jesus in terms acceptable to the pagan world.

It is clear to Prof. Klausner that there is an important difference "between the stories about the Crucifixion and Resurrection of Jesus and the stories of the pagans about the death and resurrection of their gods".[234]   There can be no doubt, however, that these stories helped to make "a Jewish Messiah" into the "Christian Son of God". But the vital question which has to be answered is: What kind of Messiah was Jesus? or what kind of Messiah did he *want* to be?

Robert Eisler has attempted to prove that Jesus was first and foremost an ecstatic revolutionary with a definite political purpose. To Eisler, Jesus is the ringleader of a revolutionary movement of a religious-nationalist character. This movement was directed against the Temple hierarchy and its Roman masters.[235] Eisler's theory is related to that of Moriz Friedländer, to whom Jesus was the leader of a popular party consisting of '*amme ha-arez*.[236] As such, Jesus stood in fierce opposition to the Pharisees. This struggle against the Pharisees became in the end a struggle against the ceremonial laws (Gesetzesbuchstaben).[237] But Friedländer explains that Jesus did not mean to abrogate the Law, he remained faithful to it, only that his attitude was that of a non-Pharisee: "Life in the spirit, but not in the letter of the Law." Such was also the attitude of all educated non-Pharisaic circles in Palestine and the Diaspora and of the Wisdom and apocalyptic literature. It was this fight against the Pharisaic interpretation of the law and its mode of life which brought Jesus to the full consciousness of his Messiahship.[238] But in reality Jesus, to Friedländer, is not a revolutionary in the usual sense of the word but rather "a religious founder". His significance lies in his emphasis upon the importance of the individual. Friedländer notices in the Gospels an all-pervading tendency to bring the individual to his own right, whom Jesus regarded "as the true bearer of religious life". This becomes specially clear in Mark 3. 28f. (the sin against the Holy Ghost) upon which Friedländer comments: "The ultimate purpose (Selbstzweck) of religion is not God nor his Messiah, but the individual who must attain to

God and his Messiah." He concludes with the words: "And for this work of man's salvation Jesus lived and died." [239]

The purely apocalyptic nature of Jesus' message and Messiahship is brought out by E. R. Trattner. Trattner takes over from Abba Hillel Silver the theory that Jesus, like John the Baptist and many other Jews at the time, believed the fifth millennium to be coming to an end ("the time is fulfilled", Mark 1. 15), and that the sixth millennium ("the Kingdom of God") was at hand.[240] "With this thought uppermost in his mind, Jesus felt a terrific inward compulsion to preach." But though he "drew heavily upon the prophetic heritage of his people", he was actually "more of an apocalyptic mystic than a prophet".[241] "The Kingdom of God" which Jesus was preaching he understood in a national sense; he believed that God in a supernatural way would intervene on behalf of his people.[242] But "only a very few shared with Jesus the conviction that the Kingdom of God was not to be established by the sword". [243] In every other way Jesus remained a faithful Jew and his attacks were not deliberately directed against contemporary Judaism, though some of his teaching contained the germs which were later developed in the "harsh anti-Pharisaic attitude of the Gospels". [244] Though some of his claims were unusual "it would be extremely difficult to imagine Jesus, even in his most sublime moods, feeling that his relationship with the Heavenly Father was based upon some sort of physical pro-creation or to believe that the words 'Son of God' were meant to be literal".[245] Jesus was a mystic, an apocalyptic, a millennarian, a man of little erudition, but of "profound insight",[246] who was preparing his people for the coming of the Kingdom of God, which, in his mind, was imminent. His aim was to "reform and purify the religion of his fellow-Hebrews"; he thus knew himself to have come, not to annul, but to fulfil the Law.[247]

Nevertheless, the Sadducean priests who delivered Jesus into the hands of the Roman Governor acted in the interests of the whole nation, for "Jesus' teaching about himself as a Messiah constituted an alarming menace fraught with the greatest jeopardy to the entire Jewish nation".[248]

Against the purely apocalyptic picture of Jesus, Enelow presents a more moderate, spiritual portrait. H. G. Enelow explains that Jesus had soon to face the two most vital questions connected with his ministry: (1) What was the

nature of the Kingdom he preached? (2) What was his own
relation to that Kingdom? These two questions created the
greatest crisis in Jesus' life.[249]   How did Jesus answer these
questions? After some inward struggle, Jesus reached a decision
which became the "ruling thought of his life": "The Kingdom
of God, he decided, was not political, it was not of this world: it
was spiritual." And because it was spiritual, it was already
present: "The Kingdom of God is already here." This was his
answer to the first question. The second question he answered
in the same spirit: "He decided, if to realize inwardly the
Kingdom of God meant to be the Messiah, the Anointed of God,
God's Son, he was the Messiah."[250]   What did this Messianic
consciousness of Jesus imply? An answer to this question lies in
Enelow's treatment of Jesus' attitude to the Law. Like most
Jewish writers, Enelow is convinced "that it was not the purpose
of Jesus to overthrow the Jewish religion, or the old law, and to
find a new one". He did not come to destroy but to fulfil the
Law. The author explains that this fulfilling of the Law meant
to Jesus "an absorption and application of its spirit, an inward
apprehension of its content and the unfoldment of its purpose in
actual life". In other words, Jesus taught that "mechanical
conformity was not enough. The Law demanded spiritual discernment and realization." Such a conception of the requirements of the Law was not a peculiarity of Jesus, but represents
the opinion of the best teachers in Judaism at all times. The
difference between Jesus and the Rabbis was not a difference of
conceptions, but "a change of emphasis, and the change was
toward the accentuation of the personal element, Jesus' own
personal interfusion with his teaching". While the Jewish
teachers "were interested in principles, in doctrines, in ideals",
Jesus was interested in the individual. They "taught imper-
sonally . . . Jesus taught personally".[251]   We have already seen
that Moriz Friedländer made a similar distinction, but Enelow
gives to Jesus' activity a purely spiritual interpretation. His view
is best described by Montefiore's phrase: Jesus was the "prophet
of inwardness".[252]   Hence the conflict between him and his contemporaries. To him Messiahship meant one thing, and to them
another thing. This involved Jesus "in the most tragic misunderstanding of his career", for which he had in the end to pay with
his life.[253]

Halfway between Eisler and Enelow stands Joseph Klausner.

To Klausner, Eisler's view, with its characteristic emphasis upon the political aspect of Jesus' activity, is unacceptable. Klausner denies that Jesus was a purely political Messiah, but he admits: "There was in the Messiahship of Jesus also a political side, even if this side was not so fundamental in it as Robert Eisler, for example, thinks." [254] Klausner, who characteristically enough opposes H. von Soden's view which makes the Acts of the Apostles out to be a kind of apology before the Roman Government,[255] holds that it actually reflects definite historical events.[256] He thus bases his view concerning the political aspect of Jesus' activity upon Acts 1. 4–8. Klausner makes the following comment on this passage: "There is here a clear indication that shortly after the Crucifixion the disciples of Jesus decided to give up the politico-national Messianic conception of the Jews, which involved a certain danger to the Roman Empire on account of its revolutionary implications, and to devote themselves solely to the propagation of the primitive Christian Messianic idea, which was abstract, mystical, and entirely spiritual—first in Palestine and afterwards in all the world." [257] But this change of policy is a later development, entirely dictated by circumstances; it does not represent Jesus' view. "Even Jesus gave consideration to the emancipation of the Jewish nation from subjection to earthly kingdoms by means of repentance and good works, by the establishment of the Kingdom 'not made with hands' through the agency of a supernatural power which God would give to the ethico-spiritual Messiah." For how otherwise can we account for the view expressed in Acts 1. 6? Klausner observes that the hope expressed in this verse "seems strange as the beginning of the story of Christianity".[258]

A similar approach we find expressed in Klausner's earlier work, *Jesus of Nazareth, His Life, Times and Teaching.* Here the author declares: "There is no reason to suppose that, like contemporary false Messiahs, he (Jesus) wished to arouse a revolt against Rome. Had such been the case, he would have met the same fate as they, and with his execution by the Romans, his ideal would have perished." No, Jesus' first objective was a spiritual revival. For this purpose he has chosen the holy city and the Day of Redemption (Passover) "when Jewish pilgrims from all the corners of the earth flocked to Jerusalem", in order to proclaim himself Messiah with the call to repentance and good works. The result of such a spiritual revival would be God's direct intervention, the overthrow of Rome, and the establishment of the Kingdom.[259]

We see thus that Klausner chose the *via media* in determining the nature of Jesus' activity. He combines the several elements into one whole; here are the three aspects woven together: the political, the mystical (apocalyptic), and the spiritual. Jesus calls to repentance, he expects as a result of it the inauguration of the New Age, which involves the defeat of Rome and national freedom. All this is implied in Jesus' claim to Messiahship.

(e) *The significance of Jesus*

We have seen that Jewish interest in the person of Jesus is entirely dissociated from all religious implications. Jesus is discussed by Jewish scholars not in the context of Christian doctrine but in the context of Jewish history. Jewish writers are not concerned with the Second Person of the Holy Trinity but with Jesus of Nazareth, the *man* and the *Jew*. What, then, is the significance of the *historical* Jesus to the Jews?

There was a time when Jesus had no significance whatsoever to Jews. His life and teaching were of no consequence in the positive sense. Later, when the spiritual benefits of Christianity became evident, he was given a place in the plan of Divine Providence as a "preparer of the way for the King-Messiah" amongst the Gentiles.[260] The question as to Jesus' significance for the Jews *themselves* is of recent origin. It was only thanks to the new circumstances in which the Jewish people found itself that such a question was raised and an answer attempted.[261] The closer contact between Judaism and Christianity necessitated by modern life made it impossible to ignore the Man under whose influence history took shape and whose moral power has endured for centuries. The fact that this Man was also a Jew is the most outstanding element in the Jewish discussion. "No sensible Jew", says Enelow, "can be indifferent to the fact that a Jew should have had such a tremendous part in the religious education and direction of the human race." [262] This knowledge is almost staggering to the Jewish mind. Trattner, in the foreword to his book, makes the following remark: ". . . it is estimated that more than sixty thousand volumes have been written about him (Jesus). Eight hundred languages and dialects tell his story." He continues: "To me—because I am

a Jew—this is an amazing thing, for nothing quite like it has ever
happened on so large a scale in the annals of man." [263]

What, then, is the significance of Jesus to the Jew?

Klausner has tried to answer this question in the last paragraph
of his book. These are his words: "To the Jewish nation he can
be neither God nor the Son of God, in the sense conveyed by
belief in the Trinity. . . . Neither can they regard him as a
Prophet; he lacks the Prophet's political perception and the
Prophet's spirit of national consolation in the political-national
sense . . . neither can they regard him as a law-giver or the
founder of a new religion: he did not even desire to be such.
Neither is he a 'Tanna' or Pharisaic Rabbi: he nearly always
ranged himself in opposition to the Pharisees. . . . But Jesus is,
for the Jewish nation, *a great teacher of morality and an artist in
parable*." [264]

Klausner's view well expresses general Jewish opinion. With
few exceptions, there is a growing desire to appreciate the person
of Jesus and to acknowledge his significance for mankind. It is
repeatedly stressed that his main value lies in the sphere of ethics,
and this not only in what he preached but in the way he lived:
Jesus is the supreme example of great human character. Graetz,
remarking on the apparent deficiency in the education of Jesus,
says: "His deficiency in knowledge, however, was fully com-
pensated for by his intensely sympathetic character. High-
minded earnestness and spotless moral purity were his undeniable
attributes; they stand out in all the authentic accounts of his
life that have reached us." [265] His great human sympathy with
the suffering and the lowly is often emphasized by Jewish writers.
Thus, Kaufmann Kohler is prepared to "admit that Jesus' great
sympathy with the outcast and despised, which was his outstanding characteristic, made him a redeemer of men and an uplifter
of womanhood without parallel in history". [266] There is also an
awareness amongst some Jewish authors that Jesus' activity marks
a new epoch in the history of spiritual development. Trattner
with great emphasis declares: "No Jewish prophet before Jesus
ever searched out the miserable, the sick, the weak, and the
downtrodden in order to pour forth love and compassionate
service. He went out of his way to redeem the lowly by a touch
of human sympathy that is altogether unique in Jewish history." [267]

Rabbi Hyman Gerson Enelow devoted the last chapter of his
book to the question of the modern Jewish attitude to Jesus. He

regards it as "a subject of absorbing interest". [268] He first calls attention to the fact that "there is no official attitude of modern Jews to Jesus. Neither the Jewish people, nor any considerable part of it, has made any formal declaration on the subject." [269] But many prominent leaders of Judaism, though speaking as individuals, have expressed their opinion. What then is their attitude? (1) Jews of all shades of opinions "whether modern or ancient, Reform or Orthodox, do not acknowledge the divinity of Jesus". "Jews could not do that and still remain Jews." [270] (2) Jews cannot acknowledge in Jesus the Messiah, "for the reason that the ideas associated in the Jewish mind with the Messiah not only were left unrealized by Jesus, but have remained unfulfilled to this day". The age "of human perfection, of human happiness, of justice and peace, as drawn by Isaiah and other Prophets" is not yet.[271] Jews thus still hope for the Messianic age. (3) "The modern Jew deplores the tragic death of Jesus." He would rather that it had not occurred. But he died the death of a true idealist, "and who knows whether it was not by this very death that Jesus gained his immortality?" (4) The modern Jew cannot "fail to glory in what Jesus has done for the growth of the ethical and spiritual life of humanity"; [272] the fact that Jesus was a Jew, that he can be only understood in connexion with his Jewish environment, adds special significance to his case.[273] (5) "The modern Jew realizes the ethical power and spiritual beauty of Jesus"; he therefore "cannot fail to appreciate Jesus as a religious and ethical teacher". On these grounds Enelow assigns to Jesus the place due to him "among the noble teachers of morality and heroes of faith Israel has produced".[274]

Looking back upon the sincere endeavour of Jewish scholarship to find the truth concerning the Man of Nazareth, a few outstanding facts inevitably strike the observer:

(1) There exists a strange unanimity of opinion amongst Jewish scholars concerning some vital historical problems. This can be seen from the almost generally accepted view regarding the "anti-Jewish" and "pro-Roman" bias in the New Testament literature, which led Eisler to look for material concerning the historical Jesus elsewhere. There is also unanimity in the matter of Pharisaism and its relationship to Jesus; in the matter of Jesus' attitude to the Law and to Judaism; in the matter of his Messiahship and its implications, etc.

(2) The preoccupation with the *teaching* of Jesus to the neglect of a closer study of his personality, its innermost motives and self-consciousness.

(3) The constant emphasis upon the *Jewishness* of Jesus, which invariably leads to an analytical study of his teaching with reference to Rabbinic literature and to minimization of his originality.

(4) The endeavour to separate Jesus from Pauline and Johannine theology, and thus from the Church. It is an effort to recover Jesus from the entanglements of Christian doctrine in order to make him presentable to the Jewish mind.

(5) The effort to relate Jesus to the religious life of his time in order to assign to him a place within the development of Judaism.

(6) The marked change in the general outlook concerning Jesus, expressing itself in sincere *appreciation* of his teaching, character, and influence.

(7) The awareness of his profound significance for humanity, which expresses itself in a desire to correlate Jesus in one way or another to modern Jewish life.

It must, however, be borne in mind that the discussion concerning Jesus, which began with Joseph Salvador after eighteen centuries of silence, is still in its initial stages. It has not yet reached maturity. So far only individual Jews have spoken, but Judaism has not yet raised its voice. The effect of Jewish study resulted rather in the breaking down of prejudice than in the building up of positive conceptions. The last word concerning Jesus of Nazareth still belongs to a future age.

CHAPTER V

PRIMITIVE HEBREW CHRISTIANITY

So FAR we have dealt with some of the features characteristic of the Jewish attitude to Jesus Christ. It is throughout a negative picture. But there is still another side which has remained unnoticed even by the most penetrating students. We are referring to the fact that throughout the ages there were numbers of Jews who submitted to the claims which Jesus made and acknowledged his Messiahship. This is important, for it is almost universally held on both sides that the Jews have rejected and the Gentiles accepted Jesus of Nazareth. This grave mistake is due to the fact that Christianity, which originally began as a movement of individuals and remained such for several centuries, subsequently became a state-patronized religion. Herein is the irony of history, that while the early triumphs of Christianity were due to the breaking down of all national ties, these very triumphs led it back into the bondage of nationalism. The main issue between the early Church and the mother religion was concerning the national prerogatives of Israel. But eventually Christianity became nationalized, for only as such could it come to terms with the State. To-day we speak of Christian nations and non-Christian nations without even suspecting the contradiction. We have become accustomed to speaking in collective terms about a movement which by its very nature concerns only individuals. If there ever were "Christian nations", the Jewish people never was one. But if amongst the nations of the world there were many *Christians*, it is our purpose to show that the same can be said about the Jews.

1. JESUS' POPULARITY

There is reason to assume that Jesus' ministry extended over a period of three years or thereabouts. The essence of his message was a familiar feature of Jewish piety. He called men to *teshubah*. Yet there was an important difference between his message and that of the Prophets. Their *yom Yahweh*, usually a future Day of Judgment, was proclaimed by him as a Day of Salvation close at hand: Ὅτι πεπλήρωται ὁ καιρὸς, καὶ ἤγγικεν ἡ βασιλεία τοῦ θεοῦ.[1] This was also John the Baptist's message.[2] But while John appeared to be retiring and unassuming, keeping himself in the background, Jesus was constantly amongst the people, and his message was strangely related to his own person. He knew himself uniquely connected with the Kingdom he preached. It reveals a good sense of realism on the part of Jewish scholars that they invariably admit the Messianic consciousness of Jesus.

But Jesus of Nazareth was not only a preacher, he was a man of action. He was constantly on the highroad, moving from place to place, "healing all manner of sickness and all manner of disease among the people". [3] A distinct feature in Jesus' activity was his chief concern with the needy and the outcasts. He knew himself sent to the sick: Οὐ χρείαν ἔχουσιν οἱ ἰσχύοντες ἰατροῦ, ἀλλ᾽ οἱ κακῶς ἔχοντες.[4] His vocation was to seek the lost: ἦλθε γὰρ ὁ υἱὸς τοῦ ἀνθρώπου ζητῆσαι καὶ σῶσαι τὸ ἀπολωλός.[5] His main mission was to preach the Gospel to the poor.[6] He ate with publicans and sinners.[7] This naturally made for the popularity of Jesus amongst the simple folk. As time went by his popularity increased. The Johannine tradition records a genuine fact when we read of the Pharisees saying amongst themselves: ἴδε ὁ κόσμος ὀπίσω αὐτοῦ ἀπῆλθεν.[8] Enelow correctly assumes that Jesus' popularity was till the very end of his life on the increase.[9]

2. JESUS' UNPOPULARITY

The fact that Jesus found a large adherence from among the multitudes, in whom he saw a flock of scattered and fainting sheep without a shepherd,[10] was one reason for the tension between him and the authorities, though not a decisive one.[11] There was more than mere jealousy which in the end led to his Crucifixion. But his unpopularity with the spiritual and religious leaders of the people is only one side of the picture. He was also unpopular with many in the crowd. The masses of the people were drawn and repelled at the same time.[12] Jewish scholars have repeatedly pointed to the double strain in the character of our Lord. We have seen how Moriz Friedländer tried to explain this disturbing duality by attributing it to the contemporary conflicting ideas regarding the Messiah prevalent at that time.[13] We would suggest another explanation. The two sides in the character of Jesus are only an apparent disharmony to the outside observer. The apparent inconsistency is not to be sought in the

character of Jesus, but in the nature of his message. A similar
case is presented by the Prophet Jeremiah. His message, as it
were, runs *against* his natural disposition. He wants to speak
comfort to his people, but it is his prophetic duty to proclaim
judgement. Herein lies the deep tragedy of the prophetic
vocation.[14] The case with Jesus is similar. His heart goes out
to the people. He is moved with compassion at the sight of their
need and frustration. He invites them to come, he brings to
them the promise of the Kingdom. He says his yoke is easy and
his burden is light. But this is only one aspect of his message.
There is another aspect of stern demand and great sacrifice.
The path Jesus is walking is that of self-denial. The way of the
disciple is a narrow way (τεθλιμμένη ἡ ὁδός; θλίβω=squeeze,
press); salvation leads through a "strait gate" (διὰ τῆς στενῆς
πύλης).[15] Discipleship entails renunciation to the highest degree:
a complete break not only with wealth but also with all family
ties for the sake of a higher purpose. It is interesting to note the
context of Luke 15. 26f: "*Great multitudes went with him* and he
turned and said unto them: If anyone come to me and hate not
his father, and mother and wife and children . . . yea, and his
own life also, he cannot be my disciple." [16] To be a disciple
meant to be persecuted, to carry a cross, and to love the Master
above everyone else.[17] He required absolute loyalty and stead-
fastness: he who puts his hand to the plough and looks back is
not fit for the Kingdom of God.[18] Such a message could not have
been popular, and it was not. It is not for nothing that the verb
σκανδαλίζειν so often occurs in the Gospels. Jesus was a two-fold
offence to those who came in contact with him: (1) he offended
people by the extreme demands of his teaching; (2) he offended
by the unique emphasis upon the importance of his own person—
"for my sake". The right to forgive sin, his strange attitude to
the Law, must have been a constant irritant to his hearers. It
was not only the Pharisees who took offence. Whatever the
cause of the sudden change may have been, John records historical
fact when he says that many of his disciples went back and walked
no more with him.[19] Thus, Jesus was popular and unpopular
at the same time. His power of personality, his beauty of speech,
his lofty teaching, his care for the simple and lowly were an
attraction. But only the small group round the Twelve and a
few outsiders, men and women, formed the inner circle of discipleship. The rest remained outside; they were only able to hear

about the mysteries of the Kingdom of God in parables. Indeed, the words of Mt. 20. 16 express the personal experience of the Master: Many be called, but few chosen. Only those who had ears were able to hear; the others were offended.

3. THE RESURRECTION-FAITH AND ITS EFFECTS

The death of Jesus created a crisis in the small circle of faithful disciples. The movement which centred round the Master's person came to a sudden end. The mood amongst his followers is reflected in the story of the two disciples on the way to Emmaus (Lk. 24. 13ff). But such was the intention of Jesus' enemies; they rightly assumed that the shameful death by crucifixion would not only remove a dangerous foe, but would also deliver the final blow to the movement which he started. Yet it was to be otherwise. Graetz has remarked of Jesus: "He is the only mortal of whom one can say without exaggeration that his death was more effective than his life. Golgotha, the place of skulls, became to the civilized world a new Sinai." [20] How did this come about? The problem how the crucified Jesus came to be the triumphant and risen Christ is the most crucial issue in the reconstruction of events. It has occupied many minds and has created a vast literature. The most perplexing fact to scholars is that Christianity is not so much the result of the teaching of Jesus as of faith in his Resurrection. The Church staked her existence upon that faith; upon it rests its whole structure.

It is universally admitted that faith in the Resurrection of Jesus was not invented by Paul, but was already a characteristic of the Jerusalem Church prior to the Apostle's conversion. On this "epilogue", as Klausner calls it,[21] hangs the Messiahship of Jesus. How did the disciples come to such a faith? To answer this question is to answer all other questions related to the problem of the birth of the Christian Church. How did Jesus, the preacher of the Kingdom of God, become himself the *object* of Christian preaching? Or, as Arnold Meyer puts it: "how did it happen that Jesus, the *subject* and bearer of a faith, became the object of faith?" [22] It has been felt that the only man to answer this question was Paul. The customary method was to place the Apostle to the Gentiles between Jesus and the subsequent Church. Steck has pointed out that Paul gradually removed himself from Hebrew-Christian influence until he became its bitter opponent. He traces the line of growing opposition from Romans to Corinthians until it reaches its height in Galatians.[23]   Paul's theology, it was said, springs from a double source—Philonism (Jewish Hellenism) and Stoicism (pagan Hellenism) (so Bauer, Steck, and others).[24]   These two worlds, it is explained, became in the mind of Paul a synthetic whole: "only he could become to the Jews a Jew and to the Greeks a Greek who in his own self carried something of both." [25] A similar synthesis has been assumed by Klausner in his book *From Jesus to Paul*.   But the importance of Klausner's work lies in the strong emphasis upon the Jewish elements in Pauline thought. Klausner is thus driven back to the standpoint of Harnack who saw in Paul a true representative of Hebrew-Christianity closely related spiritually to Pharisaism: "Pharisaism fulfilled its task in the world when it sent this Pharisee into it." [26]   Paul's deeply rooted connexions with Judaism have forced Klausner to assume not a direct, *conscious* assimilation of foreign elements, but an indirect, *unconscious* appropriation of conceptions from alien sources.   Klausner holds that it was inevitable that Paul should be influenced by the "general atmosphere" which prevailed at that time.[27]   But there is one difficulty which Klausner has left unexplained, namely, how Paul, the keen thinker, in all his sharp reasoning, failed to notice the precariousness of his position? The accommodating attitude which Paul adopted towards the Gentile world had its limits for him as for all Jews.   The demarcation line was the principle of the absolute *unity* of God.   Did not Paul realize that he was encroaching upon Jewish monotheism when he exalted Jesus Christ *his* Lord?   Some scholars have therefore held that Paul made a definite and conscious departure from Judaism.   But Meyer rightly remarks: "How the man of Tarsus should suddenly change into one of the most free-thinking spirits nobody attempts to explain." [28]   This is an important point.   There are no signs in the Pauline Epistles of an intentional break with Judaism.   Faith in the Messiah, to Paul, did not imply a renunciation of the past, but its *fulfilment*.   There is thus no satisfactory explanation either way: it is difficult to hold with Klausner that Paul yielded to pagan influence to the extent of endangering Monotheism; it is also impossible to accept the radical view which assumes a conscious break with Judaism. The answer to the puzzle lies in the *novum* which entered the Apostle's consciousness at his conversion: The Resurrection of Jesus.   Where did Paul get that knowledge?

The link between Paul and the historical Jesus was formed by the Church in Jerusalem. The importance of the primitive Church in the shaping of Pauline theology is now increasingly recognized.[29] Klausner regards the Jewish Church, even prior to Paul's conversion, as a decisive factor in the development of Christianity, especially singling out the person of Peter.[30] Paul received from the apostolic Church the cardinal tenets that Jesus was the Messiah, that he was crucified, and that he rose from the dead.[31] We are thus led back from Paul to the first disciples. The main question is, how did those witnesses of the Crucifixion attain to the Resurrection-faith? To this, Prof. Meyer gives the following answer: "That the offence of the Cross was overcome, that the disciples managed to regard as Messiah the Man of Sorrow whom they saw in Gethsemane tremble and dismayed, that they, Jews, who would worship nobody but the only true God, called upon the name of this man after his death in every place without interruption, can only be explained by the tremendous impression of his personality gripping the whole heart. . . . *Primitive Christianity is the result of this overwhelming and gripping impression.*" [32] But the force of this *psychological* argument is weakened by the admission that the Crucifixion of Jesus was a catastrophe terrible enough to counteract the spell of any personality, no matter how great. There is thus a gap between the experience of the disciples on Good Friday, and that of Easter Sunday. It is here that the story of the Resurrection comes into full play.

Klausner, who attaches considerable importance to the faith in the Resurrection of Jesus amongst the disciples, lessens its significance, however, by pointing to the universality of such a belief in those days.[33] But there is an all-important difference between the commonly accepted faith in *tehiyyat ha-metim*, which was to take place at some distant time, and the *actual* Resurrection of the Messiah which the disciples believed they had witnessed personally.[34] It was this that transformed in the eyes of the early disciples the *crucified* Jesus into the triumphant Messiah. Not Paul, therefore, but the *Jewish* believers in *Palestine* had already assigned a unique position to their Master which lifted him out of the limitations of mere human existence. "To be sure," says Klausner, "the beginning of the exaltation of Jesus to his high estate ('Saviour of the world', 'Lord', etc.), was made by the Twelve." [35] All that Paul did was to take these conceptions "from the first disciples and from the primitive Jerusalem community" and develop, broaden, and deepen them.[36] Such an admission by so scrupulous a scholar as Klausner is of greatest importance. It connects Gentile Christianity once again with Jewish Palestine.

The Resurrection of the Crucified Master was the turning-point in the fate of the Messianic movement. It became the corner-stone upon which the faith in the Messiahship of Jesus was built. Paul's whole theology centres round this fact. It is not the Cross but the Resurrection which is the starting-point of Pauline thought.[37] It was also the Resurrection which became the κήρυγμα of the primitive church. That Christ was risen from the dead was *their* εὐαγγέλιον. Hitherto a fainthearted and shy group of men, they became bold witnesses to their risen Lord. The amazing news of the triumph of the Messiah spread with great rapidity throughout Palestine and found ready acceptance among thousands of Jews. On one particular day about 3,000 people were added to the ἐκκλησία; at another time, we hear of 5,000 who believed.[38] During the life-time of the Master, the circle of disciples consisted of but a small group; after his Crucifixion, it rose to considerable proportions—to the extent of causing apprehension amongst the leaders of the people.[39]

4. CHURCH AND SYNAGOGUE: THE REASON FOR THE BREACH

Those who accepted the faith in the crucified and risen Messiah were faithful and pious Jews. Not for one moment did they intend to separate themselves from the rest of the people.[40] They participated in the services of the Temple and together with the "unbelieving" Jews worshipped in the synagogues. They naturally kept the Law of Moses and looked upon the high-priestly office-bearer as the highest spiritual authority.[41] Graetz gives a false impression when he says that "the picture of Jesus nailed to the cross, crowned with thorns, the blood streaming from his wounds, was ever present to his followers, filling their hearts with bitter thoughts of revenge".[42] There is nothing in the whole New Testament literature to justify such a view. On the contrary, the impression we receive from Peter's speeches in Acts and Paul's Epistles is the earnest striving of the believing Jews to heal the breach which must inevitably follow upon Israel's rejection of his Messiah. Nevertheless, Weizsäcker is justified in assuming a deep-seated antagonism between the believers and the non-believers.[43] Between them stood the person of Jesus. The Cross and all that was connected with it drew a dividing line between the two groups.

The essential difference between the believers and non-believers was that the first saw in Jesus the Messiah, in whom all promises were fulfilled, while the others were *still* waiting for the Messiah. To the outsider such a difference might have appeared of little consequence, but in actual fact it was of momentous import. For Messiahship as conceived in those days implied more than Judaism has later conceded. What did it imply?

Klausner's early work *Die messianischen Vorstellungen des jüdischen Volkes* goes to show that in the Tannaitic period the Messiah was looked upon as a political hero whose Kingdom was entirely of *this* world. Klausner remarks on the words: My Kingdom is not of this world—"such a sentence is unthinkable from the mouth of the Jewish Messiah. Not even the spiritualized Messiah of the Ψαλμοὶ Σολομῶντος could have uttered it." [44] From this study it would appear that there were almost no features in the Tannaitic period to correspond to the New Testament view of the Messiah, his significance and his work. On the main issue as to the suffering of the Messiah, Klausner emphatically declares: "In the whole Messianic literature of the Tannaitic period there is no trace to be found of a suffering Messiah." [45] The author, therefore, joins issue with scholars like Weber, Dalman, Wünsche, Schürer, and Bousset, who purport to find points of contact between the New Testament Messianism and that of early Rabbinic teaching. It may be that Klausner has proved too much, but there is certainly a conspicuous difference of outlook between the early Rabbis and the New Testament. The conclusion, however, that because of this difference the sources for the New Testament outlook are to be sought outside Judaism has proved fallacious. It was based upon the view that the controversy with Christianity began at a later period and left Judaism unaffected. But this is not so. We have already seen that the struggle between the followers of Jesus and their opponents began at the earliest period. We shall have occasion to show that the controversy with Christianity affected Judaism considerably.[46] It forced the Rabbis to change their emphasis and in some instances to alter their views. That the Tannaim are conscious

of Christian opposition Klausner himself admits.[47]   The Talmud
is therefore no reliable source for the question as to the Messianic
views at the time of Jesus Christ.   But neither are the apocalyptic
writings an infallible guide.   This has been admitted by Bousset
and others.[48]   The only source is the New Testament itself.[49]
There is an all-important difference between apocalyptic
Judaism and the New Testament outlook regarding the Messiah.
Bousset emphatically says: "The person of the Messiah is not
essential to Israel's eschatological hope and to Judaism."   But
for the New Testament the Messiah is *fundamental* and *central*.
The difference is not to be explained, however, by external
influence, as Bousset would have it,[50] but by the change of
circumstances.   It arose from the difference between hope and
fulfilment.   The followers of Jesus have not only taken over
apocalyptic conceptions, but have also adapted them to the
events which have taken place, events which have determined
their lives and outlook.   This consideration forms the starting-
point to an understanding of early Jewish-Christian relationships.

Jewish scholars have stressed that the Synagogue admitted a
large measure of freedom.   "It is a mistake to think", says
Enelow, "that all Jews had the same idea on the subject (*i.e.*
regarding the Messiah).   Uniformity was never an intellectual
or spiritual characteristic of the Jews." [51]   This is certainly true
of Judaism as far as side-issues are concerned.   But on questions
of principle, the Synagogue knew no toleration.   "Difference of
opinion was not a sin in the eyes of the Pharisees unless they were
convinced that this difference was contrary to the fundamental
principles of the Torah", says Klausner.[52]   Bousset has shown
that there existed two Messianic conceptions side by side, the
politico-national and the apocalyptic-eschatological: "Jewish
Messianic expectancy wavers between these two extreme conceptions, so that almost never does the portrait of the Messiah
appear clearly in either of these forms." [53]   Both views were
based upon Jewish tradition and were to some degree harmonized
with one another.   Bousset's contention is that, owing to the
tragic death of the Messiah, the apocalyptic view was given the
pre-eminence: "After the death of Jesus the Messianic faith of
the Primitive Church *could* take no other form but that of the
transcendental Messianic ideal (Messiasideal)." [54]   However,
even this emphasis upon the transcendent Son of Man was still
within the purview of Jewish thought and could not have been

the deciding factor in the schism. It has been maintained that Hebrew Christianity in its earliest form was a tolerated sect and only its extreme Hellenistic branch as represented by Stephen was liable to persecution: "To Stephen and his party, Jerusalem is hostile; as soon as they come into public view, their leader is killed and his friends dispersed. At the other end is James the Just, the Brother of the Lord. . . . No popular outbreak against the Nazarenes seems to touch him. . . . Between these extremes comes Peter: he had been unaffected by the persecution of Stephen, but later on he is singled out because the would-be orthodox King Herod thinks he will be a popular victim." [55] But Prof. Burkitt is well aware of the fact that it was not only Stephen but also James who died the death of a martyr. What occasion could there have been for a man of his integrity to give offence to the priestly hierarchy? Eisler's fantastic hypothesis that James was set up as a rival to the High Priest by an extreme nationalist party cannot be taken seriously. It flatly contradicts the whole spirit and tradition of the Messianic movement. Prof. Burkitt makes an interesting suggestion which, when substantiated, may well lead to a satisfactory answer. "I venture to suggest", says Prof. Burkitt, "that the abstinence of St. James was not exclusively directed to the mortification of the flesh. He may indeed have been a Nazarite from the beginning, like Samson of old, as Hegesippus implies, but he does not say that he was a vegetarian from the beginning." Burkitt means to say that James's strict asceticism was due to an effort to avoid a difficult situation. This was the only way left to a non-Pauline Christian.[56] Indeed, there seems to have been an inevitable conflict between faith that the Messiah *has* come on the one hand and the demands of the Law on the other. It is of great significance that Prof. Klausner admits that the abrogation of the Law was in one way or another connected with the Days of the Messiah.[57] It may well be that Rab Joseph's remark in *Niddah* 61b, "The ceremonial laws shall be abrogated in the world to come", where '*olam ha-ba* is given the meaning of the world (or time) after death,[58] is a reinterpretation of an earlier view. This may be borne out by the fact that in earlier times the words '*olam ha-ba* and *yemot ha-mashiah* were not so sharply differentiated as they were by the Rabbis in a later period.[59] Strack-Billerbeck carefully explain that the *torah hadashah*, which, in the view of the Rabbis, was connected with the coming of the Messiah, must not be understood in the sense that "this new Torah would push into the background the old Torah of Moses or by means of additions widen it". But they admit that though the new Torah, the *torato shel mashiah*, is still the old Torah of Moses it was expected to receive a new and deeper interpretation. They also cite instances, which seem to go beyond their own words.[60] It would appear that in at least a few cases the Rabbis expected an abrogation or alteration of some Mosaic laws. It ought to be borne in mind that the early Christian attitude to the Law was not much different. The "Old" and the "New" Law, the Law of Moses and the Law of the Messiah, were essentially the same.[61] Even Paul's famous τέλος γὰρ νόμου χριστὸς (Rom. 10. 4) does not necessarily imply the "end" of the Law, but its *completion*.[62]

It is only natural to assume that the same conflict which the Master had to face regarding the Law and its validity was inherited by his disciples. Under immediate suspicion were, of course, the Hellenistic Jews; this explains why Stephen was the first victim. But as time went on, it became clear to the Jewish leaders that even men like Peter and James were blameworthy as far as the Law was concerned. Wagenmann's view, therefore, that the first disciples remained absolutely loyal to the Law, and only their claim to be the *true* Israelites created the rift with the rest of the community, must be rejected.[63] Only a fundamental issue, such as the validity of the Law, could have created the schism.[64] If Jacob of Kefar Sekanya, of whom we read in the Talmud, may be identified with James the Brother of our Lord, a possibility which Klausner does not exclude,[65] then it would appear that his orthodoxy was, to say the least, questionable.[66] Grundmann's arguments, which are based on the assumption of a sharp discord between the Hellenistic party, centring round Stephen, whom he associates with Peter, and the Judaizing party in Jerusalem, have no real foundation.[67] There was, perhaps, a greater outspokenness on the part of Stephen, but no *fundamental* difference of view between him and the rest of the disciples. The theory that only Stephen understood the meaning of the message which Jesus preached has no support from the evidence we possess. If, as Prof. Grundmann thinks, Jesus' message was directed against the Temple and the sacrifices, it is difficult to see why only the Hellenistic and Galilean Jews should have understood its significance. The distinction he draws between Galilee and Judea is too artificial to be trustworthy.

We may, therefore, with good reason, assume a general agreement on fundamental issues, and an early discord with Judaism. The main problem was the question of the Law. The question at issue was not the validity or sanctity of the Law: nobody had any doubts about that. The problem was, whether the Messianic Age, the *yemot ha-mashiah* inaugurated by Jesus of Nazareth, could be brought into harmony with the institutions which were hitherto binding. The maintaining of both was a logical contradiction, as they virtually excluded each other: either the Messiah has come and *fulfilled* the Law, or the Law is still pointing towards him, in which case the Messiah has not yet come.

5. THE SCHISM

It must be conceded that the views concerning the deeper implications connected with the *yemot ha-mashiah* were not universally accepted. Indeed, there was no uniformity of outlook concerning the person and function of the Messiah. On this subject Rabbinic statements are confused and contradictory; [68] they were so probably not only after but also before the Destruction. The question which immediately arises is: What were the unifying factors which made for an early Hebrew-Christian view?

Naturally, a unified Christology came only slowly into existence. There is a measure of truth in Kohler's presentation that the "early Church distinguished itself little from the Synagogue. Its members, who are called Judaeo-Christians, continued to observe the Jewish Law, and changed their attitude to it only gradually." [69] Not only were ideas still in the melting-pot, but an adequate terminology was lacking. Prof. Burkitt says rightly that the disciples "were not at once provided . . . with an appropriate nomenclature for their mysterious Master". [70] But whatever other influences moulded the specific Christian outlook regarding the Messiah, two factors were of fundamental importance: the teaching of Jesus and the teaching of the Old Testament Prophets. It is surprising how little attention scholars have paid to these two powerful influences in the formation of a specific Christology in the early Church. We venture to say that the influence of the Old Testament upon the Messianic movement far outweighs all other considerations. [71] It is a striking fact that while the Pharisees and the Rabbis stand nearer to the Law, Jesus and his early followers stand closer to the Prophets. There is no evidence to prove a definite connection between the Essenes and the Messianic movement (against Graetz, Kohler and others), but there is enough internal and external evidence to show an affinity between early Christianity and the Prophetic outlook.

It is an established fact that the Old Testament presents a double strain: the prophetic and the priestly view. These two tendencies often contradict and sometimes oppose each other. Nowhere is this more evident than in the case of the sacrifices. While in the priestly opinion the sacrifices and the Temple cult are the highest forms of service, the Prophets, with strange unanimity, make light of such a view. Prof. Volz, whose judgement may well be trusted, says: "From Amos to Jeremiah Prophet after Prophet rises to oppose the public services (öffentlicher Gottesdienst): 'obedience is better than sacrifice', 'Jahwe demands moral life rather than Temple cult and sacrifice' is the pronouncement of 1 Sam. 15. 22; Am. 5. 21ff; Hos. 6. 6; Is. 1. 11ff; Mi 6. 6–8. They do not want therefore a purified cult, but something different from it. The Prophets also plainly say that they bring no innovation, but only desire to uncover the well of Moses which remained choked for centuries. They are right; the principle of Old Testament religion is the moral worship of the Spiritual God." [72]   It is difficult to believe that this far-reaching tendency, which Volz calls the "turning-point in religious history", should have disappeared from the spiritual horizon, especially after the prophetic message had, through the Canon, entered the Jewish consciousness. The *shefal-ruaḥ* and the *shefalim* of Is. 57. 15, like the *'anawim* of the post-exilic period,[73] are singularly close to the circles from which Jesus and his followers came and to those to whom the Master's message was directed.

In some respects Pharisaism was also a reaction against the supremacy of the priesthood. Bousset has called attention to this fact. He says: "The piety of the Temple and the cult is slowly replaced in the later period of Judaism by a different piety, which though related to the former is yet in its whole structure essentially different from it: the piety of the Law or observance which already existed before as an under-current, but later forced its way to the surface." [74]   He points out that on the surface it may appear that the Temple cult was still at the time of Jesus of extraordinary importance, but in reality this was not so. There was an ever growing independence on the part of the lay-people from the priestly form of worship.[75]   But there was a profound difference between the prophetic view, with its characteristic insistence upon the deeper motives of the Law, and the Pharisaic submission to its letter.

In the Tannaitic period, when the splendour of the Temple was associated with national independence, the restoration of the Temple service was paramount to the restoration of Israel. The Messianic Age, therefore, does not, according to the Rabbis, dispense with the Temple cult.[76] But this is obviously not the view of the New Testament. The best evidence we have is the Epistle to the Hebrews. Prof. Burkitt shows remarkable insight when he says: "I do not suppose that the idea of 'Christ our Passover' was exclusively Pauline." It certainly was not. The prophetic leaven has slowly worked its way into the religious consciousness. Since the days of the Prophets there was latent the tendency to disclaim the absolute efficacy of the Temple cult. The Messiah, who was to fulfil the deepest hopes, was associated with the pure and the spiritual worship of God, which would supersede the crude Temple sacrifices. The οἶκος πνευματικός, built of living stones for a holy priesthood offering spiritual sacrifices, is the finest fruit of prophetic teaching.[77]

But the other more immediate influence is of equal importance. Bousset, after hinting at the characteristic feature of Jesus' message which was directed against the outward show of piety, observes: "He comparatively seldom entered into controversy against exaggeration and over-valuation of the sacrificial cult."[78] But though references to the Temple are scarce, they are not entirely absent.

It is first to be noted that Jesus was deeply concerned with the purity of the Temple. It is to him the House of God. The record of the cleansing of the Temple is not only contained in all the Synoptic accounts, but also in John. It surely belongs to genuine Christian tradition. The story about the cleansed leper, recorded by all the Synoptics with curious unanimity, ends with the advice that he go and show himself to the priest and offer the gift which Moses commanded. In this case, a conclusion as to Jesus' attitude is made difficult by the additions εἰς μαρτύριον αὐτοῖς, which suggests that the object of the thank-offering is the reinstitution to community life. A more positive attitude, however, we find in the Matthaean tradition, which, though unsupported by the other Synoptics, is nevertheless genuine, as it only reiterates a view already expressed in connection with the cleansing of the Temple. In Mt. 23. 21, we read: καὶ ὁ ὀμόσας ἐν τῷ ναῷ ὀμνύει ἐν αὐτῷ καὶ ἐν τῷ κατοικήσαντι αὐτόν. But even from this, no definite conclusions can be made. In the related passage in the Sermon on the Mount, the same sanctity is ascribed to the *whole* of Jerusalem ὅτι πόλις ἐστὶν τοῦ μεγάλου βασιλέως (Mt. 5. 35). On the negative side the evidence is much more conclusive. First, there stands the great word of the Prophet: חסד חפצתי ולא זבח (Hos. 6. 6), which occurs twice in the Matthaean tradition (Mt. 9. 12, 12. 7), though the verse is not quoted by the other Synoptics.[79] In Mt. 5. 24, we are told that reconciliation with the brother goes *before* the offering of a sacrifice, but it is also added: καὶ τότε ἐλθὼν πρόσφερε τὸ δῶρόν σου.[80] An interesting passage is Mt. 12. 6: λέγω δὲ ὑμῖν ὅτι τοῦ ἱεροῦ μεῖζόν ἐστιν ὧδε. Some MSS read instead of μεῖζον, μείζων.[81] This verse again is peculiar to Matthew. A remarkable passage is Mk. 12. 32f, where not Jesus but a Scribe approvingly remarks that love towards God and one's neighbour: περισσότερόν ἐστιν πάντων τῶν ὁλοκαυτωμάτων καὶ τῶν θυσιῶν. Small wonder that the Master told him he was not far from the Kingdom of God.[82] Both the Scribe's remark and Jesus' answer are an eloquent example of how the Law was understood in certain circles. Our main evidence, however, comes from the accusation which was made against Jesus. It may seem odd that we should accept items of evidence described by the evangelist as ψευδομαρτυρίαι, but there is a strange persistence in Christian tradition which lends to their testimony the mark of authenticity. They were "false witnesses" not because of what they said but of *how* they said it, and their intention in saying it.[83] An echo of the accusation is contained in Jn 2. 15: "Jesus answered and said unto them, Destroy this temple and in three days I will raise it up." [84] It is quite in keeping with the behaviour of false witnesses that Matthew and Mark substantially differ in the wording of the accusation. While in Mt. 26. 61, they give witness that Jesus said: "I am able to destroy the temple of God and build it in three days"; in Mk. 14. 58, they say: "We heard him say, I *will* destroy this temple that is made with hands, and in three days will I build another made without hands." Strangely enough, later in the Crucifixion story, when the passers-by mock at Jesus, Matthew and Mark almost verbally agree: "Thou that destroyest the Temple, and buildest it in three days, save thyself!" (Mt. 27. 40; Mk. 15. 29). It is of singular interest that the accusation against Stephen is similar. Stephen is accused of uttering: ῥήματα βλάσφημα εἰς Μωϋσῆν καὶ τὸν Θεόν (Acts 6. 11). These words of blasphemy against Moses and God are presented by the "false witnesses" as blasphemous words "against the holy place and the law" (v. 13). Stephen is credited with having said: "This Jesus the Nazarene will destroy this place and change the institutions which Moses gave us." That the accusation was not entirely devoid of truth is best borne out by the speech which follows. Whatever authenticity we ascribe to it, it is a fine example of early Christian *apologia*. The veiled attack upon the whole sacrificial system by quoting Am. 5. 25 (LXX; cp. Acts 7. 42) and the remark following the mention of Solomon's temple: "Howbeit the most High dwelleth not in hand-made (temples)" (Acts 7. 48), sufficiently substantiate the accusation made against the first martyr of the Church.[85] Prof. Burkitt has drawn attention to an interesting point. According to Ebionite tradition, Jesus is supposed to have said: "I came to destroy the sacrifices."[86] To this Burkitt remarks: "This may be taken as unexceptionable evidence that some, at least, of the Jewish Christian schools of thought had a difficulty in combining the old sacrificial worship with their new belief that Jesus was the chosen of God."[87] This, of course, evokes the problem as to the interpretation by the early disciples of the death of the Messiah. That an adequate interpretation of the Crucifixion was an absolute necessity is obvious, if we are to assume that *Christian* preaching began soon afterwards. How did the first believers explain the death of their Master?

Von Weizsäcker, whose authority is still considerable, says: "There was on the whole no difference of opinion between Paul and his predecessors as to the meaning of Christ's death. We know, and not only from 1 Cor. 15. 3, that he traced his doctrine that Christ died for our sins to the tradition that had been handed down to him. But it is also evident that it was his most important line of proof, when he desired to rest his argument on a proposition contested by no one, and accepted even by his opponents. Paul's statement concerning the death of Christ, Rom. 3. 25, was undisputed; it was only his inference from it that served to refute his opponents. . . . The preaching of the Cross was everywhere recognized as the preaching of the Gospel (1 Cor. 1. 18)."[88] It is obvious that the tradition to which Paul appeals does not simply go back to that of Antioch, but to Jerusalem itself. "For the Jewish Christians", says Weizsäcker, "the suffering Messiah formed the transition to the crucified." The witness to the Messiahship of Jesus was only possible if his death was given a *religious* meaning, if it was explained as part of the scheme of salvation. This was not entirely alien to Jewish thought. To quote Weizsäcker once more: "So far as our knowledge of the contemporary Jews goes, even they were not all indisposed to the belief that the Messiah should pass through sufferings, although it met with opposition on the part of a section of them." It is, nevertheless, remarkable how little evidence there is from Rabbinic sources to show any such belief in the period under discussion. The isolated references to a suffering Messiah seem to belong to a later date.[89]   Strack-Billerbeck, however, remark: "The rejection of a suffering Messiah is somewhat remarkable when it is remembered what great importance the old Synagogue was wont to attach to suffering." [90]   It may well be that this extraordinary silence concerning a view which, as it would appear from the New Testament, is almost taken for granted, is a result of the feud which arose between the disciples of Jesus and the Synagogue.[91]   We may therefore assume that there were two opposing views concerning the Messiah: a popular view, which has survived to this time in certain quarters, and which makes the Messiah a national hero, whose main mission is the aggrandizement of Israel.[92]   Along with this, there was another view, shared only by a small group and closely akin to the prophetic idea concerning the *'ebed Yahweh*.[93]   Between the two stood the Jewish apocalyptic, offering a synthesis of the two conceptions.[94]   Its main influence, however, was confined to Hellenistic Judaism; it only affected the *prophetic* group to a limited extent and was therefore unable to bridge the cleavage. We are thus driven to the conclusion that there existed in *Palestine*, to use Prof. Burkitt's phrase, "two Judaisms": a *Pharisaic* and a *Prophetic* Judaism.[95] The latter was to some extent related to the Hellenistic Synagogue, which in many important features differed from both.[96]   The prophetic outlook has been deposited in books, like the Epistle to the Hebrews,[97] the Epistle of James,[98] and the Didache.[99] A unique example is the Matthaean Gospel, which Moore describes as "the most conservatively Jewish of the Gospels, and the most violently anti-Pharisaic".[100]   The Gospel was evidently edited at a time when one could still be both.

The process of separation began immediately after the death of Jesus, and was necessitated by an inner logic which made a compromise impossible; between the two diametrically opposed groups stood the crucified Messiah. The inevitable persecution which thus arose hastened the process. *The main issue turned round the Sacrifices.* If Jesus was the Messiah, then his death was of a propitiatory nature, and the sacrifices became superfluous; but if the sacrifices were still obligatory, then Jesus' death was of no efficacy, and thus he was not the Messiah. But because in the view of his followers, Jesus *was* the Messiah, the implications were such as made their religious existence within Judaism impossible. Had the Messianic movement fallen immediately after the Destruction, the whole situation would have been different.[101] But as it was, a breach became inevitable. The persecution against the Church, which made an early appearance, revealed more than mere fanaticism; behind it were concentrated the forces which are born out of the tension when the Old and the New meet. History has its own logic and goes its own ways. The parting of the road became a historical necessity.[102] Its significance lies in the fact that it began in *Jerusalem* and *before the Destruction of the Temple.* Joël is thus essentially right when he says: "In the first place, the estrangement had as its cause not dogmatic differences in the more narrow sense, but the dispute whether the Law was obligatory or not after the appearance of the Messiah."[103]

6. THE GROWTH OF HEBREW CHRISTIANITY

We have said that the separation between the Synagogue and the Church took place in Jerusalem and before the Destruction of the Temple. But such a statement needs certain reservations. In the first instance, there was no consciously planned act on the part of the disciples which made a schism inevitable. On the contrary, the Jewish believers in the Messiah Jesus tried for many years to maintain their position in Judaism. We have seen that this is the only explanation for the introduction of the *Birkat ha-Minim* before the end of the first century. Then, the small group of Jewish Christians regarded itself not only as an integral part of the people but also as the rightful heir to Israel's heritage. They were fighting their way, from the beginning, to the heart and the conscience of their brethren. Their efforts were not without success. Their enthusiasm, their sincerity, and their mode of life were a great attraction. Several factors must have worked for the success of the *Messianic* preaching. First, the political unrest of those days will have created a receptivity for new spiritual values, as is usually the case. Secondly, Messianic preaching had always political associations to the Jewish mind. As in the case of Jesus, at an earlier time, there will have been many who joined the new movement under a misapprehension; some were disillusioned and left, others remained.[104]   Thirdly, there was the prestige and the influence of Jesus himself. The memory of this winning personality was still fresh in many minds. Many who drifted away after the tragic Friday began slowly to return. Faith in the *risen* Messiah overshadowed the fact of his Crucifixion. One more point may be added. The early Christian community consisted mostly of simple folk, peasants and fishermen. Following the example of their Master, the disciples would have paid special attention to the poor and the lowly. Their simple message was for the humble and the oppressed. Acts records the conversion of Pharisees and even of priests, but they were naturally in a minority.[105] The good news found its way most easily to the hearts of those who were hungering and thirsting for righteousness. Thus, the most stable and tenacious elements among the people were won for the Messiah.

Owing to the hostility which the movement met, it was driven from the beginning to assume a defensive character and a measure of independence.[106]   The formation of separate Synagogues seems to have been a feature of Jewish life in Jerusalem.[107] Soon there was added a new Synagogue, that of the Nazarenes. Its existence will have scarcely created any sensation, though it was destined to become the nucleus of a world-wide Church. Its separate existence was not due to Peter, "the fickle one", as Klausner contemptuously calls the Apostle,[108] but to the difficult situation in which the disciples found themselves. The fact that James the Just became the head of the community is usually interpreted as a sign of its orthodoxy, but this rests upon a misunderstanding as to the nature of James's position. Klausner naturally vouches for the orthodoxy of James who, though recognizing Jesus as the Messiah, did not regard him as the Son of God.[109] But Klausner's position reveals an inconsistency. If James really was the strictly observing Jew he makes him out to be, how could he have had a hand in a decree which, in Klausner's own words, "yielded to the *Gentiles* on most of the ceremonial requirements, *but not on all;* and to *Jews* who had become believers in Jesus, it yielded *nothing*"?[110]   James's popularity, however, may be due to other reasons; it may simply be an indication of the esteem the Messianic movement enjoyed among the people. If Klausner's suggestion as to the meaning of the name which, according to Hegesippus, was given to James, holds good, then it would go some way to prove our point. If ὠβλίας means Father of the People, [111] then his popularity may be due as much to his position in the Messianic community as to his own personal integrity. That his esteem did not reach the upper classes is proved by his death. James was the Father of the People because the Messianic movement was essentially a movement of the *People*. This would to a large extent explain the ever-growing hostility on the part of the Jewish authorities.

It may well be that the martyrdom of James the Just and the flight of the Hebrew Christian community to Pella in Perea, east of the Jordan, are logically connected. According to Eusebius this took place in obedience to a "certain oracle that was vouchsafed by way of revelation to approved men there".[112] Epiphanius, who mentions Pella on several occasions, has nothing to say beyond the bare fact "cum Pellae discipuli omnes habitarent, a Christo de relinquenda Hierosolymorum urbe migrandoque praemoniti, quod ejus immineret obsidio".[113] Lawlor and Oulton think that both Epiphanius and Eusebius have drawn upon a common source, probably the *Memoirs* of Hegesippus.[114] But the fact itself cannot easily be called in question. It rests upon authentic Christian tradition. The motives which lay behind such a step are difficult to ascertain, and to some extent depend upon the date when the exodus took place. From Eusebius' account, it would appear that it took place *before* the beginning of the war. The war against Rome began in the year A.D. 66, following the disturbances in Jerusalem under Florus.[115] The Martyrdom of James, if we credit Josephus' account, falls in the year A.D. 62.[116] The migration to Pella must, therefore, have taken place between 62–66. But the reasons for such a desperate step at such an early date are entirely lacking. Weizsäcker rightly conjectures that the Christian community would have not lightheartedly abandoned the city, unless absolutely compelled by circumstances. Such a situation, Weizsäcker holds, arose in A.D. 67, after the Jewish victory over Cestius, when nationalist rule set in, showing intolerance to those of more moderate views. Harnack assumes an even later date. He says: "At the beginning of the first Siege of Jerusalem the Christians left the city", *i.e.* in the year A.D. 68.[117]   But it is difficult to see how the Christians were allowed to leave the city once the siege had started. Even Weizsäcker's date raises difficulties, for Perea itself was at that time a war-threatened country.[118]   Again, there is no evidence for the theory that the primitive Church was in any way politically committed, unless we accept Eisler's point of view.   But then, it is difficult to see why a *nationalist* movement of Eisler's description would be forced to quit Jerusalem.[119]   Schürer does not exclude the possibility of an earlier departure.   We would venture to suggest that it took place not long after the martyrdom of James.   The reason for such a step was probably an outbreak of persecution which did not stop with the death of James, but affected the whole community.   The migration to a foreign country was not a *voluntary* act, for this Jerusalem occupied too important a place in Jewish-Christian thought.[120]   Jewish Christians left the city when life became impossible there; it was entirely a measure of self-protection.

The persecution was instigated by the authorities.   Its aim was to deprive the community of its venerable leader and to scatter its members.   This is actually borne out by the evidence we find in Eusebius.   There seems to be more than a literary connection between the death of James, the banishment of the Apostles from the land of Judea, and the migration of the Church to Pella.   If our conjectures are right, the flight to Pella would, therefore, be another sign of the early success of Christianity upon Judean soil.   Persecution is usually an indication of success on the part of those persecuted.

The departure of the more prominent members of the Christian community,[121] the rapid deterioration of the political situation in Palestine, and the terrible struggle which followed brought the Messianic movement to a temporary standstill.   The situation changed, however, after the Fall of Jerusalem.

The year A.D. 70 marks a turning-point in the history not only of Judaism but also of Christianity.   The military defeat which ended in the Destruction of the Temple affected the young Jewish Church in several ways:

(1) The fact that the war against Rome took place without Christian participation widened the breach between the nationalistically minded Jews and the believers in Jesus Christ.

(2) The Destruction of the Temple tipped the scales in favour of the antinomian elements of Jewish Christianity and it also

solved the perplexing problem concerning Christian participation in the Temple cult.[122]

(3) It detached the Jewish Church from Jerusalem as a religious centre, and thus allowed a greater measure of freedom and independence.

(4) It provided the Messianic movement with a new and powerful weapon for propaganda purposes. It is on this last point that we will now concentrate our attention.

Soon after the Destruction of the Temple we find evidence of an increase in Jewish-Christian influence. There are two outstanding facts which point in this direction: (1) the introduction of the *Birkat ha-minim;* (2) the new frequent disputes between the *minim,* in most cases, Jewish Christians, and the leading Rabbis. The first point we have elaborated in another place.[123] In support of the second point we should like to quote the weighty opinion of George Foot Moore. Prof. Moore says: "The vehemence with which the leading Rabbis of the first generation of the second century express their hostility to the Gospel, and other books of the heretics, and to their conventicles, is the best evidence that they were growing in numbers and influence: some even among the teachers of the Law were suspected of leaning toward the new doctrine." [124] This lends support to the view that Hebrew-Christianity experienced a sudden revival after the Destruction and that its influence made itself felt to such an extent as to alarm the Jewish authorities. What was the cause of its sudden rise? This question evokes a four-fold answer.

(1) The Destruction of the Temple was naturally interpreted by the Church as an act of judgment. It was looked upon as a punishment for the rejection of the Messiah. Thus, Justin says to Trypho: "Even when your city is captured and your land ravaged, you do not repent." [125] The οἶκος ἔρημος, which undoubtedly refers to the Destruction of the Temple, is already in the oldest Christian tradition connected with the rejection of the Messiah.[126] That the Destruction was an important point in the polemic between the Church and the Synagogue may be supported from Talmudic evidence. In *pal. Sab.* 119b and *Yoma* 9b, an effort is made to provide an answer for the cause of the Destruction. In the first passage, eight reasons are enumerated which have brought about the calamity; in the second passage, three main sins are mentioned: idolatry, fornication, and the shedding of blood.[127] Schoeps accepts Marmorstein's view that

the Rabbis thus intended to contradict the Christian contention
which made the Destruction a punishment for the rejection of
Jesus.[128]

(2) The death of Jesus, after the Destruction of the Temple,
appeared in a new light. The whole of the Epistle to the Hebrews
is built up upon the thought that the Temple-sacrifices were
only an *adumbratio* or a *praefiguratio* of the perfect sacrifice of the
perfect High Priest. Whatever date we assign to the Epistle, there
can be little doubt that it was composed before the end of the
first century.[129] Even if we accept von Soden's view that the
recipients of Hebrews were Gentile Christians in Italy, the
writer himself must have definitely been a Jew, even though an
Alexandrian Jew.[130] Strangely enough, though Justin, in his
Dialogue, in several instances closely approximates to the point
of view of the Epistle to the Hebrews, he never refers to it. But
what Harnack says about Paul may be easily applied to Hebrews
also. Justin did not know the New Testament in our present
composition. All he knew were some apostolic traditions
("Erinnerungen der Apostel") and some apocalyptic frag-
ments.[131] Justin's argument concerning the Passover lamb is
typical of the Christian point of view: "God does not permit the
lamb of the passover to be sacrificed in any other place than
where His name was named; knowing that the days will come,
after the suffering of Christ, when even the place in Jerusalem
shall be given over to your enemies, and all the offerings, in short,
shall cease; and that lamb which was commanded to be wholly
roasted was a symbol of the suffering of the Cross which Christ
would undergo." [132] The same point of view we meet in the
Agnus Dei motif, and in the allusion to the spiritual worship of
God in the Johannine Gospel.[133] Paul's reference to Christ as
our passover sacrificed for us (1 Cor. 5. 7) was probably a well-
known thought in Hebrew-Christian circles as the associations
with the Lord's Supper and the paschal meal were only too
obvious. But the whole force of the argument could only be
made use of once the Temple was destroyed. Evidence that the
Messiah's sacrifice was acceptable in the sight of God and that
all other sacrifices became unnecessary was seen in the fact that
God *allowed* the Destruction. This is the meaning of the synoptic
reference to the rent veil of the Temple.[134]

(3) The prophetic utterances of Jesus concerning the Temple:
Mk. 13.1 f records an utterance of Jesus which occurs in the

other Synoptics, but which has every mark of authenticity. As Jesus was leaving the Temple in the company of his disciples, one of them draws the Master's attention to the magnificence of the building (διδάσκαλε, ἴδε, ποταποὶ λίθοι καὶ ποταπαὶ οἰκοδομαί) to which Jesus replies: οὐ μὴ ἀφεθῇ λίθος ἐπὶ λίθον, ὃς οὐ μὴ καταλυθῇ.[135] Klostermann comments upon this apocalyptic word of Jesus: "The less need it be regarded as a *vaticinium ex eventu* as something similar is warranted by 14. 58 etc." [136] He draws attention to similar prophetic utterances, like Mic. 3. 12; Jer. 33. 6. 18; and the prophecy of Jesus the son of Ananos in Jos. *Bell.* VI. 53. Such an oracle belonged to the prophetic function of the Messiah and was in keeping with accredited tradition.[137] Strangely enough, both Josephus and the Talmud know of similar premonitions attended by miraculous signs.[138] But whatever authenticity we are prepared to ascribe to Mk. 13. 1f, it undoubtedly belongs to the oldest Christian tradition and served as an important proof of the Messiahship of Jesus.

(4) The psychological effect of the Destruction was an important factor in the reaction to the Gospel preaching. The burden of the Messianic message was an invitation to those who were fainting with weariness and were heavily burdened (οἱ κοπιῶντες καὶ πεφορτισμένοι Mt. 11. 28). Jesus himself had a special word of comfort for those who mourn (Mt. 5. 4; Lk. 4. 16–20). For a people which has been bereaved of all its national hopes, which has been left like sheep without a shepherd, humiliated by a bitter and ruthless enemy, the message of the love of God, the hope for the heavenly Jerusalem, and the triumph over death through the risen Messiah, was indeed εὐαγγέλιον in the deepest sense of the word. It offered spiritual consolation at a time of great national defeat.[139] This psychological moment helped to create a situation never paralleled in the history of Judaism. The period between the Destruction of Jerusalem and the war under Hadrian saw the rise of an indigenous Jewish Christianity which, if not similar, was yet closely related to the Christianity of the Gentile Church.

If the list of Jewish bishops as enumerated by Eusebius is genuine,[140] the thirteen "bishops" or elders who are interposed between the years A.D. 107–135 would go to show how widely spread were the Jewish communities in Palestine. This may be another proof of the existence of a large number of Jewish Christians all over the country.[141]

7. JUDAIC CHRISTIANITY AND JUDAISTIC CHRISTIANITY

Prof. Harnack, who with his usual thoroughness has subjected Justin's Dialogue to close examination, has recognized the great importance of this document for our knowledge of Hebrew Christianity in the middle of the second century. Justin reveals a remarkable knowledge of the Jewish arguments against Christianity and of the Jewish-Christian position; Harnack, therefore, rightly stresses the fact that Justin's home was Samaria. He knew of Jewish Christianity from his own personal experience. At that time, says Harnack, *"Hebrew Christianity does not appear as a rudiment and historical curiosity, but still stands before Justin's eyes as a living and connecting factor between the two parties, Judaism and the Catholic Church."* [142]

Justin, addressing himself to Trypho, comments on the wickedness of the Jews, which is the cause of God's withholding from them "the ability to discern the wisdom of his Scriptures; yet (there are) some exceptions, to whom, according to the grace of His long-suffering, as Isaiah said, He has left a seed for salvation, lest your race be utterly destroyed like Sodom and Gomorrah" (ch. lv). At another place, Justin explains that God spares the Jews now, as he spared them in the days of Elijah, because of the seven thousand who have not bowed their knees to Baal; and he continues: "even so He has now neither yet inflicted judgment, nor does inflict it, knowing that daily some (of you) are becoming disciples in the name of Christ and quitting the path of error" (ch. xxxix). [143]

To Trypho's inquiry as to Justin's attitude to those Jews who both believe in Jesus and keep the Law (ch. xlvi), he receives the following answer: "In my opinion, Trypho, such an one will be saved, if he does not strive in every way to persuade other men, I mean those Gentiles who have been circumcised from error by Christ, to observe the same things as himself, telling them that they will not be saved unless they do so." Justin explains that this is his private opinion; there are, however, Christians who think otherwise and who would not "venture to have any intercourse with or extend hospitality to such persons, but I do not agree with them". But Justin's tolerance has a definite limit. He disapproves of those Jews who, though believing in Jesus Christ, compel Gentiles who are also believers "to live in all respects according to the law given by Moses"; but even those thus persuaded to practise the Law "shall probably be saved" (ch. xlvii).

What were the christological views of the Hebrew Christians Justin is referring to? On this, unfortunately, we have no clear statement, but only one or two hints. Thus, Justin, addressing himself to Trypho and his companions, remarks: "there are some, my friends of your [144] race, who admit that He is Christ, while holding Him to be man of men, with whom I do not agree" (ch. xlviii). Harnack asks the important question: "Did all Hebrew Christians think so?" He holds that a definite answer is not possible, but is inclined to assume that such was Hebrew-Christian opinion. However, it seems to us that Harnack's exegesis is somewhat biassed. There is no need to press Justin's words too much. Harnack's conclusion is based upon a very fine distinction as to the literal meaning of Justin's words: "Justin does not say 'some of the Jewish Christians' but 'some of the Jews', therefore all Hebrew Christians *could* have held this view." [145] But apart from the fact that there is some doubt as to the reading "our race" or "your race", such a view does not tally with Justin's former statement. It is difficult to imagine that he would acknowledge as brothers those who not only keep the Law, but also deny the divinity of the Messiah. Harnack himself has felt the difficulty, for in a note he cautiously adds: "It appears to me remarkable that Justin is not more severe (schärfer), but one dare not conclude too much from it." [146] If, however, Justin associated himself with the Hebrew Christians by calling them "some of *our* race", then Harnack's definition of Hebrew Christianity as Justin understood it needs correcting.

Harnack puts the question: who is a Hebrew Christian according to Justin? He answers: "A Jewish Christian is only such a Jew who believes in Christ and observes the Law. If he does not observe the Law he is as little a Jewish Christian as a Jew is a Jew who has emancipated himself from the Law." In a footnote, Harnack adds: "Reversely, a circumcised Gentile who observes the Law is a full-blooded Jew." [147] But a Jew who both keeps the Law and denies the divinity of Christ would hardly be reckoned by Justin as a member of the Church. If Justin's reference, however, was to some of Trypho's race, then, according to Harnack's definition, he is simply referring to Jews who are *outside* the Church, but hold Jesus to be the Messiah in a strictly heretical sense. But to such Justin is opposed.

The result of Harnack's inquiry into the Hebrew-Christian position and its relationship to Gentile Christians as it appears from Justin's Dialogue can be seen from the following list:

(1) There are Jewish Christians who insist that Gentile Christians keep the Law, and who refuse communion with those who do not. These Justin refuses to regard as brothers in Christ.

(2) There are Jewish Christians who keep the Law, but do not insist that Gentile Christians do likewise. Justin regards them as brothers, though other Christians do not share his opinion.

(3) There are Gentile Christians who have been misled by Jewish Christians to keep the Law, but do not refuse communion with other Gentile Christians who do not keep the Law. Justin thinks that such *may* be saved.

(4) There are Gentile Christians who, in adverse circumstances, had to deny Christ, but tried to save themselves by adherence to Judaism, in order to remain faithful to the true God. Such must return before death, otherwise they are lost.

(5) There are Jews who do not regard it as essential to join the Christian Church, on the grounds that the Church admits that faithful Jews before the coming of Christ will be saved. Justin holds that such will perish, though those who lived before Christ will be saved.

In our opinion, it is to this last group that Justin is referring in ch. xlviii. They were of Trypho's race, they held Christ to be man of men, and they remained within the boundaries of Judaism. This explains the utter indifference with which Justin is treating them.

But Harnack's list is not complete. The most important section of Christians of Jewish descent has been left out.[148] Who are those Christians referred to in ch. lv, as some laudable exceptions whom God has left as a seed for salvation lest the race be utterly destroyed? Who are those seven thousand alluded to who have not bowed their knees to Baal (ch. xxxix)? Harnack doubts whether the "τινες", those who are daily becoming disciples, are actually Jews, but it seems to us that the whole argument rests upon that fact. What connexion would there otherwise be between the Gentile converts who daily turn to Christ and the continued persistence of the Jewish people?

The fact is, that Justin's conception of "race" is such as to include all those who are knit together by the bond of a common faith.[149] Jews who were full members of the Catholic Church were of the Christian "race", and their existence was taken for granted.[150] Only those who were not within full communion of the Church, whose position had to be clarified, and concerning whom there was some difference of opinion, were the object of Justin's elucidations. We thus arrive at the following conclusion:

(1) There were Jewish Christians, members of the Catholic Church; the seven thousand who have not bowed to Baal and who constituted the remnant of Israel, the holy seed (Is. 1. 9; 6. 13).

(2) There were Jewish Christians who kept the Law and demanded of the Gentile Christians to do likewise. These were outside the Christian communion.

(3) Between these two extremes there was a third group occupying a middle position; those who kept the Law, but did not demand of Gentile-born Christians to do likewise. Concerning such, there was difference of opinion.

(4) Apart from these, there were Jews still within the Synagogue who were semi or secret believers.[151] Their position was ambiguous and Justin shows little interest in them. Such was the situation in the middle of the second century.

A remarkable feature of the picture thus obtained is its close similarity to what we know about the internal position of the Jewish Church from the Pauline Epistles and from the Acts of the Apostles. The deep-seated division between the Judaizing party on the one hand and the antinomian party on the other began in Jerusalem and goes back to the days of the Apostles.[152] There is also evidence for the existence of a moderate party, standing half-way between the two: a party which probably at one time enjoyed the greatest influence, as it could claim for itself the authority of James and Peter. Thus, the "temporary duality"[153] which the Church developed in its earliest days, endured for over a century. But now the situation was undergoing a change. The middle of the second century, *i.e.* the time when the *Dialogue* took place, marks a transition-period in Hebrew-Christian history. The change is effected by the new political situation.

After the failure of the Bar Cochba insurrection and the brutal measures adopted by the Roman authorities to quell the Jewish spirit of resistance, there is a notable change of outlook.   In the Jewish consciousness, nationalism and religion have been always closely related.   But Jewish nationalism prior to the Destruction was nurtured entirely by religious motives.   For Israel to be in subjection to heathen rule was an insult to God.   We know from Josephus that till the last moment Jewish nationalists were clinging to the hope that God would miraculously interfere to save his Sanctuary.[154]   They conceived their cause to be identical with that of God.   But after the Destruction and the final defeat under Hadrian, religion became *subservient* to the national cause. It became the means to an end, and that end was the preservation of Jewish identity.   In the changed circumstances the problem concerning the Law was lifted from its religio-theological connotation into the sphere of national emergency.   "Jewish nationalism", says Klausner, "in so far as it is connected with religion, is bound up with the ceremonial laws", for "they are a defence against assimilation by the heathen peoples which surrounded the Jews on every side." [155]   But what is a defence is also a barrier.   Thus *Judaistic* Christianity, which tenaciously adhered to the Law for the sake of the *people*, became isolated from the rest of the Church.   A part of it drifted back to Judaism, from which it was separated more by tradition than actual difference of belief.[156]   The rest was swallowed up by the strong gnostic currents until it entirely lost its Jewish-Christian connections.

"Judaic" Christianity, following the signification given by F. J. A. Hort,[157] we identify with that section of the Jerusalem Church which, from the beginning, held a liberal outlook concerning the Law.   It inclined to the Pauline view with regard to the Gentiles; it found itself in opposition to the Jewish authorities; it was compelled to take refuge in Pella, and in the Diaspora it united with the main body of the Catholic Church.   These Jewish Christians soon lost their identity through intermarriage, as there were no barriers to separate them from the Gentile Church.[158]

8. THE MINIM

Moriz Friedländer has tried to show that the *minim*, whom we meet so often in the Talmudic literature, were originally not Christians but Jewish heretics of pre-Christian times.   Their antiquity is avouched by the fact that the meaning of the word itself has been lost, as is also the case with the names Pharisees, Sadducees, Essenes: "which is to show that their origin falls at so early a time that even the oldest recorders were unfamiliar with the etymology of these names'".[159] Another proof for his theory Friedländer adduces from the fact that already in the first Christian century there was in existence "a strongly contested literature which the Pharisaic scribes laid under the anathema"; "such, however, does not come into existence overnight".[160] Friedländer, therefore, feels justified in disassociating the Hebrew Christian movement from that of the *minim*. They have nothing in common. Friedländer's conclusion is based upon the unwarranted assumption that the *minim* rejected the cardinal dogma of Christianity, *i.e.* the resurrection.[161] But Friedländer's views have found little support amongst scholars.[162] On the contrary, it is generally held that, if not in all, then in many cases the *minim* referred to in the Talmud are Hebrew Christians.[163] The fact that they were well acquainted with Pharisaism, that they knew the Scriptures, and were trained in the principles of the Jewish religion is no justification for turning them into Gnostic heretics, as Friedländer does.[164]

(a) The etymology of min

The etymology of the word *min* has for long presented a puzzle to scholars and many suggestions have been made.[165] We will now dwell upon it at some length, as in our opinion the meaning of the name is essential to a right understanding of Hebrew Christianity and its relationship to Judaism.

In the first place, it must be borne in mind that the word *min* has come to us from an opposing party, *i.e.* from an enemy source. It is, therefore, a name of derision. But as is usually the case, such nicknames are either a perversion of the real name, with the intent of giving it a malicious meaning, or else they are an entirely new invention, expressing some peculiar feature of those thus named. In other words, the name *min* must either refer to some peculiarity of the sect under discussion or else be a corruption of another name, or both. The purpose of a nickname is to provide the opponent with a derisive or negative appellation.

The majority of scholars are agreed that the word *min* is to be connected with Gen. 1. and translated to mean "species", "kind". Thus, Strack explains: "*Min* is simply the word known

from Gen. 1. *min*, γένος, kind. Just like *gôj*, nation, specially
Gentile-people, meaning 'Gentile' and Jisrael, in which Israel
received the connotation 'one of Israel' (Israelite), so *min*
signified: as (to differentiate him from the main mass of Jewry)
belonging to a special kind (of degeneracy=*Abart*), a heretic;
he who follows his own heart (instead of the authoritative words
of the teachers of the Law)." [166]   Herford holds the same view,
but he gives a more elaborate explanation in support of this
theory. He first contradicts Levy's suggestion that the word *min*
is derived from the Arabic root "*man*", to lie, speak falsely; and
the Syriac "*mania*", madness. He then suggests that because
zan and *min* are analogous, and because *zanah* in the Old Testament means unfaithfulness to the "covenant-religion with God";
zan and *min* have been combined in such a way as to mean both
"apostasy from the national religion" and also "kind", "species",
"sort".[167]   Bacher, who holds a similar view to that of Strack
and Herford, offers a more simple and therefore more convincing hypothesis. He explains: "*min* is the biblical expression
translated in Genesis 1, for instance, by γένος. The word is used
figuratively, in the sense of sect, αἵρεσις; in particular, it was
usual for the Pharisees and their adherents to speak of *min ha-
zedukim*, 'the sect of the Sadducees'." Bacher then points to
Josephus, *Antiq.* XIII. 10. 6, where we find the expression τὸ
Σαδδουκαίων γένος used in the sense of Σαδδουκαίων αἵρεσις. He
then explains: "In the course of time, *min* came to mean simply
sect, with primary reference to the sect of the Sadducees." [168]
This is a very plausible explanation but for one difficulty.

It is important to notice that the very simple word *min* occurs
sometimes in a varied orthography. Thus in *Sanh.* 37a it reads
mina, but in *Baba bathra* 25a, it reads *mini;* whereas Sifra has
entirely an orthography of its own: *m(a)in* and *m(a)inim*. Bacher
has felt the difficulty, though he only refers to the spelling in
Sifra. But he explains it as an isolated case of no further significance, due to the hand of a writer whose intention was to give to
the word a distorted meaning of his own: "The originator of
this unique spelling—it is found nowhere else—would seem to
have deliberately inserted the 'a' in the word *minim* in order to
distort it and give it a derogatory meaning. *M(a)inim* or
mi(a)nim would be the plural of *ma'en* (Ex. 7. ₊4; 9. 2; 10. 4),
or perhaps of *me'en* as in Jer. 13. 10." [169]   But the verb *ma'an*
which means to "refuse" or "disobey" neither distorts the

meaning nor makes it specially derogatory.[170] At best
we can regard it as an attempt to give some meaning to a
difficult word. Had this been the only orthography, such an
explanation could have been acceptable. But we have already
seen that there are other modes of spelling it. Bacher's explanation is, therefore, not satisfactory.

On the other hand, a few important scholars have held that
the word *min* is a corruption of *maaminim*. This explanation has
the advantage not only of restoring a reasonable *meaning* to a
difficult word, but also of relating it to the life of those thus
named. Joël rightly observes that such names are to be explained
not only "by linguistic aid, but at the same time by recourse to
life and legal practice (*Halakah*)".[171] In a footnote, Joël
adds: "It is altogether superfluous to point out the essential and
therefore name-giving significance of πίστις (*emunah*) in the New
Testament."[172] It is also possible that Derenbourgh's theory,
which explains *minim* as a contraction of the initials *maamine
Yeshua nozri* or *min* for *maamin Jeshua nozri* is by no means too far-
fetched, especially when we remember how fond the Rabbis
were of making puns and juggling with words.[173] It seems to
us that Herford dismisses such a suggestion too light-heartedly.[174]

The fact that a scholar like George Foot Moore, though declaring himself in favour of the first theory, mentions without contradiction the etymology which sees in *minim* a corruption of
maaminim, and even quotes Acts 5. 14: πιστεύοντες τῷ Κυρίῳ in
support of it, is significant enough.[175] It is also worth noting that
this is not a theory of entirely modern origin, but that it has some
measure of support in Jewish tradition. Joël mentions that
he found Mussafia (1606?–1675) to have given a similar
explanation.[176]

But even if we accept *min* as to be connected with *maamin* there
is still the question why *such* a corruption and no other? On the
other hand, if *min* meant nothing at all, it would have been use-
less as a nickname. It appears to us that both contending views
contain part of the truth. *Min* is to be understood in connection
with Gen. 1. and means γένος. It was given a negative connotation, something like "*Abart*" (Strack); this happened
because the *minim* called themselves *maaminim*. Herein lay their
distinction from the rest of the people: they were *the believers*.
By some strange coincidence, the original name has preserved
itself in Sifra. It is remarkable that but for one single letter it

presents the unmistakable reading of *maaminim*. If such an interpretation stands its ground, we have made the first step towards
identifying the *minim*.

(b) The identification of the minim

It appears from R. Naḥman's remark (*Hul*. 13b), who speaks
in the name of Rabba bar Abuha, that the word *minim* is applied
to Jewish, and not to non-Jewish sectaries: "among the Gentiles
there are no *minim*". It is generally agreed that this is the case;
the word *min* signifies a Jew tainted with heresy. But there occur
some exceptions. Herford admits that there are instances when
the term appears to be applied to *Gentiles* also. In the case of
R. Hanina, R. Hoshaia and the *min* (*Pes*. 87b) engaged in a
conversation, in which both Rabbis and also the *min* make use
of Scripture, the latter is obviously a Gentile, and probably a
Christian.[177] Who then were the *minim*?

As with the etymology of the name, so with its application,
opinion is mainly divided into two groups:

(1) Some scholars, like D. Chwolson, H. Graetz, A. Geiger,
A. Schlatter, and M. Joël, hold that *minim* are primarily Hebrew
Christians.

(2) Others, like H. Ewald, J. Hamburger, E. Schürer, A.
Wünsche, J. Bergmann, and J. Levy, regard *minim* as signifying
Jewish heretics in general, Christian or otherwise.

It must be admitted that most modern scholars are in favour
of the wider interpretation of the name. Thus, Israel Lévi defines
the term in the following words: "C'est un terme neutre, passepar-
tout, s'appliquant indifféremment à toutes les hérésies, ici aux
judéo-chrétiens, tantôt aux chrétiens (considérés comme formant
une secte juive), souvent aux gnostiques chrétiens." And again,
more emphatically: "Mais, encore une fois, jamais ce mot par
lui-même ne dénonce une hérésie déterminée; il signifie tout
simplement: hérésie." [178] It cannot be denied that the word
min has acquired a meaning for which there is enough evidence
to support Israel Lévi's wide interpretation. But even those
scholars who hold a similar view are constrained to admit a
special connexion between *minut* and Hebrew Christianity.
Thus, Strack observes that whenever the Synagogue was speaking
of *minim*, it had primarily in mind Hebrew Christians.[179] Bacher
says: "de *min* on forma l'abstrait *minut*, qui, dans un sens plus
particulier, désigne le christianisme." [180] Büchler, whose one

aim is to show that *minim* are non-Jewish heretics with no reference whatsoever either to Jesus or to Christianity, feels constrained to make the following observation: "This is not a denial
that in a number of Talmudic passages *min* is applied to Jews of
heretical views; but all these records relate to views and circumstances before the year 135 and to Judea." [181] This is an important admission on the part of Büchler. The question which
immediately arises is: what kind of heretics were those people
whose Jewish connexions Büchler reluctantly admits? His
reservation, though not completely justified, that those *Jewish
minim* belong to the period prior to A.D. 135, and that their place
of abode is Judea, is an important clue to the solution of our
problem. The height of success was reached by the Hebrew
Christian movement in the period between the Destruction of
the Temple and the Bar Cochba insurrection, *i.e.* between
A.D. 70 and 135. In the middle of these 65 years, in A.D. 90,
or thereabouts, the *Birkat ha-Minim* was introduced. The
Synagogue was striving to apply counter-measures in order to
check the heresy. The division became more and more pronounced. An important factor was the steady growth of Gentile
Christianity, which compromised the Jewish Christians in the
eyes of the Rabbis. The crisis came to a head at the outbreak of
the insurrection. Bar Cochba's authority rested upon a Messianic
claim, a claim which Hebrew Christians could not accept.
Public opinion turned against them, and they were subjected
to severe persecution.[182] This completed the process of separation. The Jewish Christians now realized that a compromise
was impossible; there was no room for them amongst their people.
Before them were three choices: (1) back to the Synagogue,
(2) membership in the Gentile Church, or (3) a separate existence. No doubt some made one choice, others made another.
That there still survived Hebrew-Christian communities, leading
a separate life, we know from Jerome, who called them *semijudaei*
and *semichristiani*, which well described their difficult position.[183]
This is in complete agreement with Moore's statement as to the
effect of Hadrian's war upon Hebrew Christianity in its relationship to the Jews.[184] But it must not be assumed, as Moore does,
that after the war every contact with the Jewish people was broken.
Prof. Moore states: "The Christianity which the Rabbis had to
do with after (the war) was Greek, and the controversy with
Catholic doctrine." [185] As in the case of Büchler, this statement

is based on the assumption that there were *no* Hebrew Christians within the Catholic Church, or approaching the view of orthodox Christianity. We shall have occasion to see that there actually were such Jews. But if Moore is right, then we have to assume that the discussions with *minim* of a later date refer either to Jewish Gnostics or to Gentile Christians. But Herford has shown that in most cases the controversy involved Christian doctrine. His conclusion with regard to the *minim* is, that they are neither Gentile Christians nor Jewish Christians, but a certain *type* of Jewish Christians who tried to keep up their connexion with Judaism, and whose theology was related to that of Hebrews.[186] These two contradictory statements make it abundantly clear that the word *minim* has been gradually widened to include both Jews and Gentiles. But the fact that Gentiles *were* included within the category of *minut* leads us again back to Hebrew Christianity. For how otherwise could Gentiles be *heretics*, unless their heresy was associated with Judaism?

Harnack makes the following observation: "The name 'Christians' is the title of Gentile-Christians; at first and probably through a long period, Jewish-Christians were never called by this name." In a footnote he explains that, to his knowledge, there is no old Christian document where Jews are called "Christians".[187] This was entirely a Gentile designation: "The Jews could not have invented the name Christians for the Christians, nor could the heathen think of speaking of 'Christians' as long as the movement remained a purely Jewish one."[188] But it appears to us that even the Hebrew equivalent of *meshiḥiim* would have been an impossible appellation, as faith in the Messiah was not only a Christian but also a Jewish characteristic. The only difference between them was that the first *believed* he had come, while the others still looked for his coming. The "Christians" were thus the *believers*, the *maaminim*. This self-designation has been derisively corrupted by their opponents into *min* and *minim*. When the Gentiles accepted faith in the Messiah, and claimed to believe in the God of Israel, esteemed the Scriptures, and looked for the Resurrection, but otherwise walked in the way of the *minim*, they were naturally, in Jewish eyes, *also minim*.

The *minim* were thus Christians: first *Jewish* Christians, then *also* Gentile Christians; later, when Christianity removed itself from the Jewish horizon, the appellation was given to *any* Jews of dissenting views.[189] It became a *terminus technicus* to describe apostasy from God.[190]

(c) *The* minim *and Judaism*

Chwolson draws attention to an interesting sentence in connection with the case of R. Eliezer ben Dama, the nephew of R. Ishmael, who was bitten by a serpent and who died because his uncle prevented his being healed by Jacob of Kefar Sama (Sekanya) in the name of Yeshu ben Pandera. To the implied question, why R. Ishmael intervened in a case of emergency, in which case there is no prohibition,[191] the following explanation is given: "With *minut* (Hebrew Christianity) it is somewhat different, because it is enticing and one may become seduced by them (*i.e.* Hebrew Christians)." [192] That *minut* had an enticing quality against which a Jew was to guard himself we know from other instances. Eliezer ben Hyrcanus, who was arrested for *minut* by the Roman authorities,[193] on R. Akiba's suggestion, suddenly remembered that he once walked along the street (upper market) of Sepphoris, where he met Jacob of Kefar Sekanya, who quoted a saying of Jesus which *pleased* him. The Rabbi thus interpreted his arrest for *minut* as a punishment for taking pleasure in a Scriptural interpretation which had Jesus as its author.[194] The actual exposition concerning the hire of a harlot (Deut. 23. 18) strangely contrasts with the sayings of Jesus we meet in the Gospels. Klausner remarks: "At first sight, this exposition . . . does not accord with the character of Jesus' teachings"; but he holds that "Pharisaic methods of exposition are by no means foreign to him". [195] Klausner therefore accepts the tradition as genuine. Strangely enough, R. Eliezer ben Hyrcanus was himself under grave suspicion of heresy. It is remarkable that he does not refute the charge, but makes, as Herford says, "a skilful evasion". There is also the fact of his excommunication by the Sanhedrin at Jabneh.[196] It is therefore possible that behind his confession to have taken pleasure in a certain exposition coming from a heretical source is more than would appear on the surface.[197] But, however the case may be, the fact is that the *minim* were a snare to one of the greatest Rabbis at the end of the first century A.D.

R. Eliezer ben Hyrcanus is by no means an isolated case. An even more interesting person is the much discussed Elisha ben Abuyah, often referred to as *Aḥer* ("the other"). Elisha, who flourished at the end of the first and the beginning of the second century, was a famous *Tanna* and the teacher of R. Meir.[198] The references concerning him are obscure and sometimes contradictory. The opinion amongst scholars as to the nature of his heresy is diverse. Some scholars hold that he became a Gnostic, others that he became a follower of the Philonian philosophy. Louis Ginzberg holds that he was simply a Sadducee. Only this, he thinks, can explain R. Meir's continued friendship with his former teacher.[199] But Ginzberg's interpretation meets with a great difficulty. There is the fact that Elisha was credited with having broken the Sabbath in the most unseemly manner.[200] Was this characteristic of Sadducean behaviour? However, it is impossible to decide what his views were.[201] But we do know that he was suspected of hiding in his clothes *sifre minim* while he was still functioning as a teacher in the schoolhouse.[202] Herford points out that Elisha, whom he calls the "arch-Gnostic of the Talmud", is never referred to as being a *min* himself; "the most that is said of him is that he used to read books of *minut*". Nevertheless, though there is no evidence for his adherence to Christianity, this may show that he took some interest in it.[203] Curiously enough, the story about Hananiah, the nephew of R. Yoshua ben Hananiah, in one feature resembles the case of Elisha ben Abuyah.

Midrash Rabbah tells the following story: Hanina, the son of R. Yoshua's brother, came to Capernaum, and the *minim* worked a spell on him and set him riding on an ass on the Sabbath. He went to his uncle Yoshua, who anointed him with oil and he recovered. (R. Yoshua) said to him, "Since the ass of that wicked person has brayed at you, you are not able to stay in the land of Israel." So he went from thence to Babylon and he died in peace.[204] Herford says: "That the *minim* here denote Christians there can be no possible doubt." "The ass of the wicked one", he interprets as a reference to Jesus. But he has some doubts as to the authenticity of the incident on the grounds that Hanina, a well-known Babylonian authority, was in a dispute with the patriarch R. Shimeon ben Gamaliel, and the incident here recorded intends to depreciate an opponent.[205] The story is only recorded in the Midrash and there is no reference to it in the Talmuds. However, Herford sees reason to believe that it goes back to old tradition. There certainly are no sufficient grounds to discredit it. As it stands the narrative gives the impression of veiled hints, and the whole incident seems to be wrapped in mystery. But several facts stand out clearly: the story refers to a famous Rabbi whose uncle enjoyed a great reputation. It seems to us that the mere quarrel with the patriarch is not sufficient ground to throw suspicion upon an important personage, as the passage unquestionably does. It is also evident that the *minim* here are Christians and that there is a reference to Jesus. The incident takes place in Capernaum, and the Rabbi is presented as a breaker of the Sabbath law—very much like Elisha ben Abuyah. Herford says: "The story represents Hanina as having been the victim of magic." The spell upon the Rabbi which his uncle so effectively removed was the result of the "braying of the ass of the wicked one". The real nature of the incident is revealed by the fact that Hanina had to leave Palestine. The spell of the *minim* spoilt his reputation.

Justin presents Trypho as having said: "I am aware that your precepts in the so-called Gospels are so wonderful and so great that I suspect no one can keep them; for I have carefully read them" (ch. X). This is an interesting admission, which undoubtedly goes back to an authentic remark of Justin's opponent; especially as the praise of the lofty Gospel-teaching is combined with genuine Jewish criticism which is strangely reminiscent of modern writers. Whether Trypho can be identified with R. Tarphon or not,[206] he was a distinguished Jew who knew the Scriptures and had read the Gospels. On his own admission, he had studied them carefully. There may be a grain of irony in his words, but it is nevertheless an admission that the Gospels are both wonderful and great. Significantly enough, the controversy between Trypho and Justin does not turn upon the teaching but upon the person of Jesus Christ and the Christian attitude to the Law. Trypho's knowledge of the Gospels reveals their popularity and the fact that they were read not only by Christians but also by Jews.[207] It is therefore natural to conclude that they presented an attraction. It is with this fact in the background that Talmudic and Midrashic evidence concerning Hebrew Christianity must be viewed. The sources at our disposal are hostile, and their aim is to misrepresent a hated opponent. To take all they say literally is to misunderstand their purpose. This becomes abundantly clear in the light of the following example:

In *Eccles. rabbah* 1. 8, following upon the story of Hanina, is the strange experience of R. Jonathan with the *minim*. One of Jonathan's disciples ran away to the *minim*. The Rabbi went to seek him and found him in subjection to them (or doing the cooking).[208] The *minim* invited the Rabbi to join them. Thereupon he fled, and they pursued him. After they had persuaded him to do kindness to a bride, he went and found them ravishing a girl. He said to them, "Is this the way for Jews to behave?" They answered with a text (Prov. 1. 14). Then he fled home and shut the door in the face of his pursuers. The story ends with the *minim* saying to R. Jonathan: "If thou hadst turned and looked upon us, instead of our pursuing thee, thou wouldst have pursued us." Herford holds that the Rabbi is R. Jonathan ben Eleazar, a Palestinian *Amora* of the third century.[209] He belonged to the circle of R. Hanina, was a pupil of Simeon ben Jose ben Lakonia, and teacher of Samuel bar Nahman. He lived in Sepphoris.[210] The *minim* here are, according to R. Jonathan himself, Jews. The fact that they lived either in Sepphoris or Capernaum points to their being Hebrew Christians.[211] The rest of the story, however, is nothing else but an exhortation to keep away from the *minim*. They are thus presented as practising immorality, which characteristically enough they justify by quoting a text from Scripture. This is undoubtedly a reference to the Christian habit of appealing to the Old Testament. They entice Jonathan's disciple and keep him in subjection. But above all, they even endanger the master himself. The mere sight of a *min* is sufficient to pervert a pious Jew.[212] All rabbinic references to Christianity bear a similar character. They are therefore misleading in any attempt at construing the conduct and beliefs of their opponents.[213] Nevertheless, there are enough hints to warrant a guess as to the main tenets of the heresy.

The fact has been noted that in the discussions between the Rabbis and the *minim* the person of Jesus is strangely avoided: "The replies are mostly indirect, they are wrapped in similitudes and make use of scarcely understandable allusions."[214] This fact led Herford to assume that the *minim* in question were "Jewish-Christians whose Christology was developed beyond the point at which the Messiahship was the chief distinction of Jesus".[215] It is not clear, however, what Herford means by that. To Christians, especially Hebrew Christians, the Messiahship of Jesus was basically important. It would have certainly been the main topic of conversation with unbelieving Jews. It appears to us that the reasons for that strange caution are to be sought in the fact, first, that we have only fragmentary notes and even these are distorted, and secondly, that the Jewish sources were not interested in providing posterity with the views and argumentations of the *minim*. There is also the obvious tendency to avoid the name of Jesus.

A characteristic feature in the dispute between Jews and the *minim* is the constant appeal to Scripture on the part of the latter. It is usually not the Rabbis but the *minim* who are the questioners, and the discussions seem always to turn round the interpretation of *texts*. In this, the *minim* adopt a method similar to that of Justin. He too clinches his arguments by quoting Scripture.[216] Now, what was the topic of their conversations? The fact that, in spite of the many references in the Talmudic and Midrashic literature, this question is not easily answered, is already significant. But, as we said, there are some hints.

The Jewish main argument against Christianity was always directed to prove its deficient view of the Godhead. It has argued that, by raising the Messiah to a position almost equal to that of God, the purity of monotheism was impaired. Some of the Rabbinic references have clearly this objection in view [217]; Trypho's contention against the Christian doctrine of the Messiah points in the same direction.[218] The question concerning the plurality in the Godhead is a prominent feature in the rabbinic discussions with the *minim*. Traces of it, it would appear, may already be found in the Mishnah.[219] One particular passage in the Talmud well illustrates the nature of the dispute; R. Johanan said: In all the passages which the *minim* have taken (as grounds) for their heresy, their refutation is found near at hand. Thus, "Let us make man in our image" (Gen. 1. 26; plur.); "and God created man in his own image" (v. 27; sing.). "Come, let us go down and there confound their language" (Gen. 11. 7; plur.); "And the Lord came down to see the city and the tower" (v. 5; sing.). "Because there were revealed (plur.) to him God" (Gen. 35. 7); "Unto God who answereth (sing.) me in the day of my distress" (v. 3). "For what great nation is there that hath God so nigh (plur.) unto it, as the Lord our God is (unto us) when we call upon him" (sing., Deut. 4. 7). "And what one nation in the earth is like thy people, (like) Israel, whom God went (plur.) to redeem for a people unto Himself" (sing., 2 Sam.

7. 23). "Till (thrones) were placed and (one) that was ancient did sit" (Dan. 7. 9).[220]

The Talmud, however, proceeds to ask, Why were these (plurals) necessary? R. Johanan's theory is: The Holy One, blessed be he, does nothing without consulting his heavenly court (*pamalya*, family). The idea being that the plurals indicate the presence of the heavenly beings who stand before God. But this does not explain the plural of the last text: "Till thrones were placed". R. Akiba's suggestion is: "One (throne) was for Himself and one for David" (*i.e.* the Messiah). But R. Jose protested: "Akiba, how long wilt thou profane the Shechinah?" R. Jose offers a better explanation: "One (throne) for justice and the other for mercy." R. Eleazar ben Azariah, however, suggests: "One for His throne and one for His footstool. A throne for a seat and a footstool in support of His feet." [221]

Akiba's remark concerning the son of David and the immediate rebuke of R. Jose, significantly enough a Galilean, in our view throws important light upon the whole discussion. Why did R. Jose think that with his remark concerning the Messiah the *Shekinah* was being profaned? Jacob Schachter answers: "By asserting that a human being sits beside Him." [222] But did not R. Akiba notice the implication of his remark? Herford has felt the difficulty. He says: "It is remarkable that R. Akiba, who was sufficiently alive to all danger of heresy, should not have detected the fault in his interpretation of the text." [223] Such an assumption is impossible. It is more natural to hold that Akiba was giving expression to an ancient view. But at that time, *i.e.* before the Bar Cochba insurrection, such a view became unpopular. The severity of the rebuke reveals the importance R. Jose attached to the case. Herford says rightly that R. Jose's explanation is "a very forced one"; so it was. It is an explanation created by an emergency. Here we meet a case where Scripture is being reinterpreted under the pressure of *minut*.[224]

We have previously noticed that the references to the Messiahship of Jesus are few. But that the Messiah was discussed and that Jesus was meant is more than a mere assumption.

R. Abbahu and a *min* discussed an anachronism in the Psalms. The difficulty for the *min* was why "the Psalm which refers to the earlier event comes after that which refers to the later one".[225] To Abbahu this is no difficulty at all. He says to the *min:* "To you, who do not interpret 'contexts', there is a difficulty; to us, who do interpret 'contexts', there is no difficulty."[226] But Abbahu proceeds to ask: "Why, then, is the Psalm concerning Absalom (Ps. 3) next to the Psalm concerning Gog and Magog" (Ps. 2)?[227] He explains: "So that should anybody ask thee: 'Is there a slave that rebels against his master?' do thou ask him: 'Is there a son who rebels against his father?' The latter has happened, and similarly will the former happen."[228]

The rebellion of the slave against his master refers to the nations rising in revolt against God (Ps. 2); the son rebelling against his father refers to Absalom's rebellion against David. So much is obvious from the text. But when we remember that R. Abbahu was speaking to a *min* and that he often engaged in disputations with Christians,[229] the conclusion that he was hinting at Jesus is near at hand. A more explicit reference to the Sonship of Jesus is contained in the *Palestinian Talmud*. Commenting on the phrase "Like a Son of God" (Dan. 3. 25), Reuben ben Aristobulos (?)[230] said: "In that hour (*i.e.* when Nebuchadnezzar uttered these words) an angel descended and struck that wicked one upon his mouth and said to him, 'Amend thy words: hath He a son?'"[231] Bacher regards this passage as a definite rebuke against the Christian doctrine of the Son of God.[232] This is also Herford's view.[233] It is difficult to say whether Reuben's censure is directed towards Gentile or Jewish Christians. But the fact that he still belongs to a comparatively early period would suggest the latter.[234]

That the Rabbis took notice of what was happening in the Gentile world can be seen by the interesting, almost modern view expressed by R. Ḥanin, who said: "Israel will not require the teaching of the royal Messiah in the future, for it says: Unto him shall the nations seek (Is. 11. 10), but not Israel." H. Friedman remarks: "For Israel will receive its teaching direct from God."[235] Bacher sees in it "a polemical point directed against Christianity and its Messiah".[236] The fact that such an explanation was necessary contradicts the view that Judaism remained indifferent to the Christian movement.[237]

The Talmud quotes a saying which seems to have been attributed to several teachers: "The son of David will not come until the whole kingdom is converted to *minut*."[238] A similar sentence is to be found in the *Mishnah*, which, though there is some doubt whether it was uttered by R. Eliezer ben Hyrcanus, belongs nevertheless to the Mishnaic period.[239] It therefore falls in the second century. *Malkut* (*i.e.* Kingdom) is usually interpreted to mean Rome. Herford explains the meaning of the utterance: "The conversion of the Empire to *minut* is merely a way of saying that the spread of heresy and the consequent decay of religion will be universal." [240] But at that early stage does it mean that the Rabbis were concerned with the "orthodoxy" of pagan Rome? There is, however, another passage about which there is some doubt as to the reading, and which Herford has therefore not included in his collection; [241] but Bacher does not hesitate to accept the reading of *minai* instead of *babliim* in the text. [242] It reads: "When thou seest the seats (*subsellia* in the schools) filled with *minim*, then look for the feet of the King Messiah. As it is said: 'He hath spread a net for my feet, he hath turned me back'" (Lam. 1. 13). [243] It is difficult to imagine that Abba b. Kahana, who is credited with this utterance, could have applied the quoted text to his Babylonian colleagues. The fact that *minim* are invading the schools of learning points to Hebrew Christians. The Rabbi is undoubtedly exaggerating. Perhaps the reference is not to pupils but to teachers, as the word *subsellia* (saphsellin) seems to suggest. We have already seen that a few of them became suspect of heresy. It reveals the alarm the Rabbis felt at the spread of the Christian heresy in their own ranks.

The Synagogue's aim was not only to separate the "sheep from the goats" [244] but also to find suitable arguments to counter Christian propaganda.

The *Midrash* contains an interesting passage which deserves to be quoted in full: "Abraham said to God: 'Sovereign of the Universe! Thou madest a covenant with Noah not to exterminate his children; then I arose and accumulated meritorious acts and pious deeds, whereupon my covenant superseded his. Perhaps another will arise and accumulate even a greater store of precepts and good deeds, and then a covenant with him will supersede Thy covenant with me?' Said the Holy One, blessed be He, to him: 'From Noah I did not set up shields of the righteous, but from thee I set up shields of the righteous. Moreover, when thy children take to transgressions and evil deeds, I will see one righteous man then who will be able to say to My Attribute of Justice, "Enough!" Whereupon I will take him and make him atone for them.'" [245] Here is Bacher's comment on this unique passage: "One cannot resist the impression that this *Agada* contains a polemical point against the 'new Covenant' alleged to

have replaced the 'old Covenant' begun with Abraham. Abraham
thus receives the assurance that the Saints (die Frommen) arising
from Israel, the 'shields' (magen) of the nation, are the warrant
for the endurance of the Covenant.   The idea of the great man
who was taken away by God for the atonement of the sinful
nation intends to emphasize against the Christian idea of the
atoning death of Jesus which forms the basis of the new Covenant,
that such atonement effected by a Saint (Frommer) of Israel
only   confirms   the   continuity   of   the   old   Covenant   with
Abraham." [246]   Now, the *Midrash* is of a late date, but incor-
porates ancient tradition.   The reference to the righteous man
whom God makes atone for the sin of Israel is puzzling.   Bacher
connects the atoning power of the death of the righteous one
with the "shields of the righteous".   This may or may not be so.
It can hardly be a reference to Jesus, whom the Christians claim
to have died an atoning death.   On the other hand, this passage
points to a time when Christian arguments were still a matter of
conscience and when adequate answers were urgently needed.
The claims of Gentile Christianity left Jewish thinking largely
unaffected.[247]   We are thus brought back again to Hebrew
Christianity.

What then were the main points under discussion?   They
concerned the interpretation of Scripture, the Unity of God,[248]
the human nature of the Messiah.   It has been argued that the
controversy was with Gentile Christianity exclusively or else with
Gnosticism.   "In no wise", says Büchler, "did the teachers of the
Mishna in the second century refer to the Son of God; their
opposition (Kampf) to him belongs to a much later time between
280 and 350."   But even in the later period, Jewish Christians
are excluded.[249]   This is a biased view, based on the conviction
that all Jewish believers in Jesus were strict observers of the Law.
Such an assumption is contradicted by the facts.[250]   To our
mind the most conclusive proof that the controversy was with
Jewish Christians lies in the effect it had upon Judaism.

The controversy with Jewish Christianity caused the Synagogue
to modify some of its views and to alter its emphasis.   The unity
of God, the most fundamental principle in Judaism, was upheld
with *renewed* insistence.[251]   The ideas concerning the Messiah
were modified and stripped of all metaphysical significance.[252]
The Torah was given a transcendent meaning by way of
reaction.[253]   Orthodoxy became more rigid in proportion to

the intolerance shown to those who dared to maintain their own point of view.[254]   The national aspect of Judaism was reaffirmed.[255]   Other, once essential, tenets were assigned only secondary importance [256]—"Jewish tradition has—this is evident from the *Dialogue*—experienced an extraordinarily strong alteration and contraction (Verengung) as a result of the struggle with the Christian daughter-religion (Tochterreligion)"[257]—with the consequence that Hebrew Christianity was pressed out of Jewish life.[258]

9. THE DECLINE OF THE HEBREW-CHRISTIAN CHURCH

Israel Abrahams has shown that the Synagogue's dealings with *minut* must be viewed as an internal affair.   Its main purpose was self-defence.[259]   For that purpose, it introduced the *Birkat ha-minim*; [260] it altered its liturgy; it changed its emphasis, especially with regard to Messianic teaching; it created barriers. As the disintegration of Jewish national life coincided with the growth of Gentile Christianity, the re-emphasis of Israel's election in face of the Christian claim was an important factor pressing for decision.   Thus, Hebrew Christianity found itself at the crossroads.   We have already said that some Jewish Christians must have returned to the Synagogue, perhaps secretly still uniting the Messianic hope with the person of Jesus.[261]   Many, of course, entered the life of Gentile-Christian communities, where they disappeared through intermarriage.   Some, though still retaining features peculiar to Jewish Christianity, stood in close relationship with the Catholic Church.   An interesting case is Hegesippus the author of the Ὑπομνήματα Πέντε.   According to Eusebius, he was of Jewish origin, a fact which is well borne out by his knowledge of Hebrew-Christian tradition.[262]   Hilgenfeld holds that Hegesippus was opposed to Pauline theology, but at that stage he could still remain within the Catholic Church.   This view, however, has been disputed.[263]   There seems to be good reason to maintain his Jewish origin, and this in spite of his strange list of Jewish heretical parties.[264]   Eusebius appeals to him as an authority on Apostolic tradition, and seems to have no doubt whatsoever about his orthodoxy.   Two other men may probably be claimed by Hebrew Christianity: it is possible that both Papias and Melito of Sardis were of Jewish origin.[265]   However the case may be, Hilgenfeld's description of Hebrew Christianity as a "Grossmacht" is certainly no exaggeration for the first decades of the second century.[266]

There is a good measure of truth in Schonfield's suggestion that the Gentile Christian attitude towards Jewish Christians, as it appears from Justin's Dialogue, had a corresponding parallel on the Hebrew-Christian side. There were those amongst the Gentiles who refused fellowship to those who kept the Law; but there were also those, like Justin himself, who did not mind, provided it was not imposed upon others. Similarly, there was a Jewish section of the Church which accepted the Virgin Birth and the Apostleship of Paul. These Hebrew Christians were satisfied that the Gentile brethren kept only the Noachian laws as laid down in Acts. There were others, however, who demanded from the Gentiles absolute submission to the Law.[267] But it seems to us that Schmidtke's important work has been too often overlooked by writers on the subject.[268] Scholars sometimes use the names Ebionites, Jewish Christians, and Nazarenes as if they were synonyms, which they are not. This fortuitous use of names not only confuses the issue, but also gives the impression that all Hebrew Christianity was heretical as far as the Catholic Church was concerned. But this is incorrect. We will therefore attempt to give a brief outline of the Hebrew-Christian situation as it appears in the last decades of the fourth century.

(a) Christians of Jewish descent

Scholars speak of Jewish Christianity as opposed to the Catholic Church. This creates the impression that all Jews believing in Jesus were outside the communion of Catholic Christianity. It is therefore important to emphasize that such a presentation fails to convey the whole truth. Schmidtke well asks: "With what right is it assumed (glaubt man) that these are other than baptized Jews who have joined the Catholic Church (Grosskirche) and who have been more closely described by Origen, Epiphanius haer. 30. 3 ff. and also by Jerome himself comm. in Tit. 3. 9 (M.L. 26, 631) as their companions?"[269]

Origen's reference to the Jew who became a fugitive for the sake of the faith in Christ;[270] Epiphanius' account concerning the experiences of Joseph of Tiberias;[271] Jerome's Hebrew teacher, whom he calls frater qui ex Hebraeis crediderat,[272] these were all Jews who became members of the Catholic Church. Schmidtke shows that Jerome clearly differentiated between catholic Jewish

Christians and heretical Hebrew Christianity: "How far the Church-Father was in reality from equalizing the names (Begriffe) of Nazarenes and Christ-believing Hebrews is illustrated by his commentary to Is. 8. 23–9. 3, where he first quotes the explanation coming from the *frater* of the Christ-believing Hebrews and immediately afterwards the exegesis offered by the Nazarenes to the same text as a contribution from completely different quarters. Under the believing Hebrews are understood in every respect orthodox Christians of Hebrew origin. . . . Jerome never thought of regarding the Ebionites and the Nazarenes as the actual representatives of the Hebrew Christians." [273] Schmidtke's opinion cannot be easily contradicted. The usual division of Hebrew Christianity into two main groups, which Wagenmann calls "a vulgar and a syncreto-gnostic Hebrew Christianity",[274] is only a distinction within *heretical* Hebrew Christianity, but it does not circumscribe the whole Hebrew-Christian situation. Not only was there an important Jewish ingredient within the Catholic Church, but there was also a section of Hebrew Christianity which, though living its own national life, was closely related to it. It stood, as it were, between Catholic Christianity and heretical Jewish Christianity: nearer to the former than to the latter.

(b) The Nazarenes

The Nazarenes and the Ebionites are sometimes taken for the same group under different names. Brandt has argued that a differentiation between them rests upon a misunderstanding due to Epiphanius' "joy of specifying".[275] He holds that Justin's failure to mention either the Nazarites or Ebionites shows how quickly the Catholic Church had lost touch with Hebrew Christianity. "In fact, however, the whole of Aramaic Christianity has never ceased to use the Nazarene name which originated in the Primitive Church (Urgemeinde): the Talmud, Gnostic literature, a self-designation accepted by the Manichæans, finally the Koran and Moslem tradition in general give evidence to this." [276] The name Nazarenes Brandt connects with that section of Hebrew Christianity which spoke Aramaic; the Greek-speaking Hebrew Christians called themselves *Christians*. Later, under the influence of the Aramaic version of Matthew and the Hebrew Scriptures, they began to call themselves Ebionites, for they were both the pious and the poor, especially those to the east of

Jordan.[277]   Brandt, therefore, does not distinguish between
Ebionites and Nazarenes as two different sects, but rather traces
the two different names back to the difference of language.
While the Nazarenes were Aramaic-speaking Jews, the Ebionites
spoke Greek.   Hilgenfeld, however, has accepted Epiphanius'
authority that the Ebionites were a split from the Nazarenes, who,
as it were, represented the more conservative branch of the heretical sect.   Their common feature was a determined antagonism
to Paul.   The Nazarenes, it would appear, stood nearer to the
Catholic Church, the Ebionites to the syncretic Gnosticism of
Elkesai.[278]   Hilgenfeld sums up the Nazarene position: "In the
Nazarenes survives (erhält sich) on the whole primitive-apostolic
Hebrew Christianity."   But Schmidtke has shown with great
ingenuity that the Nazarenes are in no way to be confounded
with the Ebionites.[279]   The Nazarenes, at least those of Beroia
(Berœa in Coelesyria), used a New Testament canon similar to
that of the Catholic Church; they included Paul amongst the
Apostles; they were anti-Pharisaic in their attitude, and though
they kept certain customs prescribed by the Law, these were
given a national and not a religious significance.[280]   In view of
these facts, it is difficult to accept Bousset's summary judgment:
"Nazarean Hebrew Christianity of Beroia with its Aramaic
translation of Matthew, its Church canon, and its general position
in complete harmony with the Catholic Church (Grosskirche), I
regard as a secondary and accidental phenomenon which has hardly
anything to do with Primitive Christianity and its development
to the East of the Jordan." [281]   It is interesting to note that
Bousset does not deny Schmidtke's findings; he only ascribes to
them secondary importance.   But how is it possible to believe
that such an important affinity between Jewish and Gentile
Christianity is the result of a mere coincidence?   Bousset suggests
the possibility that the Nazarenes in question represent a
circle of Jewish Christians who have subsequently joined the
Catholic Church.   But then they would cease to be Nazarenes.
Schmidtke's explanation is undoubtedly much more plausible.

Schmidtke denies a *direct* connection between the Nazarenes of
Beroia and the primitive Church in Jerusalem.[282]   These Nazarenes were, however, brought up under the roof of the Catholic
Church.   They were "the afterwards separated Jewish-Christian
section of the community at Beroia which originally was a
mixture of Jewish and Gentile born members like the

Community at Antioch (Gal. 2). These Christians of the Jewish people were forced by circumstances to form a union in which they could practise their national customs with the least disturbance." [283] They were thus no heretics in the accepted sense; their attitude to the Law, to Paul, and to the Gentile Church was such that they could be regarded as a branch of Catholic Christianity. Justin Martyr would look upon them as weak brethren, but nevertheless brethren. [284] The name itself is very old and probably goes back to the first Christian community in Jerusalem.

(c) The Ebionites

Hilgenfeld has worked upon the principle that to Justin a Hebrew-Christian heresy is still an unknown thing. [285] He points out that even those Hebrew Christians who would force upon the Gentiles the keeping of the Law meet only with disapproval and not with condemnation on the part of Justin. But it seems to us that the moderation in Justin's language must not be relied upon too much. The fact that he was speaking to a Jew whom he tried to win to, or at least to interest in, the Christian faith deserves due consideration. However, while Justin knows or appears to know but little about Jewish-Christian heresy, Irenæus is the first to mention the existence of the Ebionites. [286] Hippolytus seems to connect the Ἐβιωναῖοι with a certain Ebion whom he associates with Cerinthus. [287] But it is Epiphanius who appears to know most details about Ebion—he lived at Kochaba, [288] travelled to Ephesus and Rome; he amalgamated all heresies in his own person: from Jews he received his name, from the Samaritans the abomination, from the Essenes, Nazorites, and Nazarites his mind, from the Carpocratians his wickedness, and from the Christians he usurped his second name. [289] Some of the other Church Fathers seem to accept the theory that a man of such a name existed, and that he was the founder of the sect. [290] A few scholars have thus held to the existence of Ebion as historical fact. J. Lightfoot has drawn attention to *Joma* 4. 3, where a somewhat similar name occurs. [291] Hilgenfeld has pointed to *Baba Kama* 117a, where we are told that R. Huna bar Judah came to a place of the Ebionites (*lebe ebyone*). [292] He accepts the testimony of the Church Fathers as authentic on the grounds that nobody had any doubt in the old Church as to the existence of such a personage. [293] This is also Dalman's view. [294] On the other hand, it has been noted that the statements of the Church

Fathers concerning the Ebionites are confused and sometimes contradictory. Epiphanius himself, who seems to know most details about Ebion, awakes suspicion. At one time he connects the name of the Ebionites with Ebion; at another time he explains it from the poverty of the Hebrew-Christians, who sold their possessions at the time of the Apostles.[295] It has also been noticed that Epiphanius ascribes the same or similar customs to both Ebion and Elkesai, interchanging and mixing up the two heresies freely.[296] To this may be added the fact that neither Justin nor Hegesippus ever mention *Ebion*. The same is true of Irenaeus, Origen, and Eusebius.[297] Hoennicke has thus concluded on good grounds that a man of the name of Ebion never existed.[298] This is also Schmidtke's view.[299]

Who were the Ebionites?

Two parties are usually distinguished within this group: (1) Ebionites of a purely Judaistic type, emphasizing the humanity of Jesus, the importance of the Law, and rejecting the apostolic authority of Paul. This would cover what Wagenmann chooses to call "vulgar Hebrew Christianity", which he regards as a genuine continuation of the original Judaistic movement though Schoeps denies the legitimacy of such a division.[300] They have been well described as Ebionites of a Pharisaic type.[301] The nature of their christology and their attitude to the Catholic Church are difficult to define. Schmidtke has shown the extent to which the Church Fathers have mixed them up with various other heresies and the odium they attached to the name of the Ebionites.[302] Moreover, the Ebionites have frequently been confused with the Elkesites, with whom they shared certain points of doctrine.[303] But there were important differences which divided the two sects. The Ebionites rejected the Virgin Birth; they seem to have paid special homage to John the Baptist, whom they copied as their example of a vegetarian, and whom they revered as a preacher of repentance, the Baptizer of Jesus, and the descendant of Aaron.[304] As to their name, Schmidtke makes the following suggestion: "I conjecture that the consciousness of the connection with the Primitive Church (Urgemeinde) gave the first impulse to the acceptance of the name of Ebionites. For Rom. 15. 26 and Gal. 2. 10 could easily be misunderstood in the sense that the believers at Jerusalem were in the Apostolic Age already called 'the poor'." [305] The name itself appeared at a later period and probably in the Diaspora. Hoennicke makes the suggestion that it is connected with the material position in which the Hebrew Christians found themselves after their flight from Jerusalem.[306] This is, however, improbable. It is more likely that the name goes back to certain Old Testament texts, where the humble, the poor, and the righteous appear to be synonyms.[307] Schmidtke finds reason to assume that the Ebionites consisted mostly of Greek-speaking Hellenistic Jews. This creates a difficulty, as a Hebrew name presupposes a Hebrew or Aramaic-speaking community. But there is no need to suppose that Greek-speaking Jews had no knowledge of Hebrew or that the terminology of the Hebrew Old Testament was unfamiliar to them. There may, however, be another reason for their name. We have already noticed that the Ebionites held in high esteem the person of John the Baptist and that they were vegetarians. There is therefore a definite Essene element in their teaching. It may well be that a certain emphasis upon poverty was part of their doctrine. It is difficult to assume, as Hoennicke and Schmidtke do, that the name Ebionites was a self-chosen appellation. It is more natural to suppose that it was in the first instance a nickname which, gradually hallowed by tradition, became a title of honour.[308] If this be the case, we may account for the double tradition or the fusing of traditions in Ebionism: the Nazarene tradition leading back to the Jerusalem Church, and an Essene tradition with a tendency towards Gnosticism.

Though it is not possible to draw a clear line of distinction between Pharisaic and Gnostic Ebionism,[309] we may say with a measure of safety that in the more conservative (*i.e.* Pharisaic) circles the Judaic elements prevailed, while in the more progressive (*i.e.* Gnostic) circles it was the syncretistic-speculative elements. But on the whole, it seems to us, the line of division is not so much to be sought in the sphere of theology or Christology as in the sphere of national emphasis. While the Pharisaic group stressed the national importance of Israel, the religio-national significance of Jerusalem, and the Law,[310] Gnostic Ebionism had, by its very nature, assumed a more universalistic outlook. In the form or Elkesaitism, it even made an appeal to the Gentile world.[311] That both groups shared in a definite Gnostic outlook is proved by the fact that even Pharisaic Ebionism had points in common with Cerinthus.

(2) Syncretistic-gnostic Ebionism falls into many groups and is difficult to describe. Our chief authority is again Epiphanius,

and we have already seen how confused his ideas are.[312] The Gnostic Ebionites are distinguished by certain non-Jewish features from the more conservative group. However, Wagenmann asserts: "It is obvious that they are all distinguished by their affirmation of the Law and its ceremonial and ritual demands." [313] They laid great emphasis upon the Pentateuch or certain parts of it, but seem to have rejected the books of the Prophets. Their canon, however, included the historical and hagiographical books of the Old Testament.[314] They practised circumcision, kept the sabbath (perhaps also Sunday?), denounced St. Paul; they repudiated the Virgin Birth, in some instances they associated Adam with the Messiah. Jesus they held to be a mere man of great virtue. To him was united the spiritual Messiah, an eternal Being, who suffered upon the Cross, rose from the dead, and ascended into Heaven. They led a severely ascetic life; they were vegetarians and drank no wine. They strongly repudiated the sacrifices. We are inclined to think that Prof. Schoeps' description of Hebrew Christians is limited mainly to this group. We have already remarked that they had affinities with the Elkesaite system. But while Schmidtke has shown the important points where the two systems diverge, Beveridge holds "that the differences between the Essene Ebionites and the Elkesaites were small, practically the only point of divergence being the new doctrine of forgiveness".[315] Beveridge, therefore, definitely associates the Gnostic believers with the *Book of Elkesai* and the *pseudo-Clementine literature*, while Schmidtke holds the Elkesaites and the Ebionites separate. But it appears to us that the difference of opinion is due to a too rigid delimitation of both groups.

On the whole, we may say that Gnostic Ebionism was marked by a more highly speculative Christology; by a more rigid form of asceticism and a less pronounced nationalism. While to the Pharisaic group the *Messiah's* significance lay in his *perfect* fulfilling of the Law, by the Gnostic group he was given greater metaphysical importance.[316] To both, however, *Jesus* himself was only a man of great virtue, a teacher and a prophet. The asceticism of the Gnostic group is clearly of Essene origin, which expresses itself not only in a strict vegetarianism but also in the repudiation of the sacrificial system and the practice of daily lustrations.

But it is doubtful whether there is justification to speak of

distinct groups within heretical Hebrew Christianity. Hoennicke's observation, "that the Hebrew Christians were divided
in strictly exclusive sects is historically improbable",[317] deserves
our full attention; it is a warning against a too clear-cut
systematization of Ebionism.

10. THE END OF HEBREW CHRISTIANITY

Jewish Christianity, as it presents itself to us in the first three
or four centuries of the Christian era, reveals the following
picture:

(1) A proportion of the Hebrew Church, even prior to the
Destruction of Jerusalem, was swallowed up by Catholic Chris-
tianity. This Jewish element was steadily reinforced by means
of conversion and intermarriage, especially after the Fall of
Jerusalem. It is usually held that the Jewish element within the
Catholic Church was numerically insignificant. But this is
difficult to ascertain. Their influence, however, upon the
Gentile Church was of the greatest possible importance. Gentile
Christianity owes to those Jewish Christians the handing on of
the primitive tradition, the emphasis upon the moral aspect of
religion, the exegetical understanding of the Old Testament;
but above all, the Old Testament itself. It is doubtful whether
the Gentiles, without the insistence of Hebrew Christians, would
have retained the Old Testament canon. The importance of
this cannot be overestimated.[318]

(2) Apart from Jewish Christians who lived in full communion
within the Gentile Church, there was the Nazarene group, which
closely approximated to the Catholic view. The distinction between
the Nazarenes and the Gentile Christians was fundamentally of
a national and not of a theological nature. They attached
national significance to the observance of certain customs, but
did not require of the Gentile believers the keeping of the Law.
Even Graetz admits their Christology to be akin to that of the
Gentile Church.[319] To what extent they submitted to Pharisaic
principles is difficult to say. Graetz speaks of Jewish Christians
who "went yet further than the Nazarenes and gave up the
Law, either in part or altogether". We are inclined to assume
that this was actually the case with the Nazarenes themselves.
If we accept Schmidtke's arguments, and there are no good
reasons to oppose them, the Nazarenes were pro-Pauline and
anti-Pharisaic. Their separate existence was due to their national

loyalty and to a sense of duty towards their own people. Hoennicke well remarks: "For many Jews the acceptance of the
Gospel was a step of great consequences which resulted in severance from the national and religious bond." [320] The separate
existence of the Nazarenes was the result of a vain effort to
maintain the connexion, if not with the Synagogue, then at
least with the Jewish people.

(3) Ebionism in its various forms was the right wing of the
Nazarene section of the Church. The Ebionites were closer to
Judaism than to Christianity. Beveridge has defined it as "the
residuum of the struggles\ and heart-burnings of the age when
the religion of Jesus Christ shook off the trammels of Judaism".
It was an effort to combine faith in Jesus Christ with the tradi-
tional tenets of Judaism. As always, the national motive was an
important factor. Though Graetz is mistaken in identifying the
Ebionites with primitive Hebrew Christianity in its purest form,
he is right in emphasizing their strong national leanings.[321] If
W. Singer is right, the writer of the Book of Jubilees is an Ebionite
Christian who is pleading against the abrogation of the Law.[322]

However, there was no room even for Ebionism in the Jewish
Synagogue. It was this fact that drove the Ebionites ever closer
to a Gnostic non-Jewish outlook.

Thus, Judaistic Christianity, the historical episode which
depicts the attempt to graft faith in Jesus Christ upon the
essentially different Synagogue, found its slow and tragic death.
Hemmed in between the Catholic Church and Catholic Judaism,
Jewish Christianity slowly dwindled away. Between Justin
(*Dia.* c. 47) and Irenæus (*Adv. haer.* I. 42, where Ebionites are
already an obscure sect) lies the last phase of Hebrew-Christian
existence, as far as the Church was concerned.[323] For the
Synagogue, Hebrew Christianity proper ends with the Bar
Cochba insurrection, when the final act of separation was completed. Its actual existence reached to the fourth and fifth
centuries, especially in Syria. But it exerted no important
influence either upon the Synagogue or the Church.

Hoennicke suggests a few valuable points which contributed
towards the disappearance of the Judaistic party: [324]

(1) The universalism of the Christian message.

(2) The abatement of Pauline influence within the Catholic
Church: "As Pauline thought (Predigt) receded the Judaistic
movement must have lost its pungency, its particular *pointe*."

(3) The Destruction of Jerusalem.

(4) The hostility which Jewish Christians met with from their Jewish brethren.

Of these the most important is the Destruction of Jerusalem. Hebrew Christianity detached from its native soil had only two alternatives—back to the Synagogue, which entailed denial of Jesus the Messiah, or fellowship with the Gentile Church, which meant denial of the Jewish national heritage. The dilemma was a specifically Jewish one; the Gentiles were in a different position. For them the choice was entirely within the sphere of religious life; for the Jews it was both a *national* and a *religious* problem. Ebionism reveals an effort to find a compromise or to evade the issue. It went half-way in both directions, but history has proved that its path ended in a *cul de sac*.[325] Schoeps attributes its disappearance from history partly to chiliastic disappointment.[326] This may have been a contributory factor. But the real cause must be sought in its contradictory position—a half-way house between Church and Synagogue.

CHAPTER VI

CONTEMPORARY HEBREW CHRISTIANITY

ACCORDING TO a strange Jewish tradition, to the Apostle Peter is ascribed the authorship of the prayer *nishmat kol hai*, the *piyyut* for the Day of Atonement *eten tehilah*, and some other *piyyutim*.[1] The origin of such a legend is difficult to explain, but it may bear evidence to the fact that a vague memory of the Synagogue's connexion with Christianity has never left the Jewish consciousness. Not only has the Synagogue felt herself challenged by the existence of the Church, but Jews in all centuries have been both attracted and repelled by Christianity. The main fascination for the enquiring Jew was the person of Jesus Christ. To use Rabbi Enelow's words, "as a matter of fact, the interest of Jews in Jesus was never dead",[2] but only "suppressed or misdirected".[3] It was inevitable that some Jews should come into closer touch with Christianity and yield to its message. However impenetrable the fence the Synagogue erected to separate the Jews from the Gentiles, the fact that the outside world was to a large extent Christian was of no little significance to Judaism. The missionary impulse of Christianity, its non-national features, its lofty spirituality, and its affinity with Judaism on some vital points of doctrine, but, above all, the social pressure exerted upon the Jewish population, made it an ever-present danger to the Synagogue. There was never a time when there were no Jewish Christians in the Church.

To the Synagogue, naturally, every Jewish conversion to Christianity was a major calamity. It broke the closed ranks of Jewry and jeopardized Jewish existence. To this must be added the fact that some of the converts, especially in the Middle Ages, showed a fanatic hatred to Jewry and were the cause of great tribulation. Every convert was thus regarded both as a traitor and a mischief-maker. To this day *meshummad*[4] is the most contemptible appellation a Jew can conceive. It implies apostasy, faithlessness, and opportunism in one. Seldom do Jewish writers admit the sincerity of a Jewish convert to Christianity. All baptized Jews are suspected of mixed motives. The possibility of conviction is almost unanimously denied. While Jews have never had any doubts as to the sincerity of Gentiles who became Jewish proselytes, some of whom were outstanding men and abandoned high positions and wealth for the sake of Judaism,[5] they heap scorn upon every Jew converted to Christianity. Such behaviour, however, is not only the result of intolerance on the part of a minority struggling for self-preservation. While the Gentile by becoming a Jew joined a despised and persecuted religion, the Jew by becoming a Christian found himself at an obvious advantage. To this must be added the fact that the Church was sometimes guilty of employing unworthy methods, such as bribery, social pressure, etc., in order to win converts.[6] Furthermore, Jews are deeply convinced that Christianity is inferior compared with Judaism. Conversion, therefore, born out of personal conviction is ruled out as an impossibility.[7]

From the Jewish point of view, religion is not a matter left to the decision of the individual. At any rate, as far as the Jew is concerned it is not his choice or conviction, but the fact of his birth which is decisive. For the Jew there is no escape from Judaism: it is part of his destiny, if he likes it or not. Every effort at independence is equal to treason. While for the Gentile proselyte his choice is purely a religious matter, for the Jew who leaves Judaism it is both religious and national: to leave the Synagogue means to leave the people at the same time. Here lies the main reason why Judaism, while gladly admitting proselytes, calumniates every Jewish convert to Christianity.

That a great number of Jews who accepted baptism did so for other than religious motives is an undeniable fact. The social, economic, and other advantages of joining the majority are so obvious that even in the case of sincere conversion there is always the suspicion of opportunism. For this reason, many Jewish believers in Jesus Christ have never joined the Christian Church.[8] On the other hand, to deny sincerity of conviction to all Jewish converts, amongst whom were many saintly men and women, is a grave injustice. It springs out of the conscious or unconscious assumption that the difference between Jew and Gentile is such that the psychological and spiritual laws operating in the one are not applicable to the other. That such an assumption has no foundation is amply proved by the fact of Hebrew Christianity. That there is no essential psychological difference between the

Jew and Gentile goes without saying. The accident of birth must not and cannot be the determining factor in the human quest for truth. If our definition of the difference between Judaism and Christianity in terms of *inward disposition* rather than outward adherence holds good, then neither tradition nor history is a decisive factor.[9] The characteristically *Jewish* attitude is not confined to Israel nor the characteristically *Christian* attitude to the Gentiles. Before God man stands in his fallen humanity, and he stands *alone*, in all his poverty. His national traditions, his loyalty to the past, his claim upon prerogatives provide no refuge before the Judge of mankind. Man either surrenders in his helplessness, pleading no merit save God's grace, or else he asserts himself before God, falling back if not upon his own, then upon his peoples' virtues.[10] Faith in Jesus Christ, as the Church understands it, implies surrender. The underlying principle of Judaism is opposed to such an attitude, for it is based upon the fundamental Jewish assertion that man can hold his own before God.[11]

There are many Jews in the Synagogue who, though never challenged by the Christian message, have been led to acknowledge their utter helplessness by falling back upon God's grace; in this, their *inward* disposition, they are potentially Christians.[12] On the other hand, there are many Christians in the Church who faithfully adhere to traditional Christianity, but who in their self-sufficiency have assumed an attitude of *independence* vis à vis God; in this, their inward attitude, they are *Jews*.[13] To the first Jesus Christ says: "He that is not against us is for us" (Mk. 9. 40); to the latter he says: "The last shall be first and the first last" (Mt. 20. 16). It is from this position of *inwardness* that the demarcation line between Church and Synagogue becomes fluid. The real test lies not in the rigid adherence to tradition but in the inward attitude of the individual believer.[14] To deny this fact is to deny not only a vital Christian truth but the basic principle of *true* religion.

There is, however, one more point which must be borne in mind. In the Christian view that characteristic attitude of surrender, which is only the reverse side of *humble acceptance* of salvation from the hands of God, is due not to human humility but to God's grace. Man cannot save himself, he must *be* saved. Even man's acceptance of salvation is due to God and not to man. This is the meaning of "prevenient grace". The source

of faith itself is God and not man.[15]   Conversion, therefore, is
always a miracle of God's grace. Man does not convert himself;
he *is* converted by the Spirit of God. That conversions can and
do happen is upheld not only by the missionary experience of the
Church but by the miracle of her own existence. It is the fact
of conversion which holds the secret of the continual *renewal* of
Christianity.   Franz Rosenzweig has clearly recognized conversion as an important characteristic of the Christian Church.
Missionary enterprise is thus an integral part of the Christian
faith. Its life depends upon it. The Church began its existence
by calling individual men into fellowship with Jesus Christ, and
it still addresses itself primarily to the individual.[16]   In her
missionary vision the Church knows of no geographical or racial
limitations. In her claim and profession she is still the *ecclesia
catholica*. If not in practice, in theory at any rate her missionary
obligation towards Jews and Gentiles was never abandoned. Jewish
converts are thus the result of the missionary effort of the Church
which knows herself called to preach to *all* men. What appears
to the Synagogue as interference is for the Church an expression
of her loyalty and faith. To leave out the Jew from the missionary
obligation is to the Church not religious tolerance but betrayal of
her cause and denial of her faith. Without the Jews, the Church
is incomplete.[17]

Thanks to the missionary impulse of the Church, Hebrew
Christianity [18] has really never totally disappeared. At no time
was the Church entirely without converts from Judaism. There
is, however, an important difference between Hebrew Christianity
prior to A.D. 135 and after that date. While Hebrew Christianity
till the Bar Cochba insurrection was a phenomenon taking place
within the life of the Jewish people, after the Bar Cochba incident
it first lived in separation and later in estrangement and even in
hostility to the Jews. The revival of modern Hebrew Christianity
is marked by the attempt on the part of Jesus-believing Jews to
regain entrance into Jewish society.

1. THE MISSIONARY APPROACH

The missionary approach to the Jewish people is as old as the
Church itself. Its beginnings go beyond the opening chapters of
the Acts. Johannes Weiss has shown that traces of the missionary
activity immediately after the death of Jesus are still recognizable
in the Gospels.[19]   In one sense the first and greatest missionary

to the Jews was Jesus himself, who addressed his message primarily to the Jewish people.[20]   The disciples followed their Master's example, limiting their missionary effort to their own kinsmen. Even Paul, the "Apostle to the Gentiles", seems to have carefully followed the rule "to the Jew first".[21]   Only by degrees were the Gentiles included; St. Paul's Apostleship to the Gentiles was the result of circumstances rather than design.   It was under pressure that he turned to non-Jews with his Gospel,[22] though he was not the first to approach the Gentile world with the message.   Nevertheless, the main attention of the early Church was fixed upon Israel.

(a) The Old Testament

The burden of the missionary message was the Messiahship of Jesus. This was supported by Old Testament texts. Christian interpretation of the Old Testament was, from the beginning, an important factor in the missionary witness of the Church.   In the case of the two disciples of Emmaus, it was Jesus himself who, "beginning from Moses and from all the Prophets", interpreted to them the Scriptures concerning his own person.[24] κατὰ τὰς γραφάς (1 Cor. 15. 3. 4) was an important phrase in the vocabulary of early Christianity.[25] The appeal to the authority of the Canon was a powerful weapon, especially as far as the Jews were concerned. It is for this reason that the controversy with the Synagogue was primarily exegetical in character.[26] The knowledge of the important proof-texts and their right interpretation formed the basic education of the Christian missionary. As there were, however, no *professional* missionaries in our modern sense, the knowledge of Messianic passages was a universal acquirement in the Christian community. Everyone was expected to be able to give an answer concerning the hope cherished by the believers (1 Pet. 3. 15). It was for this purpose that manuals containing selected texts, the so-called Books of Testimonies, came into existence.[27]

The method of finding the Messiah predicted in the Old Testament is not a Christian invention. It belongs to the ancient tradition of the Synagogue. The Rabbis held that "all the prophets prophesied only of the days of the Messiah". [28] The identification, however, of Jesus with the Messiah was the distinctly *Christian* interpretation of Scripture. For this purpose incidents in the life of the Messiah were made to tally with Old

Testament prophecies; and, *vice versa*, prophetic utterances were applied to the Person of Jesus as the promised Messiah.[29]   A classical instance is Philip's interpretation of Is. 53 to the Ethiopian eunuch.[30]   The connection between the suffering Servant of God and the crucified Messiah was only too obvious.   But here, again, it was not Philip's ingenuity that created the parallel. Is. 53 has undoubtedly had important Messianic significance for the Synagogue, though it is not possible to ascertain how early this chapter was interpreted as referring to the Messiah.[31] καθὼς γέγραπται (Mk. 14. 21), ὅτι γέγραπται (v. 27), ἵνα πληρωθῶσιν αἱ γραφαί (v. 49) and the various other references to the fulfilment of Scripture belong to the genuine tradition of the primitive Church and undoubtedly go back to Jesus himself.[32]   It is for this reason that we have to repudiate Lee Woolf's assertion that the Messiahship of Jesus was only of local significance.[33]   Without the Old Testament and the deeply-rooted Messianic tradition of the Synagogue, Jesus' claims would have been without a background.[34]

The Old Testament, therefore, was of the greatest possible assistance to Christian preaching.   All missionary preaching, especially to the Jews, was substantiated by an appeal to Scripture.   The speeches in Acts attributed to Peter, Stephen, and Paul all make reference to the Old Testament.   Apollos, who was "mighty in the Scriptures", showed by the same that Jesus was the Christ.[35]   The importance attached to the Old Testament appeal can be judged from the dialogue between Justin and Trypho.   Here every claim Justin makes for Jesus he tries to prove by Scripture, even to the name of the Messiah, which he identifies in some curious way with the name of God (ch. LXXV). He also accuses the Jews of having removed passages from Esdras and Jeremiah.   He alleges that from Ps. 96. 10 they have removed the phrase "from the Tree", which in Justin's opinion contained a reference to the Cross (ch. LXXIII).[36]   Another exegetical curiosity is the famous passage in the Epistle of Barnabas, where it is made out, first, that Abraham circumcised 318 men of his household and, secondly, that this number contains the initials of the name of Jesus (IH) and a reference to the Cross (T).[37]   But such ingenious exposition was by no means foreign to the methods with which the Synagogue was acquainted.   The Church Fathers soon learned from the Rabbis how to make use of the text for their own purposes.[38]   Evidence of the ingenuity of both is amply provided by the Talmud, the Midrash, and the patristic literature. The reason why the Church Fathers in some instances appear to outbid the Rabbis lies in the fact that in most cases they entirely relied upon the Greek text.[39]   But however forced the exegetical methods may appear to our modern mind, the importance of the appeal to the Old Testament in discussions with Jews cannot be overestimated.   It gave the Christian missionary the first point of contact, it created a mutual platform, and made it possible to point to the essential unity between the Old and the New Testaments.   The allegorical method of spiritualizing the ceremonial law and the sacrifices which we meet throughout the patristic literature, *e.g.* in the *Epistle of Barnabas*,[40] was practised, though with greater restraint, in certain Jewish circles, especially in the Diaspora.[41]   In one form or another, it was known and used by the Rabbis in Palestine itself.[42]   To a large extent it was this method of allegorical or typological interpretation which dominated the missionary approach of the Church.   It is still widely used, with a certain measure of success.

Dr. Hertz in a note on the "alleged Christological references in Scripture" makes out that some passages traditionally held by the Church as referring to the Messiah, like Gen. 49. 10 (Shiloh), Ps. 2. 12 ("Kiss the Son"), Is. 7. 14 ("a virgin shall conceive"), and Is. 53 (the Suffering Servant), have become untenable under the pressure of modern scholarship.[43]   He therefore holds that only illiterate Jews, ignorant of Scripture, can be impressed by the argumentations of Christian missionaries. But the fact is that in many instances not the ignorant, illiterate Jews, as the late Chief Rabbi alleges, but men of great learning have accepted the Christian interpretation of the Messianic texts contained in the Old Testament, and have acknowledged Jesus to be the promised Messiah.[44]   It was with this fact in mind that the late Prof. Franz Delitzsch wrote his famous missionary tract: *Ernste Fragen an die Gebildeten jüdischer Religion.*[45]   Christian missionaries to the Jews have always paid special attention to the educated representatives of Judaism.[46]   It was with them that an adequate discussion concerning the Christian claims was possible.   These claims were for the most part based upon the Old Testament.   It was here that the Church found its supreme witness to the truth, as she knew it in Christ Jesus.   It was handed down to her by Jewish hands.   They were Jews who first connected the Messianic passages in the Old Testament with Jesus the Messiah, and throughout the centuries the appeal to the Hebrew Scriptures remained the most convincing argument for the Messiahship of Jesus. Saul, the converted Pharisee, was "proving" (συμβιβάζων) [47] to the Jews of Damascus that Jesus was the Christ; J. Lichtenstein, the old Rabbi of Tapio Szele, Hungary, was "proving" to his brethren, since the days of his conversion, that Jesus was the *promised* Messiah.[48] Both Rabbi Saul of Tarsus in the first century and Rabbi Lichtenstein of Tapio Szele in the nineteenth were appealing for evidence to the same Old Testament.[49] The Hebrew Scriptures are still of fundamental importance in the proclamation of the Christian message. Without them Christianity is inexplicable.[50] However much our exegetical methods have changed, the appeal to the Old Testament is still an essential part of Christian evidences. The discussion between Jews and Christians must of necessity centre round the interpretation of Scripture.[51] It may be that the "New Israel", as the Christian Church calls itself, "did not precisely grow out of an 'Old Israel' ", to borrow a phrase from S. A. Cook,[52] but without the one the other would have been impossible. The embryo of Christianity is deeply embedded in the Old Testament and this not merely in the sense of a progressive understanding of spiritual truth, as is now commonly held,[53] but in the deeper sense of promise and fulfilment.

The experience of the Dutch poet Isaac Da Costa was the experience of most sincerely converted Jews. Da Costa, in the preface to the English edition of his book *Israel en de Volken*, tells us that it was through the study of the Old Testament that he was led to the New Testament and finally to Jesus Christ.[54] Elsewhere Da Costa confesses that he owes his conversion to the testimony of the great Dutch poet William Bilderdijk (1756-1831), who spoke to him of the Old Testament and directed his attention "to the prophecies, to the promises given to the fathers, to the portions of revealed truth preserved even in the traditions of the Rabbis (Messiah ben David and Messiah ben Joseph, etc.)".[55] For the religious Jew converted to Christianity, the Old Testament has been the infallible guide leading in a straight line from Moses and the Prophets to Jesus and the Apostles. To the Hebrew Christian the connexion between the Old Testament and the New Testament is of most vital importance. Unless the two Testaments complement and explain each other, faith in the Messiahship of Jesus becomes a purely subjective conviction without anchorage in historical revelation.[56]

(b) Mysticism

It is unfortunate that excess of zeal on the part of Jewish missionaries, especially converts,[57] has led to extending the field of evidence from the Old Testament first to the Talmud and then to Jewish mysticism. In the search for a starting-point the temptation to elaborate any affinity of ideas is very natural. Paul in Athens seized upon the inscription Ἀγνώστῳ Θεῷ in order to make known the God who revealed himself in Jesus Christ; he even quotes a Stoic poet to give force to his argument against idolatry.[58] But occasional reference to a familiar quotation from an alien source is one thing and the adducement of proof that the source is only apparently alien is another.

Christian apologists have sometimes committed the mistake of going to Rabbinical literature for evidence in support of Christian doctrine. Pablo Christiani appears to have been one of the first to use this sort of argumentation in his famous public discussion with Nachmanides,[59] while Raymund Martini followed the same path in his *Pugio Fidei*.[60] Later, when the mystical literature of the Synagogue became more widely known amongst Christian scholars, the apparent affinity with Christianity led to the conviction that it actually contained in esoteric language the doctrines of the Church. Thus, the *Zohar* was held to be an important witness to the truth of the Christian faith.[61] Some resemblance to the Christian doctrines of Atonement, Mediation, the Holy Trinity, etc., and the metaphysical speculations of the Cabbalah has led to the assumption of an internal harmony between Christianity and Jewish mysticism. Medieval scholasticism was specially attracted by the speculative, fanciful method of exegesis employed in the *Zohar*. Fascination for Jewish mysticism has survived to our days. Jeḥiel Zebi Lichtenstein, a Jewish-Christian missionary, has tried to prove in his book *Limmude ha-Nebiim* (1869) the extent of harmony between the teaching of the Cabala and that of the New Testament.[62] Dr. P. P. Levertoff, a great exponent of *ḥasidic* thought, has devoted his energies to working out the essential unity between Jewish (viz. *ḥasidic*) [63] and Christian points of view in matters of worship and doctrine.[64] Lev Gillet, who appears to be influenced by Levertoff, has demonstrated in his book that there are fundamental elements in the Rabbinical tradition which are common both to the Church and the Synagogue.[65] To Gillet, the strongest link between Judaism and Christianity is to be found in Jewish mysticism, especially in the doctrine of the *Shekinah*.[66]

Christian writers have rightly found in Jewish mysticism the weakest spot in the armour of the Synagogue which is ever ready to defy the missionary propaganda of the Church.   But while older writers have worked on the principle that good evidence from any source may be used for missionary purposes,[67] modern apologists work on the principle that Judaism is not a false but only an incomplete religion: "Nothing of the true Jewish tradition", says Gillet, "needs to be altered in order to adjust itself to the Gospel: it needs only to be complemented.   The Christian doctrines of the Word, the Son of God, the Messiah, the Mediator, the Holy Spirit and the Community are legitimate interpretations and extensions, not only of Scriptural, but also of Rabbinical Judaism." [68]   Underlying this approach is the principle of progressiveness in religion.   On this premise there must be a way back to the source from which Judaism and Christianity sprang.   From the historical point of view such retrospect in the sphere of comparative religion is a logical possibility. Christianity explained in terms of religious growth is deeply anchored in Jewish tradition.   If it is possible to retrace the thread to the place from which both Church and Synagogue originally started, the fact that it is mainly in the mystical domain of Judaism that any affinity of ideas can be discovered ought to caution Christian writers.   The association of *Cabbalah* with Christian theology throws a shadow of suspicion upon the Church.   Christianity is more than speculative mysticism. The mystical elements in the Christian tradition are not the main characteristics of the Church.   Besides, the *Cabbalah* itself owes some debt to Christian ideas, having drawn upon a large variety of sources.[69]   Orthodox Judaism, on the whole, has looked upon its mystical speculations with suspicion.[70] Judaism, though making room for a certain amount of mysticism, is essentially a religion of law and reason.[71] Mystics in Judaism, as in every other religion, have always been a small minority.   The affinity between Jewish and Christian mysticism is explained not only by the derivation from common sources but also by the fact that mysticism is essentially universal—it follows the same law and strives towards the same goal.   To describe the origin of Christianity as the result of suppressed mysticism is an aberration.[72] Every religion possesses a mystical element, if we understand mysticism as the expression of inwardness. But mysticism proper is infinitely more than religious inwardness. It is rebellion against historical revelation, and as such both Judaism and Christianity are opposed to it. While there is an undeniable affinity of outlook between Jewish and Christian mysticism, Jewish mystical speculations cannot serve as a bridge leading to Christian orthodoxy.[73] The underlying principles of Judaism and Christianity are such that they automatically exclude each other. A. Fürst has shown the precariousness of the missionary approach via Jewish mysticism.[74] The divergence between Jewish mysticism and the Christian Faith is fundamental. Spiegel rightly says: "The Kabbala teaches nothing less than that this deliverance of God can be brought about by man and by man alone."[75] It is here that the disparity appears in all its force.

(c) Criticism

The most common method in missionary propaganda was the direct assault upon Judaism. Christian preachers and writers have set themselves to prove the inferiority of the Jewish religion as compared with Christianity. The starting-point of this method was the attempt to show the Jews their misunderstanding of the Old Testament.

St. Paul, in an effort to explain the unbelief of his brethren, spoke of the "veil of Moses" which lies upon the heart of Israel so that they cannot see Christ.[76] The reference to the Spirit in the context (v. 17), suggests that the veil of the Law which hides Christ from the eyes of the Jewish people is caused by their faulty understanding of Scripture. This was an ancient view in the Church; thus, Jn. 5. 39 reads: Ἐρευνᾶτε τὰς γραφὰς . . . ἐκεῖναί εἰσιν αἱ μαρτυροῦσαι περὶ ἐμοῦ. The reason why the Jews could not see Jesus Christ in the Old Testament was because they clung to the letter which killeth, while neglecting the Spirit which giveth life.[77] It was with this fact in view that the Epistle of Barnabas carries on its strange exegetical argumentation. Here every Old Testament ritual is made to pre-figure Christ, and is given a spiritual significance. Thus, the red heifer is a type of Christ,[78] and circumcision has meaning only when interpreted in the spiritual sense.[79] Even the Mosaic prohibition of certain foods the author finds possible to explain in a spiritual fashion. The reason why the esoteric meaning of the Old Testament is clear to the Christians but obscure to them (*i.e.* the Jews) is "because they did not hear the voice of the Lord". This mode of argument is common to all ancient Christian writers.[80]

To the old Church, Judaism was an error born out of unbelief and lack of spiritual insight. It was not and could not be the religion of the Old Testament. Between the Rabbis and Moses was a gap. Both the Law and the Prophets foretold Christ, but the Jews rejected him; they have thus disobeyed the laws.[81] Tertullian tells us that in the dispute between a Christian and a Jewish proselyte, it was the Gentile who vindicated God's Law and not the Jew of the stock of Israel.[82] For Israel has misunderstood the meaning of the Law and has fallen away from the faith as represented in the Old Testament.[83] Tertullian explains elsewhere that, "in former times, the Jews enjoyed much of God's favour, when the fathers of their race were noted for their righteousness". But having trusted in their noble ancestry and being puffed up, they have fallen away from God and become impious.[84] As a merited punishment for their sin, they are unable to understand the Lord's first advent,[85] still waiting for their own Messiah to come in glory, while rejecting the humble appearance of the Son of God.[86]

The mind of the Church with regard to Judaism has been clearly put forth by Cyprian. In the first of his three books, *Ad Quirinum*, the noble bishop of Carthage proves from Holy Writ the utter rejection of the Jewish people; their incapability of understanding the Scriptures; the annulment of the Law; the abolishment of the priesthood; the passing away of the Temple; the acceptance of the Gentiles instead of the Jews, etc.[87] Cyprian, however, does not end in this strain: the Jews still can obtain pardon from their sins "if they wash away the blood of Christ slain in his baptism, and passing over to his Church obey his precepts". He supports this view by quoting Is. 1. 15 ff.: Wash you, make you clean, etc. This may appear a harsh view judged objectively. But for the Church Fathers, Judaism was not adjudged on its merits or demerits, only on its attitude to Jesus Christ. The fact that it was hostile to him whom the Church believed to be the Christ stamped it as an error. They therefore sharply differentiated between the Synagogue and the Church of the Old Dispensation. In arguments with the Jews this has been repeatedly brought up by Christian apologists. Tertullian explains that the veil which was on the face of Moses was only a figure of the veil which is still on the heart of the Jewish people, "because even now Moses is not seen by them in heart, just as he was not then seen by them in eye".[88] An interesting attempt to reconcile Jewish unbelief in the Messiah and Israel's adherence to the Law is contained in the *Clementine Homilies*. The author explains that the things which belong to the Kingdom have been hidden from Israel, but the way which leads to the Kingdom "that is, the mode of life, had not been hid from them". For Moses said: Behold, I have set before you the way of life and the way of death; and the Teacher (*i.e.* Jesus), when asked how one can inherit eternal life, pointed to the commandments of the Law.[89] Here the Law itself is not repudiated, but the Jewish interpretation of it. It is for this reason that the author quotes Mk. 12. 24, adding: "Wherefore every man who wishes to be saved must become, as the Teacher said, a judge of the books written to try us." For the Old Testament contains spurious matter which only the believer in Christ knows how to separate from what is genuine.[90]

The argument of the *Clementine Homilies* is unique. The more usual line followed by Christian apologists is to show the inconsistency of Judaism. The fact that the Jews cling to the promises of the Old Testament, still expecting the coming of the Messiah, while all the time rejecting Jesus, in whom the prophecies were fulfilled, appeared to the Church an inconsistency which could only be explained by obduracy and which Origen held to be in keeping with human nature generally [91] and most specially with the character of the Jewish people.[92]

A certain disparity between the Old Testament and Rabbinic Judaism has been noticed by Christian apologists from the beginning. It underlies all Christian arguments directed against Judaism. The frequent accusation "that the Jews understand the words of the prophets in a carnal manner and explain them falsely", [93] is already implied in the New Testament literature. The most natural step was to separate Rabbinic Judaism from the Old Testament altogether and to discredit it as an aberration. The essential difference between Judaism and Christianity was seen in the fact that while Christianity is closely linked to the Old Testament, Rabbinism is a departure from it. Writers like

J. Georg Walch (1693–1775), P. J. Martin Gläserner, Paul Anton (1661–1730), H. Stuss and J. Christoph Georg Bodenschatz (1717–1797), have all worked on this principle. Martin Rudolf Meelführer, though convinced that Judaism holds much in common with Christianity, stresses that it has strayed away from Biblical truth.[94] Writers like John Lightfoot (1602–1675),[95] Johann Christian Wagenseil (1633–1705),[96] Johann Christian Schöttgen (1687–1751),[97] and many others have held similar views. A Jewish Christian writer, Philipp Ernst Christfels (born 1671), in his book *Das neue Judentum* (1735–1738) sharply distinguishes between the Old Testament, which he proves to be closely related to Christianity, and the "new" Judaism, entirely an invention of the Rabbis. Most pronounced are the views of Johann Andreas Eisenmenger (1654–1704), the notorious enemy of the Talmud. In his *Entdecktes Judentum*, he declares the Talmud to be nothing else but "an invention of the Rabbis consisting purely of man-made precepts, a work wherein the commandment of Deutr. 4. 2 f. is expressly transgressed".[98] Eisenmenger explains: "The reason however why the Jews deal with Holy Scripture in so unusual and perverse a manner is their great blindness and obduracy."[99] The fact is often obscured that Eisenmenger wrote in a missionary interest; Chapter XVIII deals with the reasons why so few Jews are converted, and he ends his book with a prayer that God would remove the veil of Moses from the Jewish heart, so that both Jews and Gentiles would become united in the Messiah.

The last great missionary writer, whose book marks, as it were, the end of the period of the older method of approach, is Prof. Alexander McCaul. His *Old Paths*, which first appeared in sixty weekly instalments, beginning 15 January, 1836, and has since seen several editions and translations, is based on the principle of absolute disparity between Rabbinism and Old Testament teaching. The author uses Rabbinic sources in order to show the utter inadequacy of Judaism. In his preface to the first edition, he carefully explains that it is not his purpose "to ridicule any man's superstition, but to instruct those whom Moses and the Prophets would have declared to be in error". Eisenmenger's tone is abhorrent to the pious writer, and he expresses the hope that his readers will know how to distinguish between Judaism and the Jewish people. His controversy is thus not with the Jews, but with their religion.[100]

Prof. McCaul explains at the beginning of the first chapter that the opposition between Judaism and Christianity is not that of a Jewish to a Gentile religion, but of two Jewish creeds: "It must never be forgotten that the latter is as entirely Jewish as the former." Accordingly, the writer defines Christianity as the Old Testament explained by the New Testament, while Judaism is the Old Testament explained by Rabbinic law, *i.e.* by *torah she-be'al peh*. It is, therefore, obvious that Rabbinism is a departure from the Old Paths, *netibot 'olam* (Jer. 6. 16). In conclusion of this rather elaborate study (over 650 pages), McCaul arrives at the following points: (1) Judaism is a false religion; (2) Judaism has for its authors wicked men, unworthy of credit; (3) hence their testimony against Christianity is of no value; (4) finally, in all those points wherein the Oral law is weak, the New Testament is strong.

The last point is important, for it reveals to us the main principle upon which missionary propaganda was based, namely, the exaltation of Christianity at the expense of Judaism. The result of such an approach invariably led away from the main purpose of Christian witness into the inconclusive discussion as to which "religion" is superior. Thus, McCaul says in all earnestness: "If there be one sign of true religion more satisfactory than another, it is the placing of holiness of heart and life as the first great requisite, at the same time that it does not undervalue any of God's commandments. Now this mark Christianity has, and Judaism wants." [101] What would a Jew answer to such criticism? Isn't the moral law the very essence of the Jewish faith? McCaul appeals to his readers to compare the New Testament with the Talmud and judge for themselves. Montefiore, however, has pleaded convincingly that the counterpart to the Talmud is not the New Testament but the patristic literature.[102] Furthermore, Nachmanides, in his controversy with Paulus Christiani, has already explained that nothing in the Talmud but *Halakah* is binding for Judaism.[103] It is true that McCaul resorts to the Jewish Prayer Book in order to establish the authority of the Oral law from it, but his digressions are such that they seem to include every possible superstition in order to show the absurdity of Rabbinism.[104] There is still another point which immediately strikes the impartial observer in a presentation of Christianity such as McCaul's. There is complete absence of reference to historical fact as far as the Church is concerned. In view of Church history, it almost sounds like mockery when McCaul declares that had Judaism power it would convert the nations with the edge of the sword.[105]

A definite reaction against such one-sided and partisan presentation of Christianity marks the modern missionary approach. Here Judaism is presented not as an erroneous religion, devoid of all truth, separated in letter and spirit from the Old Testament, but as of the same essence as Christianity, yet at a less developed stage. It is stressed that "Judaism and Christianity are not so far apart as some imagine . . . Christianity is the completion of Judaism, not the destruction of its fundamental truths."[106] G. H. Box, after referring to the view which holds the two creeds as "hopelessly divergent", explains that "such an attitude can only be looked upon as unhistorical". To him, Christianity is nothing more than "the flower and perfection of Judaism in its most vigorous and spiritual phase".[107] Not only are there Christian strains in Judaism,[108] but it is even possible to speak of a "latent Christianity" within the religious life of the Synagogue.[109] Another author reminds us that "Judaism is of divine origin", [110] and in his recent book, Lev Gillet urges the full use of Rabbinic theology in an attempt to translate Christianity in terms comprehensible to the Jewish mind.[111] Even in the official document of the findings of the Budapest Conference, "the difference in the religious approach between the followers of other non-Christian religions and of Judaism" is stressed.[112] An increasing appreciation of the value of Judaism marks modern Jewish-Christian relationship.[113]

(d) Conversion

For the old Church, conversion meant a radical break with the convert's former religion. In the case of the Jew, owing to the fact that all national customs had religious significance and also because of the ever-present fear of "Judaising", he was expected to break away completely from his former traditions, even from contact with his people. Origen's answer to the Jew whom Celsus quotes as accusing converts from Judaism to Christianity of having forsaken the Law of their fathers, is somewhat ambiguous. He draws attention to the Ebionites whose very name is derived from the "poverty of the Law", and who strictly keep to the traditions of the fathers, but makes no reference to the other Jewish Christians who were within the Catholic

Church. His scornful remark concerning the Law and his explanation of the Apostles' adherence to it show clearly that the Jewish believer was not expected to remain in subjection to the old customs.[114] At a later stage of his argument, Origen proves to Celsus that it is not impious to do away with ancestral laws when these laws are unreasonable and harmful.[115] In the case of the Mosaic law, it was neither unreasonable nor harmful, but superseded by the new dispensation.

The convert who left Judaism and became a Christian assumed a new loyalty to the community into which he entered. He left behind "the unbelieving and ignorant Jews",[116] who have been disinherited by God for rejecting Christ,[117] to become a member of God's people. The severity of the restrictions and the imposition of a solemn renunciation of the Jewish faith, as practised in the early Middle Ages, was the result of suspicion attached to the Jewish convert.[118] The national motive was of little consequence to the Church. The Christian faith created a new brotherhood. The controversy between the Church and the Synagogue was at such a pitch that the two faiths were held to be totally incommensurate, the one entirely excluding the other.

Historical research and the comparative study of religion has effected an important change of attitude towards Judaism. Careful investigation of the Jewish religion in the New Testament period has revealed a certain association of ideas common to the Rabbis and the primitive Church. Early Rabbinic writings became an indispensable factor for a better understanding of the New Testament.[119] The steady growth of Rabbinic knowledge amongst Christian scholars shed new light upon the faith of the Synagogue and brought Judaism and Christianity into closer contact. The decline of orthodoxy and the modern tendency towards relativism have made a more sympathetic understanding of Judaism easier. The gap which once divided the two creeds has considerably narrowed, and in some instances has actually been bridged. The characteristic emphasis upon religious experience on the one hand and ethics on the other has pushed dogmatic thinking into the background. It is held in certain circles that a common platform is possible on a purely religious and moral basis.[120] In these circumstances, the missionary effort of the Church is looked upon as antiquated. It is asserted that in the case of so highly developed a religion as Judaism, there is nothing Christianity can offer. Judaism itself has a contribution to make to the life of the Christian Church.[121]   Some scholars would even hold that Judaism is closer to Jesus and Paul than is the Gentile Church: "For Christians to wish to turn Jews into Gentiles", says Parkes, "is to ignore the facts that the religion of Jesus and of Paul was Judaism, and that neither of them envisaged the creation of a rival body. . . ."[122]   We have already seen that in the less radical view, Christianity and Judaism meet at many important points, only that the Church supplements the Synagogue and takes it a step further.   "The change from Christianity to Judaism", it is asserted, "is less a conversion than a progress. It requires little of destructive work, but something of building on the old foundation, and the acceptation of the fulfilment of promises foretold."[123]   It is on this premise that the idea of a Christianized Synagogue is founded, a Synagogue wherein all *national* rites and ceremonies are retained, *super-adding* to these "the distinctively Christian observances".[124]   "Conversion", in the sense of an absolute break with the spiritual traditions of the Synagogue and with Jewish nationalism, has thus become obsolete.

But the *rapprochement* of Christianity and Judaism has led to a further development.   The whole idea of conversion itself has undergone a profound and significant change.   Judaism knows of no conversion in the Johannine or Pauline sense.   *Teshubah* is a much-used term in the Synagogue's vocabulary, but παλιγγενεσία is not.[125]   Though the term is Greek and can only with difficulty be translated into Hebrew,[126] the notion itself must be sought in the Old Testament and the ancient Synagogue.[127]   In the New Testament the idea occurs under a variety of expressions and is closely associated with faith in Jesus Christ.   In this connexion, it is a characteristic peculiarity of early Christianity.[128]   The New Life, the Life from above, the Second Birth is the consequence of faith in the Son of God.   Conversion in terms of καινὴ κτίσις (2 Cor. 5. 17) is more than repentance, moral reform, or renewed religious endeavour: it is an inward quickening by an act of grace.   It is because this possibility does not occupy a fundamental place in Judaism that the Jew is forced to explain conversions to Christianity either by hypocrisy or opportunism.[129] But that Christian writers should overlook a phenomenon of such vital importance to the Christian faith and to which even modern psychology has paid due attention,[130] reveals the extent of departure from basic New Testament teaching.   Lev Gillet tells us that the word conversion implies "that one is brought over from an error to a truth, either dogmatic (as in the conversion of the heretic or the unbeliever) or moral (as in the conversion of the sinner)". But as far as the pious Jew is concerned neither of the two cases is applicable. Judaism is not an error, nor is the pious Jew a sinner. The word "conversion" ought therefore to be avoided.[131]

This overlooks the fact that conversion has still another meaning, namely that of regeneration. Whatever the missionary approach of the Roman Catholic or the Greek Orthodox Church has been,[132] Evangelical missions to Jews and Gentiles were born of the conviction that conversion in the sense of regeneration is the basis of all Christian life; that it is a miracle, and a miracle wrought by God.

In the last resort, the basic principle underlying the missionary witness of the Church is not founded upon exegetical proof, nor the community of religious ideas, but solely upon faith in the miracle of conversion. The challenge which Jesus Christ presents is not answered in terms of doctrine, but of life. The Gospel message comes to the Jew, as it comes to the Gentile, not merely as a call to augment his religion but to transcend it. The Church does not regard her missionary witness as a participation in the general contest of religions in which the better wins.[133] Her message is not a religious system, but Jesus Christ. Her witness is carried by the conviction that in him is an abundance of life which in quality and intensity transcends all religious forms (her own included), and brings men face to face with the eternal reality of God. This is certainly a subjective view which can be easily gainsaid. But all faith has the quality of subjectivity. The missionary work of the Church is the expression of her faith.

2. MISSIONS TO JEWS

We have already remarked that in one sense missionary work amongst the Jews never really ceased. If not carried out by the Church at large, there were always individual Christians who tried to win Jews for Jesus Christ. The methods employed differed according to the spirit of the age. The motives behind the missionary attempt were, alas, not always spiritual. Impatience, greed, fanatical zeal, and religious intolerance have often obscured the more noble impulse on the part of individual Christians. It is noteworthy that the stimulus to renewed effort frequently came from converted Jews,[134] sometimes with results which brought more harm than good. This was one of the reasons why the converted Jew was so dreaded by the Jewish community. Most of the famous converts of the later Middle Ages were in one way or another engaged in winning their brethren to their new faith. Abner of Burgos (1270–1348), John of Valladolid (1335), Joshua ibn Vives al-Lorqui (Geronimo de Santa Fé, 15 c.), Peter Alphonsi (1062–1110), Peter Ferrus,[135] Diego de Valencia, Juan d'Espana, Juan Alphonso de Baena, Francisco de Baena— they all sought to win the Jews to Christianity. Astruc Raimuch (=Francesco Dios Carne) is described as "an ardent proselytizer among the Jews."[136] The greatest of them all is the famous bishop of Burgos, Paulus a Sancta Maria (Solomon ha-Levi c. 1351–1435), who in his *Scrutinium Scripturarum* (Fürst calls it a "Jewish-Christian *More Nebuchim*"),[137] has set himself the task of removing the difficulties which stand in the way of the Jew acknowledging Jesus Christ. Even men like Donin and Pfefferkorn were, in their own crude ways, interested in the conversion of their former co-religionists.[138]

On the Gentile side there were numerous attempts at converting the Jews, and not always by means of coercion. The saintly Gilbert Crispin wrote a Dialogue between a Jew and himself on the Christian Faith.[139] Nicolas de Lyra wrote to prove that the time of Christ's coming corresponds with the time prophesied in the Old Testament, and also that according to the same Scriptures the Jewish Saviour was to be both God and man. He also wrote a treatise to refute the allegations of a certain Jew who criticized the Gospel according to St. Matthew.[140] Some of the Dominican preachers, especially men like Raymund de Peñaforte, Raymund Martini, and Raymund Lull,[141] have done much both as controversialists and also as inspirers of others to carry on the work. Ignatius Loyola founded in Rome the first Jews' Society with a strictly missionary purpose. But on the whole mission work remained "spasmodic and unorganized".[142] The systematic and organized effort to preach the Gospel to the Jews is strictly connected with Protestant Christianity, and especially with the religious revival of the eighteenth century in Germany and in England. The pioneer country for missions to Jews in the modern sense is Germany,[143] but the establishment of the London Society for promoting Christianity amongst the Jews (1809: now Church Missions to Jews) made England the champion of the Jewish missionary cause.[144]

There is an important difference between the earlier missionary enterprise of the Church and evangelical missions of our modern age. It is marked by the difference of spirit which divides the Middle Ages from our own times. Its first characteristic is the new attitude towards the Jewish people and a better understanding of Judaism. Instead of maintaining, as the old Church did, that the Jewish people is utterly rejected by God,[145] it was now recognized that Israel had still a great future. This change was to a large extent effected by the revival of eschatological interest and the intensive, though biased, study of prophecy which accompanied the pietist movement in Germany and the Evangelical revival in England.[146] One of the first champions of the prophetic view regarding the Jewish people was William Gouge.[147] A number of tracts dealing with the Jews and their attitude to Christianity appeared in quick succession.[148] The dispute about Jewish disabilities and the ever-growing "prophetic" outlook fixed Christian attention upon the Jewish people. A theology in which the Jews played a vital part came into existence.[149]

The next important feature resultant from the spirit of the New Age was the abandonment of all forms of coercion. This came about only slowly, and reflects the steady advance from medievalism to modernism. Even Edzard (1629–1708), otherwise a great friend of the Jews,[150] was still under the influence of the medieval point of view. He kept close watch that the Jews complied with all the restrictions imposed upon them by law, which in those days were many. In Hamburg they were only admitted on sufferance and had to promise that they would build no synagogues and refrain from practising circumcision. Edzard saw to it that these and other restrictions were strictly observed.[151] The authorities, on the other hand, quite in accordance with medieval Christianity, deemed it proper to order Jews to attend sermons in Christian churches.[152] In Holland, where in the seventeenth century there was an unusual interest in missionary work amongst the Jews,[153] John Hoornbeck, though missionary-minded, was still in favour of heavy restrictions. The same may be said of Richard Kidder (1630?–1703), Bishop of Bath and Wells, who is described as "more formidable against the unbelieving Jew than the credulous Romanist".[154] Though opposed to the use of force, he advocated a method by which Jews were to be made to listen to sermons.[155] But the spirit of the age was rapidly changing. Christians realized that the only method worthy of

Christianity was that of friendly intercourse. A real step towards
a warmer and more humane missionary approach was made by
the staunch French Protestant Philippe de Mornay (1549–1623).
His book *De veritate religionis*, which has seen many translations
and editions, breathes a new spirit and forecasts the approach of
a new age in the Church's dealing with the Jews.[156]   In 1698
Charles Leslie (died 1722) wrote *A Short and Easy Method with the
Jews*,[157] which in approach and argument is a definite break
from the crudity of less enlightened times. But the great pioneer
in this direction was Philipp Jacob Spener (1635–1705), who was
the first to work out a detailed missionary plan of the Christian
approach to the Jews. Its main significance was the renunciation
of all forms of coercion. The only method he approved was that
of prayer and the use of the Word of God. Spener himself
prayed daily for the conversion of the Jews and firmly believed
in their ultimate redemption. It is, however, interesting to note
that even Spener only gradually arrived at the conviction that,
as Roi puts it, "the good must also be brought into effect in a
good way".[158]   Spener went so far as to advocate complete
freedom for the Jews in the exercise of their own religion. This
was an entirely novel idea even for pietistic Germany.[159]

The fact that modern missions to Jews were the outcome of a
religious revival, such as Pietism in Germany and Methodism in
England, with their characteristic emphasis upon personal conviction, had profound influence upon missionary preaching.
Whereas in the past "conversion" in most cases expressed itself
in conforming to the dogmas of the Church, the emphasis now
was upon personal religious experience. This had immediate
effect upon the quality of the converts and the methods of the
missionaries. It reduced the number of hypocritical conversions;
it also removed the temptation of using unworthy methods on
the part of the missionaries. It shifted the Christian witness
from learned controversy with the few to the common Jewish
people.[160] Mission work was not any more the specialized job
of the scholar, but the duty of every professing Christian.

To this must be added another feature which distinctly marks
modern missions to Jews from the medieval attempt in this
direction. It is the increasing recognition on the part of the
Church that Jewish converts must not be segregated from the
rest of their people. This is a novel point of view inconceivable
to the medieval Church. In the past the Jewish convert was

made to break all ties with his former life. Any retention of Jewish tradition would have been regarded as a lapse from the faith. A man like Paulus of Burgos could say to his son with pride, "*Nobis ex Levitico sanguine descendentibus*," but his attitude to his Jewish brethren was nothing but hostile. He contented himself with remaining an outsider. This was taken for granted both by the Church and by the Synagogue. The Church insisted upon complete separation. The recognition that the missionary effort must not aim at "Gentilizing" the Jew was an entirely new development.[161]

It has been remarked already that the modern missionary approach is distinguished by a better understanding of Judaism. The older method of ridiculing the Jewish religion has become obsolete.[162] The search for points of contact has rather tended to obscure the deep division which separates the two faiths.[163] The attempt to present the Gospel in terms less alien to the Jewish mind has its inevitable dangers. But however the case may be, the effort at an honest appreciation of Judaism has had a salutary effect upon the whole missionary enterprise. The repeated admonitions by eminent scholars like Franz Delitzsch, Hermann Strack, Gustaf Dalman, G. H. Box, W. O. E. Oesterley, A. Lukyn Williams, who have pressed for a closer study of Judaism, have not been in vain.[164] The result was not only a more adequate presentation of Christianity to Judaism and Judaism to Christianity, but, what is more important, a deeper understanding of the significance of the Gospel. The juxtaposition of Judaism and Christianity has made it clear that the Christian contribution to the Synagogue is not in the sphere of religion or ethics, but in an honest presentation of Jesus Christ. The missionary message has thus become more Christocentric and less doctrinal. The keynote of missionary preaching became a call to discipleship rather than to Church membership.[165] Herein lies the greatest difference between the medieval and the modern presentation of the Gospel.

The last 150 years have witnessed an ever-growing effort on the part of the Protestant Churches to evangelize the Jews. At the beginning of this century (1902), Prof. Dalman, in an address delivered in Scotland, said: "The century that has just come to a close has been emphatically one of Jewish missionary work. A great system of missionary stations has been spread over many lands, where Jews are settled. A considerable number of missionaries are at work." [166]   Israel Cohen records that at the International Missionary Conferences at Budapest and Warsaw (1927) there were represented 47 societies, employing 724 missionary workers at 169 stations, adding: "but these numbers do not by any means comprise the entirety of evangelists of all the various Christian denominations and do not include any at all of the Catholic Church." [167]   This organized missionary effort testifies to what has been called "the changed heart of the Church" [168] and to the discovery that the Jew can and must be reached with the Gospel message.[169]   Thus, the missionary effort once maintained by small groups of pious Christians is increasingly becoming the concern of the Christian Church.[170]   The above-mentioned conferences at Budapest and Warsaw proposed the creation of a special department working in conjunction with the International Missionary Council.   The proposal was discussed and accepted at the meeting of the Council at Jerusalem in 1928, with the result that there is now in existence an International Committee on the Christian Approach to the Jews, enjoying the support of all Protestant Churches.   This fact is of great significance for the future development in the mission-field.[171]

3. CONVERTS

To the Synagogue every Christian convert appears indiscriminately as a traitor.   The possibility of conviction is almost entirely ruled out.   Geiger, puzzled as to the reasons which led to the conversion of Paul (Rabbi Solomon ha-Levi) of Burgos, could only explain it by his loss of common sense.[172]   The more usual explanation, however, is the desire for material gain or social advantage.   That such was the case in many instances nobody can deny.   It will be difficult to dispute Mr. Cohen's judgment: "Instances of conversion for conscience' sake may occur, for even Jewry has its mystics; but they are difficult to prove, as the acceptance of baptism is invariably accompanied by a material advantage." [173]   The nature of the case lends force to such an allegation.   The fact that the converted Jew leaves a despised minority for the camp of the majority is, or appears to be, in itself an advantage.   In countries where religious discrimination prevails, the temptation to leave a persecuted religion is very great, especially in the case of Jews whose attachment to Judaism is only formal.   To this must be added the fact that in the past the Jews have suffered considerably at the hands of unscrupulous converts. Rabbi Leo Jung, however, greatly exaggerates when he says: "The Jewish apostates, from Saul who became Paul, have been a source of profound trouble to Jewry. Many became informers, blackmailers, defamers of Jews and Judaism, relentless enemies, who by their machinations and falsifications caused countless massacres, burning of Jews and of Jewish books, exile and other misfortunes." [174]   It is difficult to see how Paul the Apostle can be included amongst such traitors. That some converts in the past have behaved treacherously, there is no denying. In some cases, however, enemies of Judaism have been suspected of Jewish origin without good foundation. Thus, Alfonso de Spina, described by Newman as "one of the inveterate foes of Spanish Jewry", was of pure Spanish origin.[175]   To what extent Luther was indebted to converts for his anti-Jewish tracts is difficult to say. The fact that he quotes Antonius Margaritha's *Der ganze jüdische Glaube* (1530) and that he was in touch with a few Jewish converts does not explain his sudden change towards the Jewish people.[176] On the other hand, no less an authority than Dr. H. C. Lea, the historian of the Inquisition, observes: "From early times the hardest blows endured by Judaism had always been dealt by its apostate children, whose training had taught them the weakest points to assail and whose necessity of self-justification led them to attack these mercilessly." [177]   Thus it was in the past. In more recent times, however, the attitude of Christian converts has radically changed. This has been frankly admitted by Kaufmann Kohler: "Most modern converts, unlike the apostates of former centuries, have retained in their heart of hearts love for the faith and the history of their nation, and in critical hours many have stepped forth in its defence." Kohler calls them, therefore, *mumerim le-teabon*, in Rabbinical terminology, such as have yielded to desire, or as he interprets the term, "such as apostatized for personal motives".[178]   The fact that amongst those who defended the Jews were sincerely converted men, such as Johann August Wilhelm Neander (1789–1850), the great Church historian [179]; the famous Roman Catholic priest Johann Emanuel Veith (1788–1876) [180]; Paulus Cassel (1821–1892) [181]; Michael Salomon Alexander (1799–1845), the first Anglican bishop in Jerusalem, who headed the list of protesting Hebrew Christians in England against the blood libel at Damascus [182]; and many other less prominent Hebrew Christians, carries little weight with Jewish writers. The Jewish policy towards Christian converts has remained substantially unchanged. Every member of the community, without regard to the degree of his own religious adherence, is expected to refrain from any form of intercourse with a converted Jew.[183] In this respect Jewry, though often pleading religious tolerance, is seldom prepared to yield to the same principle.[184] This is true not only of orthodox, but also of reformed and even of liberal Jews, to a large extent. As always in Judaism, the motives for such action are not purely religious. Baptism has proved the greatest danger to continued Jewish existence. It is the first step towards assimilation. This is borne out by the fact that in spite of the steady flow of Jewish converts to the Christian Church, there has been so far no Hebrew-Christian tradition possible. Prof. Dalman once remarked: "If all the Jews who have embraced Christianity had remained a distinct people instead of being absorbed by the nations among whom they dwelt, their descendants would now be counted by millions." [185] But Jewish Christians, so far, have not been able to retain their identity. The implications of the Christian faith, with its definite denationalizing tendency,[186] the social ostracism on the part of the Jews which invariably leads to intermarriage with Gentiles,[187] and the infallible law that a minority ultimately succumbs to the majority, makes Hebrew-Christian survival a remote possibility.[188] The several millions of "non-Aryans" victimized by the German National Socialist State bear sufficient evidence to the rapidity of the process of assimilation once the religious barriers are removed.

But while Jewry still judges Hebrew Christianity by past experience, certain developments in the outside world have completely changed the complex of problems associated with conversion to Christianity.

(a) Religious discrimination

The most important change in the structure of social life in Europe was the progressive weakening of the religious factor. In Western Europe discrimination on religious grounds has largely ceased. Where it exists, it is only as a subterfuge for anti-Semitism. Religious considerations only seldom decide social relations. In Russia, where religious pressure upon the Jews was strongest and where baptized Jews enjoyed special privileges,[189] the religious factor has completely disappeared. There are few countries left where baptism constitutes an advantage.

(b) The rise of racial philosophy

The rise of nationalism in modern Europe was accompanied by a steady growth of anti-Semitism, which reached its final triumph in the race-philosophy of Nazi Germany. Its effects have extended beyond the borders of the Reich and have determined Gentile-Jewish relationship considerably.[190] The racial outlook, with its strong appeal to human selfishness, has put the baptized Jew at a definite disadvantage. He finds himself excluded from Gentile society by virtue of his race and from the Jewish community by virtue of his religion. This is a position which removes every illusion of gain from submission to baptism.

(c) The national revival

The rebirth of Jewish nationalism has strangely affected the outlook of Protestant Christianity. Long before political Zionism made its appearance, it was held in Evangelical circles on the strength of Old Testament prophecies that there will finally come a time for Israel's national restoration. The gathering in of the Scattered Nation was an important element in the eschatological scheme in these circles.[191] The appearance of political Zionism was thus followed with keen interest. The attempt to return to Palestine was interpreted by a certain section of the Church as a definite fulfilment of prophecy. This gave a new stimulus to missionary activity and made the Church realize the national coherence of Jewish life. As this coincided with a growing national consciousness in the Gentile-Christian world, especially in Germany, the baptized Jew was not any more expected to break away from his people. On the contrary, it was insisted upon that the convert remained a loyal member of the Jewish nation.[192] It was this new development that made modern Hebrew Christianity possible.

(d) Freedom of conscience

The right to personal conviction is an acquirement of our modern age. Tribal loyalty militates against the private opinion of the individual. In primitive society obedience to the religion of the clan was a supreme duty to which every member had to submit. The difference between collectivism and individualism

is the difference between savagery and civilization.[193] Owing to
the peculiar political situation of Jewry, the survival of a certain
tribal strain in Judaism is a fact which cannot be easily denied.[194]
Loyalty to the community takes precedence of loyalty to personal
conviction. The disintegration, however, of Jewish communal
life and the decline of orthodoxy brought the Jew into the stream
of modernism, where the assertion of the right of the individual
is regarded a sacred duty. In these new circumstances religious
conviction is increasingly becoming the private concern of the
individual.

These four factors—the disappearance of religious discrimination and the substitution of racial discrimination, together with
the insistence on the part of the Church upon the convert's
loyalty to his people and the modern assertion of the right to
personal conviction—have fundamentally changed the whole
position of the Jewish convert. Whereas in the past the acceptance of baptism offered a definite advantage, at present it does
not. On the contrary, the position of the convert is socially more
complex than that of the Jew. On the other hand, those Jews
who desire to assimilate themselves to their surroundings and seek
the opportunity of intermarriage may do so without the inter-
mediation of the Church. In countries where civil marriages are
not yet sanctioned and intermarriage necessitates the formal
acceptance of Christianity, such baptized Jews sink all peculiarities
and soon disappear amongst the Gentiles. They can hardly be
regarded as "converts" in any real sense.

4. HEBREW CHRISTIANS

In the Jewish view the term Hebrew-Christian is a *contradictio
in adjecto*. One can either be a Jew or a Christian. To be both
at the same time is to attempt the impossible. A Jewish writer
tells us that "the term 'Jewish-Christian' challenges logic".[195]
Another writer restricts the right to existence of Jewish Christians
to the time of Primitive Christianity, apart from which they constitute an anachronism.[196] The reason for such a view is two-
fold: first, it is based upon the conviction that the Jewish people
and Judaism form an inseparable unity [197]; secondly, it is held
that Christianity is alien to the mental and psychological make-up
of the Jews.[198] To some Jewish writers Hebrew Christianity
suggests either a compromise or a fusion of Judaism and Christianity. Thus, S. S. Cohon tells us that "the past nineteen

centuries have shown that such a fusion has been impossible". He adduces proof from early Christianity to demonstrate that a "dual allegiance is as undesirable in religion as it is in politics".[199]

The confusion arises from the fact that, with the exception of a few representatives of liberal Judaism,[200] most Jewish writers are not clear in their own mind as to the exact definition of the terms "Jew" and "Judaism". Sometimes, the word "Jew" is given a purely national (or racial) connotation and sometimes a purely religious meaning; sometimes Judaism is taken to describe the *Jewish* religion,[201] at other times it is used to describe Jewish civilization, religion included.[202] The position of the Hebrew Christian depends to some extent on the answer to the question whether a Jew who ceases to practise Judaism still retains his status amongst the Jewish people. In this connection an important passage from an orthodox writer deserves to be quoted: "When some of our brethren reject the authority of the Oral Law, while others refuse even to recognize the authority of the Written Law; when some set aside the Divine precepts out of convenience, and others from principle, and still others from ignorance; when some limit their Judaism to the nominal membership of the Jewish race, and others to a negation of other creeds: are all these Jews?" Rabbi M. Friedländer replies: "Whatever the answer to this question may be from a practical, political, social and communal point of view, the fact is that they are Jews."[203] This is a correct statement and in accordance with the Rabbinic view that the privilege of belonging to Israel is a birthright: "the Jew is born a Jew",[204] and the fact of birth cannot be annulled. The Hebrew Christian is thus a Jew, but an apostate Jew.[205] By accepting another allegiance, he has put himself outside the Jewish community. For there cannot be any doubt about the fact that Judaism is a *national* religion: "Without Jews there would be no Judaism."[206] It is at this point that the Jewish position, measured by Western standards, becomes indefensible.[207] Montefiore once said, though in a different connexion: "If the Jews are a nation, then it must be possible for the members of that nation to include believers in many creeds; and if Judaism is more than a tribal religion, then it must be possible for the believers of that religion to include members of many nations."[208] With regard to the second half of the quotation, we would say that *de jure* there is limited room for members of other nations to enter the Jewish community in the form of proselytes; [209] but as to the first half of the sentence, we must say that "the co-extension of nationality and religion" which Mr. Montefiore deplores in Czarist Russia is an inherent feature of historical Judaism. The survival of this form of tribalism in the Jewish community is more the result of necessity than choice. In the peculiar political situation in which Jewry finds itself, the sacrifice of personal freedom for the sake of national survival is the only price which makes continued Jewish existence possible. It is a price which all Jews have to pay. It is only from this angle that the problem of the Hebrew Christian can be properly understood.

Church historians refer generally to Hebrew Christianity as to a heretical branch of the early Church. It is thus described as the Judaizing movement which sought to bring about a compromise between loyalty to Jesus and loyalty to the Synagogue. Harnack insists that the term "Hebrew Christianity" may only be limited to those Jews who, because of religious scruples, refused communion with Gentile Christians; thus Peter, in the second period of his activity, ceases to be a Hebrew Christian.[210] We have already seen, however, that this is too narrow a definition, as it does not describe the whole situation of the *Jewish* Church. There were Jewish Christians who, though loyal to the Catholic Church and its doctrine and in full communion with it, yet lived their separate life as the *Jewish* branch of that Church. Modern Hebrew Christianity, as we understand it, is a revival of the old tradition. It is therefore necessary that we clearly define the meaning of the term "Hebrew Christian".

A "Hebrew Christian", to give sense to the term, must acknowledge himself both a *Hebrew* and a *Christian*.[211] It means that a Jew who accepts baptism with a view to losing his identity is not a Hebrew Christian, though he may be a Christian. It also means that a Jew who accepts baptism without conviction is not a Hebrew Christian, but a renegade. Both types are frequently associated with traditional Christianity. There are Jews who have accepted baptism out of conviction, but who refuse to associate with the Jewish people and do everything to hide their identity. There are also Jews who have become baptized for other than religious reasons and are obviously not Christians. Thus, the suggestion made by J. Singer, that in order to solve the Jewish problem, the Jews should accept baptism; call their synagogues churches, their Rabbis pastors, and themselves

Christians; give up the Sabbath for the Sunday and together with it the food restrictions and the Talmud, on the conditions that the spirit of pure monotheism be maintained and that these new "Christians" still maintain their national unity until such time as humanity has outgrown all national limitations,[212] is not Hebrew Christianity as we understand it. The writer, either purposely or out of ignorance, fails to appreciate the gulf that divides the two creeds.[213] He also fails to understand that there is such a phenomenon as *Jewish* Christians in the truest sense of the word. His assertion that it can be statistically proved that there never was a case of a Jew becoming a Christian out of conviction is more than an exaggeration, it is a misrepresentation of fact.[214]

Whether it is acknowledged by Jewry or not, it is an established fact that there are Jews who believe in Jesus Christ, and who have become members of the Christian Church out of conviction. Biographical notes of such Jews have been collected on the Roman Catholic side by Rosenthal [215] and on the Protestant side by De le Roi and others.[216] The uprightness, integrity, and sincerity of conviction of men like Isaac da Costa, Dr. Abraham Capadose, Prof. A. Neander, Prof. C. P. Caspari, Dr. J. H. Biesenthal, Prof. P. S. Cassel, F. C. Ewald; of the great missionaries, Joseph Wolff,[217] Aaron Adolph Saphir; [218] of the three Jewish bishops, Alexander, Hellmuth, and Schereschewsky; of the fine Jewish scholars, Dr. Alfred Edersheim, Isaac E. Salkinson, and a host of others, will not easily be gainsaid. It is not our purpose to provide proof of their conviction. Their lives, their books, and the influence they exerted both upon the Christian Church and the Jewish people are evidence enough. It is, however, our intention to point out that apart from the bond of blood there is a spiritual experience common to all Hebrew-Christians which is the basis of their essential unity. In the centre of this experience is the person of Jesus Christ. The nature of the experience can be described but cannot be explained. How a Jew becomes a Christian is as much a mystery as how a heathen becomes a Christian, but the fact is that he does. There may be psychological, theological, and other causes which affect conversion, but these are secondary. When Paul of Burgos said *Paulus me ad fidem convertit*,[219] he meant that Paul helped him to see Jesus Christ; the object of his faith was not Paul but Jesus. When Rabbi J. Lichtenstein described his strange experience on

first reading the New Testament, after having been in possession
of the book for thirty-three years, he does not exalt the lofty
idealism of the book, but the person who stands in its centre,
namely Jesus the Messiah.[220]   A striking case is that of O. V.
Aptekman, a young medical student in the stream of the Nihilist
movement in Russia, who, while trying to enlighten a nurse of
peasant origin, was himself converted through her witness and
accepted baptism.   Nadejda Gorodetzky tells us that he "abandoned a successful university career and went to work under a
carpenter, who finally advised him to use his knowledge rather
than his hands".[221]   The intermediary causes effecting conversion are varied, but the result is always the same: Jesus Christ
becomes the object of faith, trust, and personal devotion.   Many
Jews have become believers through reading the New Testament
and comparing it with the Messianic predictions in the Old.
Others have been led to believe by the humble and quiet witness
of Christian friends.[222]   There is an instance on record of a Jewess
who entered a church "in utter spiritual darkness seeking for
truth", bought a Prayer-Book, and by comparing the Athanasian
Creed with the Bible, became converted.[223]   There is also the
fact that some Jews who for other than religious motives have
accepted baptism, have later become convinced believers.   An
interesting case is that of Christlieb von Clausberg (1689–1751),
who was knighted by King Christian IV of Denmark and awarded
the highest order.   In a conversation with missionaries from the
Institutum Judaicum, he admitted that he had been a Christian
by name for thirty years, and that only now was he beginning to
realize the true meaning of the Christian faith.[224]   Here must
also be mentioned those who never left the Synagogue, but who
have been convinced of the Messiahship of Jesus.   Some of them
believed secretly,[225] a few of them, like Rabbi J. Lichtenstein,[226]
expressed their views openly, though they never accepted
baptism.[227]

Not a few of these converted Jews have shown great depth of
character and true saintliness.   Apart from men like Neander,
Caspari, or Edersheim, who have become famous not only as
scholars but as Christians, there were many humble believers of
whom the world knows nothing, but who have faithfully followed
their Master.   There is the story of the Polish Rabbi Abraham
Schwarzenberg, who, after having read some missionary literature
and the New Testament, became convinced of the Messiahship of

Jesus. He first baptized himself and later was baptized by the great Jewish missionary of the London Jews Society Alex. McCaul, at the age of sixty-four. After baptism he retained his distinctive Jewish garb, "in order to prove to his brethren that no mere worldly motive had induced him to renounce Rabbinism".[228] He gave his few possessions to his son, earning his own living by selling fruit in the streets of Warsaw. He never missed an opportunity of preaching Christ and distributing missionary literature in the Jewish quarters of the city. Once when the Russian police were beating up a Jewish crowd for mishandling the old man, Schwarzenberg knelt down in the street and would not move until the police left off punishing his enemies. He died in 1842 at the age of eighty.[229] An even more remarkable character was the beautiful daughter of Johann Navrazky (or Naferowsky),[230] who became a leading member of the Herrnhuter community. She is the authoress of several well-known hymns, notably the hymn: *O Lord, in whom so many Jews hope*. Roi tells us that she is still remembered amongst the Brethren by the name of Esther.[231] Many Hebrew Christians were not only greatly honoured in the Churches to which they belonged but have been held in esteem amongst their former co-religionists. Of S. S. Jacobsohn (1810–1871), a devoted missionary of the Berliner Judenmission, it is said that even the Jews had to admit "he became out of conviction a Christian".[232]

But Hebrew Christianity, to deserve its name, must not only express the religious conviction of certain Jews but must also imply a *positive* attitude towards the Jewish people. It is here that the vast difference appears between the modern Hebrew Christian and the baptized Jew of the Middle Ages. Modern Hebrew Christianity is impelled by a desire to remain loyal to the Jewish people so long as such loyalty does not clash with its religious convictions. It is essentially a movement *towards* the Jewish people and is marked by the effort to find a place in its life.

5. THE HEBREW-CHRISTIAN POSITION

The Hebrew-Christian problems are in some ways similar to those of other converts. They too are struggling to build up a tradition, to adapt themselves to the new circumstances, and to create for themselves an atmosphere of trust amongst those whom they have left behind and also amongst those whom they have joined. But owing to the difficult position in which the Jewish people has been destined to live, the Hebrew-Christian problem shows peculiar features of its own. While in the heathen mission-field the issue between the converts and the rest of the people is mainly of a religious nature, though the tribal element is by no means absent, in the case of the Jewish convert it is both religious and national, but mainly national. The reason for this is, first, because the religious element does not any more dominate Jewish life as it did in the past; secondly, because the Jewish people is at present witnessing a surge of nationalism; and thirdly, because the Jews, as a minority struggling for survival, react more intensely at any attempt at surrender to the opposite camp.

The second consideration in estimating the position of the Hebrew-Christian is his relationship with the Gentile world. Baptism cuts him off from the communal life of his own people. He becomes a member of a *Gentile* Church. He comes to it as a stranger (and herein lies the main difference between the heathen convert's position and the Jewish convert: in the case of the heathen, it is the missionary who is the stranger and the convert the *indigène*), brought up against a different background, and in a different atmosphere. His first problem is that of adaptation. But the decline of religious life in the Western world and the intensity of nationalist sentiment, so characteristic of the present age, makes the process of adaptation more than difficult. The Jewish convert finds not only a divided Church but also an intensely nationalist Church.[233] In such an atmosphere the stranger feels ill at ease. To make it worse, the influence of the Church is rapidly diminishing; the vast multitude of religiously indifferent Gentiles look with suspicion upon a man who left the faith of his fathers for a religion in which they themselves have ceased to believe. To them, he is still a Jew, and a bad Jew at that. To the average Gentile, therefore, the Hebrew Christian appears as an interloper, who has trafficked with his soul in order to gain some social advantage. The natural reaction on the part of the Jewish convert is an attempt to find a way back to his own people. It is the struggle for a place in Jewish life which marks modern Hebrew Christianity, in contradistinction to the baptized Jews of the past, who moved in the opposite direction.

(a) The Hebrew Christian and the Jewish people

Schwarzenberg, the old Polish Rabbi who accepted baptism at the advanced age of sixty-four, by his behaviour and attitude may be styled the Father of modern Hebrew Christianity. To quote his own words: "The Jews often think that persons are baptized in order to escape reproach, or to live in Christian quarters of the city, or to walk in the 'Saxon Garden' (from which Polish Jews were then excluded), but I will show them that none of these things moves me. I am a Jew still—formerly I was an unbelieving Jew, but now I am a believing Jew; and, whatever inconvenience or reproach may result, I wish to bear it with my brethren." In order to prove his words, he refused to shave his beard or to change his dress, and continued to live in the midst of his people. On this account he was denounced before the police, being accused of "Judaizing habits". He wittily defended himself before the magistrate, saying that Christ's command was not to baptize the clothes, but the heart.[234] But the outstanding figure in the history of Hebrew Christianity is Joseph Rabinowitsch (1837–1899), the head of the Jewish-Christian community in Kishineff (Bessarabia), called "Israelites of the New Covenant".[235]

The importance of the movement initiated by Rabinowitsch lay in that it was Catholic, as far as Christian doctrine was concerned, and Jewish at the same time. Herein lies Rabinowitsch's greatest achievement. There were other leading men in Hebrew Christianity, notably C. Theophil Lucky, of Stanislawów, and Jechiel Zebi Lichtenstein (Herschensohn), of Leipzig, who have united faith in Jesus the Messiah with a profound love for the Jewish people. But their over-emphasis of Jewish tradition made them suspect of Judaistic tendencies. We have, however, the authority of Prof. Franz Delitzsch and Prof. G. Dalman vouching for the orthodoxy of Rabinowitsch's views.[236]

Joseph Rabinowitsch was singularly fitted for his task. He had a winning personality, a warm heart, a deep religious disposition, and a great love for his people. As a speaker, he made a singular appeal to the Jews. Roi says of him: "His speech often reminds one of the Prophets; everything in it is original, nothing artificial. Spirit and mind are equally attracted by him; he speaks in notes of love and friendship which have a peculiar charm." [237] Rabinowitsch spoke Hebrew fluently and was contributor to the Hebrew periodical *Hamelitz* and the Yiddish journal *Kol-Mebasser*, both edited by his friend Alexander Zederbaum. He joined early the *haskalah* movement, and in the controversy which followed Jacob Prelooker's tracts, advocating a drastic reform of Judaism, Rabinowitsch sided with the latter.[238] But while Prelooker's programme for his *Novy Israel* (New Israel) was an eclectic religion consisting of all the best elements of all existing religions,[239] Rabinowitsch's spiritual development led him into fellowship with Christ.

Rabinowitsch was deeply concerned about the welfare of his people. Russian Jewry at that time was groaning under the oppressive hand of the Czarist régime. Many Jews realized that they needed both a social and religious reform. Rabinowitsch himself advocated in an article in the Hebrew journal *Ha-Boker Or* a drastic reform of the Rabbinate and the Jewish return to agriculture. In Elizabethgrad the "Bible Brotherhood" (Bibleitzy) came into existence, founded by Jacob Gordin in 1879.[240] They were recruited mainly from the working class, and one item of their programme was the repudiation of the Talmud and of the Jewish ceremonial law.[241] The movement had in view an *approchement* to the Greek Orthodox Church. The outburst of pogroms in Odessa in 1871 and the defeat of France in 1870 combined to disillusion those Jews who staked their hope upon the progress of humanity and the triumph of liberalism. Rabinowitsch became an ardent supporter of the early Zionist movement in Russia, and went to Palestine. But even here he found no peace, until he came to the conviction that Jesus Christ holds the key to the Jewish problem.[242] Decisive for Rabinowitsch's future became a copy of a Hebrew New Testament handed him by his youthful friend Jechiel Zebi Herschensohn, the later missionary Lichtenstein. In later years Delitzsch's translation of the New Testament became his inspiration and guide. Delitzsch said of him: "Rabinowitsch lives and moves in our Hebrew version of the New Testament." [243] His motto became, "Jesus our Brother".

Rabinowitsch, on his return from Palestine, published his thirteen theses addressed to Russian Jewry, in which he put forth his faith in the Messiahship of Jesus. He soon gained adherents in Kishineff and in other Bessarabian towns. In 1885 he published his Hebrew-Christian creed, consisting of seven articles. Prof. Franz Delitzsch was deeply interested in the movement and admits that the confession of Faith which Rabinowitsch has drawn up "exhibits throughout a familiar acquaintance with and conformity to the Church's symbols".[244]   In fact, it is almost a paraphrase of the Apostolic Creed, with an emphasis upon justification through faith, forgiveness of sin through baptism, and the resurrection from the dead.   But Rabinowitsch, though strongly repudiating the Talmud,[245] maintained his Jewish right to national customs, and even thought it necessary to retain the rite of circumcision.   He advocated the keeping of the Sabbath, giving to it no religious, but only national significance.   To the end of his life he remained a warm nationalist.

The remarkable thing about the Kishineff movement was that it originated from within Jewry itself without outside help.[246] Rabinowitsch's influence expanded wide over the Russian Empire as far as Siberia.   Seldom were such masses of Jews reached by the Gospel message.[247]   Rabinowitsch managed, Roi says, "to place Jesus from the periphery into the actual centre of Jewish life". [248]   Though the Russian government refused his request to allow the establishment of a Hebrew-Christian community, such a community came actually into existence.[249] Opposition on the part of Jewry was fierce.   Rabinowitsch met with hostility on every side.   After his death the movement began to disintegrate.   Thus Rabinowitsch, of whom Roi says that he was a Jew "in whom every fibre is and remains Jewish", found himself pushed out from Jewish life and his dream remained unrealized.   The terrible pogrom in Kishineff, on Easter Day, 1903, must have helped considerably to undo Rabinowitsch's work.

Rabinowitsch's importance for the future missionary policy of the Church cannot be overestimated.   Though it had been realized before that the Gospel ought to be brought to the Jews in more congenial terms, the issue as to the Christian approach was brought to a head by the leader of the Hebrew-Christian community in Kishineff.   Rabinowitsch reserved himself the right to give to his faith his own specific Jewish expression, though affirming his membership of the Catholic Church.   He naturally met with opposition, and there were some who suspected the reappearance of heretical Hebrew Christianity.   But in the end he triumphed.   The most enlightened section of the Protestant Church stood by him.   In the venerable Prof. Franz Delitzsch, Rabinowitsch found a great and sympathetic friend.   The question concerning a Hebrew-Christian Church and a Hebrew-Christian liturgy, raised by G. H. Box, C. J. Ball, and others, was largely due to the influence and example of this remarkable man.[250] The subject has been repeatedly discussed ever since.[251] Box suggested the creation of a liturgy "which should be at once both Jewish and Christian".[252] For this purpose he proposed that a *Hebrew-Christian* Liturgiological Society be formed "with a view to formulating out of existing material (*a*) a Hebrew-Christian Prayer Book; (*b*) a Hebrew-Christian Liturgy (Communion Office)".[253]

The Bishop of Salisbury suggested the creation of a special Saturday evening Service to usher in the Lord's Day, corresponding to the Friday evening service of the Synagogue.[254] Bishop Popham Blyth, in an article on the revival of the Church of the Hebrews, expressed the view that "the Jew cannot, by the missionary distinction imposed by Christ, be incorporated into any Gentile form of Christianity".[255] G. H. Box, one of the most enthusiastic propagators of a Hebrew-Christian branch within the Catholic Church, worked out a tentative form of Evensong "for the use of Hebrew-Christians on the Eve of the Lord's Day".[256] Even Canon Hastings Kelk, who opposed the idea of a distinct Hebrew-Christian Church, advocated the formation of Hebrew-Christian congregations and admitted that allowances ought to be made for "Jewish idiosyncrasies, manners and customs".[257] The matter was discussed at the Budapest-Warsaw Conference of 1927 and at the Atlantic City Conference of 1931, but without much result.[258] The greatest difficulty involved is that at present, owing to diaspora-life, the Hebrew Christians belong to a multitude of denominations, which creates the danger of a Church coming into existence with branches "as numerous and variegated as all the rest of the Church combined".[259]

Amongst Hebrew Christians themselves, opinions are divided. P. P. Levertoff, Morris Zeidman of Canada, and others hold that a Hebrew-Christian Church is the only solution of the social problems which the Jewish Christian has to face on the Jewish and the Gentile fronts.[260] Others, like Pastor Christlieb T. Lipshytz, hold an opposite opinion. The reasons which Lipshytz gives against a Hebrew-Christian Church deserve attention. They are: (1) The content of the Christian faith is independent of a distinct national consciousness; (2) the present economy is

that of the (universal) Church; (3) the Jewish-national consciousness is the consciousness of a people which has rejected
Jesus Christ.[261]

Many hold, and with good reason, that a Hebrew-Christian
Church in the dispersion is an utter impossibility. A native
Hebrew-Christian Church can only come into existence under
conditions of independent national life. This is increasingly
being recognized by both Gentiles and Jews. Canon Hastings
Kelk has already argued that the conditions for a Hebrew-
Christian Church "are a Hebrew-Christian people, and a land
in which they are the supreme authority".[262] In a recent article,
Mr. H. Poms, a Hebrew Christian, has clearly recognized that
the whole Hebrew-Christian movement depends upon the
national re-establishment of Jewish life. Without the existence
of a real Jewish nation, Hebrew Christianity hangs in the air.[263]
On the Jewish side it is admitted that owing to the political
changes taking place in Palestine "a revival of the Judeo-
Christian phenomenon is not impossible".[264]

As long as the state of dispersion lasts, a Hebrew-Christian
Church appears to be not only impracticable but also undesirable.
For the creation of such a Church would be the first step towards
the establishment of a new denomination. The existence of a
distinctive national Church is conditioned by geographical and
linguistic limitations; otherwise it is a sect and not a branch of
the Church Catholic. No such limitations exist in the Diaspora.
To create a Hebrew-Christian Church in the dispersion would
be an admission that the middle-wall of partition between Jew
and Gentile still exists. There is and there must be room for the
scattered Jewish Christians in the universal Church of Christ.[265]
But there is a further point which calls for attention. It is sometimes argued that only the existence of a Hebrew-Christian
Church will overcome Jewish suspicion and remove the accusation that baptism leads to assimilation. This is the main line
of Philip Cohen's book *The Hebrew-Christian and his National
Continuity*. "Our contention, therefore, is", says Mr. Cohen,
"that if Christianity is to become a lasting and conquering power
among Israel, it must lose its Gentile form and colour, and it
must become as much a Hebrew religion to the Hebrews as the
Protestant religion is English to the English, German to the
German, etc." [266]   But so far history has proved that no attempt
on the part of the Hebrew Christian to force his way into Jewish

life has been successful. Neither Rabinowitsch nor Salkinson nor
Levertoff has been admitted into Jewish society. The pre-
carious position of J. Lichtenstein was due to the fact that he
had never accepted baptism. Roi says that Rabinowitsch had
shown to his people "how specially for the Jew Christ brings to
perfection all that is holy, great and precious to him".[267]
But the fact remains that his efforts were depreciated and his
name slandered. Neither Rabinowitsch's love for his people
nor Salkinson's mastery of Hebrew [268] nor Levertoff's admiration
for Jewish mysticism has won them a place in Jewry.

(b) The Hebrew Christian in the Gentile Church

When Hans Herzl, the son of the great Zionist leader, after
having become a Roman Catholic committed suicide, Prof.
Einstein is supposed to have remarked: "This shows the terrible
danger of cutting oneself off from the community." [269]   Perhaps
more correctly the great scientist ought to have said "of being
cut off from the community". However, this is the first and
greatest problem the Hebrew Christian has to face the moment
his baptism becomes known amongst other Jews. Together
with the expulsion from community-life arises the economic
problem. The individual Jew is to such an extent dependent on
the community, especially where Jews live in larger groups
together, that severance from it spells economic ruin. This has
been and still is the greatest deterrent to an open profession of
faith. In order to remedy the situation, the Christian Church
felt it its duty to offer help to those who have thus suffered for
their faith. The reluctance to offer such help Eisenmenger
includes amongst the reasons why so few Jews are converted.[270]

The necessity of offering help to many converts is naturally a
source of great danger and raises grave problems. First, it provides the Jews with the standard accusation of the use of bribery.
This is a widely spread view amongst the Jewish people. There
was hardly a convert who had not to face it. Even Rabbi
Lichtenstein, who had formally never left the Synagogue, was
constantly accused of having been bribed by the missionaries.[271]
Israel Cohen, following the mathematical calculations of Kaufmann Kohler, alleges that it cost the London Jews Society in
1894 between £600 and £3,000 to make a single convert.[272]
Secondly, it has a demoralizing effect even upon sincere believers,
in that it makes them rely upon other people's help. Thirdly,

it is apt to attract unworthy men who are willing to barter their religion for material advancement. Nothing has done greater harm to the name of Hebrew Christian and to the missionary cause among Jews than the presence of such individuals. Lastly, it constitutes an additional burden upon the Christian community and also tends to degrade the convert in the eyes of the Gentile Christian.

In the Middle Ages the economic position of the Jewish convert was even more aggravated by the custom of depriving him on his baptism of all his property. The reason for this lay in the fact that Jewish property belonged to the king, who stood in danger of losing it once the Jew became a Christian.[273] The establishment of the *Domus Conversorum* in London by Henry III, in 1232, may have been an effort to compensate in some measure the material loss, but its prime purpose was to encourage those who were inclined to accept Christianity by assuring them of shelter and food.[274] The expenses were mainly borne by the royal treasury with the help of gifts from pious Christians, though the Jewish community had to contribute towards it.[275] In more recent times, the idea of a similar home for converts was conceived by Johann Philipp Fresenius. He was the founder of such a home in Darmstadt in 1738, which, however, had a very short history, for it was discontinued after Fresenius left the place to take up a professorship at Giessen.[276] As the missionary zeal of the Protestant Churches increased and the number of converts grew, their situation became more and more difficult. The Jewish community refused them every aid and the Christians stood aloof. Many of these converts were wandering about, with their baptismal certificates in their hands as evidence of their "conversion", begging.[277] The Herrnhuter Brethren were amongst the first to extend help and encouragement to Jewish converts. The missionary societies felt it their duty to remedy the situation, and various plans were conceived and executed with a view to bringing material and spiritual help to Hebrew Christians.

Already in the early days of the London Jews Society, a weaving shop, a small printing press, and other branches of industry were created in order to provide employment for Hebrew Christians. But these were short-lived.[278] Later other institutions were created, notably an industrial establishment in Palestine for training converts in carpentry and joinery, inaugurated in 1843. It soon developed into a home and a workshop "in which the converts and enquirers were housed, maintained, and instructed in Christianity, during the time they were learning a trade".[279]   Similar homes for Jewish enquirers were founded by the Rev. Ridley Haim Herschell, the father of Lord Herschell, also by another Hebrew Christian, Erasmus H. Simon, at Camden Town. A much more ambitious plan was conceived by Adelbert Graf von der Recke-Volmerstein. It consisted of creating a seminary for Hebrew Christians as future missionaries and a home for Jews who wanted to be baptized. This was to be the nucleus of a future Hebrew-Christian colony.[280] A similar idea was conceived by Dr. H. Lhotzky, the assistant missionary to Pastor Faltin in Bessarabia. He purposed to establish an agricultural settlement where Jewish enquirers and Hebrew Christians could work together on the soil. He was encouraged by the fact that German farmers had already employed at various times Hebrew Christians in farm work. Lhotzky rented a piece of ground of 200 morgen at Strembeni-Oneshti, in 1886, for the period of twelve years. Dr. Lhotzky himself, assisted by an experienced farmer, stood at the head of the establishment. Seven young Jews and two Jewish families were settled on the farm. Unfortunately, the Russian authorities intervened, as there was a law prohibiting Jewish settlement upon land. Only the baptized members of the colony were allowed to stay; the others were dragged back to the town like criminals. Finally, the project had to be given up. The establishment of an agricultural colony in Palestine was seriously contemplated by the London Jews Society, though its main purpose was to help the distressed Jews who were at that time fleeing from Russian persecution. The moving spirit behind the enterprise was a missionary of the Society, a Hebrew Christian, Hermann Friedlander.[281] For this purpose, in 1883, the Refugees' Aid Society was founded under the patronage of the Earl of Aberdeen, with the result that 1,250 acres of land were purchased to the southwest of Jerusalem and a number of families settled. Unfortunately this plan too met with little success, for various reasons.[282] In many other ways, the London Jews Society has tried to help Jewish converts. The "Operative Jewish Converts' Institution", an establishment for teaching converts and candidates for baptism printing and book-binding, was founded in 1829 by the great friends of the society, Simeon, Marsh, Hawtrey, and Sir

G. H. Rose.[283] This institution, originally established in Palestine Place,[284] was later transferred to Hackney.[285] It continued for a number of years and proved a great help in giving employment and shelter to many Jewish Christians.[286] There was also in existence the Jewish Converts' Relief Fund for the purpose of helping Jewish Christians in distress.

The economic problem connected with the open profession of the Christian faith is still one which frightens many Jewish believers. On the other hand, missionary societies, unless they are prepared to deteriorate into philanthropical institutions, are unable to make themselves responsible for the upkeep of converts. Many believing Jews, therefore, have been refused baptism until their economic position was secured. Thus, following the work of Pastor Faltin in Kishineff, so many Jews offered themselves for baptism that only the unmarried could be accepted because of the impossibility of providing support for the others. This policy has been followed by other missionary societies where it is increasingly recognized that philanthropic activity is no solution of the problem.

(c) The Hebrew-Christian Alliance

The Hebrew-Christian Alliance grew out of an effort on the part of Hebrew Christians themselves to solve some of their difficulties. It is not a union of baptized Jews, but of Jewish *Christians*. The rules laid down by the Hebrew-Christian Alliance of Great Britain require, therefore, of its members: (1) public confession of their faith in Jesus Christ; (2) the acknowledgment of Jesus Christ as personal Saviour and Redeemer; (3) faith in the Atonement and vicarious suffering wrought upon the Cross; (4) faith in Christ's Divinity and Resurrection; (5) adherence to the Scriptures of the Old and New Testaments as the supreme rule of faith and life.[287] Its first aim is "to foster a spirit of fellowship and co-operation among Hebrew Christians throughout the world".[288]

The beginnings of the Hebrew-Christian Alliance go back to 1813, when the first Hebrew-Christian Association, under the name of *bene Abraham*, was formed in the Jews' Chapel, London, with a membership of forty-one. They undertook to meet for prayer twice a week, to attend divine service, to visit sick members, etc.[289] Carl Schwartz, a Hebrew Christian, originally from Poland and sometime missionary of the London Jews Society, was the first to conceive the idea of a Hebrew-Christian Alliance on a wider scale, which he organized in 1866.[290]   But a more immediate connexion with the present Hebrew-Christian Alliance is to be found in the Hebrew-Christian Prayer Union, which came into existence in 1882, largely due to the exertions and devoted service of the Rev. J. B. Barraclough, Chaplain to Palestine Place until 1891. "Its objects were the promotion of unity, piety, and brotherly feeling amongst Jewish converts, by means of mutual prayer and religious intercourse." [291]   The first president of the Union was the veteran missionary H. A. Stern.   Each member pledged himself to pray for the Union every Saturday.   On the Day of Atonement a meeting was arranged to offer prayer for the salvation of the Jewish people.   In 1886, 393 Hebrew Christians belonged to the Union; later the number rose to 536, and in 1890, 600 members were on the list, amongst whom were the names of the two Jewish bishops Hellmuth and Schereschewski and outstanding Hebrew Christians like A. Saphir, P. Cassel, Herschell, Lucky, Margoliouth, Rabinowitsch, Schönberger, etc. Branches of the Union were formed in Germany, Norway, Roumania, Russia, Palestine, and the United States.

In America there came into existence a Hebrew-Christian Alliance in 1915.   Representatives of the American Alliance and the Hebrew-Christian Prayer Union in Great Britain issued a joint appeal inviting Hebrew Christians of all countries to an International Conference, which took place at Islington, London, on September 5th–12th, 1925.   The outcome of this conference was the formation of an International Hebrew-Christian Alliance. A resolution carried unanimously read: "That we Hebrew Christians from different parts of the world standing for the Evangelical Faith now met in Conference, reaffirm our living faith in the Lord Jesus as our Messiah and our oneness in him; and do hereby declare that we now form ourselves into an International Hebrew-Christian Alliance." [292]   The late Samuel Schor was its first president, and he was followed by the late Sir Leon Levison of Edinburgh.

The spiritual and material welfare of scattered Hebrew Christians has remained the main concern of the International Hebrew-Christian Alliance, whose president is now (1946) the veteran missionary, the Rev. A. Frank, D.D., formerly of Hamburg.   The official organ of the Alliance is a quarterly magazine called the Hebrew Christian.

The importance of the International Hebrew-Christian Alliance lies not only in the valuable service it renders to individual Hebrew Christians in need. It strives to promote the sense of unity amongst the scattered Hebrew-Christian members and to encourage their Christian witness to their own people. It presents the Hebrew-Christian cause to the Gentile Church and a united front before the Jewish people. By keeping together, Hebrew Christians demonstrate to the Jews that they are determined, as far as in them lies, to maintain their loyalty to their own people.

The existence of the International Hebrew-Christian Alliance refutes the notion that Christianity is a purely Gentile prerogative.

(d) Hebrew-Christian influence

The Jew in the dispersion, on becoming a Christian, naturally enters one of the existing Gentile Churches. Owing to the divisions within Christendom, the choice which denomination to join is not an easy one. Rabinowitsch was determined to become a member of the Church Catholic and not of one particular Christian denomination. On March 24th, 1885, he was therefore baptized in the Bohemian Church in Berlin, by Prof. Mead, of Andover, America; but that was all he could do. Most Jews, however, join the denomination either of the mission where they were converted or the national Church of the country in which they live. Many of them have assimilated themselves to a remarkable degree to the theological outlook of their particular Church. Others have only superficially accepted a denominational colouring, remaining strangers to its traditional past. In an anonymous article an Anglican High Churchman, obviously a Gentile, complains bitterly of the "undenominationalism" of the Hebrew-Christian Alliance and Prayer Union. The writer reasons as follows: "If a Jew is converted as a Plymouth Brother, he must remain a Plymouth Brother if he is sincerely convinced that that form of faith be the true one; to pretend to be in communion with the Church would be hypocrisy on his part, because the Church teaches as vital truths things which a Plymouth Brother regards as utterly unnecessary; the same applies to members of each of the sects."[293] This gives some indication of the convert's position within the Church of his choice. He is naturally expected to identify himself with the theology, tradition, and mode of life of the community.

From the foregoing it is obvious that there can be no question of a distinctive Hebrew-Christian contribution to the life of the Gentile Church. This can only be possible when there comes into existence a Hebrew-Christian branch, living its free and independent life. The important influence exerted by converts from Judaism upon the Church was only due to their remarkable ability at adaptation. Their greatness lay in the fact that in spite of their Jewish descent they managed to attain positions of prominence. They acted not as Hebrew Christians, but as typical representatives of each particular Church. Thus, Neander represents the orthodox Lutheran view and Dr. Ludwig Jacoby that of a typical Methodist.

The Hebrew-Christian contribution to the life of the Church was mainly in two directions: within the sphere of theology and in the mission field.

(i) THEOLOGY

There is no Hebrew-Christian theology or school of thought, nor can there be, considering the circumstances. But individual Hebrew Christians have made important contributions to learning, especially in the Protestant Church. It is a remarkable fact that the greatest Hebrew-Christian names are associated with a vigorous affirmation of orthodoxy. Only seldom have Jewish Christians moved in the opposite direction. This is the more noteworthy as it is frequently held that the Jews are a revolutionary element in every movement.

One of the most outstanding Hebrew Christians was undoubtedly the great orientalist and translator of the Scriptures, Emmanuel Tremellius (1510–1580). His importance as a biblical scholar in the Reformation period cannot be overlooked. He produced a Syriac New Testament with a Latin translation, to which he added a Syriac and Chaldee grammar. He also wrote a Hebrew grammar, a Hebrew Catechism, and a commentary on the Prophecy of Hosea. But his greatest work is the celebrated Latin translation of the Bible published in 1575 with the help of Francis Junius. The *Real. Encycl. für protest. Theol. und Kirche* says with good reason that Tremellius was "a well-known theologian and an outstanding expert on the Hebrew language". He is looked upon as one of the most learned scholars in oriental languages of his time.[294]

Tremellius had an adventurous life and took an active part in the Reformation movement. He held the chair of Hebrew at various universities on the Continent and was for a short time Professor of the Old Testament at Cambridge. Together with his great friend Vermilius, he came to England, following an invitation by Cranmer. He helped with the framing of the Thirty-nine Articles and the compilation of the Book of Common Prayer. It is thus of special interest that a Jew had some part in the doctrinal and liturgical constitution of the Anglican Church.

Two other Hebrew Christians belonging to the same period deserve to be mentioned, though their importance is entirely confined to the field of Biblical scholarship. Johannes Isaac Levita Germanus (1515–1577), who strangely enough, though originally baptized in the Protestant Church, became a Roman Catholic and was appointed Professor of Hebrew at Cologne; he wrote a Hebrew Grammar and edited Maimonides' work on astrology and Moses ibn Tibbon's commentary on Aristotle's physics. Matthæus Hadrianus, the other Hebrew Christian, a man of great scholarship, was highly praised for his learning by Erasmus, Reuchlin, and Luther.[295] In the field of Biblical scholarship and the Hebrew language converted Jews have made valuable contributions. Charles Singer points out that of the four Latin Christians in the Middle Ages who have left any written records to show their Hebrew scholarship, one was probably and the other certainly (namely, Paul of Burgos) a converted Jew.[296] To mention a more recent name, Christian David Ginsburg (1831–1914) is looked upon as "one of the greatest biblical scholars of his day".[297] His massoretic studies have made an important contribution to the fixation of the Hebrew text.

Perhaps the man to whom the Protestant Church owes most was the remarkable scholar Jacob ben Chayim ibn Adonyah (died 1537), who was employed by the famous printer Daniel Bomberg and "who was mainly responsible for the *editio princeps* of the Rabbinic Bible, and wrote the Introduction to it".[298] There is some reason to suppose that he became a Christian.[299] It was the Hebrew Bible which stood in the centre of the Reformation movement and the scientific publication of the massoretic text still in use was mainly due to the labours of this great scholar.[300] Another Hebrew Christian who worked for Bomberg was Felix Pratensis, the editor of the *Biblia Veneta* (Venice, 1418).[301]

It is unnecessary to enumerate all the Jewish Christians, many of whom were fine Hebrew scholars and not a few of them teachers at various European universities, but one more name deserves special mention. A man of great prominence, of whom Delitzsch spoke as being an ornament to the Christian Church,[302] was Moses de Krakovia, who after his conversion assumed the name of John Kemper (died 1714). He taught Judaica at the university of Upsala and is the author of some works dealing with subjects related to the *Zohar*. He also translated the New Testament, and wrote notes.[303]

It is a remarkable fact that in the age of growing rationalism some Hebrew Christians rank as the foremost defenders of orthodoxy. On the Roman Catholic side, one of the most representative Jewish Christians was undoubtedly Dr. Theodor Kohn, the archbishop of the ancient see of Olmütz. Kohn was an expert on Roman law, and an energetic defender of the faith. But as an apologetic writer for positive Christianity, Don Juan Josef Heydeck is a unique phenomenon in the Roman Church. His work, *Defensa de la religion Christiana* (three volumes, Madrid, 1792), is designed to refute the attacks upon Christianity by Voltaire, Rousseau, and others. Both Abraham Capadose and Isaac Da Costa were greatly helped by this work.[304]

On the Protestant side there are several great Hebrew-Christian names, especially in Germany. Foremost amongst them is Prof. August Neander, who stood firmly on the ground of positive Christianity. Neander became professor at Berlin university at the early age of twenty-three, and for many years he exercised an amazing spiritual influence upon German youth. It was largely thanks to the example and teaching of this noble Hebrew Christian that Germany witnessed a new spiritual revival. Roi boldly asserts, and with good reason: "It is in a special measure due to him (*i.e.* Neander) that there came a new awakening of religious life at the German universities in that century."[305] As a thinker, Neander combined Schleiermacher's theology with the warmth of personal conviction and nobility of character.[306] His favourite motto reveals the importance of the personal element in his theological thinking: *Pectus est quod theologum facit.* The *Encyclopædia Britannica* says of him: "He rested with a secure footing on the great central truths of Christianity."[307] As a Church historian, he had an amazing grasp of his subject and a good psychological understanding of the intricacies of human nature, the decisive factor in historical events. Neander has written much and on many subjects, but experts regard his great work *Die Allgemeine Geschichte der christlichen Religion und Kirche* (five volumes; the sixth volume was edited posthumously by K. F. Th. Schneider) as of epoch-making importance.[308]

In answer to Strauss' *Leben Jesu*, Neander wrote *Das Leben Jesu Christi in seinem geschichtlichen Zusammenhange u. seiner geschichtlichen Entwickelung dargestellt* (1837). The finest evidence of his deep conviction is afforded by his noble behaviour with regard to Strauss' book. Answering a request by the Prussian authorities with a view to suppressing the book, Neander advised that the only way of procedure was to answer the challenge in a scientific manner. Neander was convinced that scholarly research would in the end overcome Strauss' evidence and help to confirm the Christian faith.[309]

Another Jewish Christian whose influence was perhaps more perceptible, but less profound, was Friedrich Julius Stahl (1802–1861), a great leader in German politics and a convinced and firm Christian.

Stahl was the founder of the German Conservative Party and its leader in the Prussian Upper House. Kohut regards him, with some justification, as the father of the German national-Christian philosophy for which he fought all his life.[310] Both as a political leader and as professor of law at Erlangen and Würzburg, but chiefly at Berlin, he exercised immense influence upon German life. In the opinion of some he is held to have had a more lasting influence and to have been possessed of greater political skill than Disraeli.[311] He was, perhaps, the most ardent defender of Lutheran orthodoxy of his time, and as such he opposed Hegel's philosophy, stressing the importance of revelation above reason. There is a consistent apologetic strain in defence of orthodox Christianity in all his numerous writings.[312] He is the author of the famous sentence "Science must return (to God)". Stahl betrays his Jewish upbringing by his characteristic insistence upon Christianity pervading the totality of human life, refusing to distinguish between Church and State.

In this connexion, the names of Friedrich Adolf Philippi (1809–1882), professor of theology at Rostock; Karl Paul Caspari (1814–1892), professor of theology at Christiania; and, last but not least, the Dutch poet Isaac Da Costa, deserve our mention.

Philippi was an ardent defender of the Church, and his

Glaubenslehre (1853) became a standard work of Lutheran theology. Roi says of him: "it was specially thanks to his influence that rationalism abated in the Grand-Duchy." [313] Caspari enjoyed great esteem in Norway and is still known as an outstanding Old Testament scholar. He was held to be one of the most learned Lutheran theologians of his time.[314] Da Costa occupies a unique position in Dutch literature, both as a poet and as a theologian. The *Encyclopædia Britannica* affirms that "da Costa ranked first among the poets of Holland after the death of Bilderdijk".[315] But besides poetry, he wrote many books on theological and missionary subjects. His outlook was definitely Calvinistic and he exerted a decisive influence upon the Reformed Church of Holland. From the day of his baptism (1822) to the end of his life, he remained a faithful champion of orthodox Christianity.

(ii) MISSION WORK

The greatest contribution Hebrew Christians have made to the life of the Church is undoubtedly in the sphere of missionary activity, especially in the Jewish field. The remarkable array of great missionaries within the short period of scarcely a hundred years is a unique phenomenon in the history of missions. The often asserted view that the Jewish people is specially gifted for mission work finds some support in the fact that many of the converts have proved to be missionaries of outstanding quality. However the case may be, the missionary zeal on the part of many leading Hebrew Christians is more than a "necessity for self-justification", as Dr. H. C. Lea would suggest. The position of many of those Hebrew Christians who showed sincere concern with the spiritual welfare of their own people was such that self-justification on their part was unnecessary. What need for self-justification could there be for men like Da Costa, Caspari, or Adolf Janasz? The fact that men like these showed so much zeal and self-sacrifice in their missionary endeavour ought to caution Jewish writers against indiscriminately condemning all Jewish missionaries as opportunists.

The father of modern missions to Jews is undoubtedly Christian Friedrich (Joseph Samuel) Frey (1771–1851). He was the prime mover in the establishment of the London Jews Society (1809). A. Fürst says convincingly: "Had he accomplished nothing else in his life but the establishment of the *London Society* he would have deserved already the gratitude and fame of Christ-believing posterity." [316] Frey's importance in the history of Jewish missionary work cannot be overestimated. Roi, who is not given to exaggeration, says of him: "For the history of Jewish missions he remains one of the most important personalities, for he is the actual father of the present missionary work." [317] It was Frey who conceived the plan for the creation of a society, which was destined to become the stronghold of all missionary work among the Jews. Thanks to Frey's remarkable tenacity and perseverance against many difficulties, the plan of an independent society was ultimately crowned with success. In his far-sighted policy he was often misunderstood and he had to fight hard battles, first with the committee of the London Missionary Society, in whose employment he stood, and later with the committee of the new Society. His broadly conceived plan became the foundation for the Society's centre, the famous Palestine Place.[318]

Frey, though originally a qualified shoemaker, was a man of intellect and considerable learning. His missionary book *Joseph and Benjamin*, written in the form of letters, treats of almost all the controversial points between Rabbinic Judaism and Christianity. It saw several editions in England and America [319] and may still be consulted with some profit by Jewish missionaries.

It is remarkable that not only the great English Society but that also German missionary work amongst the Jews owes its existence in some measure to the missionary zeal of a Hebrew Christian.[320]

The name of Dr. Heinrich Christian Immanuel Frommann is closely connected with the early history of the Institutum Judaicum in Halle. Thanks to Frommann's enthusiasm while still a young medical student, the little printing-press was established which became the nucleus of the later famous Institute. Roi generously admits: "The fact that the Mission in Halle came into existence is in no small measure due to Frommann." [321] Frommann remained to his life's end a faithful champion of Jewish missions. For this purpose he translated parts of the New Testament into Yiddish. His Hebrew translation of Luke has been highly praised by Delitzsch.[322] Dr. Biesenthal brought to light a Rabbinic commentary on St. Luke written by Frommann, which he revised and edited.[323] Frommann was a good doctor, a pious Christian, and a noble character.[324]

An unusual man was Adolf Janasz. He was the son of a rich

landowner near Warsaw. Both he and his father were baptized in the Protestant Church. Janasz married the daughter of a Hebrew Christian missionary of the London Jews Society named Rosenthal. After the abortive Polish insurrection of 1863 he founded an orphanage for destitute Jewish children, and attached to the orphanage was a home for Jewish inquirers. Janasz employed at his own expense a Bible woman and two colporteurs to bring to the Jews of Warsaw the Gospel message. Later, the British Jews Society sent him the Hebrew-Christian missionary, Paul Dworkowicz. A Polish nobleman, Count Wengerski, was keenly interested in Janasz's work and helped him to finance it. Dworkowicz left in 1877 for another field, but Janasz faithfully continued his missionary effort single-handed. London Jews Society missionaries in Warsaw found in him a devoted friend, and he remained a generous supporter of the Society all his life. He is the author of a tract called *Die Zukunft des Volkes Israel* (Berlin, 1882).[325] His name is now largely forgotten, though at one time he was a well-known figure to many Jews in Warsaw. There is still a market-place in the Jewish quarter of the city bearing the name of Janasz; the property once belonged to the family.

Many other Hebrew Christians have played a decisive rôle in the Church's endeavour to preach the Gospel to the Jews. Some of them, like Da Costa in Holland, Dr. C. H. A. Kalkar (1803–1886) in Denmark,[326] and Caspari in Norway, have profoundly stirred their respective Churches to the Christian missionary obligation in general, though the Jewish missionary cause was closest to their heart. Neander himself was a great supporter of missions to the heathen, though he lacked understanding for the work amongst the Jews. He regarded the existence of the Church as a great enough challenge, making direct missionary enterprise to the Jewish people superfluous.

Hebrew Christians have also made some contribution to the Church's missionary endeavour at home. Dr. Abraham Capadose, Da Costa's close friend, took great interest in home evangelization, and was one of the founders of the Dutch Protestant Union for Evangelization.[327] Ridley Haim Herschell (1807–1864), already referred to, was not only one of the founders of the British Society for the Propagation of the Gospel amongst the Jews (founded 1842), but had also some share in the founding of the "Evangelical Alliance",[328] which came into existence mainly by the efforts of Edward Bickersteth in 1845, in order to bring the nonconformists into closer touch with the evangelical party.[329] In Paris he helped to establish a union for the distribution of Christian literature, and in many other ways he showed keen interest in home missions. His funeral was attended by three hundred police officials who used to attend his weekly Bible readings.[330]

The greatest contribution, however, that Jewish Christians have made, is in the actual mission field itself. Herein lies a marked difference between the Jewish and the heathen field. While only few heathen converts have shown qualities required of a great missionary, the Jewish field has provided a continuous succession of great and efficient missionaries. It is not possible to enumerate all outstanding Jewish missionaries, but a few names of special merit must be mentioned.

The first place undoubtedly belongs to Joseph Wolff (1795?–1862), the greatest of modern Jewish missionaries. Wolff was no missionary in the ordinary sense; he was a great traveller and a great adventurer as well. Few missionaries have travelled so extensively, have met with greater adventures, and have enjoyed greater success than Wolff.[331] Without any exaggeration, Wolff belongs to the greatest missionary pioneers of all times. A man of great courage, of profound scholarship and gifted with many tongues, he was described by Lewis Way, the benefactor of the London Jews Society, as "a comet without any perihelion, and capable of setting a whole system on fire". Wolff was an extraordinary character, passionately active, in constant need of motion, and consumed with zeal to preach the Gospel. He knew of no obstacles, was capable of superhuman endurance, and was a born leader. Way describes him thus: "A man, who at Rome calls the Pope 'the dust of the earth', and at Jerusalem tells the Jews that 'the Gemara is a lie'; who passes his days in disputation, and his nights in digging the Talmud; to whom a floor of brick is a feather-bed and a box is a bolster; who makes or finds a friend alike in the persecutor of his former or of his present faith; who can conciliate a pasha or confute a patriarch; who travels without a guide, speaks without an interpreter, can live without food, and pay without money; forgiving all the insults he meets with, and forgetting all the flattery he receives; who knows little of worldly conduct, and yet accommodates himself to all men without giving offence to any." Wolff had a great love for his people and a greater love for Jesus Christ.

Like all great men, he acknowledged no fetters. Way accurately says of him: "He knows of no church but his heart, no calling but that of zeal, no dispensation but that of preaching." [332] His *Travels and Adventures* and his *Missionary Journal and Memoir* [333] give some indication of his eventful life and his great missionary efficiency.

Next to Wolff we would place Joseph Rabinowitsch, who, though less spectacular, was possessed with an equal zeal, a great vision, and profound love for his people. While Wolff was the wandering preacher, aptly called in missionary circles "the meteor", Rabinowitsch was a great organizer. His merit is to have been the founder of the first modern Hebrew-Christian community without any outside assistance. As such, he will always occupy the first place in the history of modern Hebrew Christianity. As a man of great Christian virtues, as a great preacher, and, above all, as a leader, Rabinowitsch will remain for long the finest example of a Hebrew-Christian missionary.

In this connection we must make mention of Dr. Joachim Raphael Heinrich (Hirsch) Biesenthal (1804–1886), who, though different from Wolff and Rabinowitsch, stands out as the exemplary scholar-missionary. Both Strack and Schlottmann have confessed that they owe to him their missionary zeal and their love for the Hebrew language. Biesenthal's merits are mainly literary, but all his writings are inspired by a great missionary zeal and profound scholarship. Delitzsch regarded his books as the best of all missionary literature. He was also appreciated, for honest scholarship, Rabbinic knowledge, and Hebrew style, by Jewish writers like the historian Jost and the grammarian Dr. Julius Fürst. [334]

Both as a missionary and a writer, he exerted great influence upon Gentiles and Jews alike. Under the pseudonym of Karl Ignaz Corvé, he defended his Jewish brethren against the Blood libel. [335] Of his many works, his *Zur Geschichte der christlichen Kirche in ihrer ersten Entwickelungsperiode bis zum Anfang des 4. Jahrhunderts* (1850) deserves special attention from the missionary point of view. This book was written for the Jewish people, intending to demonstrate the utter "Jewishness" of the early Christian movement. His *Chrestomathia Rabbinica etc., cum Versione Latina et Vitis Scriptorum* (1844) earned him the D.D. of the university of Giessen. The London Jews Society may be proud to have counted this great man amongst its missionaries.

Of Hebrew Christians who laboured in the heathen field, the most famous is Dr. Joseph S. Schereschewsky (1831–1906), to whom the Church in China owes a lasting debt. His Christian character, his devotion to duty, but, above all, his amazing perseverance, are a lasting monument of the triumph of spirit over matter.

Schereschewsky was a missionary of the Episcopal Church of America in China. During the hostilities with the United States, he was one of the few European missionaries who refused to leave the country, earning his livelihood by teaching. Twice he was appointed bishop, but refused to accept the office, until finally he conceded in 1877, becoming bishop of Shanghai. Already as an ordinary missionary he had translated the Psalms into the colloquial language of China and together with Bishop Burdon compiled the first Mandarin Prayer Book; he was also a member of the committee entrusted with the task of translating the New Testament. In 1865 he undertook the translation of the Old Testament into Mandarin and completed the task in eight years. Later he translated the Prayer Book into classic Chinese (*Wen-li*) and began the translation of the Apocrypha, when he was suddenly seized with paralysis. It was during his illness, being able to use only his two middle fingers on a typewriter, that the bishop accomplished his greatest task, namely the translation of the whole Bible, including the Apocrypha, into the *Wen-li* dialect. For twenty years he laboured on this work, which he completed not long before his death. Thus, a Hebrew Christian brought the Bible "to the two-hundred and fifty million Mandarin-speaking Chinese, as well as to the mass of readers in China".[336]

Bishop Schereschewsky was also the author of several Chinese grammars and dictionaries. He translated the Gospels into Mongolian and prepared a dictionary of that language. Prof. Max Müller regarded him as one of the most learned orientalists; as a Sinologist he certainly occupies a prominent position.

Of the many other missionaries of the house of Israel, the names of Salkinson, Cassel, Lucky, the two Lichtensteins, Schönberger, Joseph Immanuel Landsmann, and Dr. P. P. Levertoff may all provide material enough for interesting biographical studies. They can all be characterized by devotion to the missionary cause, simplicity of faith, and great Talmudic learning. The most original of them all was undoubtedly Theophilus Lucky, the editor of *Eduth le Israel*. Lucky was possessed of a phenomenal memory and could speak with expert knowledge on almost any subject. He was deeply religious and a great Jewish nationalist. It was his conviction that organized missionary activity is harmful and he consequently refused every help from outside. He lived the life of an orthodox Jew, keeping the Mosaic commandments, but firmly convinced of the Messiahship of Jesus. His attitude to the Church has sometimes been called in question. Dalman and Roi regard him as an Ebionite of the heretical type,[337] but Bernstein asserts that he was "thoroughly orthodox with regard to the cardinal doctrines of Christianity".[338] His observance of the Rabbinical laws was rather an expression of loyalty to his people than of doctrinal significance.

Lucky managed to collect a circle of Jesus-believing *hasidim* both in Stanislawów and Lwów, and the movement which he started in some ways resembled the one of Kishineff led by Rabinowitsch. After his death a few of his disciples joined the Protestant Church; others lapsed to Judaism.[339]

Thus, Hebrew-Christian missionaries have brought valuable psychological and Rabbinic knowledge to the missionary task of the Church. They have insisted that the Gospel be brought to the Jews not in Greek but in its original Hebrew dress, and have made no small contribution both to the interpretation and translation of the Christian Faith in terms familiar to the Jewish people. Not a few of them have had a share in introducing Hebrew as a means in the missionary approach. This has proved of utmost importance, for together with the Hebrew language came a new understanding of Judaism and the Jewish people in general. Modern missions to Jews are closely connected with the history of the Hebrew New Testament. As long as the Church saw fit to preach to the Jew in an alien tongue, Christianity remained a subject of controversy between a few learned Rabbis and priests. It was the New Testament offered to the Jew in the sacred tongue which opened the way to the heart of the Jewish people.

Tremellius clearly recognized the great importance of approaching the Jew in his own language and not in a foreign tongue.[340] It was with this purpose in view that he published in 1554 his Hebrew Catechism, which contains an exposition of the Apostles' Creed, the Ten Commandments, the Lord's Prayer, and the two Sacraments, and finishes with some prayers.[341] To what extent Tremellius' opinions have influenced others it is difficult to say, but it is remarkable that in this period the first efforts were made to bring the New Testament to the Jews in the Hebrew language. In the first place of this pioneer work stands the Strassburg professor, Elias Schadaeus, who established a special printing press for the purpose of publishing parts of the New Testament in Hebrew script.[342] It was Elias Hutter (1553–1605?) who translated the New Testament into Hebrew for the polyglot Bible (Nürnberg, 1599).[343] There soon followed a whole series of translations, not only of parts of the New Testament, but also of other important Christian documents, such as the *Augsburg Confession* by Philipp Gallus (1588) and *Luther's Catechism* by Theodosius Fabricius. Even Christian hymns were translated into Hebrew and adapted to well-known Jewish melodies (Leipzig, 1662). The Rev. Thomas Ingemethorp, in the diocese of Durham, translated the Anglican cathechism in 1633, and W. Robertson corrected Hutter's Hebrew New Testament. A Hebrew Christian by the name of Abraham Bar Jacob made the first translation of the Book of Common Prayer in 1717, which, however, was never published. But together with the translation by another Hebrew Christian named Czerskier, made about one hundred years later, it served as the basis for the Hebrew translation published by the London Jews Society in 1834–1836, for which McCaul and Reichardt were responsible. This translation was in use at Palestine Place from 1837 and in Jerusalem from 1838.[344]

There are at least three standard translations of the New Testament used by the various missionary societies. The first was published by the London Jews Society between the years 1814–1817.[345] It is to a large extent the work of Hebrew Christians. It was partly made by a German Jew named Judah d'Allemand, and the committee which was responsible for its revision in 1838 and 1866 consisted mostly of Hebrew Christians.[346] The second is Prof. Delitzsch's masterly translation,[347] which appeared complete in 1877, having the Sinaiticus as its basis. It has since seen many editions. The last translation is that by Salkinson, published posthumously by the learned Dr. C. D. Ginsburg in 1886. It is entirely the work of a Hebrew Christian, and though perhaps less accurate than Delitzsch's translation, it far surpasses it in beauty of style and the easy flow of language.[348]

6. THE HEBREW-CHRISTIAN FUTURE

Standing mid-way between the Gentile and the Jewish world, Hebrew Christianity performs a double function: it interprets Judaism to Gentile Christianity and Christianity to Judaism. But its existence is of still greater significance.

The crisis of the twentieth century in which the Church and the Synagogue are both involved, has its roots in a philosophy which has placed man in the centre of the universe. Strange as it may be, such exaltation of man is neither contrary to Greek philosophy nor to the spirit of Judaism. It is, however, alien to the essence of Christianity, which is based upon the notion of human inadequacy. The prevailing humanism of our age has thus greatly reduced the distance which once divided Church and Synagogue. The faster the Church is moving in the direction of Greek philosophy, especially Platonism, the closer it approximates the Jewish point of view. The gap which still divides the two creeds is increasingly bridged by the common religious denominator. The emphasis upon religious experience has created a platform for all religiously-minded men, irrespective of creed. "Proselytizing" is thus increasingly becoming a sign of intolerance, and is looked upon as outrageous to the religious instinct. On the Jewish side, the lack of active missionary propaganda on the part of the Synagogue is regarded as a virtue. On the Christian side, the theological implications of the central doctrines of the Church are giving place to the mystic experience of the individual, thus rendering missionary activity pointless. In this general atmosphere of syncretic religiosity, the Hebrew Christian is a curiosity, a disquieting phenomenon to both sides. At a time of doctrinal indifference, when adherence to an historic creed is more an expression of loyalty than personal conviction, the presence of the Jewish Christian is a strange reminder of a bygone age. To leave the Synagogue, with its many and great religious traditions, appears not only to the Jew but to many a Gentile Christian an act of betrayal. Again, in our age of intense nationalism, when the Christian Faith has been perverted to a tribal religion of various ethnic groups, conversion from Judaism to Christianity appears to some Gentiles as an intolerable intrusion. This will become obvious when we remember that to many Church people to be a Christian is a Gentile prerogative. In spite of the fact that the Gentile world is increasingly becoming indifferent to the Christian profession, it is still taken for granted that the Gentiles have accepted and the Jews have rejected Jesus Christ. It is thus almost expected of the Jew to remain loyal to the religion in which he was born.

The position of the Hebrew Christian is one of great loneliness. He finds himself outside both camps, standing mid-way. He is torn in two directions, between the Gentile Church and the Jewish people. We now understand the reason why so many prominent Jewish Christians have championed the cause of orthodox Christianity. Positive Christianity can provide the only justification for the grave step a Jew takes when accepting baptism. Religious experience is no Christian prerogative; it can be attained within the walls of the synagogue. If a Jew leaves his kindred and his father's house and becomes a stranger, there must be a great and compelling reason. True Hebrew Christianity is thus founded upon loyalty to Jesus Christ. It is for Christ's sake that the Jewish Christian is called upon to make this great sacrifice. Nobody who has read the revealing memoirs of a convinced Roman Catholic Jew, a Polish lawyer, can remain unmoved by the clash of loyalties in which the Hebrew Christian is involved.[349] His first loyalty is to the Church, whose spiritual son he is; his second loyalty is to his people, to whom he belongs and whose memories and traditions are deeply buried in his heart. Jewish Christians have sometimes held that there need be no clash of loyalties. They argued that, like the Frenchman or the Englishman who manages to be loyal to his nation and remain a good Christian, the Jewish Christian ought to be able to be both a Jew and a Christian. Such reasoning, however, overlooks two fundamental facts: (1) The age-long division between the Synagogue and the Church, with its manifold implications; (2) the political position of Jewry, which demands every sacrifice for the preservation of Jewish existence. But there is yet a greater truth involved. Historic Christianity avoided the conflict between loyalty to Jesus Christ and the demands of the world by a compromise. It made peace with the world by giving to Cæsar what legitimately only belongs to God. There can be little doubt that national selfishness, which inevitably involves political intrigue, has been the misfortune of the Church. In essence, Christianity stands opposed to the world, cutting right across all national aspirations. Philip Cohen, arguing for the national continuity of the Hebrew Christian on the basis "that the acceptance of Christianity does not involve denationalization", was unfortunate in the choice of his example. He says: "Japanese Christians have given a practical illustration to their people that loyalty to the national cause and love of Christ are not incompatible".[350] Subsequent events, however, have given the lie to this statement.[351] The Church in Japan was made to choose between the two loyalties, and like the rest of Gentile Christianity, it chose nationalism. Cohen's plea on behalf of Hebrew Christians, "to be allowed to exercise the same law of self-preservation, as far as our nationality is concerned, as others are allowed to do",[352] may be justifiable on historical grounds, but spiritually it cannot be so. The uniqueness of the Hebrew Christian's situation lies in the fact that he is put in a position where choice becomes inescapable. Only two possibilities are left to him: on the one side is Jesus Christ, but loyalty to him spells the forfeiture of national rights; on the other is the Jewish people, demanding the denial of personal conviction, for the sake of its continued existence. There is no way out of the dilemma. The creation of the much discussed Hebrew-Christian Church or separate Hebrew-Christian communities will not solve the problem. At best it can bring the Jewish Christian to the position Gentile Christianity occupies at present, adding another sect to the manifold divisions of the Church.

In the Hebrew Christian, thus, the drama of Primitive Christianity is re-enacted. Loyalty to Jesus Christ becomes to him the supreme test of discipleship. He is called upon to go outside the camp "bearing His reproach", having no abiding city in this world (Heb. 13. 13 f.). This was the price both Jews and Gentiles once had to pay for their faith. The Jewish Christian still pays the price. From the national point of view, the Hebrew Christian has no future. H. Loewe reflects this opinion when, alluding to the *Birkat ha-minim*, he says, "for the Jewish Christians there can be no hope".[353] National continuity of Hebrew Christianity will only be possible when the Jewish people lives its own life upon its own soil, and can afford to grant to its members the luxury of personal conviction without endangering its separate existence. Until then there is no way out of the impasse. Every effort at a solution must break at the person of Jesus Christ. Only men for whom to belong to Jesus means more than to belong to a nation are fit for the Kingdom of God. "This is the experience of every Jew who yields to the challenge of the Gospel message. The tragedy of the Church is that this is no longer the experience of the Gentile Christian." [354]

In the unique position of Hebrew Christianity, the conflict between faith in the One Catholic and Apostolic Church and the spirit of national separatism breaks out in all its acuteness. In the Hebrew Christian the tension which exists between the Church and the world reaches a climax. Discipleship means once again carrying a cross and fellowship in suffering. Faith ceases to be intellectual acquiescence and becomes once more a hazardous venture. Abraham's experience is the experience of every true Jewish Christian. This over-accentuation of the implications of the Christian Faith is a constant irritant to self-centred Christianity. Herein lies the significance of Hebrew-Christian existence to the Church. By the sacrifice of national loyalty for the sake of a higher good, the Hebrew Christian demonstrates before the Church and the Synagogue that the flesh profiteth nothing; it is the Spirit which giveth Life (Jn. 6. 63).[355]

CHAPTER VII

JUDAISM AND CHRISTIANITY

W E H A V E already had occasion to notice that the controversy between the Church and the Synagogue centres in the person of Jesus Christ. The problem for the Jew is, What place can be assigned to Jesus in Jewish thought without endangering the fundamental principles of Judaism? It has become increasingly obvious to Jewish thinkers that the traditional attitude of aloofness is not only impossible in modern conditions of life but also harmful to the cause of Judaism.[1] Yet room for the Master of Nazareth within the structure of Jewish thought is only possible on the condition of a clear distinction between the Christ of the Christian dogma and Jesus the *Jew*. Jesus can enter the sanctuary of the Jewish heart only divested of all his supernatural glory. Is such a distinction possible? Jewish writers say, yes. It is not only possible, but absolutely essential for the sake of Divine truth.[2] The Christian perception of Jesus in terms of the Holy Trinity to them rests upon a tragic misunderstanding. Such differentiation between the historic Jesus and the Christian Christ is a modern development, and was made possible by the influence of advanced scholarship. The rehabilitation of the "historic Jesus" at the expense of the orthodox Son of God is the logical answer on the part of progressive Jewish writers, after critical study had reduced the Divine Saviour to the plebeian position of a Jewish Rabbi. But what need is there, one would ask, to attach so much importance to the restoration to a place of honour of a man thus reduced to insignificance? Is it just to satisfy the modern Jewish craving to reaffirm the Jewish origin of important personages?

John Cournos, an enthusiastic champion of the reclamation of Jesus by the Jews, has no real answer to that question. He holds that for a Jew to deny Jesus is "to reject the Jewish heritage, to betray what was best in Israel".[3] But, we would ask, is it not possible to claim that heritage, minus Jesus? Has not Judaism assimilated the teaching of the Prophets without paying special attention to the Prophets themselves? To Judaism there can be no religious significance attached to *any* historic person. It is *not* the man who brings the message but the *message* which he brings that is decisive.[4] So far, our study has clearly shown that Jewish scholars are unable to discover in all honesty any objective truth by which Judaism could have been enriched by Jesus. Cournos tells us that "Christ's essential Jewishness has been admitted by Jewish scholars and divines".[5] But in the light of our investigation this sentence requires careful examination. "The Jewishness of Jesus" admitted by Jewish scholars refers to the background of Jesus' life, which existed in its self-sufficiency *before* Jesus and remained essentially *unaffected* after his coming. Jesus owes a debt to Judaism, but Judaism owes *no* debt to Jesus. Such is the general view of Jewish scholarship. It is obvious that the Jesus whom Cournos has stripped of all theological and dogmatic significance, in order to make him acceptable to the Jewish taste, has simultaneously lost all his peculiar uniqueness, which both attracts and repels the Jew. Jesus, secularized and divested of all his religious meaning, ceases to be important. Rabbi Enelow and John Cournos thus defeat their own ends: a Jesus whom the Jews do *not* reject need not be reclaimed! The controversy regarding Jesus left on the plane of humanitarian idealism inevitably works itself to a standstill. It ends in the resolve to admit the Man of Nazareth to the venerable assembly of the geniuses belonging to the Jewish race. Such admittance entails no obligations and makes no demands.

The *real* controversy regarding Jesus takes place, not on the plane of secularized idealism but on the plane of religious truth. It is essentially a *theological* controversy which can only be carried on in its full significance between the Synagogue and the Church. The nature of their mutual relationship, their historic interdependence, their common hope, their profound divergence, and their deep-rooted opposition to each other, make them, and them only, legitimate partners in the discussion. The dialogue which has taken and still takes place between Synagogue and Church is more than mere theological quibbling; it is a *necessity* upon which their life depends. In juxtaposition to each other, they learn the meaning of their own existence. Confronting each other in question and answer, they perpetuate their decision and affirm their faith.

The divergence between the Church and the Synagogue is fundamental and covers the whole sphere of human-Divine relationship. At no point do these two divergent circles intersect. It is only a vague and diluted Christian theology which imagines it possible to come to terms with Judaism. In reality, there is no understanding between the two faiths: they possess no common denominator which could form the basis for a "bridge theology".[6] They can only compromise by surrender: either the Church becomes the Synagogue or the Synagogue the Church. But in their separateness their only legitimate relationship is that of continuous interrogation. They can, nay, they *must* question each other until the end of time.[7] Their existence side by side puts both simultaneously under a question mark. The theme of their conversation is thus as to the why and wherefore of their separate life. The answer to this question leads to the person of Jesus Christ. Between Church and Synagogue stands the Crucified. Church and Synagogue derive their existence from their attitude to Him. The Synagogue perpetuates her existence in her *continued* negation, and the Church in her *continued* affirmation of the claims which Jesus made.

1. THEOLOGICAL ISSUES

Mr. Montefiore has hinted at the possibility of an understanding between liberal Judaism and Christianity on the basis of the Sermon on the Mount.[8] He even went one step further. In his book *The Old Testament and After* he makes a remark which has been severely criticized on the Jewish side. His words are: "It will be needful for the liberal Jewish theologians to consider the new modern interpretations of the doctrine of the Trinity"; and: "Nor does it follow that because the doctrine has been, and even is, in frequent danger of degeneration into Tritheism, or has often so degenerated, it is therefore not true."[9] But whatever opinions Montefiore may hold about the philosophical significance of the Trinitarian doctrine, it has no bearing upon the person of Jesus. Not even in its diluted Unitarian form is the Christian emphasis upon the importance of Jesus acceptable to a liberal Jew.[10] An approach to the Church is therefore made impossible for any form of Judaism as long as the Christian faith has Jesus at the centre. That Montefiore is well aware of the difficulty can be seen from an earlier remark: "The centre of the teaching of the historic Jesus is God: the centre of the teaching of the Church is he" (*i.e.* Jesus himself).[11] It is this peculiar attitude to Jesus which divides for ever the Church from the Synagogue. By working out the implications of faith in Jesus Christ, we automatically draw the demarcation line which divides Judaism from Christianity. But because we are writing from the Christian point of view, we will reverse the process by stating primarily the Jewish position.

(a) The unity of God

The essence of Judaism is the doctrine of the absolute and unmodified unity of God. Prof. Moore's masterly definition of the Jewish conception of that unity can hardly be surpassed. He calls it, "the numerically exclusive and uncompromisingly personal monotheism".[12] With it, Judaism stands and falls. Indeed, the absolute unity of the God of Israel together with the Torah, *i.e.* the revelation of this one and only God, form the heart and essence of Judaism. The rest of Jewish thought and practice is of secondary importance when compared with these two fundamental truths. Though liberal Judaism has only retained the first pillar upon which the Synagogue rests and has substituted for the unchangeable Torah a progressive conception of revelation commensurate with reason,[13] yet in its emphasis upon absolute monotheism and in its conception of Law it is still in spirit and essence Judaism[14]

This characteristic emphasis upon the oneness of God, which forms the basis of the Ten Commandments and has found its classic expression in the Old Testament literature, differentiates the Synagogue from all other religions. But the Rabbinic interpretation of the Old Testament conception of the unity of God is such that it runs contrary to the Christian conception of the Messiah. This most vital tenet, as conceived by orthodox and liberal Judaism alike, stands thus in direct opposition to the Trinitarian doctrine of the Christian Church. It is at this point that the gulf between the Church and the Synagogue opens before us in all its depth and significance. On this issue, Judaism has never faltered. It still speaks with one united voice. Dr. J. H. Hertz,[15] an orthodox Jew, and Kaufmann Kohler,[16] a liberal, unequivocally say the same thing. The teaching of the divinity of Jesus Christ is an unpardonable offence in the eyes of Judaism. It is for this reason that Judaism could never proclaim whole-heartedly the Christians to be Monotheists; at best they were looked upon as "semi-proselytes";[17] while

Mohammedanism was always regarded as more closely related to the mind of Judaism.[18]

The puzzle which confronts the historian in his study of the inner causes which led to the division between the early Christian Church and the Synagogue, resolves itself into a simple question when viewed from this fundamental theological aspect. Did the disciples in Jerusalem, i.e. Jews upon Jewish soil, claim for Jesus divinity? This question is difficult to answer, and we have seen that even Bousset hesitates.[19] But there can be little doubt that the first *believers* in Jesus claimed for the Master a unique importance which gradually lifted him out of the ranks of mere humanity.[20] Against this, Judaism could not but protest with all its strength. Even the suggestion that Jesus' position was unique amongst men, a claim which was upheld by every shade of Hebrew Christianity, no matter how it differed in every other respect, could not be anything else but an offence to the Synagogue.[21] Such an admission would inevitably break the closed ranks of humanity and set Jesus upon a plane outside history. It is for this reason that Judaism can admit neither the authority, the uniqueness, nor the perfection of Jesus. It consequently rejects even the Unitarian point of view.

Ferdinand Weber has shown that the Synagogue's conception of the unity of God underwent a change under the influence of Christianity. He maintains that the conception of God in the older Targums is more closely related to that of the Old Testament. But even there he finds "a certain monism and transcendentalism which renders it incapable of conceiving the inter-divine movement of life (innergöttliche Lebensbewegung) underlying the Trinitarian conception of God, incapable also of doing justice to the entry of God into history as it is demonstrated by the Old Testament".[22] Such criticism, however, may appear to overlook the great tradition of Jewish piety and the strongly developed Jewish awareness of God's interference in human life. So much may be said in defence of Judaism. But it will be noticed that an appeal to *experience* removes the discussion from the theological plane on to empiricism. Philosophically, however, and theologically the Jewish conception of *aḥdut elohim* (unity of God) reveals an abstract monism and a cold transcendentalism which strangely contrasts with the in-dwelling richness of the Christian view.[23] We have already referred to Montefiore's remark regarding the Christian conception of the Trinity, which goes to show that he was aware of that fact. But Judaism as long as it confronts the Christian Church is irrevocably committed to such a position. The slightest retraction from rigid monotheism makes room for the Christian conception of the Christ. But such a conception runs directly contrary to the whole structure of Jewish thought. This can be seen from Husik's comment on Maimonides' conception of the Godhead. He says: "God is conceived as absolutely transcendent and unknowable. No positive predicate can apply to him so as to indicate his essence. We can say only what he is not, we cannot say what he is. There is not the faintest resemblance between him and his creatures. And yet he is the cause of the world and of all its happenings. Positive attributes (*e.g.* life, power, knowledge) signify that God is the cause of the experience denoted by the attributes in question." [24] From this description it can be clearly recognized wherein lies the difference between the Christian and the Jewish conceptions of God. The God of Jewish theology, especially under Maimonides' influence, is reduced to a philosophical principle. The active and intervening God of Old Testament Scriptures assumes here the form of the *First Cause*. His absolute otherness removes him entirely from the world of his Creation. But while the infinite difference between man and God is also the starting-point of Christian thinking, God's transcendence is overcome not by the arbitrary act of human piety but by the self-chosen and self-willed manifestation of God in the person of Jesus Christ; in Judaism it is overcome by *man himself*. This is the most significant difference between Church and Synagogue.

Closely connected with the unity of God is the Jewish conception of man. Here it is well to remember that philosophical and theological thinking is never suspended in the abstract air of pure logic, but has a generic relationship to the *concrete* facts of life. It is a remarkable fact that the Jews, a small people, living for centuries in most difficult circumstances, exhibit a positivism to life and an optimism about man which is peculiarly their own. There is an interesting connexion between the Jewish outlook and the actual historical experience of the Jewish people.

It seems to us that Jewish life, which for centuries has entailed humiliation and suffering, has coloured Jewish thought in a peculiar way. The natural result of oppression is the development of an inferiority complex. But by way of compensation that sense of inferiority has been turned into a positive tendency to assertiveness. In Jewish thought this expresses itself in an exaggerated emphasis upon the importance of Israel in particular and of man in general.

We hold that there is an inner connexion between the Jewish conception of man and the Synagogue's attitude to the Christian concept of the Messiah; we will thus turn to consider Jewish anthropology.

(b) The Jewish conception of Man

Dr. Dienemann has seen aright when he said that the most characteristic difference between Judaism and Christianity "is the doctrine about man, the view concerning his nature and essence".[25] This is by no means an exaggeration. At first sight, it would seem that the fundamental difference between Judaism and Christianity lies in their respective conceptions of God. But this is not so. Man's conception about God reflects his view about himself. Feuerbach's contention that the idea of the Godhead is a projection of the human mind undeniably contains some truth.[26] The starting-point of man's thinking is *man* himself.[27] It cannot be otherwise. Thus, the genesis of the division between Church and Synagogue is of an anthropological nature. Because the Church and the Synagogue radically differ on this point, they differ on all other points.

What is man? Upon the answer to this question depends the philosophical outlook and ultimately the theological direction of both faiths. Needless to say, both Synagogue and Church try to answer this question in the light of Scripture. Their difference lies in the emphasis, but it is a difference of far-reaching consequences. The Synagogue emphasizes the *Imago Dei* in man; the Church stresses man's fall. The result is that the Synagogue offers a lofty humanism which is essentially idealistic and optimistic in its outlook. The Church, on the other hand, by emphasizing the depravity of human nature and the impotence of man to save himself presents a negative, ascetic attitude to the world. It is thus in direct opposition to that frame of mind of which humanism is the expression.

There have naturally been attempts to combine the two views in a synthesis, as both apparently contain elements of truth, and on the surface seem to supplement each other. Indeed, the history of Christian thought, viewed from this angle, reveals repeated attempts in one form or another to find a compromise.

But in reality a synthesis is impossible. The *Imago Dei* concept, which ultimately dispenses with the need for man's restoration, or adoption, as Paul would call it, destroys the most central fact of the Christian faith, namely the Incarnation. If man is essentially good, then the difference between him and Jesus is only a difference of degrees in the scale of perfection. Then there is no *actual* difference between him and us. He only *is* what we *shall* be. Upon the ladder of human perfection Jesus merely occupies a higher rung. He has attained while we are still striving. But even such a relativization between Jesus and the rest of humanity is unbearable to Judaism. As Montefiore puts it: "There have been many men who were very good and very wise; there never has been, and there never can be, a man who was perfectly good and perfectly wise".[28]   Here we meet with the inexorable logic of Judaism. To admit perfection on the part of one man means to detach him from the rest of the human race, and thus to break the closed circle of humanity. In essence it amounts to the deification of one man.[29]   The only other alternative is to assume that so perfect a man is not *man* in the ordinary sense of the word. But against such an assumption, Judaism revolts, for underlying it is the thought of human impotence. If God revealed himself in history through his Son, as the Christian Church claims, then his appearing amongst us is an indication of human helplessness; it is the greatest crisis in the history of man. Such a crisis Judaism cannot admit, for in the light of the *Imago Dei* concept the line between God and man is not *really* broken; it is only marred. It is still within the power of man to ascend heavenwards. It is for these reasons that Judaism is able to accept, without restriction or qualification, the doctrine of the Fatherhood of God and from it the deduction of the brotherhood of man. The equality of men is thus a logical corollary to the Jewish outlook. Hence the democracy of the Synagogue. It is a democracy with a positive sign.

It is at this point that the bridge is built between the transcendental and eternal God and finite man. God's transcendence is not overcome by God himself, in that he condescends to dwell amongst men, but by man, in that he reaches out God-wards. Thus, the barrier which divides man from God is broken down not by an act of God, as the Christian believes, but by the self-sufficiency of man.[30]   Buber has admirably defined the position, by contrasting Judaism with Christianity: Judaism, he said, is based upon the belief that there is a way from earth to heaven, from below, upwards. It is the faith that struggling man, in his moral effort, can climb the steep hill which leads to God. Christianity, on the other hand, holds the opposite view. It is based upon the belief that there is no way from earth to heaven, from man to God. Unless God in his mercy stretches out his hand from above, man can never reach him. Hence the Incarnation, which teaches that in the person of Jesus Christ God came from heaven to earth to find and to save mankind.[31]

Judaism is built upon the assumption of man's unlimited resources to attain to the highest. "If you wish to stand under the special protection of special Providence", says Rabbi Wise, "you must exert your energies to rise, to climb, to ascend and come as near to your God as you can." [32] But what if man cannot? The Synagogue does not admit such a possibility: Judaism is essentially a religion for those who *can*. We quote Dr. Wise again: "To rise to self-conscious immortality and happiness is in man's power exclusively; it depends on no circumstances and no outer influences. Man is to all intents and purposes a free and independent being." [33]

It is obvious that the Fall of man, which occupies a central position in Christian theology, reverses the picture which Judaism draws. The corollary of the Fall is that the original relation between man and God is broken. Henceforth man stands before God not as a child before the father but as a creature before the Creator, as guilty before the Judge. The Church thus speaks in terms of unredeemed humanity. Without this fact, the Incarnation becomes superfluous. The Cross, which in the eyes of the Church is the symbol of Salvation, otherwise becomes a mere tragedy and the Christian Faith the result of a misunderstanding.

Indeed, the Church also knows about the Fatherhood of God, but this is conditioned by an act of adoption on the part of God of which Jesus Christ is the pledge and token. For man to claim relationship with God, without the Cross, without forgiveness, is to overlook the grim fact of sin; it is an act of supreme presumption.

(c) *Free will*

From what has been said already about Jewish anthropology, it is an easy inference that the teaching of free will is an important element in the whole conception. Indeed, Jewish thinkers from the earliest times invariably assert the absolute freedom of the human will.[34] This is already implied in the well-known sentence: *ha-kol bide shamayim ḥuẓ miyirat shamayim*.[35] The meaning of this adage is, that though God, by virtue of his position, controls the affairs of man, his control is not such as to override human choice. The assumption being that man is capable of choosing for himself and choosing aright.

The doctrine of free will plays a prominent part in Jewish thought. It is constantly asserted by Jewish divines and has been claimed to be a fundamental principle of Judaism. Husik says: "So fundamental has it seemed for Judaism to maintain the freedom of the will that no one hitherto (*i.e.* till Crescas, *circa* 1340–1412) had ventured to doubt it. Maimonides [36] no less than Judah Halevi, and with equal emphasis Gersonides, insist that the individual is not determined in his conduct. This seemed to be the only way to vindicate God's justice in reward and punishment." [37] But in actual fact, the insistence upon human freedom has deeper reasons than the vindication of divine justice. The whole concept about man and his relationship to God makes freedom of will a logical necessity for Judaism. Husik is well aware of this.[38] The main difficulty which Jewish thinkers have felt was that the idea of human freedom clashes with the doctrine of God's omniscience. They have been thus forced either to restrict human freedom or God's omniscience; or else, as in the case of Maimonides, evade the problem by a reference to God's transcendence.[39] Crescas' position is exceptional for Judaism. But even in his case the tension is lessened by a dialectical distinction between determinism and fatalism.[40] On the whole, it may be said that the natural trend in Jewish theology is towards an emphasis upon the human side. But while medieval thinkers still restricted human freedom so as to relate it to God's sovereignty,[41] moderns assert unqualified freedom of will.[42]

Judah Halevi explained that free will, which by its nature belongs to the class of intermediary causes, is linked up with other causes "which reduce it, chain-like, to the Prime Cause". Human action is thus, in one way or another, related to God's omniscience. The final choice, however, is not compulsory, but *potential*: "the mind wavers between an opinion and its opposite, being permitted to turn where it chooses. The result is praise or blame for the choice".[43] This may be contrasted with the advanced views of modern writers. Rabbi Dienemann, pointing out the Christian conception of grace which man requires not only in order to abstain from evil, but also to do good, observes: "Jewish ideology (*Anschauung*) holds tenaciously to the thought of the complete *independence* of the moral personality." [44] But Dienemann actually goes further than this. In the interests of ethics, on the grounds that "moral renewal must grow out of one's own strength", and that man in himself must therefore carry the sources of moral regeneration,[45] he does not hesitate to place man *opposite* God: "Next to the grandeur and limitless grace of God stands as an equally important religious value, the dignity of Man." [46] The Jewish conception of man and the characteristic emphasis upon human action provide the background for this sentence. It is the logical conclusion of a theology which is essentially anthropocentric. That Dienemann by no means occupies an isolated position may be judged from the words of another writer, who represents a somewhat different school of thought. The leader of the Neo-Kantian school in Judaism, Hermann Cohen, explaining the connexion between free-will and ethics, says: "Man's task is to choose the good. Freedom of choice is the basic condition of moral judgment (*Vernunft*). For it, for the freedom of the human as the moral will, there can be no limitation in God. The Will of God, the Essence of God demands the freedom of the human will." [47] At this point, the border-line between Judaism and Christianity becomes visible. Whatever *freedom* the Christian assigns to himself, whatever worth he ascribes to human personality, in view of the Cross he stands incapacitated, *i.e.* he cannot save *himself*. Salvation is a gift from God: in the last resort, man undergoes salvation; he does not attain to it. But such is not the Jewish view.[48] God indeed acts, but his action is conditioned by human behaviour. Israel's redemption *depends* on Israel's repentance: R. Eliezer said: "If Israel repent, they will be redeemed; if not, they will not be redeemed. R. Joshua said to him, If they do not repent they will not be redeemed. But the Holy One, blessed be he, will set up a king over them, whose decrees shall be as cruel as Haman's, whereby Israel shall engage in repentance, and he will thus bring them back to the right path." [49] Against this may be put the words of the Apostle, which by contrast reveal in a remarkable way the profound difference between the Christian and the Jewish idea of redemption: "While we were yet sinners, Christ died for us" (Rom. 5. 8).

The whole idea of salvation in the Christian sense is foreign to Judaism; and naturally so. The Synagogue knows of two kinds of redemption; national redemption *i.e.* the redemption of Israel, and redemption from sin. Israel's redemption depends on Israel's repentance; redemption from sin is understood in terms of forgiveness: it is God's prerogative to save man from sin. This he does by an act of forgiveness. Hermann Cohen thus makes forgiveness of sin "the particular speciality of God's goodness".[50] Judaism, therefore, emphasizes not Salvation but Atonement. The Day of Atonement occupies a central place in the calendar of the Synagogue. Characteristically enough, Hermann Cohen's great book on Judaism (*Die Religion der Vernunft*) has a chapter on Atonement (*Versöhnung*), but no chapter on Salvation. Wherever Salvation is referred to, its meaning is that of Atonement.

The prerequisite to Atonement is repentance. The Rabbis had an extraordinary estimation of repentance. The Mishnah teaches that repentance atones for lesser transgressions of the Law, while the punishment for greater transgressions is, thanks to repentance, suspended until the Day of Atonement.[51] But in later Rabbinical writings the importance of repentance is even more magnified. A fine example of the place *teshubah* occupies in Rabbinic thought is offered by Pesikta de Rab Kahana, where one section deals exclusively with repentance (*Piska* XXV).[52] R. Juda Nishraja said in the name of R. Juda bar Simon: "When a man shoots an arrow, how far does it go? The length of a field (required) for the sowing of one cor of corn, or two fields (required) for the sowing of one cor of corn. But great is the power of repentance, for it reaches to the throne of Glory." [53] There is no crime for which repentance cannot atone. Even Cain's sin was forgiven because he repented.[54] Kaufman Kohler says: "Repentance occupies a very prominent position in all the ethical writings of the Middle Ages." [55] It is still the corner-stone of Jewish piety.[56]

Montefiore seems to be in agreement with Delitzsch's estimate of the difference between the Jewish and the Christian conception of repentance. "According to the Jewish doctrine," says Delitzsch, "God lets himself be reconciled through repentance; according to the Christian doctrine, he is reconciled (*versöhnt*) through the mediation (*Mittlerwerk*) of Christ, and the individual man is reconciled to God (*versöhnt*) when in faith and repentance he

accepts the mediation, which is common and general for all
mankind. The New Testament method of salvation (*Heilsord-
nung*) has the same sound as (*lautet auch wie*) *jer. Maccoth* 1. 6:
ya'aseh teshubah we-yitkaper lo ('let him repent and receive atonement'), but repentance is 'not the factor which atones (*das
Sühnende selbst*), but only the way to receive atonement (*der Weg
zur Versöhnung*).'' [57]   It seems to us that in this subtle distinction
lies the whole difference between the Church and the Synagogue
with regard to human freedom and divine grace. For the main
point under discussion is not what is intended by repentance (on
this Church and Synagogue are agreed) but the question what
efficacy we ascribe to the act. In the estimation of Judaism,
forgiveness is conditioned by repentance; according to the
Church, forgiveness has its foundation in the Cross. The centre
of gravity is thus for Judaism on the human side, and for Christianity on God's action which precedes repentance.

We restate the case: according to Judaism, it is man who takes
the first step towards reconciliation, and not God; hence the
utter importance of repentance. In the act of contrition, man
expresses his willingness to amend his life and to ask for forgiveness. That God will forgive is taken for granted. It is on these
grounds that Maimonides can pronounce without hesitation:
"Now in our days, when the house of the Sanctuary exists no
longer, and when we have no atoning altar . . . repentance
atones for all transgressions.'' [58]   This actually goes beyond the
Mishnah, where forgiveness is still to a certain degree tied to the
efficacy of the Day of Atonement. But even in the Mishnah, the
reference to the Day of Atonement does not lessen the importance
of repentance: "death and the Day of Atonement effect atonement if there is repentance''. [59]   It is therefore quite true to the
spirit of Judaism when Leo Baeck says, "Atonement too is *ours,
our task and our way*''. [60]   Dr. Dienemann has not over-
accentuated the Jewish position by differentiating between the
Christian conception of Salvation and the Jewish conception of
Atonement: the Jew stands in no need of Salvation, all he requires
is Atonement (*Versöhnung*): "*in the act of Atonement,*'' however, "*both God and man co-operate . . . . but in the forefront
stands the work of man accomplished by his own strength*''. [61]
Klausner explains that Paul's doctrine of predestination, which
he calls a "mystico-religious determinism'', puts man in a
position where the chance to determine his own fate is taken

from him. Such a doctrine is unacceptable to Judaism, which is characterized by profound faith in life and a strong optimism.[62] In the Jewish view, human dignity requires that man be free, with an absolute freedom, for only thus can he be held responsible for his deeds. It is for this reason that in the Jewish conception sin does not totally affect human nature; man only sins, but is *not sinful*.

(d) The Jewish conception of sin

Closely related to the problem of free-will is the problem of evil. Judaism, with its characteristic emphasis upon morality and law, is naturally conscious of the fact of evil. The Synagogue knows of sin and human depravity. It often speaks of the *yeẓer tob* and *yeẓer ha-ra'* fighting for supremacy within the human heart. But the Jewish conception of *yeẓer ha-ra'* is totally different from the Christian conception of sin. The difference is logically connected with the doctrine of free-will.

Evil and good are ever-present potentialities in human life. Man is constantly put to the test by being offered the choice between right and wrong. He carries in his bosom the tension between two dispositions. But his human dignity requires that he be free to tip the balance in either direction. The final decision is with him. Deut. 30. 19 plays an important part in Jewish thinking: "I have set before thee life and death, blessing and cursing; therefore choose life that thou mayest live." Dr. J. H. Hertz comments on this text: "Jewish ethics is rooted in the doctrine of human responsibility, that is, *freedom of will*." Dr. Hertz, however, knows that the human will is conditioned by heredity and environment; nevertheless, he holds that "in the moral universe, man ever remains his own master". This is an axiom to Judaism; on it depends its whole structure. Maimonides rightly regarded the doctrine of free-will as the pillar of the Law and the Commandments.[63] The enacting of Commandments postulates the possibility of keeping them; they presuppose human freedom. I. M. Wise puts it: "The Sinaic revelation is the proof for the immortal and God-like nature of man." [64] It is then obvious that for Judaism there can only be sins, but no sin in the Christian sense.[65] Its main concern is with *'aberot*, trespasses and the safeguarding of the Law, but not with the redemption of sinners as the Church understands it.

Original sin was unknown to the old Synagogue [66] and it is of no consequence in the teaching of Judaism. The Rabbis taught that man at his birth is given by God a pure and holy soul; [67] and though man possesses the latent possibility towards evil or good, the inclination towards good is stronger than the inclination towards evil.[68] Thus, man at the outset starts with a *plus* and not with a *minus*.[69] Dienemann has shown that the existence of evil is not a postulate of Judaism. It is not something that man finds already present on entering the world, but is of his own creation. Judaism denies the *a priori* character of evil.[70] "And if thou wilt now ask", says a Midrash, "why did then God create the *yezer ha-ra'*, God replies: 'Who makes him a *yezer ha-ra'*? only thou thyself.'" [71] Sin is therefore not an inherent characteristic of human nature, it is only acquired. To quote Dienemann again: "Sin is according to Jewish teaching therefore no necessity, nothing that is inborn in man and inseparable from him." [72] Hence, sinfulness to Judaism is not a state to which man is confined, but rather "a transient and passing repression (Hemmung)".[73] Or, as Rabbi Wise puts it: "A sin, according to Rabbinical definition, must be an action." [74]

If we understand Hermann Cohen's difficult discourse on the origin of evil aright, sin is essentially a *means* for the individual to develop into an Ego and thus to find his completion. Cohen guards himself against the thought that there is an inherent inclination (Anlage) within man towards evil. On the contrary, man carries in his bosom the holy spirit.[75] Man by nature, however, is bound up socially with the rest of humanity: he is, therefore, only an individual, but not an Ego. Sin serves as a medium by which man develops into a self-conscious "I". Cohen strongly differentiates between social sin and sin before God. Religious sin, *i.e.* sin before God, is the refusal on the part of man to rise to the state of isolated existence as an Ego. To use his own words for the sake of clarity: "Only this kind of sin of the individual do we acknowledge as sin before God by means of which the human individual is lifted up to the human Ego." [76] Sin thus understood serves a *positive* end. It becomes a ladder which leads man to his highest existence. It is not something from which man must be *saved*, it is something which man is called upon to *overcome*. Without it, man is deprived of the means of attaining his highest end: "Sin before God", Hermann Cohen explains, "leads us to man as Ego. Sin before God leads us to redemption by God. Redemption by God leads us to man's atonement with himself. And this in the last instance to the atonement of the Ego with God. It is the atonement with God however that finally brings the individual to maturity as an Ego."[77]

The involved philosophical reasoning of H. Cohen need not obscure the fact that his structure is built upon the foundations of Judaism. The whole Jewish outlook is marked by a deep-seated optimism. Judaism is fundamentally at peace with the world. It affirms life and existence and is determinately opposed to every form of other-worldliness.[78] 'Olam ha-ba, which plays such an important part in Rabbinic thought, is not the expression of renunciation of this world, but the longing for an improved form of present existence. Leo Baeck rightly regards this inveterate affirmation of life as a peculiarity of Judaism, which he calls "the religion of ethical optimism". [79] Not that Judaism is unaware of the wrongs and tragedies of human existence. A denial of evil is impossible in face of the accumulation of Jewish experience. But Jewish optimism is founded upon the belief that evil is not a necessary prerequisite of life, but only a deficiency which man has the power to remedy. "The optimism of Judaism", says Baeck, "consists in a *belief in the good* which *wills* the good. It is the belief *in* God, and consequently the belief *in man*, in God through whom the good finds reality, and in man who is able to realize the good. All the ideas of Judaism can be traced back to it." [80]

Now, in the opinion of some Christian writers, "the other-worldly aspect of Christianity needs to be balanced by the incorrigible optimism of the Jews with regard to this world".[81] That may be so. Pessimism which expresses itself in retreat and seclusion is alien to the Christian spirit. Christianity is also essentially optimistic. But its optimism springs from a different source. The basic note of the Easter message is victory, but not *man's* victory; it is *God's* victory. God's victory, however, is man's *defeat*. Not so to Judaism: here, man's victory is God's victory; it is man who *helps* God to triumph. It cannot be otherwise; any other position for Judaism would mean the denial of its fundamental proposition—the inherent self-sufficiency of man.

The difference here between Judaism and Christianity is fundamental. While to Judaism sin is only a latent disposition or an acquirement easily corrected, to Christianity sin is an all-pervading principle in life. It has cosmic significance and expresses itself in the human attitude of inward rebellion against

God: *Eritis sicut Deus* (Gen. 3. 5).[82] In the Christian view, man
stands as a usurper of God's glory and a rival to his power; he
is thus guilty of high treason. Sin is a power which enslaves man,
incapacitates his will, pushes him irresistibly towards evil, and
puts him in a state of utter helplessness. To the Church man is
sinful before he has yet done anything; to the Synagogue, man
is sinful when he is full of sins. Consequently, in the eyes of the
Church even the best of men needs salvation; in the view of
the Synagogue, the *transgressor* needs only amendment of life.
Hence, Christianity speaks in terms of regeneration, Judaism in
terms of moral conduct.[83]   What Strack-Billerbeck say about
the old Synagogue well applies to Judaism in general: "The old
Jewish religion is thus completely a religion of self-salvation; it
has no room for a Saviour-Redeemer who dies for the sins of the
world." [84]

(e) *Mediation*

The concept of sin determines the question as to the human
approach to God. To Judaism, man's access entirely depends
upon his moral integrity (cf. Ps. 24. 3 ff.). "The essence of
Judaism is ethics." [85] Or, as Baeck puts it: "It is the right deed
alone which always places man in the presence of God." [86] The
attention of the Synagogue is arrested upon man in his moral
endeavour. It is for this reason that Judaism is unable to accept
the doctrine of the Incarnation, for such a doctrine implies the
need for mediation. Mediation, however, implies the inadequacy of the human effort to reach out Godwards. Judaism
is founded on the premise that man is capable by virtue of his
moral effort of approaching God. Hence, God's coming to man's
aid not only becomes superfluous, but actually interferes with
the progress of human development.

To Judaism the way from man to God is open.[87] All that man
needs is to amend his ways and return to God: "If he has sinned
he is always able to become different, he is able to find his way
back . . . he can hallow and purify himself again, he can make
atonement." [88] This possibility is not only a Jewish prerogative:
"The righteous of all nations have a share in the world to
come." [89] Jewish writers are proud of this sentence and quote
it frequently.[90] The meaning of it is that not faith but works
decide. God judges man according to his deeds. Though man
transgress and fall away from God, he never can fall so as not to

be able to stand up again. The guarantee for his ability to rise is the Imago Dei, which man has imprinted upon his soul. Thus "the covenant of God with man is never broken"; [91] contact between God and man is always possible: "Everybody can draw near to his God, and a way to God proceeds from every soul." [92] It is no exaggeration to say, that the Synagogue's motto is: *man is able*.

This almost unlimited confidence in human ability pervades the whole Jewish outlook. There is an interesting passage in *San.* 97b: "Rab said: 'All predestined dates (for Messiah's coming) have passed, and the matter (now) depends only on repentance and good deeds.' But Samuel maintained: 'It is sufficient for a mourner to keep his (period of) mourning.'" H. Friedman explains Samuel's words to mean: "Israel's sufferings in the *Galuth* in themselves sufficiently warrant their redemption, regardless of repentance." [93] Thus Israel's redemption, in the opinion of both sages, actually depends on Israel himself. The only difference is that in one case it is Israel's repentance and in the other Israel's suffering that effects his redemption. But to both Rabbis Israel himself is the decisive factor. *Mediation*, therefore, is foreign to the spirit of Judaism. Kaufmann Kohler rightly says: "Judaism recognizes in principle no mediatorship between God and man." [94] This directness of approach is a definite departure from the Old Testament position. It is here, if nowhere else, that we recognize the difference between the Synagogue and the Old Testament religion.

Mediation in the Old Testament plays an important part in religion. The priest, the prophet, the angels who act as messengers of God—they all stand between sinful man and the Lord of Hosts.[95] The Torah itself was received by Israel *'al-yede-sarsor* (through a mediator). This was still the view of the Old Synagogue.[96] Philo's *Logos*, which assumes such importance in his conception of God, has its root not only in Greek philosophy but also in the Old Testament.[97] It rests upon the principle that between God and man there is a gap. Judaism, however, with its characteristic predisposition towards the unitary view of life and its emphasis upon human action, has gradually departed from the doctrine of mediation. An important factor will have been opposition to the teaching of the Church, which made mediation an absolute necessity. There is a characteristic remark by Abraham ibn Ezra which singularly well describes the Jewish tendency: "The angel that mediates between man and God is reason." [98]   Behind these words lies concealed the thought that man, by virtue of his God-given faculties, is able to bridge the gulf which divides him from his Creator. The whole trend of modern Jewish thought is in this direction.[99]

How then does sinful man, we ask, find approach to the holy and invisible God? "First", says Rabbi Wise, he must "find and understand the loftiest and surest standard of rectitude." This standard Judaism finds in the Torah. The second step is exemplified in the words Israel spake at Sinai: *na'aseh we-nishm'a*, "we will do and obey". In this manner man returns to God, and in doing so he "obliterates his own sins . . . he changes and reforms his character . . . he rises to the dignity of manhood". [100]   Communication between man and God is made possible by the fact that man participates in God's spirit. The unity between them is therefore never broken. The Holy Spirit belongs as much to man as to God: "The Holy Spirit can neither be altogether God nor man, even less God and man at the same time, but an attribute of the two conceptions or rather the union of both." [101]   In other words, the Holy Spirit is conceived not in the sense of Hypostasis but in terms of *function*; it is the result of the meeting between God and man. Cohen calls it "the uniting link of correlation". Relationship between God and man does not so much postulate the existence of the Holy Spirit as the equality of partnership.[102]   The spirit comes into evidence not only when God speaks to man, but also when man speaks to God. It is the self-same spirit in-dwelling in both. The reason for declaring the spirit a *function* is obvious. The purpose is to exclude every form of mediation. "Union precludes mediation", says Cohen.

Man occupies a position in the Jewish view which makes mediation not only superfluous but unbearable. It is an intrusion which violates man's rights and injures his dignity. Righteousness, to Judaism, cannot be imputed, it must be attained. "Righteousness", says Rabbi Wise, "is the ability or state of man to live and act in exact conformity with the highest standard of rectitude within his reach." [103]   Judaism does not require the impossible of man; what it requires is within the sphere of human ability. Man is able to stand by himself; herein lies his dignity. "Nobody stands between him and God; no mediator or past event, no redeemer and no sacrament." [104]   The whole idea of vicarious atonement, Rabbi Wise declares, is a "product of the

Christianity of history". Neither in Scripture nor in philosophy can he see the reason for it.[105] The whole conception is directly opposed to Jewish thinking. "What need have I of a God-Man when I myself have God within me?"[106]

The gulf which divides man from God is of man's creation. Thus, only he himself can restore the divine-human relationship. By virtue of the *Imago Dei* dwelling in him, he is able to do so, if he wills. "Every man", says Miss Lazarus, "has to bridge the gulf for himself";[107] nobody can do it for him. Man must do it himself by means of his moral endeavour. Here the divergence between Judaism and Christianity becomes very clear. These are two worlds diametrically opposed to each other. The XIIIth of the *Thirty-nine Articles* of the Church of England provides a classical example of the wide divergence between the two faiths: "Works done before the grace of Christ and the inspiration of his Spirit are not pleasant to God, for as much as they spring not of faith in Jesus Christ. . . . Yea rather, for that they are not done as God willed and commanded them to be done, we doubt not but they have the nature of sin (*peccati rationem habere non dubitamus*)."[108]

In the Christian view nothing therefore, no human endeavour, no good deeds, can restore man to sonship. Sin is so grave that atonement can only be made by God himself.[109] Jesus Christ stands as Mediator between man and God by virtue of his sacrificial death. The believer through faith identifies himself with the Crucified Saviour. There is no *direct* approach to God, it leads over Calvary. In Christ Jesus God has stretched out his hand to *save* mankind. Underneath the Cross man stands condemned and pardoned; in it is revealed human *helplessness* and God's power, human sinfulness and God's eternal Love.

(f) The Messiah

From the preceding remarks, it is obvious that the Jewish conception of the Messiah must differ fundamentally from that of the Church.

To start with, it is well to remember that faith in a personal Messiah does not belong to the fundamental tenets of Judaism.[110] This is the more curious when we consider that Maimonides has included it in the Creed[111] which is still in use in our day, and that Jewish hopes were for centuries associated with the coming of Messiah. No doubt in the old Synagogue the Messianic hope was adhered to with great fervour, though Bousset has shown that in the pre-Christian era the Messiah did not occupy as central a position as is usually assumed.[112]   It appears to us, however, that the apocalyptic literature must not be solely relied upon for our judgment concerning the Messianic views of that period.   But even that literature contains enough evidence to show the place the Messiah occupied in Jewish thinking.[113]   At a later period, especially after the decline of the Hasmonean dynasty, the Messianic hope came to new life again.   In the post-Christian era, it became the subject for many speculations, and Rabbinic literature is full of references to the Messianic age and the person of the Messiah.[114]   There are reasons, however, why the person of the Messiah was never emancipated so as to occupy a central place in Judaism.   The first is an external reason, and is connected with the appearance of Christianity.   Some Rabbinic sayings, like that of Joḥanan b. Torta, addressed to Akiba on his proclaiming Bar Cochba the Messiah, "Akiba, grass will sprout through your cheeks ere the son of David comes", may have been prompted by its rise.   The context, however, makes this doubtful.[115]   A more likely case is that of Rabbi Hillel, who declared: "There shall be no Messiah for Israel, because they have already enjoyed him in the days of Hezekiah." [116]   This strange remark has been sometimes connected with the story recorded by Epiphanius about Hillel the Patriarch, who is supposed to have accepted baptism before his death.[117]   But it seems to us that Rabbi S. Mendelsohn's explanation is more plausible.   He suggests that Hillel "may have been prompted to this declaration by Origen's professed discovery in the Old Testament of Messianic passages referring to the founder of Christianity".[118]   In later times, Jewish views concerning the Messiah's functions have been greatly modified.   This can be seen from Rashi's remark that the Almighty himself will redeem Israel and reign over him.[119]   This can also be seen from Maimonides' utmost caution in describing the position of the Messiah: "The king who is to arise out of the seed of David will be wiser than Solomon and he will be a great prophet near (karob) unto Moses our Rabbi." [120]   The second reason is of an internal nature.   The hegemony of the Law conflicts with the idea of a Messiah who may command supreme authority.   Even the Messiah can only occupy a place near Moses and is under obligation to obey and keep the commandments. The Targum already conveys this idea plainly.[121]   The Rabbis spoke of the *torato shel mashiaḥ*, but the Messiah's Torah was essentially Moses' Torah.[122] The abrogation of the Torah by the Messiah is totally alien to the Rabbinic view. Strack-Billerbeck observe: "Such an assumption is excluded from the beginning by the firmly established doctrine (Glaubenssatz) that just as the Torah of Moses pre-existed in eternity, so it was given to Israel for all eternity and nobody has the right to add anything to it or subtract from it." [123] The Messiah not only obeys the Torah, but also studies it and expounds it.[124] In the days of the Messiah, the Torah will assume new significance and will be universally obeyed, the theatres and circuses of Edom will be turned into schools of study. Thus, the centrality of the Torah in Jewish thought has forced the Messiah into the background. This has already been recognized by Albo. "Faith in the Messiah, according to Albo, would prejudice the redemptive significance (Heilsbedeutung) of the Law." [125] "The nomistic principle", as Weber calls it, determined Jewish Christology. The supremacy and the immutability of the Torah, which is fundamental for Rabbinic thinking, has necessarily forced Jewish theology to assign to the Messiah a secondary place.

Nevertheless, hope in the Messiah's coming and the establishment of a Messianic age played an important part in Jewish life and worship and still sways the imagination of Jewry. It forms the backbone of Jewish eschatology. It must be remembered, however, that the Rabbis have never worked out a consistent and systematic theory concerning the Messiah, his person, his coming, and his reign. Their ideas are confused, often contradictory and vague. On the whole, it may be said that Rabbinic notions connected with the coming of the Messiah show more signs of the play of imagination than of serious theological thinking. Against modern liberal views, however, it may be safely affirmed that the Rabbis never detached the Messianic age from the person of the Messiah. The two were inseparable. They conceived the Messiah not as an ideal but as a real historical person.[126] The Messianic function, however, was conceived to be primarily political. His chief mission was to free Israel from bondage. Klausner's description well states the case: "The Jewish Messiah", he says, "is above all a redeemer of his nation from subservience to foreign rulers." [127] That this was the case can be seen from Akiba's behaviour towards Bar Cochba. It is, however, noteworthy that not all the Rabbis shared Akiba's enthusiasm. No doubt the Synagogue expected more than political leadership from the Messiah. Even Klausner admits so much.[128]

Dr. S. Schechter has worked out four main points under which the Rabbinic ideas concerning the Messianic age can be summarized; these notions reveal their view concerning the person of the Messiah himself. All the other features attached to the Messiah by various Rabbis are only of secondary importance. They are of a mystical nature (like the pre-existence of the Messiah, the creation of his name before the creation of the world, etc.), and have never seriously affected Judaism. Dr. A. Cohen rightly remarks: "The Talmud nowhere indicates a belief in a super-human Deliverer as the Messiah." [129] Dr. Schechter's points are: (1) The Messiah is a descendant of the house of David and his purpose is to restore the kingdom of Israel and extend it over the whole world. (2) In a last terrible battle the enemies of God will be defeated and destroyed. (3) The establishment of the Messiah's kingdom "will be followed by the spiritual hegemony of Israel, when all nations will accept the belief in the unity of God, acknowledge his kingdom and seek instruction from the law". (4) The Messianic age will bring material and spiritual happiness, death will disappear and the dead will rise.[130] For the sake of clarity, however, it must be added that the Messianic concepts of the Rabbis contain other important elements. One of the most striking is that of suffering. The passages referring to the suffering Messiah have been studiously collected by Strack and Billerbeck in their great Commentary.[131] The most striking of these, which show remarkable likeness to the Christian conception of vicarious suffering, come from the *Pesikta Rabbati*.[132] But three things must be borne in mind: (1) Though the Rabbis were acquainted with the thought of sacrificing one's life "whether voluntarily or involuntarily for the sake and the benefit of others", *vicarious* suffering on the part of the Messiah was unknown to them.[133] (2) The occasional allusions to a suffering Messiah have a definite nationalistic colouring. It is Strack's and Billerbeck's opinion that "only Israel's sin is atoned by the Messiah. The thought that the Messiah carries the sins of the world, therefore also those of the non-Israelites (Jn. 1. 29), we meet nowhere in old Rabbinical literature." [134] With this statement Mr. Montefiore is inclined to agree.[135] (3) The Messianic kingdom of the future is, according to Rabbinic views, essentially this-worldly. It is a kingdom within history and time and is ultimately superseded by the final end.[136]

We see, then, that whatever similarity there might be between the Jewish and the Christian conceptions of the Messiah and the Messianic age, on three most vital points they totally differ. The Christian faith is founded upon the belief in the vicarious suffering of the Messiah; this suffering benefits *all* nations; the Messianic kingdom, though conceived to take place upon *earth*, is not *totally* of this world; it brings history to an abrupt conclusion and starts a New Order.[137] But there is a further point of even greater importance. In Christian faith the Messiah occupies a *central* position. He commands obedience, he makes claims upon loyalty, he forgives sin, he mediates between man and God, he redeems men, he renews their spirit, he reveals God and His love. And furthermore, this Messiah is identified with a *historical* person whose name is Jesus of Nazareth.

The divergence between liberal Judaism and orthodox Christianity is even greater.

Liberal Jewish theology has completely abandoned the idea of a personal Messiah. Leo Baeck, a typical representative of liberal thinking, interprets the prophetic conception of the Messiah as a symbolic form of speech. He explains that Hebrew genius, being averse to the abstract form of expression, invested the Messianic ideal in a concrete person. But later, Judaism shifted the emphasis from the *person* upon the *time*: it began to speak more of "the days of the Messiah" and of "the Kingdom of God" than of the Messiah himself.[138] Thus, liberal Judaism has completed the process of evolution. It detached the Messianic ideal from the person of the Messiah, and looks forward to the realization of the Messianic age. "The future man", says Rabbi I. M. Wise, "will need no Messiah." [139] To liberal Judaism the Kingdom of God is no gift from Heaven; it is the result of the slow but steady progress of humanity. It is brought about by "the uninterrupted work of humanity upon itself".[140] The establishment of the kingdom depends on the final triumph of human reason and the highest human aspirations; "it is not given, but achieved".[141] The Kingdom of God is not God's kingdom, but man's kingdom where God has been made King.

It is obvious that though the orthodox and liberal conceptions regarding the Messianic age appear to differ on a vital point, in essence they are agreed. With the Messiah or without the

Messiah, to Judaism the Kingdom of God is in our hands; it is
for us to *establish* it upon this earth.[142]   The idea that Israel
himself is the Messiah is not far removed from the Jewish mind.
Dr. K. Kohler's view will meet with approval from many on the
orthodox side that the Kingdom of God is not the work of an
individual Messiah but of Israel as a whole.   Kohler says,
"Deutero-Isaiah stated it for all time, Israel, the Servant of God,
the Messiah of the nations, working amid woe and suffering",
will ultimately bring "the divine kingdom of righteousness and
peace on earth." [143]

(g) *The Torah*

Felix Perles in a short essay on *Die Autonomie der Sittlichkeit im
jüdischen Schrifttum* points out that the importance of Hermann
Cohen's work lies in showing that the concept of moral autonomy
stands in opposition to religion, and therefore also to Judaism.[144]
The writer traces the anomaly to the Philonian influence upon
Rabbinic thinking.   He holds that the Rabbis did not realize the
existing contradiction "between Philo's teaching of the autonomy
of ethics and the Jewish conception (Anschauung) of God as the
only Law-giver ": [145] a contradiction which, when thought out
to the last consequences, destroys the very basis of religious faith.
Naïvely enough, Perles thinks that the Rabbis could not have
been aware of this fact before Kant had explained the meaning
of "autonomy".   But to regard this phenomenon as a mere
result of faulty thinking appears to us to overlook the whole
nature of Judaism.   The autonomy of ethics in Jewish thinking
has its roots not in speculative metaphysics but in the concrete
conception of man.   The absolute validity of the moral act
vis à vis God postulates freedom on the part of man and therefore the autonomy of ethics.   The whole structure of Jewish
religious thinking depends upon it.   The depreciation of the
validity of moral action strikes at the foundations of Judaism,
underlying which is the conception of law and justice.

Jewish scholars have rightly protested against the erroneous
view that "Torah" and "Law" are synonyms.   Torah is a much
wider and more comprehensive conception than the word νόμος
conveys.   "The legalistic element," says Dr. S. Schechter, "which
might rightly be called the Law, represents only one side of the
Torah." [146] Torah itself covers the whole sphere of Judaism, as
it expresses itself both in doctrine and practice.   Torah, then, is

the norm against which Jewish life is measured, and it fulfils, in a sense, the purpose the dogmas do in the Church. But here lies a significant difference. H. Loewe has with fine insight recognized that the difference between Judaism and Christianity expresses itself in that the former insists upon *orthopraxy* and the latter upon *orthodoxy*.[147] Behind this fact lies concealed the gulf which divides the two faiths.

Jewish scholars often dwell upon the peculiarity of the Church in that it insists upon orthodoxy, *i.e.* the adherence to a creed and to dogmas.[148] That Judaism, however, has no dogmas is a view which has been repudiated by Dr. S. Schechter.[149] There is, however, a good deal of truth in H. Loewe's statement. The main emphasis in Judaism is upon the *right deed*. Leo Baeck hardly exaggerates when he says: "Judaism too has its Word, but it is one word only—'to do'; [150] hence the multiplicity of commandments. They all pursue the same end—the guiding of human life into the channel of *right* action. It is through the medium of the moral act that the Jew finds his approach to God."[151] Indeed, Baeck goes so far as to say that obedience to the law of God is prior to any comprehension of God himself. It is only when men become "conscious of the *moral unity*" that they can "comprehend the *unity of God*".[152] It is from such insistence upon the right deed that the Law is put in its proper perspective.

The significance of Torah as Law and Commandment is the most characteristic feature of Judaism. It is for this reason that Moses occupies a unique position in Rabbinic thought,[153] and that the Pentateuch stands above the rest of the canon.[154] What Weber says about the Scriptures in general applies primarily to the *torat Mosheh*; it is the *norma normans* of all Rabbinic thinking.[155] The Torah is looked upon as the greatest and most perfect gift that God has bestowed upon Israel.[156] In it is embodied "the will and purpose of the perfect God—perfect in wisdom, perfect in righteousness, perfect in loving-kindness". [157] It forms the sure guide under all conditions of life and its purpose is the purification and the sanctification of man.[158] Israel, therefore, owes his loyalty to the Torah, and he expresses his obedience by keeping the Commandments. By doing so he ratifies the covenant established at Mount Sinai between the chosen people and the God of Israel. Thus, the Torah occupies a central place in the Jewish faith.[159]

The late Chief Rabbi, Dr. Hertz, in a speech said with great emphasis that the second fundamental principle of Judaism (the first being the Unity of God) was morality and law. "It proclaimed the divine origin of the moral law; that there was an everlasting distinction between right and wrong, an absolute 'Thou shalt' and 'Thou shalt not' in human life, a categorical imperative in religion." [160]   This connexion between moral action and faith in God is upheld by Christianity as well as by Judaism. St. Paul's antinomy between faith and works has never been understood by the Church as a dispensation from the human obligation to do right. It seems to us that Schoeps mispresented St. Paul's position when he implied that the Apostle misunderstood the purpose of the Law, namely the sanctification of the *will* of God.[161] Schoeps' well-chosen passages to show that the Rabbis too knew of the value and greatness of faith have nothing to do with the main issue. The Apostle would have been the last to deny to the Synagogue the claim to the possession of faith.[162] There is also no hint in the Epistles of St. Paul to show that he repudiated the right of the Law to make demands upon men. On the contrary, he affirms the divine origin and the justice of the Law;[163] to him the Law is the law of God.[164] He too knows that not the hearers but the *doers* of the Law shall be justified.[165]

The extent of the misunderstanding on the Jewish side can be gathered from Montefiore's suggestion that the antinomy between the Jewish emphasis upon works and the Christian emphasis upon faith may be combined in a synthesis, for "we need them both: each possesses its measure of truth". Montefiore continues: "I cannot help believing that this old point of difference between Judaism and Christianity may gradually be done away with. Each will recognize that the fuller truth lies in a combination of doctrines hitherto thought opposed and alien to each other." [166] To this we might ask: did the Apostle Paul ever oppose and does the Church oppose *faith* to *work* in the sense that one excludes the other? Such an allegation we would emphatically deny. There is no antinomy between faith and works; this is made impossible by the fact that in the Christian view they both belong to different *spheres*. In Christian thought faith and work are held separate, the one relating to God, the other to human relationship. Herein lies the *duality* at the heart of Christian thinking to which Benzion Kellerman draws attention.[167] Such *duality* is conditioned by the singular position which Jesus Christ occupies in the Church.

Man's relationship to God depends, in the Christian view, not upon right *action* but upon a right attitude to *Jesus Christ*. This is the meaning of faith in the Pauline epistles; a striking example is offered by the strange phrase in Gal. 3. 23 and 25: πρὸ τοῦ δὲ ἐλθεῖν τὴν πίστιν .... ἐλθούσης δὲ τῆς πίστεως ... Paul does not mean to imply that *before* the appearance of Christ there was no faith, but that faith *now* centres in the person of the Messiah. Herein lies the reason for the characteristic emphasis upon the creed, which Kohler calls the *conditio sine qua non* of the Christian Church.[168] The creed, as the intellectual deposit of faith, is the only criterion, whether a man affirms or denies the claims the Church makes for Jesus of Nazareth.[169]

But there is still one further point to be considered.

Montefiore severely criticizes Christian theologians for presenting Judaism as a religion of external Law-observance and *Lohnsucht* (passion for merit).[170] This mistaken view has arisen from the position which the Law occupies in Judaism. Montefiore himself agrees with Weber that the Law forms the centre of the Jewish religion: "All radiates out from the Law, and from it all depends." [171] The supremacy of the Law goes right through the whole history of Judaism. Even in Hermann Cohen's religious philosophy the emancipation of religion from ethics has not taken place. Cohen was not able to overcome the supremacy of the Law as completely as Felix Perles seems to imply.[172] Faith and Law, religion and ethics are inter-twined to a degree which makes any attempt at separation impossible. This utter dependence of religion upon ethics puts man in a position of independence *vis à vis* God which in the Christian view is nothing else but rebellion, for it ultimately implies that man is *able* to stand before God on his own merits. This the Church categorically denies.

Schoeps rightly regards St. Paul's assumption that man is unable of himself to keep the Law as alien to the spirit of Judaism.[173] "Every Jew", says Dienemann, "is convinced that 'faith in the moral power of man' and 'Law,' upon the fulfilment of which that faith depends, are both inseparably connected." [174] It is here that the difference reveals itself. The discussion, as throughout, turns round man's position *before* God. To the Synagogue man appears as an independent agent capable of holding his own: "Thou canst" is its constant cry.[175] Pauline theology, on the other hand, begins with the assumption that man is *unable* to keep the Law; he thus stands condemned before God. God in His mercy, however—and herein lies the meaning of the Gospel—sent His Son to die for sinners: "While we were yet sinners, Christ died for us" (Rom. 5. 8). It is thus that God becomes the Justifier of the ungodly (Rom. 4. 5). Rom. 10. 4, τέλος γαρ νόμου Χριστὸς εἰς δικαιοσύνην . . ., does not imply, therefore, arbitrary abrogation of the Law on the part of the Apostle. The end of the Law is in its completion, in the fact that God has accomplished on behalf of man what man was unable to do for himself. The "righteousness" of the believer is not his *own*; he owes it to God through the Messiah. Kohler says that loyalty to the Torah is an "all-penetrating principle of the Synagogue".[176] What the Jew owes to the Torah, the Christian owes to Jesus Christ. But the difference lies not merely between loyalty to a *person* and loyalty to a *code*. Underneath the Cross man stands in the position of crisis, asking for grace; under the Scrolls of the Law, man stands in a position of self-assertiveness, giving *his* best.[177] Thus the difference between Judaism and Christianity lies in the difference of *attitude*.

(h) Revelation

The connexion between Torah and revelation is obvious. Traditional Judaism has always claimed faith in revelation as a fundamental tenet of the Synagogue. The inference from the principle of revelation is the immutability of the Law. Maimonides, Hasdai, Albo, and others regard this as an essential belief of Judaism.[178] The rigidity which such a tenet would inevitably impose upon Jewish thinking has been remedied by the conception of tradition. Next to the written Law (*torah she-beketab*) is the oral Law (*torah she-be'al peh*), in the orthodox view both originating from Moses and enjoying equal sanctity. This principle of oral tradition accompanying the written Law provides Judaism with the possibility of growth and adaptability to circumstances.[179] The rational tendency and the idea of progress are thus organically connected with the concept of revelation. This wide conception of Torah is already present in the teaching of the old Synagogue. When two schools of thought, like that of Hillel and Shammai, differed on a vital point, both claiming the right to *halakah*, the Talmud simply declared both right: "All words come from the same shepherd." [180]   The

Rabbis worked on the principle that the words of the Torah "are fruitful and multiply".[181]   Torah thus assumes a much wider meaning than the principle of immutability would imply. Indeed, the Rabbis went so far as to maintain that all which was to be taught in the future was already communicated to Moses on Mount Sinai: "The doctrines of the Rabbis were the harvest from the seed which was sown at the time of the original Revelation." [182]

This fluid and broad conception of revelation lends to Judaism a unique power of adjustment to the ever-changing concepts in human development.[183]   All manifestations of the human spirit—all wisdom, all philosophy, all science—become thus, as it were, a diffusion of Torah, being related to the revelation of God.   Once again we meet here the underlying principle of unity between God and the world.   The totalitarian tendency of Judaism to extend religion to all spheres of life springs from this source.   The division between the secular and the holy, the material and the spiritual is thus reduced to a minimum.   The connexion between Spinoza's philosophy and the Jewish conception of revelation becomes evident.   There is an undeniable pantheistic strain in Judaism which manifests itself in the narrow margin separating God from man.   Hermann Cohen, who is determined to draw a clear dividing-line between his ethical monotheism and Spinoza's pantheism, is only able to establish his case within the sphere of ethics.[184]   There is no denying that Spinoza's *amor intellectualis* and the categorical imperative derived from the Law of Moses differ both in intensity and quality.   But it is significant that the dividing-line appears most prominently within the sphere of ethics as nowhere else.   The reason for this lies deeply embedded in the fibre of Judaism.

It is true that Judaism is deeply aware of God's transcendence; it is equally true that the Immanence of God is a vital element of Jewish piety.   "Resting on this twofold anchorage", says Abelson, "Rabbinical Judaism was saved from destruction.   Its outwardness and its inwardness were both necessary for its preservation." [185]   But the vital question which concerns us is, by what *means* does the transcendent God become immanent?   In other words, under what conditions does the finite meet with the Infinite?   To this Judaism has only one answer: *man* creates those conditions himself.[186]   By his piety, by his earnest endeavour, by his striving upwards he reduces the distance which divides him

from the Holy One.   The immanence of God is thus obtained
by intrusion: it is left to man to break down the barrier which
keeps him separate from God.

Here we come upon the internal connexion between Spinoza's
philosophy and the Jewish conception of revelation.   The great
philosopher in his *Short Treatise on God, Man, and his Well-being*
asks the important question: how can God make himself known
to man?   Does it happen by means of the spoken word or by
direct communication through himself?   To this he answers:
"We consider it to be unnecessary that it should happen through
any other thing than the mere essence of God and the understanding of man; for, as the Understanding is that in us which
must know God, and as it stands in such immediate union with
him that it can neither be nor be understood without him, it is
incontrovertibly evident from this that no thing can ever come
into such close touch with the Understanding as God himself
can." [187]   Spinoza's point is that the affinity between the human
and the divine Spirit is such that any intermediary instrument is
not only unnecessary, but impossible: "Because we can never
attain to the knowledge of God through any other thing (*i.e.*
words, miracles or any other created thing), the nature of which
is necessarily finite . . . for how is it possible that we should
infer an infinite and limitless thing from a finite and limited
thing?"   Only on the assumption, therefore, that man and God
partake of the same infinity is revelation possible.   The process
itself takes place *within* the soul of man.[188]   With this we should
like to compare the statement made by the great Jewish theologian Kaufmann Kohler.   In his article on "Revelation" in the
Jewish Encyclopaedia he describes the process as "the gradual
unfolding of the divine powers in man".[189]   The difference
between Israel and the other nations lies in that the Jewish race
"has been endowed with peculiar religious powers that fitted it
for the divine revelation".   In view of these two statements it is
difficult to see how Dr. Kohler can assert that the essential
feature of revelation "is not merely a psychological process in
which the human imagination or mental faculty constitutes the
main factor".   Can the "divine powers in man", we would ask,
be legitimately segregated from the intellectual life of any
individual?   That Kohler's conception of revelation is a purely
subjective one, and this in spite of his remark "that man is but
the instrument upon which a superhuman force exerts its power"

can be judged from his concluding remark. He finishes the article by saying: "Whether 'Torah' has not frequently a far broader and deeper meaning in the prophetic and other inspired books—denoting rather the universal law of human conduct, the Law of God as far as it is written upon the heart of man in order to render him a true son of God—is a question at issue between orthodoxy and reform."

The difference, however, between the orthodox and reformed conception of Torah is only a *formal* one. It turns round the *position* of the written Law within the wider concept of revealed Truth. While orthodoxy relates all truth in some way or another, to the Mosaic Law, liberal Judaism does not hesitate to brush the Law aside when it conflicts with reason. Montefiore thus bluntly declares: "Liberal Judaism no longer teaches the eternal validity of the Pentateuchal laws or law; we teach a progressive religion, a progressive apprehension and unfolding of the will of God." [190] But, strange as it may seem, there is no *essential* difference between the liberal and orthodox view. We shall find this affirmed by the example of H. Loewe, who describes himself as orthodox, but not as a "fundamentalist".

In his introduction to the *Rabbinic Anthology* he dwells upon the subject of revelation. "Judaism", Mr. Loewe explains, "whether orthodox or liberal, old or modern, teaches that God's Law is universal as well as immutable What is true in nature is true in religion; what is false in science cannot be true in religion. Truth is one and indivisible. God is bound by his own laws." [191] Between Torah and the laws of nature there is then no essential difference. Not only the Holy Scriptures, says Mr. Loewe, but also history and archaeology "have been vouchsafed to us by revelation".[192] Revelation, he thus concludes, "is the silent imperceptible manifestation of God in history"; or to be more precise, "God in history is the definition of Revelation".[193] If we ask in what relation then stands the Torah to this concept of revelation, Mr. Loewe has a twofold answer: (1) "Judaism regards the Torah as capable of expansion." [194] He provides proof from Rabbinic literature to show that this is by no means a novel view. According to the Rabbis "God's word", we are told, "is not an antiquated διατάγμα, but one which is ever new, which men run to read. The Torah is 'your life', and like life, it grows".[195] (2) Side by side with the doctrine of the immutability of the Torah "there is in Judaism a basic

principle of the most potent mutability, the doctrine of progress".[196]

It is clear to us that Mr. Loewe has sufficiently demonstrated
the essential unity between the orthodox and the liberal view.
On this subject, to use his own words again, "there is no difference between liberal and orthodox Jews".[197] This fact is of the
utmost importance, as it warns us from drawing too clear a line
of demarcation between the two schools of thought.

It is evident then that between the Jewish and the Christian
conception of revelation is a deep cleavage. The cleft appears
not in the question as to the primacy of the Bible or value of
Biblical criticism, but over the problem of history. In the Jewish
view history is essentially the manifestation or unfolding of
God's will. It is on these grounds that revelation and history
can be linked up in one straight line. "In Judaism", says Leo
Baeck, "the Kingdom of God is not a kingdom above the world,
or opposed to it, or even side by side with it. It is rather the
answer to the world . . . the reconciliation of its finiteness
with its infiniteness." [198] Between the Kingdom of God and this
world there is no qualitative difference, but only a difference of
degree. Human history progressively unfolds God's purpose.
All that happens within the experience of man serves a higher
end. History becomes thus the supreme test of good and evil.
What survives is good, what is unable to survive is evil.[199] It is
for this reason that thinkers like Rosenzweig, Buber, Schoeps, [200]
and others have included Christianity within the general scheme
of salvation. It withstood the test of history; it thus proved its
value and is therefore God-willed.[201]

The Christian position, however, is diametrically opposed to
such a view. Revelation, to the Christian Church, is not something that runs alongside the world, and certainly not something
that merges with it; it is something that stands *opposed* to it. The
word of God is primarily a word of judgment, a condemnation
of history. Between God and the world stands the Cross of Jesus
Christ. The meaning of the Incarnation is that the continuity
of history has been broken at a definite point. Whatever progress
can mean for mankind, it *cannot* mean that man is able to advance
to a position *beyond* the place where Jesus Christ stood. In the
Christian view revelation is thus concentrated in his person.
The value of the Bible is that it points to him. It is for
this reason that the Church could maintain the unity between

the Old and the New Testament.[202] The very fact that the Old and New Testaments were knit together into one whole refutes the view of a progressive unfolding of God in history. The idea of endless evolution is excluded not merely by the fact of the Canon but by the position which Jesus Christ occupies in the Christian Faith.

The existence of a *new* Testament never meant to the Church that the *old* one had been outgrown, but that it had reached its culminating point in the Messiah. In the words of Luther: "*Christus universae scripturae scopus est.*" [203] Schleiermacher's opinion, therefore, that Christianity is a new and different religion, detached from the Old Testament, does not represent the view of the historic Church.[204] Mr. Davies' *via media*: Christianity grew out of Judaism, but "in the marvellous personality, life and teaching of Jesus, we have a new beginning", also fails to understand the Christian point of view. His underlying principle is the idea of evolution, which extends not only in the sphere of human existence, but to God's dealing with man.[205] The view the Church has taken is perhaps best expressed in Prof. Macmurray's words: "Jesus is at once the culmination of Jewish prophecy and the source of Christianity. These are not two different aspects of the life of Jesus. They are the same things referred backwards into the past and forward into the future." [206]

Revelation, as far as God's dealing with man is concerned, the Church finds not outside but *inside* the Canon. The Canon forms, as it were, the periphery of revelation, its centre being Jesus Christ. This unique position assigned to the Messiah runs contrary to the whole Jewish conception. "That word from the burning bush", says Buber, " 'I will be present as the one who will be present' (*i.e.* as the one I am ever present), makes it for us impossible to accept something that happened but once as the final revelation of God." [207]

The reasons for objecting to the singling out of *one* person and attaching to him revelational significance are not difficult to find: (1) Jewish anthropology demands absolute equality of the human race. *All* men stand basically in the same relation to God. At no point may the chain of humanity be broken. (2) The superiority of the Torah and Israel's unique position in the process of revelation cannot admit revelation to be vested in an individual person. (3) The concept of revelation understood in terms of continuous growth contradicts all claims to finality: "The richness of the religion is not contained in a single one. . . . The whole content of Judaism truly lies in its unended and unending history." [208]

Modern Jewish thought, deeply impressed by the idea of evolution, inevitably tends to deny absolute validity to religious values. The Christian emphasis upon the historical, the concrete, the individual, clashes with the basic principle of evolution.[209] Herein modern Judaism differs vitally from the old Hebrew attitude to history. A-historical thinking in terms of the general and the abstract is alien to the Bible. It always speaks in terms of *concrete* events. To regard the concrete individual case as a mere manifestation of the general and the abstract, a mere fraction of the pattern which is to evolve by way of endless evolution, is Greek and not Hebrew. It is for this reason that Greece had no real sense for the historical; instead of concrete history it developed an abstract mythology, where the heroes of history became shadows or symbols of an idea.[210]

Christianity, by its very nature, is anchored in history. The Christian Messiah is not a mythological abstraction but a historical person. He lived, taught, died at a definite moment in history. It is on behalf of a *historical* person that the Church makes stupendous claims. These claims have the nature of finality: there will never be a person to bring to mankind a more complete revelation or a greater truth. It is on this issue that Judaism and Christianity part.

2. ISRAEL AND THE NATIONS

Apart from the main theological issues already discussed, there is still one important problem to be considered. It concerns Israel's position in the world. The significance attached to Israel's election; the meaning of Jewish destiny; Jewish close proximity to the Bible; the Jewish position in the history of Revelation; the Jewish claim to the sole heirship of the prophetic tradition—these are factors which have vitally determined the structure of Jewish thought.

It is not possible to understand Jewish thinking without paying full attention to the basic principle underlying all Jewish theology: Israel's singular position in the history of mankind. The division, therefore, between the Church and the Synagogue opens a far wider issue than can be expressed in terms of theology. It concerns the very existence of the Jewish people. Israel's opposition to the Church is dictated by something more elemental than theological divergency, namely, by the instinct of self-preservation. The Christian claims are such that the whole meaning of Jewish destiny is at stake. The existence of the Church throws a threatening shadow upon Jewish life. Two vital factors are here involved: (1) The spiritual destiny of Israel; (2) the safety of Israel's national life.

The relation between Jewish separate existence and Israel's spiritual significance is such that a threat to either is a threat to both. In the Jewish view, Judaism and Jewish nationhood are interdependent: there is no Judaism without the Jewish people and there is no Jewish people without Judaism. The modern distinction between religion and nationhood is for three reasons inapplicable to the Jewish situation: (1) the unitary tendency of Judaism allows of no separation between the religious and the secular; (2) the political position of Jewry makes religion the only unifying factor of Jewish life; (3) Jewish experience as a scattered minority has shown that any loosening of the religious bond opens a wide door to assimilation. But the disappearance of Israel amongst the nations is tantamount to the betrayal of his spiritual vocation. Israel and Israel's message are inseparable; the message is vested in the people and the people exists by the message. Israel, in order to fulfil his historical vocation, must exist. It may be observed, however, that the liberal Synagogue, especially in England and America, has made strenuous efforts to overcome the national implications of Judaism. Whether it will be able to survive in the recast, universalistic form only the future will show. Older liberal theologians, like Kaufmann Kohler and Leo Baeck, recognized the indivisible unity between the people and the message, and have thus held to the doctrine of Israel's unique significance amongst the nations of the world. We will now turn to consider the Synagogue's attitude to the nations and its teaching about Israel.

(a) Jewish universalism

The question whether Judaism is a universalistic or particularistic religion has been discussed at great length in recent years. Christian writers have adduced evidence from Jewish sources to prove the particularistic attitude of Judaism. Jewish writers have, from the *same* sources, given proof of the opposite. The undeniable fact is that both tendencies exist side by side in the Synagogue.[211] To a large extent Jewish feeling towards the other nations was governed by the circumstances under which the Jews lived.[212] Montefiore's contention that the real attitude of the Rabbis must be judged not from isolated instances but against the general historical background to which they belong, is a just plea.[213]

There is still a further point to be considered. It has been the practice of Christian scholars to contrast Rabbinic teaching with that of the New Testament. We have seen how Montefiore has contested the fairness of such a comparison. The counterpart to Rabbinic writings, he points out, is not the classical literature of the New Testament but that of the Church Fathers.[214] This is an important point worth bearing in mind.

To deny to Judaism a strong universalistic tendency, as some Christian scholars have done, is to overlook the mass of evidence contained in Rabbinic literature. The concern with the Gentile world is much older than the Synagogue and goes back to the Prophets of Israel. Is. 19. 29 f, where Israel is given the *third* place, standing side by side with Egypt and Assyria, his hereditary enemies, is the finest testimony to prophetic universalism. A similar spirit permeates many of the Psalms. From the New Testament writings we know that the Jews busied themselves with what we would now call foreign missions.[215] It may well be that it was the missionary need which led to the translation of the Hebrew Scriptures.[216] When Paul went out with the Gospel message, he found a well-prepared field; the pioneer work had already been done by Jewish teachers and missionaries. The debt the Church owes in this respect to the Synagogue is inestimable.[217] The Rabbis in later centuries often showed a similar concern for the Gentile world.[218] Such an attitude was not only prompted by the prophetic spirit of the Scriptures, but was implicit in the monotheistic faith of Judaism. The God of Israel, being the One and Holy God, was inevitably the Lord of the Gentiles also. There is the touching sentiment expressed by R. Johanan, who declared that God does not rejoice over the downfall of the wicked: when the ministering angels wanted to sing a hymn at the destruction of Egypt, God said: "My children lie drowned in the sea, and you would sing." [219]

By its very nature, Judaism was at first a religion deeply rooted in nationhood. The history of the Jewish people was at the same time the history of its religion. Their customs were religious customs and therefore national; their book was a national book and therefore religious. Prof. Moore has pointed out: "The Jews were both in their own mind and in the eyes of their Gentile surrounding, and before the Roman law, not adherents of a peculiar religion, but members of a nation." [220] It was as such that they carried with them wherever they went their religion and their mode of life. But Prof. Moore has drawn attention to a peculiar feature which is of great importance in the development of Judaism. The fact that the *ger*, who previously was an *advena* in Jewish territory, becomes after the fall of the kingdom an *advena* to the Jewish religion, testifies not only to the change of political circumstances but to an important change in the outlook of Judaism.[221] Dr. A. Marmorstein has noted the fact that the word *'olam*, at a certain period of Jewish history which cannot be chronologically fixed, changed its meaning from the restricted sense as used in the Bible to its world-wide signification in Rabbinic writings. This inner change in the word *'olam* testifies to a change in Hebrew thinking in the direction of universalism.[222]

Characteristic of the spirit of some Rabbis are the often quoted words of R. Simeon ben Azzai. Against R. Akiba's suggestion that love for one's neighbour is the greatest principle of the Torah, Ben Azzai said that the words in Gen. 5. 1, "This is the book of the generations of Adam . . . in the likeness of God made he him", contains a still greater principle. The inference being that the common origin of humanity imposes the duty of mutual love.[223] Leo Baeck makes the following claim for Judaism, which will not easily be refuted: "Judaism created the fellow-man or neighbour, and with it the conception of humanity in its true sense. . . . In Judaism, neighbour is inseparable from 'man'." [224] This, of course, is an over-statement in that it includes *all* exponents of Judaism. But that many Rabbis have taken so noble a view cannot be questioned. The fact that such lofty views were often held in spite of the adverse circumstances under which Jews had to live enhances their nobility in the eyes of mankind. It must also be borne in mind that the distance which separated the faithful Jew from his heathen neighbour was not conducive to a universalistic outlook. The natural feeling of superiority, both by reason of the great spiritual tradition and the moral purity when compared with heathen life, must have made it very difficult indeed for the Jew to regard the pagan as his equal.

Nevertheless, if in the eyes of the pious Jew his pagan neighbour could hardly be his equal, it must be said to the credit of Judaism that it made honest attempts to raise him to equality. Prof. Moore has stressed that the principle of absolute equality between the *ger* and the born Israelite runs right through the traditional Law. The moment the Gentile underwent circumcision and baptism, he was duly received into the religious community, "having all the legal rights and powers and being subject to all the obligations of the Jew by birth." [225] Even if he lapsed afterwards, he was still looked upon as an apostate Jew and not as a heathen. It is true that we sometimes meet with slighting references to proselytes. It was alleged that they cause misfortune, that they postpone the coming of the Messiah, that they are like leprosy to Israel. [226] But these sentiments are easily explained by the inevitable disappointments that accompany all missionary efforts. On the other hand, the *ger zedek* was held in great esteem; he was looked upon as specially beloved by God; he was to be treated with deference; his origin was not to be cast in his teeth; his failings were to be borne patiently. The Midrash contains the touching parable about a stag which joined the king's herd. The king was told about it; but he felt affection for the stag and ordered that it be treated with special care. When the servants enquired the reason for his special affection for a wild creature, the king explained: "The flock have no choice; whether they want or not it is their nature to graze in the field and to come in at even to sleep in the fold. The stags, however, sleep in the wilderness. It is not in their nature to come into places inhabited by man. Shall we then not count it as a merit to this one, which has left behind the whole of the broad, vast wilderness, the abode of all the beasts, and has come to stay in the courtyard?" The Midrash continues: "In like manner, ought we not to be grateful to the proselyte who has left behind him his people and all the other peoples of the world, and has chosen to come to us?" It is for this reason that God provides the proselyte with special protection and exhorts Israel to do likewise. [227] "The names of the proselytes", said the Holy One, blessed be he, "are as dear to me as the wine of libation which is poured out upon the altar." [228]

God gave the Torah to Israel not for the purpose of keeping it

to himself, but of sharing it with the Gentiles. This is the meaning of a comment to Is. 45. 19: God did not wait to give the
Torah until Israel entered the Holy Land, but gave it in the
wilderness, lest Israel claim it for himself and exclude the
nations.[229] The Gentiles too have a claim upon it: R. Jeremiah
said: "Whence can you know that a Gentile who practises the
Law is equal to the High Priest? Because it says: 'Which if a
man do he shall live through them' (Lev. 18. 5). And it (also)
says: 'This is the Torah of man' (2 Sam. 7. 19). It does not say
the Torah of Priests, Levites, Israelites, but *Torath ha-Adam*. . . .
And it does not say: 'Open the gates, and let the Priests and
Levites and Israelites enter', but it says: 'Open the gates that a
goi ẓaddik may enter' " (Is. 26. 2).[230]

In Pirkê de Rabbi Eliezer,[231] there is the following eschatological reference: "Ten kings ruled from one end of the world
to the other"; "The first King was the Holy One, blessed be
he"; the second king was Nimrod; the third king was Joseph;
the fourth Solomon; the fifth was Ahab; the sixth was Nebuchadnezzar; the seventh was Cyrus; the eighth king was Alexander
of Macedonia; the ninth king is King Messiah, "who in the
future will rule from one end of the world to the other. The
tenth king will restore the sovereignty to its owner.[232] He who
was the first king will be the last king, as it is said: 'Thus saith
the Lord, the King . . . I am the first and the last; and beside
me there is no God', and it is written, 'and the Lord shall be
king over all the earth'." [233] In this passage we receive a glimpse
of the Rabbinic vision, which was based upon the faith of the
ultimate vindication of God's righteousness and the extension of
his Kingdom over the whole world. The passage reveals close
affinity with the Pauline hope when God will be τὰ πάντα ἐν
πᾶσιν (1 Cor. 15. 28).

We may therefore say with some assurance that Israel's
Messianic hope had always a universal aspect. In the Messianic
age the Gentile world will join the true worshippers of God.
Meanwhile it was incumbent upon the faithful Jew to preach
repentance and to make proselytes. "By these means", says
Schechter, "the Kingdom of Heaven, even in its connexion with
Israel, expands into the universal Kingdom to which sinners and
Gentiles are invited." [234] Here, however, one important feature
must be noticed. The Kingdom of God is closely connected with
the triumph of Israel. Not until the Jewish people has regained

its freedom and established the divine order in the Holy Land
can salvation come to the rest of the world: "Israel is the
microcosm in which all the conditions of the kingdom are to find
concrete expression." [235]   Not before redemption has come to
Israel can it come to the world; until then, even the Shekinah
is in exile. [236]

(b) Jewish particularism

It is an undeniable fact that side by side with the universalistic
outlook runs a strong particularistic trait through the whole
history of Judaism. Jewish scholars have tried to explain it, and
we take into consideration the suggestions they make. The fact,
however, remains with all its consequences. There is no necessity
to refute Dr. A. Cohen's statement that "in the sphere of morals"
the Rabbinic outlook "was universal and not national". [237] The
point is that it is not in the moral sphere that Jewish particularism
appears. Its roots are to be sought in the consciousness of the
Jewish people. In the Rabbinic view the difference between the
Jew and the Gentile arose not merely from the difference of moral
standards. It is true that to the Rabbis the Torah made a fundamental difference between Israel and the nations. "Torahless
universalism", as Schechter calls it, would have been abhorrent
to the leaders of the Synagogue. It is equally true that to the
Rabbis Israel was not a nation in the ordinary sense. It was not
race but the Torah that made Israel a people. [238] This fact of
spiritual prerogative, however, was not always interpreted in the
sense of special grace, but of merit. [239] The Gentile world refused
the Torah, while Israel accepted it. [240] There was a certain
unspecified inherent quality in Jewish blood, a connexion with
the Patriarchs, a special favouritism on the part of God, which
placed Israel in a singular and unique position. [241] The best the
Gentile could do was to *join* Israel, but he could not become
Israel. [242]

Prof. Moore explains that "equality in law and religion does
not necessarily carry with it complete social equality", and that
"the Jews would have been singularly unlike the rest of mankind
if they had felt no superiority to their heathen converts". It was
for this psychological reason that the proselytes were put at the
end of the list in Jewish society. Indeed, sometimes so low that
they ranked lower than bastards and *Nithinim* (descendants of
old Temple-slaves) and only above the heathen slaves who had

been freed by their Jewish masters.[243]   Social conventions are
certainly persistent and must not be made the criterion of religious
standards.   There are, however, deeper reasons which affected
the Jewish attitude to the Gentile world.

It is essential to bear in mind that in the Jewish view between
Israel and the nations there existed an abyss which could not be
bridged.   There could be no compromise between Israel and the
Gentiles, as there could be no compromise between the God of
Israel and the idols.   Faithfulness to God already implied hostility
to idolatry, and therefore to idolators.   The harsh sayings against
Gentiles are primarily prompted by religious scruples.[244]   There
was something so terrible in idolatry for the Jewish mind that to
conceive the possibility of a radical change within the lifetime
of one generation was impossible.   "We do not believe a proselyte
until seven generations (have passed), so that the waters should
not return to their source." [245]   A Jew could in no circumstances marry a non-Jew.   There was no social intercourse
between them, "for whosoever eateth with an uncircumcized
person is as though he were eating flesh of abomination".[246]   If
a Jew showed kindness to a Gentile, it was only *mipne darke
shalom*.[247]   Faithfulness to Judaism required a measure of hostility
towards the pagan world.   To this must be added the important
point that the Gentiles, who by reason of their idolatry were
enemies to the God of Israel, were also, by reason of their political
superiority, enemies to God's people.   Guignebert affirms with
good reason that even in cases where the Messianic ideal tended
towards universalism, "its fundamental idea was still the restoration of Israel, that is to say, the triumph of Jewish nationalism".[248]
This was only natural, for in the Jewish view the triumph of
Israel was tantamount to the triumph of God.   The primary
function of the Messiah, the true son of David, was the restoration of Israel's independence and the defeat of his enemies.
Maimonides quotes the Talmudic saying: "There is no difference
between this world (*i.e.* as it is now) and the days of the Messiah,
except only submission to (foreign) government." [249]   It must
not be overlooked that Jewish universalism was crippled by
the growing hostility of the Roman Empire and the tragic end
of national life.   It is for this reason that the universalist utterances of the Old Testament have been given a restricted
meaning.

Bousset admits that Judaism was conscious of a world-mission,

but he holds it was hindered by its deeply rooted nationalism.[250]
The only way, therefore, to reach out to the heathen world was
to join the Gentiles to Israel: "he who truly joined the Jewish
religion became a Jew".[251] It was in this peculiar form of
universalism that the Synagogue differed from the Church.
Both were conscious of a message and both made claims upon the
Gentile world. But while Christianity, thanks to the labours of
St. Paul, became completely detached from nationhood, Judaism
could not afford to do so. The Jewish message could therefore
only come to the Gentile world in its national dress. The reasons
for this lie deeply rooted in Jewish history. But two main factors
must be mentioned in order to account for the course Judaism
had taken.

(i) THE NATIONAL MOTIVE

It is a peculiar fact about Judaism that religion and nationhood
are inseparably welded together. This characteristic feature,
which almost creates the impression of tribalism, is not only
explained by the tendency of monotheism towards the total
unification of life. The religious development of the Synagogue
must be placed against its proper political background to do full
justice to it. It must be constantly borne in mind that Judaism
has laboured under abnormal political conditions. The Rabbis
who faithfully watched over the Synagogue were not only the
religious leaders but also the guardians of national life.[252] Only
at the expense of deeply cherished principles could Jewish life
continue. Everything that served towards preservation of the
Jewish people became hallowed by religion. Judaism became
the means of preserving the Jewish people. While in natural
circumstances Israel would have lived for his religion, under
abnormal conditions, Israel's religion became subservient to
Israel's national existence.[253] Such use of religion for the purpose
of nationalism could have only taken place where the national
and the religious cause were looked upon as identical. But such
was the case in Judaism: the people of God and the God of the
people were inseparably united. Subservience of the religious to
the national cause was no departure from the main principles of
Judaism. It may well be doubted whether the Rabbis were
even conscious of the fact. To them the preservation of Israel's
identity was a *religious* task. They therefore never hesitated to
use religion as the most potent means for the preservation of

national life. It is for this reason that the demands of Judaism aim primarily at national preservation.[254]

(ii) THE JEWISH RELIGIOUS CONSCIOUSNESS

We have observed already that, according to the Rabbis, Israel occupies a singular position. The Jewish people differs from all other peoples upon earth. Such a view was, in the first place, prompted not by an exaggerated form of nationalism but by the religious consciousness of the Synagogue. God's dealings with Israel have both national and religious significance. God called his people: he saved it from the house of bondage; he gave it his Torah; he brought it to the Promised Land; he was and is Israel's King. *Abinu malkenu* is a familiar phrase in the Synagogue's liturgy.[255]

To have Abraham as a father, to claim God's promises, to keep his Commandments, to belong to the commonwealth of the Chosen People were the *religious* prerogatives of the Jew. The fact of his birth was not fortuitous, but a God-given privilege, an act of grace. It is for this reason that the Jew thanks God for not having been made a heathen, a slave, or a woman.[256] To have been born a Jew had religious significance. Even the Jewish sinner was in a different position from the Gentiles: no Jew goes to Gehenna, as there is no Israelite without some good.[257] Such notions had their root in the conviction that Israel stands in unique relationship to God. "God's love is primarily for Israel as a whole." [258] Israel's election stands for eternity.[259]

To this must be added the fact that the Law of Moses in its Rabbinic interpretation imposed severe restrictions upon Jewish life. Hoennicke has paid attention to this important factor: "The Law (interpreted) as custom and observance exerted decisive influence upon the life of every Jew." [260] It stood as the middle wall of partition between Jew and Gentile.

These two factors, the national and the religious, have decided the Jewish attitude to the Gentile world. In spite of its many and noble efforts, Judaism was unable to break down the barriers; it remained essentially a national religion. Even the Hellenized Jews of the Diaspora have only loosened but not thrown off the fetters of national exclusiveness.[261] Such an attitude, if detached from its religious motives, could easily lead to extreme pride and a perverse form of nationalism. No doubt many Jews did not escape the danger.[262] Racial pride is a failing common to man. In Judaism, where the national and the religious are so closely knit together, the danger is even greater. Montefiore frankly admits the fact. "I do not deny", he says, "that the old Rabbis' religion was prevailingly particularistic. The enemies of Israel were the enemies of God." [263] The utter impossibility of separating the national cause from the religious inevitably made for a certain national arrogance. It led to utter contempt for the Gentile world. Though the door to Judaism was left open,[264] the masses of the Gentiles remained outside. For them the Synagogue had no hope.[265]

It is for these reasons that it is difficult to speak of Jewish universalism; for this, Judaism was too deeply anchored in its national life. The universalistic tendencies of Judaism "are nothing more than an extension of particularism, implying the absorption of the Gentile world by the chosen people" [266] This is not an unjust description; it tallies well with the facts. The way to the God of Israel led *via* Israel; the Synagogue could not conceive of any other way. Prof. Schoeps' essay fully bears out this view.[266a]

The great sacrifice the hour demanded Judaism was unable to make. The Kingdom of God remained closely knit to Israel's national ambitions. Weber does not exaggerate when he says: "Jewish religious consciousness stands therefore in irreconcilable opposition to the thought of the universality of the Kingdom of God." [267] Between the God of Israel and the Gentile world stands the Jewish people. To come to God meant primarily to come to the Jews. Without *first* coming to Israel, the way to God remained barred. Leo Baeck has tried to exonerate the exaggerated importance of Israel by explaining that "the greatest duty always carries with it at the same time the greatest promise". He therefore asks: "Should not that power which made special demands of Israel grant it also special promise?" [268] This question we cannot answer. How God rewards faithfulness is his own secret. Jesus Christ, however, once said: "When ye shall have done all those things which are commanded you, say, we are unprofitable servants" (Lk. 17. 10). It may be that such an attitude is alien to the spirit of Judaism. The fact remains that Judaism continued a national religion; the Gentile world stayed outside the Synagogue.

Jewish writers have sometimes implied that Christianity bought its success at the price of a compromise. "Compromise between Judaism and Hellenism, between Israel and the pagans," says

Klausner, "is the foundation and basis of all Christianity." [269] But it seems to us that whatever foreign elements may have been admixed with the Gospel which Jesus preached, the success of Christianity is not fully explained by the principle of adaptation. Klausner maintains that Paul, though unconsciously and unintentionally, "made his Christianity acceptable to the minds of the best of the pagan world". [270] But, we would ask, was the Gospel which Paul preached really *acceptable* to the pagan world? Furthermore, were those who received it the best of the Gentiles? Perhaps part of the answer lies in Klausner's admission that Paul "took from the Jewish Messianic idea its universalistic side, and ignored—consciously or unconsciously—its politico-national side". [271] That Paul's behaviour, however, was conditioned by a reconciliatory policy towards the Roman authorities we would strongly repudiate. Klausner himself admits that the two aspects of the Messiah, the "politico-national" and the "universalistic-spiritual", existed side by side in the minds of the Jewish people. [272] If Paul was to preach to the Gentile world at all his choice was already predetermined, without any ulterior motives to decide. Only a Gospel unhampered by nationalistic ambitions and broad enough to include mankind could break down racial prejudice and make room for the Christian Church. Herein lay the strength of Christianity and the weakness of Judaism. [273]

(c) Israel's election

Jacques Maritain, in his fine small book on anti-Semitism, refers to Israel as a *corpus mysticum*. He holds that "the bond which unifies Israel is not simply the bond of flesh and blood, or that of an ethico-historical community; it is a sacred and supra-historical bond, of promise and yearning rather than of possession." [274] This is Israel's election viewed from the Christian point of view. The Jewish view is somewhat different.

The Jewish religious consciousness is deeply aware of Israel's election; "*atah behartanu*" [275] is to the Jew more than a pious phrase. It expresses faith in Israel's unique significance and mission to the world. Israel's election precedes the creation of the world and extends for everlasting. [276] This belief, which Schechter calls "an unformulated dogma", [277] for it is not contained in Maimonides' creed, is of basic importance for Jewish religious thought. Faith in Israel's election has determined the Synagogue's attitude to the Gentile world and was an important

factor in the Pauline controversy. Its foundation is the Old
Testament. Passages like Deut. 14. 2, "For thou art an holy
people unto the Lord thy God, and the Lord hath chosen thee to
be a peculiar people unto himself, above all the nations that are
upon the earth",[278] have naturally lent themselves to an interpretation in the sense of *unconditional* election. It is for this reason
that God is first and foremost the God of Israel: *ejn ani nikra elohe
kol ha-ummot ella elohe Yisrael* (I am not called the God of all the
nations, but the God of Israel). [279]   Israel's future is dependent
on this supreme fact. It is on the strength of this that we are
told, "All Israel will have a share in the world to come". For
Is. 60. 21 says: "They shall all be righteous." [280]   It is, however,
important to observe that such a certainty does not entirely rest
upon Israel's own merits, but rather upon God's gracious dealing
with his people. George Foot Moore remarks on this passage:
"A lot in the World to Come is ultimately assured to every
Israelite on the ground of the original election of the people by
the free grace of God, prompted not by its merits, collective or
individual, but solely by God's love, a love that began with the
Fathers." [281]   Here we must note an important deviation from
the Christian conception of election.

To the Church, election applies to the *individual*. It is only
because the Church consists of elected members from *all* races
that the Church claims election for herself. The Church as a
body is elect in as much as its members believe themselves to have
been called by God. This is not so in the Synagogue. It is not
in the first place the individual Jew who claims for himself election: it is the *people*, the *keneset Yisrael* (congregation of Israel),
whom God has chosen for an eternal heritage. Israel is, as it
were, the repository of God's grace, and the individual partakes of
it only by virtue of belonging to the community. Even the bad
individual has thus still a share in the united effort of the whole
people. "What the community does or as the community as a
whole acts can affect for good or for evil the individuals of whom
the community is composed. . . . The unity of the community
is a unity which is an advantage to its evil members." [282]   God's
dealing is primarily with the congregation of Israel, and through
the congregation with the individual Jew. This is not, however,
a denial of individual providence; it simply emphasizes the
collective and social aspect of election over against the individual.
"It must be remembered", says Montefiore, "that the com-

munity of Israel, and even each local congregation, were more important to the Rabbis, and, as they believed, more important even to God, than any individual Israelite. The Rabbis never abandoned the 'collective' point of view of the Old Testament, even though they had also adopted and intensified the later individualism. The community of Israel (*kelal Israel*) forms a sort of real, if mystical, personality. It is because the community is known to, and loved by, God, that God knows and loves each individual who composes it." [283] There is much truth in J. Abelson's opinion that Judaism is, as he calls it, an "amalgam of a Jeremiah and an Ezekiel" [284]: both elements, that of communal adherence to the religious traditions and also individual piety, are present. But there can be no doubt that the Synagogue's traditional emphasis is upon the collective side of religion. This fact is of far-reaching consequences. The collective aspect of Judaism counteracts the Christian conception of *personal* salvation, and also places the Synagogue in a different position from the rest of humanity. We will now turn to the more recent restatements of the doctrine of Israel's election.

It is the firm belief of the Synagogue that God's dealing with Israel is not merely an example, as is the Christian view, of His dealing with mankind. [285] Israel's history is essentially on a different plane. There are, as it were, two histories: the history of the Jewish people and the history of the rest of mankind. Such a view is born out of the conviction of Israel's unique mission to the world. Judah Halevi expressed it in the following words: "God has a secret and wise design concerning us, which should be compared to the wisdom hidden in the seed which falls into the ground, where it undergoes an external transformation into earth, water and dirt, without leaving a trace for him who looks down upon it." The seed, however, which thus disappears, produces a tree which bears fruit; so also Israel. [286] Israel's supreme mission is to stand as a witness to monotheism. Ziegler, referring to the determined Jewish opposition to Paul, asks the question, would it ever have come to a trinitarian doctrine had the Jews been less adamant towards the Apostle? Ziegler's answer is that there was no other solution, no compromise would have satisfied Christianity; to yield to the Gentile Church would have meant the end of the Jewish people, and therefore also of monotheism. [287] Providence had endowed Judaism, at a moment of great peril, with leaders whose only aim in life became "*the preservation of the religion by means of the nation*".[288]   It was for this higher purpose that the Synagogue had made use of religion to preserve Jewish identity. This is a constant Jewish plea.

Ziegler himself admits that the tenacious holding to the Law on the part of the Jews was prompted not only by religious but also by national motives.[289]   It is for this reason that H. Loewe insists upon the importance of the ceremonial side of Jewish life: "It prevents the disappearance of Judaism in its environment . . . the discipline of the Torah is so powerful a shield that it could be laid aside only at grave risk." [290]   The religious fence which Judaism has built up between itself and the world was a measure of self-protection. Its purpose was, and still is, to maintain "its individuality in the midst both of a hostile and a friendly world".[291]   To the Synagogue both are of equal danger; the one uses force and the other enticement to destroy Israel's separate existence. Bousset has clearly recognized the national significance of religion in Judaism; he calls it "the most important means for preserving the peculiarity of Jewish nationhood".[292]

Is such a use of religion justified? From the Jewish point of view it is, and this for two reasons: (1) From the peculiar Jewish conception of history, the ceremonial fence built round the Jewish people has served a purpose and has therefore vindicated itself. For "in history everything which fulfils a definite and required task is necessary; that which accomplishes something, and remains within the domain of the good, is justified." [293]   (2) The maintenance of Israel's separate existence is not an end in itself. The main purpose is the Jewish mission. The law serves as an iron wall to keep Israel separate from the rest of the world, because on his existence depends the existence of monotheism: "Only a full-blooded Jew", says Ziegler, with great emphasis, "is able to be a real monotheist."[294]

Thus the Synagogue makes a unique claim on behalf of the Jewish people. It demands a position which places Israel outside the wider circle of humanity. The Jewish people occupies a place to itself, by virtue of its election. No fusion is possible between Israel and the rest of mankind. He must remain what he is, "something non-recurring, unique, to be classified under no species, to be arranged under no category".[295]   To Buber, Israel is neither a nation nor a religion, in the usual sense of the words; he constitutes "a unity of Faith and Nationhood which is unique".[296]   It is this indivisible unity between nationhood

(*Volkheit*) and faith which closes the circle round Israel and keeps him apart from the nations. The outsider can only join, but not really enter into Israel's election.[297]   Schoeps accepts Judah Halevi's opinion that Israel's election is "*spermatically circumscribed*".[298]   Kaufmann Kohler's liberal view is not much different. He explains the difference between Judaism and Christianity, that while one can *become* a Christian, one has to be *born* a Jew. It is possible to cut oneself loose from Church membership, but "the Jew is born into it and cannot extricate himself from it even by the renunciation of his faith".   The original German is even more explicit: "In Judaism the community of race to that extent forms the basis of the community of faith that even the disbelieving Jew still remains a member of Jewry." [299]   Leo Baeck takes a similar view.   He claims that both the peculiarity and the difference which distinguishes Israel from all the other nations "rests on a clear and permanent possession".[300]   Franz Rosenzweig, however, has gone to the full length, and with indeflectible logic has built up a *racial* theology.   His weighty book, *Der Stern der Erlösung*, is based on the idea of Israel's mystical blood-relationship.   This, according to Rosenzweig, differentiates between the Jewish and all the other peoples: "The nations of the world cannot rely entirely on blood-relationship; they drive their roots into the night of the dead yet live-spending soil. . . . We alone trust to blood. . . ." [301]   In Rosenzweig's racial theology the Jewish people is assigned a place of self-sufficiency which borders on apotheosis.[302]   It lives by its *own* salvation; it partakes of eternity ("*Es hat sich* (i.e. *das Volk*) *die Ewigkeit vorweggenommen*"); its growth is accomplished; it has reached its goal; it stands "beyond the antithesis of peculiarity (Eigenart) and world history, Fatherland and Faith, Earth and Heaven".[303] Augustine's concept of unity between *fides* and *salus*, which is still the dream of the nations, has already been attained by Israel.[304]   Herein lies for Rosenzweig the difference between Judaism and Christianity.   It is essentially a difference of direction: "Christian life leads the Christian outside himself". Christianity is outside him: "He is never a Christian, though Christianity is". [305]   Christianity *denationalizes* the believer; but "Jewish (life) leads the Jew deeper into his Jewish nature (Art)".   It is here that the essential cleavage between the two faiths reveals itself: the greatest difference between the Jew and the Christian, says Rosenzweig, is in that the Christian "is genetically or at least by reason of birth a Gentile but the Jew a Jew".[306]

Against this attitude the whole Christian assault breaks down. The Gospel has nothing to offer. The fact that a man belongs to Israel is already good news in itself. While the heathen becomes a son of God by adoption (υἱοθεσία), the Jew is already a son by birth.[307] He stands in an everlasting covenant with God because he is a son of Abraham: "Abraham, the ancestor, and the individual (Jew) only in Abraham's loins has heard the call of God and answered it with his 'here am I'. From now on the individual is born a Jew and needs therefore no more to become one in some decisive moment of his individual life." [308]

It is obvious from this that the whole Christian conception of salvation falls to the ground. For the Jew there can be no personally acquired salvation. He already partakes in it by reason of his birth. Salvation is consequently limited to the national restoration of Israel. There is profound significance in the fact that to Judaism the Messiah is primarily a national hero.[309] "Regeneration" in the Christian sense is foreign to the Synagogue. The Jewish word for παλιγγενεσία is teshubah; the erring Jew needs only to return to the forsaken position. Rosenzweig rightly explains that for the Jew "Regeneration is not something personal but the transformation of his people to the freedom of the Covenant of God's revelation. The people and the individual in it, not he personally as such, has thus experienced his second birth." [310] The real meaning of St. Paul's struggle appears in all its significance at this point of our discussion. G. Foot Moore remarks that Paul and the Church had substituted for the Jewish national election "individual election to eternal life, without regard to race or station".[311] It may be doubted whether this was a Pauline substitution, as a tendency towards individualism is already present in the Old Testament. But it fell to the Apostle to draw the last consequences from the prophetic teaching.[312] The profound difference between Paul and the Synagogue ultimately turned round the question of the meaning of "Jew". To Paul, a Jew is not defined by race and tradition, but by the moral qualities which link him spiritually with Abraham: a *true* Jew, one can only be ἐν τῷ κρυπτῷ (Rom. 2. 28f.).[313] Israel to Paul is not defined in terms of race or colour, but faith. In Christ Jesus, the Gentiles are Abraham's seed and heirs of the promise (Gal. 3. 29). Here all national limitations are broken down the

New Israel knows of no differences and admits no prerogatives. Before God all men stand in *equal* need and therefore have equal rights.

The whole Pauline attitude towards the Law must be viewed from the angle of human equality before God. The Synagogue accepted a graduation of standards which was unbearable to the Apostle. There were Israelites, full proselytes, semi-proselytes, and God-fearers. Their status was dependent upon the degree of adherence to the Mosaic Law as interpreted by the Rabbis. Such a classification presupposed a scale of merits according to which God's attitude to man was determined.[314] This view ran contrary to the Gospel message, which proclaimed the good news of God's free grace revealed in the Messiah. Before the Cross not only the heathen stranger but also the pious Jew stood condemned and in need of pardon. It is for this reason that the Cross was to the Jew an offence. The complete levelling down of Jew and Gentile was an outrageous act of insolence in the eyes of the Synagogue. There can be no equality between the Chosen People and the pagans. Israel is pledged to the Law, the nations are not. While it is enough, therefore, for a Gentile to keep the seven commandments of Noah, it is incumbent upon a Jew to keep the *whole* Law. From Paul's position of equality, such a situation was intolerable. If the Law is necessary for salvation, then it must be the *whole* Law for *all* men; or else no Law for anyone. The manifesto of the Kingdom of God consisted for St. Paul in the announcement of *free* grace for *all* men through faith in the Messiah. Not even Israel could enter the Kingdom *cum privilegio*. It is not enough to be a son of Abraham in order to be a son of God.

It is important to note that this new and revolutionary conception of election is a recurring principle in the pronouncement of Jesus himself. "The first shall be last, and the last first" is the motto of his Kingdom.

(d) *Israel and the Church*

By God's providence the majority of the Jewish people were destined to live in the midst of Christendom. The Church and the Synagogue have been facing each other for nearly 2,000 years. They both constituted a challenge to each other. They both claimed the same privileges, lived by the same hope, worshipped in their own way the same God. Moreover, both have claimed to be Israel, the chosen people, the people of God. While Israel, however, has violently disputed the right of the Church, strange as it may seem, the Church has never disputed the right of the Jew. What is Israel to the Church?

(i) THE CHRISTIAN VIEW CONCERNING ISRAEL

The Christian view concerning Israel has been moulded by the Bible; especially by St. Paul's Epistle to the Romans. However individual Christians may have behaved towards the Jewish people, the Church, at least in her doctrinal aspect, has never denied to the Jew the right to election. She could not do so in view of the Bible. Rom. 9–11 has been deeply imprinted upon the mind of Christianity.[315]   Israel was and remained an important witness to God's revelation. The facts that Jesus Christ was a Jew, that the Church first took root upon Jewish soil, and that the historical background of the Bible is the people of Israel, have deeply penetrated the Christian consciousness. St. Paul's words acknowledging Israel's unique position the Church has accepted without demur: They are Israelites, theirs is the adoption, and the glory, and the covenants, and the giving of the Law, and the service of God, and the promises (Rom. 9. 4). Israel's obdurate refusal to accept the Messiah is a mystery to the Church which she cannot explain. But Israel's ultimate restoration, though not an article of faith, is yet a constituent part of the Church's hope. The Church knows herself incomplete without the Jewish people.[316]

Does the Church then accept the claims the Synagogue makes on her own behalf? We think the answer is definitely no. The significance the Church attaches to the Jews over and above any other people is not occasioned by what the Jews are in themselves, but by what God is. The faithfulness of God the Church does not call in question: God's gifts are without repentance (Rom. 11. 29). Blindness in part has fallen on Israel, but this is not God's final word. God's purposes are never defeated and his triumph is the last. It is because the Church clings to the God of Israel that she also clings to Israel. Israel in himself, however, stands not outside, but within the family of nations. God's dealing with the Jewish people reveals his dealing with man. The sole advantage the Church concedes to the Jew is that of *primus inter pares*. All that happens in history can only happen consecutively—this is the meaning of time. The Jew,

therefore, stands *first*, but he does not stand *alone*. The beautiful
collect for Good Friday in the Anglican Prayer Book admirably
expresses the Christian attitude to the Jewish people. There the
Church prays for the Jews, the Turks, and the Infidels. The
Jew stands amongst the Turks and the Infidels, but he stands
first. His is the first claim upon the Christian Church, though
they all stand together. And for all of them the Church prays,
"fetch them home, blessed Lord, to thy flock".[317] For obvious
reasons, however, the Church is specially concerned with the
Jews.[318] Without them, as Charue has beautifully put it, "so
long as the Chosen Nation has not been integrated into the
Church, the Church remains mutilated, as though one of its best
limbs had been cut off". And he adds in hope and faith: "This
hour will strike and when the fullness of the Gentiles and the
fullness of the Jews have thus come, the final resurrection will
usher in the true era of the Kingdom."[319]

(ii) THE JEWISH VIEW CONCERNING THE CHURCH

The Synagogue's attitude to the Church in some respects widely
differs from the Christian attitude to the Synagogue. Judaism,
however, has in recent years undergone a profound change in its
attitude to Christianity, and we shall have to take full account of
this change.

Traditional Judaism looked upon Christianity as it looked upon
Mohammedanism, as an error. We have already observed elsewhere that in some measure Jewish criticism of Christianity was
justified.[320] From the beginning the Christian attitude to Jesus
Christ raised grave doubts on the part of the Synagogue. Trypho
already accused the Christians of worshipping a man.[321] Apart
from this the Christian attitude to the Law confirmed the Jewish
view that Christianity is a terrible delusion, worse than paganism.[322] Characteristically enough, Justin is told by Trypho:
"it were better for you still to abide in the philosophy of Plato
. . . cultivating endurance, self-control, and moderation, rather
than to be deceived by false words. . . . For if you remain in
that mode of philosophy, and live blamelessly, a hope of a better
destiny were left to you; but when you have forsaken God, and
reposed confidence in man, what safety still awaits you?"[323]
The righteous heathen stands a better chance to inherit '*olam
ha-ba* than the Christian. This view is interesting as it confirms
the Rabbinic opinion concerning the righteous Gentile.[324] It

is only natural that the claims of the Church appeared to the Jew preposterous. The Church was usurping Israel's privileges and lawlessly entering upon his heritage. The levelling down of the essential difference between Jew and Gentile was an attack upon the Synagogue's prerogative and was violently opposed.[325] We have, however, seen that in later centuries an attempt was made to interpret Christianity, as well as Mohammedanism, in a more positive sense. Both were looked upon as a preparation of the way for Israel's Messiah.

This was the position till recently. In the last years an important change has taken place. Schoeps explains the *novum* in the history of the Jewish-Christian controversy as the result of the modern conception of relativity. For the first time it has been acknowledged on both sides that truth is subjective, and that Judaism and Christianity can be fully understood only from the *inside*. This led to what Schoeps calls "reciprocal recognition".[326]

In the past the controversy between Church and Synagogue was marked by mutual condemnation. Since the controversy between Franz Rosenzweig and the Christian professor of the history of Law, Eugen Rosenstock,[327] there has taken place an important development. On the Jewish side the subjective and objective truth of Christianity has been fully acknowledged. This became possible not only thanks to the recognition that an outsider is unable to fathom the ultimate truth of his opponent, but also because of the characteristic Jewish conception of history.[328] Schoeps explains: "It is the Jewish opinion that in view of the *reality* of historical events Christianity and its revelation must be regarded as the God-effected (*Gottgewirktheit*) way of salvation for the Gentile world outside Israel." This view, though not *halakah* in the traditional sense, is since Rosenzweig and Buber increasingly becoming a *minhag*.[329] "We regard Christianity", says Buber, "as something of which the mystery of its coming upon the Gentile world we cannot penetrate." [330] It is, therefore, incumbent upon the thinking Jew to take Christianity seriously, and though he cannot see its significance for the Jewish people, he must acknowledge its profound meaning for the Gentiles. The Jew takes this view in recognition of the historical significance of Christianity and also out of respect for the faith of the non-Jew.[331] Schoeps is therefore prepared to recognize both the Old Testament and New Testament as God's word directed towards humanity. He is the same God who speaks in both, and what he says is the *same* truth; but his *mode* of revelation is *different* (unterschiedlich).[332] He spoke to the Jew at Sinai and to the Gentile in Jesus Christ. The word spoken to Israel is not for the Gentiles and the word meant for the Gentiles is not for Israel. Rosenzweig thus says: "As regards the significance of Christ and his Church in the world we are agreed: Nobody comes to the Father but through him. Nobody *comes* to the Father—it is different, however, for the one who needs no more to come to the Father because he *is* already with him." And this is the case with Israel (though not with the individual Jew).[333] For the Gentile, the way to God is only through Jesus Christ; it is the way of faith and regeneration in the Holy Spirit. The Jewish way is a different one: "The people of Israel is spared the round-about way of faith." [334] Israel walks "without a Mediator" in the light of God's Countenance.[335] There can be no New Covenant for the Jew, for the Israelite "is thanks to his physiology already *in the Covenant*". Both Church and Israel, though walking different ways, move towards the same goal. Torah and Gospel (*Evangelium*) relate facts of sanctified history "in which transcendent reality became real".[336] Both testify to God's dealing with humanity. But Israel's destiny is to walk his *own* way. The Church calls it unbelief and looks upon Israel as rejected by God, but Israel knows that he is not rejected.[337] His lonely path is not obduracy, but faithfulness.[338]

(iii) THE JEWISH AND THE CHRISTIAN MISSION

The recognition of the unique position in which Israel finds himself bears directly upon the understanding of his missionary task in the world. The logical conclusion of the essential difference between the Jew and the Gentile puts an end to all proselytizing. Judaism is not for the Gentiles. Baeck consequently explains: "Judaism, however much it is a universalistic religion, universalistic both in vision and will," is yet tied to the Jewish people in a way which makes it impossible to become a universal religion.[339] Montefiore, we have noticed, regards this as the weakest point in Rabbinic Judaism.[340] But this is not the general view of Jewish writers. They rather see in Israel's peculiar position a source of strength. Baeck explains that exclusiveness is only the other side of universalism, that "only a people which felt its own individuality in its soul could feel what its importance was to be for others".[341] Israel's mission is not to convert the world to Judaism, but to be *himself*. As Ben-Chorin put it: "Israel's mission rightly understood is an existential one. Only by way of going inwards can we recruit outwardly." [342] Rosenzweig has carefully explained the Jewish position: he compares Christianity to an everlasting way which demands continual expansion. Missionary activity is the Christian form of self-preservation. The case with the Jew is different: "He who was begotten a Jew affirms (*bezeugt*) his faith by continuing to beget the everlasting nation. He does not believe on something, he is himself faith." [343] While the Jew has already reached the goal, the Christian is still on the march. [344] He is the "everlasting beginner" [345] who in hating the Jew hates his own incompleteness. [346] Christian life, therefore, leads *outward* (*nach Aussen*), Jewish life leads inward (*nach Innen*). [347]

Judaism, as understood by modern Jews, is therefore not a missionary religion in the proper sense. [348] The Noachidic movement, which is connected with the names of Rabbi Elie Benamozegh, professor of theology at the Leghorn Rabbinical Seminary, and the French proselyte Aimé Pallière, is not an attempt at proselytizing. Its aim is to help the Gentiles to lead a righteous life by keeping the seven Noachian Commandments. [349] The Noachide does not even join the Community of Israel; he only adheres to the main principles of morality founded upon monotheism. There is no need for him to walk the Jewish way; he *remains* an outsider.

There are thus two ways to God: the Jewish way for the Jewish people *only*, and the non-Jewish way for the nations of the world. This does not mean a denial of the universalistic outlook on the part of the Synagogue. Schoeps points out: "It only means that Judaism confesses a *universal* God and a *universal* will of God as well as a universal goal for mankind, but it cannot go *its* way through history as a missionary religion." And Schoeps gives the reason why Israel's way *must* be different: "for the sake of the Covenant between the one God and the one People which at the end of time will be joined by one humanity". [350] As the people of revelation (*das Volk der Offenbarung*) [351] Israel is destined to walk apart from the rest of mankind.

The significance of the new attitude lies in the fact that Christianity is not ruled out as a fatal error, as was the case in the past. It is emphatically affirmed that Jesus Christ is God's revelation to the Gentiles, but not to the Jews. Sholem Asch has given dramatic expression to the modern Jewish view in his great book on Jesus. "This Rabbi's doctrine", explains Nicodemon to his sorely tried disciple, Judah Ish-Kariot, "is good and great for those who are born without the spirit, or for such as would deny the spirit. But we that are born in the spirit . . . how shall *we* be born again without denying the spirit? For the people of the world, for those who are born only in the flesh and not in the spirit, he has been sent to bring them close to our father in heaven. . . . He has been appointed the prophet of the nations." [352] It may be noted that Trypho already accepted the doctrine of the *double* way. He says to Justin: "Let him be recognized as Lord and Christ and God, as the Scriptures declare, by you Gentiles. . . . But we who are servants of God that made this same (Christ) do not require to confess or worship him." [353] These words may be compared with H. Loewe's remark to the effect that "the world needs both the Church and the Synagogue"—it is wrong to affirm that Jesus had none of the Holy Spirit, but as far as the Jew is concerned, there is no need for him to go outside his faith "in order to supplement his own religion".[354] The famous story about the two rings admirably illustrates the Jewish position.[355] Martin Buber has defined it with masterly precision: "God's doors are open for all. In order to come to God the Christian need not go through Judaism nor the Jew through Christianity." [356]

The Synagogue's contention, therefore, is that the Church should recognize the peculiar Jewish position and refrain from missionary work amongst the Jewish people. Judaism, on the other hand, is prepared to leave to the Christian Church the missionary task amongst the nations,[357] in the conviction that both ways ultimately lead to the same goal, namely the Father of mankind. Israel's mission is thus to be himself; the mission of the Church is to convert the nations. It is on these grounds that Jewish writers object to the missionary activity of the Church in so far as it is directed towards the Jewish people. It is argued that the acceptance of Christianity will have a disintegrating influence upon Jewish life and will thus interfere with the fulfilment of Israel's historic mission. "Jesus is the extra grain in the composition of Judaism which radically changes its whole nature." [358] S. S. Cohon argues that "to tear away a person from the religion of his people to which he is linked with all the fibres of his being, both physical and psychical, amounts to cutting him off from the source of life and idealism." [359]

Kaufmann Kohler declares that "in the opinion of unbiased observers" great harm is done by those who endeavour "to uproot the faith of a race admired for its steadfast loyalty".[360]   The nature of the argument, in its theological significance, however, appears in Franz Rosenzweig's explanation that: "anchorage in its deepest self" is the secret of the Everlasting People.[361]   Israel fulfils his mission by his existence.   His vocation is to remain true to himself.[362]

(iv) THE EVERLASTING DIVISION

It is the Jewish contention that no religion can claim absoluteness.   "Judaism", says Kohler, "denies emphatically the right of Christianity, or any other religion, to arrogate to itself the title of 'absolute religion'."[363]   S. S. Cohon in his article on Christian missions argues that there must be more than one way "in which the human heart can reach out after the Holy One".[364] The truth, says Schoeps, is *one* truth, but the mode of human perception differs.   He is the *same* God who manifested himself to both Jews and Christians: "according to *the* aspect which God revealed to Israel at Sinai and to the world on Golgotha".[365] Edwyn Bevan, replying to Cohon's article, argues that the Jew cannot "consistently base his plea for 'tolerance' on the ground that Judaism and Christianity are equally good religions, Judaism for Jews and Christianity for Gentiles"; for if Christianity is not true "it must be a grievous spiritual harm to Christians that they should hold it".[366]   This argument is based on the premise that there is equality between the Jew and Gentile; what is therefore harmful to the one is also harmful to the other.   But the Jewish position, as represented by Rosenzweig, Buber, Schoeps, and others, does not admit such a supposition.[367]   Israel claims to be pledged by an eternal Covenant to God, but this is not the case with the Gentile world.   His loyalty to the Torah demands that Israel goes his own way.   God's dealing with the Jews is different from his dealing with mankind.   It is not that "truth" is denied to Christianity, but that it is not *Jewish* truth.

Can the Church accept such a duality?   Can there be two ways of salvation, one for the Jew and one for the Gentiles?   Is the word spoken on Golgotha essentially a word to the Gentiles and not to Israel?   Can the historical fact of Israel's refusal be construed as God's will and not as human guilt?

An answer to these questions the Church finds not in herself, and not in Israel, and certainly not in history, but by listening to her Lord. Ben-Chorin has rightly recognized that the command to the Church to go to all the world (Mt. 28. 19), and specially to the lost sheep of the house of Israel (Mt. 10. 6), makes it incumbent upon the Christian to preach the Gospel to both Jews and Gentiles. To neglect this duty is to betray the message, which means to betray the Master.[368] It is thus for the sake of her own loyalty, for the sake of her life and her hope, that the Church must deny any *difference* between the Jew and the Gentile.

God is no respecter of persons. Before Him, the Holy One, men stand not as *Jews* and Gentiles but as sinners who are in need of grace. Jesus the prophet may be speaking to the Gentiles; but Jesus the Son of God speaks to mankind. Jesus the martyr may be *appealing* to some and not to others; but Jesus the Lamb of God challenges the whole human race. God's word is *one* word, and God's way is *one* if it is *the* way of God.

Thus, Church and Synagogue face each other; between them stands Jesus Christ. The Synagogue's no and the Church's yes, is not no and yes to each other, but no and yes to Jesus of Nazareth, the Son of God. The Synagogue's theology and Israel's national position are both conditioned by the Jewish attitude to Jesus Christ. The Jewish conceptions about God, Man, Sin, the Messiah and Revelation, and Israel's unique claim, are not only the cause but also the result of the opposition to the Christian view.[369] Buber rightly brings down the difference between Church and Synagogue to the central point—the Messiah: "The Church stands upon the Faith of the advent of Christ as a result of which the salvation of God has been imparted to mankind. We of Israel are unable to believe it." [370] To the Church, however, Israel's unbelief is not part of his election but part of his humanity. It is not *Israel's* unbelief but human unbelief. The fact that it is *Israel* who disbelieves, stands as an everlasting warning before the eyes of the Church.[371] In Israel she sees her *own* faithlessness and unbelief.[372] In her prayer for the Jew she prays for herself. Inasmuch as the Church claims to be Israel, the prophetic words, "You only have I known of all the families of the earth, therefore will I visit upon you all your iniquities",[373] are as much applicable to the Christian as to the Jewish situation. In our common humanity, in our common failure, in our common faithlessness to God the Jew and the Christian, though standing apart, yet stand together.

The line which divides the Church from the Synagogue is not a horizontal but a vertical line.

As historical entities, between Church and Synagogue there is no *essential* difference. They both fall under the category of religion. Both express the same human cry for God and the same need of forgiveness and grace. Their difference is rather due to historic contingency than to elemental principle. In different modes they both express the same basic truth: finite man in quest of eternity. On the religious plane, therefore, whatever features distinguish the Church from the Synagogue, these are only of an accidental nature. There is no horizontal line to draw a clear-cut division. Church and Synagogue intersect and touch at many points.[374] The segregation into "Jews" and "Christians" is not spiritually but historically conditioned. Many a Jew could have lived his religion in the Church and many a Christian in the Synagogue.[375]

The *vertical* line dividing the Church from the Synagogue is *faith*. In the last resort neither Judaism nor Christianity can be adequately defined in terms of history. A person is not a Jew or a Christian in the true sense of the word by merely following the example of his parents, but by the acquisition of the habit of mind which is characteristically Jewish or Christian.[376] In both cases it is the expression of an *attitude* rather than a tradition. The Jewish or the Christian *attitude* can neither be the result of history nor of race, but entirely depends upon the personal response to Jesus Christ. Christian theology is the result of faith in Jesus of Nazareth, the Son of God. Jewish theology is the negation of that faith. The dividing line is not between Jews and Gentiles in the racial sense, but between men who accept and men who reject the Christian claim. The division between Jews and Christians on a historical basis is thus fictitious. There is only one division: between the man who in his *actual*, existential situation says yes and the man who in his *actual*, existential situation says no to the challenge which Jesus Christ presents.

Trattner closes his book with the following words: "The intelligent Jew enjoys the Jesus of the Synoptics; the Churches adore the Christ of the Fourth Gospel. And so the grand division goes on between the brethren of Jesus and his followers." To the Church, however, the division which separates Christianity from Judaism is only part of the division which separates the Church from the world. It is the division between faith which knows and unbelief which also knows.

NOTES TO CHAPTER I

1. Quoted from a small tract by E. S. Greenbaum, *What Modern Jews think of Christ*, London, 1926.

2. The initial letters of these three words make ישו —the traditional Rabbinic spelling of the name of Jesus; cf. Ch. II, n. 288.

3. Quoted by Lindeskog, p. 27.

4. This generally accepted fact has been contested by a few modern writers: cf. Klausner, *Jesus of Nazareth*, p. 233. One of the first to advocate the Aryan descent of Jesus was Houston Stewart Chamberlain (*The Foundations of the Nineteenth Century*, Engl. 1910); Emil Jung's book, *Die Abstammung Jesu im Lichte freier Forschung* (Engl. *The Ancestry of Jesus*, 1933), is a pseudo-scientific attempt to present Jesus to racially minded Germans.

5. Mt. 9. 20; 14. 36; 23. 5, suggest that the "border" of the garment were the traditional ציצית prescribed by the Law (cf. Num. 15. 38 ff., Deut. 22. 12); LXX transl. ציצית with τὸ κράσπεδον. For the Rabbinic interpretation of the rite, see M. Friedländer, *The Jewish Religion*, p. 329; A. Edersheim, *Life and Times*, I, p. 277, n. 1; Oesterley and Box, *Religion and Worship of the Synagogue*, pp. 450 ff.; Klausner, *Jesus*, p. 364, n. 7.

6. Lk. 23. 27.

7. Cf. pp. 42 ff.; 163 ff.

8. Cp., however, H. Kosmala, *The Jew in the Christian World*, pp. 47 ff.

9. Cf. Leon Simon, *Studies in Jewish Nationalism*, London, 1920, pp. 12 ff.

10. Cf. Lindeskog, pp. 96 ff.

11. Cf. Lindeskog, p. 250; cp. pp. 323 f.

12. Cf. *In Spirit and in Truth*, p. 275.

13. Cf. Klausner, *From Jesus to Paul*, p. 117; cf. Ignaz Ziegler, *Der Kampf zwischen Judentum und Christentum*, p. 58.

14. *Vide infra*, pp. 203, 321 f.

NOTES TO CHAPTER II

1. Cf. Leo Baeck, *The Essence of Judaism*, p. 4.

2. Herbert Loewe, *J. E.*, art. "Judaism"; also *Judaism and Christianity*, I. p. 155; cf. also Israel Abrahams' valuable little book, *Judaism*, pp. 23 ff.

3. Joseph Bonsirven, *On the Ruins of the Temple*, p. 106.

4. Cf. S. Schechter, *Studies in Judaism*, I, pp. 179 ff.

5. Cp. pp. 235 ff.   6. Cf. Bonsirven, p. 70.

7. Cf. *Kitab al Khazari*, IV. 10 and 11.

8. Cf. *Mishneh Torah*, Kings 11. 4; also *Responsa* (ed. Leipzig), § 58; cf. also *Jud. and Christianity*, II, pp. 233 ff. and notes.

9. C. G. Montefiore, *In Spirit and in Truth*, p. 330.

10. Rabbi J. Gould, *Jewish Chronicle*, Jan. 16, 1942; cf. the correspondence in the same paper concerning Jewish attendance of Christian Services, Nov. 28, 1941, and subsequent numbers; but cf. Friedländer, *The Jewish Religion*, p. 313, where עכום is expressly not applied to Christians.

11. F. Ch. Ewald, *Abodah Sarah*, p. xxv.

12. Cf. Nachmanides, *Derashah*, 5; Judah ha-Levi, *Khazari*, IV. 11.

13. Cf. R. Isaac of Troki, *Chizzuk Emunah*, I. 49 and 50.

14. *A Manual of Christian Evidences*, I, p. 231.

15. Cf. *Jud. and Christ.*, II, pp. 206 ff.

16. Cf. Jastrow, *in loc.*; cp. also Danby, *Mishnah*, p. 796.

17. Cf. Joseph S. Bloch, *Israel und die Völker*, pp. 50–64; 77–97; Gösta Lindeskog, p. 18; Montefiore, however, admits: "It is difficult to say precisely what the Rabbis thought of Christians. Did they fall under class I (*i.e.* worshippers of idols), or 2 (*i.e.* enemies of Israel), or 3 (*i.e.* heretics and sceptics and deniers of the perfection and immutability of the Law)? I do not know" (*Rabbinic Anthology*, p. xxxi); cp. also Kosmala, *Intern. Rev. of Miss.*, July, 1941, pp. 380 ff.

18. Cf. Lindeskog, pp. 310 ff.; Ignaz Ziegler, *Der Kampf zwischen Judentum und Christentum*, p. 73 f.

19. Cf. Klausner, *Jesus of Nazareth*, pp. 46 f.

20. *The Conflicts of the Early Church*, pp. 55 f.

21. *The Martyrdom of Jesus of Nazareth*; Rabbi Wise goes so far as to deny the historicity of the Crucifixion altogether. For this he finds support in Acts, where it is said that Jesus was hanged on a tree, and also in the fact that the Basilidians denied that Jesus was ever crucified (*ibid.*, pp. 108 f.).

22. Adolph Danziger, *Jewish Forerunners*, p. 46.

23. Montefiore, *Synoptic Gospels* (1909), p. 346; cf. Klausner, *Jesus*, pp. 340 ff.

24. Montefiore, *S. G.*, p. 363; he accepts Loisy's extreme view of an anti-Jewish and pro-Roman bias, cf. *ibid.*, p. 355.

25. John 11. 48.   26. So Klausner, *Jesus*, pp. 152 f.

27. *Ibid.*, p. 168; cf. *ibid.*, p. 336.

28. I. M. Wise, *The Martyrdom of Jesus*, p. 30.

29. Montefiore, *S. G.*, p. 382.

30. Cf. Lindeskog, p. 150, n. 3; p. 267, n. 3.

31. Cf. Leszynsky, *Die Sadduzäer*, p. 280.   32. *Ibid.*, p. 286.

33. Cf. D. Chwolson, *Das letzte Passamahl*, whose whole construction is based on the controversy between the Pharisees and the Sadducees as to the interpretation of the phrase ממחרת השבת in Lev. 23. 11, 15, 16, etc.

34. Leszynsky, pp. 61 and 302.   35. *Ibid.*, pp. 295 ff.   36. *Ibid.*, p. 297.

37. *Ibid.*, 280; there is undoubtedly an apologetic reason why Jewish investigation is mainly devoted to Pharisaism (cf. Lindeskog, p. 143). Paul Goodman writes: "The political and religious views of the Sadducees have no living interest to modern Judaism, except as an example to be avoided" (*The Synagogue and the Church*, p. 242).

38. Cf. *Studies in Pharisaism*, I, p. 16.   39. Cf. Klausner, *Jesus*, p. 222.

40. *Das letzte Passamahl*, p. 86.   41. *Ibid.*, p. 98.   42. *Ibid.*, p. 125.

43. An extreme example of prejudice is the book by Giovanni Rosadi, *The Trial of Jesus*. Thanks to Jewish criticism there is a definite turn in the opposite direction, cf. Principal Curtis' warm appreciation of Pharisaic ideals in his recent book *Jesus Christ the Teacher*, pp. 26 f.; for a rediscussion of the trial of Jesus, see Karl Ludwig Schmidt, *Der Todesprozess des Messias Jesus*, Judaica, Heft 1, März 1945.

44. *Jesus, Paul and the Jews*, p. 53.   45. *Ibid.*, pp. 92 f.
46. *Jud. and Christ.*, 1, p. 159.   47. *Jesus*, p. 222.
48. Klausner, *Jesus*, p. 335.   49. Montefiore, *S. G.*, p. 462.
50. Cf. Gerald Friedlander, *Hellenism and Christianity*, p. 49.
51. Klausner, pp. 125 f. Streeter's date for Luke is "not later than
A.D. 85, more likely about A.D. 80". He puts Mark at about A.D. 65, and
Matthew at about A.D. 85 (cf. *The Four Gospels*, pp. 485 f., 529). "Proto-
Luke" in Streeter's view is as early as Mark itself, "a conclusion of considerable
moment to the historian" (*ibid.*, p. 200).
52. S. Schechter, *Documents of Jewish Sectaries*, 1, p. xxi, note; the reference
is to Geiger's hypothesis in his book, *Urschrift und Übersetzungen der Bibel in ihrer
Abhängigkeit von der inneren Entwickelung des Jundentums*, Breslau, 1857, according
to which Pharisaism went through two definite stages of development. In an
older period it showed important connexions with Sadduceeism, traces of
which are still left in the *Mechilta*, *Sifre*, and the *Jerusalem Targum*. The second
period is characterized by a complete breach with the views of the opposing
party. Geiger has thus endeavoured to show the existence of an older and a
younger Halachah. Elsewhere Geiger observes: "Der immer in den Hinter-
grund gedrängte Sadducäismus erhielt sich jedoch kümmerlich in einer
Richtung, welche sich oppositionell der Einwirkung der Geschichte verschloss,
nämlich im Samaritanismus, und er verjüngte sich später in einer Opposition,
welche sich dem überwuchernden Pharisäismus entgegenstellte, und zwar im
Karaismus" (*Sadducäer u. Pharisäer*, Breslau, 1863, p. 6); for a survey of the
controversy provoked by Schechter's book, see Bentwich, *S. Schechter*, pp. 263 ff.
53. Leszynsky, p. 302.
54. Cf. *Studies in Pharisaism*, 1, pp. 12, 135; cf. also A. T. Robertson, *The
Pharisees and Jesus*, pp. 4 ff.
55. But even Friedländer holds that Jesus' opposition was not directed
against the observance of "hergebrachter religiöser Bräuche . . . sondern
gegen den Missbrauch, den eine den Markt beherrschende und heuchlerische
Klasse von Pharisäern mit denselben trieb" (*Die Relig. Beweg.*, p. 320).
56. Klausner, *Jesus*, p. 215.   57. *Studies in Pharisaism*, 1, p. 87.
58. *The Teaching of Jesus*, p. 37; Gerald Friedlander goes so far as to deny
such a possibility. In his opinion, "Mr. Montefiore has not only erred in
making this admission, but also in limiting his criticism to the single case of
Luke's parable" (*The Jewish Sources of the Sermon on the Mount*, p. 36); cf.,
however, W. A. Curtis, *op. cit.*, pp. 42 ff.
59. Cf. *Jud. and Christ.*, 1, p. 171
60. Lindeskog, p. 149; the whole paragraph is important, pp. 144–150;
cf. also pp. 272 ff.; Loewe argues that if the description of Pharisaism as
found in the Gospels were correct, "the system must have died out" (*Jud. and
Christ.*, 1, p. 179). A similar argument is brought forth by Parkes (cp. *Jesus,
Paul and the Jews*, p. 66). But survival in itself is no proof of greatness.
61. Cf. Klausner, *Jesus*, pp. 277 ff.; cp. also Trattner, p. 108; the writer,
however, holds that Jesus was so close to Pharisaism that the exact nature of
Pharisaic opposition is difficult to state.
62. Chowlson, in concluding his study, arrives at eleven points, ten of
which bear directly upon the relationship between Jesus and the Pharisees:
    (1) The teaching of Jesus is in no way opposed to Pharisaic teaching.

(2) In principle, there is no difference between Jesus and the Pharisees in respect to the religious customs and ceremonies.

(3) Jesus was only opposed to certain Pharisaic views which have been rejected by Judaism and have been left unrecorded by tradition.

(4) Jesus was opposed not to Pharisaism itself, but only to the corruption of the same (Auswüchse).

(5) Jesus was opposed only to those Pharisees who "aus übertriebener Kirchlichkeit" became a menace to true religion. The Rabbis did the same.

(6) Jesus, like the Rabbis, used exceedingly strong language against the *false* Pharisees.

(7) At that time the Sanhedrin was entirely ruled by the Sadducees, the Pharisees being in a minority.

(8) According to Pharisaic principles, Jesus neither said nor did anything deserving capital punishment.

(9) The procedure of the trial contradicts the rules laid down by the Rabbis.

(10) The Pharisees appear as the defenders of Christians in the trial of the Apostles, of Paul, and in the case of the martyrdom of James (cf. *op. cit.*, pp. 120 f.).

63. R. Travers Herford, *Pharisaism, its Aim and its Method*, London, 1912; *The Pharisees*, London, 1924.

64. A. T. Robertson, *The Pharisees and Jesus*, London, 1920.

65. *Jesus, Paul and the Jews*, p. 55; cp. Charue, *L'Incrédulité des Juifs*, pp. 73, 78, 81.

66. *Ibid.*, p. 72; cf. Lindeskog, p. 274 f.

67. Cf. Hugh M. Scott's art. on "the Pharisees" in *Hast. Dic. of Christ and the Gospels*, II, pp. 351 ff.; especially § 3.

68. Cf. Paul Goodman, *The Synagogue and the Church*, pp. 281 f.; Klausner, *op. cit.*, pp. 373 f.

69. Jewish scholars have protested against the equation of "Torah" with "Law". They rightly point out that Torah comprises more than the legal aspect of Judaism (cf. Loewe, *In Spirit and in Truth*, pp. 231 f.; S. Schechter, *Some Aspects of Rabbinic Theology*, pp. 117, 127; cf. also Herford, *Jud. and Christ.*, III, p. 94). We are, therefore, using the word bearing in mind its wider connotation.

70. *The Teaching of Jesus*, p. 44.   71. Klausner, *op. cit.*, p. 291.

72. Klausner, p. 368; cf. also Geiger, *Sadducäer und Pharisäer*, pp. 31 f.

73. Cf. Lindeskog, p. 250; cf. also C. J. Cadoux, *The London Quarterly and Holborn Review*, July, 1935, pp. 306 ff.

74. Cf. *Studies in Pharisaism*, I, pp. 131 ff.   75. *Ibid.*, pp. 134 f.

76. Klausner, *Jesus*, p. 369; this admission brings the discussion regarding the connection between Jesus and Paul in line with the more positive Christian view (cf. Branscomb, *Jesus and the Law of Moses*, pp. 278 f.; T. W. Manson, *Jud. and Christ.*, III, pp. 131 ff.; J. Gresham Machen, *The Origin of Paul's Religion*, pp. 117 ff.).

77. Klausner, *op. cit.*, p. 374; contrasting Jesus with Paul, Klausner says: "Ethical extremism is an outstanding characteristic of the teaching of Jesus . . . ethical compromise and adaptation to reality go hand in hand with

extremism in religious belief" in the teaching of Paul. (*From Jesus to Paul*, p. 431.)

78. Herford, *Pharisaism* (1912), p. 146.

79. Cf. H. Loewe, *Jud. and Christ.*, I, p. 161.

80. Klausner, *Jesus*, p. 255.

81. Branscomb, *Jesus and the Law*, p. 265.

82. *Ibid.*, p. 174.   83. *Ibid.*, p. 264.   84. *Ibid.*, p. 268.

85. T. W. Manson, *Jud. and Christ.*, III, pp. 129 f.

86. τίς σοι τὴν ἐξουσίαν ταύτην ἔδωκεν. Cf. Mk. 11. 28 ff.; Mt. 21. 23 ff.; Lk. 20. 1 ff. Elsewhere Prof. T. W. Manson explains the conflict between Jesus and the Pharisees as a "conflict between the prophetic spirit and the legal". The opposition springs from two different conceptions of virtue: "For Jesus, good living is the spontaneous activity of a transformed character; for the Scribes and Pharisees, it is the obedience to a discipline imposed from without" (*The Teaching of Jesus*, pp. 295, 300). This view, however, overlooks the objective authority of the Law as it appeared both to Jesus and the Pharisees.

87. *Jud. and Christ.*, III, p. 131.

88. Cf. Prof. W. Manson's recent book, *Jesus the Messiah*, pp. 106 ff.

89. *S. G.* (1909), p. 92.

90. Cf. Lk. 17. 21; we accept ἐντὸς ὑμῶν to mean ἐν μεσῷ ὑμῶν; Montefiore, however, follows Loisy's suggestion, substituting ἔσται for ἔστιν, as ἐροῦσιν is future. The sense would then be, "but suddenly will the Kingdom appear and be among you" (cf. *S. G.* (1909), pp. 1014 f.).

91. Cf. *S. G.*, pp. 99 f.

92. Constantin Brunner (Leopold Wertheimer), *Unser Christus, oder das Wesen des Genies*, Berlin, 1921, pp. 98 ff.; 382 and throughout.

93. It is important to note that Klausner admits the existence of an ancient view according to which the ceremonial laws will be abrogated in the Messianic Age (cf. *From Jesus to Paul*, p. 321, n. 13).

94. Streeter, *Four Gospels*, p. 256.

95. Cf. Montefiore, *S. G.* (1909), pp. 487 ff.

96. Streeter, *op. cit.*, p. 256.

97. Streeter, however, explains the presence of Mt. 11. 13 by the theory of two contradictory sources, Q and M.

98. Montefiore, *S. G.*, p. 487; the attitude of the early Church concerning the Law is well expressed by Tertullian in his treatise *De Oratione*: "For everything that had been in the past, was either changed, as, for example, Circumcision, or completed, as the rest of the Law, or fulfilled, like prophecy, or brought to perfection, as faith itself" (A. Souter's transl.).

99. Strack-Billerbeck, I, p. 241.

100. Cf. Mt. 3. 15; cf. Fr. Vincent McNab, *Jud. and Christ.*, III, pp. 212 ff. Thomas Aquinas has thus given expression to a view universally held by the Church.

101. *S. G.*, pp. 487 ff.   102. *Ibid.*, p. 494.

103. Harnack is inclined to regard Mt. as more original, but he significantly adds: "Aber für ihn (*i.e.* Lukas) spricht, dass die Stellung der Sätze bei ihm natürlicher als bei Matth. ist." He asks: "Entscheidet das?" (*Sprücheund Reden Jesu*, p. 16.)

104. For the difficulty connected with βιάζειν see Dalman, *The Words of Jesus*, pp. 139 ff.

105. Cf. Prof. W. Manson, *Jesus the Messiah*, pp. 80–82.

106. Harnack's remarks concerning Stephen's attitude to the Law and the Temple are important: "Stephanus hat", says Harnack, "nicht wider den Temple und das Gesetz gesprochen, um ihren göttlichen Ursprung zu bestreiten, sondern er hat die begrenzte Dauer dieser Einrichtungen behauptet" (*Mission*, p. 35). We feel convinced that the view concerning the Law the early Church derived from Jesus himself.

107. Prof. T. W. Manson, like most modern scholars, finds it inconceivable that the same person, while showing the greatest respect for the Law (cf. Mt. 5. 17, 19 f.), and even for the oral tradition (cf. Mt. 23. 1 f.), could at the same time display by far the greatest animus against the Scribes and the Pharisees (*The Teaching of Jesus*, p. 36). But surely we ought to be able to distinguish between theory and practice. Jesus had nothing against Pharisaic teaching, in so far as it was in accordance with the spirit of the Scriptures; he castigates their deeds!

108. Cf. W. O. E. Oesterley, "Judaism in the Days of Christ" (*The Parting of the Roads*, p. 100).

109. *S. G.*, p. 490.

110. As an example of such misunderstanding we would quote Bertram Lee Woolf, *The Authority of Jesus and its Foundation*, London, 1929, p. 261: "Jesus found essential only what was truly ethical, having to do with the inner self in its immediate relation with God. All the rest He treated as relatively indifferent."

110[a]. Cf. *Aus frühchristl. Zeit*, p. 219.

111. Cf. Lindeskog, pp. 217 ff.

112. Abraham Geiger, *Das Judentum und seine Geschichte*, Breslau, 1864, pp. 111 f.

113. *The Synagogue and the Church*, pp. 271 f.

114. *S. G.* (1927), 1, p. cxxxv; Montefiore, however, clearly recognizes the originality and the superiority of Jesus over the Rabbis, cf. *The Religious Teaching of Jesus*, pp. 55 ff.; *Origin and Growth of Religion*, p. 551, note.

115. *S. G.*, p. cxli. f.; cf. *Religious Teaching of Jesus*, pp. 85 f.

116. *S. G.*, p. civ. 117. *Rabbinic Literature and Gospel Teachings*, 1930, p. 85.

118. *The Old Testament and After*, p. 241. 119. *S. G.* (1927), 1, p. cxxxv.

120. *The Old Testament and After*, p. 286.

121. "Jesus' view was, 'unless you become as little children', it was a kindergarten teaching, needed for a kindergarten class. The Rabbis did not wish this to be given to those who had grown older, and had passed to a higher stage" (Montefiore, *Rabbinic Literature and the Gospel Teachings*, pp. 205, 379).

122. Ignaz Ziegler, *Der Kampf zwischen Judentum und Christentum*, p. 22; cf. I. M. Wise, *The Martyrdom of Jesus*, p. 30; cf. also Chwolson, *op. cit.*, p. 87.

123. Ziegler, pp. 25 f.

124. Klausner holds Herod to have made a claim to Messiahship and that the "Herodians" were those who upheld such claim. Klausner finds an allusion to Herod's false Messiahship in the Sibylline Oracles (cf. *From Jesus to Paul*, p. 145). Ziegler's view would therefore derive some probability from Klausner's theory.

125. Klausner, *Jesus*, p. 255; cf. also *ibid.*, pp. 264–272.

126. *Op. cit.*, p. 335.

127. Dr. G. Hollmann, *The Jewish Religion in the Time of Jesus*, pp. 129 f.; cf. also Hugh Scott's article in *Hast. Dict. of Christ and Gospels*, II, pp. 351 ff.

128. Parkes, *Jesus, Paul and the Jews*, p. 21.

129. *Ibid.*, p. 72.　　　　130. *Ibid.*, p. 78.

131. *Ibid.*, p. 88.　　　　132. *Op. cit.*, p. 95.

133. Montefiore, *Rabb. Anthol.*, p. xx; cf. *The Old Testament and After*, p. 166; cf. also Gerald Friedländer, *Hellenism and Christianity*, p. 82.

134. Cf. Louis I. Finkelstein, *The Pharisees*, 2 vols., Philadelphia, 1938.

135. Cf. *In Spirit and in Truth*, pp. 302 f.

136. Vladimir G. Simkhovitch, *Toward the Understanding of Jesus*, p. 41; We include Prof. Simkhovitch amongst Jewish writers, on Lindeskog's authority (cf. his bibliography).

137. *Ibid.*, p. 56.　　　　138. *Ibid.*, p. 60.

139. *Ibid.*, p. 75.　　　　140. *Ibid.*, pp. 71, 73.

141. Cf. Adolf Schlatter, *Die Geschichte Israels*, p. 262; Parkes, *Jesus, Paul and the Jews*, p. 67.

142. Cf. *Studies in Pharisaism*, I, p. 27.

143. Cf. Josephus, *Antiq.*, XVII. 11. 4.

144. Cf. F. Foakes-Jackson, *Josephus and the Jews*, p. 264. Foakes-Jackson suggests two factions within the Pharisaic party; a nationalist, and a "Herodian" group; cf. *ibid.*, p. 33.

145. Cf. Klausner, *Jesus*, p. 373.

146. *The Pharisees*, p. 33; for social divisions cf. *ibid.*, p. 344.

147. Cf. *Jud. and Christ.*, I, pp. 122 ff.

148. James Moffatt, *The Approach to the New Testament*, Hibbert Lectures, 1921, pp. 34 f.

149. *Jesus the Messiah*, p. 85.　　150. *Ibid.*, pp. 89–93.　　151. *Ibid.*, p. 153.

152. W. A. Curtis, *Jesus Christ the Teacher*, p. 168; cf. p. 205.

153. Cp. B. H. Streeter, *The Four Gospels*, p. 292.

154. Adolf Schweitzer, *Geschichte der Leben-Jesu-Forschung*, Tübingen, 1921, p. 4; "So fand jede folgende Epoche der Theologie ihre Gedanken in Jesus, und anders konnte sie ihn nicht beleben." "Und nicht nur die Epochen fanden sich in ihm wieder: jeder einzelne schuf ihn nach seiner eigenen Persönlichkeit." Cp. also Montefiore, *The Teaching of Jesus*, p. 122. Montefiore thinks that the great diversity of views is partly due to the fragmentary nature of our sources.

155. E. Hermann, *Eucken and Bergson*, p. 117.

156. Lindeskog, pp. 251 f.

157. Cp. Montefiore, *S. G.* (1909), p. cxxii; Klausner, pp. 237, 251–257.

158. Montefiore, *The Teaching of Jesus*, p. 120.　　159. *Ibid.*, p. 161.

160. *Ibid.*, pp. 124 f. Cp. also Montefiore's commentary on the Messianic passages in his *Synoptic Gospels*.

161. Montefiore, *The Teaching of Jesus*, p. 161.

162. Klausner, pp. 256 f. This is also Chwolson's view, cp. Chwolson, *Das Letzte Passamahl Christi*, p. 91, n. 2.

163. H. Loewe, *Jud. and Christ.*, I, p. 161; cp. also pp. 164 f.

164. Montefiore, *S. G.* (1909), p. 105.

165. J. K. Mozley, *The Heart of the Gospel*, London, 1925, pp. 172 f.

166. H. P. Chajes, *Markus-Studien*, 1899, p. 11. Klausner does not actually accept the suggestion, but thinks it is worth noting (Klausner, pp. 264 f.). Abrahams is opposed to it, and prefers A. Wünsche's suggestion that ὡς ἐξουσίαν ἔχων points to the Rabbinic idiom מפי הגבורה (Abrahams, I, pp. 13 f.). Both S. Schechter and Montefiore accept the phrase as authentic. Schechter connects it with *Ben Sira* 3, 10 (S. Schechter, *Studies in Judaism*, 2nd series, 123), but cf. T. W. Manson, *The Teaching of Jesus*, p. 106, n. 1. Montefiore's remark is noteworthy: "His teaching is fresher and more instinct with genius than that of the Rabbis, of whose teaching we have records in *Talmud* and *Midrash*. It is more inspired. It is grander. It is more prophetic. It seems to claim 'authority', just as the prophets claimed it, because they were convinced that their words were from God. Such a consciousness of inspiration Jesus also must have possessed " (Montefiore, *S. G.*, 1909, p. 555).

167. S. Schechter, *Studies in Judaism*, 2nd Series, p. 117.

168. Montefiore, *S. G.* (1909) p. 499. Montefiore resorts to the usual method, not that Schechter is wrong, but that the antithesis is added by a later hand in the passages where Schechter's explanation is inapplicable.

169. Montefiore, *The Teaching of Jesus*, p. 124.

170. "Les Pharisiens avaient tenu, pendant le siècle et demi qui précède notre ère, un rôle utile, et parfois glorieux", but "même au temps du Christ, si beaucoup n'étaient plus que le vinaigre d'un vin généreux, les epigones d'une race héroïque, une imposante minorité n'avait pas péché contre la lumière" (André Charue, *L'Incrédulité des Juifs dans le Nouveau Testament*, Gembloux, 1929, p. 23).

171. D. Chwolson, *Das letzte Passamahl Christi*, p. 87. The most recent effort to explain the death of Jesus was made by Solomon Zeitlin in his book, *Who crucified Jesus?* Zeitlin is driven to assume the existence of two Sanhedrins: one, independent and entirely concerned with the religious life of the people; the other, political, a tool in the hands of the Romans and concerned with legal questions and the relationship to the Roman Empire. It was the latter, in complicity with Pilate, which became guilty of the death of Jesus. The theory of two distinct Synhedria was propagated by Büchler, *Das Synhedrium in Jerusalem*, 1902. Abrahams is prepared to accept the view; cp. Abrahams, *Studies in Pharisaism*, I. p. 9.

172. J. Gresham Machen, *The Origin of Paul's Religion*, p. 15.

173. Cp. *op. cit.*, p. 88.   174. H. Loewe, *Jud. and Christ.*, I, p. 187.

175. Dr. Parkes, though not a Jewish Rabbi, but strangely adverse to "theological ophthalmology", whatever that may mean, apparently disputes Barth's right to discuss Pharisaism; a privilege reserved for the historian only (!) (cp. *Jesus, Paul and the Jews*, p. 19).

176. Mt. 21. 28–32.

177. οἱ πτωχοὶ τῷ πνεύματι, עניי הרוח, are the *anawim* of Is. 61. 1.

178. Montefiore, *S. G.* (1909) p. 87.

179. Rom. 3. 9 ff. Such a statement, however, runs contrary to modern Jewish sentiment.

179ª. For a discussion on the charge of blasphemy, see Schoeps, *Aus frühchristl. Zeit*, p. 292.

180. Prof. W. Manson enumerates five important points in connection with the claims of Jesus; cp. *Jesus the Messiah*, p. 98.

181. Cp. Lee Woolf, *The Authority of Jesus*, pp. 260 ff.

182. Cp. A. Taylor Innes, *The Trial of Jesus*, a legal monograph, Edinburgh, 1905, p. 43.

183. Simkhovitch, p. 81.

184. Cp. Lindeskog, pp. 275 f. Schoeps is a notable exception. Cf. *Aus frühchristl. Zeit*, p. 219.

185. Lee Woolf, *op. cit.*, p. 216.

186. It is characteristic of Dr. Lee Woolf's presentation that he describes Jesus as "a mighty soul at one with God" (*op. cit.*, p. 242). An identical expression is used by R. T. Herford! (Cf. *Jesus Christ*, London, 1901, a two-penny tract.) Dr. Lee Woolf's attitude to the question of Messiahship is the result of a complete neglect of the Old Testament as a background for Jesus' life and ministry. (On the importance of the O.T., see E. C. Hoskyns, "Jesus the Messiah", *Mysterium Christi*, 1930, pp. 69–89, a collection of essays edited by G. K. A. Bell and Adolf Deissmann; cf. also W. Manson, *Jesus the Messiah*, p. 48).

187. Dr. Lee Woolf, *op. cit.*, p. 215: "(Jesus) was not Messiah prior to and apart from this task. If He had not undertaken this special work, if He had not answered this divine call to service, He would not have been Messiah at all. The function gave the title and not the title the function".

188. Cp. W. Bousset, *Kyrios Christos*, Göttingen, 1921, p. 100; *Jesus der Herr*, Göttingen, 1916, pp. 30 ff.; *Kyrios Christos*, Göttingen, 1921, p. 260: "Die Frage, ob und wie weit das genuine (bezw. auch das Gnostisch bestimmte) Judenchristentum sich auf den Boden des Kyrioskultes der hellenistischen Gemeinden gestellt habe, muss aus Mangel an allen genaueren Quellen unbeantwortet bleiben" (cp. also n. 2).

189. Gustaf Dalman, *The Words of Jesus*, p. 326.

190. Cp. J. Gresham Machen, *The Origin of Paul's Religion*, pp. 293 ff.

191. John Reid explains that to Jewish Christians Jesus was known as the "Messiah", to Jews of Hellenistic origin, Jesus was "the Christ", but to the Gentile Christian, he was "the Lord" (*Dict. of Chr. and the Gospels*, II, p. 56a). But cp. Machen, *ibid.*, pp. 300 ff.

192. Cp. Parkes, *Jesus, Paul and the Jews*, pp. 124 f.; Oesterley: "the distinguishing feature of the Hellenistic faction was its presentation of Judaism as a religion of Hope, while to the orthodox party Judaism was, above all things, a religion of Law" (*The Parting of the Roads*, p. 87). Whether this was so, we cannot tell; to what extent Hellenistic Judaism had departed from the Palestinian point of view is a matter of controversy. Klausner's view appears to be indefinite. On the one hand, he assumes that Hellenized Judaism of the Alexandrian type "produced an eclectic system" which was "unacceptable to original Judaism" but favourable to early Christianity (*From Jesus to Paul*, p. 14); on the other hand, he disputes Moriz Friedländer's opinion that Judaism of the Diaspora was more liberal in its outlook (*ibid.*, pp. 27 f.). How the orthodox Jewish Diaspora could form a bridge to Pauline Christianity (*ibid.*, p. 25) Klausner does not explain.

193. Cf. G. F. Moore, *Judaism*, I, pp. 243 f. Cf. now Schoeps, *Aus frühchristl. Zeit*, pp. 144 ff.

194. Cp. *Yoma* 9a—for parallel passages and other explanations, cp. Strack-Billerbeck, I, 366, 882, 937; II, 253; IV, 205. Schoeps gives a different interpretation; cf. *op. cit.*, p. 151.

195. Cp. my article in *Der Weg*, Nr. 3, Warsaw, May/June, 1938—The cause of the destruction of the Second Temple (Yiddish).

196. Dr. Rabbi Ignaz Ziegler, *Der Kampf zwischen Judentum und Christentum*, pp. 52 f.

197. *Ibid.*, p. 56; cp. also pp. 73 f.

198. Rabbi Ziegler often prints with fat, big letters, statements whose historical accuracy is questionable. This emphatic presentation cannot make up for the lack of evidence. We are thus told with every possible emphasis the art of printing can provide: "dass das Judentum und seine Vertreter, gegen Jesus persönlich vorzugehen keinerlei Ursache hatten und es tatsächlich auch nicht taten. In dem Augenblicke aber, in welchem Paulus die Befreiung vom Gesetze, von der Beschneidung u. den Speise Gesetzen, aussprach, entbrannte sofort der Kampf . . ." (*ibid.*, pp. 73 f.). What evidence is there in support of such a dictum?

199. Israel Abrahams, *Studies in Pharisaism*, II, pp. 56 ff.

200. Cp. Harnack, *Die Mission*, pp. 40 f.

201. Norman Bentwich, in an essay on Philo-Judaeus (*Aspects of Hebrew Genius*, ed. by Leon Simon, London, 1910), refers to Hebrew Christianity as a section of the Jewish people "which separated itself from the general body of the community and formed the Christian Church, which, starting as a heresy from Judaism, became more and more hostile to the parent body" (*ibid.*, pp. 20 f.). Such a presentation of facts is not historically accurate. There is evidence to prove that the Jews who believed Jesus to be the Messiah *persisted* in remaining within the Jewish community. Only under great pressure did they leave the Synagogue. Reflexion upon the unforeseen results of the Synagogue's intolerance may perhaps have found expression in the words of an old *Baraita*: Let thy left hand ever repel and thy right hand invite. Not like Elisha who repelled Gehazi with both hands, nor like R. Yehoshua ben Perachya who repelled Yeshu (the Nazarene) with both hands (*Sanh.*, 107b; cp. Klausner, pp. 24 ff.).

202. Cp. pp. 235–239.

203. Cp. Chwolson, *op. cit.*, pp. 104 ff. But it is probable that in the case of Rabbi Jehudah Hakadosh, the compiler of the Mishnah (*c.* 135–220), the Min represents a shade of Hebrew Christianity closely related to Judaism. It seems to us that Chwolson is trying to prove too much. This, as other instances, must be balanced by the passages which manifestly reveal a spirit of hostility.

204. For Rabbinic references, see Strack-Billerbeck, IV, pp. 332 f.

205. *pal. T. Shab.* 13. 5. For further parallels see Strack-Billerbeck, III, p. 11. Strack refutes Bacher's suggestion that גליונים here refer to Euangellion (cp. Bacher, *Tann.*, II, p. 258). The Talmudic rule is:

הגיליונים וספרי המינים אינן מטמאות את הידים

(*Shab.* 116a), which Strack understands to mean that the books of the Minim are to be treated like the *giljonim*, to which applies the injunction that they be burned. The Rabbis have cacophemistically altered the word εὐαγγέλιον to mean אָן גליון (Strack: "*Unheilsrolle*"; Jastrov: "falsehood of blank paper") or עֵן גליון ("scroll of sin"). The word גליון (plur. גליונים) itself is according to George Foot Moore: a blank leaf, or margin, before, after or on the sides of a volume (roll) (so also Strack; cp. also W. Bacher, "Le mot 'Minim' dans le Talmud", *Revue des Études Juives*, 38, p. 40). But Rashi remarks:

רבי מאיר קרי לספרי המינים און גיליון לפישהם קורין את אותן אונגילא

(Ewald, *Ab. Zarah*, p. 121). Bacher, therefore, accepts the view that ספרי מינים are not the books of heretics as Friedländer takes it, but simply "des copies de la Bible faites par les Minim, qui servaient à leur usage". But this rule does not apply to *Hagiga* 15b and *Sanh.* 100b (cp. *op. cit.*, p. 42).

206. *Chul.* 13a: R. Eliezer (A.D. 90) said that he who eats the bread of a Samaritan is as if he ate pork.

207. *pal. T. Chul.* 2, 20 f.

208. *Jewish Studies in memory of Israel Abrahams*, New York, 1927, p. 210. Herford uses the example of the earth and the moon to illustrate the relationship between Judaism and Christianity: "Judaism continued to move on in the same direction as it had formerly done; Christianity, from its point of origin, moved in a quite different direction". "The moon began to move in a new orbit, at first not far removed from that of the earth, but in course of time diverging further and further from it" (p. 213). Such a picture belies the laws of physics. But H. guards himself against the inadequacy of the example. As a matter of fact, Judaism was as vitally affected by the appearance of Christianity as the earth was by the appearance of the moon (cf. Montefiore, *The Old Testament and After*, pp. 164 ff.).

209. *Op. cit.*, p. 211.

210. Moore, *Judaism*, III, n. 110.

211. R. Travers Herford, *Christianity in Talmud and Midrash*, pp. 200 ff.; cf. also p. 122.

212. *Tractate Berakot*, 7a. A. Cohen's excellent translation and notes Cambridge, 1921; cf. *infra* p. 185.

213. Cp. W. O. E. Oesterley and G. H. Box, *A short survey of the Literature of Rabb. and Med. Judaism*, London, 1920, p. 118; Bacher, *Paläst. Amoräer*, II, pp. 552 ff.

214. Cp. Bacher, *Agada der Amoräer* I, 555 f.; also *Midrash Rabbah*, Gen. 8. 9 (transl. by Rabbi Dr. H. Freedman, London, 1939). Cp. also *Midrash Rabbah* to Gen. 1. 1—where the plural is explained as referring to God consulting the Torah; and *Sanh.* 38b—where, on the authority of R. Johanan, it is explained that the plural signifies that The Holy One, blessed be He, does nothing without consulting His heavenly Court (lit. "family", פמליא).

215. Minim once asked Rabban Gamaliel "whence do we know that the Holy One, blessed be He, will resurrect the dead?" He answered: "from the Torah, the Prophets and the Hagiographa". But they refused to accept his proofs (*Sanh.* 90b). Herford rightly points out that this is not a case of Minim rejecting the doctrine of the Resurrection, but only the warrant for this doctrine in Scripture. Herford takes them to be Christians for whom the Resurrection of the dead "was subsequent on the resurrection of Christ" (cf. *Christianity in Tal. and Midrash*, pp. 231 ff.).

216. A. Mishcon suggests that this might have been in lieu of an honorarium for his work (a) either as a teacher of the Minim (cp. Herford, pp. 267 f.); (b) or as an assistant-collector of imperial taxes (so Bacher, *Agada d. Paläst. Amor.* II, pp. 96 ff.); (c) or as a scholar (cp. *Babyl. Talmud*, ed. by I. Epstein, *Seder Nezikin*, p. 14, note).

217. *Abodah Zarah*, 4a. A. Mishcon explains that "others" refers to the Rabbis of Babylonia. There Christianity was only known from hearsay.

218. Cp. Bacher, *Agada d. Pal. Amor.*, II, p. 141, note. There are numerous traces of the influence of Christian thought upon Judaism. Referring to *Jalkut, Chukkat* § 764, where Adam is spoken of as having brought death into the world by his fall, Friedländer remarks: "This idea has found its way into the Midrash from Christian sources" (Gerald Friedländer, *Rabbinic Philosophy and Ethics*, London, 1912, p. 236, note).

219. Joël, *Blicke*, p. 36.

220. Cp. Abrahams, *Studies in Pharisaism*, I, p. 9. See also the important note by Schoeps, *Aus frühchristl. Zeit*, p. 166, n. 1.

221. S. Singer's *Annotated Daily Prayer Book*, pp. ci f.

222. Louis Finkelstein, *The Pharisees*, p. 65.

223. Oesterley and Box, *Short Survey of Literature of Rabb. and Med. Jud.*, p. 159. It is interesting to note that to this day the Decalogue is not part of the Synagogue's liturgy.

224. W. L. Knox, in *Jud. and Christ.*, II, pp. 86–88; Knox draws attention to *Antiq.*, III, 5. 4, where Josephus declares it prohibited to repeat the actual words of the Decalogue, presumably implying that they are the words of God Himself.

225. W. L. Knox thinks that such a view is already implied in Stephen's speech, Acts, 7. 38 (?). Cp. *Didascalia*, VI, xvi, 7. The *Apostolical Constitutions*, which in its first part is a mere enlargement of the *Didascalia* (cp. Otto Bardenhewer, *Patrologie*, p. 319) simply say: "Now the Law is the Decalogue, which the Lord promulgated to them with an audible voice, before the people made the calf which represented the Egyptian Apis". But after that event "he bound them for the hardness of their hearts, that by sacrificing, and resting, and purifying themselves, and by similar observances, they might come to the knowledge of God, who ordained these things for them" (VI, IV, 20).

226. The Decalogue contains 620 letters: It was therefore regarded as the "Crown" of the Torah (Crown=כתר=620) which was explained as containing the 613 (תרי״ג) מצוות (of which 365 are prohibitions and 248 positive commandments) plus the 7 Rabbinical commandments (cp. Herbert Loewe, *Jud. and Christ.*, I, p. 111, n. 1; W. L. Knox, *Jud. and Christ.*, II, p. 87, note).

227. This is also Dr. P. P. Levertoff's view; cp. *Liturgy and Worship*, S.P.C.K., 1936, p. 63.

228. The *Shema*, the most important section of the liturgy, is composed of three parts: Deut. 6. 4–9; Deut. 11. 13–21; Num. 15. 37–41. It derives its name from the first word of the first section: *Shema Yisrael*. It is recited three times daily: twice at morning and twice at evening prayer and once at bedtime. In old times, the custom seems to have been to recite the *Shema* twice only, at the beginning and at the end of the day. Cp. Strack-Billerbeck, IV, part I, p. 198.

229. *Berakot*, I, 5.

230. Joël, I, p. 36; *Ber.* 12b: Why was the Parashah of Fringes (Num. 15. 37 ff.) included in the *Shema*? Five reasons are given, one of which is *Minut*. It is then asked: but where is there a reference to *Minut*? The answer is: "after your heart" means heresy; for thus the Scriptures state: "The fool saith in his *heart*, there is no God."

231. H. Loewe holds that "the sectarian motive underlying the choice of extracts accounts for the dropping of the Decalogue in the Synagogue and emphasizing the Shema" (Montefiore and Loewe, *Rabbinic Anthology*, p. 641).

232. For the doxology, see Singer's *Prayer Book*, p. li. For Talmudic references, see Strack-Billerbeck, IV, part I, pp. 194 f.

233. The present writer knows an analogous case. Some of Theophilus Lucky's *Chassidim*, who used to attend faithfully the Synagogue Services, made it a practice, at the end of each prayer, to utter under their breath: בשם ישוע המשיח אדנינו.

234. Cp. *Sotah*, 9, 14; "during the war of Titus", reads according to the Cambridge text "Quietus", who was governor of Judea in A.D. 116 or 117. Danby, *Mishnah*, p. 305, note. Cp. Strack-Billerbeck, IV, p. 406. The traditional day of the translation of the LXX, 8th Tebeth, came to be regarded as an evil day (cp. Strack-Billerbeck, IV, 414). This marks a definite regression from a more liberal position. Schlatter interprets the prohibition as not referring to the language itself, but to Greek literature and rhetoric. Its purpose was not so much revenge on Israel's enemies, as an attempt to sever the ties between Palestine and Hellenistic Judaism, for political reasons (cp. A. Schlatter, *Die Tage Trajans und Hadrians*, pp. 89 ff.).

235. Cp. *Dial.*, Chaps. LXXI, LXXII, LXXIII.

236. Cp. Joël, I, p. 41 f.

237. Cp. A. Schlatter, *Geschichte Israels*, pp. 364 f. For sources concerning Aquila's life, *ibid.*, n. 356.

238. Vallentine's *Jewish Encycl.*, p. 100.

239. Joseph Reider, *ibid.*, p. 99. Theodotion's translation, which was prior to that of Aquila, was really a revision of the LXX but still under its influence; cp. Schlatter, *op. cit.*, p. 364.

240. *The Parting of the Roads*, p. 306.

241. Cf. Fr. Buhl, *Canon and Text of the Old Testament*, 1892, pp. 25 ff.

242. *Ibid.*, p. 28.

243. *Rabbinic Anthology*, p. 161.

244. Quoted from *Rabbinic Anthology*, p. 161.

245. A similar passage is to be found in *Num. R.*, 14, 10: "The Holy One, blessed be He, gave Israel two Torot, the written and the oral. He gave them the written Torah in which are six hundred and thirteen commandments in order to fill them with precepts whereby they could earn merit. He gave them the oral Torah whereby they could be distinguished from the other nations. This was not given in writing, so that the Ishmaelites should not fabricate it as they have done the written Torah and say that they are Israel." Dr. A. Cohen recognizes in this passage a reference to the Christians (cp. *Everyman's Talmud*, pp. 155 f.).

246. S. M. Lehrman, Vallentine's *J. E.*, p. 598.

247. *Berakot*, 28b; English translation by A. Cohen, Cambridge, 1921; the original text reads:

תנו רבנן שמעון הפקולי הסדיר שמונה עשרה ברכות לפני רבן גמליאל על הסדר ביבנה אמר להם רבן גמליאל לחכמים כלום יש אדם שיודע לתקן ברכת המינים עמד שמואל הקטן ותקנה׃

248. A body of men, referred to in Talmudic literature as the spiritual leaders of Judaism during the period from Ezra to Simeon the Just (end of fourth century B.C.).

249. Levine observes in a footnote that under Gamaliel II (*c.* A.D. 90) "the question of excommunication was brought to the fore" (*The Parting of the Roads*, p. 302). But it is not clear whether this stands in any relationship to the Jewish-Christian controversy. Strack-Billerbeck emphasize that the חרם was not used as a means of excluding from the Synagogue till the ninth century (cp. Strack-Billerbeck, IV, p. 331). (Or does Levine, perhaps, refer to the *Birkat ha-Minim?*)   250. Singer's *Prayer Book*, p. lxiv.

251. Cp. Chwolson's *Anhang* to *Das letzte Passamahl Christi*, especially pp. 99 ff.

252. Cp. Montefiore, *Rabbinic Literature and Gospel Teachings*, p. 99.

253. Abrahams, *Pharisaism*, II, pp. 61 f.

254. Singer's *Authorized Prayer Book*, p. 48.   255. Abrahams, *ibid.*, p. lxv.

256. Abrahams says: "The text has been modified again and again, owing to the whims of censors"; cp. also Montefiore, *Rabbinic Literature and Gospel Teachings*, p. 99.

257. S. Krauss, The Jews in the works of the Church Fathers, *Jewish Quarterly Review*, V, pp. 131 f. The Church Fathers in question are: Justin, *Dial.*, Chaps. 16, 96; Origin. *Hom. in Jer.* 18. 2; Epiphanius, *Haer.* 29. 9; Jerome *in Jes.* 2. 18, reads: "Sub nomine Nazaraeorum anathematizant vocabulum Christianum"; and *ibid.*, 49. 7: "Christo sub nomine Nazaraeorum maledicunt"; also *ibid.*, 52. 4: "sub nomine, ut saepe dixi, Nazaraeorum ter die in Christianos congerunt maledicta, etc.". Krauss corrects Schürer's opinion that Epiphanius' phrase ὅτε τὰς εὐχὰς ἐπιτελοῦσιν means "at the conclusion of the prayers" (Schürer, *Geschichte des jüd. Volkes*, II, p. 387), but rather, "while they read the prayers". But cp. Strack-Billerbeck, IV, part I, p. 219.

258. Schechter's text reads:

למשומדים אל תהי תקוה ומלכות זדון מהרה תעקר בימינו, והנוצרים והמינים כרגע יאבדו, ימחו מספר החיים ועם צדיקים אל יכתבו: ברך אתה יה״ מכניע זדים;

Genizah Specimens, Jew. Quarterly Review, X, p. 657.

259. Prof. Dr. Hermann Strack, *Jesus, die Häretiker und die Christen nach den ältesten jüdischen Angaben*, Leipzig, 1910, p. 67. Cp. also Dr. Alexander Marx, "Untersuchungen zum Siddur des Gaon R. Amram," in *Jahrbuch der jüdisch-literarischen Gesellschaft*, V, pp. 341 ff.

260. *Tos. Ber.*, III, 25: "The Eighteen Benedictions which the Majority have ordered correspond to the eighteen times that the Lord is mentioned in the Psalm beginning 'Give to the Lord, O ye Sons of the mighty' (Ps. 29). One combines (the Benediction about) the *Minim* with that about the Pharisees . . ." Canon Lukyn Williams explains re Pharisees: "The word does not occur in either of the two forms of the Shemoneh Esreh, though in the best text of the Babylonian 'the pious' (*hachasidim*) are mentioned in

No. 13", *i.e.* the following benediction. A. Lukyn Williams, *Tractate Berakoth*, S.P.C.K., 1921, p. 43.

261. Dr. Emil Schwaab, *Historische Einführung in das Achtzehngebet*, pp. 124 f.
261ª. Cf., however, Schoeps, *Theologie*, p. 140 and notes.
262. Schwaab, *op. cit.*, pp. 118 ff.
263. Cp. Strack-Billerbeck, IV, pp. 208 ff.   264. Schwaab, p. 123.
265. Strack-Billerbeck, I, pp. 407 f.
266. Cp. Strack-Billerbeck, IV, pp. 208 f.
267. Strack-Billerbeck translate "zwei oder drei Augenblicke", so also Schwaab. Schwaab thinks it impossible that Samuel would have been kept waiting for two or three hours. He also refuses to see anything mysterious in the fact that he forgot the prayer. The reason for it Schwaab explains by the fact that before the insertion of the 12th benediction the 11th was followed by the 13th. He therefore understands the word בסופה "at the end" (*jer. Ber.* v, 3), meaning at the end of the whole Tefilla (*i.e.* after having skipped the *Birkat ha-Minim* altogether and not merely the words מכניע זדים (Schwaab, p. 142). Cp. also Strack-Billerbeck, IV, part I, p. 219.

268. *Ber.* 28b.   269. Joël, *Blicke*, I, pp. 24 f., and note.
270. Cp. Schwaab, p. 155.   271. Chwolson, pp. 99 f., n. 3.
272. Klausner, Abrahams, Strack-Billerbeck, etc.
273. Cp. Bacher, *Tann.*, I, 76 f.; also Derenbourgh, *Histoire de la Palestine*, 1867, pp. 306 ff.
274. Schürer, II, 4th ed., p. 544.   275. Schwaab, p. 149.
276. Schlatter, *Beiträge*, II, 3, p. 18.   277. Schwaab, p. 151.
278. Gustav Hoennicke, *Das Judenchristentum*, pp. 387 f.
279. Schwaab, p. 152.
280. Some hints to the above discussions are contained in Canon Danby's book, *The Jew and Christianity*, London, 1927, pp. 11–13.
281. Cp. Klausner, pp. 35, 38, 42, 46.   282. Klausner, *Jesus*, pp. 18 f.
283. Heinrich Laible, *Jesus Christus in Talmud*, Berlin, 1891, p. 88. (English translation by A. W. Streane, Cambridge, 1893, p. 96.)
284. Klausner, p. 19.   285. Cf. *Ant.*, XVIII, v, 2.   286. Danby, p. 37.
287. *Yeb.* IV, 13: Danby's translation; R. Joshua's definition of a bastard: (The offspring of any union) for which the partakers are liable to death at the hands of the court. Cp. Klausner, pp. 35 f.
288. Klausner explains that ישו is an abbreviated form for ישוע or יהושע He categorically denies the allegation that ישו is a nickname for יהושע and made up of the initials: ימח שמו וזכרו. See Klausner, p. 229 and note. Cp. also Hugh J. Schonfield, *According to the Hebrews*, London, 1937, who thinks that "Jeshu" is a north-Palestinian contraction of Jeshua, where the letter *ayin* was not sounded (p. 221).
289. Cp. Klausner's note on Hebrew Sources, *op. cit.*, p. 18; also G. Dalman's appendix to Laible's *Jesus Christus im Talmud*, Berlin, 1891.
290. Cp. Klausner, pp. 21 ff. For an interpretation of *Stada* see Schoeps, *Aus frühchristl. Zeit*, pp. 240 ff.   291. See Klausner, pp. 22 f.
292. See Klausner, pp. 22 f.   293. *Ibid.*, pp. 23 f.
294. The tradition that Jesus was a sorcerer is very old; there are hints of it already in the Gospels, cp. also Justin, *Dial.*, c. 69.
295. "Yeshu ha-Nozri burned his food in public."

296. R. T. Herford, "Christianity in Jewish Literature", in *Hast. Dict. of Christ and Gospels*, II, pp. 877 f. Cp. also Herford, *Christianity in Talmud and Midrash*; also Klausner, *op. cit.*, pp. 18–47. Klausner denies, however, that Balaam is a pseudonym for Jesus, as it seems on good grounds (cp. Klausner, pp. 32–35).

297. The names of the disciples are given as: Mattai (Matthew), Naqai (Luke, so Krauss), Nezer (pun on Nozrim, Klausner, or Andrew, Krauss), Buni (Nicodemus, cp. *Taan.* 20a ; or John, so Klausner) and Todah (Thaddeus).   298. Klausner, p. 19.

299. Edgar Hennecke, *Handbuch zu den neutestamentlichen Apokryphen*, Tübingen, 1914, p. 71. The whole chapter: "Jesus, Jesu Jünger und das Evangelium im Talmud und verwandten jüdischen Schriften," pp. 47–71, is very useful; for the few references to Jesus in the Zohar and the liturgy of the Synagogue, see A. W. Streane, *Jesus Christ in the Talmud*, etc., 1893.

300. The book was known in Jewish circles under several titles, like *Ma'aseh Talui*, *Ma'aseh do'otho v'et bno*, etc. Wagenseil, *Tela ignea Satanae*, Altdorf, 1681, offers a good Hebrew text, together with a Latin translation. An earlier version of the *Tol'dot* is contained in *Pugio Fidei*, by Raymundus Martinus (1220?–1284?), published in 1278.

301. Samuel Krauss, *Das Leben Jesu nach jüdischen Quellen*, Berlin, 1902.

302. Hugh J. Schonfield, *According to the Hebrews*. A new translation of the Jewish Life of Jesus (the *Tol'dot Jeshu*), with an inquiry into the nature of its sources and special relationship to the lost Gospel according to the Hebrews, London, 1937.

303. Hennecke, *Handbuch*, p. 71: "Die Toledoth sind nur in den niederen Kreisen des Judentums beliebt gewesen."

304. Krauss, p. 172.

305. *Ibid.*, p. 242. Schonfield apparently contradicts this view. He makes out that the author of the Tol'dot has purposely confused Simon Magus, the arch-enemy of the Christian legend, with the person of Jesus. *Ben Stada* of the Talmud, he identifies with Simon the *Stadios*, the Standing One, spoken of in the Clementine Homilies (II, 22) who was only later confused with *Ben Pandera* (cp. Schonfield, p. 120).

306. Krauss has not in mind the present *Yosippon* (first published in the tenth century, see Klausner, p. 52), but an earlier Yosippon, referred to by an Arab writer, Ibn Hazm (d. 1063), and the author of *The Chronicles of Yerachmeel*, but Klausner gives good reasons why this view is untenable (see Klausner, pp. 51 f.).

307. Schonfield, p. 23.   308. Schonfield, pp. 174 f.
309. *Ibid.*, p. 191.   310. *Ibid.*, p. 226.
311. Krauss, p. 246.   312. Schonfield, pp. 30, 219.

313. Klausner, p. 51. For Agobard's evidence to the *Tol'dot Yeshu*, see A. Lukyn Williams, *Adversus Judaeos*, p. 352, § 3. Klausner calls it a "book", but actually it was an epistle addressed to the Emperor Charlemagne, "recapitulating the Canons of Councils and the decrees of Kings, and enumerating at some length the grievous superstitions of Jews in general" (Lukyn Williams, p. 351).

314. Klausner, p. 53.   315. Schonfield, p. 219.
316. Klausner, *op. cit.*, pp. 47–54; for fuller details, see Krauss. Useful

notes and a good summary are contained in Travers Herford's article on "Christ in Jewish Literature," *Hast. Dict. of Christ and the Gospels*, II, p. 878, § II.

317. Travers Herford, *ibid.*, p. 879b.   318. Klausner, p. 48.

319. Nit'l, a corruption of *natalis*.   320. *Jewish Encycl.*, VII, p. 170.

321. S. Krauss, *Jewish Quarterly Review*, V, p. 143 (1893).

322. In fairness to the Jew, it must be admitted that the Church's guilt is immeasurably larger. Canon Danby rightly remarks: "Centuries of Christianity of a kind have made it a Christian instinct to loathe the Jew." The Jews, on the other hand, unable to repay in kind, "retorted in the only way that remained open to them—the rendering of Christianity ridiculous and contemptible within their own circle" (Herbert Danby, *The Jew and Christianity*, pp. 41, 55).

323. Cp. Danby, *op. cit.*, pp. 103 ff.; also Lukyn Williams, *The Doctrines of Modern Judaism considered*, London, 1939, pp. 50 ff.

324. The sentence in italics comes from an article in the American Jewish weekly *Ha-Doar* occasioned by the appearance of Klausner's book: quoted by Danby, *op. cit.*, p. 118.

325 Cf. Aḥad Ha'am's *Essays on Zionism and Judaism*, transl. by L. Simon, pp. 223 ff.

326. Cp. Danby, p. 113; the extent of ignorance concerning Jesus even on the part of a modern Jew is dramatically described by an anonymous Jewish writer; cp. *The Atlantic Monthly*, Feb. 1945, pp. 91 ff.

NOTES TO CHAPTER III

1. James Parkes, *The Conflict of the Church and the Synagogue*, London, 1934, especially pp. 371 ff.

2. Harnack rightly stresses the fact that Paul was not the first missionary to the Gentiles and that he never made such claims. The importance of Paul's influence: "Er hat das Recht der Mission und die Pflicht wirklich begründet, und er hat die Bewegung aus unsicheren Anfängen zur Weltumspannenden Mission erhoben". (*Die Mission*, pp. 33 f., and n. 2; p. 37; cf. also Klausner, *From Jesus to Paul*, p. 343).

3. For the status of Jewish proselytes and their different degrees of attachment to Judaism, see F. C. Porter's article in *Hast. Dict.*, IV, pp. 134 ff.; cf. Harnack, *Die Mission*, p. 37; cf. also Klausner, *From Jesus to Paul*, pp. 34 ff.; pp. 42 f.

4. Cf. Harnack, *op. cit.* p. 37, n. 4; pp. 294 ff.

5. S. C. Gayford, *Hast. Dict.*, I, p. 385a.

6. Gal. 2. 4. Cp. 2 Cor. 11. 26.

7. Machen, *The Origin of Paul's Religion*, p. 105.

8. Cp. pp. 45 ff.; cp. also pp. 155 ff.

9. A. S. Peake, "Paul and the Jewish Christians" (reprinted from *The Bulletin of John Rylands Library*, XIII, Nr. 1, Jan. 1929), pp. 17 f.

10. So Peake; Klausner holds that the Decree does not justify speaking of "food-laws". "James yielded to the Gentiles in the matter of *Terephah*, but not in the matters of *Nebelah* and the eating of blood, both of which were abominable to an Essene and observing Jew like James" (*From Jesus to Paul*, p. 368, n. 18).

11. καί ὅσα μὴ θέλετε ἑαυτοῖς γίνεσθαι ἑτέρῳ μὴ ποιεῖν. D also adds after εὖ πράξετε: φερομενοι ἐν τῷ ἁγίῳ πνεύματι. Cp. Alford's *Greek N.T.* in loc.

12. Cp. E. Nestle, *Introduction to the Textual Criticism of the Greek N.T.* (English translation), p. 232.

13. Gotthold Resch, *Das Aposteldekret nach seinem ausserkanonischen Textgestalt*, 1905.

14. Cp. Nestle, *ibid.*, p. 232.

15. A. v. Harnack, *Beiträge zur Einl. in das N.T., Die Apostelgeschichte,* Leipzig, 1908, pp. 190 f.

16. Harnack changed his mind "trotz vielem Sträuben und nach langer Überlegung". For reasons, see *ibid.*, pp. 193–96.

17. Kirsopp Lake, The Council of Jerusalem described in Acts 15, in *Jewish Studies in memory of I. Abrahams*, p. 253, note.

18. *Jewish Studies in memory of I. Abrahams*, p. 253. But Lake admits that to the Jewish mind there was nothing wrong in "putting 'blood' into the same category with idolatry and forbidden marriages".

19. Cp. Harnack, *Untersuchungen zu den Schriften des Lukas*, Leipzig, 1908, pp. 153 ff., 156. As against Zahn's view that Luke only acted as a copyist, Kirsopp Lake, like Harnack, favours the view that the Decree itself is historically authentic. The fact that Paul makes no reference to it either in Galatians or in 1 Corinthians, signifies that he purposely ignored it. For to accept them "would have been an abnegation of his own claims" (Lake, *op. cit.*, p. 262).

20. Kirsopp Lake, *op. cit.*, p. 262.

21. Cp. *Sanh.* 56b; *Ab. Zara*, 64b; *Gen. R* to 8. 17; *Dt. R* 2 (198b).

22. Cp. Paul Goodman, *The Synagogue and the Church*, pp. 89 ff.

23. Maimonides *H Mel.* 8. 10.

24. Jewish sources differ as to the number of the Commandments and the particular clauses; cp. Strack-Billerbeck, III, pp. 37 f.

25. Peake points out that the Decree did not provide for a situation which arose at Antioch: "Nothing had been said as to the relation in which Jewish Christians stood to the Law" (*Paul and the Jewish Christians*, p. 23). But cp. F. C. Burkitt, *Christian Beginnings*, London, 1924, p. 134: "It was a law regulating the diet and social behaviour that Gentile Christians must adopt if Jewish Christians were to feel free to eat with them."

26. Conrad Henry Moehlman describes the position of the early Church: "The Judaistic Christians desired to convert all Christians to Judaism and all Jews to Christianity. The Peter-James group desired to convert all Jews to a conservative type of Christianity. Paul sought to convert Jews and Gentiles to a liberal Christianity . . ." (*The Christian Jewish Tragedy*, New York, 1933, pp. 189 f.). This is an over-simplification of the case, but describes the position. It is, however, still questionable whether Peter and James differed from Paul in principle. Moehlman's allegation that Paul despised the Law has no foundation.

27. Cf. Klausner, *From Jesus to Paul*, p. 48.

28. Harnack, *Mission*, pp. 31 f., 40 f.; Abrahams, *Studies in Pharisaism*, II, p. 56.

29. Cf. Justin, *Dialogue*, CXXXI; CXVII; Eusebius on Is. 18. 1 f.; Origen *against Celsus*, VI, p. 27; Tertullian, *Ad nationes*, I, 14; see also Harnack, *Mission*, pp. 40 f., n. 3. But Abrahams shows with good reason that some

evidence has no historical basis, as in the case of the *Martyrdom of Polycarp*. Jews could not have been preparing wood and faggots on a day which is stated to be the Great Sabbath (cp. Abrahams, *op. cit.*, II, pp. 67 ff.); there is also no evidence that the Jews were guilty of the Neronian persecution. The fact that Poppaea, Nero's second wife, was friendly towards the Jews (cp. Joseph, *Antiq.*, XX, VIII, 11) is not sufficient ground for such a statement. On the other hand, Prof. W. D. Niven makes an important observation concerning the difference of behaviour between the Jews in Palestine and those in the Diaspora. Whereas in Palestine they were held responsible for public disorder, abroad there was no such restraining influence. "The rousing of mob violence against Christians was therefore vastly easier outside Palestine than in it" (*The Conflicts of the Early Church*, p. 67). Dr. James Parkes takes an opposite view, cp. *Conflict*, Ch. IV, pp. 121–150.

30. Gerald Friedländer, *The Jewish Sources of the Sermon on the Mount*, p. 34.

31. Cp. Ephraim Levine, The Breach between Judaism and Christianity, in *The Parting of the Roads*, p. 296.

32. J. Weiss, *Das Urchristentum*, Göttingen, 1917, p. 123.

33. Cf. Justin, *Dial.*, Ch. VIII.

34. Trypho asks Justin: "Tell me, do you really admit that this place, Jerusalem, shall be rebuilt; and do you expect your people to be gathered together (there)?" This Justin admits (Ch. LXXX). In Ch. LXXXI Justin explains that this hope is based on Is. and Rev.

35. Harnack, "Judentum und Judenchristentum in Justin's Dial. mit Trypho," *Texte und Untersuchungen*, XXXIX, p. 92.

36. Euseb., III, 5. 3. The authenticity of this information is difficult to assess, its source is probably Hegesippus; cp. *Notes on Eusebius* by H. J. Lawlor and J. E. L. Oulton, London, 1928, II, p. 82.

37. Akiba's behaviour with regard to Bar Cochba's (his real name was Simeon) claim to Messiahship has always been a puzzle. For a possible explanation, see Schlatter, *Die Tage Trajans und Hadrians*, p. 93.

38. Justin, *Apol.* I, 31.

39. Cf. Streeter, *The Primitive Church*, p. 42.

40. For the difference between "Judaic" and "Judaistic", see F. J. A. Hort, *Judaistic Christianity*, p. 48.

41. Prof. H. L. Goudge, in *A New Commentary on Holy Scripture*, S.P.C.K., 1928, part III, p. 441a.

42. James Parkes, *Jesus, Paul and the Jews*, p. 129.

43. Cp. Parkes, *Conflict*, pp. 104 f. Cf. also O. S. Rankin, *The Origins of the Festival of Hanukkah*, Edinburgh, 1930, p. 202, n. 2. T. K. Cheyne, *The Origin and Religious Contents of the Psalter*, London, 1891, p. 19 and note. Chanukkah, *the Feast of the Dedication of the Temple after the Maccabaean victory* (cp. 1 Mac. 4. 56; Jn. 10. 22), was held by the Christian Church for several centuries. Cp. also Abrahams, *Judaism*, p. 64.

44. Cp. Parkes, *ibid.*, pp. 161 f.; cf. also Theophania, English translation by S. Lee, Cambridge, 1843, pp. 165, § 18; 166, § 20; 169, §§ 25, 26, 27; in fairness, however, it must be noted that Eusebius regards Christ-believing Jews as the true *remnant* of Israel. The Church of Christ consists for him of Jews and Gentiles; cp. *ibid.*, pp. 259 f.

45. *Dial.* Ch. XXIX.

46. *Dial.*, Ch. XXIX. The question, "Are you acquainted with them, Trypho?" is clearly rhetorical; Justin most obviously assumes that both draw upon the same sources. Cp. Lev Gillet,"Dialogue with Trypho", *Intern. Review of Missions*, April, 1942, pp. 172 ff.

47. Cf. Harnack, *Texte und Untersuchungen*, xxxix, Leipzig, 1913, pp. 49 f. Harnack stresses the fact that Justin's home was in Samaria; he therefore had intimate knowledge of Hebrew Christianity.

48. The moderating influence of Hebrew Christianity upon the Gentile Church is well reflected in the words of the *Clementines*, viii, 7: "Neither, therefore, are the Hebrews condemned on account of their ignorance of Jesus, by reason of Him who has concealed Him, if, doing the things (commanded) by Moses, they do not hate Him whom they do not know." R. H. Snape describes the author as a "Christian heretic—an Essene Ebionite, who regarded the Law as still binding" (*Rabbinic Anthology*, by Montefiore and Loewe, p. 639); Bardenhewer suspects Elchasaistic tendencies (*op. cit.*, p. 67); but it is generally accepted that the author was a Hebrew Christian (cp. Hort, *Clementine Recognitions*, pp. 83 ff.).

49. Jerome, *Ep.* cxxi.

50. Cp. *The Jew in the Medieval Community*, London, 1938, p. 12. The word *conciliabulum* (*concilio*) itself is inoffensive, and simply means a place of assembly. The offensive meaning is only found in Plautus.

51. Cp. Canon A. Lukyn Williams, *Adversus Judaeos*, pp. 132 ff.

52. *Ibid.*, p. 133; Dr. Otto Bardenhewer thinks that these homilies are not so much against the Jews "als vielmehr gegen die Christen gerichtet, welche mit den Juden religiöse Feste feierten" (*Patrologie*, Freiburg/B, 1910, p. 305).

53. Cp. Lukyn Williams, *ibid.*, p. 133, n. 2.

54. Cp. Lukyn Williams, *ibid.*, p. 136.

55. Dr. Otto Bardenhewer's point that the Homilies were not so much directed against the Jews as against those Christians who celebrated Jewish festivals and observed Jewish customs (*Patrologie*, 1910, p. 305), has been sympathetically brought out by A. Fürst in his short chapter Chrysostomus' Reden wider die Juden, *Christen und Juden*, Strassburg, 1892, pp. 20 ff. Interesting material on the nature of the controversy between Church and Synagogue is contained in Aphrahat's homilies, cp. Georg Bert, "Aphrahat's des persischen Weisen Homilien," *Texte und Untersuchungen*, Leipzig, 1888. Specially important is homily XI on circumcision, XIII on the Sabbath, XV on the distinction of foods, XVI on the twelve tribes among the Gentiles who have taken the place of the people (of God), and, above all, XVII on Christ, that he is the Son of God. For a short summary see A. Lukyn Williams, *Adversus Judaeos*, pp. 95 ff.; also Bardenhewer, pp. 333 ff.

56. Cp. Louis Israel Newman, *Jewish Influence on Christian Reform Movements*, New York, 1925.

57. Lord Macaulay, in his famous speech on Jewish disabilities, before the House of Commons in 1830, said with characteristic frankness: "During many ages we have, in all our dealings with them, abused our immense superiority of force . . ." (see *Essay and Speech on Jewish disabilities by Lord Macaulay*, ed. by Israel Abrahams and S. Levy, Edinburgh, 1909, p. 57).

58. Parkes, *Conflict*, p. 158.

59. There may have been another Pope of Jewish descent; but whether John XXI (XX?) (1276–77), whose name was Petrus Hispanus and who is chiefly known for his work on logic, *Summulae Logicae*, and some books on medicine, was of Jewish origin is now impossible to ascertain (cp. Brewster, p. 45, n. 1). The fact that he came from Portugal; that he practised medicine; and that he was unpopular in the Church (cp. Platina, II, pp. 106 f.), may, however, lend some support to this view. Cf. Joachim Prinz, *Popes of the Ghetto*, 1968.

60. James F. Loughlin, *The Catholic Encycl.*, I, p. 447.

61. Platina naturally regards Anacletus as the anti-pope and Innocent II as the legally instituted pope (cp. B. Platina, *The Lives of the Popes*, English translation, II, p. 39). But the fact is that Anacletus had the greater right to the See, the majority of cardinals being in his favour. That the schism revealed more than personal ambition on the part of Pierleoni can be seen from the fact that after his death (Jan. 25, 1138), another anti-pope, Victor IV, was elected.

62. L. I. Newman, *Jewish Influence on Christian Reform Movements*, p. 250. Cf. *Letters of St. Bernard*, transl. by Bruno Scott James, 1953, p. 210: "Just as if to the injury of Christ that a man of Jewish race has seized for himself the See of Peter, so it is against the interests of Caesar that any one should make himself the king of Cicily."

63. Newman says: "The central issue in this warfare was that Anacletus belonged to a Jewish family" (*ibid.*, p. 248).

64. Cp. Newman, *ibid.*, p. 250.

65. This sentiment, however, may perhaps be balanced by an incident of a later date. When Pope Eugenius IV heard that Don Alphonso, Bishop of Burgos, the famous son of his famous father, Paulus a Sancta Maria, was intending to visit Rome, he declared publicly "that in presence of such a man he felt ashamed to be seated in Peter's chair" (cp. Brewster, *op. cit.*, p. 48). *Ep.* 139 (c. 1135).

66. For a summary of the Discussion, see Lukyn Williams, *Adversus Judaeos*, pp. 141 ff.

67. There is enough evidence to prove that the Jews were not inactive in making proselytes. Jewish influence was considerable. An interesting case is Bodo, the chaplain to Louis the Pious, who was converted to Judaism and assumed the name of Eleazar (cf. Solomon Katz, *The Jews in the Visigothic and Frankish Kingdoms of Spain and Gaul*, Cambridge, Mass., 1937, pp. 45 f.; cf. also *ibid.*, pp. 53 f.).

68. Cp. Maurice Fishberg, *The Jews: a study in race and environment*, London, 1911, p. 422.

69. Parkes, *Conflict*, p. 214; for similar instances of Gregory's behaviour towards the Jews, see Solomon Katz, p. 28.

70. Quoted by Gustav Pearlson, *Twelve Centuries of Jewish Persecution*, Hull, 1927, p. 169.

71. James K. Hosmer, *The Jews, ancient, mediaeval and modern*, London, 1917, pp. 193 f.

72. Gustav Pearlson, p. 172.　　73. Parkes, *Med. Community*, p. 135.

74. Fishberg, *op. cit.*, pp. 419 f.

75. Parkes, *Med. Community*, p. 14. It is a curious fact that the Jews fared

better under the reign of the Vandals and the Arian section of the Church than under Catholic Christianity. They were justly treated in Italy by the Ostrogoths, and in Spain by the Visigoths. The Vandals left them free to exercise their religion. It was not until the conversion of Recared to Catholicism in 589, or, more accurately, until the accession of Sisebut in 612, who resolved to enforce Recared's anti-Jewish laws, that the situation changed. Cf. Katz, *op. cit.*, p. 11; for the Jewish position in the Middle Ages, see Cecil Roth, *The Jews in the Middle Ages*, Cambridge Medieval History, VII, pp. 632 ff.

76. Parkes, *Conflict*, pp. 178 f. 77. *Ibid.*, p. 181.

78. *Ibid.*, p. 182. 79. *Conflict*, p. 185.

80. See T. W. Crafer, *The Apocriticus of Macarius Magnes*, English translation and notes, S.P.C.K., 1919, pp. xiii, xix.

81. Several suggestions have been made concerning the heathen philosopher whose objections Macarius attempts to answer. Harnack suggested Porphyry (233–304?), the famous Neoplatonist, Duchesne is in favour of his later disciple, Hierocles. The latter is also Crafer's choice. Cp. *ibid.*, p. xv.

82. See Crafer, p. 103. 83. *Ibid.*, p. 66.

84. Lord Macaulay, in his famous speech on the Civil disabilities of the Jews, remarked with great insight: "When once you enter on a course of persecution, I defy you to find any reason for making a halt till you have reached the extreme point". Macaulay, *Jewish Disabilities*, ed. by I. Abrahams and S. Levy, p. 45). These words of great wisdom have been adequately illustrated by Jewish history in ancient and modern times.

85. Cf. Graetz, English translation, III, pp. 3 f.

86. Cp. Parkes, *Conflict*, p. 234. In later ages, the wealth of the Jews, ostentatiously exhibited, was a grave source of provocation; cp. E. N. Adler, *Auto de Fé and Jew*, 1908, p. 47.

87. M. L'Abbé Fleury, *Eccl. Hist.*, A.D. 400–429, English translation, Oxford, 1843, p. 149.

88. Cp. L'Abbé Fleury, *op. cit.*, pp. 265 ff.

89. Cp. Parkes, *Conflict*, pp. 366 ff. Katz, however, admits that the Jews were involved in a plot against the state to the advantage of the Moors (cp. Katz, *op. cit.*, p. 21; cf. also pp. 116 f.).

90. Parkes, *Med. Community*, p. 40; cp. Katz, p. 85. It must, however, be borne in mind that the Jewish position was only partly affected by religious considerations. Their status was, to a large extent, determined by the fact that they were foreigners. But the fact that they *remained* foreigners was determined by their religion (cf. Katz, *ibid.*, p. 84).

91. Cp. Adler *Auto de Fé*, p. 46.

92. Cp. Parkes, *Med. Community*, p. 108. It is not mere coincidence that the last city to eliminate the Ghetto in Europe was Rome (1870). I. Abrahams points out that at first "the Ghetto was rather a privilege than a disability, and sometimes was claimed by the Jews as a right when its demolition was threatened" (*Jewish Life in the Middle Ages*, London, 1896, p. 65).

93. Parkes, *Med. Community*, p. 41.

94. Parkes, *ibid.*, pp. 81, 106.

95. H. P. Stokes, *Short History of the Jews in England*, S.P.C.K., 1921, pp. 8 f. It became legally fixed that "the Jews and all their property belong to the King"; or as a Spanish King put it: "The Jews are ours and the peculiar

patrimony of the royal treasury" (Parkes, *Med. Com.*, p. 107).

96. A well-known example is Spain.

97. For a brief survey of these enactments, see Parkes, *Conflict*, Appendix, pp. 384 f.

98. Vallentine's *J. E.*, p. 146a; cf. Katz, *op. cit.*, pp. 11 ff., and throughout; as far as Spain was concerned, Jewish influence was so strong that many of the anti-Jewish enactments found only spasmodic application; cf. Brewster, *op. cit.*, pp. 157 f.

99. Cp. Newman, *op. cit.*, pp. 363 ff.

100. Cp. Hermann L. Strack, *The Jew and Human Sacrifice*, English translation, 1909, pp. 250 ff. Rabbi Benjamin Ben Jonah of Tudela in Navarre, a Jewish merchant whose extensive travels took him almost round the then known world, draws a pleasant picture of Jewish life in Rome. He must have visited the "metropolis of all Christendom" in *c.* 1159–60. Rome at that time had a Jewish community of about 200. We learn that some of these Jews were "officers in the service of Pope Alexander". One of them, R. Jechiel, "frequents the pope's palace, being steward of his household and minister of his private property". Another Jew, R. Menachem, is spoken of as the president of the University. We are told that the whole Jewish community was greatly respected and paid tribute to no one (*The Itinerary of Rabbi Benjamin of Tudela*, English translation by A. Asher, New York, p. 38).

101. A typical case is the strange "conversion" of the Jews at Magona (Port Mahon) in Minorca, after their Synagogue had been plundered and burnt in *c.* A.D. 418 (cp. M. L'Abbé Fleury, *op. cit.*, pp. 328 ff.).

102. Parkes, *Med. Community*, p. 189.

103. I. Abrahams, *Jewish Life in the Middle Ages* (New Edition by Cecil Roth, London, 1932), p. 442.

104. *Ibid.*, p. 442.   105. Cp. Newman, *op. cit.*, p. 375.

106. Cf. Katz, *op. cit.*, pp. 10–31. This is an important chapter for the Church's dealings with the Jews at that period.

107. Parkes, *Med. Community*, p. 37.

108. From the fact that Gamaliel the Patriarch was deposed in 415, on the charge, amongst other accusations, of having built new synagogues, Dr. Parkes adduces the existence of an even earlier law (cp. *Conflict*, p. 182; cf. also Katz, p. 74).

109. Parkes, *Conflict*, p. 238.

110. *Ibid.*, p. 250; the legal position with regard to synagogues thus confiscated was that once they have been used for Christian worship they remained the property of the Church (cf. Katz, p. 74).

111. Parkes, *ibid.*, p. 187.   112. *Ibid.*, p. 263.

113. Fleury, *op. cit.*, p. 330.   114. Parkes, *Conflict*, p. 335.

115. There is, however, some suspicion attached to the authenticity of the case, cp. Parkes, *Med. Community*, p. 39.

116. Parkes, *Conflict*, p. 358. On forced baptisms, cp. Newman, *op. cit.*, pp. 363 ff. Cf. Eduard Roditi, *Judaism*, Fall, 1970, pp. 436 f.

117. Parkes, *Med. Community*, pp. 79 f.   118. Parkes, *ibid.*, pp. 142 f.

119. Newman, *op. cit.*, p. 365.

120. *Ad Scapulam*, Ch. II: "it is a fundamental human right, a privilege of nature, that every man should worship according to his own convictions. . . . It is assuredly no part of religion to compel religion. . . ."

121. *Contra Celsum*, VII, 26.   122. Book V, Ch. XX.

123. Cp. *Ep. ad Vincentian*, 93; Quid est enim pejor, mors animae quam libertas erroris? asks Augustine (*Ep.* 166).

124. Joseph Blötzer, *The Catholic Encycl.*, VIII (1910), art. "Inquisition".

125. Cp. Parkes, *Conflict*, p. 268. In the reign of the Emperor Honorius, it was decreed in *c.* 412 "that neophytes who through any external cause had become Christians might return to Judaism" (Newman, p. 364). Augustine asks Christians to proclaim the message to Jews with love and humility and not "proudly glory against the broken branches" (*Adversus Judaeos*, ch. 10 (end).

126. Cf. Blötzer, *op. cit.*   127. Newman, *op. cit.*, p. 363.

128. *Ibid.*, p. 376.

129. Newman, pp. 360 ff. Mr. Laurie Magnus quotes the words of a bishop, an eye-witness of forced baptism upon Jewish children: "I have seen many dragged to the font by the hair, and the fathers, clad in black, with bowed heads, accompanying their children to the altar, to protest against these inhuman baptisms. I have seen still more horrible and indescribable violence done them" (*The Jew in the Christian Era*, London, 1929, p. 236).

130. Alexander IV, in Nov., 1259; Clement IV, in Nov., 1265, etc.

131. Henry Charles Lea, *History of the Inquisition in the Middle Ages*, 3 Vols., 1888; *A History of the Inquisition of Spain*, 4 Vols., New York and London, 1906-7.

132. E. N. Adler, *Auto de Fé and Jew*, p. 43.   133. *Ibid.*, p. 43 f.

134. The Inquisition was spoken of as the *Sanctum Officium*.

135. The inscription upon the banner of the Inquisition at Goa; cp. *Jew. Encycl.*, VI, p. 601. Raphael Sabatini in his book *Torquemada and the Spanish Inquisition*, London, 1913, reproduces a facsimile taken from Limborch's *Historia Inquisitionis*, representing the more popular banner of the Inquisition: a big cross in the centre; to the right of the cross, a sword; to the left, an olive branch; surrounding the whole are the words: *Exurge Domine, et Judica causam Tuam*. Ps. 73 (=Ps. 74, 22); *ibid.*, facing p. 272. See also Adler, facing p. 164.

136. Cp. Adler, *op. cit.*, pp. 80-88, 168.

137. Since the Bull *Ad exstirpanda*, issued by Pope Innocent IV in 1252 and repeatedly endorsed by his successors, Alexander IV (1254-61); Clement IV (1265-68); Nicholas IV (1288-92); Boniface VIII (1294-1303), etc., the civil authorities under pain of excommunication were obliged "to execute the legal sentences that condemned impenitent heretics to the stake" (Blötzer, *op. cit.*).

138. Adler, *op. cit.*, pp. 81 f.

139. Judaism and Sorcery were often synonyms in medieval phraseology. Usury became the main trade of the Jews (cp. Parkes, *Med. Community*, where the problems connected with usury are fully discussed).

140. Parkes, *Med. Community*, p. 140.   141. *Ibid.*, p. 139.

142. Cp. Newman, *op. cit.*, p. 317.

143. The title "Catholic Monarchs" was granted to Ferdinand and Isabella in 1495 in recognition of their fanatical zeal for the purity of the Church; see Adler, p. 55.

144. In Jewish literature, the Marranos are referred to as Anusim (=אנוסים, the outraged; אנס="the victim of an accident, unavoidably prevented", so Jastrow). The term Marrano is disputed—some hold it means swine, others that it refers to 1 Cor. 16. 22, where by some curious mistake ἀνάθεμα and μαρὰν ἀθά were taken to be synonyms. This is still the case in the Polish

version of the New Testament, printed by the Brit. and For. Bible Society; for the story of the Marranos, see Cecil Roth, *A History of the Marranos*, Philadelphia, 1932.

145. Raphael Sabatini, *op. cit.*, p. 392. The author says of Torquemada: "His honesty of purpose, his integrity, his utter devotion to the task he had taken up are to be weighed in the balance of historic judgment against the evil that he wrought so ardently in the unfaltering conviction that his work was good." This is certainly a mild estimation of a man who was guilty of so much human misery and untold suffering.

146. Adler assumes an earlier date, see *op. cit.*, p. 61; Frey Tómas must not be confused with Cardinal Don Juan de Torquemada who was of Jewish origin; cp. Brewster, *op. cit.*, p. 52, n. 1.

147. There is considerable difference of opinion as to the number of victims penalized by the Inquisition. An exact computation is impossible, as much of the procedure was in secret and many documents have been lost. For general statistics, see Adler, *op. cit.*, pp. 39 f., 99 ff.

148. Joseph Blötzer, art. "Inquisition" in *The Catholic Encycl.*, 1910.

149. Some idea of the relentless cruelty shown by the Inquisition can be gained from an edict published in the Netherlands in order to prevent the spreading of Protestantism there: "Women who have fallen into heresy shall be buried alive. Men, if they recant, shall lose their heads. If they continue obstinate, they shall be burnt at the stake . . ." Quoted from James Anthony Froude, *Short Studies on Great Subjects*, 1879, I, pp. 49 f.

150. Adler, pp. 48 f.

151. Cecil Roth, Vallentine's *J. E.*, art. "Inquisition".

152. Cecil Roth, *ibid.*, art. "Marranos"; cp. also his *History of the Marranos*, pp. 371 f.

153. H. Danby, *The Jew and Christianity*, p. 38.

154. מחזור מכל השנה כמנהג פולין, with English translation by David Levi, London, I, p. 116.

155. Vallentine's *J. E.*, art. "Amnon of Mayence".

156. *Kusari*, v, 25. So Hirschfeld, the Hebrew text does not quite give the same meaning, cp. Cassel, p. 432.

157. Quoted by A. C. Adcock, Renaissance and Reformation in *Jud. and Christ.*, II, pp. 261 f (Ginsburg, *Introduction to Levita's Massoreth Hamassoreth*, London, 1867, p. 6). A longer version of the same letter is quoted by Graetz, *op. cit.*, IV, pp. 293 ff.; Graetz dates the letter 1454.

158. Parkes, *The Jewish Problem in the Modern World*, Home University Library, p. 16.

159. Louis Golding, *The Jewish Problem*, Penguin Special, 1938, p. 97.

160. Luther's attitude to the Jews remains somewhat of a puzzle. From his pamphlet *Jesus was born a Jew*, published in 1523, to his *Tischreden*, where the Jews are pictured in the darkest colours, Luther seems to have undergone an unusual change. The cause of this change is difficult to explain. It is sometimes held that at the beginning of his career he hoped to rally the Jews round him, but in later years, when his hopes failed to materialize, he became a hardened enemy. That he gave up hope of converting the Jews is testified by his words: "Das jüdische Herz ist Stock=Stein=Eisen=Teuffelhart, das mit keiner Weise zu bewegen ist". Newman's suggestion that Luther's hos-

tility was due to the influence of converted Jews is entirely unsubstantiated (cp. Newman, *Jewish Influence on Christ. Reform Movements*, pp. 625 ff.). The fact that Luther appears to be quoting from works of Jewish converts like Antonius Margaritha is no evidence in itself, for his anti-Judaism left the plane of religious controversy and became personal antipathy to the race.

161. Jacques Maritain, *Antisemitism*, 1939, p. 27.

162. A definite distinction must be made between Continental and British Christianity. The Churches of the British Isles, the Scandinavian Churches, the Church of Holland and to a large measure the Swiss Churches have shown a spirit of charity and tolerance in keeping with their great liberal traditions. But cp. for Italy, C. Roth, *The Hist. of Jews in Italy*, 1946, pp. 539 ff.

163. S. H. Hooke, in *Jud. and Christ*, i, p. 254.

164. A. Fürst, *Christen und Juden*, p. 103.

165. *Ibid.*, p. 108.   166. Cf. p. 424.

167, Lev Gillet, *Communion in the Messiah*, London and Redhill, 1942; cf. p. 277.

168. Significantly enough, the Hebrew Bible ends with the last chapter of the 2nd book of Chronicles. It virtually has no end.

169. See Dr. J. H. Hertz, Alleged Christological References in Scripture, one volume ed. of his *Pentateuch and Haftorahs*, London, 1938, pp. 201 f. The late chief Rabbi's exegetical arguments do not meet the point; the main point is that to the Church the importance of the Old Testament lies in its witness to Jesus Christ.

NOTES TO CHAPTER IV

1. The Jews refer to him as Rashi. He was born in Troyes in 1040 and died there in 1105; cp. Kaufmann Kohler, *Jewish Theology, systematically and historically considered*, New York, 1918, p. 427; cp. also p. 329.

2. His name has been Latinized to Maimonides. Jews refer to him as Rambam. He was born at Cordova in 1135 and died at Fostat (Old Cairo) in 1204, where he was court physician to the Caliph; for his attitude to Christianity, see p. 12, and Ch. II, n. 8.

3. For Jewish influence upon the Renaissance and Reformation, see Charles and Dorothea Singer, The Jewish factor in Medieval thought; also G. H. Box, Hebrew Studies in Reformation Period and After; in *The Legacy of Israel*, Oxford, 1927. Cp. also M. I. Schleiden, *The Importance of the Jews for the Preservation and Revival of Learning during the Middle Ages*, English translation, London, 1911.

4. Special attention to the Jewish influence upon the Reformation is given by L. I. Newman, *Jewish Influence on Christian Reform Movements*, New York, 1925.

5. *The Legacy of Israel*, p. 498.

6. *The Jewish Encycl.* pointedly remarks: "The external history of the Talmud reflects in part the history of Judaism persisting in a world of hostility and persecution" (xii, p. 22).

7. To our knowledge, however, the Talmud was never on the *Index librorum prohibitorum*. It was thus not a prohibited book in the strict sense of the word. The Church only raised objections to certain passages referring to Jesus and Christianity.

8. For a short description of the Controversy, see Danby, *The Jew and*

Christianity, pp. 48 ff.; cf. also the excellent article by S. A. Hirsch, John Pfefferkorn and the Battle of the Books, *J. Q. R.*, IV (1892), pp. 256 ff.

9. Cp. A. C. Adcock, Renaissance and Reformation, in *Jud. and Christ.*, II, pp. 263 ff.

10. O. Zarek, quoted by Lindeskog, p. 30, n. 3. Husik, *op. cit.*, p. 429: "The material walls of the Ghetto and the spiritual walls of the Talmud and the Kabbala kept the remnant from being overwhelmed and absorbed by the hostile environment of Christian and Mohammedan." Husik connects the decline of the political and economic conditions of the Jews in the fourteenth and fifteenth centuries with the growth of mysticism and obscurantism.

11. R. Moses ben Nachman is usually referred to as Nachmanides; amongst Jews he is known as Ramban, from the initial letters of his name. He was known to non-Jewish scholars under the name of Bonastruc de Porta, which led in the past to the assumption of two distinct persons. Cp. *Jew. Encycl.*, IX, pp. 87 ff.

12. Cp. I. Ziegler, *Religiöse Disputationen im Mittelalter*, Frankfurt, 1894. The account of the discussion between Pablo Christiani and Nachmanides is contained in Wagenseil's *Tela Ignea Satanæ*, 1681; but Wagenseil's text is corrupt with many interpolations. A more trustworthy version is given by Steinschneider, *Sefer Wikuach ha-Ramban*, Berlin, 1860 (Hebrew). Cp. Lukyn Williams, *Adversus Judaeos*, p. 245, n. 3; for a short summary, see S. Schechter, *Studies in Judaism*, London, 1896, pp. 125 ff., with useful bibliographical notes, *ibid.*, p. 423; cp. also *The Legacy of Israel*, pp. 295 ff.; Graetz, *History of the Jews*, Engl., London, 1891, III, pp. 617 ff.; Geronimo de Santa-Fé was assisted by another Jewish convert, Andreas Beltran, a native of Valencia, and afterwards Bishop of Barcelona; cp. Brewster, p. 50.

13. Graetz, who calls Pablo Christiani "the first missionary preacher for the conversion of the Jews", holds that Pablo is to be held responsible for the banishment of his adversary. This, however, is doubtful. Graetz himself, comparing this dispute with the one held at Paris between Rabbi Yechiel ben Joseph of Paris and Nicholas Donin (1240), says: "The Rabbi of Paris and the Dominican Donin fought like two fierce pugilists, who assailed each other with heavy blows of the fist, accompanied by words of abuse: the Rabbi of Gerona and the Dominican Pablo, on the other hand, met like two well-cultured noblemen, who dealt their blows with an air of politeness, and with due observance of the etiquette of refined society" (*op. cit.*, III, p. 618).

14. Cp. Kaufmann Kohler, *Jewish Encycl.*, IV, p. 617. Cp. also Hans Joachim Schoeps, *Jüdisch-christliches Religionsgespräch, in 19 Jahrhunderten*, Berlin, 1937, pp. 63 ff.

15. ספר חזוק אמונה, *Befestigung im Glauben*, Hebr. with German transl., by Rabbi David Deutsch, Sohrau and Breslau, 1873; also Wagenseil, *op. cit.* For a short discussion of this work see Lindeskog, pp. 19 ff.

16. Cp. Lukyn Williams, *The Chizzuk Emunah as it appears to an Englishman*, London, 1909, introduction; also *Manual of Christian Evidences*, 1911, I, p. 4; cp. also Schoeps, *op. cit.*, pp. 78 ff.

17. Frederick the Great; cp. Shalom Spiegel, *Hebrew Reborn*, London, 1931, p. 52.

18. It is significant that, at Lafayette's suggestion, the French Declaration began with the words: "Les hommes naissent et demeurent égaux en

droits . . .", words borrowed from the American Declaration (cp. René Fülöp-Miller, *Leaders, Dreamers, and Rebels*, London, 1935, p. 127).

19. Cp. G. F. Abbott, *Israel in Europe*, p. 296.

20. Maurice Fishberg, *The Jews: a study in Race and Environment*, London and Felling-on-Tyne, 1911, p. 431.

21. William Zukerman, *The Jew in Revolt*, London, 1937. This book offers an interesting study of the relationship between anti-Semitism and the capitalist system. The following passage is characteristic: "The Jew stands out as the most prominent symbol of the hateful system, as the living personification of the people's trouble, and it is upon him that their wrath is poured down first. It is not a coincidence that the outbursts of anti-Semitism occur always in times of economic depression and among nations most deeply steeped in economic despair. . . . For anti-Semitism is primarily economic unrest, misdirected, misguided, following the wrong clue, but nevertheless not without some plausible, understandable, erring human reason" (p. 248).

22. A. Montefiore Hyamson, art. "Anti-Semitism," in Vallentine's *J. E.*, p. 40a. Cp. also the small pamphlet, *The Psychology of Antisemitism*, by A. Cohen, London, 1942.

23. Dr. Parkes writes: "According to Germanic Custom, a stranger was an object without a master. In so far as he was not protected, either by a powerful individual, or by inter-tribal or international arrangement, he did not enjoy the most elementary rights. He could be killed, and his murderer could not be punished; any man who gave him lodging was responsible for his actions; his property was ownerless, and his heir had no right of inheritance" (*The Jew in the Med. Community*, pp. 102 f.).

24. Political motives are an important factor in all anti-Semitic agitations. A good example is furnished by the riots in Budapest which the Austrians staged in order to counteract the effects of the liberal-nationalist propaganda carried on by the famous Magyar leader Louis Kossuth (1802–1894); cp. Otto Zarek, *Kossuth*, Engl. by L. Hudson, London, 1937, pp. 226 ff.

25. "Die wichtigste Folge der Emanzipation ist die Selbstbefreiung des jüdischen Geistes aus dem Zwange des Ghetto-daseins und die damit zusammenhängende *Assimilierung* an die abendländische Kultur, was negativ die Entnationalisierung des Judentums bedeutete" (Lindeskog, *op. cit.*, p. 33).

26. *Haskalah* is derived from שכל, reason, in modern Hebrew, "Enlightenment". Protagonists of the Haskalah are called *Maskilim*. Cp. P. Wiernik's art. in *J. Encycl.*, VI, pp. 256 ff.; for the whole movement see Dr. Josef Meisl, Berlin, 1919. On the Haskala cf. Lucy S. Dawidowicz, *The Golden Tradition*, 1967, ch. II.

27. Leon Simon, art. *Haskalah*, Vallentine's *Jew. Encycl.*, p. 267, a, b.

28. Spiegel, *op. cit.*, pp. 54 f.

29. *The Pentateuch* (1780–83); *the Psalms* (1783); *the Song of Songs* (1788). The significance of Mendelssohn's work can hardly be overestimated. M. Samuels aptly says of Mendelssohn: "*Moses* the son of *Amram* delivered his brethren from bodily slavery; the glorious task of emancipating their *minds* was reserved for *Moses* the son of Mendel" (*Memoirs of Moses Mendelssohn*, London, 1825, p. 110).

30. So Spiegel, *op. cit.*, p. 45.   31. Cp. Lindeskog, pp. 34 f.

32. Cp. the excellent art. by J. Lestschinski, "Apostasie", in *Encycl. Judaica*, II, pp. 1209 ff.

33. Mendelssohn's own attitude towards Christianity he has defined in his famous controversy with J. C. Lavater, cp. H. J. Schoeps, *Jüdisch-christliches Religions gespräch in 19 Jahrhunderten*, Berlin, 1937. Cp. also Dibre Emeth, 1877, 121, containing an account of a conversation between Mendelssohn and a missionary called Litzki; cf. also M. Samuels, *op. cit.*, pp. 44–67.

34. Israel Cohen, *Jewish Life in Modern Times*, London, 1929, 2nd ed., p. 270.

35. *Ibid.*, p. 270. Mr. Cohen fails to mention, however, that such action was taken by the authorities on the request of the Jewish orthodox party which was bitterly opposed to every sign of Reform (cp. David Philipson, *The Reform Movement in Judaism*, New York, 1907, pp. 34 f.).

36. Jewish history tends to show that outside pressure has often been the cause of stronger national cohesion and intenser spiritual life; cf. L. Simon, *Stud. in Jew. Nationalism*, pp. 20 f., 43 f.; Spiegel, *op. cit.*, p. 206; Brewster, *op. cit.*, pp. 94, 97.

37. Cf. Cohen, *op. cit.*, p. 270; *ibid.*, p. 277.

38. Mr. Cohen's partisan spirit has led him to many overstatements where Christian missions are concerned, and to several inaccuracies. Thus, quoting the authority of "Die Allgemeine Zeitung des Judentums", 1897, p. 317, he credits De le Roi with the saying: "Never has a Jew become baptized through conviction". But the fact is that De le Roi has written three volumes to prove the opposite! (Cf. Cohen, *op. cit.*, pp. 273 f.; cf. De le Roi, *Die evangelische Christenheit und die Juden*, 3 vols. Berlin, 1884–92; cf. specially his Introduction.) For the high quality of some of the converts, see Meisl, *op. cit.*, pp. 160, 197.

39. Cp. J. F. A. de le Roi, *Die evangelische Christenheit und die Juden*, II, pp. 28 f.

40. Israel Cohen devotes a whole chapter to "*Drift and Apostasy*" (*op. cit.*, pp. 268–283).

41. Berlin, 1799; cp. Schoeps, *op. cit.*, p. 98; David Philipson presents the incident between Friedländer and Teller in a different light, cp. *The Reform Movement in Judaism*, New York, 1907, pp. 15 f.; but Schoeps' presentation is more accurate.

42. W. A. Teller, *An einige Hausväter jüdischer Religion. Von einem Prediger in Berlin.* Berlin, 1799. De le Roi records that Teller used to avoid at Jewish baptisms the traditional baptismal formula by saying: "Ich taufe dich auf das Bekenntnis Christi, des Stifters einer geistigeren und erfreuenderen Religion, als die der Gemeinde, zu welcher du bisher gehört hast". We are told that such [alterations were a frequent occurrence in those days (cp. De le Roi, *op. cit.*, II, p. 34).

43. Philipson, *op. cit.*, p. 37.

44. Cp. Philipson, pp. 14 f.; Lindeskog, p. 38: "The primary object of Reform has been to save the modern Jew for Judaism and Judaism for the modern Jew". Adolph Lichtigfeld, *Twenty Centuries of Jewish Thought*, London, 1937, p. 163.

45. Israel Cohen divides lapsed Jews into two groups:
    (a) Those who leave the Synagogue without entering the Church.
    (b) Those who become nominal Christians.
(Cp. *op. cit.*, p. 269.)

46. For the history of the movement, see D. Philipson, *op. cit.* For a short summary of the main difference in points of doctrine see G. Gottheil, *The development of religious ideas in Judaism since Moses Mendelssohn*, a paper read before the World Parliament of Religions, Cincinnati, 1895, pp. 26 ff.; most valuable is Montefiore's book, *Outlines of Liberal Judaism*, London, 1912.

47. S. Formstecher, *Die Religion des Geistes*, eine wissenschaftliche Darstellung des Judentums nach seinem Charakter, Entwicklungsgange und Berufe in der Menschheit, Frankfurt/M., 1841; for a short summary, see Lichtigfeld, pp. 144 f.

48. Vallentine's *J. E.*, p. 522b.

49. Israel I. Mattuck, *What are the Jews?* London, 1939, p. 239. Liberal Judaism is the extreme wing in the Reform movement. There is a marked difference between Liberal and Reform Judaism, especially in Germany; cf. J. H. Hertz, *Affirmations of Judaism*, London, 1927, pp. 124 ff. (esp. p. 125, n. 10); some Liberal Synagogues, notably in the U.S.A., have pushed reform to the extreme: The Beth Israel Congregation at Houston, Texas, has by a large majority of votes adopted the principle to bar from active membership those who adhere to "the Rabbinical and Mosaic laws which regulate diet". It has also been decided to require from members the repudiation of the Hebrew language as "unintelligible to the vast majority of our co-religionists" (*Jew. Chronicle*, Jan. 7th, 1944). The opposition to Zionism on the part of American Rabbis is very considerable.

50. Philipson points out the difficulty of translating the German "Wissenschaft des Judentums". But he says: "if the word 'science' be understood in its original and larger meaning of knowledge and not in the more restricted significance of physical science, the phrase 'science of Judaism' may stand as the equivalent of the German" (*op. cit.*, p. 38, note). It is in this sense that we make use of the phrase, following Philipson's example.

51. Lindeskog, *op. cit.*, p. 41.

52. So Spiegel, *op. cit.*, p. 67.

53. Cp. C. G. Montefiore, *Outlines of Liberal Judaism*, pp. 284 ff.; also Israel I. Mattuck, *What are the Jews?*

54. Cp. Meisl, *op. cit.*, pp. 192, 202.

55. Spiegel, p. 206.   56. *Ibid.*, p. 201.

57. Vallentine's *J. E.*, p. 251a.   58. Spiegel, p. 206.

59. The definition of political Zionism was left to a Western Jew, Theodor Herzl (1860–1904) (*Der Judenstaat*, 1896). Herzl was the founder of the Zionist World Organization.

60. Cp. J. H. Hertz, on Brotherhood in Israel, *op. cit.*, pp. 121 ff.

61. Cp. Hans Joachim Schoeps, *op. cit.*, pp. 116 ff., 121 ff., 129 ff.

62. Cp. Joseph Bonsirven, *On the Ruins of the Temple*, English translation, London, 1931, p. 73.

63. Cp. *Affirmations*, pp. 21 f., 93 f., 125, 179.

64. J. D. Eisenstein (*Ozar Wikuhim*, 1928, p. 20), quoted by A. Lukyn Williams, *The Doctrines of Modern Judaism considered*, S.P.C.K., 1939, p. 50; cp. also the appended note by Herbert Danby, *The Jew and Christianity*, p. 118, n. 13, where similar views are expressed by "a Hebrew writer of considerable repute".

65. To call Dr. Klausner's work "a vindication of Christianity" betrays

a mind of more than ordinary prejudice. Does Mr. Eisenstein know that Jesus enjoyed the reputation of a great teacher *before* Klausner's book was written? For a Christian scholarly criticism of Klausner's work, see C. J. Cadoux, "Dr. Klausner's estimate of Jesus", *The London Quarterly and Holborn Review*, July, 1935, pp. 306–321.

66. *Affirmations*, p. 93, n. 16.

67. Paul Goodman, *The Synagogue and the Church*, London, 1908, p. 230.

68. *Ibid.*, p. 233.

69. *Ibid.*, p. 242; this is a widely held view amongst Jewish scholars; cp. Klausner, p. 202. Graetz defines Christianity: "Essenism, interwoven with foreign elements" (*History of the Jews, from the earliest times to the present day*, English translation, London, 1891, II, p. 142; cp. also II, pp. 171 f.).

70. Goodman, *op. cit.*, p. 243.   71. *Ibid.*, p. 263.   72. *Ibid.*, p. 264.

73. Paul Goodman, *The Synagogue and the Church*, p. 267. This is the view of almost all Jewish scholars. Ernest R. Trattner attempts to show "that Jesus was not an isolated phenomenon, a self-contained organism utterly unrelated to his fellow-men, but a product of Jewish life" (*As a Jew sees Jesus*, New York and London, 1931, p. 35).

74. Goodman, *op. cit.*, p. 271.

75. *Ibid.*, p. 274. The impracticability of Jesus' ethical teaching is often stressed by Jewish writers; cp. Klausner, *op. cit.*, pp. 373 ff.

76. Goodman, *op. cit.*, p. 277.

77. *Ibid.*, p. 281: "No healthy state of society has ever been built on purely Christian principles".

78. *Ibid.*, pp. 290 f.

79. Gerald Friedlander, *The Jewish Sources of the Sermon on the Mount*, London, 1911, pp. 1 ff.; cp. also his preface, pp. xxiii ff.

80. *Ibid.*, p. xviii.

81. *Ibid.*, p. xxi; cp. also G. Friedlander, *Hellenism and Christianity*, London, 1912, pp. 49 ff. It is, however, characteristic of Jewish scholarship to insist on the historicity of Jesus: "Wenn wir die Literatur überblicken, finden wir dass die allermeisten jüdischen Autoren von der Geschichtlichkeit Jesu fest überzeugt sind" (Lindeskog, p. 207). But there are a few exceptions: Samuel Lublinski, *Das Werdende Dogma vom Leben Jesu*, Jena, 1910, advocates "die mythologische Richtung". Lublinski's aim is to work out a positive and synthetic picture of the "Erlösungsmythos" and to emphasize the magnificence of the symbol which forms its background. He therefore reduces the whole Synoptic tradition to mythology. Wherever two persons show any affinity or similarity, they instantly become "Doppelgänger", *e.g.* Mary and Martha, Lazarus and John, etc.; cp. also Georg Brandes, *Jesus-Sage*, Berlin, 1925.

82. Friedlander, *op. cit.*, p. 4.   83. *Ibid.*, p. xxii f.

84. *Ibid.*, p. 23; this is a common feature of most Jewish writers. Abraham Geiger already said: "Sind die Äusserungen, die in den reinsittlichen Verhältnissen der Menschen gegen einander wurzeln, wirklich treu berichtet (*i.e.* in the Gospels), so finden wir in ihnen entweder nichts Neues, oder das Neue tritt in einer gewissen krankhaften Weise auf, wie es einer kranken Zeit gehört" (*Das Judenthum und seine Geschichte*, Breslau, 1864, p. 113). Lindeskog calls it the "Nihil novi" attitude, cp. *op. cit.*, pp. 217 ff. and footnotes. Montefiore thinks that the majority of educated Jews would insist that the teaching

of Jesus, "where good was not original, and where original was not Jewish or good" (*In Spirit and in Truth*, p. 316).

85. Friedlander, *Jew. Sources*, p. xxvii; *Test. Issachar*, v, 2.
86. *Ibid.*, p. 266.   87. Cp. pp. 264 f.
88. Cf. Lindeskog, p. 250.   89. Friedlander, p. 262.
90. Friedlander, p. 265.   91. Friedlander, pp. 262 f.
92. Martin Buber, *Der Heilige Weg*, Frankfurt/M., 1920, p. 14. It must be noted that Buber is neither a Zionist nor a Socialist in the ordinary sense. He explicitly says: "Nationalismus als isolierte Lebensanschauung und Sozialismus als isolierte Lebensanschauung sind dem echten Judentum gleich fremd" (*ibid.*, p. 19).
93. *Ibid.*, p. 15.
94. *Ibid.*, p. 16.
95. Buber singles out two main features of Judaism: "Die erste grosse werbende Eigentümlichkeit der jüdischen Lehre war diese ihre Alloffenheit, die zweite war ihre Richtung auf die positive Tat. Sie wollte nicht wie etwa der Buddismus, von der Welt weg, sondern ins Herz der Welt führen; sie forderte von dem tätigen Menschen nicht, dass er auf das Tun verzichte, sondern dass er das Rechte tun lerne" (*Vom Geist des Judentums*, Leipzig, 1916, pp. 32 f.).
96. Buber, *Vom Geist des Judentums*, pp. 33 f.; Buber explains that Christianity has conquered the West in its syncretistic form: "wohl hat sie (*i.e.* Christianity) vom Hellenismus mehr angenommen als Bilder und Worte; aber das dauernd Zeugende im Christentum war jüdisches Urgut" (*ibidem*). The greatest weakness of Christianity is its dualism which has its origin in Pauline theology (cp. *Der Heilige Weg*, pp. 44 ff.). Prof. Buber has thus anticipated Klausner's last book, *From Jesus to Paul* (cp. pp. 204 f., 522, and throughout).
97. Buber, *Der Heilige Weg*, p. 40.   98. *Ibid.*, p. 41.
99. *Ibid.*, pp. 48 f. Saul, the man of Tarsus, whom Buber calls a "representative Jew", has deflected the essential Jewishness of Jesus' message, in his effort to hand it over to the Gentile world. Over and against the ever-present attempt of Judaism to positive action, stands the Pauline conception of human impotence. Buber calls Paul's attitude the "titanic renunciation" (titanischer Verzicht).
100. Buber, *Die Stunde und die Erkenntnis*, Berlin, 1936, pp. 159 f.
101. ". . . an Stelle dieses echt jüdischen Wissens tritt die Annahme einer grundsätzlichen und unüberbrückbaren Zweiheit von Menschenwillen und Gottesgnade". (*Der Heilige Weg*, p. 45.)
102. *Der Heilige Weg*, p. 47.
103. Quoted by Levertoff, *Der Weg*, Jan.–Feb., 1933, p. 8 (Yiddish).
104. "Dies, dass Gott in der Welt . . . verwirklicht werden will . . . dieses abgründliche Wissen ist Jesu tiefstes Judentum" (*Der Heilige Weg*, p. 41).
105. *Ibid.*, p. 44.
106. It may be that Prof. Buber would object to such a statement. But the general trend of his reasoning makes such an assumption possible.
107. *Ibid.*, p. 18.   108. Cp. Lindeskog, pp. 170 f.
109. "The Jew must change his attitude before the world, and come into spiritual fellowship with those around him. John, Paul, Jesus himself, we can

claim them all for our own. We do not want 'missions' to convert us. We cannot become Presbyterians, Episcopalians, members of any dividing sect, 'teaching for doctrines the opinions of men'. Christians as well as Jews need the larger unity that shall embrace them all, the unity of spirit, not of doctrine" (Miss Josephine Lazarus, "The Outlook of Judaism", in *Judaism at the World's Parliament of Religions*, Cincinnati, 1894, p. 303).

110. The emphasis upon the *Jewishness* of Jesus is common to all Jewish writers, with the exception of the ultra-orthodox. By placing Jesus of Nazareth within the line of religious development, the edge of his *uniqueness* is broken and he can be dealt with as a phenomenon belonging to the manifold manifestations of the spirit of Judaism.

111. C. G. Montefiore, *The Synoptic Gospels*, 2 Vols, London, 1909 (I. Abrahams contributed a third volume of Additional Notes, *vide infra*) ; 2nd ed. 1927. For an earlier attempt by Rabbi Elie Soloweyczyk, see Lindeskog, pp. 123 f.

112. "Montefiores *interpretatio evangelica* innerhalb der Grenzen des religiösen Liberalismus und des konsequenten Historismus bezeichnet einen Höhepunkt in der Geschichte der neutestamentlichen Exegese" (Lindeskog, pp. 241 f.).

113. *Synoptic Gospels*, 1927, appended note at the end of the second volume.

114. Lindeskog, p. 241.

115. "The teaching of Jesus, which has had such gigantic effects upon the world, is more and other than a dissected list of injunctions. It is not merely the sum of its parts; it is a whole, a spirit." *S. G.*, 1909, pp. civ f.; cp. *Some Elements of the Relig. Teaching of Jesus*, 1910, pp. 85 f.

116. Lindeskog, pp. 236 f. Though Montefiore was not the first to hold this view, Lindeskog says of him : "Er scheint mir das Problem geschickter und bewusster als andere gestellt und gelöst zu haben." The greatest merit of Montefiore's work is his honesty in controversy and his fine sense of justice. An outstanding example of these great qualities is his essay, "Jewish Views of Christianity" (*In Spirit and in Truth*, pp. 311 ff.).

117. Cp. Montefiore's short art. "What a Jew thinks about Jesus", written late in life, *Hibbert Journal*, XXXIII, 1934–35, pp. 511 ff.

118. *Some Elements of the Teaching of Jesus*, p. 20, cp. *S. G.*, p. cxxxiv: "His teaching is a revival of prophetic Judaism, and in some respects points forward to the Liberal Judaism of to-day."

119. "What a Jew thinks about Jesus," *H. J.*, XXXIII, p. 516.

120. *The Teaching of Jesus*, pp. 55 ff.

121. *Ibid.*, pp. 89 ff. Montefiore holds that while the Talmud and other Rabbinic literature are opposed to Christian trinitarian doctrine, yet there is no contradiction "between the religious and ethical teaching of Jesus and the best religious and ethical teaching of the Rabbis" (*Rabbinic Literature and Gospel Teachings*, London, 1930, p. 161). At another place, Montefiore remarks: "Jesus was not so far from the Rabbis, nor were the Rabbis so far from Jesus" (*ibid.*, p. 195).

122. *Ibid.*, pp. 125 ff., 132; Montefiore, though admitting what he calls "a marked personal element" in the teaching of Jesus, thinks that this has been unduly emphasized by tradition and editors ; cp. *ibid.*, pp. 154 ff.

123. *Ibid.*, p. 131.

124. *Ibid.*, p. 141.

125. "To the hardest excellence of all even Jesus could not attain. For it was far easier for him to care for the outcast than to care for his opponent . . ." (*ibid.*, p. 53). In this respect he did not differ from the Rabbis (cp. Montefiore and H. Loewe, *A Rabbinic Anthology*, London, 1938, p. xxix).

126. *Ibid.*, p. 146.

127. Montefiore holds that though the evidence is conflicting Jesus inclined to the universalistic view, cp. pp. 70 f.

128. *Ibid.*, p. 139. Montefiore admits that a subjective element enters into the task of textual criticism; cp. passages where he expresses the hope that certain utterances are unauthentic because they conflict with his own views, p. 164.

129. Cp. pp. 143, 145, 147, 152, 156, 159, etc.

130. *Ibid.*, p. 143; cp. pp. 146 f.; cp. *S. G.*, 1927, II, pp. 624 f.

131. *Ibid.*, p. 159; cp. *S. G.* (1927), II, pp. 176 f.

132. "Rabbinic Judaism and the Epistles of St. Paul," an address delivered before the St. Paul Association, Nov. 21, 1900 (*J. Q. R.*, Jan. 1901, p. 167).

133. *J. Q. R.*, Jan. 1901, pp. 168 f. But Montefiore does not altogether reject Paul. H. Loewe, in his introduction to the *Rabbinic Anthology*, objects to Montefiore's opinion that "there are no such religious geniuses and innovators as Jesus, Paul and the author of the Fourth Gospel among the Rabbis". In Loewe's view, Hillel's introduction of *Prosbul* and Simeon ben Shetach's invention of *Ketubbah* make them of equal importance to society. The Rabbis have, therefore, also a claim to the title "religious innovators" (pp. xcix f.).

134. "The Significance of Jesus for his own age," *Hibbert Journal*, xx, 1911–12, pp. 773, 779.

135. Cp. Kaufmann Kohler, *Grundriss einer systematischen Theologie des Judentums auf geschichtlicher Grundlage*, Leipzig, 1910; English translation: *Jewish Theology, systematically and historically considered*, New York, 1918, p. 428; cp. also *The Origins of the Synagogue and the Church*, New York, 1929, p. 261.

136. "The Synoptic Gospel and Jewish Consciousness", *Hibbert Journal*, III, 1904–5, p. 660; cp. also *Liberal Judaism and Hellenism, and other essays*, London, 1918, pp. 93 ff.

137. *H. J.*, III, 1904–5, p. 657; in his later work, *Rabbinic Literature and Gospel Teachings*, Montefiore has made an even stronger case for the originality of Jesus; cp. *ibid.*, pp. 162 f.

138. *Outlines of Liberal Judaism*, London, 1912, p. 319. On the subject of Jesus' limitations, cp. *S. G.* (1909), pp. 140, 633; *The Teaching of Jesus*, pp. 151 f.

139. Cp. Kaufmann Kohler, *The Origins of the Synagogue and the Church*, New York, 1929, p. 218, 230; Klausner, *op. cit.*, pp. 373 ff. (German ed., 1934, p. 416).

140. *Liberal Judaism and Hellenism, etc.*, pp. 104 ff.

141. *Synoptic Gospels* (1909), p. 594.

142. *Liberal Judaism and Hellenism, etc.*, p. 128. (The whole chapter, Liberal Judaism and the New Testament, gives a clear outline of Montefiore's position and also contains some of the most striking tributes to Jesus Christ.)

143. *Liberal Judaism and Hellenism, etc.*, pp. 126 f.

144. *Outlines of Liberal Judaism*, p. 313.

145. *Hibbert Journal*, XXXIII, 1934–5, p. 520; cp. O. Lazarus, *Liberal Judaism and its standpoint*, London, 1937, pp. 85 f.

146. Kaufmann Kohler, *The Origins of the Synagogue and the Church*, edited with a Biographical Essay by H. G. Enelow, New York, 1929.

147. *Ibid.*, p. 215.   148. *Ibid.*, p. 217.

149. *Ibid.*, p. 205; *Antiq.*, XVIII, 3. 3.

150. *Ibid.*, pp. 227 f.; cp. Kohler's art., Jesus in Theology, *J. E.*, VII, pp. 166 ff.

151. *Ab. de R. Nathan*, ed. by Schechter, Vienna, 1887, p. 56; for Jesus' connection with the Essenes, see Kohler, *op. cit.*, pp. 238 ff.; *Jew. Encycl.*, VII, p. 256b; but cp. *Lexikon für Theologie und Kirche*, I, p. 643a.

152. "Judaism and Christianity (or the Synagogue and the Church)", an address delivered before the Religious Congress in Chicago, 1893; cp. *Judaism at the World's Parliament of Religions*, Cincinnati, 1894, pp. 114 ff.

153. *The Origins of the Synagogue and the Church*, pp. 218, 230.

154. *Ibid.*, p. 230.   155. *Ibid.*, p. 223.   156. *Op. cit.*, p. 231.

157. *Origins of the Synagogue and the Church*, pp. 217, 229 f. It is interesting to observe that a similar criticism is made by Klausner with regard to Judaism. Klausner points out that Judaism by its tendency to give to all accidents of life a religious bent has made the development of politics impossible. That is the reason why "the Arabian, Abyssinian and Cuzarite kings, who embraced Judaism in the Middle Ages, found themselves unable to survive" (Klausner, *Jesus*, p. 226); in opposition to the Rabbinic striving for "a higher synthesis", however, Jesus fully accepted a duality alien to the spirit of Judaism (cp. *ibid.*, pp. 373 f.).

158. Israel Abrahams, *Studies in Pharisaism and the Gospels*, first series, 1917; second series, 1924.

159. *Op. cit.*, pp. VI f.   160. *Ibid.*, p. 16.

161. *Ibid.*, p. 134; cp. the Rabbinical formula in *Yoma*, 85a: לפקוח נפש שדוחה את השבת.

162. *Ibid.*, p. 142.   163. *Ibid.*, p. 149.

164. *Ibid.*, p. 146; cp. *Abot*, III, 20 (Danby, III, 16). Abrahams explains the Pharisaic position as an effort "to hold the balance between man's duty to *strive* to earn pardon and his inability to attain it without God's gracious gift of it" (*ibid.*, p. 147). Strangely enough, the Pauline words of Phil. 2. 12 f. entirely escaped the author.

165. *Ibid.*, p. 156.   166. *Ibid.*, p. 88.

167. Paul Goodman, *op. cit.*, p. 291.

168. Montefiore, *Outlines of Liberal Judaism*, p. 304.

169. Joseph Salvador, *Jésus-Christ et sa doctrine; Histoire de la naissance de l'Église, de son organisation et de ses progrès pendant le premier siècle*, Tome 1–2, Paris, 1838; cp. Lindeskog, pp. 96 ff.

170. For a survey of the literature, cp. Lindeskog, Chs. V, X, and his exhaustive bibliographical list, pp. 328 ff.

171. Klausner complains with justification of A. Schweitzer's inadequate attention to Jewish writers. Salvador's work, to which Klausner attaches great importance, Schweitzer mentions in a short footnote, carelessly misspelling his name (cp. *The Quest of the Historical Jesus*, Engl., 2nd ed., London, 1926, p. 162, n. 2). See Klausner, *Jesus of Nazareth*, Engl., p. 107.

172. Robert Eisler, *The Messiah Jesus and John the Baptist, according to Flavius Josephus' recently rediscovered 'Capture of Jerusalem' and the other Jewish and Christian Sources*, Engl., London, 1931, p. x: "I was actuated almost exclusively by a boundless curiosity and a passionate desire to get at the real truth."

173. K. Kohler, *The Origins of Church and Synagogue*, p. 232.

174. Klausner, pp. 9, 369 ff.; cp. also Klausner's recent book, *From Jesus to Paul*, English translation by W. F. Stinespring, New York, 1943, p. ix.

175. Ernest R. Trattner, *As a Jew sees Jesus*, New York and London, 1931, p. 55.

176. Graetz, *History of the Jews*, Engl., II, p. 155.

177. Trattner, *op. cit.*, p. 49.   178. *Ibid.*, p. 50.

179. H. Graetz, *History of the Jews*, Engl., II, p. 142; cp. Klausner, pp. 275, 371.

180. Martin Buber, *Die Stunde und die Erkenntnis*, Berlin, 1936, pp. 159 f.

181. This is the burden of Klausner's recent book, *From Jesus to Paul*.

182. Enelow, *A Jewish view of Jesus*, p. 159; Montefiore says of Paul that he was "a religious genius of the first order" ("Rabbinic Judaism and St. Paul", *J. Q. R.*, Jan. 1901).

183. "Paul", says Graetz, "conceived Christianity to be the very opposition of Judaism. The one was founded on Law and compulsion, the other owed its origin to freedom and grace" (II. p. 231); cf. S. Schechter's attitude to Paul and Paulinism, N. Bentwich, *Solomon Schechter*, Cambridge, 1938, pp. 102, 176, 290.

184. Graetz, *ibid.*, II, pp. 224 f.; but cp. Klausner, *op. cit.*, pp. 275 f.

185. Kaufmann Kohler, *The Origins of the Synagogue and Church*, p. 260; cp. Enelow, *op. cit.*, p. 159.

186. But cp. Solomon Grayzell, Vallentine's *J. E.*, p. 463a. Dr. Grayzell says: "The Epistles of Paul are permeated with Jewish concepts and Jewish modes of thought." But elsewhere, Grayzell says that Paul could not have been for any length of time a pupil of Gamaliel "since his subsequent writings show no evidence of an understanding of Pharisaism" (*ibid.*, p. 505b); Montefiore holds Paul's opposition "of work and faith, and of merit and grace" as inapplicable to Rabbinic Judaism, which is an "unsystematic mixture of works and of faith, of grace and of merit" (*J. Q. R.*, Jan. 1901, p. 183).

187. But cp. Klausner, *From Jesus to Paul*, p. 309; Klausner says: "it seems to me that there is evidence, even if it is not absolutely conclusive, that Paul *was* a pupil of Rabban Gamaliel".

188. *The Origins of the Synagogue and Church*, p. 261; cp. also Kohler's article on "Paul", *J. E.*, XI, pp. 79 ff.; cp. also Klausner, *From Jesus to Paul*, pp. 304 f. Klausner says: "If Paul could without sufficient grounds assign Jesus to the house of David, why could he not assign himself to the house of Saul?" Klausner explains that he called himself a Benjaminite on the grounds that his namesake King Saul also belonged to that tribe (!).

189. *The Origins of the Synagogue and Church*, p. 262; cp. Klausner, *From Paul to Jesus*, pp. 467 ff. Many of Kaufmann Kohler's views occur in Prof. Klausner's book.

190. Dr. Isaac M. Wise, *The Martyrdom of Jesus of Nazareth*, Cincinnati, 1874, p. 107. Klausner repeatedly stresses the opportunism of Paul; he calls him "a thorough-going opportunist", *op. cit.*, p. 429; cp. p. 506.

191. *Ibid.*, p. 127. Dr. Wise's denial of the actual Crucifixion of Jesus is

based upon the apparent similarity between the martyrdom of Jesus and that of Antigonus who was scourged and crucified by the Romans under Antony. Paul made use of the death of the latter because there was great sympathy amongst the peoples of the east for him. Cp. also Salomon Reinach, *Orpheus, A history of religions*, London, 1931, pp. 245 f., 249 f.

192. Reinach, *Orpheus*, p. 253; cp. p. 257 f. A peculiar view is that of Moriz Friedländer, who sees in Paul a representative of Jewish Hellenism which was opposed to the Pharisaic point of view. Though Paul thought himself a Pharisee, "ein richtiger Pharisäer ist er dennoch niemals gewesen". When Paul first heard Apollos preach in Ephesus "da wurde er inne, dass der Inhalt seiner Predigt sich mit dem gottgeoffenbarten Evangelium Jesu decke". This would, of course, mean that the essence of the Gospel message existed independently of the preaching of Jesus. Indeed, Friedländer says of Apollos: "Dieser predigte, ohne noch von Jesu Kenntnis zu haben, sein hellenistisches Judentum frei in den Synagogen der griechischen Diaspora." *Die religiösen Bewegungen*, pp. 342 f.; cp. also pp. 344, 349 ff.

193. Klausner, *From Jesus to Paul*, p. 119.   194. *Ibid.*, pp. 311 f.

195. Cp. *ibid.*, p. 310; *Shab.* 30b. In a note Klausner explains that "there is no good basis for the conclusion that the Rabban Gamaliel, who discoursed about the Messianic Age, was Rabban Gamaliel II (Rabban Gamaliel of Jabneh), as Bacher asserts against I. S. Bloch" (p. 311, n. 40); cf. Strack-Billerbeck, III, p. 856, note.

196. The reference is to *Shab.* 30b where, to Gamaliel's teaching regarding the Messianic age, somebody referred to as "that pupil" is supposed to have laughed and to have quoted Eccl. 1. 9: There is no new thing under the sun; cp. Klausner, *From Jesus to Paul*, pp. 600 f.; *Abot*, III, 12, contains this striking passage: R. Eleazer of Modiim said: "If a man profanes the Hallowed Things (some texts read 'the Sabbaths') and despises the set feasts, and puts his fellow to shame publicly, and makes void the covenant of Abraham our father (*i.e.* circumcision) and discloses meanings in the Law which are not according to *Halakah*, even though a knowledge of the Law and good works are his, he has no share in the world to come" (cp. A. Jellinek, Zur Geschichte der Polemik gegen das Christentum, *Orient*, x (1847), p. 413; G. Kittel, Paulus im Talmud, *Rabbinica*, Leipzig, 1920).

197. *Ibid.*, p. 312; cp. p. 465. Klausner explains that Paul, influenced by his environment, created a religion "which was Judaism and non-Judaism at the same time. Such a religion", the author says, "could not have been created or founded by Jesus, who, with all the strange, non-Jewish elements that came to him, perhaps from the schismatic Jewish sects founded by apocalyptists, or, more correctly, from a very vivid expectation of 'the end of days', was nevertheless a Jew rooted in the soil of Palestine".

198. *Ibid.*, p. 466; a similar view is expressed by M. Friedländer. He describes Paul as "der Diasporajude, in dessen Brust zwei Seelen wohnten, zwei Kulturen, die jüdische und die griechische, miteinander rangen" (*Die relig. Beweg.*, p. 371).

199. *Op. cit.*, p. 581.   200. *Ibid.*, pp. 581 f.

201. *Ibid.*, p. 588.

202. Jesus' teaching already contained the germ for the future rise of Christianity, cp. *Jesus of Nazareth*, p. 371.

203. *Ibid.*, p. 590; it is to be noted that Klausner attaches considerable importance to the influence of the primitive Jewish Church upon the views of Paul. The germs of some characteristic tendencies in Pauline thought are already present, according to Klausner, in primitive Christianity, while still on Jewish soil. If this were not so, it is difficult to see, Klausner says, the reason why James the brother of Jesus was executed in A.D. 62. He thus ignores Eisler's hypothesis which gives a political interpretation to the death of James. This Eisler does by connecting the brother of the Lord with the ultra-nationalist party which, apparently dissatisfied with the pro-Roman policy of the priestly hierarchy, acclaimed Jesus to the high-priestly office. Ananus, however, profiting "by the interregnum in the Roman governorship after the death of Festus" had James executed (Robert Eisler, *The Messiah Jesus and John the Baptist*, Engl., London, 1931, pp. 540 ff.).

204. Quoted by Lindeskog, p. 27.

205. Cp. Lindeskog, pp. 269, 276. "Like the Prophets of old, Jesus unhesitatingly criticized the religion of his people; but no more than they, did he dream of instituting any independent organization or of becoming the founder of a new faith" (Trattner, p. 46).

206. Moriz Friedländer, *Die religiösen Bewegungen*, p. 317.

207. Enelow, *op. cit.*, p. 73.

208. Graetz, II, p. 156; cp. Trattner, p. 55   See also p. 323, n. 5

209. Cp. Graetz, II, pp. 149 ff.; Moriz Friedländer's view, according to which Jesus acted in conscious opposition to the Pharisees and stood on the side of the *Amme ha-arez*, found little support among Jewish scholars (cp. Klausner, p. 116); for Friedländer's view concerning the *Am ha-arez*, see Lindeskog, p. 153.

210. Cp. Klausner, pp. 224 f.; cp. also his remark concerning Delitzsch's book, *Jesus und Hillel*, Leipzig, 1879, p. 224, n. 99; sometimes Jesus conformed to the views of the School of Shammai (*ibid.*, p. 374).

211. Cecil Roth, *A short history of the Jewish people*, London, 1936, p. 140.

212. Moriz Friedländer, *op. cit.*, p. 316.

213. Trattner, *op. cit.*, pp. 50 f.

214. Enelow, p. 85.

215. Enelow, *op. cit.*, p. 86; cp. pp. 93, 137; cp. Kohler, *Origins of Church and Synagogue*, p. 218.

216. Adolph Danziger, *Jewish Forerunners of Christianity*, London, 1904, p. 32. Danziger comments on the death of Jesus: "Jesus died for the essence of all religion; for purity, charity and holiness; for a cause in which death itself is a godly thing" (*ibid.*, p. 51).

217. Cp. *Die Relig. Bewegungen*, p. 340: "Es bestimmt nicht den geistigen Adel einer grossen Persönlichkeit, aus dem Nichts zu stammen . . . Aber deswegen ihr das Verdienst der Initiative absprechen und ihr Werk in eine Summe von Massenwirkungen aufheben . . . hiesse Ursache und Wirkung kritiklos durcheinander werfen und das Wesen der geschichtlichen Kausalität arg missdeuten".

218. I. M. Wise, *The Martyrdom of Jesus*, p. 133. The author refers to his own book, *Judaism, Its Doctrines and Duties*, 1872; Wise compares his book with the Gospels and naïvely claims superiority for his own work on the grounds that it contains no reference to Satan, etc.

219. *Ibid.*, p. 132; cp. also the view of S. Reinach, *Orpheus*, p. 153.

220. Enelow, *op. cit.*, pp. 14 f.

221. Montefiore, *Rabbinic Literature and Gospel Teachings*, London, 1930, p. 85; cp. also *ibid.*, pp. 47, 52, 102 f., 221 f., 254 f., etc.

222. Enelow, *op. cit.*, p. 18; cp. p. 26.   223. Klausner, *Jesus*, p. 374.

224. Graetz, II, p. 368.   225. Klausner, *From Jesus to Paul*, p. 261.

226. Graetz, *op. cit.*, II, p. 150; cp. Klausner, pp. 110 ff.

227. Klausner, *ibid.*, p. 211; cp. p. 202.   228. Klausner, pp. 211, 245.

229. Cp. Trattner, *op. cit.*, p. 41.   230. Cp. Lindeskog, pp. 251 ff.

231. Cp. Lindeskog, p. 252.

232. Klausner, in a prefatory note to his most recent book, *From Jesus to Paul*, remarks: "I came to the conclusion, after much research, that Jesus considered himself to be the Messiah, and that, by means of the repentance and the morality which he preached in Jewish cities, he expected to bring redemption to Israel"; p. ix; cp. pp. 4, 255 ff., etc.

233. R. T. Herford, *Jesus Christ* (small pamphlet), London, 1901, p. 18. Herford holds that the final step of the deification of Jesus was taken by "John", by identifying him with the Divine Word (*ibid.*, p. 20).

234. *From Jesus to Paul*, p. 107.

235. Eisler's main argument seems to rest upon the fact of Jesus' Crucifixion as an "auctor seditionis" (cp. *op. cit.*, pp. 510 ff.); the reconstruction of his sources, his treatment of the so-called *Testimonium Flavianum*, and his use of the Slavonic *Bellum Judaicum*, has met with severe criticism; cp. Gustav Pfannmüller, *Jesus im Urteil d. Jahrhunderte*, Berlin, 1939, pp. 399 ff.; cp. also Lindeskog, *op. cit.*, pp. 193 f.

236. *Am ha-arez* in Friedländer's view is not the "idiotische Pöbel" of a later period, but the land-gentry which stood in opposition to the Pharisaic party; cp. *Die relig. Bewegungen*, pp. 78 ff.; but cp. I. Abrahams' notes on the *Am ha-arez* appended to Montefiore's commentary, 2nd ed.

237. Friedländer sees the mission of Jesus in the attempt to break the power of Pharisaism which hindered Judaism from becoming a world-religion. But Paul went one step further; the Apostle broke the letter of the Law of Moses; cp. *op. cit.*, p. 354.

238. Moriz Friedländer, *Die relig. Bewegungen*, pp. 318 ff. It is interesting to note that Friedländer, like other Jewish scholars, feels the harmony of the person of Jesus disturbed by the double strain in his character (severity and humility, love and rigour, etc.). But Friedländer ingeniously explains the double presentation of the character of Jesus by the double conception people had of the Messiah: "bald als eine von himmlischer Liebe überquillende, bald als eine kriegerische, die Welt in Schrecken setzende, mit dem Hauch seines Mundes tötende Persönlichkeit". This duality "ist eine Schöpfung der Evangelisten"; it does not belong to the historical Jesus. It only betrays the close connexion between primitive Christianity and the Apocalyptic literature. But the historical Jesus by far outdistances (überragt) the mythological portrait (*ibid.*, pp. 323–328).

239. M. Friedländer, *op. cit.*, p. 339; it may be noted that Klausner attributes the emphasis upon the individual, not to Jesus, but to Paul, and regards it as a departure from traditional Jewish teaching, cf. Klausner, *From Jesus to Paul*, pp. 119, 535.

240. Cf. Abba Hillel Silver, *A history of Messianic Speculation in Israel from the 1st through the 17th Centuries*, New York, 1927, pp. 6ff.

241. Ernest R. Trattner, *As a Jew sees Jesus*, New York and London, 1931, p. 45.

242. *Ibid.*, p. 64. 243. *Ibid.*, p. 66.

244. *Ibid.*, p. 111; "after his death, his disagreements with contemporary Judaism were magnified in the interests of Gentile propaganda" (p. 50).

245. *Ibid.*, p. 78; cp. also pp. 145 f. Trattner explains that Jesus' emphatic "I say unto you"—"is merely ... a very old and approved Rabbinical method" (p. 86); cp. *supra*, p. 37.

246. *Ibid.*, p. 95. 247. *Ibid.*, p. 49. 248. *Ibid.*, p. 133.

249. Enelow, *op. cit.*, p. 128. 250. *Ibid.*, p. 130.

251. Enelow, *op. cit.*, p. 101.

252. Montefiore, *The teaching of Jesus*, p. 20; S. G. (1927), p. 25; cp. D. Chwolson, *Das Letzte Passamahl Christi*, p. 89; "Der Kern und die Quintessenz der Lehre Christi besteht, wie allgemein erkannt wird in der Vergeistigung der Religion".

253. Enelow, *op. cit.*, pp. 131 f.; cp. p. 92

254. Klausner, *From Paul to Jesus*, pp. 266, 267 f.

255. Cp. H. von Soden, *Die urchristliche Literaturgeschichte*, Berlin, 1905, Engl. *The History of Early Christian Literature*, 1906, pp. 227 ff., 234.

256. Cp. Klausner, *op. cit.*, p. 213.

257. *Ibid.*, p. 212; it is difficult to see what Klausner means by the phrase "the disciples decided". Does he visualize some sort of a conference which resulted in a change of policy? The author is actually trying to evade unobtrusively a problem of the greatest importance. It involves the question: how did the Messianic movement, with its national implications, become a purely mystical movement continued by Paul? On Klausner's own evidence, the change began not with the Apostle of the Gentiles, but with the primitive Church in Palestine (cp. *ibid.*, pp. 343 *et al.*)

258. *Ibid.*, p. 268; cp. also pp. 437 f.

259. Klausner, *Jesus of Nazareth*, pp. 312 f.

260. Maimonides, *Mishneh Torah (Yad ha-Hazakah)*, *Hilkhot Melakhim*, XIV, 4; cp. *supra*, pp. 13 f.

261. Cp. Enelow, *op. cit.*, pp. 168 f.

262. Enelow, *op. cit.*, p. 9.

263. Trattner, *op. cit.*, foreword.

264. Klausner, *Jesus of Nazareth*, pp. 413 f.

265. Graetz, *op. cit.*, II, p. 149.

266. Kohler, *The Origins of the Synagogue*, p. 231.

267. Trattner, *op. cit.*, p. 40; cp. Montefiore, *The Religious Teaching of Jesus*, pp. 56 ff.

268. Enelow, *op. cit.*, p. 167.

269. *Ibid.*, p. 170; Schalom Ben-Chorin, in his preface to the booklet containing George L. B. Sloan's address on the Christian view on the O. T. and his own answer, well remarks: "Die protestantische Kirche, ebenso wie die Synagoge, kann heute nicht durch einen Sprecher verbindlich vertreten werden. Was allein möglich scheint in dieser Weltstunde, ist ein Glaubensgespräch zwischen Juden und Christen. Das heisst also zwischen *Einzelnen*, die

als *Einzelne* sprechen, nicht als Delegierte einer Gruppe" (*Das christliche Verständnis des Alten Testaments und der jüdische Einwand*, Jerusalem, 1941).

270. *Ibid.*, pp. 171 f.

271. *Ibid.*, pp. 172 f.; cf. Buber, *Die Stunde und die Erkenntnis*, p. 153: "Wir wissen aber auch, wie wir wissen, dass Luft ist . . . dass Raum ist . . . tiefer, echter wissen wir, dass die Weltgeschichte nicht bis auf ihren Grund aufgebrochen, dass die Welt noch nicht erlöst ist. Wir *spüren* die Unerlöstheit der Welt."

272. *Ibid.*, p. 179; cp. p. 181.   273. Cp. *ibid.*, p. 43.

274. *Ibid.*, pp. 176,178.

NOTES TO CHAPTER V

1. Mk. 1. 15; cf. Lk. 4. 20 f.

2. Cp. Mt. 3. 2: Prof. F. C. Burkitt may be right, however, in pointing out that the words ἤγγικε γὰρ ἡ βασιλεία τῶν οὐρανῶν in Mt. 3. 2, are a Matthæan addition, as they are lacking in Luke. If so, then "the message of John was comprised in the single word 'Repent' "! (F. C. Burkitt, *Christian Beginnings*, London, 1924, pp. 15 f.)

3. Mt. 4. 23; cp. 9. 35.   4. Mt. 9. 12 and parallels.   5. Lk. 19. 10.

6. Mt. 11. 5.   7. Mt. 9. 11 and parallels.   8. Jn. 12. 19.

9. Enelow, *op. cit.*, p. 138.   10. Mt. 9. 36.

11. The deeper reasons for the antagonism which finally led to our Lord's death, we have discussed elsewhere, see *supra*, pp. 34–42.

12. Edmond Fleg (Flegenheimer) has shown fine psychological insight in portraying the double effect which Jesus exerted, upon the common people; cf. *Jesus: told by the Wandering Jew*, London, 1934.

13. Cf. *supra*, Ch. IV, n. 238; Montefiore, who admits the double strain in Jesus' character and often refers to his inconsistency (cp. *The Teaching of Jesus*, p. 53), speaks at the same time of his character as "finely balanced and tempered" (cf. *S. G.*, 1909, p. 182); cp. also Cecil Roth, *A history of the Jewish people*, p. 140.

14. Cp. Jer. 20. 7–9.

15. Mt. 7. 13 f.; cp. Lk. 13. 24: ἀγωνίζεσθε εἰσελθεῖν διὰ τῆς στενῆς θύρας.

16. Lk. 14. 25 ff.   17. Cp. Mt. 10. 37 f.   18. Lk. 9. 62.

19. Jn. 6. 66.   20. Graetz, *op. cit.*, II, p. 166.

21. Klausner, *Jesus*, p. 356.

22. Prof. Arnold Meyer, *Die moderne Forschung über die Geschichte des Urchristentums*, ein Vortrag gehalten auf dem ersten religionswissenschaftlichen Kongresse in Stockholm, 1. Sept. 1897, Freiburg in B., 1898, p. 6.

23. Cp. Meyer, *ibid.*, p. 16.

24. W. Bousset, *Kyrios Christos*, Göttingen, 1921, p. xiii—Paul the Pharisee must have come in contact with Greek-pagan thought and speculations which he carefully stored up in his mind, and which came to the surface under the impact of the new faith: "Und wie bei einem Eisbruch die träge Masse in Fluss gerät und die Eisschollen sich stossen u. schieben und über einander türmen, so ist nun die Gedankenmasse des Paulus in Fluss geraten und hat sich zu wunderlichen Massen aufgetürmt, und das Ergebnis war—die paulinische Theologie".

25. Meyer, *ibid.*, p. 20.

26. Harnack, quoted by Meyer, *op. cit.*, p. 36.

27. Klausner, *From Jesus to Paul*, pp. 464 f.; and elsewhere. It is of interest to note that Klausner's detailed analysis of Philonian conceptions related to Pauline theology yield negative proof against the author's intention. It seems to have escaped Prof. Klausner that he is actually proving the opposite. For example, he points out that Philo's goal was the advancement of supreme happiness for the human race (*De Virtutibus—de Caritate* II, 395)—but was this Paul's goal? Paul, who worked upon the principle of eternal predestination! Again, he tells us that Philo speaks of man as "having come into being as a copy or fragment or ray of that blessed nature" ("the divine spark" idea) (*De Mundi Opificio*, I, 35)—this "modernist" conception is foreign to Paul, to whom man is only related to God by *adoption*. Again, to show the high opinion Philo entertained about man, Klausner quotes his sentence: "Assuredly there is in the soul of every man, however undistinguished he may be, a detestation for evil" (*De Specialibus Legibus*, III, M II, 312)—but this is not Paul's opinion about fallen man in whom sin reigns unto death (cp. Rom. 5. 21). The "delight in the law of God after the inward man" in Rom. 7. 22 applies only to the awakened sinner or the struggling saint. The others are dead in their sins till they are quickened with the risen Lord (Col. 2. 13). Pauline theology reveals a *low* opinion of man. Again, Philo's mysticism which Klausner describes as the attainment to the highest knowledge, the "sober intoxication" (μέθη νηφάλιος), "the state in which man's knowledge of himself is fused with the heavenly light which is shed from deity into the soul of man" (Klausner, p. 196), is different from the life ἐν Χριστῷ Ἰησοῦ (cp. Gal. 2. 20) of which St. Paul speaks. This *unio mystica* of which Klausner speaks is not easily applied to Paul, as Deissmann has shown. Herein the Apostle differs from the mystics of the Middle Ages. In Pauline theology no "fusion" is possible; its feature is the dying with Christ in order to be raised with Him (cp. Rom. 6. 8 ff.; Col. 3. 1; cp. also Adolf Deissmann, *Paul*, Engl., London, 1926, pp. 147 ff.). That Philo's conception of the Messiah is entirely different from the Christian view, Klausner admits himself: "at this point Christianity was not able to borrow anything whatever from Philo" (*op. cit.*, p. 198).

With regard to pagan Hellenism, Klausner finds only minor affinities, apart from the idea of the sacraments and the conception of the Son of God. Its importance, he sees, not so much in the influence of explicit doctrine as in the general tendency, the "colour", and the atmosphere (cp. *op. cit.*, pp. 464 ff.). On the main issue, as to the faith in the risen Christ, Klausner definitely dissociates the early Church from the influence of pagan cults: "The differences between the stories about the crucifixion and resurrection of Jesus and the stories of the pagans about the death and resurrection of their gods are so numerous and so great, the possibility of death by crucifixion, at the hands of the Roman procurator, for anyone who claimed to be the Messiah was so near certainty, and belief in the resurrection of the dead was so widespread in Israel in the period of the Second Temple that all three of these reasons force us to conclude that the fate of Jesus is not just a reflexion of the fate of the gods Osiris, Attis, Adonis, Mithras, and other such divinities" (Klausner, *ibid.*, p. 107).

28. Meyer, *op. cit.*, p. 17. Klausner is well aware of the difficulty; after

strongly affirming that "*there is nothing in all the teaching of Paul, as there is nothing in the teaching of Jesus, which is not grounded in the Old Testament, or in the Apocryphal, Pseudepigraphical, and Tannaitic literature of his time*" (p. 482; Klausner's italics), he adds: "Nevertheless, it is difficult to explain the adoration, amounting almost to deification, with which Paul regarded Jesus merely as an intensification of the Jewish Messianic idea" (p. 484). It is on these grounds that Klausner is driven to assume the influence of "pagan-philosophic" ideas "which *hovered in the air* in the Hellenized cities in which Paul lived and preached".

29. Cp. Carl von Weizsäcker, *The Apostolic Age of the Christian Church*, English translation, London and New York, 1894, I, pp. 124, 130 f.; cp. Bousset, *Die Religion des Judentums*, 1906, pp. 307 f., n. 2.

30. Cf. Klausner, *From Jesus to Paul*, p. 270.   31. Cf. 1 Cor. 15. 3 ff.

32. Meyer, *ibid.*, p. 69; cp. also p. 65. Klausner, *op. cit.*, p. 261: "If Jesus had not been a remarkable personality, who did remarkable deeds and spoke remarkable words, he would have faded from the memory of his disciples after a shameful death on the cross, as faded the memory of the rest of the 'false Messiahs', that is to say, the saviours who did not succeed in saving."

33. Cp. *supra*, note 27.

34. Cp. *supra*, p. 149. Faith in the Resurrection was now related to the person of Jesus, cp. Acts 4. 2.

35. Klausner, *op. cit.*, p. 437.   36. Cf. Klausner, *ibid.*, p. 440.

37. Schäder has rightly stressed the fact that the Cross with Paul does not lead to death, but to Resurrection and life. The Apostle knew of the meaning of the Cross in the light of the Resurrection (cp. Meyer, *op. cit.*, p. 31).

38. Acts 2. 41; 4. 4.

39. Graetz explains the success of the early Church by the fact that the message was chiefly intended for the simple and dejected, whom the Law deprived of their rights "while Christianity opened the Kingdom of Heaven to them" (*op. cit.*, II, p. 367). But this is not borne out by Christian tradition which includes amongst the believers men like Nicodemus and Joseph of Arimathea and many priests and Pharisees.

40. But cp. Johannes von Walter, *Die Geschichte des Christentums*, Gütersloh, 1932, pp. 26 ff., where separation is already contemplated by Jesus.

41. Cp. Jn. 11. 49–51; Acts 23. 5. Jn. attributes to the High Priest the gift of Prophecy and Paul acknowledges him to be the ruler of the people. (There must have been an old tradition which attached the gift of prophecy to the high-priestly office. Strack-Billerbeck quote some passages where prophecy is uttered unawares, but have nothing to show for the connexion between the high-priesthood and the gift of prophesying.)

42. Graetz, II, pp. 171 f. From the context it would appear that he is actually speaking of the early Christians (? !).

43. Weizsäcker, *op. cit.*, I, p. 130.

44. Dr. Joseph Klausner, *Die messianischen Vorstellungen des jüdischen Volkes im Zeitalter der Tannaiten*, Berlin, 1904, p. 2; cp. p. 119.

45. *Ibid.*, p. 14 (Klausner's italics).   46. Cp. *infra.*, p. 189 f.

47. Klausner, *op. cit.*, p. 117; W. Bousset admits that after the Destruction of Jerusalem "scheint das Interesse an der Gestalt des Messias dann allerdings sehr stark zurückgetreten zu sein", and he refers to Klausner's work (cp. *Die*

Religion des Judentums im neutestamentlichen Zeitalter, Berlin, 1906, pp. 257 f., n. 3). But Bousset offers no explanation for this strange phenomenon. Cp. also Paul Volz, *Jüdische Eschatologie von Daniel bis Akiba*, Tübingen und Leipzig, 1903, pp. 198 ff.

48. Bousset, *op. cit.*, pp. 255 f.: "Wenn nicht noch andere Quellen neben denen der jüdischen Apokalyptik vorlägen, namentlich die neutestamentlichen Schriften, könnte man zu der Anschauung kommen als hätte in der Hoffnung des Spätjudentums die Gestalt des Messias kaum noch existiert"; cp. also Burkitt, *op. cit.*, p. 27.

49. Cp. W. Bousset, *Kyrios Christos*, p. 2. But Bousset limits the evidence of the N. T. to the Synoptic Gospels.

50. Cp. *ibid.*, pp. 151 ff.   51. Enelow, *op. cit.*, pp. 114 f.

52. Klausner, *From Jesus to Paul*, p. 313.

53. Bousset, *Kyrios Christos*, p. 2.   54. Bousset, *ibid.*, p. 17.

55. Burkitt, *op. cit.*, pp. 104 f.; cp. Prof. Walter Grundmann (Jena), *Das Problem des hellenistischen Christentums innerhalb der Jerusalemer Urgemeinde* (*Zeitschrift für die neutestamentliche Wissenschaft*, herausg. von H. Lietzmann, u. W. Eltester, Bd. 38/1939), p. 65: "Es ist ein beredter Hinweis auf die Tiefe dieser Spaltung (*i.e.* between the Hellenists and Judaizing Hebrew Christians), wenn die Zwölf und ihre Anhänger in der Stadt bleiben können, während die Sieben und die Hellenisten sie verlassen müssen" (Wetter's words quoted by Grundmann).

56. Burkitt, *op. cit.*, pp. 62 f.

57. Klausner, *From Jesus to Paul*, p. 321, n. 13.

58. Cp. Klausner, *ibid.*, p. 496.

59. Cp. Strack-Billerbeck, Exkurs 29: *Diese Welt, die Tage des Messias*, etc., IVB, pp. 814 ff.   60. Cp. *ibid.*, IVA, pp. 1 ff.

61. 1 Jn. 2. 7: οὐκ ἐντολὴν καινὴν γράφω ὑμῖν, ἀλλ' ἐντολὴν παλαιὰν; cp. Bousset, *Kyrios Christos*, p. 293.

62. W. Bousset presents Paul as "the great opposer and destroyer of the Law" (*Die Religion des Judentums im neutest. Zeitalter*, p. 138). But such a view rests upon a misunderstanding. Paul never called in question the sanctity of the Law. See Schoeps' discussion of the subject in *Aus früchristl. Zeit*, pp. 221 ff.

63. Cp. Julius Wagenmann, *Die Stellung des Apostels Paulus neben den Zwölf in den ersten zwei Jahrhunderten*, Giessen, 1926, p. 26.

64. For the central importance of the Law, see Bousset, *Die Relig. d. Judentums im neutest. Zeitalter*, pp. 136 ff.

65. Cf. Klausner, *Paul*, p. 281; *Jesus*, p. 41.

66. Cf. *Ab. Zarah*, 16b–17a.   67. Grundmann, *ZNW*, 38/1939, pp. 65 ff.

68. Cp. George Foot Moore, *Judaism*, II, p. 376.

69. Kaufmann Kohler, *Jewish Theology*, p. 427.

70. Burkitt, *op. cit.*, pp. 46 f.

71. Cf. the important essay by Edwyn Clement Hoskyns, "Jesus the Messiah", *Mysterium Christi*, ed. by G. K. A. Bell and A. Deissmann, 1930, pp. 69 ff. Cf. also Schoeps, *Theologie*, pp. 406 ff.

72. Paul Volz, *Der Prophet Jeremia*, Leipzig, 1928, pp. 103 f.; cp. also *Jesaia II*, Leipzig, 1932, pp. 45 f. Ben-Chorin, however, holds that the prophets did not oppose the cult itself "sondern seiner Überbetonung und der Irrlehre,

dass Opfer genüge und den Menschen vom Halten der Gesetze entbinde, welche die Gebiete von *zedek* und *mischpath* berühren. . . ." (*op. cit.*, p. 46). But Hermann Cohen holds a different view. In his book *Die Religion der Vernunft aus den Quellen des Judentums*, Leipzig, 1919, he says: "Unter den Wundern, welche für die geschichtliche Auffassung mit dem Wunder des Monotheismus verbunden sind, steht doch vielleicht an erster Stelle der Kampf der Propheten gegen das *Opfer*" (p. 200). "Die Geschichte des Prophetismus verläuft beim Opfer in zwei Wegen. Der eine hält sich in der Verwerfung des *Opfers*, der andere hingegen geht auf seine Verwandlung . . ." (p. 205).

73. Cp. Volz, *Jesaia* II, p. 218.

74. Bousset, *Die Religion des Judentums*, p. 124 (his italics).

75. Bousset, *ibid.*, pp. 128 ff. Bousset quotes three facts to prove this important point:

(1) The existence of the Essenes, who, though universally esteemed for their great piety, did not participate in Temple-cult, at least not in the animal sacrifices.

(2) The general tendency of Jesus' message, directed against the outward ceremonial.

(3) The fact that after the destruction of the Temple Judaism remained unshaken.

76. Cp. Klausner, *Die messianischen Vorstellungen*, pp. 117 f.; Schlatter has shown that there existed some form of Temple-service even after the Destruction, cp. A. Schlatter, *Die Tage Trajans und Hadrians*, pp. 55 ff.

77. Cp. 1 Peter 2. 5. 78. Bousset, *Die Religion des Judentums*, p. 130.

79. E. Klostermann regards the quotation both in Mt. 9. 13 and 12. 7 as not original, entirely due to the "Biblizist Mt." and interfering with the context (*Handbuch z. N.T.*, *Das Matthäusevangelium*, Tübingen, 1927, pp. 81, 105).

80. Cp. *Yoma* 8. 9: For transgressions that are between man and God, the Day of Atonement effects atonement, but for transgressions that are between a man and his fellow, the Day of Atonement effects atonement only if he has appeased his fellow (Danby). Cp. also Thomas Walker, *Hebrew Religion between the Testaments*, London, 1937, pp. 117 f.

81. Klostermann says that μεῖζον "geht (wie Mt. 11. 9; 12, 41 f.) doch nicht auf ein wirkliches Neutrum." The meaning of the passage is: "kann der Tempel schon seine Diener vom Sabbatgebot entbinden, wie viel mehr der Messias seine Jünger" (Klostermann, however, thinks the whole text out of place here, cp. *op. cit.*, p. 105).

82. But cp. Klostermann, *Das Markusevangelium*, Tübingen, 1926, p. 142.

83. Klostermann points to an important difference between Mt. and Mark concerning the "false witnesses"; he says of Mt.: "Durch die (weitere) Auslassung von Mc. 59 (Ch. 14) und durch die ausdrückliche Betonung von ὕστερον und δύο (=die erforderlichen zwei, die Mt. also übereinstimmen lässt) scheint er die Aussagen über das Tempelwort nicht wie Mc. als weiteres Beispiel der ungültigen ψευδομαρτυρίαι zu rechnen, sondern als ein gültiges Zeugnis, dessen schwerwiegender *Inhalt* nun den Hohenpriester zu einer direkten Frage veranlasst" (*op. cit.*, p. 215). Erwin Preuschen remarks: "jede Christus feindliche Aussage galt als ψευδομαρτυρία (*Handbuch z. N.T.*,

Die Apostelgeschichte, Tübingen, 1912, p. 38). For Schoeps' view, see *Theologie*, p. 444 n. 3. His objections are ill-founded.

84. Eisler for some reason regards John as having preserved the more genuine text (*op. cit.*, p. 496).   85. Cp. Preuschen, *op. cit.*, p. 38.

86. Ephiphanius, *Haer.* xxx, 16: ἦλθον καταλῦσαι τὰς θυσίας—ad abroganda sacrificia veni—Migne, xli, 431; it is a remarkable fact that in Jewish legend the birth of the Messiah is placed on the day of the Destruction of the Temple. Gressmann says: "die Zerstörung und der Neubau des Tempels (ist) mit dem Erscheinen des Messias aufs engste verknüpft" (*Der Mess.*, p. 449, n. 5). He leads this tradition back to Menaḥem ben Hiskia, who led the insurrection in A.D. 66 (cp. Jos. *Bell.* II, 17. 8–9). Menaḥem could have easily been singled out as the cause of the destruction (cp. Gressmann, pp. 458 ff.). There is, however, some difficulty as to the connexion between the coming of the Messiah and the destruction of the Temple. The reading is uncertain (cp. A. Cohen, *Midrash R. Lamentations*, p. 137, nn. 1, 2). בּרגליה (עַל רֵיגְלִיוֹ—Buber) may mean *because* of his coming; or *through* him (so Geiger) or, for his sake. Gressmann remarks: "die dritte Auffassung, wonach dieser (*i.e.* the Messiah) als Ursache gedacht ist, setzt Mk. 14. 58 voraus". It is therefore quite possible that the view which connects the Messiah with the destruction of the Temple goes back to a much older tradition (cp. *Jer. Talmud Ber.*, II, 4 fol. 5a; *Midrash Rabbah, Lamentations*, to 1. 16).

87. Burkitt, *op. cit.*, pp. 62 f. Cf. also the interesting admission of Schoeps', *Theologie*, p. 224.

88. Carl von Weizsäcker, *The Apostolic Age*, Engl., 1894, I, p. 159.

89. Cp. Strack-Billerbeck, II, pp. 282 f.; cp. Klausner, *Die mess. Vorstellungen*, p. 119. But cp. Prof. Schoeps' conclusion in *Aus frühchristl. Zeit*, pp. 107 ff.

90. *Ibid.*, II, p. 274.   91. Cp. Volz, *Jüdische Eschatologie*, p. 237.

92. Cp. Strack-Billerbeck, II, pp. 292 f., 297; cp. Bousset, *Die Religion des Judentums*, 1926, 3rd ed., pp. 206, 215.

93. For the *Ebed Jahve* and his messianic features, see Hugo Gressmann, *Der Messias*, Göttingen, 1929, pp. 308–323.

94. It is remarkable how little reference there is to the suffering Messiah in the apocalyptic literature (cp. Strack-Billerbeck, II, p. 282, n. 1).

95. Cp. also W. Baldensprenger, *Die messianisch-apokalyptischen Hoffnungen des Judentums*, Strassburg, 1903, pp. 88 ff. Baldensprenger takes over Schürer's simile and speaks of two poles in Judaism: Nomism and Messianism. In the ordinary way these two trends counterbalanced each other, but under special circumstances, *e.g.* under the influence of a powerful religious personality the balance could be upset. This does not, however, imply a conscious opposition to the Law, but a latent tendency in this direction (Unterströmung), cp. p. 215.

96. We have already pointed out Klausner's failure to establish a connexion between Paul and Philo. The same may be said of Moriz Friedländer. Friedländer connects all the great truths in Paul's Epistles with Jewish Hellenism. This includes his teaching about the Law, the Resurrection, Grace, Election, etc. For parallels he naturally goes to Philo. But his quotations rather tend to show the opposite. Friedländer, like so many other scholars, overlooks the fact that both Philo and Paul have at least one important source

in common, the O. T. It is also to be noted that not only Philo, but the Rabbis too, knew about the resurrection, grace, election, etc. (cp. Friedländer, *op. cit.*, pp. 349 ff.). For the relationship between Christian and apocalyptic writings see Baldensprenger, *op. cit.*, pp. 164 ff., 174 ff. His estimate of this literature is important: "Im Unterschied zu den prophetischen Messianismus bedeutet die Apokalyptik nicht Fortsetzung, sondern Abbruch, nicht Abschluss, sondern Antithese, nicht potenzirtes Erdenleben, sondern Gericht über das Vergangene und neuer Ansatz, sie ist nicht ein *Finale,* welches an ein früheres Motiv anklingt, sondern ein *neues Lied in höherem Chor*" (p. 174). In that it is detached from history and other-worldly, it essentially differs from the prophetic outlook. "Es gibt keinen anderen Punkt, in welchem sich das apokalyptische Judentum so scharf von der älteren Religion abhebt als die Vorliebe für die transzendente Welt."

97. Hoennicke assumes that Hebrews was written by a Jew for Jewish Christians, before the destruction of the Temple (Gustav Hoennicke, *Das Judenchristentum im ersten und zweiten Jahrhundert,* Berlin, 1908, p. 95); but see Hermann von Soden, *The History of Early Christian Literature,* Engl., 1906, pp. 248 ff. Herford, *Christianity in Talmud,* p. 384; "Hebr. is a sort of declaration of independence on the part of the Minim".

98. Cp. Hoennicke, *op. cit.,* pp. 90 ff. Hoennicke regards James as a document of the time when Hebrew Christians still participated in the Service of the Synagogue. 2.2 refers to the Synagogue and not to the ἐκκλησία, which has a Christian connotation.

99. Cp. Moore's excellent analysis of the *Didache, op. cit.,* I, pp. 188 f. He dates it at the beginning of the second century, and regards as its source a Jewish Christian community.

100. Moore, *ibid.,* I, p. 186; Prof. T. W. Manson says: "The strong antipharisaic tendency seems to belong both to the first evangelist and to his special source" (*The Teaching of Jesus,* 1935, p. 330, Additional Notes). Arnold Meyer justly calls attention to Rev., which shows "wie eng das Christentum mit der apokalyptischen Erwartung des Judentums, also mit den stärksten und innersten Fasern des jüdischen Lebens zusammenhängt . . ." (*Die moderne Forschung über die Geschichte des Urchristentums. Ein Vortrag,* p. 56).

101. Joël maintains that the "Yom Trajanus" in the *Megilla Ta'anit* 18b, which is a day of rejoicing, was due to the fact that at first Trajan declared himself willing to allow the rebuilding of the Temple. Such an attempt, however, was frustrated by the influence of the antinational and antinomistic section of Hebrew Christianity, as for them it was a question of to be or not to be (*Blicke,* p. 15; cp. also pp. 30 f.) The Destruction of the Temple was certainly of great consequence to Hebrew Christian theology, but Joël has no evidence for Hebrew Christian interference: (1) The "Yom Trajanus" is connected with the escape of Pappus and Luliani (Julianus); (2) it is doubtful whether טורײנוס can be identified with Trajan in view of the fact that the latter died a natural death. There is a suggestion that the incident refers to Trajan's general Lusius Quietus, who was executed by Trajan (cp. Schürer, I, p. 660, n. 62); (3) Trajan's record and his attitude to the Jewish people was not such as to show willingness for the restoration of its religious-national centre. Samuel Krauss suggests that the "Yom Trajanus" was to commemorate a Jewish victory over the Roman army (cp. *J. E.,* XII, 218b); this is also

Schlatter's view (cf. *Die Tage Trajans und Hadrians*, pp. 95 f.). The whole subject was recently re-discussed by Dr. Hans Bietenhard, Die Freiheitskriege d. Juden, *Judaica*, 1948, Hefte 1–3.

102. Though Samuel Lublinski represents the opposite view to our own, he has a sentence which deserves quoting: "Die Absonderung der jungen Kirche vom alten Stamm war eine Entwicklungsnotwendigkeit, die ohne wilde Kämpfe und Krämpfe und ohne Krisen nicht vollzogen werden konnte. Hier lässt sich die Schuld und Unschuld nicht mit der Elle messen" (p. 148).

103. Joël, *op. cit.*, II, p. 87. Grundmann expresses somewhat similar thoughts with regard to the Temple, but his presentation is too radical and includes *only* the Hellenistic element of the Church in Jerusalem (cp. "Das Problem des hellenistischen Christentums innerhalb der Jerusalemer Urgemeinde," *ZNW*, Bd 38/1939, p. 65). If Schoeps is right his description of Hebrew Christian views regarding the law can only apply to a certain section and a later age. Cf. *Theologie*, pp. 211 ff.

104. Joël's judgement, "Das Christentum enstand als Verwirklichung gerade der *nationalen* Hoffnung, die damals Israel hegte . . ." (*op. cit.*, pp. 25 f.), is an overemphasis of the national element. But that there were national motives which came into play need not be denied.

105. According to Graetz, Jesus chose to work amongst the lowly and the outcast because the middle class was already good enough (!) and the rich would not listen in any case (cp. *op. cit.*, II, p. 152).

106. It is difficult to see how Moehlman can assert: "The earliest Christian records (then) reveal no break between Jerusalem Jew and Christian prior to C. E. 66" (*op. cit.*, pp. 189 f.).

107. Cp. Erwin Preuschen's commentary to Acts: *Die Apostelgeschichte* (*Handbuch z. N. T.*), Tübingen, 1912, p. 37.

108. Klausner, *From Jesus to Paul*, pp. 271 f.

109. *Ibid.*, p. 280.   110. *Ibid.*, p. 369; cp. p. 368, n. 18.

111. Cp. Euseb. *H. e.*, II, 23. The passage reads: ('Ιάκωβος) ἐκαλεῖτο ὁ δίκαιος καὶ ὠβλίας, ὅ ἐστιν ἑλληνιστὶ περιοχὴ τοῦ λαοῦ, καὶ δικαιοσύνη. Klausner suggests three interpretations, of which the last seems to be the most natural: (1) ὠβλίαμ—עוֹפֶל עַם "strong tower of the people." (2) ὠβλίαμ—עוֹז לְעַם "strength of the people". (3) ὠβλίαμ אַב לְעַם "Father of the people." cp. Klausner, *op. cit.*, p. 279. But cp. the notes by H. J. Lawlor and J. E. L. Oulton to Euseb., II, p. 74. Burkitt says: "Oblias means nothing at all"; *op. cit.*, p. 58, n. 1. The whole subject is again discussed by Schoeps but inconclusively. Cp. Schoeps, *Aus frühchristl. Zeit*, pp. 120 ff and 301.

112. Euseb., *ibid.*, III, 5: κατά τινα χρησμόν τοῖς αὐτόθι δοκίμοις δι' ἀποκαλύψεως ἐκδοθέντα.

113. Epiphanius, *Adversus haer.* 29. 7; cp. 30. 2.   *De Mensuris et Ponderibus* 15: "discipuli omnes ab angelo moniti sunt, ut ex ea urbe migrarent".

114. Lawlor and Oulton, II, p. 82; or Julius Africanus, cp. Harnack, *Mission*, p. 413; cp. also Schmidtke, *Texte und Untersuchungen*, xxxvii.

115. Cf. Schürer, *The Jewish People*, Engl., 1890, Div. I, II, p. 208.

116. Cp. Lawlor and Oulton, II, p. 73. Cf. Guy Schofield, *In the Year 62*, The Murder of the Brother of the Lord and Its Consequences, 1962; also Jean Danielou, *The Theology of Jewish Christianity*, Vol. I, 1964.

117. Harnack, *Mission und Ausbreitung*, p. 413.

118. Schürer, Div. II, 1, p. 230.

119. Joël extends the nationalist tendency of the Messianic movement to the period of Simon Clopha (cp. Euseb. *h. e.*, III, 32). He says: "Simon Clopha teilte wie alle Judenchristen damals noch die nationalen Hoffnungen der Juden, und das Jahr seiner Hinrichtung 116 ist ja eben bezeichnend genug" (*Blicke*, p. 32, n. 1).

120. The importance which primitive Christianity attached to Jerusalem can be seen from Justin's *Dial.* Trypho asks Justin with understandable curiosity: "Tell me, do you really admit that this place, Jerusalem, shall be rebuilt; and do you expect your people to be gathered together . . .?" To this, Justin replies that for his part he has such a hope, though others "who belong to the pure and pious faith, and are true Christians, think otherwise" (*Dial.*, Ch. 80; cp. also Ch. 81). Cp. also Julius Wagenmann, *Die Stellung des Apostels Paulus neben den Zwölf in den ersten zwei Jahrhunderten*, Giessen, 1926, p. 28.

121. Harnack interprets the evidence from Eusebius and Epiphanius to mean that the *whole* Christian community left for Pella. He therefore feels himself entitled to assume that the Church consisted of a very small minority (cp. *Mission u. Ansbr.*, p. 413, and n. 5). But the evidence of Acts is against such an interpretation. It is therefore more reasonable to assume that only the leading members of the Church left the city. Hoennicke also assumes a very small Christian community in Palestine (*Das Judenchristentum im ersten und zweiten Jahrhundert*, Berlin, 1908, p. 175). But the fact of persecution is evidence for the growth of a movement.

122. Joël attributes to the Destruction of the Temple one of the main causes which brought about the separation of Christianity and Judaism (cp. *op. cit.*, II, pp. 85 f.); a similar view is expressed by Travers Herford (cp. *Christianity in Talmud and Midrash*, London, 1903, pp. 383 f.).

123. Cp. *supra*, pp. 51–57; cp. also I. Abrahams, *Studies in Pharisaism and the Gospels*, p. 59.

124. George Foot Moore, *Judaism*, 1, p. 244.

125. *Dial.*, Ch. 108; cp. Ch. 40. For the whole subject see now Schoeps, *Aus frühchristl. Zeit*, pp. 144 ff.

126. Mt. 23. 38; Lk. 13. 35: ἰδοὺ ἀφίεται ὑμῖν ὁ οἶκος ὑμῶν.

127. *Shab.*, 119b: Abaye said: Jerusalem was destroyed only because the Sabbath was desecrated therein; R. Abbahu said: Jerusalem was destroyed only because the reading of the (shema) morning and evening was neglected; R. Hamnuna said: Jerusalem was destroyed only because they neglected (the education of) schoolchildren; Ulla said: Jerusalem was destroyed only because they (its inhabitants) were not ashamed of each other; R. Isaac said: Jerusalem was destroyed only because the small and the great were made equal; R. Amram, son of R. Simeon b. Abba said in R. Simeon ben Abba's name in R. Ḥanina's name: Jerusalem was destroyed only because they did not rebuke each other; Rab Judah said: Jerusalem was destroyed only because scholars were despised therein; Raba said: Jerusalem was destroyed only because truthful men ceased therein.

128. Cp. H. J. Schoeps, *Jüdisch-christl. Religionsgespräch*, p. 41; "Kein Christ", says Harnack, "mochte es auch ein eifernder Judenchrist sein,

konnte die Katastrophe des jüdischen Staates, seiner Stadt und seines Heilig-
tums, für etwas anderes halten als für die gerechte Strafe des Volkes, das
seinen Messias gekreuzigt hatte" (*Mission*, pp. 44 f.); cp. A. Marmorstein,
Religionsgeschichtliche Studien, H. 2, pp. 3 f.

129. Von Soden puts the date between A.D. 92–96, on the grounds that the
persecution hinted at in the Epistle refers to the reign of Domitian; cp. *op. cit.*,
pp. 271 f.; cp. also H. Windisch, *Der Hebräerbrief*, Tübingen, 1913, pp. 114 f.

130. Von Soden seems to doubt the author's Jewish origin (cp. *op. cit.*,
pp. 271 ff.), but cp. Hans Windisch, *Der Hebräerbrief*, p. 114.

131. Harnack, "Judentum u. Christentum in Justins Dialog mit Trypho,"
Texte u. Untersuchungen, XXXIX, 1913, p. 51.

132. *Dial.*, Ch. 40.

133. Jn. 1. 29; 4. 23 f.: cp. 11. 51; H. Loewe says that "the stress laid in
the Church on the Agnus Dei motif . . . made the Jews look for a parallel".
They found it in the *Akedah*, the binding of Isaak. *Rabb. Anthol.*, p. ci.

134. Mt. 27. 51; Mk. 15. 38; Lk. 23. 45. According to Jewish tradition, the
veil of the Temple Titus cut with his sword; cp. Strack-Billerbeck, I, p. 1044.

135. Cp. Mt. 24. 1 f.; Lk. 21. 5 f.

136. Erich Klostermann, *Das Markusevangelium*, p. 147.

137. Cf. Montefiore, *S. G.*, 1909, p. 300.

138. Cp. Strack-Billerbeck, I, pp. 1045 f.

139. V. G. Simkhovitch's remarks concerning the application of Jesus'
message to the political situation of his time has greater force for the post-
Destruction period (cp. *Toward the Understanding of Jesus*, New York, 1937).

140. Streeter, *The Primitive Church*, London, 1929, pp. 92 ff.; cp. Lawlor
and Oulton, II, pp. 167 ff.

141. Hoennicke has rightly argued that 13 bishops within the space of 28
years implies that they did not hold office in consecutive order but several of
them simultaneously (cp. Hoennicke, pp. 106 f.).

142. Harnack, "Judentum u. Judenchristentum in Justins Dialog mit
Trypho," *Texte u. Untersuchungen*, XXXIX, 1913, pp. 49 f. (Harnack's italics).

143. Harnack observes: "Dass unter den τινες, die noch täglich zu Christus
bekehrt werden, geborene Juden zu verstehen sind, ist nicht gewiss, aber
wahrscheinlich" (*ibid.*, p. 84, n. 2). But this is an unnecessary caution, as the
whole sense of Justin's argument would otherwise fall to the ground.

144. Some read "of our race" (cp. *Ante-Nicene Christian Library*, II, p. 149,
n. 1), but "your race" seems to be more natural, as Justin is now addressing
himself to the whole company.

145. Harnack, *op. cit.*, p. 89.   146. *Ibid.*, p. 89, n. 2.

147. *Ibid.*, p. 84 and note.

148. Harnack's omission is due to his narrow definition of Hebrew Christianity, according to which not Jewish descent, but adherence to the national
character of Judaism, is the determining factor. Thus Paul, because of
Rom. 11 is a *Jewish* Christian, while Papias, the author of the Didache, and
Hermas are not (cp. Harnack, *Abriss der Dogmengeschichte*, 1893, pp. 42 f.).

149. Cp. *Dial.*, Ch. 119: "After that the righteous One was slain we
bloomed forth as another people. . . . This is that nation which God promised
of old to Abraham". The Christians spoke of themselves as "a new nation"
and "the Christian nation"; cf. Euseb., *Hist.*, I, 4. 2; IV, 7. 10; cf. Lawlor

NOTES TO CHAPTER V

and Oulton, ii, p. 52; for the Christians as *tertium genus hominum,* see Weiss, *Das Urchristentum,* 1917, p. 481.

150. The Nazareans with whom Jerome stayed in Aleppo seem to have been orthodox Christians; cf. Lawlor and Oulton, ii, pp. 97 f.

151. To such secret or semi-believers the Talmud refers:

טעה...בברכת המינים מעלין אותו חיישינן שמא מין הוא;

Berach. 29a; also *Mishnah Ber.,* v, 3 (cp. *Ber.* 34a; *Megilla,* 25a). According to Joël this is evidence to "die noch nicht vollzogene Trennung zwischen Juden und Christgläubigen" (*op. cit.,* p. 34, note).

152. Cp. Walter Grundmann, *Das Problem des hellenistischen Christentums innerhalb der Jerusalemer Urgemeinde* (*ZNW,* Bd. 32/1939, p. 60); p. 63: "Die Eigenständigkeit des Christentums des Hellenistenkreises ist schon in Jerusalem offenbar".

153. So Hort, *Judaistic Christianity,* p. 83.

154. Josephus, *Wars,* vi, 5. 2.

155. Klausner, *From Jesus to Paul,* p. 530.

156. Chwolson's Talmudic references, showing close relationship between Jewish Christians and pious Jews, bear out our theory. Chwolson finds it remarkable that the Mishnah very rarely refers to *Minim.* He thus concludes that Judaism only opposed gnostic Hebrew Christians; but as to the others: "Man stimmte zwar ihrem Glauben an die Messianität Christi nicht bei, aber man verdammte sie nicht deshalb". R. Judah, the compiler of the Mishnah, Chwolson suggests, must have known only such Hebrew Christians who in everything shared the religious life of the Jews, and were thus treated as members of the community. Hence the lack of reference to them (cp. *Das letzte Passamahl,* pp. 110 f.). The story in *Hullin* 87a where Judah (usually referred to as Rabbi, died A.D. 193) sat down to a meal with a Min, the Min insisting upon the privilege of pronouncing the blessing upon the wine (כוס של ברכה), is a remarkable example of such friendship (cp. *ibid.,* pp. 104 f.). Schoeps' construction of Hebrew-Christianity from the Clementine literature, if correct, can only apply to a remote Gnostic sect.

157. Hort, *op. cit.,* p. 48.

158. Harnack well observes: Das Judenchristentum, welches in Lebensgemeinschaft mit den Heidenchristen trat, hob sich damit selbst auf . . ." (*Mission,* p. 43).

159. M. Friedländer, *Die religiösen Bewegungen,* p. 171 (cp. also *Der vorchristliche jüdische Gnosticismus,* 1897; *Der Antichrist,* 1901).

160. *Op. cit.,* p. 172.   161. *Ibid.,* p. 178.

162. Cp. R. Travers Herford, *Christianity in Talmud and Midrash,* London, 1903, p. 122, n. 2; p. 145, n. 1, etc. In a later essay Herford accepts M. Friedländer's contention that there is a connexion between Minim and pre-Christian gnostics, but he holds that "when it becomes a term of reprobation and acute controversy it denotes Jewish-Christians" (*Jewish Studies in Memory of George A. Kohut,* N.Y., 1935, pp. 359 ff.). Some of Friedländer's grave mistakes which occur in his book, *Der vorchristliche jüdische Gnosticizmus,* have been pointed out by W. Bacher; cp. "Le Mot 'Minim' dans le Talmud", *Revue des Études Juives,* xxxviii, pp. 38 ff.

163. In a few instances, such Minim may have been Gentile Christians or

other heretics. Thus Moore says: "That by the Minim who are so often named in the Talmuds and Midrashim, Nazarenes or Christians are always intended is going much beyond the evidence and sometimes contrary to it" (*op. cit.*, III, p. 68). Cp. also Herford, *op. cit.*, p. 122: "A Min as such is not necessarily a Christian; but as a matter of fact, most of the heretics who came into strained relations with Jews were Christians, and more particularly Jewish Christians". A. Schlatter perhaps goes too far when he makes all the Minim to be Christians (cp. *Die Kirche Israel's vom Jahre* 70–130, 1898, pp. 7 f.

164. Cp. *ibid.*, pp. 177 f. That there were Gnostic Minim, nobody can deny. Some of them may have existed in pre-Christian times, but whether they were called *Minim* before the advent of Christianity we seriously doubt. (But cp. H. L. Strack, *Jesus, die Häretiker und die Christen nach den ältesten jüdischen Angaben*, Leipzig, 1910, p. 47; Strack speaks of pre-Christian Minim, Minim at the time of the appearance of Christianity, and Minim who are Hebrew Christians of a later time.)

165. Cp. Herford, *op. cit.*, pp. 362–365. Büchler does not even attempt "das noch immer rätselhafte Wort מין zu erklären" (A. Büchler, "Über die Minim von Sepphoris u. Tiberias im zweiten u. dritten Jahrhundert," *Festschrift zu H. Cohens siebzigsten Geburtstage*, Berlin, 1912, p. 272).

166. H. Strack, *op. cit.*, p. 47.

167. Herford, *op. cit.*, p. 363; J. Wiesner, *Scholien zum babylonischen Talmud* I, 1859, p. 35, explains the etymology of מין with μηνύτων=μηνύειν =to betray: "so wurden die Christen im ersten Jahrhundert genannt, weil es wahrscheinlich nicht selten vorkam, dass die Anhänger der neuen Sekte ihre früheren Glaubens und Leidensgenossen bei den römischen Gewalthabern verleumdeten und anschwärzten". (?) But why should the Jews go to Greek for a Christian nickname?

168. W. Bacher, *op. cit.*, p. 45; cp. also Israel Lévi, "Le Mot 'Minim'", *Revue des Etudes Juives*, XXXVIII, 1899, pp. 214 ff.; Isaac Broydé, *J. E.*, VIII, pp. 594 f.; G. F. Moore, *op. cit.*, III, pp. 68 f.; Schwaab, *op. cit.*, pp. 145 f.; G. Hoennicke, *op. cit.*, p. 386, n. 2.

169. *Ibid.*, p. 45, n. 2.

170. Cf. Brown, Driver and Briggs, *Hebr. Lex.* ad loc.

171. Joël, *Blicke*, II, p. 90.   172. *Ibid.*, II, p. 90, n. 2.

173. Cp. J. Derenburgh, *Essai sur l'histoire et la géographie de la Palestine*, I, 1867, pp. 354 f.

174. Herford, *op. cit.*, p. 365: "This is ingenious, but nothing more". (?) Joël draws attention to a few similar corruptions, like בי אבידן (*be Abidan*) which he thinks stands for the meeting-place of the Ebionites; and בי נצרפי (*be Nazrefe*) for the meeting-place of the Nazarites (cp. *ibid.*, II, p. 91, n. 2). But this is doubtful. However, there are other examples: The corruption of the word εὐαγγέλιον, which R. Meir called Aven-giljon (אָוֶן גִּלָּיוֹן) and R. Yochanan called Avon-giljon (עָוֹן גִּלָּיוֹן). *Shab* 116a; or else the corruption of ἐκ παρθένου into ἐκ πορνείας, which Krauss identifies with the Talmudic פנדרא applied to Jesus. Cf. *J. Q. R.*, v, pp. 143 f.

175. Moore, *op. cit.*, III, pp. 68 f.   176. Cp. Joël, II, p. 188.

177. Cp. Herford, *op. cit.*, pp. 247–250. A. Büchler has tried to show "dass in Galiläa im zweiten und dritten Jahrhundert Min in erster Reihe ausserjüdische Sektirer bezeichnet . . ." (Über die Minim von Sepphoris und

Tiberias im zweiten und dritten Jahrhundert, *Festschrift zu Hermann Cohens siebzigsten Geburtstage*, Berlin, 1912, p. 273.)   But such is not the general view.   Büchler's main proof rests on the assumption that no Hebrew Christians have ever accepted the divinity of Christ (cp. *ibid.*, p. 289).   But we shall see that this is unwarranted.

178. Israel Lévi, "Le Mot 'Minim'", *Revue des Études Juives*, XXXVIII, 1899, p. 206.

179. Strack, *op. cit.*, p. 47.   180. Bacher, *op. cit.*, p. 45.

181. Büchler, *op. cit.*, p. 293.   Against Büchler's view may be put that of I. Abrahams: "The Jewish sources have a good deal to say about Christians, but almost invariably it is *Jewish* Christians that are the subject of castigation" (*Studies in Pharisaism*, II, p. 56; cp. also *ibid.*, appended note 1).

182. Cp. Justin, *Apology*, I, 31.   Schlatter has shown that Akiba was not the only one to acclaim Simeon (Bar Cochba) King Messiah.   There were other leading Rabbis who followed Akiba's example.   Cf. *Die Tage Trajans u. Hadrians*, pp. 50 ff.

183. Cp. Harnack, *Mission*, p. 45.   Jerome, in his epistle to Augustine (Ep. 89), says: "usque hodie per totas Orientis synagogas inter Judaeos haeresis est, quæ dicitur Minaeorum, et a Pharisaeis usque nunc damnatur, quos vulgo Nazaraeos nuncupant, qui credunt in Christum filium Dei, natum de virgine Maria, et eum dicunt esse, qui sub Pontio Pilato passus est et resurrexit; in quem et nos credimus, sed dum volunt et Judaei esse et Christiani, nec Judaei sunt nec Christiani".   Schmidtke, however, has shown with some reason that the whole passage depends upon Epiphanius, *haer*, 30, 9— cp. Alfred Schmidtke, "Neue Fragmente u. Untersuchungen zu den judenchristlichen Evangelien, Leipzig", 1911, *Texte u. Untersuchungen*, XXXVII, pp. 252 f.

184. "The war under Hadrian brought about a complete separation of the Nazarenes from the body of Judaism, and after the war the animosity diminished with the danger of the spread of infection within the Synagogue" (Moore, *Judaism*, I, 244; cp. also pp. 90 ff.).

185. *Ibid.*, I, p. 173.   186. Herford, *op. cit.*, pp. 380 f.

187. "Ich kenne ein bisher nicht publiziertes altchristliches Fragment, in welchem sich der Ausdruck χριστιανοί τε καὶ 'Ιουδαῖοι χριστὸν ὁμολογοῦντες findet" (*Mission*, p. 38, n. 1).   188. Harnack, *ibid.*, p. 37, n. 5.

189. "Der *Min* Judenchrist ist zu unterscheiden einerseits vom Nochri Heiden, der den 'Völkern der Welt' angehört und ein unzweifelhafter Götzendiener ist, anderseits vom *Kuthi*, Kuthäer (2 Kg. 17. 24, 30) oder Samariter, der des Götzendienstes verdächtig ist.   Der Min ist ürsprünglich Jude, er hat aber den Monotheismus nach dem Urteil der Synagoge aufgegeben, indem er sich dem christlichen Trinitätsglauben ergab und gilt als Häretiker" (Ferdinand Weber, *Die Lehre des Talmud*, Leipzig, 1880, p. 147).

190. *Sanh.* 38b.   Adam is called a מִין, for it is written, And the Lord God called unto Adam and said unto him, Where art thou? (Gen. 3. 9) *i.e.* whither has thine heart turned? R. Isaac said: He practised epiplasm, for it is written, But like man, (Adam) they have transgressed the covenant (Hos. 6. 7). This passage may, however, contain a hint to Hebrew Christianity. (?)

191. *Abodah Zarah* 27a permits to receive medical treatment from a *min* if it is not done בפרהסיה, *i.e.* secretly (ἐν παῤῥησίᾳ).

192. Chwolson's transl., p. 102 (Chwolson also refers to A. C. Toetter-mann, *R. Eliezer ben Hyrkanos*, Leipzig, 1877; cp. *ibid.*, p. 101, n. 4); cp. *Abodah Zarah*, 27b; A. Mishcon translates the sentence in the same manner: "It is different with the teaching of *Minim*, for it draws, and one (having dealings with them) may be drawn after them" (*Abodah Zarah*, London, 1935, p. 137): שאני מינות דמשכה דאתי לממשך בתרייהו.

193. *Tosefta Ḥull.*, II, 24; cp. Klausner, *Jesus*, pp. 39 f.

194. *Abodah Zarah*, 16b–17a.

195. Klausner, *ibid.*, pp. 42 f.; cp. Herford, p. 145.

196. Cp. *J. E.*, v, p. 114; Strack, *Introduction to Talmud and Midrash*, English, 1931, p. 111.

197. *Yoma*, 66b, R. Eliezer was once asked whether פלוני is worthy of the world to come. But he obviously tried to evade the question by saying: "have you only asked me about פלוני?" Dr. Leo Jung remarks that *all* his answers are evasive (cp. *Yoma*, London, 1938, p. 311, n. 1); but Klausner has shown that פלוני refers to Jesus (cp. Klausner, *Jesus*, p. 37); cp. Hoennicke, *op. cit.*, pp. 389 ff.; cp. also Chwolson, p. 101. *Ber.* 28b, Eliezer became ill and his pupils asked him to teach them the way of life. He advised them that their children be restrained from reading (the Scriptures?). Goldschmidt transl. הגיון "nachsinnen" (cp. *Der Babylonische Talmud*, Bd. I, p. 124, n. 67). But if Löw is right, then הגיון ought to read הגליון=εὐαγγέλιον (?). Cp. Bacher, *Die Agada der Tannaiten*, 1903, I, p. 98, note. This may be an attempt to rehabilitate a great teacher, suspected of heresy (?) (cp. Hoennicke, p. 392, n. 1).

198. Cp. Wilhelm Bacher, *Die Agada der Tan.*, II, pp. 5 ff.

199. L. Ginzberg, *J. E.*, v, p. 139.

200. Cp. *jer. Ḥagg.*, II, 1 (77b); Schlatter interprets the story of R. Meir's seeing his former teacher on the Sabbath at Tiberias on horseback, metaphorically, the horse being a symbol for wealth (cf. *Die Tage Trajans*, p. 26).

201. Cf. Herford's short essay, Elisha ben Abujah, *Essays presented to J. H. Hertz*, London, 1942, pp. 215 ff.

202. *Hagigah*, 15b: "It is told of Aḥer that when he used to rise (to go) from the schoolhouse, many *sifre minim* used to fall from his lap". May there not be some significance in the fact that R. Meir, R. Akiba's greatest pupil and "Aḥer's" devoted disciple, is credited with the pun on εὐαγγέλιον= "אָוֶן גליון" which Joḥanan further developed into "עֲוֹן גליון"? (See Bacher, *Agada der Tannaiten*, II, p. 36, note.)

203. L. Ginzberg doubts whether the note in *Ḥag.* 15b is genuine as it is lacking in the Jerusalem Talmud; he also suggests that owing to the changes made by the censors, the original may have referred not to Minim, but to Sadducees (*J. E.*, v, p. 138b). This may be so or may not.

204. *Midrash Rabbah*, Ecclesiastes, I, 8 (A. Cohen's transl., London, 1939; we quote with slight alterations).

205. Cp. Herford, *Christianity in Talmud and Midrash*, p. 213 f.

206. A few Christian scholars, notably Schürer, have identified Trypho with R. Tarphon; Jewish scholars oppose this view (cp. Schürer, *Geschichte*, II³, pp. 378, 555 f.; cf. Strack's *Introduction to Talmud and Midrash*, Philadelphia, 1931, p. 309, n. 44). Schlatter supports the Jewish view, cp. *Die Tage Trajans*, p. 98.

207. There are several hints in Rabbinic literature which show a knowledge of the N.T.:

Reference to the three hours' darkness and the rending of the veil; cp. Joël, *op. cit.*, pp. 6 f.

Reference to the rock (1 Cor. 10. 4; Rom. 9. 33). Cp. Gerald Friedlander, *Rabbinic Philosophy and Ethics*, London, 1912, p. 249, note. In *Midrash* to Is. 51. 1 and *Jalkut Num.* § 766 fol. 243 c. (ed. Venedig), Abraham is referred to . . . הרי מצצאתי פטרא; on this, see Krauss, *op. cit.*, p. 270; *J. Q. R.*, XII, April, 1900, p. 428 (Schechter); Edersheim, *Life and Times*, II, p. 83. Reference to Gal. 3. 10; cp. G. F. Moore, *op. cit.*, III, pp. 150 f.

208. Cp. A. Cohen, *Midrash rabbah, Eccl.*, London, 1939, p. 20, n. 4.

209. Cp. Herford, *op. cit.*, pp. 216 ff.

210. Cf. Strack, *Introduction*, p. 120.

211. Cf. Herford, pp. 216 f.

212. Herford's analysis of this, as of many other stories, suffers from a too literal adherence to the text. His presentation presupposes historical accuracy; he thus tries to interpret every feature, while most of it is allegory with the intent to sermonize.

213. Cp. Herford, *op. cit.*, p. 391. There is also another factor to be considered, and this is the alterations made owing to Christian censorship. Cp. Hoennicke, *op. cit.*, pp. 282 f.

214. So Schoeps, *op. cit.*, p. 25, n. 3. 215. Herford, pp. 379 f.

216. Cp. Schoeps, *op. cit.*, p. 27.

217. אדם נברא באחרונה ולמה נברא באחרונה שלא יהו המינין אומרין שותף "Man was created last. And why was he created last? That היה עמו במעשהו the Minim might not say there was a partner with him in his work". *Tosephta Sanh*, 8, 7 (*Tosephta* ed. by Dr. M. S. Zuckermandel, 2nd ed., Jerusalem, 1937). Cp. the prologue to John's Gospel; cp. also *Midrash rabbah* to Gen., I. 1.

218. *Dial.*, Ch. 49: Trypho: "Those who affirm him to have been a man, and to have been anointed by election, and then to have become Christ, appear to me to speak more plausibly than you who hold those opinions which you express. For we all expect that Christ will be ἄνθρωπος ἐξ ἀνθρώπου . . ."; cp. Ch. 67, where Trypho hints that the Christian doctrine concerning the birth of the Messiah resembles the Greek myth about Perseus and Danae, the virgin.

219. *Megillah*, IV, 9: האומר יברכוך טובים הרי זה דרך המינות. Danby takes טובים to refer to man, "Good men shall bless Thee"; Rabbinowitz translates in the same manner: "The good shall bless Thee"; the heresy thus being "in the implication that God is blessed only by 'the good' and not by all His creatures". This is Rashi's view. But the Jerusalem Talmud, Rabbinowitz admits, "interprets טובים ('the good') as referring to the Deity", in the sense: "May the beneficent powers bless thee" (cp. Joseph Rabbinowitz, *Mishnah Megillah*, London, 1931, pp. 130 f.). If this were the case, Rabbinowitz thinks to detect Zoroastrian dualism here, which he identifies with "the chief doctrine of the anti-Jewish Christian Gnostics". Did the Parsees, however, invoke a *blessing* of Ahriman as well as of Ormuzd? It seems to us that there is no need to go beyond the text, especially as in the phrase מודים מודים, Rabbinowitz seems to admit a reference to two powers (cp. *ibid.*, p. 132). Schoeps, however, may be right in the interpretation of

טוכים as a self-chosen name on the part of some Hebrew Christians. Cf. *Theologie*, pp. 280 ff.

220. R. Samuel b. Naḥman said in R. Jonathan's name: When Moses was engaged in writing the Torah, he had to write the work of each day. When he came to the verse: "And God said, let us make man", etc, he said: "Sovereign of the Universe! Why dost Thou furnish an excuse to heretics?" "Write", replied He, "whoever wishes to err may err" (*Midrash Rabbah*, to Gen. 8. 8). Evidence of how the Christians understood this passage is to be found in the Epistle of Barnabas. Here the writer represents God saying to the Messiah at the foundation of the world, "Let us make man, etc." (*Barn.*, Ch. 5; cf. Ch. 6).

221. *Sanh.*, 38b.

222. Jacob Schachter, one of the translators of *Sanhedrin*, London, 1935, I, p. 245, n. 7.

223. Herford, p. 297.

224. For other instances concerning the unity of God, the "Two Powers", etc., see Herford, *op. cit.*, pp. 291–307.

225. Cf. Herford, p. 273.

226. The reference is to Semukin (סמוכין) which Herford transl. "contexts", *i.e.* "The law of Biblical exegesis which is based on the fact that two passages are found together in the text and are therefore to be connected in interpretation" (A. Cohen, *Berakot*, Cambridge, 1921, p. 429. Semukin ="connected"; A. Cohen translates: "juxtaposition", cp. *ibid.*, p. 58).

227. Cp. A. Cohen, *ibid.*, p. 41, n. 4.   228. *Ber.* 10a.

229. Cp. Strack, *Introduction*, p. 125.

230. So Herford, p. 303; Strack calls him Reuben ben Isterobeli or Esterobeli. Nothing is known about him; it is assumed that he belongs to the Tannaitic period and that he lived in Rome (cp. Strack, pp. 116, 314, n. 45).

231. *J. Shab.* 8d.

232. Bacher, *Agada d. paläst. Amoräer*, III, p. 80; cp. also p. 362.

233. Herford, pp. 302 f.; cp. also the following passage on the same theme, *ibid.*, pp. 303 f. The passage from *Agadat Bereshit* c 31 (end) concerning the death of the son of God belongs to a later period (4th c.); cp. Bacher, *Agada d. paläst. Amoräer*, III, p. 690.

234. For similar passages, see Schoeps, *op. cit.*, p. 29.

235. H. Friedman, *Midrash Rabbah, Genesis*, London, 1939, II, p. 957, n. 8.

236. Bacher, *Agada d. paläst. Amoräer*, III, p. 91, n. 3. ר' חנינא Bacher reads ר' חנין; cp. *ibid.*, p. 86, n. 4. An Amora perhaps identical with Chanin of Sepphoris? cp. Bacher, *ibid.*, p. 88.

237. Cp. Edgar Hennecke, *Handbuch zu den neutestamentlichen Apokryphen*, Tübingen, 1914, p. 71.

238. אין בן דוד בא עד שתהפך כל מלכות למינות *Sanh.* 97a; for parallels, see Herford, p. 207.

239. Cp. *Mishnah Sotah*, 9, 15.

240. Herford, p. 209. Abrahams suggests the following explanation: "The refusal of the Jewish Christians to join (in the latter's) revolt against Rome and the triumph of Rome over the Jewish nationalists, may well have appeared to Judah b. Ilai (acc. to *Sanh.* 97a, he is credited with this utterance) an indication that the 'Kingdom shall be turned to *minut*', and that another

than Bar Cochba must be looked for as Messiah" (*Stud. in Phar.*, II, p. 63.) But in view of the fact that Abrahams insists that *Minut* is a purely *Jewish* heresy, the only inference possible is that the passage contains a reference to the success of Christianity. One of the most famous rabbis, Ben Zoma, 2nd c. tanna, is suspected of being a Christian (cf. S. H. Levey, *Judaism*, 1972, pp. 455 ff.).

241. Cp. *ibid.*, p. 209, n. 1.

242. Cp. Bacher, *Agada d. paläst. Amoräer*, II, p. 481, n. 5.

243. אם ראית ספסלין מלאין מלאין מינאי צפה לרגלי מלך המשיח שנאמר פרש רשת
Midrash Rabbah, Lam. I. 13; cp. Song of Songs *R*. 8. 9 (10); לרגלי השיבני אחור
A. Cohen and Maurice Simon (*Midrash Rabbah*, London, 1939), have both accepted the reading "Babylonians".

244. Abrahams, *Stud. in Pharis.*, II, p. 59; for "test-passages", see Montefiore-Loewe, *Rabb. Anthol.*, pp. 335, 369; cp. also *ibid.*, p. 12 (§ 21).

245. *Midrash Rabbah*, Gen. 44. 5. Dr. H. Friedman's translation, London, 1939.

246. Bacher, *Die Agada d. paläst. Amoräer*, I, p. 470, note.

247. To the same category belongs the passage quoted by Schoeps from *Midrash* Sam. v, 4: "Wenn du das Daleth in dem Worte 'Echod' (Deut. 6. 4) zu einem Resh machst, zerstörst du die Welt". *Echod* would thus become *Acher*="an other one". This is the reason why Prayer Books and Bibles have the dalet printed in double size and fat type (cp. Schoeps, p. 29, n. 1).

248. "Der Kampf zwischen den Juden und den Judenchristen bewegt sich um die Einheit Gottes" (F. Weber, *op. cit.*, p. 148).

249. Büchler, *op. cit.*, p. 293.

250. *Mishnah Megillah*, IV, 8, makes some mysterious reference to the דרך המינות and דרך החיצונים—it is difficult to decide who are meant. It is in connexion with the performance of public prayer, and Graetz and Herford and Moore have assumed that the reference is to Hebrew Christians (cp. Herford, pp. 199 ff., 361 ff.; cp. Moore, *Judaism*, I, pp. 365 f.).

251. "Our Rabbis taught: Adam was created on the eve of Sabbath. And why? Lest the Sadducees say: The Holy One, blessed be He, had a partner in his work of creation" (*Sanh.* 38a; cp. also *Sanh.* 37a).

252. Cp. the case with R. Akiba and R. Jose. Cf. Schoeps, *Theologie*, p. 90, n. 3.

253. The Torah declares: "I was the working tool of the Holy One, blessed be He"; God consults the Torah in the creation of the world—the Torah itself being created before the world (*Midrash Rabbah*, Gen. I. 1; cp. *J. Q. R.*, III, pp. 357 ff.). Cf. also Schoeps, *Theologie*, p. 177.

254. Scrolls of the Law, *tefillin*, *mezuzzot*, written by a Min were burned (*Git.* 45b; *Ab. Zarah* 40b); relatives of a Min were not permitted to observe the laws of mourning after his death and were required to wear festive garments and to rejoice instead (*Semahot*, II, 10). But considering the late date of Ebel Rabbati (euphemistically called Semahot), the custom may belong to a much later period.

255. Leo Baeck points out that R. Simon bar Yochai's saying that together with Israel is also the Shekinah exiled, is directed towards the Christian Church; also R. Juda ben Simon's utterance about the dwelling-place of the Shekinah in Israel's midst points in the same direction (cp. Schoeps, *op. cit.*, p. 36, n. 1).

256. *Taanit*, 7a: R. Abbahu said: "Greater is the day of the fertilizing rain than the resurrection of the dead; for this is only for the pious, but the rain for pious and wicked". A strange utterance from the mouth of a Pharisee! (cf., however, Loewe, *Rabb. Anthol.*, p. 369.) Cf. also Schoeps, *Theologie*, p. 85.

257. Harnack, *Texte und Untersuchungen*, XXXIX, p. 91.

258. The prevailing temper towards the Minim can be seen from the following story: A *Min* said to Beruriah: It is written "Sing, O barren, thou that didst not bear" (Is. 54. 1). Is the woman to sing because she did not bear? This is her answer: "Sing, O community of Israel, who art like a barren woman that hath not borne children for Gehinnom—like you" (*Berakot*, 10a). Beruriah was the wife of R. Meir and the daughter of R. Hanina ben Teradjon. It must be borne in mind that her father was executed during the persecution under Hadrian. Her husband was a disciple of R. Akiba, another martyr. This may account for some of the bitterness to people who refused to partake in the national struggle. The Min here is certainly a Christian, and probably a Jewish Christian. Herford remarks: "Her answer shows clearly enough the hostility felt by Jews towards the Christians, in the second century, at a time when the latter were steadily increasing in numbers" (*ibid.*, p. 239).

259. I. Abrahams, *ibid.*, II, p. 56.

260. Joël rightly says it represents the first attempt on the part of the Synagogue "das Judentum gegen das überhandnehmende Christentum abzugrenzen" (Blicke, pp. 61 f.).

261. It is possible that *Mishnah Megillah*, IV, 8. 9, where reference is made to those who place their phylacteries on their foreheads (in a way not prescribed by the Rabbis) and on the palms of their hands (instead of the traditional way on the inner side of the left arm), has in mind Hebrew Christians (cp. Herford, pp. 200–204). It would be a means of detecting those with heretical tendencies. Perhaps the practice arose in an effort to symbolize the manner of death of the Messiah? It may well be that those referred to in *Midrash* Ps. 31. 23, who say "Amen against their will in faithfulness", are secret believers in Jesus (but cp. *Rabb. Anthol.*, p. 355). That some Gentile Christians have also left the Church and joined or rejoined the Synagogue may be assumed. An outstanding example is that of the translator of the O. T. from Hebrew into Greek, Aquila. Both Jewish and Christian tradition connect Aquila with the Church and the Synagogue (cp. Ephiphanius, *De Ponderibus et Mensuris*, XIII–XVI; Git. 56b and 57a; see also *J. E.*, II, pp. 37 f.). Aquila is supposed to have been a Christian who apostatized for Judaism and became a pupil of R. Akiba.

262. Cp. Euseb. *h. e.* IV. 22. 8; cp. Lawlor and Oulton, II, p. 144; *J. E.*, VI, p. 318a.

263. Adolf Hilgenfeld, *Die Ketzergeschichte des Urchristentums*, Leipzig, 1884, p. 445; cp. *ibid.*, p. 33, n. 47. Hilgenfeld bases his view upon the testimony of Stephanus Gobarus quoted by Photius. Carl Weizsäcker, however, suggests that his remark on 1 Cor. 2. 9 may well refer not to Paul, but to a Gnostic Apocryphon. For, indeed, the words of Paul in 1 Cor. 2. 9, and the words of Jesus (Mt. 13. 16) which Hegesippus is supposed to have quoted to contradict them, express the same thought (cp. Weizsäcker, *Realencykl. für protest. Theologie u. Kirche*, 3rd ed., VII, p. 534).

264. Weizsäcker's main reason for denying Hegesippus' Jewish descent.

265. Cp. Hoennicke, *op. cit.*, p. 141, n. 1.

266. Hilgenfeld, *op. cit.*, p. 445.

267. Hugh J. Schonfield, *According to the Hebrews*, London, 1937, pp. 253 f.

268. Wilhelm Bousset refers several times to Schmidtke's work. For his criticism, see *Kyrios Christos*, pp. 21 f.; cf. also A. F. Findlay, *Byways in early Christian Literature*, pp. 54 ff.

269. Schmidtke, *op. cit.*, pp. 247 f. Schoeps, however, makes frequent reference to "Grosskirchliche Judenchristen."

270. Origenes, *Hom.* xx *in Jer* : καὶ πρῶτον χρήσομαι παραδόσει Ἑβραϊκῇ, ἐληλυθυίᾳ εἰς ἡμᾶς διά τινος φυγόντος διὰ τὴν Χριστοῦ πίστιν . . .

271. Epiph., *haer.*, 30. 9; Graetz has naturally nothing good to say about Joseph whom Constantine raised to the dignity of Comes. As to his story about the Patriarch who accepted Christianity on his death-bed, Graetz calls it "a thoroughly incredible tale" (*op. cit.*, II, p. 572); but cp. F. Heman, *Geschichte des jüdischen Volkes seit der Zerstörung Jerusalems*, Stuttgart, 1908, pp. 57 f.

272. Hieronymus, *Ep.* 125 *ad Rusticum* § 12; cp. also *Ep.* 18 § 10.

273. Schmidtke, *op. cit.*, pp. 248 f. 274. Wagenmann, *op. cit.*, p. 142.

275. Wilhelm Brandt, *Elchasai*, Leipzig, 1912, p. 53.

276. *Ibid.*, p. 54.

277. *Ibid.*, p. 57. Cf. Schoeps' splendid essay on Israel's election, *Aus frühchristl. Zeit*, pp. 184 ff.

278. Hilgenfeld, *op. cit.*, pp. 445 f. 279. Schmidtke, *op. cit.*, pp. 118 ff.

280. Schmidtke, *ibid.*, pp. 108 ff. 281. Bousset, *Kyrios Christos*, p. 22.

282. "Zwischen ihr (*i.e.* the Nazarene community of Beroia) und der Jerusalemischen Urgemeinde hat ein Zusammenhang bloss in der Phantasie des Epiphanius bestanden" (*ibid.*, p. 124).

283. Schmidtke, *ibid.*, p. 125.

284. Cp. *ibid.*, p. 125, n. 1. Origen, in referring to those Israelites who, though converted to Christianity, have not abandoned the law of their fathers, has probably such Nazarenes in mind (cf. *C. Cels.*, Ch. 3).

285. Cp. Hilgenfeld, *op. cit.*, p. 21.

286. Irenaeus, *Haer*, I, 26, 2; cf. also Hort, *op. cit.*, p. 197.

287. Hippolytus, *Philosophumena*, 7, 23.

288. Cp. Schmidtke, pp. 230–232.

289. Epiphanius, *Haer*, 30. 1. Σαμαρειτῶν μὲν γὰρ ἔχει τὸ βδελυρὸν, Ἰουδαίων δὲ τὸ ὄνομα, Ὀσσαίων δὲ καῖ Ναζωραίων καὶ Νασαραίων τὴν γνώμην, Κηρινθιανῶν τὸ εἶδος, Καρποκρατιανῶν τὴν κακοτροπίαν, καὶ χριστιανῶν βούλεται ἔχειν τὴν προσηγορίαν.

(Nam samaritanorum impuram superstitionem affectavit. A Judaeis porro nomen accepit; ab Ossaeis, Nazaraeis et Nasaraeis dogmata. Cerinthianorum deinde formam, Carpocratianorum nequitiam, Christianorum denique appellationem usurpare contendit), Migne, XLI, p. 406.

290. Cf. Tertullian, *De praescriptione haer.* Chs. 10, 33; *de carne Christi*, Ch. 14; *de virginibus velandis*, Ch. 6; *Hieronymus*, Gal. 3. 14; Tit. 3. 10, etc.; cp. Schmidtke, *op. cit.*, pp. 191 ff., 247 ff.; Hoennicke, pp. 228 ff.

291. J. Lightfoot, *Perergon de excidio urbis*; cp. Hoennicke, p. 229.

292. Hilgenfeld, p. 426, n. 725. Cp. J. Levy, *Neuhebräisches Wörterbuch*; also Jastrow, *ad loc.* It has been suggested that *Baba Kamma*, 117a, corresponds with *Shab.* 116a, where בי אבידן and בי נצרפי occur. These being corruptions

of אביונים and נצרנים; cp. Hoennicke, p. 229, n. 2; cp. also *ibid.*, p. 175, n. 15. Schoeps denies that these were Jewish Christians; cp. *Theologie*, p. 140.

293. "An Ebion als Stifter der Ebionäer hat in der alten Kirche niemand gezweifelt" (Hilgenfeld, p. 423).

294. Dalman, *The Words of Jesus*, Engl., p. 52, n. 3.

295. Epiphanius, *haer.*, 30, 17; cf. Hilgenfeld, pp. 432 f.

296. Cf. Brandt, *op. cit.*, pp. 74 f.; Schmidtke, pp. 187 ff., 213 f. Other ancient writers do the same; cp. *ibid.*, p. 241.

297. Origen explains the name Ebionites: πτωχεία τῆς διανοίας (*De princ.*, IV, 22; cp. also *Contra Cels*, II, 1; cp. Euseb. *h. e.*, III, 27).

298. "Viele Gründe sprechen dafür, dass Ebion eine fingierte Persönlichkeit ist . . ." (Hoennicke, *ibid.*, p. 231.)

299. Schmidtke has shown that Epiphanius, the chief witness for the existence of Ebion, had almost no personal knowledge concerning the Ebionites. He is entirely dependent upon other writers whose data he reconstructs according to his own intuition (cp. *ibid.*, pp. 215 ff.; cp. also pp. 204 ff., where Schmidtke describes the sources of Ephiphanius' knowledge).

300. Wagenmann, *op. cit.*, p. 143. But cp. Schoeps, *Theologie*. pp. 12 and 57.

301. Cp. W. Beveridge, art. "Ebionism", *Encycl. of Religion and Ethics*, V, pp. 139 ff.

302. "Bekanntlich man in der alten Kirche sogar die Lehren eines Arius, Photin, Paul von Samosata und Nestorius als ebionitisch bezeichnet, und Hieronymus hat den jüdischen Bibelübersetzer Theodotion wiederholt bloss wegen seiner Version von Jes. 7. 14, als Ebionäer eingeführt" (Schmidtke, p. 235; cp. *ibid.*, pp. 236 ff.). Prof. Schoeps' learned contribution explains only part of the problem.

303. Cp. Schmidtke, pp. 241 f.; cp. also W. Beveridge, *op. cit.*, p. 144a.

304. Cp. Schmidtke, pp. 227 ff.

305. *Ibid.*, p. 233.   306. Hoennicke, p. 232.

307. Cp. Brandt, *op. cit.*, p. 90; Findlay explains the name "partly with reference to their outward condition, and partly through their sense of unity with the pious in Israel who in the Old Testament were often so called" (*op. cit.*, p. 309). Cf. the important chapter by Schoeps, *Theologie*, pp. 196 ff. and pp. 279 ff.

308. Cp. also W. Beveridge, *op. cit.*, p. 139.

309. A clear-cut distinction between the Pharisaic, *i.e.* non-Gnostic, and the Gnostic or Essene Ebionism, is not possible (cf. J. C. Lambert, art. "Ebionism", *Hast. Dic. of Christ and Gospels*, I, p. 505a). For Essene influence upon the Ebionites, see Beveridge, *op. cit.*, p. 143a.

310. Cf. Irenaeus, *haer.*, I, xxvi, 2.

311. Cf. Beveridge, *op. cit.*, p. 144a. For this reason, Schoeps' view if correct can only apply to one specific section of Hebrew Christians.

312. Schmidtke came to the following conclusion with regard to Epiphanius' statements: "So viel steht nunmehr unbedingt fest: die meisten und eindruckvollsten Nachrichten von *haer.* 30 sind nicht nach eigenen Erforschungen in ebionäischen Gemeinden niedergeschrieben, sondern aus dem vermeintlich total ebionäisch verfälschten Klemensroman herausgezogen" (*ibid.*, p. 199).

313. Wagenmann, p. 145.

314. Irenaeus, *adv. haer.*, I, 62; cp. Schmidtke, pp. 225 ff.

315. Beveridge, *op. cit.*, p. 144a; cp. Schmidtke, pp. 227–235.

316. Beveridge mentions the following three points which differentiated the Gnostic Ebionites from the Pharisaic type: (a) their Christology, while fundamentally alike, is mixed with elements of Gnostic speculation; (b) their asceticism is rigid, except on the point of marriage; (c) for their abandonment of the sacrificial system, the annals of Pharisaism contain neither precedent nor preparation (*ibid.*, p. 143a).

317. Hoennicke, p. 240.

318. Hoennicke has recognized the absolute importance of the O. T. to the young Gentile Church: "ohne das Alte Testament wäre es schwerlich so schnell zur Verbreitung des Evangeliums gekommen. Das Alte Testament so wie die Predigt der Judenchristen trug dazu bei, dass bei den Heidenchristen das Evangelium sich nicht verflüchtigte oder auflöste in asketische Theorien, in Libertinismus oder philosophische Spekulationen" (*op. cit.*, p. 176).

319. "The Nazarenes . . . acknowledged the power of the Jewish law in its entirety; but they explained the birth of Jesus in a supernatural manner . . . and ascribed to him godlike attributes" (Graetz, II, p. 373).

320. Hoennicke, p. 175. 321. Cp. Graetz, II, p. 373.

322. W. Singer, *Das Buch der Jubiläen*, 1898; but cp. Hoennicke's criticism, *op. cit.*, p. 225, n. 2.

323. Cp. B. H. Streeter, *The Primitive Church*, pp. 42 f.

324. Hoennicke, pp. 241 ff.

325. Hilgenfeld has described Ebionism as "Entwicklungsunfähig" (*op. cit.*, p. 445), but its basic problem, in our view, was not doctrinal, but national.

326. Schoeps, *Theologie*, p. 86 f; see also *op. cit.*, p. 295.

NOTES TO CHAPTER VI

1. The prayer is called ברכת השיר and is recited at the end of the first section of the Sabbath morning prayers in the Synagogue and at the home service for the two Passover nights (cp. Singer, pp. 125 ff.). The peculiarity of the prayer is that it forms a "nominal acrostic", giving the name of שמעון written backwards. For the tradition, cp. Samuel Krauss, *Das Leben Jesu*, pp. 226 f.; cp. also *Monatschrift für Geschichte u. Wissenschaft des Judentums*, 1858, p. 461; 1861, p. 212; 1870, p. 237; cf. also Baring-Gould, *Lost and Hostile Gospels*, pp. 91, 101; also G. H. Box, "Peter in the Jewish Liturgy," *Expository Times*, xv (Oct. 1903–Sept. 1904), pp. 93 ff. Box describes the tradition as "nothing more than a passing Jewish fancy". For St. Peter in Jewish legend, see August Wünsche, *Midrash Ruth Rabba*, Leipzig, 1883, pp. 88 ff. (Drei Petrussagen).

2. Enelow, *op. cit.*, p. 167. 3. *Ibid.*, p. 168.

4. שמד, Hif. השמיד to destroy.

5. Cp. Lev Gillet, *Communion in the Messiah*, pp. 236 f.

6. Raymund de Peñaforte, on the authority of Gregory I, held that Jews and Saracens ought to be provoked to accept the Christian faith with the

help of "authorities, reasonings and allurements" (*auctoritatibus, rationibus et blandimentis*); quoted by L. Williams, *Adv. Jud.*, p. 243, n. 2.

7. Leo Baeck, after deploring the methods the Church employed in order to win over Jews to the ruling religion, asks with obvious irony: "Who are they, for the most part, who left Judaism, in order to belong to another religion?" Here is his answer: "They were too often 'believers', who went over to the other religion, in which they did not believe, or in which they *also* did not believe. . . . Seldom has *conviction* ever caused anybody to turn his back on Judaism, seldom has conversion shown a spirit of courageous *sacrifice*. Usually the conversion has been an act of materialism" (*op. cit.*, pp. 284 f.; cf. also S. Daiches, *Aspects of Judaism*, London, 1928, p. 133).

8. Henri Bergson explained in his will that he decided not to accept baptism as he felt it impossible to leave the Jewish people at a time of rising anti-Semitism. Cf. Jacques Maritain, *Redeeming the Time*, London, 1943, p. 89, note; cf. also *Jewish Chronicle*, Jan. 16, 1942. Alfred Engländer, one of the two heroes in Franz Werfel's novel *Barbara*, undoubtedly expresses the author's own experience when he confesses the reason for his not accepting baptism: "Ich war ein Sklave der Menschenfurcht, ich war zu eitel, mich durch einen scheinbar vorteilhaften Tausch in den Verdacht des Opportunismus zu setzen. . . ." (*Barbara*, p. 514).

9. Cf. *infra*, pp. 321 f.

10. A. Marmorstein, *The Doctrine of Merits in Old Rabbinical Literature*, London, 1920, has shown that the emphasis upon Israel's merits was due to the Synagogue's controversy with the Church (cp. pp. 79, 86, 96 f., 106, 128, etc.). It appears, however, that the whole concept of merit is much older than the Jewish Christian controversy, and is closely connected with the Jewish view concerning the value of human action.

11. Cp. *infra*, p. 270.

12. R. Isaac's opinion; "Everybody is in need of God's grace, even Abraham on whose account grace surrounds the whole world", expresses an essential Christian attitude (cf. Marmorstein, *The Doctrine of Merits*, p. 13; cf. also *ibid.*, pp. 10, 12, etc.).

13. An extreme example of an essentially Jewish attitude is provided by the person of Pelagius. His emphasis upon human freedom, upon the natural goodness of man (*naturalis sanctitas*), human sufficiency, etc., is characteristic Jewish teaching (cf. W. J. Sparrow-Simpson, *The Letters of St. Augustine*, pp. 126 ff.).

14. The present writer found an anonymous note in a copy of Dienemann's book, *Judentum und Christentum*, belonging to the New College Library, Edinburgh. The note was written by a German Jew who once left the Jewish community out of "cowardly motives". As time went by, he found deeper reasons for separating himself from Judaism. Though eclectically inclined, he was drawn towards Christianity. But for the fact that the Christian Church is "zu sehr im Buchstabenglauben gefangen", and therefore does not incorporate the teaching of Jesus, he would have become a Christian. His remarks are important, as an illustration that the characteristic *Christian* attitude is no Gentile prerogative.

In contradistinction to Dienemann's emphasis upon the goodness, autonomy and self-sufficiency of man, the writer remarks:

(1) I believe that man is sinful. I need Christ as a Symbol, as Mediator between me and God. To me, the Jewish teaching concerning Jewish election is inconceivable. The conception of the eternal value and the continued existence after death is entirely different in Judaism and Christianity.

(2) Concerning grace: When I do anything good, my first reaction is gratitude for having been allowed by the Almighty to do it, and not the consciousness of my own strength.

15. Cf. Augustine, *Retractiones*, XIII, 2; cf. *de praed*. 2. 5; 2. 7.

16. "Der Christ ist ewiger Anfänger; das Vollenden ist nicht seine Sache—Anfang gut, alles gut. Das ist die ewige Jugend des Christen; jeder Christ lebt sein Christentum eigentlich noch heutigen Tags, als wäre er der erste" (*Rosenzweig Der Stern der Erlösung*, p. 451; cf. p. 497).

17. Cf. *infra*, p. 314; cf. also Gore's *Com. to Rom.*, London, 1920, II, p. 62.

18. We use the term Hebrew Christianity, not in the narrow sense which Harnack assigns to it, but in the wider sense, describing Christians of Jewish descent.

19. Weiss, *Das Urchristentum*, p. 99; cf. Harnack, *Mission*, p. 31.

20. Cf. Mt. 10. 5 f.; 15. 24. These passages express more than the much spoken-of Judaistic tendency of Mt. Streeter's comment to Mt. 10. 23, may well include the above verses also: "It is not that Gentiles cannot or ought not to be saved, but the time will not be long enough to preach to all, and Israel has the first right to hear" (*Four Gospels*, p. 255). Cf. also Hort, *Judaistic Christianity*, p. 34.

21. Rom. 1. 16; 2. 9. 10; cf. Lightfoot, *Gal.* p. 26.

22. Acts 13. 46: στρεφόμεθα εἰς τὰ ἔθνη; in the usage of Acts τὰ ἔθνη are the Gentiles, as distinct from ὁ λαός, the Jews; cp. Harnack, *Die Apostelg.*, Leipzig, 1908, pp. 54 f.; Hort, *Jud. Christ.*, p. 59.

23. Harnack: "Paulus ist nicht der Erste gewesen, der die Heidenmission begonnen hat . . ." (*op. cit.*, p. 211).

24. Lk. 24. 27.

25. Rev. 19. 10: ἡ γὰρ μαρτυρία τοῦ 'Ιησοῦ ἐστι τὸ πνεῦμα τῆς προφητείας; which Weymouth translates beautifully: Testimony to Jesus is the spirit which underlies Prophecy (Moffatt reads the sentence differently).

26. Cf. *supra*, pp. 46 f.

27. Canon Lukyn Williams, *Adversus Judaeos*, briefly discusses the theory as suggested by Edwin Hatch and later developed by Rendel Harris (cp. *op. cit.*, Ch. I).

28. *Sanh.*, 99a; *Ber.*, 34b.

29. Cf. Mt. 2. 5 f. 15, 17 f., etc. Edersheim's insistence upon the conception of unity between Israel and the Messiah is important to the understanding of the Gospel references to the O. T., especially in Mt. Cf. *Life and Times*, I, pp. 161 f.; cf. also *Church and Synagogue Quart.*, VI, p. 45; for the use of O. T. prophecy in the early Church, see V. H. Stanton, *The Jewish and the Christian Messiah*, Edinburgh, 1886, pp. 177 ff., 370 ff.

30. Acts 8. 35.

31. Cf. Strack-Billerbeck, I, p. 481; under the stress of the controversy with Christianity, Is. 53 has been reinterpreted as a prediction of the sufferings of Israel (cf. Bergmann, *Jüdische Apologetik*, p. 57; cf. also Dr. Montalto, *A Jewish tract on the 53rd ch. of Isaiah*, transl. from Portuguese, London, 1790).

386   THE JEWISH PEOPLE AND JESUS CHRIST

32. Cf. Lk. 4. 21; 18. 31; Mt. 26. 24.

33. Cf. Lee Woolf, *op. cit.*, p. 219; cf. *supra*, pp. 41 f.

34. Cf. E. C. Hoskyns, Jesus the Messiah, *Mysterium Christi*, ed. by G. K. A. Bell and Adolf Deissmann, p. 70. Against the background of the O. T., Jesus' significance becomes that of the Messiah; "if this be the case, we must then abandon a merely tentative ascription to Jesus of Messianic claims . . ."

35. Acts 18. 24, 28.

36. Prof. F. C. Burkitt refers to it as "a curious interpolation which long survived in Latin Psalters" (*Legacy of Israel*, p. 87, n. 2). "Wood" as a reference to the Cross appears to have been an important item in Christian evidences. Tertullian sees in almost every O. T. reference to it a prediction of the Cross (cf. *Adv. Judaeos*, Chs. X, XIII); the accusation that the Jews have tampered with the text is a frequent feature of Christian apologetics (cf. Origen, *Ep. to Julius Africanus*, Ante-Nicine Lib., x, pp. 377 ff.). The Jewish convert David Aboab makes similar accusations against his former co-religionists (cf. his Preface to *A Short, plain and well-grounded Introduction to Christianity*, London, 1750).

37. Cf. *Barn.*, Ch. IX; cf. R. H. Snape, *Rabb. Anthol.*, p. 619; Lukyn Williams, *Adv. Jud.*, pp. 24 f. A somewhat similar result was obtained by the Rabbis on the number 318 (Gen. 14. 14) by way of *gematria*; cf. Lev Gillet, *Com. in the Mess.*, p. 53.

38. Lukyn Williams observes: "Christian Jews only carried on the methods of Biblical interpretation which they had used before their conversion, and Gentile Christians naturally followed suit" (*Adv. Jud.*, p. 17). The infinite ingenuity of exegetical skill can be seen from the way in which a newly converted Jew, David Aboab, manages to translate the words ונשמחה בישועתך "we shall rejoice in thy Jesus" (!) (*op. cit.*, p. x), first having inserted these words in Ps. 145. 13; the Vulg. transl. אגילה באלהי ישעי (Hab. 3. 18) "exsultabo in Deo, Jesu meo". (!)

39. Cf. Lukyn Williams, *Adv. Jud.*, pp. 63 f.; cf. also Burkitt, *Legacy of Israel*, pp. 87 f.; James Parkes, *Jud. and Christ.*, II, p. 123.

40. Cf. Lightfoot, *The Apostolic Fathers*, p. 239.

41. Cf. Strack-Billerbeck, III, p. 386 and parallels; Klausner, *From Jesus to Paul*, pp. 28 ff.; M. Güdemann, *J. Q. R.*, IV, p. 353.

42. Strack-Billerbeck, III, p. 388; cf. Lev Gillet, pp. 53 ff.; H. Loewe, *Jud. and Christ.*, II, p. 11; Strack-Billerbeck point out the important difference between the Alexandrian method of interpretation and that of the Rabbis. The latter, probably under the stress of the Jewish-Christian controversy, warning against the dangers of allegorizing (*ibid.*, III, pp. 397–399); the same warning is sounded by Hayyim ben Musa of Bejar who advises his co-religionists to keep to the literal text and reject allegory when engaging in Christian controversy (cf. A. Neubauer, *The Expositor*, 3rd series, VII, p. 194).

43. Cf. *The Pentateuch*, abridged ed. p. 202; cf. M. Friedländer, *Jewish Religion*, pp. 225 f.

44. Prof. M. Philippson (1846–1916) has frankly acknowledged the fact that many Christian converts were men of outstanding quality. These are his words: "Man ist häufig geneigt, sich über den um sich greifenden Abfall zu trösten indem man sagt, es seien nur faule, kranke Zweige, die von dem uralten Baume abbröckeln.—Allein das ist leider unrichtig; vielmehr ver-

lassen uns zahlreiche geistig und materiell potente, sogar sonst sittlich hochste-
hende Elemente" (quoted by A. Frank, *Zeugen aus Israel*). A similar admission
is made by Graetz, who says: "By the conversion of learned and educated
men, physicians, authors, poets, Judaism was deprived of many talents; some
of them were possessed of a zeal for conversion, as if they were born Dominicans" (Geschichte, VIII, p. 83; quoted from *Enc. of Missions*, 2nd ed., 1904,
p. 356b); cf also Schechter's view: Bentwich, *S. Schechter*, p. 101.

45. Franz Delitzsch, *Ernste Fragen an die Gebildeten jüdischer Religion*, Leipzig,
1888. (*Institutum Judaicum*, Nrs. 18, 19.)

46. Cf. the answer by the Rev. M. M. Ben-Oliel to a similar allegation
made by Claude G. Montefiore, in a letter to *The Times*, April 26th, 1902
(*Church and Synagogue Quart.*, IV, p. 118); Mr. Ben-Oliel, addressing himself
directly to Montefiore, points out that seven members of his own family circle
have become Christians; cf. also C. P. Sherman who, in an article on Isaac
Salkinson's translation of *Paradise Lost*, says: "The Mission to Jews can
boast of having from the days of St. Paul gained the ear and heart of many
brilliant sons of Israel who shine as stars in the firmament" (Milton and
Salkinson, *Church and Synagogue Quart.*, XI, p. 85).

47. Acts 9. 22.

48. Cf. A. Bernstein, *Some Jewish Witnesses*, p. 338.

49. J. Lichtenstein, in an open letter to his Jewish brethren, declared with
great solemnity: "als ein im Amte ergrauter Rabbiner, als alter gesetzestreuer
Jude bekenne ich nun laut: Jesus ist der geweissagte Messiahs Israels . . ."
(*Eine Bitte an die gelehrten Leser*, Budapest (no date), p. 4).

50. Charles Kingsley, in a letter to Adolph Saphir, truly stresses this point;
cf. *Church and Synagogue Quart.*, VI, p. 74.

51. The greater part of the Chizzuk Emunah is concerned with the interpretation of O. T. passages. Lukyn Williams' answer to R. Isaac of Troki is
an exposition of the same passages from the Christian point of view (cf. Lukyn
Williams, *Christian Evidences*, Vols 2, 1911–1919).

52. S. A. Cook, *The Old Testament, A Reinterpretation*, p. 222.

53. Cf. *ibid.*, p. 221.

54. Dr. Isaac Da Costa, *Israel and the Gentiles*, Engl. by Mary J. Kennedy,
London, 1850; cf. also Dr. Abraham Capadose's experience, Brewster, *op. cit.*,
p. 174.

55. Quoted in full by Bernstein, p. 178.

56. Kingsley has truly recognized the importance of the O.T.: "if we
once lose our faith in the Old Testament", he wrote to Saphir, "our faith in
the New will soon dwindle to the impersonal spiritualism of Frank Newman,
and the German philosophers" (*Church and Synagogue Quart.*, VI, p. 75).

57. Cf. A. Fürst, *Christen und Juden*, pp. 225 ff.

58. Acts 17. 22 ff.

59. Cf. S. Schechter, *Studies*, I, p. 126; Lukyn Williams, *Adv. Jud.*, p. 247;
Pablo was not the first to introduce this method of argumentation, cf. *Adv.
Jud.*, p. 244, n. 2; 247, n. 1.

60. For a description of the *Pugio Fidei* and the line of argument it takes,
see Lukyn Williams, *op. cit.*, pp. 248 ff.; cf. also the learned art. by
A. Neubauer, "Jewish Controversy and the *Pugio Fidei*" (*The Expositor*,
3rd series, VII, pp. 81 ff., 179 ff.). Neubauer shows, against Schiller-Szinessy,

that Martini was well versed in Rabbinic literature and that not Pablo, but he himself, was the author of the *Pugio Fidei*.

61. Cf. G. H. Box, *Legacy of Israel*, pp. 328 ff.; A. C. Adcock, *Jud. and Christ.*, II, pp. 292 ff.; one of the most outstanding pupils of the Cabbalah was Pico di Mirandola (1463–94); Reuchlin attached great importance to the Messianic conceptions of Jewish mysticism, cf. Kayserling, *J. E.* art. Cabala, III, pp. 470 f.

62. Cf. Bernstein, *Jewish Witnesses*, p. 337; Delitzsch called Lichtenstein's book upon which the author has laboured for twelve years "das gelehrteste und eigentümlichste, was je ein Judenchrist geschrieben", describing it as "gnostischebionitisch" (Saat auf Hoffnung, 1868/69, p. 189); Lichtenstein's later Commentary, however, shows greater restraint in the application of esoteric teaching (cf. Zöckler, *Aus Jechiel Lichtensteins hebräischem Kommentar*, Leipzig, 1895, p. 6); another famous Hebrew Christian, Joachim Biesenthal, uses the *Zohar* to adduce proofs for the doctrine of the Trinity and other Christian dogmas (cf. *Auszüge aus dem Buche Sohar*, 1837).

63. "'Christianity expressed in Jewish terms', has always meant to Levertoff, 'Chassidic terms'". (O. T. Levertoff, "The Jewish-Christian Problem", *Judaism and Christianity*, ed. by L. Gillet, p. 99); cf. also *Comm. in the Messiah*, p. 203.

64. Cf. his study in the conception of love in Chassidism and the Johannine Gospel (*Love and the Messianic Age*, London, 1923); cf. also his liturgy, *Missale Judaeorum Fidei Christianae*; Paul Schorlemer, *Eine Judenchristliche Liturgie;* Olga Levertoff, "Paul L. and the Jewish Christian Problem", in *Judaism and Christianity*, ed. L. G., pp. 57 ff., 71 ff., 93 ff.

65. Gillet, *Communion*, p. 97; Gillet observes, however, "One must categorically repudiate the naïve endeavours to find in Jewish tradition the present Christian dogmas of the Trinity, Incarnation and Redemption".

66. *Ibid.*, pp. 81 ff. ("Questions concernant la Chekinah", in *Judaism and Christianity*, ed. by L. G., pp. 33 ff.)

67. Cf. Lukyn Williams, *Adv. Jud.*, p. 251. Of older writers, G. Ch. Sommer, Heinrich Michaelis and J. Chr. Schoettgen may be mentioned.

68. *Communion in the Messiah*, p. 186; J. Douglas Lord: "The change from Judaism to Christianity is less a conversion than a progress" in *Church and Synagogue Quart.*, 1 (1898), p. 213.

69. Cf. A. Lukyn Williams, *Church and Synagogue Quart.*, VI, p. 9, cf. J. Abelson, Vallentine's *Jew. Encycl.*, p. 121; L. Gillet, *Communion in the Messiah*, p. 64. A short summary of Cabbalistic teaching is to be found in Joseph Bonsirven's book, *On the Ruins of the Temple*, Ch. XII, pp. 250 ff. For the description of Jewish mystical literature, see Oesterley and Box, *A short Survey of the Liter. of Rabbinical and Medieval Judaism*, pp. 235–254; cf. also S. Spiegel, *Hebrew Reborn*, pp. 136 ff.

70. Cf. A. Fürst, *Christen und Juden*, pp. 223 f. The Chassidic Movement of Israel b. Eliezer Baal Shem-Tob (Besht) met with fierce opposition on the part of Talmudic Judaism; cf. S. Schechter, The Chassidim, *Studies in Judaism*, I, pp. 19 ff. For an understanding of Jewish mysticism, see T. Ysander, *Studien zum B'estschen Hasidismus*, Uppsala, 1933, pp. 17–37.

71. Cf. Abrahams, *Judaism*, pp. 68, 76 f. Heinrich York-Steiner's verdict: "von Mystizismus will die jüdische Religion absolut nichts wissen . . .", is

obviously an exaggeration. Torsten Ysander speaks rightly of a double trend in Judaism, one tending towards rationalism, the other towards mysticism. The trend towards rationalism is, however, in preponderance.

72. "Der unterdrückte Mystizismus wurde ein Ferment des entstehenden Christentums . . ." (York-Steiner, p. 114).

73. It is interesting to note that Nachmanides and Buber, both no mean mystics, are strongly opposed to Christianity.

74. A Fürst, Die Kabbala und ihre Ausschreitungen auf dem Gebiete der christlichen Apologetik, Christen u. Juden, pp. 222 ff.

75. Spiegel, op. cit., pp. 137 f.   76. 2 Cor. 3. 13–15.

77. 2 Cor. 3. 6; cf. M. Güdemann, "Spirit and Letter in Judaism and Christianity", J. Q. R., April, 1892. Güdemann holds that the Rabbis, too, were willing to sacrifice the letter for the sake of the spirit. They opposed Paul, because the spirit with which he was concerned was not the spirit of the Biblical text, but a spirit foreign to it: "The Jewish teachers felt themselves compelled to retain their hold upon the letter, *not for the sake of the letter, but for the sake of the spirit*" (ibid., pp. 354 f.).

78. Cf. Barn., Ch. 8; the writer speaks of "the calf of Christ". The whole chapter is an example of how far-fetched the allegorical method can become.

79. Barn., Ch. 9.

80. Cf. Cyprian's treatise, Testimonies against the Jews, Bk. I, §§ 4, 5.

81. Hippolytus, Refutation of all heresies, Bk. IX, Ch. 25

82. Adv. Jud., Ch. I.   83. Cf. ibid., Ch. XIII.

84. Apologeticus, § 20.   85. Ibid., § 21.

86. Tert., Ad. Jud., Ch. XIV; Hippolytus says of the Jews that "up to this day they continue in anticipation of the future coming of Christ", whom they expect to be "a warlike and powerful individual" (Haer., Ch. XXV).

87. Testimonies against the Jews, Bk. I; cf. Origen, C. Cels, Bk. II, Ch. VIII.

88. Tert., Adversus Marcionem, Bk. V, Ch. XI.   89. Homily, XVIII, 17.

90. Homily, XVIII, 20; the usual method of dealing with difficult texts in the O. T. was by means of allegory. A past master in this method of exegesis was Origen. Dr. R. B. Tollinton says of him: "His whole exegesis rests upon the principle that Scripture says one thing and means another . . ." (Selections from Comm. and Homilies of Origin, p. xxvi).

91. C. Cels., Bk. II, Ch. VIII.   92. Ibid., Bk. II, Ch. LXXIV.

93. Cf. Peter Alphonsi, Dialogus Petri; Lukyn Williams, Adv. Jud., p. 234; cf. A. Fürst, pp. 47 ff.

94. Meelführer wrote a little book, Jesus in Talmude sive Dissertatio Philologica, etc., Altdorf, 1699, in which he discusses the well-known passages referring to Jesus with special attention to the Tol'dot Yeshu; but his Consensus veterum Hebraeorum cum Ecclesia Christiana, 1701, and Causae Synagogae errantis, 1702, contain his views concerning Judaism and its relationship to the Church.

95. The author of Horae Hebraicae et Talmudicae, in his Manipulus spicilegiorum, has a section specially intended for the Jews, showing how the Law of Moses foretells the function of the Messiah which has been fulfilled by Jesus Christ.

96. Joh. Christophorus Wagenseilius, Tela Ignea Satanae, etc., 1681.

97. J. Chr. Schoettgen, *Horae Hebraicae et Talmudicae in universum Novum Testamentum*, Leipzig, 1733.

98. Johann Andreas Eisenmenger, *Entdecktes Judentum, oder Gründlicher und Wahrhaffter Bericht welchergestalt die verstockte Juden die Hochheilige Drey-Einigkeit Gott Vater, Sohn und Heil. Geist, erschrecklicher Weise lästern und verunehren, etc., etc.*, Königsberg/Pr., 1711, p. 302; cp. *ibid.*, pp. 453 ff.; another work akin to it though less known is that by M. Sigismundo Hosmann, *Das Schwer zu bekehrende Juden-Herz/Nebst einigen Vorbebereitungs-Mitteln zu der Juden Bekehrung/Auf Veranlassung der erschröcklichen Gottes-Lästerung, etc., etc.*, Zelle und Leipzig, 1725.

99. Eisenmenger, p. 492.

100. *The Old Paths* (Nethivoth Olam) was translated into Hebrew by a Jewish Christian, Stanislaw Hoga of Kazimierz, Poland. In 1857 the Jews replied to it in a Hebrew book, *The voice of Judah*, where it is alleged that McCaul is a Jew by the name of Judah, the son of Rabbi Israel of Brody, near Lwow; that he was given 100,000 marks for his work; that he went to America and there returned to Judaism. Later, Isaac Ber Levinsohn (1788–1860) and Lazar Zweifel (1815–1888), have also written against it (cf. Roi, III, p. 56); for Levinsohn's reply to McCaul, see Meisl, *op. cit.*, p. 119.

101. *Old Paths*, p. 652.

102. Cf. *J. Q. R.*, Jan. 1901, p. 170.

103. Cf. Lukyn Williams, *Adv. Jud.*, p. 247; cf. also A. Neubauer, *Expositor*, 3rd series, VII, p. 194.

104. Cf. *Old Paths*, p. 178 ff.   105. *Ibid.*, p. 654.

106. *Church and Synagogue Quart.*, I, p. 378; cf. *ibid.*, p. 213.

107. *Church and Synagogue Quart.*, III, p. 54.

108. *Ibid.*, p. 55 (K. T. Cheyne quoted, *Expositor*, 3rd series, I, 1885, pp. 401 ff.).

109. *Ibid.*, p. 58.

110. H. E. K. Fry, *Church and Synagogue Quart.*, III, p. 181.

111. *Communion in the Messiah*, p. 186.

112. *The Christian Approach to the Jew*, Report of the Budapest-Warsaw Conferences, April, 1927, London, 1927, p. 19. § 3.

113. There is, however, an important difference in the appreciation of Judaism between those who look upon it as opposed to Christianity and those who regard it merely as on a lower stage of development. Thus, Dalman in a missionary talk once said: "Let us not despise Judaism as a religion. Some missionaries have tried to make Jewish religious thoughts, books, and customs ridiculous. This is an entirely wrong method of procedure, and will only be resorted to by ignorant people. Among the non-Christian religions of the world, none deserves more respect, none is of greater interest or more worth studying than the Jewish—wrong though it is" (*Church and Synag. Quart.*, IV, p. 105); against this may be put Lev Gillet's view that Christianity is merely a continuation or the completion of Judaism (cf. *Communion in the Messiah*, pp. 180, 186). The difference between these two outlooks is connected with the conception of progressive revelation. To Gillet, the Messiah has not only come in history, but is still coming; his coming is "a long-drawn-out historical process" (*ibid.*, p. 110).

114. *C. Cels.*, Bk. II, Ch. I.   115. *Ibid.*, Bk. V, Ch. XXV.

116. Clement Alex., *Stromata*, Bk. II, Ch. V.

117. Cf. Lactantius, *Epitome div. inst.*, Ch. XLVIII; cf. Gregory Thaumaturgus, *On the Annunciation to Mary, Ante-Nicene Lib.*, xx, pp. 134 f.

118. Cf. Parkes, *Conflict*, p. 395, § 2; Rabbi Moses Scialetti, an Italian Jew who was baptized in London in June 1663, in his tract, *A letter written to the Jews*, London, 1663, gives us the questions and answers on condition of which baptism was administered. One question reads: Do you renounce the errors of Judaism and with all your heart embrace the doctrine of Christianity? Another question: Are you heartily sorry . . . for the errors and obstinacy of your nation, whereby they approve the malice of their forefathers, and are guilty of the death of our Lord and Saviour Jesus Christ? (*Ibid.*, pp. 16 ff.)

119. William Surenhusius, the famous Amsterdam Hebraist, held that a worthy disciple of Christ must either become a Jew or else learn thoroughly the language and culture of the Jews (cf. Graetz, v, p. 199 f.). For the influence of Rabbinic Studies upon modern Christian thought, see G. H. Box, "Hebrew Studies in the Reformation Period and After," *Legacy of Israel*, pp. 315–375.

120. R. E. Strahan, in an article, *Evangelistic work among the Jews*, points to the strong bond of unity between the English Christian and the Jew on the religious basis. Judaism already possesses "the great elements of religion" (cf. *Church and Synag. Quart.*, viii, p. 30).

121. Cf. Gillet, *Communion in the Messiah* ("The Mission of Israel to the Christian Church"), pp. 191–195.

122. *Jesus, Paul and the Jews*, pp. 151 f.; cf. also his article, "A Christian looks at the Christian Mission to the Jews," *Theology*, xlvii, No. 292, Oct. 1944.

123. J. Douglas Lord, *Church and Synag. Quart.*, i, p. 213.

124. G. H. Box, "The ideal of a Hebrew Christian Church", *Church and Synag. Quart.*, vi, p. 40; but H. Heathcote, "The Anglican Church and the Jews" (*Church and Synag. Quart.*, iv, pp. 43 ff.), warns against the creation of another Church which will soon become a denomination. He holds that "the Synagogue reformed in the direction of Christianity" will not meet the need. "The Anglican Church can offer the Jew nothing less than the Catholic faith in its entirety" (cf. G. H. Box's answer, *ibid.*, p. 55).

125. The idea itself is not entirely absent in Judaism, and occurs under the term of בריה חדשה; cf. Dalman, *Words of Jesus*, p. 178.

126. Dalman, p. 177.

127. Cf. Vernon Bartlett, *Hast. Dict. of Bible*, iv, p. 215a.

128. Cf. James Denney, *Hast. Dict. of Christ and the Gospels*, ii, p. 489a.

129. J. Douglas Lord records a significant fact: "The orthodox Jew looks upon a sincere acceptance of Christianity as a moral and inherent impossibility, and attributes in every case base motives" (*Church and Synag. Quart.*, i, p. 213). In the majority of cases this is also true of the non-orthodox Jew. For Jewish views concerning converts, see *J. E.*, art. "Apostasy", ii, pp. 12 ff.; also "Conversion to Christianity", *ibid.*, iv, pp. 249 ff. Kaufmann Kohler repeats the ridiculous story about a certain Jewish convert of the thirteenth century called Everard, canon of St. Andrew's in Cologne, who is supposed to have said: "As little as the dog will ever cease running after the hare and the cat after the mouse, so little will the Jew ever become a true Christian". The Haggadic origin of the whole story is clearly recognizable. (!)

130. See William James, *The Varieties of Religious Experience*, 1902.

131. Gillet, *Communion in the Messiah*, pp. 195 f.; Gillet, however, takes up a much more positive attitude in his reply to Parkes' article on "Missions to Jews", cf. *Theology*, XLVII, Oct. 1944, pp. 224 ff.

132. It is significant that Fr. L. Gillet is a member of the Greek Orthodox Church.

133. The polemical or apologetical factor is thereby not excluded and has its place as part of the human effort to say what can only be said adequately by God Himself. The missionary may thus follow the example of the great Apostle (cf. Oesterley, *Church and Synagogue Quart.*, XI, pp. 67 f.).

134. Jo. Christoph Wolf, in his *Bibliotheca Hebraea*, gives a list of over eighty Jewish converts who have written on behalf of Christianity before the year 1721: *Scriptores anti Judaici ex Judaei, op. cit.*, pp. 1003–1013. The list contains ninety-one names, but a few do not appear to have been of Jewish descent. A. Neubauer remarks that it was usually learned converts "who provoked the official discussions" (*op. cit.*, p. 88).

135. Bernstein says of him: "He was a poet of ability, but lacked discretion as well as charity in his poems with regard to the Jews" (*op. cit.*, p. 45).

136. L. I. Newman, *Jewish Influence*, p. 552; an unusual exchange of views took place between Paulo Alvaro of Jewish descent and Bodo, the royal chaplain to Louis le Débonnaire, who became a Jewish proselyte and assumed the name of Eleazar, cf. Lukyn Williams, *Adv. Jud.*, pp. 224 ff.

137. A. Fürst, *Christen u. Juden*, p. 69.

138. Pfefferkorn's character has been repeatedly discussed. Few have tried to defend him, amongst them Geiger. For the whole case see S. A. Hirsch, "John Pfefferkorn and the Battle of the Books," *J. Q. R.*, IV, pp. 256 ff.; cf. also Danby, *The Jew and Christianity*, pp. 48 ff.

139. *Disputatio Judaei cum Christiano de Fide Christiana*; Lukyn Williams dates the tract some time before A.D. 1098; for a description, see *ibid.*, pp. 375 ff.

140. Cf. Lukyn Williams, *Adv. Jud.*, pp. 409 ff., 412 ff.

141. For Peñaforte, Martini and Lull, see E. Allison Peers, *Ramon Lull, A Biography*, London, 1929.

142. W. T. Gidney, p. 2. Italy was the scene of an intensive missionary effort in the sixteenth century due to the influence of Pope Paul III, who established a house for Jewish enquirers in 1550 and who was a great friend of the Jews, cp. Heman, p. 299.

143. In 1728, the Institutum Judaicum in Halle came into existence, founded by Prof. John Henry Callenberg. It was the result of coincidence rather than design. Johannes Müller of Gotha wrote a booklet *Das Licht am Abend*, which a Hebrew-Christian student of medicine called Immanuel Frommann translated into Yiddish-German, and for lack of a publisher offered to act as compositor (Bernstein attributes the authorship of the tract to Frommann himself, but this is a mistake). In March 1728 the first 1,000 copies were printed. Frommann put on the title page the Hebrew translation of Müller's name: Jochanan Kimchi. The booklet was a tremendous success and was translated into many languages. Soon two other Hebrew Christians were engaged in the printing press. Thus the Institute was born. On Nov. 16th, 1780, the first two theological students, Johann Georg Widmann and Johann

Andreas Manitius went out as wandering missionaries to reach the Jews. Not long after, other students followed their example. Roi regards Callenberg as the father of Jewish missions of the evangelical Church (cf. *op cit.*, 1, p. 246). At the end of a little book, *A short account of the wonderful conversion to Christianity of Solomon Deitsch, with Preface and Remarks* by the Rev. Mr. Burgmann, London, 1771, the writer, a missionary of the Halle Institute, gives a short description of its early history. The Institute was established "for the good of Jews and Mohametans".

144. An interesting tribute to the importance of C.M.J. comes from the Jewish side: "Until the beginning of the nineteenth century", says Israel Cohen, "the efforts of missionaries to convert the Jews were carried on only sporadically, but since the establishment in 1809 of the London Society for the Propagation of Christianity among the Jews, missionary societies have sprung up in all parts of the world" (*Jewish Life in Modern Times*, p. 271).

145. The dispersion of the Jews was a favourite argument for the truth of Christianity, cf. Augustinus, *Ep.* 232, § 3.

146. In German pietistic circles, the general conversion of the Jews became a universally accepted dogma, only opposed by a few theologians (cf. Roi, 1, p. 239). Roi mentions that in 1748 the theological discussion as to the final salvation of Israel stirred so much strife amongst the Danzigers, that the authorities had to forbid any further discussion of the subject.

147. *The Calling of the Jews, a present to Judah and the Children of Israel*, London, 1621.

148. John Grindley, *The Farmer's Advice to the Unbelieving Jews*, Shrewsbury, 1717; the writer makes three points: (1) He gives proofs that the promises in the O. T. apply to Jesus; (2) that Jesus whom the Jews put to death has fulfilled these promises; (3) he demonstrates that both Scripture and reason prove Jesus to be the promised Messiah. *The Jews impartially considered*, London, 1754; the writer explains that the Jewish people is not to be considered in the same category with the rest of mankind "but as a People now dispersed abroad by the Hand which at first collected them together, and under correction of that Hand for a very flagrant Enormity" (p. 3). They must thus remain monuments of God's displeasure till they "acknowledge the divine Mission of Jesus". Richard Parry, *The Genealogies of Jesus Christ in Matthew and Luke explained; and the Jewish objections removed*, London, 1771. J. Bicheno, *A Friendly Address to the Jews*, London (about 1787); the writer gives Scriptural proofs for the Messiahship of Jesus and also an answer to a letter by a certain Mr. Levy in connection with the letters by Dr. Priestley addressed to the Jews (see *ibid.*, pp. 70 ff.). *The Case of the Jews, considered with Respect to Christianity*, anonym., London, 1755 (the same writer is the author of another tract called *Deism Refuted: or, the Truth of Christianity Demonstrated*, London, 1755); for further literature, see Roi, *op. cit.*, 1, pp. 421 ff.

149. Paul Lewis, *A Treatise of the Future Restoration of the Jews and Israelites to their own Land . . . Address'd to the Jews*, London, 1747; the writer frequently speaks of the Messiah, but avoids mentioning the name of Jesus Christ; he calls the Jewish people to cleanse themselves from their iniquities and to make themselves worthy of God's wonderful promises to His people. Joseph Eyre, *Observations on the Prophecies relating to the Restoration of the Jews* (1777); Charles Jerram, *An essay tending to show the grounds of Scripture for the*

future restoration of Israel (1796). A literary curiosity is the strange story told by S. Bret, a supposed eye-witness of a council of Jews to examine the Scriptures concerning the Messiah: *A true Relation of the Proceedings of the Great Council of the Jews*, assembled the 12th of October, 1650, in the Plains of Ajayday, in Hungary, about 30 leagues distant from Buda, to examine the Scriptures concerning Christ (the account is incorporated in a little book called *A looking-glass for the Jews: or, The Credulous Unbelievers*, London, 1753; it contains the story of Shabbethai Zevi and a brief account of 21 other false Messiahs). William Pinchion of Springfield (N. England), wrote *The Jews Synagogue, or a Treatise concerning the ancient Orders and manners of worship used by the Jews in their Synagogue-Assemblies*, London, 1652; the writer proves that the "Synagogue-Assemblies" were true visible Churches of Jesus Christ and thus some of their customs before their "Apostasie" may prove profitable for Christianity, such as prayer and preaching without any levitical ceremony, weekly lectures, the use of the common tongue, etc.; the *Monthly Magazine*, 1796, published an article by a certain Meiron, putting forth the theory of blood-relationship between the Old Britons and the Hebrews.

150. Esdras Edzard is held by some to have been of Jewish descent, but this is doubtful.

151. Cf. Roi, I, p. 107.   152. Cf. Roi, I, p. 103.

153. The Dutch Church has made an early contribution to the missionary cause amongst the Jews. Her Synod was the first to propose the training of missionaries and the creation of an adequate missionary literature. In its missionary zeal, it went as far as removing pictures from churches which might appear offensive to the Jews. It also instituted special prayers for the conversion of the Jewish people and Israel's salvation became the topic of many sermons. The University of Leyden created a chair for Jewish controversy. The most outstanding champion of the missionary cause was the famous Arminian Hugo Grotius (1583–1645), a personal friend of Rabbi Menasseh ben Israel (cf. Roi, I, pp. 147 f.). Another Leyden professor, Simon Episcopius, an ardent Arminian, took an anti-Trinitarian view, holding that this doctrine was the greatest obstacle to Jewish conversion.

154. *Imperial Dict. of Universal Biography*, III, p. 89.

155. Richard Kidder, *A demonstration of the Messiah in which the truth of the Christian Religion is proved especially against The Jews;* in two parts, London, 1684 and 1699. In the second part, the author sets out to give reasons why the Jews ought to believe in Jesus: "it is not my business to speak in diminution of Moses, or to question his Divine Mission, but only to show that the Jew hath the same reason to believe Jesus sent from God, and greater reason also" (*ibid.*, II, p. 17). Eisenmenger includes "die allzu grosse Freiheit, welche den Juden gegeben wird" (!) and "derselben Beförderung zu Ehrenaemtern" (?) amongst the obstacles which hinder Jewish conversion (cp. *op. cit.*, p. 990).

156. Roi says of him: "Der Ton aber, welchen er den Juden gegenüber anschlägt, ist ein ungemein ansprechender. Die Worte kommen aus einem liebewarmen Herzen und aus einem für das Heil der Seelen glühenden Eifer" (*op. cit.*, I, p. 141).

157. This tract was reprinted by L. J. S. in 1812.

158. Roi, I, p. 208.

159. Sigismund Hosmann wrote a tract, *Das schwer zu bekehrende Judenherz*

(1701), in which he advocates coercion as the only means of breaking Jewish opposition to Christianity. Julius Stahl (1802–1861), himself a convert from Judaism, professor of Law and Philosophy and leader of the conservative party, was opposed to the idea that Jews should hold public office in a Christian State (*Der Christliche Staat und sein Verhältniss zum Deismus und Judentum*, Berlin, 1847; cf. Roi, II, pp. 236 ff.).

160. Modern Jewish writers still complain of unworthy methods employed by missionaries in order to make converts. In a letter to the editor of *The Times* (April 26th, 1902) C. G. Montefiore complains of the missionary activities of the Church in the East End of London. He calls it "a remarkable thing that the proselytizing activities of the various conversionist societies seem to limit the sphere of their operations to the poorer and less cultivated class of Jews". Israel Cohen alleges that missionary work is carried on by means of cunning enticement and prying on Jewish misery and poverty (cf. *Jewish Life in Modern Times*, pp. 272 ff.). A similar allegation is made by S. Daiches (cf. *Aspects of Judaism*, pp. 132 ff.). That missionary societies have tended to concentrate their effort upon the poorer Jews cannot be denied (cf. Dalman, *Church and Synag. Quart.*, IV, p. 99); that missionary work has a philanthropical side to it is inevitable, but the Jewish contentions are not only exaggerated, but also unfair. The Gospel message was from the beginning primarily for the poor and needy.

161. The great champion of this new understanding of the Jewish national tradition was undoubtedly the French professor A. F. Pétavel (1791–1870). In his *Discours prononcé dans l'assemblée générale des missions* (1834), he insists that converted Jews be encouraged to remain in close touch with their people. Hebrew Christians must not be an offence to their brethren and must continue their life within Jewry. Roi calls these "sonderbare Ideen" (?) (cf. Roi, *op. cit.*, II, pp. 280 f.), but Pétavel's views have quickly gained recognition. A few sentences from a sermon by the great Jewish missionary, Gustaf Dalman, may be quoted: "We have not to Germanize or to Anglicize but only to Christianize them. . . . Jewish missionaries are called upon to endeavour to preach the gospel in as Jewish a shape as its essence permits, and so to respect the peculiarity of the Jewish nation. . . . At all events, let us not help to kill the spirit of Jewish nationality by our missions!" (*Church and Synag. Quart.*, IV, pp. 101 f.) Charles Kingsley, in a letter to Adolf Saphir, says: "I would, therefore, intreat you, and every other converted Jew, not to sink your nationality, because you have become a member of the universal Church. . . ." (*Church and Synagogue Quart.*, VI, p. 75).

162. Cf. *The Christian Approach*, p. 19: "In the religion of Israel there are ideas of culture and principles of morality which are not to be found in other non-Christian religions".

163. In this respect German writers have been more cautious than their English counterparts. J. Fr. Buddeus has already stressed the difference between Judaism and Christianity in the conception of sin which makes a Saviour to the Synagogue superfluous (cf. Roi, I, p. 232). Gustaf H. Dalman, fully appreciating Judaism, was convinced that "true evangelical Christianity must be placed in opposition to Judaism, without any watering down and without disguise" (*Christianity and Judaism*, transl. by G. H. Box, London, 1901, p. 25 f.). English writers, on the other hand, have tended towards

reconciliation at the price of toning down Christian doctrine. Another feature is the appeal from modern Judaism to Rabbinic sources as Oesterley has done in his study of the Jewish and Christian doctrine of Mediation (cf. *Church and Synag. Quart.*, X–XII); cf. also H. E. K. Fry's criticism of Dalman's essay (*Church and Synag. Quart.*, III, pp. 179 ff.).

164. Dalman, in an address delivered in Scotland in Jan. 1902, severely censured missionaries who speak to the Jews "as if they were addressing non-Jewish Christians, without importing into their words anything specifically Jewish or calculated to appeal specially to Jews as such" (*Church and Synag. Quart.*, IV, p. 95). Lukyn Williams pleaded for a scientific study of Missions to the Jews and his programme includes a thorough knowledge of Judaism (cf. *Church and Synagogue Quart.*, IX, p. 11); cf. also *The Christian Approach*, p. 41, § 11b.

165. Cf. *The Christian Approach to the Jew*, pp. 18 f.: "Our message to the Jews is the love of God revealed in Jesus Christ. . . ."

166. *Church and Synagogue Quart.*, IV, p. 105. For a description of the various Jewish Missionary Societies, see *Encycl. of Missions*, 1904, pp. 356 ff.

167. *Jewish Life*, p. 271; cf. the official report of the Conference, *The Christian Approach*, pp. 79 ff., 198 ff.

168. Cf. *The Christian Approach*, p. 5.

169. Cf. *ibid.*, p. 7: "the Jew, as never before, has been discovered to be reachable—we believe, gloriously reachable". At the Conference at Atlantic City in May, 1931, under the auspices of the International Missionary Council, a resolution was passed in the form of a "unanimous acceptance of a statement on the supreme Christian responsibility of sharing with the Jew the faith in Christ and knowledge of God in Him which is the supreme treasure of the Christian Church" (*Intern. Rev. of Miss.*, XXI, 1932, p. 344).

170. The influence of men like Graf Nicolaus Ludwig Zinzendorf (1700–1760) and Prof. Franz Delitzsch (1813–1893) upon the Protestant Church cannot be overestimated. Thanks to the spirit of Zinzendorf, the Herrnhuters were the first to introduce prayers in their litany for Israel's conversion; to pray for the Jews on the day of Atonement; to insert special hymns in their hymnary remembering the Jews. Their finest missionary was Samuel Lieber-kühn (1710–?), who may be called the first *modern* missionary to the Jews. He adapted himself to those to whom he preached to such an extent that the Dutch Jews called him Rabbi Samuel (cf. Roi, I, p. 366). Prof. Delitzsch, by his example and his writings, has stimulated to missionary activity not only the Lutheran, but the Protestant Church at large (cf. Roi, II, p. 132). To these friends of Israel must be added the name of the great Englishman, Lewis Way, whose importance for the London Jews Society cannot be over-estimated; for the story of his life, see A. M. W. Stirling, *The Ways of Yesterday*, London, 1930.

171. Cf. *International Review of Missions*, XXI, 1932, pp. 342 f.

172. Cf. A. Fürst, p. 60.   173. *Jewish Life in Modern Times*, p. 269.

174. Vallentine's *J. E.*, p. 45b.

175. Cf. Lukyn Williams, *Adv. Jud.*, p. 277.

176. Newman mentions Victor von Carben, Emmanuel Tremellius, Jochanan Isaac and his son Stephen, as Luther's special friends. To a former Rabbi Jacob Gipher, called Bernhard, Luther sent his tract, *That Jesus was*

born a Jew. With Matthew Adrian, Hebrew professor at Wittenberg, and Johann Boeschenstein, Luther came to grief (cf. Newman, *op. cit.*, pp. 625 ff.).

177. Quoted by Adler, *Auto de Fé*, p. 49; also Roi, *op. cit.*, I, pp. 404 ff. A notable exception was the convert Dr. Carl Anton, a former pupil of Eibeschütz, who defended the Jews against Eisenmenger (cf. *ibid.*, p. 403). Newman mentions also Martin of Lucena as friendly disposed towards the Jews (cf. *op. cit.*, p. 371). But such were exceptions. What the Jew expected from the converts we can guess from the Chassidic story about the baptized Jew who becomes a bishop but is brought back to the fold by the mystic power of Baalshem. The former bishop confesses: "I was filled with hatred against my own belief, and this grew every day. But in the nights, when I was defenceless, the shame of my apostasy came upon me. In the day I took revenge for the unrest of my nights, and persecuted my people" (M. Buber, *Jewish Mysticism*, p. 108) ; *Anti-Judaice ex Judaei* (cp. Elkan N. Adler, *About Hebrew Manuscripts*, 1905, p. 118).

178. Cf. *J. E.*, IV, pp. 249 ff.

179. Neander's Jewish name was David Mendel. Already in 1805, on leaving school, he made a Latin speech deploring the difficult position of German Jewry and pleading for equality (*De Judaeis optima conditione in civitatem recipiendis*). He remained a friend of the Jews all his life: "He emphatically denounced the Blood Accusation in 1840" (Vallentine's *J. E.*, p. 457b).

180. Veith, who was a great preacher, a prolific writer and a good physician, defended the Jews in the Damascus Blood Libel of 1840, as Neander had done. According to the Jewish press, he was supposed to have taken a solemn oath from the pulpit with the Crucifix in his hand, denying the use of blood by Jews for religious purposes (cf. A. Jürst, pp. 289 f.; Adolph Kohut, *Berühmte israelitische Männer u. Frauen*, II, p. 357).

181. Paulus Stephanus Cassel (Selig Cassel) is described as "an active opponent of anti-Semitism" (Vallentine's *J. E.*, p. 132b). At the time of the rise of anti-Semitism in Germany, Cassel raised his voice with great effect on behalf of his people. He wrote: *Wider H. v. Treitschke für die Juden; Die Antisemiten und die evangelische Kirche*, and many articles against Adolf Stöcker. Roi disapprovingly remarks: "Alle seine Kundgebungen auf diesem Gebiete sind mit der vollsten Einseitigkeit der Partei behaftet" (II, p. 191). But Roi's judgment is in itself biased, though in the opposite direction. He denies the Jews the right to citizenship (cp. *ibid.*, II, p. 259) and defends Stöcker's anti-Semitic activity (cp. *ibid.*, II, p. 263).

182. For the full list of names, see the Magazine of the London Jews Society, *The Jewish Intelligence*, Aug. 1840, pp. 240 f.

183. Cf. A. Fürst, p. 60: "In dieser Beziehung sind unsere modernen Juden um kein Haar besser gesinnt als ihre Vorfahren". J. Lichtenstein bitterly complains that religiously indifferent Jews are his most ardent opponents (*Eine Bitte*, pp. 9 f.).

184. There are, naturally, laudable exceptions. Dr. Blau of Frankfurt/M, in an attack upon apostatized Jews and those who maintain social relations with them, makes it plain "that he has no quarrel with persons who may become converted to Christianity from conviction" (*Jewish Chronicle*, March 26th, 1909).

185. Quoted by C. M. Robinson, *History of Christian Missions*, 1915, pp. 473 f.; the Capadose family affords a good example of the rapidity of the process of assimilation; cf. Brewster, *op. cit.*, p. 186, n. 1.

186. The insistence upon the significance of the individual as against the nation (Judaism) is one of the main denationalizing causes of Christianity. "Historically", says J. H. Oldham, "the creation of this sense of the value of the individual was largely the work of Christianity" (*Christianity and the Race Problem*, p. 221). It is the belief of the Church that in Jesus Christ there is established a new human relationship which transcends all human divisions (cp. *ibid.*, pp. 253 f.).

187. Lukyn Williams, *Missions to Jews: A Historical Retrospect* (S.P.C.K., 1897), p. 54: "If a Jew is converted, he, from want of sufficient choice among Jewish women, marries a Gentile, while his children for a certainty, and even he himself for a probability, become assimilated to Gentile surroundings, and practically become indistinguishable from the English, Germans or French among whom they dwell".

188. A. Hastings Kelk, in an article on "A Hebrew Christian Church," admits the fact that the rapid assimilation of the Hebrew Christians to their surroundings is "a great hindrance to their brethren of the Synagogue" (*Church and Synagogue Quart.*, IV, p. 143).

189. A Ukase signed by Czar Alexander I on March 25, 1817, ruled that (1) all magistrates ecclesiastical and civil afford protection and assistance to all Jews seeking baptism; (2) that settlements of such Jews be facilitated with sufficient land provided by the Government; (3) that a Society of Christian Jews be established; (4) that a board be formed to supervise these settlements; (5) that this board report periodically to the Czar.

The rules respecting the Society of Christian Israelites provide:

(1) Free land provided by the Crown to Christian Israelites and their posterity.

(2) On these lands they may organize their communal life in perfect freedom.

(3) Full and perfect liberty of confession regardless of denomination to all Jewish Christians entering the Society.

(4) Apart from the Committee in Petersburg, nobody is to exercise any authority over them.

(6) All civil rights granted to them throughout the whole empire.

(10) Members of the Society are exempt from all military and civil service and this applies both to them and their posterity.

(12) Members of the Society of Christian Israelites are exempt from all kinds of duties and taxes for the space of twenty years.

(13) Foreign Jews who have embraced Christianity and desire to become members are given all rights and privileges granted to the Society.

(For the full text in English, see *Three letters to the Hebrew Nation*, Anon., London, 1817, pp. 117 ff.)

190. Cf. Frederick A. Aston, The Menace of Anti-Semitism in America To-day, *The Hebrew Christian Quart.*, April, 1940, pp. 12 ff.

191. One of the early missionaries in Callenberg's Institute, Johann Georg Widmann, was the first to conceive the idea of a Hebrew Christian settlement in Palestine. His plan was to settle on the land with a group of converted

Jews in order to await the Lord's Return which he expected to be imminent (cp. Roi, I, p. 285). Most of the missionary literature in the subsequent period had a similar eschatological bias.

192. G. H. Box: "So long as Christianity is presented to the Jew in such a way that its acceptance involves severance of racial ties and ultimate absorption, it can hardly be wondered at if the great mass of Jewish people refuses to consider such a possibility. In the face of such a phenomenon as present-day Zionism . . . it is hardly necessary here to insist on this point further" (*Church and Synagogue Quart.*, III, p. 53). G. H. Dalman, referring to the discussion of a Jewish Christian Church, explains that it is not the missionary purpose to make Jews into non-Jews or Gentiles, but rather "bad Jews into true Jews" for God "wills not that Israel should be absorbed among the nations" (*Church and Synagogue Quart.*, III, p. 109).

193. Cf. Sir James George Frazer, *Folk-Lore in the O. T.*, II, p. 227.

194. Montefiore admits that Judaism is a national religion *de facto* though not *de jure* (cf. *Liberal Judaism*, p. 286). E. Bevan has described Judaism as "a strange survival in the modern Western world—a survival of a type of community which in primitive times was general" (*Intern. Review of Missions*, XXII, 1933, p. 490).

195. H. Loewe, *In Spirit and in Truth*, p. 262.

196. Franz Rosenzweig: "Die Judenchristen haben ihr Recht geschichtlich im Urchristentum, so sie alsbald abstarben, als die Heidenkirche des Paulus wuchs, und dogmatisch in der christlichen Eschatologie. Dazwischen sind sie in der ersten Hinsicht ein Anachronismus und in der zweiten eine Paradoxie" (Quoted by Schoeps, p. 134).

197. The soul of the Jewish people is Judaism, "without which it cannot possibly live" (S. S. Cohon, *Intern. Review of Missions*, XXII, 1933, p. 473; cf. Klausner, *From Jesus to Paul*, p. 535).

198. J. Singer, *Sollen die Juden Christen werden?* Wien, 1884, p. 23: "der getaufte Jude glaubt nicht an die Dogmen des Christenthums, er steht ihnen so fremd, vielleicht noch mehr fremd gegenüber als früher . . ."; Heinrich York-Steiner says of the Christian conception of Original Sin, that it stands "dem jüdischen Wesen und der jüdischen Lehre wesensfremd gegenüber" (*op. cit.*, p. 128).

199. *Op. cit.*, p. 477.

200. Cf. Montefiore, *Liberal Judaism*, p. 292; Mattuck, *What are Jews?* p. 254.

201. Cf. M. Friedländer, *The Jewish Religion*, p. 2.

202. Cf. Felsenthal, p. 212: " 'Judaism' and 'Jewish religion' are not synonymous terms. . . . Jewish religion is only part of 'Judaism'. . . . Judaism is the sum total of all the manifestations of the distinctively Jewish national spirit".

203. Friedländer, *The Jewish Religion*, p. 236. 204. Felsenthal, p. 218.

205. Cf. Felsenthal, p. 220, § VII; but cp. M. Gaster, *Zionism and the Jewish Future*, ed. by H. Sacher, 1916, pp. 91, 94; Dr. Gaster categorically declares: "There cannot be Christian and Jewish Jews".

206. Felsenthal, p. 214; cf. *ibid.*, pp. 233 f., 256.

207. Edwyn Bevan, in his answer to S. S. Cohon's plea against Christian interference with Judaism, finds it difficult to see "why a member of the

Jewish community who embraces it (Christianity) should be considered to have abandoned Judaism" (*Intern. Review of Missions*, XXII, 1933, p. 490). E. Bevan apparently uses the word "Judaism" as synonymous with the Jewish community (?).

208. Montefiore, *Truth in Religion*, p. 33.

209. We say *de jure* first, because active missionary endeavour has largely ceased, and secondly, because we hold with Felsenthal and others that in the Rabbinic view even the *ger zedek* was not a Jew in the true sense of the word (cp. Felsenthal, p. 221, § VIII). Cf. *infra*, pp. 302 ff.

210. Harnack, *Mission*, p. 43.

211. Cf. Lukyn Williams, *The Hebrew Christian Messiah*, London, 1916, p. 205.

212. J. Singer, *Sollen die Juden Christen werden?* pp. 36, 38. The assimilationist tendency of the tract is obvious. It is a plea for unity between Jews and Christians and was occasioned by the intermarriage dispute in the Hungarian Parliament. The writer is in favour of intermarriage. A somewhat similar attitude was taken by the founder of the New Israel movement in South Russia, Jacob Prelooker (1860–1935). Cf. S. Dubnow, *History of the Jews in Russia and Poland*, II, p. 344; *J. E.*, IX, p. 343; Vallentine's *J. E.*, p. 460b.

213. Singer differentiates between Christianity and Church. Church is a corruption of Christianity; over the ruins of the Church, Christianity can find its way back to its old mother—Judaism, who will be willing to forgive. In essence both Judaism and Christianity are identical, for did not Lord Beaconsfield say: "Christianity is Judaism for the multitude, but it still is Judaism"? (*ibid.*, p. 24 and note; cf. also p. 34).

214. "Man könnte nämlich statistisch nachweisen, dass bisher noch kein Convertit aus innerer Ueberzeugung die Religion das Judentums verlassen habe; es geschah aus Feigheit oder anderen, noch gemeineren Motiven" (*ibid.*, p. 7).

215. David August Rosenthal, *Convertitenbilder aus dem neunzehnten Jahrhundert*, Schaffhausen, Weisenburg, 1866–70.

216. J. F. A. de le Roi, *Die evangelische Christenheit und die Juden*, 3 vols., Berlin, 1884–1892; cf. also A. Bernstein, *Some Jewish Witnesses for Christ*, London, 1909; *Zeugen aus Israel*, ed. by A. Frank, Hamburg (no date); *Engl. Witnesses from Israel, Life-stories of Jewish Converts to Christianity*, Edinburgh and London, 1903; J. Littell, *Some Great Christian Jews*, Keene, U.S.A.; various biographical notes can be found in *Saat auf Hoffnung, Zeitschrift für die Mission der Kirche an Israel*, founded by Franz Delitzsch and C. Becker in 1863; *Church and Synagogue Quarterly* founded in 1896 and ed. by Oesterley and Box; *The Jewish Missionary Intelligence*, the official organ of the London Jews' Society, and in the many other missionary magazines.

217. A new biography recently appeared by H. P. Palmer, *Joseph Wolff*, London, 1935.

218. For the life of Saphir see Gavin Carlyle, *A Memoir of Adolph Saphir*, London, 1893.

219. Cf. A. Fürst, p. 55.

220. Cf. Rabbi J. Lichtenstein, *Judaism and Christianity*, Engl. by Margaret M. Alison, with a preface by John Alison, convener of the Jewish Miss. Comm. of Church of Scotland, Edinburgh, 1893, p. 21: "I felt myself peculiarly and

wonderfully taken possession of. A sudden clearness, a light flashed through my soul. . . . I looked for thorns and gathered roses, I discovered pearls instead of pebbles—heavenly treasure. . . ."

The old Rabbi makes the following confession: "Surely, whoever knows Him must love Him, whoever loves Him must honour Him, whoever honours Him must adore Him, and whoever adores Him understands Him when He says, 'I and my Father are One'" (*ibid.*, p. 104).

221. N. Gorodetzky, *The Humiliated Christ in Modern Russian Thought*, London, 1938, p. 90; Aptekman, however, was in sympathy and outlook a Russian rather than a Jew (cp. *ibid.*, pp. 87 f.).

222. Pastor R. Faltin's missionary interest in the Jews was due to the faithful witness of a pious old woman. When Rabbi Gurland became a Christian, it appeared that the same woman had been praying for his and his wife's conversion for eighteen years. Frey, who is the actual founder of the London Jews Society, was converted through the witness of a Christian tanner called Michaelis.

223. Cf. *Church and Synagogue Quart.*, VI, p. 146.

224. Cf. Roi, I, p. 430; von Clausberg is reported to have humbly remarked: "Allein das wahre Leben habe ich noch nicht erfahren gehabt, darin bin ich jetzt noch ein kleines Kind".

225. Gustaf Dalman revealed the story of a union of secretly baptized Jews in Amsterdam about the year 1770. At one time the famous Rabbi Jonathan Eibeschütz (1690–1764) is supposed to have stood at the head of this movement (cf. *Saat auf Hoffnung*, 1890, pp. 18 ff.). Roi thinks that the movement began somewhere about 1680–90 and was the sequence of the Shabbethai Zevi (1621?–1676) fiasco. Only recently a secret union of believers in Palestine was recorded by Abram Poljak, cf. *The Cross in the Star of David*, London, 1938, pp. 41 ff. The evidence for this, however, is very slender. The present writer has occasionally met and also heard of Jews who were secret believers.

226. Lichtenstein, after attaining full conviction, never hid his views from his congregation, yet he remained within the Synagogue to the end. The Rabbis at a conference at Pesth tried to induce him to recant his views or to leave the Synagogue, but he firmly refused to do either.

227. A remarkable case is that of Philipp Jaffé (born in 1819 near Posen, d. 1870). He taught history at the Berlin University. Roi says that he belongs to the most outstanding scholars of the history of the Middle Ages. Jaffé was near to the Christian faith, but refused baptism out of fear that he might be accused of ulterior motives. Finally he accepted baptism, but committed suicide two years later under the delusion that he was being persecuted as a result (cf. Roi, II, pp. 218 f.).

228. T. W. Gidney, *History of the London Jews Society*, p. 222. The present writer knows of at least two instances when Jews have baptized *themselves* in the name of the Messiah Jesus, one of them in the Vistula, and the other in a bath.   229. Cf. Roi, III, p. 123.

230. The story of Navrazky is unusual. As a child he was forcibly baptized in the R. C. Church and was kept by a Polish nobleman under appalling conditions. In the end he was exchanged for a dog and became the property of a Saxon officer. His new master was a kind and religious man and Navrazky himself became "ein wahrhaft frommer Christ" (Roi, I, p. 370).

231. After the early death of her first husband, the sculptor Michael Grünbeck, Magdalene Augusta Navrazky married the Hebrew Christian, David Kirchhoff (1716–1789), and received from Zinzendorf the additional name of Esther.

232. Roi, II, p. 152.

233. E. Bevan truly remarks: "a great multitude of men in all Christian countries do practically lapse into the ethnic view". *Intern. Mission. Rev.* XXII, 1933, p. 493; cf. Morris Zeidman, *Christians and Jews*, p. 91; cf. also the interesting article by a German Hebrew Christian, Otto Salomon, "We Jewish Christians", in *The Hebrew Christian Quart.*, Oct. 1942, pp. 66 ff.

234. Cf. Gidney, p. 222.

235. Literature for Rabinowitsch's life and work: *Die Schriften des Institutum Judaicum*, Nrs. 4, 5, 9, 16; H. Strack, *Nathaniel*, 1885, pp. 149 ff.; G. A. Krüger, *Une Eglise Judéo-Christienne en Bessarabie*, Lausanne, 1885; A. Frank, *Zeugen*, pp. 73 ff.; *Church and Synag. Quart.*, I, pp. 45–59; S. M. Dubnov refers to Rabinowitsch's community as a "puny Congregation of New Testament Israelites" consisting of ten members (*History of the Jews in Russia and Poland*, Engl. Philadelphia, 1918, II, p. 335), but Prof. Dubnov's views are naturally biased.

236. Cf. Franz Delitzsch's introduction to Rabinowitsch's autobiography, *Church and Synag. Quart.*, I, pp. 45 ff.; Gustaf Dalman, *Christianity and Judaism*, p. 26, note.

237. Roi, II, p. 349.

238. It is believed that Prelooker's ultimate intention was to "unite a reformed synagogue with the dissenters from the Greek Orthodox Church—the Molokans, Stundists, and Dukhobortzy" (Peter Wiernik, *J. E.*, IX, p. 343).

239. Cp. Jaakoff Prelooker, *Under the Czar and Queen Victoria*, pp. 21 f., 196–209.

240. Cf. *J. E.*, VI, p. 46.   241. Cf. *J. E.*, III, p. 197.

242. Roi records that the Jewish community in Jerusalem was a great disappointment to Rabinowitsch; he also relates that Rabinowitsch, before leaving Jerusalem, went up the Mount of Olives, and as he looked down upon the ancient city, he was subject to a strange experience; he was suddenly seized by the conviction that "the keys to the Holy Land lie in the hands of our brother Jesus".

243. *Church and Synagogue Quart.*, I, p. 47.

244. *Ibid.*, I, p. 46; cf. also "The First-ripe Fig", Articles, Creed and Form of Worship of Joseph Rabinowitsch, transl. by J. Adler (no date).

245. It is interesting to note that Delitzsch, the Gentile scholar, speaks disapprovingly of Rabinowitsch's attitude to the Talmud and the Midrashic literature; cf. *ibid.*, p. 48.

246. The work of Pastor R. Faltin in Kishineff, however, must not be underestimated (cf. Gidney, pp. 442 f.). His greatest success was the conversion of the Rabbi Rudolf Gurland, who was baptized together with his wife on Easter Sunday, 1864. Faltin's work was financially supported by the London Jews Society.

247. Cf. Roi, II, p. 353.   248. Roi, II, p. 350.

249. He was only given permission to maintain a prayer-house, where he

had the right to lecture and carry on mission work. According to Prelooker, the reason for the official disfavour was Rabinowitsch's baptism in the Protestant Church. Pobiedonostzeff, the procurator of the Holy Synod, regarded this as an ungrateful act (cf. Prelooker, *Under the Czar*, p. 150).

250. G. H. Box makes direct reference to Rabinowitsch and the Kishineff community (cf. *Church and Synagogue Quart.*, III, pp. 52 f.).

251. Opinion amongst those keenly interested in missionary work amongst the Jews was divided. It is, however, noteworthy that men like Godet in Switzerland; Delitzsch, Faber, Müller and Pastor Wiegand in Germany; G. Krüger, Nogar and Eynard in France, were all keen advocates of a Hebrew-Christian Church. On the other hand, De le Roi and to some extent G. Dalman were opposed to the idea. For the controversy between Roi and Wiegand, and other material, see the interesting article by A. Bernstein, "The Formation of a Hebrew Christian Church: is it desirable?" *Jew. Missionary Intelligence*, May, 1902.

252. *Ibid.*, III, p. 44.

253. *Church and Synagogue Quart.*, III, p. 59; with regard to the latter suggestion, Dr. P. P. Levertoff's Order of the service of the Meal of the Holy King has laid the foundation for a future Communion Office in the Hebrew-Christian Church.

254. Cf. *Church and Synagogue Quart.*, IV, pp. 50 ff.

255. *Ibid.*, IV, p. 3. For criticism of Bp. Blyth's views, see W. Ewing, "Bishop Blyth and the Jewish Mission Problem", *Expository Times*, XIII, pp. 333 f. (1902).

256. *Ibid.*, IV, pp. 16 ff.

257. *Ibid.*, IV, p. 143.

258. Cf. *The Christian Approach to the Jew*, 1927, p. 109; *Christians and Jews*, 1931, pp. 52, 60, 73, 91.

259. Rennie MacInnes (Anglic. Bp. in Jerusalem), *The Christian Approach*, p. 175; for doctrinal difficulties, see Lukyn Williams, *The Hebrew-Christian Messiah*, pp. 210 ff.

260. Cf. *Christians and Jews*, p. 91; Olga Levertoff, *The Wailing Wall*, p. 119. For Dr. Levertoff's attitude to the question, see Olga Levertoff's article, "The Jewish Christian Problem" in *Judaism and Christianity*, ed. by L. Gillet, pp. 98 f.

261. Christl. T. Lipszytz, *Der Ebionitismus in der Judenmission, oder Christentum und national-jüdisches Bewusstsein* (Ein Vortrag gehalten auf der Internationalen Judenmissions Konferenz zu Stockholm am 9 Juni 1911); *Schriften des Institutum Judaicum in Berlin*, Nr. 41; the last point is important, as few Christian writers have paid attention to it.

262. *Church and Synag. Quart.*, IV, p. 143; cf. also Lukyn Williams, *The Hebrew-Christian Messiah*, p. 213, § III.

263. H. Poms, "Thoughts on Hebrew Christianity", *The Hebrew-Christian Quart.*, April, 1944, pp. 12 ff.; this important point has entirely escaped the notice of Lev Gillet.

264. I. Abrahams, *Studies in Pharisaism*, II, p. 57.

265. Against L. Gillet, who, for unexplained reasons, holds that "the adhesion of a Jew to one of the Gentile Churches" is neither normal nor desirable (*Communion in the Messiah*, p. 191).

For the significance of the Hebrew-Christian position, see the author's article in. *The Hebrew-Christian Quart.*, April, 1945, pp. 11 ff.

266. Philip Cohen, *The Hebrew Christian and his National Continuity*, London (no date), p. 43; cf. also Lukyn Williams, *The Hebrew-Christian Messiah*, pp. 206 f.

267. Roi, II, p. 350. Cf. also M. J. Levy, *Hebr. Chty. and Jewish Nationalism*, 1931.

268. Shalom Spiegel appreciatively says of I. E. Salkinson that "he translated the Gospels, Milton and Shakespeare into magnificent Hebrew". To Spiegel, it is a matter of surprise "how incredibly deep and genuine a love for Hebrew the baptized minister still had in his heart" (*Hebrew Reborn*, p. 173). For a fine criticism of Salkinson's literary merits as a translator, see C. P. Sherman, "Milton and Salkinson", *Church and Synag. Quart.*, XI, pp. 84 ff.

269. Cf. O. Levertoff, *The Wailing Wall*, pp. 120 f.

270. Eisenmenger, *op. cit.*, p. 990: "Die Verlassung der Bekehrten, indem man ihnen nicht mit nöthiger Hülffe an die Hand gehet". This is also Lull's view, cp. Allison Peers, p. 74.

271. Cf. Lichtenstein's introduction to the English transl. of *Judaism and Christianity;* Lichtenstein, in self-defence, says: "It is indeed an open secret to all my acquaintances that my former happy, prosperous circumstances were overcast directly after the publication of my writings, and rapidly got worse" (*ibid.*, p. 12).

272. Cf. *Jewish Life in Modern Times*, p. 272; cf. Kaufmann Kohler, "Conversion to Christianity", *J. E.*, IV, pp. 249 ff.; an excellent answer to similar allegations in an article which appeared in the *Saturday Review*, "Costly Converts", is given by Franz Delitzsch; see *Saat auf Hoffnung*, 1863, Nr. 3, pp. 15 ff.

273. Cf. Parkes, *The Jew in the Med. Community*, pp. 143 f. The Church has tried to remedy the situation, but with little success. Pope Alexander issued a Bull ordaining that baptized Jews should no more forfeit their property, but the custom continued for some time.

274. Cp. *J. E.* in loc.; also *Transactions of the Jewish Historical Society of Eng.*, I, 1893/94, pp. 15 ff.; H. P. Stokes, *Short History of the Jews in England*, pp. 37 f.

275. Jews, from the age of twelve, had to pay a poll-tax (chevage), in support of the Converts' Inn; cf. Stokes, p. 50; *J. E.*, IV, pp. 636 f.).

276. Cf. Roi, I, p. 355.

277. Cf. Roi, I, pp. 406 f.; the report of the Sitzung des Ausschusses der Allgemeinen Judenmissionskonferenz, held in Berlin, Oct. 15, 1901, under the chairmanship of Prof. Dalman contains the following note: "Zum Zwecke besserer Kontrolle der Missionsbettler werden die Gesellschaften, Missionare und Leiter von Proselytenhäusern gebeten, über solche in ihrem Gebiete aufgetretene Leute (abgewiesene, aus Heimen entlassene Proselyten oder Taufbewerber, Bettler, Betrüger u. dergl.) einer *Centralstelle* Nachricht zu geben, die dann die nächstbeteiligten Gesellschaften unterrichtete."

278. Cf. Gidney, p. 40.

279. *Ibid.*, p. 237.

280. Cf. Roi, II, pp. 130 f.

281. Cf. Roi, III, pp. 192 f.

282. Cf. Gidney, pp. 453 f.

283. Gidney, p. 76 f.

284. Gidney, p. 42.

285. *Ibid.*, p. 534.

286. In the now sadly depleted library of Church Missions to Jews, we

have found a number of books bound at the Institution. Some of these were most expertly done.

287. *Hebrew-Christian Alliance of Gt. Britain* (no date), p. 1.

288. *Constitution and Bye-laws of the International Hebrew Christian Alliance* (no date), § II.

289. Gidney, p. 43.   290. Cf. Roi, III, p. 341; Bernstein, p. 469.

291. Gidney, p. 424. In New York a similar effort was made as early as 1855; cf. *The Journal of Sacred Literature & Biblical Record*, I, 1855, 497.

292. Quoted from a tract: *The Intern. Hebr. Christ. Alliance. What it Is and What it Does* (no date).

293. *Church and Synagogue Quart.*, III, p. 187; an example for the complete disregard of denominational loyalty on the part of some Hebrew Christians is Joseph Wolff; cf. Palmer, *op. cit.*, pp. 98, 190, 200.

294. *Real Encycl. für protest. Theologie*, 2nd ed., XV/XVI, p. 3.

295. Cf., however, Newman's remarks about Matthew H. Adrian's strained relationship with Erasmus and Luther (*op. cit.*, pp. 626 f.).

296. *Legacy of Israel*, pp. 313 f.

297. Vallentine's *Jewish Encycl.*, p. 246a.

298. G. H. Box, Hebrew Studies, *Legacy of Israel*, p. 336.

299. Cp. Box, *op. cit.*, p. 337.

300. Dr. M. I. Schleiden truly says: "Without Hebrew no Reformation; without Jews no Hebrew, for they were the only teachers of the language" (*The Importance of the Jews*, p. 30).

301. Box, *op. cit.*, p. 338; the Hebrew text for the *Complutensian Polyglot* (1514-1517), printed by Cardinal Ximenes, was arranged by three learned Jewish Christians; cp. Brewster, *op. cit.*, p. 57, n. 1.

302. Cf. Roi, I, p. 194.

303. "Novum Testamentum hebraice convertit cum brevibus notis, sed non edidit" (Wolf, *Bibl. Hebr.*, I, pp. 894, n. 1, 648).

304. Cf. A. Fürst, p. 202; A. Bernstein, pp. 147 f.

305. Roi, II, p. 200; the great German divine, Friedrich A. G. Tholuck, owed his positive Christian outlook to Neander of whom he always spoke with the greatest love and devotion (cf. *Imper. Dict. of Univers. Biogr.*, III, p. 1135b).

306. "Neander war nicht nur eine tieffromme Persönlichkeit, sondern auch ein durch und durch vornehmer Charakter" (Schweitzer, *Geschichte d. Leben Jesu Forsch.*, p. 102, note).

307. *Encycl. Brit.*, 11th ed., XIX, p. 321.

308. "His Church History remains the greatest monument of his genius" (*Encycl. Brit.*, 11th ed., *in loc.*). "Dieses Werk bezeichnet eine neue Epoche der Kirchengeschichtsschreibung" (Roi, II, p. 201).

309. Cf. Schweitzer, p. 104.   310. Cf. Kohut, II, p. 298.

311. Cf. *Letters of Lord Acton to Mary, daughter of the Rt. Hon. W. E. Gladstone*, ed. by Herbert Paul, London, 1904, pp. lxxvi and 97.

312. Kohut remarks with amusement that it was left to two converts from Judaism, Neander and Stahl, to become the classical defenders (Träger) of ecclesiastical orthodoxy in Germany (*op. cit.*, II, p. 297).

313. Roi, II, p. 205.   314. Cf. Roi, II, p. 189.

315. *Encycl. Brit.*, 11th ed., VII, p. 728.   316. A. Fürst, p. 274.

317. Roi, III, p. 19; Roi, who never praises *Jews* undeservedly, holds that

it is only thanks to Frey that there are in existence modern Missions to Jews (cp. *ibid.*, p. 10).

318. For an estimation of the importance of the London Jews Society (Church Missions to Jews), see Roi, iii, p. 249. For Palestine Place, see Gidney, pp. 42 f., 279 f.

319. Joseph Samuel Christian Frederick Frey, *Joseph and Benjamin: a series of letters on the controversy between Jews and Christians.* . . . Fifth edition, 2 vols., New York, 1837.

320. The Barbican Mission to Jews owes its existence to a Hebrew Christian, P. J. Warschawski; some other missionary societies have been founded by Jewish Christians.

321. Roi, i, p. 390.

322. Cf. Roi, i, p. 392.

323. Frommann's N. T. was prefaced with a few words in Latin to the Christian reader, dated Halle, July 9, 1735; Biesenthal's edition with the Rabbinic commentary is dated בשנת תצ״ה לפק (=A.D. 1735).

324. "Frommann gehört zu den edelsten Gestalten unter den Proselyten nicht bloss seiner Tage, sondern aller Zeiten" (Roi, i, p. 393).

325. The present writer found a MS. in the library of the late Joseph I. Landsman, written by Janasz, which has never been published.

326. Dr. Kalkar became president of the Danish Missionary Society in 1861 and held the post to the end of his life. He is the author of several important books on the history of Missions. His valuable work, *Israel og Kerken*, Copenhagen, 1881, is often quoted.

327. Cf. Roi, ii, p. 300: "Niederländisch evangelisch-protestantischer Verein für Evangelisation".

328. Cf. *J. E.*, vi, p. 363.

329. Cf. G. R. Balleine, *Hist. of the Evangelical Party*, p. 167.

330. A. Frank, *Zeugen aus Israel*, pp. 41 f.

331. Cf. H. P. Palmer, *Joseph Wolff*, London, 1935, p. 217: "Wolff was more a pioneer than an ordinary Missionary".

332. Quoted by Gidney, p. 105.

333. Joseph Wolff, *Travels and adventures of J. W.*, second edition, London, 1860; *Missionary Journal and Memoir of the Rev. J. W.*, written by himself, *Revised and edited by J. Bayford*, London, 1824; 2nd ed., 3 vols., London, 1827–29.

334. Cf. Roi, iii, p. 91; cf. also *J. E.*, iii, p. 209b.

335. Cf. Bernstein, p. 130.

336. Bernstein, p. 464; Roi, iii, p. 382: "ihm ist es zu danken, dass die Schrift in weite Kreise der Chinesen gelangte". For a full biography, see Muller, J. A., *Apostle of China: Samuel Isaac Joseph Schereschewsky, 1931-1906*, 1937. On the Roman Catholic side Fr. Francis Libermann (1802-52) occupies an important position as a great missionary. In recognition of his labours he was beatified in 1868; cf. Henry J. Koren, *The Spiritans*, 1958; also Adrian L. van Kaam, *A Light to the Gentiles*: the Life Story of the Venerable Francis Libermann, 1959.

337. Cf. Gustaf H. Dalman, *Christianity and Judaism*, p. 26, note; cf. Roi, iii, pp. 388 f.

338. Bernstein, p. 348.

339. The present writer, on a visit to Lwow, had occasion to meet personally a few of Lucky's former disciples.

340. We notice that the great Roger Bacon (1214–1292?), as in so many other things, anticipated a more modern age. In his *Opus Majus*, III, § 13, he stresses the importance of preaching to the Jews in their own language and interpreting the Scriptures according to their literal meaning.

341. ספר חנוך בחירי יה *Instruction of the Chosen of the Lord* has seen several translations and many editions. It was last published by L. J. S. in 1820.

342. M. Elias Schadaeus published five books: Luke, John, Acts, Romans and Hebrews, of Luther's translation, "in Idioma Germanicum translatos Veste Judaica, id est, Literis Hebraicis in Judaeorum gratiam indutos Typis sumptibusque propriis Mundo tradidit" (Introduction to M. Christianus Müller's *Novum Testamentum Hebraeo-Teutonicum*, Frankfurt/Oder, 1700).

343. Sebastian Münster (1489–1552), professor of Hebrew at the university of Basel, was the first to translate a part of the N. T. in Hebrew, namely the Gospel of St. Matthew which appeared in Basel in 1537 (cf. *Legacy of Israel*, p. 334); according to A. Neubauer, there was a Hebrew transl. of the N. T. made by Shem-Tob ben Shaprut (cf. *Expositor*, 3rd Series, VII, p. 194).

344. Cf. Roi, III, p. 16.

345. It was the L. J. S. edition of the Hebrew N. T. which brought Samuel Isaac Schereschewsky and Joseph Rabinowitsch in touch for the first time with the Christian message.

346. Of nine members on the committee, at least six were Hebrew Christians: The Rev. John Henry Brühl (1823–1893), Dr. R. Neumann (1788–1865), Bishop Alexander (1799–1845), S. Hoga, Dr. Biesenthal, and the Rev. J. C. Reichardt (cp. Gidney, p. 535). Roi attributes the translation to Thomas Fry (Frey?) and Dr. Collyer, both honorary secretaries of L. J. S. between 1810–1814; but cf. Gidney, p. 55.

347. Delitzsch in his transl. of the N. T. relied upon the help and advice of Jechiel Lichtenstein; for his criticism of Salkinson's translation, see *The Expositor*, 3rd Series, IX, pp. 135 ff., 310 ff.

348. Cf. *Church and Synagogue Quart.*, XI, pp. 88 f.

349. The book appeared under the *nom de guerre* of Gabriel Jehuda ibn Ezra, the writer being a descendant of the ancient family, under the title: *Chrześcijańskiego Żyda—wspomnienia łzy i myśli*, Poznan, 1929, pp. 256; for a review, see *Der Weg*. Sept./Oct. 1929 (Yiddish).

350. *The Hebrew Christian and his National Continuity*, pp. 142 f.

351. Cf. *World Dominion*, Nov./Dec. 1941, *Clash of Loyalties in Japan*, pp. 359 ff.; cf. also *ibid.*, May/June, 1941, *Sun Goddess of Japan*, pp. 149 f.

352. Cohen, *op. cit.*, pp. 131 f.   353. *In Spirit and in Truth*, p. 262.

354. *International Review of Missions*, XXXI, July, 1942, p. 363.

355. Cf. J. Jocz, "The Significance of the Hebrew-Christian position", *The Hebrew-Christian Quart.*, April, 1945, pp. 11–14.

NOTES TO CHAPTER VII

1. Cp. Montefiore, *S. G.*, 1927, p. 437.

2. Cf. Trattner, *op. cit.*, p. 180 (end); cp. also John Cournos, *Hear, O Israel*, London, 1938, pp. 17, 22, etc.

3. *Ibid.*, p. xv.

4. *Rabbinic Anthology*, p. xcix: "Judaism stresses the message but neglects the messenger".   5. Cournos, *op. cit.*, p. 15.

6. On Lev Gillet's attempt to construct such a theology, see p. 210.

7. Cf. Hans Joachim Schoeps, *Jüdisch-christliches Religionsgespräch in* 19 *Jahrhunderten,* p. 13.

8. Cf. *S. G.,* 1927, I, p. cxliv; cf. also Kaufmann Kohler, *The Origins of the Synagogue and the Church,* p. xxxv.

9. Montefiore, *The Old Testament and After,* London, 1923, pp. 28 and 561; cp. J. H. Hertz, *Affirmations of Judaism,* 1927, pp. 19 f.

10. Cp. Montefiore, *Hibbert Journal,* XXXIII, 1934/1935, pp. 511 ff.; O. Lazarus, *Liberal Judaism and its Standpoint,* 1937, p. 85.

11. Montefiore, "The Significance of Jesus for his own age", *Hibbert Journal,* XX, 1911/1912, p. 779.

12. Moore, *Judaism,* I, pp. 364 f.

13. Cf. Montefiore, *Outlines of Liberal Judaism,* p. 317.

14. Cf. Loewe's introduction to *The Rabbinic Anthology,* p. lxix; the difference between orthodox and reform Judaism has undoubtedly been overemphasized by some writers (cf. *Church and Synagogue Quart.,* XII, p. 36).

15. Dr. Hertz says of Jewish Christians, they "darkened the sky of Israel's monotheism by teaching a novel doctrine of God's sonship, by identifying a man born of a woman with God, and by advocating the doctrine of a Trinity" (*Affirmations,* p. 17).

16. Kaufmann Kohler, *The Origins of the Synagogue and the Church,* 1929, p. 140: "The absolute Unity of God, the fundamental and central belief of Judaism, became the question of life or death for the Synagogue from the time when the Christian Church placed Jesus, her Messiah, upon the throne of God, either as His son or His equal. . . ."

17. Isaac ben Sheshet's *Responsa,* 119.

18. Kaufmann Kohler, *Jewish Theology,* 1918, p. 427; cp. also p. 329.

19. Cp. Ch. II, n. 188.

20. Weber's opinion may still be counted with, despite his obvious apologetic interests. He says: "Die Einheit Gottes ist das Grundbekenntnis des Judentums gegenüber dem heidinschen Polytheismus. . . . Aber auch zum trinitarischen Gottesbegriff der Christen ist der jüdische Monotheismus in Gegensatz getreten. Und zwar kommen unter den Christen zunächst in Betracht die Judenchristen, welche in der talmudischen und midrasischen Literatur den Namen *Minim* מינים tragen" (Ferdinand Weber, *Die Lehre des Talmud,* Leipzig, 1880, p. 147).

21. It appears to us that even in the case of those Ebionites, of whom Hippolytus records that they saw the significance of Jesus in his absolute fulfilment of the whole Law, and that they themselves, if they fulfilled the commandments, could attain to the same dignity, they still assigned to the Messiah a unique and singular position (cf. Hippolytus, *Philosophumena,* Bk. VII, Ch. 22).

22. Weber, *op. cit.,* p. 147.

23. "Der Mangel an der Erkenntnis, dass Gott in der Heiligkeit die sich selbst mitteillende, entgegenkommende, dem Anderen einwohnende Liebe ist, hinderte die Erfassung des trinitarischen Gottesbegriffs" on the part of the Synagogue (Weber, *op. cit.,* p. 149). The classical definition of the אחדות אלהים comes from the master of religious Jewish philosophy, Maimonides:

"This God is One God; He is neither two nor more than two but One to whose Unity there is no comparison among the individual units in the universe; not like the unit of a genus which embraces many individual units, nor like the unit of a body which is divisible into parts and particles, but a Unit to Whose Unity no other unit in the universe is like". *Yad Hachazakah*, ספר המדע, I, 7 (Engl. by Rabbi Simon Glazer, New York, 1927).

24. Isaac Husik, *A history of Medieval Jewish Philosophy*, p. xlv; the otherness of God as conceived by Maimonides in some ways resembles Barthian theology, but the difference is immense. Barth knows about the Deus Absconditus from underneath the Cross, Maimonides from philosophical reasoning.

25. Rabbi Max Dienemann, *Judentum und Christentum* (Einleitung).

26. Cf. Ludwig Feuerbach, *Das Wesen der Religion*, Berlin, 1913, p. 147: "Ein Gott ist . . . das verselbständigte und vergegenständigte Wesen der menschlichen Einbildungskraft".

27. This is essentially different from the famous "cogito, ergo sum" (Cartesius). Thought presupposes existence, and existence determines its mode and substance.

28. *Outlines of Liberal Judaism*, p. 304.

29. The emphasis must be placed on the "one". Judaism, and especially Liberal Judaism, does not hesitate to ascribe a measure of divinity to the *whole* human race. This is an inevitable result of the over-emphasis of the *Imago Dei* concept.

30. O. Lazarus explains that "the gulf between the divine and the human", in the Jewish view, "can never be closed". And yet the gulf must be bridged if communion with God is to become possible. Her answer is: "Judaism believes that the gulf is bridged by man's prayers and study, by his thoughts and his actions" (*Liberal Judaism and its Standpoint*, p. 86).

31. The writer heard Buber lecture on *Judaism and Christianity* in Frankfurt/M, in 1933. The citation is a free rendering from memory.

32. I. M. Wise, *Judaism and Christianity*, Cincinnati, 1883, p. 62.

33. *Ibid.*, p. 95.

34. Though the views of the Rabbis on the subject have varied, the assertion of freedom of choice is predominant. Cp. Strack-Billerbeck, I, pp. 8 ff.; IV, pp. 4 ff.

35. A saying accredited to R. Chanina (c. A.D. 225); *Ber.*, 33b.

36. Maimonides, in *Yad Hachazakah*, says:

רשות לכל אדם נתונה אם רצה להטות עצמו לדרך טובה ולהיות צדיק הרשות
בידו ואם רצה להטות עצמו לדרך רעה ולהיות רשע הרשות בידו.

37. Husik, *A History of Medieval Jewish Philosophy*, p. 396.

38. Cf. Husik, *op. cit.*, p. xv.

39. To the question how human freedom can be reconciled with divine sovereignty, Maimonides replies, that it so pleased God to endow man with this gift. As it is inherent in the nature of fire and air to ascend, and of water and earth to descend, so is it inherent in human nature to be free.

40. Cf. Husik, *op. cit.*, p. 396.

41. R. Akiba already said: "Everything is foreseen but free will is given" (*Abot*, III, 15).

42. Cf. Lukyn Williams, *The Doctrines of Modern Judaism Considered*, p. 70 and references.

43. *Al Khazari*, v, 20.   44. Dienemann, *op. cit.*, p. 38.

45. Dienemann, *op. cit.*, pp. 49 f.   46. Dienemann, *op. cit.*, p. 40.

47. Hermann Cohen, *Die Religion der Vernunft*, p. 482.

48. Cf. Bonsirven, *op. cit.*, p. 111.

49. *Sanh.* 97b; *Pesikta* 103b: If the whole of Israel unitedly performed one day of repentance, deliverance would come through the Messiah. *Shabb.* 118b: If Israel kept two Sabbaths properly they would be delivered at once; according to *Wajikra Rabba*, Ch. 2, even one Sabbath would suffice. For other references, see A. Cohen, *Everyman's Talmud*, p. 373.

50. Hermann Cohen, *op. cit.*, p. 245.   51. *Yoma*, VIII. 8.

52. August Wünsche's transl., *Pesikta des Rab Kahana*, pp. 224–240.

53. Wünsche, *ibid.*, p. 235.   54. Wünsche, *ibid.*, p. 230.

55. *J. E.*, x, p. 379a. His whole article on Repentance is important.

56. Cp. Leo Baeck, *The Essence of Judaism*, pp. 168 ff.

57. Quoted from Montefiore's article on "Rabbinic Judaism and the Epistles of St. Paul", *Jew. Q. Review*, Jan., 1901, p. 204.

58. *Yad Hachazakah*, הלכות תשובה, 1, 3: בזמן הזה שאין בית המקדש «
קיים ואין לנו מזבח כפרה . . . תשובה מכפרת על כל העבירות . . .»

59. *Yoma*, VIII. 8.   60. Leo Baeck, *op. cit.*, p. 169.

61. *Op. cit.*, p. 50. Dienemann's own italics.

62. Cf. Klausner, *From Jesus to Paul*, pp. 524 f.

63. Dr. J. H. Hertz, *The Pentateuch*, abridged ed., p. 882.

64. I. M. Wise, *op. cit.*, p. 90.

65. Cp. J. H. Hertz, Jewish View of the "Fall of Man", *op. cit.*, p. 196.

66. Cf. Strack-Billerbeck, IV, 9 and references; cf. also Klausner, *From Jesus to Paul*, p. 517.

67. Cf. Montefiore and Loewe, *Rabbinic Anthology*, pp. 22, 311 f.; and the important note, pp. 689 f.

68. Older Jewish thought shows, however, greater restraint and is inclined towards a more pessimistic view. Cf. Strack-Billerbeck, *Exkurs*, 19: *Der gute und der böse Trieb.*, IV, pp. 466 ff.; F. Weber, pp. 216 f.; cf. also Oesterley, *Church and Synagogue Quart.*, VIII, p. 157.

69. The Rabbis, however, held that יצר הרע is older than the יצר טוב, for while the first begins with the earliest youth, the latter appears at a later stage (cp. Strack-Billerbeck, IV, pp. 468 f. For the question how early יצר הרע appears, cp. *Gen R.* 8, 21).

70. Dienemann, p. 22.

71. *Tanhuma, Bereshit*, 4b; cp. also *ibid.*, 10a; *Bereshit Rabba*, 21; *Niddah*, 16b; *Maimonides Hil. Teshubah*, 5, 4.

72. Dienemann, *op. cit.*, p. 19; cf., however, the article *Yetzer hara* in *J. E.*, XII, pp. 601 f.

73. *Ibid.*, p. 24.

74. I. M. Wise, *Jud. and Christ.* p. 66; cf. Bonsirven, pp. 113 f.; Oesterley, *Church and Synagogue Quart.*, VIII, pp. 154 f.

75. Hermann Cohen, *op. cit.*, p. 214; cp. p. 119. Montefiore's collection of Rabbinic texts bears out H. Cohen's view (cf. *Rabbinic Anthology*, pp. 295–314).

76. *Op. cit.*, p. 219.   77. *Ibid.*, p. 222.

78. It is for this reason that mysticism has always met with considerable opposition on the part of the Synagogue.

79. Baeck, *op. cit.*, p. 79.   80. *Ibid.*, p. 81.

81. W. W. Simpson, *Jews and Christians to-day*, p. 76.

82. Friedrich Nietzsche expressed a sentiment which may well serve as a commentary to the enticing words of the serpent: "Wenn es Götter gäbe, wie hielte ich's aus, kein Gott zu sein! Also giebt es keine Götter" (*Also sprach Zarathustra*, Taschen-Ausgabe, Leipzig, 1906, p. 124).

83. Leo Baeck, *op. cit.*, p. 164: "The word 'sin' to Judaism is not a word of fate, but a word of judgment, of judgment concerning human action".

84. Strack-Billerbeck, IV, p. 6; Rabbi Dienemann observes that Christian piety begins with the sense of sin, Jewish piety begins "durch das stete Anknüpfen an die Kraft des Menschen" (*op. cit.*, p. 25).

85. Lindeskog, *op. cit.*, p. 84.

86. Baeck, *op. cit.*, p. 50; "Judaism is not merely ethical, but *ethics constitutes its principle, its essence*" (*ibid.*, p. 52).

87. Baeck, p. 165.   88. *Ibid.*, p. 164.

89. *Tos. Sanh.* XIII, 2; cf. *Rabb. Anthol.*, pp. 603 f.; cf. also Maimonides, *Mishneh Torah*, to Sanh. 10. 2; cf. the references given by Morris Joseph, *Judaism in Creed and Life*, 1903, p. 154; Strack-Billerbeck, III, p. 142; Maimonides, however, adds the clause: "provided they do not observe them, as mere precepts of nature, but as laws specially revealed by God".

90. Cf. Baeck, *op. cit.*, pp. 64 f.; Hermann Cohen, *op. cit.*, pp. 388 f.; and others. Schoeps is one of the few to stress the physical importance of Jewish election, cf. *Aus frühchristl. Zeit*, pp. 202 f and elsewhere.

91. Baeck, p. 166.   92. *Ibid.*, p. 39.

93. *The Babylonian Talmud*, ed. by Rabbi I. Epstein, London, 1935; *ad loc.*

94. Kaufmann Kohler, *J. E.*, VIII, p. 406b (art. *Mediator*).

95. Cf. C. H. Toy, *Judaism and Christianity*, London, 1890, pp. 90 f. But Toy remarks on pp. 228 f.: "This idea of mediation for the sinner by men or angels, though a perfectly natural one, does not find frequent expression in the Old Testament or in the Apocryphal books". It appears to us, however, that mediation is an underlying principle of the O. T. The Priesthood, the Temple cult, the prophetic Office are all closely connected with the idea of mediation; cf. Oesterley, "The Jewish and the Christian Doctrine of Mediation", *Church and Synag. Quart.*, X (1908), pp. 34 ff.; also his book *The Jewish Doctrine of Mediation*, London, 1910.

96. Cf. Strack-Billerbeck, III, p. 556; cf. also Oesterley, The Doctrine of Mediation in Rabbinic Writings, *op. cit.*, pp. 98–116; but Oesterley observes: "In spite of the clear enunciation of the doctrine of Mediation to be found in the Old Test., the Apocrypha, and Pseudepigraphic writings, and even the Targums, yet there are pointed instances in which this doctrine is combated in Talmudic writings. . . ." (*ibid.*, p. 115).

97. That there was external influence need not be denied, cp. Toy p. 431, note.

98. Quoted by K. Kohler, *J. E.*, VIII, p. 409a; cf. Erwin I. J. Rosenthal's remarks about Maimonides, *Jud. and Christianity*, III, pp. 192 ff.

99. Montefiore explains that Judaism "brings together in close relation man and God, and it declares that there is, and need be, and can be, no other being or thing to act as bridge or go-between or intercessor" (*Outlines of Liberal Judaism*, p. 306).

100. I. M. Wise, *op. cit.*, p. 68.   101. H. Cohen, *op. cit.*, pp. 121 f.

102. The close proximity between Judaism and Unitarianism is revealed in the question of mediation. R. T. Herford, in a small booklet entitled *Jesus Christ*, London, 1901, says: "The supposed necessity of a God-man to be the means of communication between God and man only arises when God and man are supposed to be *unlike* each other, unable to communicate with each other directly" (p. 23).

103. I. M. Wise, *op. cit.*, p. 65.   104. Baeck, *op. cit.*, p. 169.

105. I. M. Wise, *op. cit.*, pp. 101 f.

106. Ziegler, *op. cit.*, p. 87; Oesterley has shown that the idea of Mediation has been dropped by the Synagogue as a result of its controversy with Christianity; cf. *Church and Synagogue Quart.*, XI (1909), p. 120; for the modern Jewish attitude, cp. *ibid.*, XII, pp. 17 ff., 68 ff.

107. O. Lazarus, *op. cit.*, p. 86.

108. There is a similar view expressed by the Rabbis: in R. Eliezer's opinion "all charity and kindness done by the heathen is counted to them as sin, because they only do it to magnify themselves". *Baba Batra*, 10b.

109. This is the underlying thought of Anselm's *Cur Deus Homo*. Prof. T. W. Manson, writing on the question of forgiveness as Jesus conceived it, remarks: "It may be observed that there is no suggestion of the debt being paid by a third party. It is simply cancelled. Whatever view we take of the Atonement, it must be confessed that the notion of the payment of man's debts to God by a third party is one which finds no support in the teaching of Jesus himself. That teaching is perfectly plain, and it is that the debts are not paid by anyone, but wiped out by God's free grace" (*The Teaching of Jesus*, p. 310, note). Prof. Manson's interpretation of "Son of Man" which includes both Jesus *and* his followers makes such a statement necessary. On his own evidence the connexion between the Son of Man and the Passion in the second part of Jesus' ministry is well attested (cp. *ibid.*, p. 227). But it occurs to us, that even allowing for a wider interpretation of "Son of Man" vicarious suffering may still be within the scope of Jesus' teaching. Prof. Manson's references to the Pauline Epistles would bear this out.

110. Though K. Kohler's view is biased by his liberal outlook, his assertion that the final redemption and the establishment of the Kingdom of God is not the work of the Messiah but God's, is essentially a Jewish view (cf. *op. cit.*, p. 144).

111. Maimonides' 13 articles of faith are to be found in his Introduction to his Commentary on the 11th chapter of *Mishnah Sanh.;* also in the various Jewish Prayer Books. The 12th art. reads: אֲנִי מַאֲמִין בֶּאֱמוּנָה שְׁלֵמָה בְּבִיאַת הַמָּשִׁיחַ וְאַף עַל פִּי שֶׁיִּתְמַהְמֵהַּ עִם כָּל־זֶה אֲחַכֶּה־לּוֹ בְּכָל־יוֹם שֶׁיָּבֹא. (Singer, p. 90).

Hasdai ben Abraham Crescas, however, does not include faith in the Messiah amongst the six fundamental dogmas of Judaism (cp. Husik, p. 392), but amongst the non-fundamentals (*ibid.*, p. 402); so also Joseph Albo (Husik, p. 415).

112. Wilhelm Bousset, *Die Religion des Judentums im neutestamentlichen Zeitalter*, Berlin, 1903, pp. 209 f. Bousset gives two reasons for this: (1) the widening of the Jewish horizon so as to conceive the eschatological hope in terms of a

general catastrophe; (2) the priestly ascendency at the time of the Maccabees which put the tribe of Judah with whom the Messiah was associated in the shade.

113. Cf. Bousset, *op. cit.*, pp. 216 ff.

114. Cf. Weber, *op. cit.*, pp. 333–347; Dr. A. Cohen, *Everyman's Talmud*, London, 1932, p. 367; Strack-Billerbeck,throughout.

115. Cf. *Rabbinic Anthology*, p. 262 (*p. Taan.*, 68d).

116. *Sanh.* 99a.   117. Cf. F. Heman, *op. cit.*, p. 57.

118. *J. E.*, VI, p. 401b.   Without throwing doubt upon Epiphanius' account, we hold that here two distinct persons are involved; in Epiphanius' case, the reference is to the Patriarch, Hillel II (330–365) who was the son of Judah III; the author of the adage was the son of Gamaliel III and the brother of Judah II.

119. See H. Freedman's note 5 to *Sanh.* 99a (Dr. I. Epstein's ed. *Sanh.* II, p. 669). K. Kohler's views regarding the Messiah may thus make a claim upon traditional authority (cp. *Origins of the Synag. and the Church*, pp. 143 f.).

120. Bernard translates "nearly as great" (cp. H. H. Bernard, *Yad Hacha-zakah*, Cambridge, 1832, p. 312).

121. Cf. Strack-Billerbeck, III, pp. 570 f.

122. Cf. *ibid.*, III, p. 577.   S.-B. remark that the phrase תורתו של משיח they have only met once!

123. *Ibid.*, IV, p. 1.

124. Cf. Strack-Billerbeck, IV, pp. 878, 883, 918.

125. Weber, *op. cit.*, p. xxxi; Nachmanides, in the famous disputation with Pablo Christiani, has, in full accord with the spirit of Judaism, explained that the doctrine of the Messiah does not occupy a central place in Jewish theology. Cf. S. Schechter, *Studies in Judaism*, 1896, p. 128; Lukyn Williams, *Adv. Jud.*, p. 246.

126. S. Schechter observes: "The statement by some moderns, to the effect that Rabbinism did not hold the belief in a personal Messiah essential, is unscientific and needs no refutation for those who are acquainted with the literature" (*Some Aspects of Rabbinic Theology*, p. 101, n. 2).

127. Klausner, *From Jesus to Paul*, p. 526; cf. M. Friedländer, *The Jewish Religion*, pp. 164 ff.

128. *Ibid.*, p. 469.   129. A. Cohen, *Everyman's Talmud*, p. 368.

130. Cf. Schechter, *Some Aspects of Rabbinic Theology*, p. 102.

131. Strack-Billerbeck, II, pp. 279 ff.; IV, pp. 771, 1045, 1049, etc.; cf. also Aug. Wünsche, *Die Leiden des Messias*, Leipzig, 1870, pp. 55 ff.

132. These passages have been collected by Montefiore and Loewe in their *Rabbinic Anthology*, pp. 584–586; cp. also Montefiore, *Rabbinic Literature and Gospel Teachings*, pp. 306 ff. The likeness between the Christian and Jewish conceptions regarding the Suffering Messiah is so great that George Foot Moore has suggested that we have here an "appropriation of Christian doctrine for a Jewish Messiah" (*Judaism*, I, p. 551).

133. Montefiore, *Rabbinic Literature and Gospel Teachings*, p. 305; cp. also Weber, *op. cit.*, p. 346.

134. Strack-Billerbeck, II, p.292.

135. Cf. *Rabbinic Literature and Gospel Teachings*, p. 309; cf., however, S. Schechter's view; Bentwich, *S. Schechter*, p. 71.

136. Cf. Schechter, *Some Aspects*, pp. 103 ff.

137. Hermann Cohen's conception of the Messianic Kingdom strikingly approaches the Christian view on this point: the relationship between present reality and messianic future is that of opposition. The Messianic hope (Messianismus) puts in place of the present world-order (sinnliche Gegenwart), "eine neue Art von Übersinnlichkeit . . . nicht eine überirdische, sondern die der Zukunft. Diese Zukunft schaft eine neue Erde und einen neuen Himmel, also eine neue Wirklichkeit" (*op. cit.*, p. 342).

138. Cf. Baeck, *op. cit.*, pp. 250 ff.   139. Wise, *op. cit.*, p. 102.

140. Dienemann, p. 61.   141. Baeck, p. 126.

142. O. Lazarus, *op. cit.*, p. 89. The liberal Jew believes "that it is within man's power to bring God's kingdom upon earth".

143. K. Kohler, *Origins of the Synagogue and Church*, p. 144.
Mr. Hans Kosmala has kindly drawn my attention to an important point in the Jewish-Christian controversy. It concerns the question of *unfulfilled* Messianic promises. Thus Buber significantly remarks: "Wir wissen aber auch, wie wir wissen, dass Luft ist . . . dass Raum ist . . . tiefer, echter wissen wir, dass die Weltgeschichte nicht bis auf ihren Grund aufgebrochen, dass die Welt noch nicht erlöst ist. Wir *spüren* die Unerlöstheit der Welt" (*Die Stunde und die Erkenntnis*, p, 153). The same sentiment is used by other Jewish writers. Rabbi Isaac ben Abraham of Troki has collected these unfulfilled hopes under eight points: (1) Universal reign of the Messiah; (2) universal religion; (3) disappearance of idolatry; (4) disappearance of evil; (5) universal peace; (6) peace in the animal world; (7) prosperity of Israel; (8) restoration of Israel and renewal of the Covenant (cf. חזק אמונה, Ch. I; Deutsch's ed., pp. 33–37). Such objections, however, presuppose an almost magic transformation of human nature which is at variance with the New Testament conception of personal regeneration.

144. In the *Festschrift, Hermann Cohen*, p. 103.

145. *Ibid.*, p. 107; L. Treitel, however, appears to deny Philo's influence upon Rabbinic thinking, cp. *ibid.*, pp. 177 ff.

146. *Some Aspects of Rabbinic Theology*, p. 117; for the meaning of תורה as "religion" see M. Friedländer, *The Jewish Religion*, p. 4.

147. Cf. art. "Judaism" in Vallentine's *J. E.*, p. 336b.

148. Cf. Loewe, *Jud. and Christ.*, I, p. 153: "Pharisaism laid more stress on life and conduct, Christianity on belief", cp. Baeck, *op. cit.*, pp. 4 ff., 261.

149. S. Schechter, cf. *Studies in Judaism*, I, pp. 179 ff.; Loewe admits a certain minimum of dogma prerequisite to Judaism, cp. *Jud. and Christ.*, II, p. 42, note.

150. Baeck, *op. cit.*, p. 50; *Kiddushin*, 40b: R. Tarphon and the Elders were at a meal in Lud where the question arose: Is study great or is the deed great? R. Tarphon said: The deed is great. R. Akiba said: Study is great. Then all present rose to their feet and said: תלמוד גדול שהתלמוד מביא לידי מעשה (Study is great for study leads to deeds). Cp. Oesterley, *Church and Synagogue Quart.*, VIII (1906), p. 158.

151. *Ibid.*, pp. 31, 91; cf. I. I. Mattuck, "The Jewish Approach to God", *In Spirit and in Truth*, pp. 32 ff.

152. *Ibid.*, pp. 92 f.

153. Cf. A. Cohen, *Everyman's Talmud*, p. 130; Albo regards the superiority

of Moses over against the other prophets as one of the eleven principles every true Jew must hold (cp. Husik, p. 415).

154. A. Cohen, *ibid.*, p. 132.

155. Cf. Weber, *op. cit.*, pp. 96 f.; Oesterley and Box, *Relig. and Worship of the Synagogue*, pp. 161 ff.

156. Cf. Montefiore, *Rabbinic Literature and Gospel Teachings*, p. 240.

157. *Ibid.*, p. 319; cp. A. Cohen, *Everyman's Talmud*, p. 141.

158. Cf. A. Cohen, *op. cit.*, p. 160. Dr. Cohen quotes an interesting passage from *Gen. R.* 44. 1, which testifies to the rational aim underlying the commandments.

159. The central place which the Scrolls of the Law occupy in the Synagogue expresses the centrality of the Law in Jewish thought and worship (cf. Oesterley and Box, pp. 337 f.; cf. also Oesterley, *Church and Synag. Quart.*, VIII (1906), pp. 1 ff.; M. Friedländer, *Jewish Religion*, p. 424).

160. Cf. *Jewish Chronicle*, Dec. 24, 1943 (*Fundamentals of Judaism*). S. Daiches has shown that Kant misunderstood Judaism by asserting that reward was its main motive for keeping the commandments, whereas the Rabbis said: שכר מצוה מצוה (*Aspects of Judaism*, London, 1928, pp. 60 f.).

161. Cf. Schoeps, *op. cit.*, p. 51. 162. Cf. Rom. 10. 2.

163. Rom. 3. 31; 7. 12, 14. 164. Rom. 7. 22. 165. Rom. 2. 13.

166. *Outlines of Liberal Judaism*, p. 309.

167. Cf. Benzion Kellermann, Die philosophische Begründung des Judentums, *Festschrift, Hermann Cohen*, pp. 101 f. Franz Rosenzweig has clearly perceived the inner cause of what he calls Christian dualism, "Erst an der Hand des Sohnes wagt der Christ vor den Vater zu treten; nur durch den Sohn glaubt er zum Vater kommen zu können. . . ." The Christian life thus expresses itself in a two-fold motion: from the Son to the Father, and from the Father to the Son (*Der Stern der Erlösung*, p. 439; cp. also pp. 440 ff.).

168. Kaufmann Kohler, *Jewish Theology, systematically and historically considered*, New York, 1918 p. 6.

169. Cf. Rom. 10. 10.

170. Cp. Rabbinic Judaism and St. Paul, *J. Q. R.*, Jan. 1901, pp. 176 ff.

171. *Ibid.*, p. 173.

172. H. Cohen's position may be judged from the following sentences: "Die Religion hat Eigenart, keineswegs aber der Ethik gegenüber Selbständigkeit. Der Anteil, den sie an der Vernunft hat, bindet sie an die Ethik. Der methodische Zusammenhalt mit der Ethik war immer der Kompass der jüdischen Religionsphilosophie" (*op. cit.*, p. 497). The Kantian postulate of the categorical imperative subordinates religion to ethics.

173. Cf. Schoeps, p. 53. 174. Dienemann, p. 69.

175. Cf. Baeck, *op. cit.*, p. 129; Prof. Felix Adler's (1851–1933) philosophy and the Society for Ethical Culture which he founded in New York (1876) is the logical consequence of the emancipation of ethics from religious belief. Adler's motto is: Not by thy Creed, but by thy Deed. For a description of the movement and its relation to Judaism and Christianity, see A. Bernstein, "Ethical Judaism: A study of a recent form of Jewish thought", *Church and Synagogue Quart.*, XI (1909), pp. 162 ff.

176. *Origins of Synagogue and Church*, p. 141.

177. The absence of the sacramental aspect in Judaism is significant. The

Christian in the sacramental approach to God expresses his human need, he stands as a recipient. The Jew, by keeping the Law, gives of his best.

178. H. Loewe regards the words in the *Yigdal* prayer: "God will never alter nor change His Law, to everlasting, for any other", as a polemical reference to Christianity (cf. *Rabbinic Anthology*, p. lxix).

179. Cf. Schechter, *Studies in Judaism*, I, pp. xx f.

"The *Torah* is for all time, but revelation is progressive" (H. Loewe, *In Spirit and in Truth*, p. 254).

180. *Pes. R.* 8a; cp. *Rabbinic Anthology*, note 71 (p. 683).

181. *Chagigah*, 3b.

182. A. Cohen, *Everyman's Talmud*, p. 157 and references.

183. Cf. Leo Baeck, *The Essence of Judaism*, pp. 14 f., 22: "Judaism experiences a continuous renaissance".

184. Cf. H. Cohen, pp. 262, 468, etc.

185. Cf. J. Abelson, *The Immanence of God in Rabbinical Literature*, London, 1912, pp. 374 f.

186. Rosenzweig, who traces back the Christian dualism to a consciousness of God's love and God's justice, makes the revealing remark: "Jene blitzschnell unerwarteten Umschläge aus dem Bewusstsein der göttlichen Liebe in das der göttlichen Gerechtigkeit und umgekehrt, wie sie für das jüdische Leben wesentlich sind—der Christ kennt sie nicht . . ." (*op. cit.*, p. 440). If Rosenzweig is right the reason for it lies in the fact that the Christian knows about God's love and justice, not from his consciousness, but from the Cross.

187. Spinoza's *Short Treatise on God, Man and his Well-being*, Ch. XXIV; Engl. by A. Wolf, London, 1910 (pp. 141 f.). "Judaism", says Abrahams, "wavers between the two opposite conceptions: absolute transcendentalism and absolute pantheism. Sometimes Judaism speaks with the voice of Isaiah; sometimes with the voice of Spinoza" (*Judaism*, 1910, p. 40).

188. Dr. J. H. Hertz speaks of a "psychic experience of a direct communion with God" vouchsafed to Moses and the whole people at Sinai (*The Pentateuch*, p. 403). Felsenthal regards "natural religion in the soul of man" as "the kernel of Judaism" (*B. Felsenthal, Teacher in Israel*, p. 250; cf. also *ibid.*, pp. 269 f.).

189. *J. E.*, x, pp. 396 ff.

190. Montefiore, *Outlines of Liberal Judaism*, p. 317.

191. *Rabbinic Anthology*, p. lxix. That God is bound by his own laws is an important premise in Spinoza's philosophy; cf. Will Durant, *The Story of Philosophy*, London, 1926, pp. 187 ff.

192. *Rabbinic Anthology*, p. lxvi.

193. *Ibid.*, p. lxxiii: cp. M. Friedländer, *The Jewish Religion*, pp. 46 f.

194. *Ibid.*, p. lxvii.

195. *Ibid.*, p. lxx.

196. *Ibid.*, p. lxx; S. Schechter, the leader of Neo-Orthodoxy, expresses a similar view on the subject of revelation; cf. Bentwich, *S. Schechter*, p. 285.

197. *Ibid.*, p. lxvi: Dr. J. H. Hertz, who repudiates the notion that human reason or the human personality is the *source* of revelation, does not seem to differ essentially from Loewe's view. The late Chief Rabbi explains revelation as the result of the "close spiritual relationship between God and man" and the

"interplay of spiritual forces and energies, whereby the human soul responds to the Self-manifesting Life of all Worlds. . . ." (*The Pentateuch*, one vol. ed., p. 402).

198. Baeck, *op. cit.*, p. 251.

199. In uniformity with this function assigned to history, H. Loewe explains that the survival of the dietary laws seems to indicate that they serve a purpose (*ibid.*, p. ciii).

200. Cf. Schoeps, pp. 130 ff.

201. Gamaliel's wise words, Acts 5. 34 ff., express a deep-seated Jewish conviction; cf. *Abot*, v, 17.

202. The Christian view regarding the O. T. has been admirably restated by G. L. B. Sloan in his recent controversy with Sch. Ben-Chorin (*Das christliche Verständnis des Alten Testaments und der jüdische Einwand*, Jerusalem, 1941).

203. Sloan, *op. cit.*, p. 7.

204. Schleiermacher's *Reden über die Religion*, Gotha, 1888, Rede v, p. 308: Judaism is not the forerunner of Christianity: "Ich hasse in der Religion diese Art von historischen Beziehungen; jegliche hat für sich ihre eigene und ewige Notwendigkeit, und jedes Anfangen einer Religion ist ursprünglich".

205. Cf. T. Witton Davies, "The relation between Judaism and Christianity", *Transactions of the Third International Congress for the History of Religions*, Oxford, 1908, II, pp. 303 ff.

206. Macmurray, *The Clue to History*, p. 42.

Gustaf Dalman, in an essay on *Judaism and Christianity* (transl. by G. H. Box, London, 1901), has a note on the relationship between the Old and the New Test. He explains that in older times the O. T. "was put on the same level with the N. T. The plan which was possible then can no longer be pursued, now that the O. T. is understood in accordance with its own special spirit, and merely serves to illustrate the New" (*ibid.*, p. 37). These words reveal the inroads the idea of evolution has made upon the mind of so positive a Christian scholar as Dalman. The R. C. writer, Prof. B. Bartmann, takes a similar view, disrupting the connection between the Old and New Test.: "Jesus denkt und operiert nicht geschichtlich, sondern prophetisch-vertikal"; "Er (*i.e.* Jesus) weiss sich als *absoluter Anfang*" (Hartmann, *Der Glaubensgegensatz zwischen Judentum und Christentum*, Paderborn, 1938, pp. 74 f.; cp. *ibid.*, pp. 78 f.).

207. Martin Buber, *Die Stunde und die Erkenntnis*, Berlin, 1936, p. 154. M. Buber, in *Ich und Du*, has a few remarkable sentences which at first sight create the impression of an affinity with the Barthian view regarding revelation. But on closer examination there appears an important divergence. Buber observes regarding Revelation: "Der Mensch empfängt, und er empfängt nicht einen 'Inhalt', sondern eine Gegenwart, eine Gegenwart als Kraft . . . ," (*ibid.*, p. 127). And again: "Das ist die ewige, die im Jetzt und Hier gegenwärtige Offenbarung. . . . Ich glaube nicht an eine Selbstbenennung Gottes, nicht an eine Selbstbestimmung Gottes vor den Menschen. . . . Ich bin der Ich bin. . . . Das Offenbarende ist das Offenbarende. . . . Das ewige Du kann seinem Wesen nach nicht zum Es werden" (*ibid.*, p. 129). The main difference between Buber and Barth is in their attitude to the historical element in revelation. For Barth, "die im Jetzt und Hier gegenwärtige Offenbarung" cannot be anchored in the subjective *experience* of the believer, but in *history*.

Schoeps is quick to notice the meaning of the a-historical conception of revelation, and warns against it (cp. Schoeps, *op. cit.*, pp. 140 f.).

208. Baeck, p. 37.   209. Cf. Lindeskog, p. 88, n. 2.

210. Cf. Edwyn Bevan's important remark in *The Legacy of Israel*, Oxford, 1928, p. 56; cf. also J. H. Hertz, *Pentateuch*, abridged ed., p. 935.

211. Cf. Klausner, *From Jesus to Paul*, p. 444.

212. Cf. H. Loewe's remarks in *Rabbinic Anthology*, pp. lxxxii ff.

213. Cf. Montefiore, *Rabbinic Literature*, p. 100.

214. Cf. Montefiore, *J. Q. R.*, Jan. 1901, p. 170.

215. Cf. Strack-Billerbeck, I, pp. 924 ff.; but cf. Ch. Guignebert, *The Jewish World in the time of Jesus*, 1939, p. 157. The writer, referring to Mt. 23. 15, says: "Our evidence, however, for the alleged zeal of the Pharisees is very slight, and it is probable that the Palestinian Jews of that day, even the least bigoted of them, could only conceive of a *universalism* which was compatible with their own deep-rooted particularism".

216. Prof. W. Curtis makes the interesting suggestion that the name for the Greek transl. "Seventy" (LXX) is not a reference to the legendary translators, but to the Rabbinic notion of the seventy nations of the world for whom the book was meant (cf. *Jesus Christ the Teacher*, 1943, p. 24).

217. Klausner's remarks on the pre-Christian propaganda of Judaism are very important (cf. *From Jesus to Paul*, pp. 29 ff., 162, and throughout).

218. Klausner holds, with good reason, that the concern for the nations of the world is no exclusive right of Christianity; "it was anticipated by Judaism, even by Palestinian Judaism. . . ." (*From Jesus to Paul*, p. 177).

219. Cf. *Rabbinic Anthology*, pp. 52 f., 465.

220. Moore, *Judaism*, I, p. 233.   221. Cf. Moore, *op. cit.*, I, p. 329.

222. Cf. A. Marmorstein, "Judaism and Gentile Christianity in the third Century", *The London Quarterly and Holborn Review*, July, 1935, p. 364.

223. Cf. A. Cohen, *Everyman's Talmud*, p. 225; the whole chapter on Brotherly Love contains a fine summary of best Rabbinic teaching.
Strack-Billerbeck: "Ben Azzai dürfte der erste Lehrer der alten Synagoge sein, der für das Verhalten gegen Nichtisraeliten dieselbe Norm aufstellt wie für das Verhalten gegen einen israelitischen Volksgenossen . . ." (*ibid.*, I, p. 358; cf. also Schechter, *Some Aspects*, p. 120).

224. Baeck, p. 193; against this ought to be placed Strack-Billerbeck's remarks concerning the Jewish attitude to strangers (cf. Strack-Billerbeck, I, pp. 353 ff.).

225. Moore, *Judaism*, I, p. 332.   226. Cf. Strack-Billerbeck, I, p. 930.

227. *Num. R.* VIII, 2.   228. *Ibid.*, VIII, I.

229. Cf. Schechter, *Some Aspects*, p. 131, n. 3.

230. *Sifra*, 86b; cf. *Rabb. Anthol.*, p. 564; Schechter, *Some Aspects*, p. 133.

231. The date of this work is the 8th or 9th century, though it may contain old traditions.

232. Accepting the alternative reading instead of "owners", cf. G. Friedländer, p. 83, n. 6. Klausner remarks in connexion with this passage: "Without a sympathetic, and more than sympathetic attitude toward the proselytes on the part of Israel, it would be impossible to explain the success of Judaism among the Gentiles" (*From Jesus to Paul*, p. 37).

233. Ch. XI, Friedländer's transl., pp. 80 f.

234. *Some Aspects*, p. 106.   235. Schechter, *ibid.*, p. 114.
236. Cf. *Rabb. Anthol.*, pp. 64, 104.   237. *Everyman's Talmud*, p. 226.
238. S. Schechter quotes an interesting sentence from R. Saadia: כי אומתינו אינגה אומה אם כי בתורותיה ("Because our nation is only a nation by reason of its Torah"). *Some Aspects of Rabb. Theology*, p. 105.

239. Though Schechter remarks: "Even those Rabbis who tried to establish Israel's special claim on their exceptional merits were not altogether unconscious of the insufficiency of the reason of works in this respect, and therefore had also recourse to the love of God, which is not given as a reward, but is offered freely" (*op. cit.*, p. 61).

240. Cf. Schechter, *Some Aspects*, pp. 131 f. and references; it is interesting to note that J. H. Hertz speaks of a "predisposition in the nature of the Jewish people to receive the message of Sinai" (*Pentateuch*, abridged ed., p. 403, § v).

241. The Rabbis thought of a double relation between God and humanity. "He is the Lord of all nations, while his name is specially attached to Israel" (so Schechter, *op. cit.*, p. 63; cp. also note 2). "God is in a special sense the God of Israel; but He is unequivocally, too, the God of all flesh" (Abrahams, *Judaism*, p. 41).

242. Cf. Schoeps, p. 128: "Judaism for the Jew may almost be claimed as a principle of orthodox Judaism" (Abrahams, *Judaism*, p. 42); for Schechter's view, see Bentwich, *S. Schechter*, pp. 304, 347.

243. Moore, *op. cit.*, I, p. 335 and references.

244. The whole Mishnaic tractate *Abodah Zarah* reveals the extent of Jewish aversion to idolatry.

245. Gerald Friedländer, *Pirke de Rabbi Eliezer*, p. 208. Cf. *Sanh.* 94a.

246. *Ibid.*, p. 208. Another reading is: "as though he were eating with a dog". G. Friedländer, for some curious reason, refers to Phil. 3. 2, and Eph. 2. 11, as "parallel N. T. teaching". Does the translator imply that Paul refused to eat with Gentiles? For further strange use of the N. T., see *ibid.*, pp. 208, n. 7, and 209, n. 1.

247. Cf. Weber, pp. 71 f.

248. Ch. Guignebert, *The Jewish World in the time of Jesus*, Eng. by S. H. Hooke, 1939, p. 157; cf. also Bousset, *op. cit.*, p. 223.

249. *Yad Hachazakah*, תשובה, I, Ch. 9 (end); cf. *Shabb.* 63a.

250. W. Bousset, *Die Religion des Judentums im Späthellenistischen Zeitalter*[3], Tübingen, 1926, p. 77.

251. *Ibid.*, p. 79; Hoennicke, *op. cit.*, p. 77: "Nur durch Israel bekommen die Heiden am Heil Anteil. Das ist der Grundgedanke".

252. Saul Lieberman has tried to show that there existed a closer relationship between the Rabbis and the Gentile world than is usually assumed. But he admits that "the learned Rabbis were conscious of their great task of guarding the true faith, the high ethics and the pure family life of the Jews against any outside contamination; they made hedge upon hedge around the Law in order to protect it and to preserve it in its entire purity" (*Greek in Jewish Palestine; Studies in the life and manners of Jewish Palestine in the II–IV Centuries C.E.*, New York, 1942, pp. 89 f.).

253. Cf. Leon Simon, *Studies in Jewish Nationalism*, pp. 16 ff.

254. Cf. Bousset, *op. cit.*, p. 92: "Ihre Grundforderungen sind in erster

Linie darauf gerichtet, das Volkstum in seiner Sonderheit zu bewahren".
The interdiction to marry heathen, the insistence upon circumcision for
proselytes, the restrictions upon social intercourse on the grounds of ritual
defilement, interdiction to learn Greek, etc., all served the national purpose,
according to Bousset.

255. Cf. Abrahams' note in Singer's *Prayer Book*, pp. lxxiii f.

256. Cf. Singer, pp. 5 f. and note pp. xvi f.

257. Cf. Weber, pp. 51 f. and references.

258. Montefiore, *Rabbinic Anthology*, p. xxxii.

259. Cf. Weber, *op. cit.*, pp. 56 ff.   260. Hoennicke, p. 76.

261. Cf. Bousset, *op. cit.*, p. 92; cf. also Hoennicke, pp. 60 ff.; cf. also
Klausner, *From Jesus to Paul*, pp. 177 f.

262. "The Covenant made the Jew self-confident and arrogant, but these
very faults were needed to save him" (Abrahams, *Judaism*, p. 11).

263. *Rabbinic Anthology*, p. 614; but cf. H. Loewe's note, *ibid.*, pp. 649 f.

264. Cf. Schechter, *Some Aspects*, p. 106.

265. Weber, *op. cit.*, p. 76: "Während so Einzelne aus der Heidenwelt
bald in geringer, bald in grösserer Zahl durch freiwilligen Anschluss an Israel
gerettet werden, hat die Völkerwelt als solche keine andere Zukunft, als die
des Gerichtes".

266. So Guignebert, *op. cit.*, p. 157.

266ᵃ. Schoeps, *Aus frühchristl. Zeit*, pp. 204 ff.

267. Weber, p. 67.   268. Baeck, *op. cit.*, p. 63.

269. Klausner, *From Jesus to Paul*, p. 203; cf. pp. 178, 188, 205: "Christianity took elements from Judaism and Hellenism and of the two compounds
something new which was neither one nor the other" came into existence.
Cf. also Ziegler, *op. cit.,*, p. 75: "nur mittels Konzessionen" was the new
religion able to succeed.

270. *Ibid.*, p. 80.   271. Klausner, *ibid.*, p. 446.   272. *Ibid.*, p. 445.

273. Montefiore, *J. Q. R.*, Jan. 1901, p. 182: "Particularism was the great
weakness and defect of the Rabbinic religion, though it was accompanied by
qualities too commonly overlooked or denied in the customary descriptions
of Judaism".

274. Jacques Maritain, *Antisemitism*, p. 18; cf. also *Redeeming the Time*, p. 130.

275. Cf. Singer, p. 227: · · · אתה בחרתנו מכל־העמים, cf. Deut. 10. 15;
14. 2, etc.

276. Cf. Weber, pp. 56 ff.; Schechter, *Some Aspects*, p. 59.

277. Schechter, *ibid.*, p. 57.

278. Cf. Deut. 7. 6; 10. 15; 29. 13; 32. 9; 33. 29; and the many passages
where Israel is spoken of as *God's* people; *His* people; *My* people, etc.

279. *Ruth Rabba*, introduction (פתיחה), R. Simeon ben Yochai taught,
etc. (27c); English transl. by Rabinowitz, p. 3.

280. *Sanh.* 10. 1.   281. Moore, *Judaism*, II, p. 95.

282. *Rabbinic Anthology*, p. 225.   283. *Rabbinic Anthology*, p. 351.

284. J. Abelson, *The Immanence of God*, p. 374.

285. H. Cohen, however, denies this. Translating סגלה with "Vorbild",
he regards Israel as a "Symbol der Menschheit" (*op. cit.*, p. 174). Israel
exemplifies in himself what Monotheism could mean for humanity.

286. *Al Khazari*, IV, 23.

287. Ziegler, *op. cit.*, p. 75. 288. *Ibid.*, p. 76. Ziegler's italics (fat).

289. Cf. *ibid.*, p. 79; cf. also pp. 84 ff.; Martin Buber, in the introduction to his small volume on Jewish Mysticism, says: "The longer the exile lasted, and the more terrible it became, the more necessary did the maintenance of religion seem to be for the maintenance of the race; and so much the stronger grew the power of the Law" (*Jewish Mysticism*, Engl. by Lucy Cohen, London, 1931, p. xxii).

290. *Rabbinic Anthology*, p. xcvi.

291. Baeck, p. 278. 292. Bousset 1926, p. 92.

293. Baeck, p. 278. This peculiar sentence is strangely reminiscent of Jesuit thinking!

294. Ziegler, *op. cit.*, p. 78; cf. pp. 80, 82, 86, etc.

295. Martin Buber, *Die Stunde und die Erkenntnis*, Berlin, 1936, 148 f. (cf. *Theologische Blätter*, Sept. 1933).

296. *Ibid.*, pp. 156 f.

297. Cf. Judah Halevi, *Al Khazari*, I, p. 115. Cf. Weber, pp. 282 ff.

298. Cf. Schoeps, p. 73; commenting on Rosenzweig's attitude, Schoeps explains that Israel's election is based on God's promise to Abraham: "die laut gnädiger Zusage des Ewigen physisch geknüpft bleibt an den Samen Abrahams" (*ibid.*, p. 127); a similar view is taken by Isaac Breuer, who regards both the Jewish people and Erez-Israel as integral parts of God's revelation to men (cf. A. Lichtigfeld, *Twenty Centuries of Jewish Thought*, London, 1937, p. 150; cf. also Schoeps' recent essay in *Judaica*, Heft 3, Okt. 1946: "Weiteres zur Auserwählung Israels").

299. K. Kohler, *Grundriss einer systematischen Theologie des Judentums*, Leipzig, 1910, p. 6; Schoeps, therefore, contends that the comparison ought not to be between Church and Synagogue, but between Church and the people of Israel (cf. Schoeps, *ibid.*, p. 149).

300. Baeck, p. 55.

301. Franz Rosenzweig, *Der Stern der Erlösung*, pp. 376 f.; cf. also pp. 377 ff.

302. Cp. p. 505; the gravitation of Jewish life is inwards: "Weil sie sich ewig aus sich selbst ernährt, sammelt sie die Glut zugleich ins Innerste zu höchstem inbrünstigem Brand".

303. *Ibid.*, p. 413. 304. *Ibid.*, p. 416. 305. *Ibid.*, pp. 497 f.

306. *Ibid.*, p. 511.

307. Christianus fit, non nascitur; it is the opposite with the Jew, says Rosenzweig (cf. *ibid.*, p. 497); H. Loewe protests against the racial interpretation of Judaism. He says: "Nationalism is the declaration that racial descent is equal to belief in God as a test of Judaism" (*Rabbin. Anthol.*, p. lxxx). But we doubt whether he would be prepared to emancipate Judaism from its peculiar national connexion.

308. Rosenzweig, pp. 496 f.

309. Cf. Klausner, *From Jesus to Paul*, p. 526 and throughout.

310. Rosenzweig, p. 496. 311. Moore, II, p. 95.

312. St. Paul's importance in the struggle cannot be overestimated. But for him the Church would have succumbed to the demands of the Judaistic party; cf. Harnack, Judentum u. Judenchristentum. *Texte u. Untersuchungen*, xxxix, p. 88.

313. Klausner has fully recognized the implications of Pauline teaching.

It was due to Paul that Israel's position of "splendid isolation" was broken down (cf. *From Jesus to Paul*, pp. 531 ff.).

314. "Judaism as a theology stood or fell by its belief that man can affect God" (Abrahams, *Judaism*, p. 47).

315. The influence of Rom. Chs. 9–11 upon the Christian attitude to the Jews can hardly be overestimated. Origen who, like the rest of the Church Fathers, does not hesitate to appropriate all the promises given to Israel, for the Church, remembering, however, the Apostle's words concerning his own people, still clings to the hope that at the last hour all Israel shall be saved. Origen entreats God on Israel's behalf, that finally he may attain to salvation (Comm. in *Ep. ad Rom.* 8, 1).

316. The Roman Catholic, Prof. Bernhard Bartmann, in answer to Schoeps' book, affirms that St. Paul regarded the promises given to the Old-Israel as *transferred* to the New-Israel, *i.e.* the Church (cp. *Der Glaubensgegensatz zwischen Judentum und Christentum*, pp. 30 f.). But this is unwarranted as it cannot be deduced from his epistles. However the Church Fathers may have interpreted Israel's position, for the Apostle only hardening in part had befallen Israel, until the fullness of the Gentiles be come in (Rom. 11. 25). Dr. Bartmann's position is conditioned by the R. C. view concerning the O. T. which, apart from its prophetic-testimony (Weissagungsbeweis), appears to be of no further significance (cp. *ibid.*, pp. 70 ff.); for a more positive interpretation see Jacques Maritain, *Redeeming the Time*, pp. 123–157; and Prof. Walter Zimmerli, Biblische Grundlinien zur Judenfrage, *Judaica*, Heft 2, Juli, 1945.

317. Lev Gillet pleads for a proper Christian understanding "of Israel's function in the divine economy" (*Communion in the Messiah*, p. 183). But Israel's significance as far as the Church is concerned is not independent of or outside the *Communion in the Messiah*. The admission of a double relationship, in view of the Pauline Epistles, is impossible. God deals with man and not with Jews *and* Gentiles.

318. Cf. H. Kraemer, *The Christian Message in a Non-Christian World*, pp. 227 f.

319. Charue, *op. cit.*, pp. 341 f.   320. Cf. *supra* pp. 13 f.

321. Cf. *Dial.*, Ch. 68; cf. also Harnack, *Texte u. Untersuchungen*, xxxix, p. 75, n. 5.

322. Antinomian excesses must have often compromised the Church in the eyes of the Synagogue (cf. S. Baring-Gould, *The Lost and Hostile Gospels*, 1874, pp. 26 ff., 40 f.). It may be, however, that the author is exaggerating the antinomian effect of Pauline preaching.

323. *Dial.*, Ch. 8.   324. Cf. *supra*, pp. 301 f.

325. We have already referred to the discussions between Rabbis and Minim on the subject, who is *true* Israel, cf. pp. 188 f.; cf. also H. Loewe's note, *Rabbinic Anthol.*, pp. 161 f; also Wolfgang Trilling, *Das Wahre Israel*, 1958, p. 200.

326. Schoeps, p. 88; Buber, *Die Stunde u. die Erkenntnis*, p. 155: "Das Geheimnis des anderen ist innen in ihm und kann nicht von Aussen her wahrgenommen werden. Kein Mensch ausserhalb von Israel weiss um das Geheimnis Israels. Und kein Mensch ausserhalb der Christenheit weiss um das Geheimnis der Christenheit. Aber nichtwissend können sie einander im Geheimnis anerkennen". Sch. Ben-Chorin expresses a similar thought: "Die Offenbarung Christi aber in den Seelen der seinen ist das Geheimnis der

christlichen Seele, von dem Israel nichts weiss. Ich wage nicht dieses Geheimnis anzutasten, aber ich habe nicht Teil daran" (Sloan and Ben-Chorin, *op. cit.*, p. 47).

327. For the discussion itself, see Schoeps, pp. 120–134.

328. "Wenn neues, sachbezogenes Denken etwas lehrt, dann doch wohl dieses, dass geschichtliche Wirkung nur von geschichtlicher Wirklichkeit ausgehen kann und es unsachlich ist, ein Ergebnis—zumal ein heiliges—anders erklären zu wollen, als es sich selber erklärt" (Schoeps, *op. cit.*, p. 147).

329. Schoeps, *op. cit.*, pp. 146 f.

330. Buber, *Die Stunde und die Erkenntnis*, p. 153.

331. Schoeps, p. 131; cf. p. 153: "Das grundsätzliche Neue nun—und damit auch die äusserste Grenze des Möglichen—ist dieses, *dass* wir es ihnen glauben".

332. Cf. Schoeps, pp. 10 f.   333. *Ibid.*, p. 131.   334. *Ibid.*, p. 150.

335. *Ibid.*, p. 129.   336. Schoeps, p. 149.

337. Buber, *Die Stunde und die Erkenntnis*, p. 148.

338. Cf. Schoeps, p. 123 (Franz Rosenzweig).

339. Leo Baeck, *Wege im Judentum*, Berlin, 1933, p. 211.

340. Cf. p. 306, n. 273. In two interesting sermons on "The Missionary element in Judaism", he severely criticizes the non-missionary attitude of modern Judaism; cp. Montefiore, *Truth in Religion*, pp. 15 ff.

341. Baeck, *The Essence of Judaism*, pp. 60 f.

342. Sloan and Ben-Chorin, pp. 29 f.. To Klausner, the basic principle of Judaism is: "*nationality for the sake of universality*" (*From Jesus to Paul*, p. 536).

343. *Der Stern der Erlösung*, p. 429.

344. *Ibid.*, pp. 425 f.   345. *Ibid.*, p. 451.

346. *Ibid.*, p. 517: "Hass gegen die eigene Unvollkommenheit, gegen das eigene Nochnicht".

347. *Ibid.*, p. 436.

348. Cf. Rabbi I. Epstein, *Judaism*, pp. 11 f.; the non-missionary attitude was forced upon Judaism by circumstances (cp. Abrahams, *Jew. Life in Middle Ages*, new ed., by C. Roth, 1932, p. 73); modern Jewish writers, however, have made of it a virtue. Menasseh ben Israel in his *Vindiciae Judaeorum* takes up this attitude and Moses Mendelssohn naturally endorses it (cp. M. Mendelssohn, *Jerusalem*, Engl. transl. by M. Samuel, London, 1838, I. pp. 58, 152 f.).

349. Cf. Hans Kosmala and Robert Smith, *The Jew in the Christian World*, p. 95; L. Gillet, *Communion in the Messiah*, p. 237. For Aimé Pallière's life and conversion, cf. his autobiography, *Le Sanctuaire Inconnu*, 1926; Engl. *The Unknown Sanctuary. A Pilgrimage from Rome to Israel*, New York, 1928.

350. Schoeps, p. 128; Montefiore has, however, recognized the inconsistency of such an attitude, for Monotheism involves universalism and missionary expansion (cf. *Liberal Judaism*, pp. 285 f.; *Truth in Religion*, pp. 19 f.).

351. Cf. K. Kohler, *Grundriss*, p. 33.

352. Sholem Asch, *The Nazarene*, London, 1939, pp. 612 f.

353. *Dial.*, Ch. 64.   354. H. Loewe, *In Spirit and in Truth*, pp. 252 f.

355. Cf. Danby, *The Jew and Christianity*, p. 61. A somewhat similar story, but with a different application, is contained in *The Hasidic Anthology*, arranged by L. I. Newman, p. 46, § 2.

356. Quoted by Schoeps, p. 145.   357. Cf. Schoeps, p. 132.
358. S. S. Cohon, *International Review of Missions*, xxii (1933), p. 477.
359. *Ibid.*, p. 475.   360. *J. E.*, iv, pp. 249 f.
361. Rosenzweig, p. 436.
362. Israel's mission is fulfilled "in a calm and dignified silence" (The late Chief Rabbi, quoted by Montefiore, *Truth in Religion*, p. 26); cf. also Felsenthal, *op. cit.*, p. 247.
363. Kohler, *Jewish Theology*, p. 18.
364. "The Jew and Christian Evangelization", *International Review of Missions*, xxii, 1933, p. 474.
365. Schoeps, p. 11.
366. Edwyn Bevan, "Considerations on a complaint regarding Christian propaganda among Jews, *Intern. Review of Missions*, 1933, p. 490.
367. Salis Daiches' argument against Christian missions to Jews is based not on the essential difference between Israel and the world, but on the fact that Christianity is alien to the Jewish disposition (cp. *Aspects of Judaism*, p. 135); cf. also H. Loewe: "Judaism and Christianity have, each of them, that conception of God that is best suited to their spiritual mentality" (*In Spirit and in Truth*, p. 262).
368. Cf. Sloan and Ben-Chorin, *op. cit.*, p. 28.
369. It is here that we differ fundamentally from L. Gillet. To him, "the negation of Jesus' Messiahship commonly associated with Judaism is super-added to the few articles of the authentic Jewish creed, but forms no part of it" (*Communion in the Messiah*, p. 196). To us the *denial* of Jesus' Messiahship is implicit in the Jewish creed; Judaism as it devolved in the Christian era is the result of the controversy with the Church, particularly with Hebrew Christianity.
370. *Die Stunde und die Erkenntnis*, p. 153.   371. Cf. Rom. 11. 21.
372. We have expressed similar thoughts in a little book, *Is it Nothing to You?* pp. 63 f.
373. Am. 3. 2.
374. Cf. W. Curtis, *Jesus Christ the Teacher*, pp. 209, 237 f.
375. A somewhat similar thought is expressed by Pascal; cf. Hans P. Ehrenberg, "The rediscovery of the Jew in Christianity", *The Intern. Review of Missions*, xxxiii, Oct. 1944, pp. 402 f.; cf. also K. E. Kirk, *The Vision of God*, 2nd ed., pp. 132, 134, 139, 174.
376. Jewish writers, like Rosenzweig, Schoeps and others, who define Judaism in terms of race, introduce a mechanical element which is at variance with spiritual life. Against it must be placed the Pauline definition of "Jew". Dr. J. H. Hertz' conception of Judaism as a "religious civilization" lacks the individual element of all true religion (cf. *Affirmations*, p. 35; cf. also *Bernh. Felsenthal, Teacher in Israel*, p. 212; but Felsenthal, with characteristic emphasis of the Liberal Jew, breaks the traditional limitations of Judaism: "Gladly we admit", he says, "that Judaism is not confined to a particular country, nor to a particular people, nor to a particular period and stage of culture", *ibid.*, p. 130; Felsenthal, however, is divided in his views, as his definition of Judaism indicates; cf. *ibid.*, pp. 232 f.).

BIBLIOGRAPHY

Abbott, G. F., *Israel in Europe*, London, 1907.

Abelson, J., *The Immanence of God in Rabbinical Literature*, London, 1912 (*Vallentine's Jewish Encyclopedia*).

Aboab, David, *A short, plain and well-grounded Introduction to Christianity*, London, 1750.

Abrahams, Israel, *Jewish Life in the Middle Ages*, London, 1896 (new ed. by Cecil Roth, London, 1932). *Judaism*, London, 1910. *Studies in Pharisaism and the Gospels*, first series, Cambridge, 1917; second series, 1924.

Adcock, A. C. (*Judaism and Christianity*, II).

Adler, Elkan Nathan, *Auto de Fé and Jew*, 1908. *About Hebrew Manuscripts*, 1905.

Ante-Nicene Christian Library, ed. by Alex. Roberts and James Donaldson, 24 vols., Edinburgh, 1867–1872.

Asch, Sholem, *The Nazarene*, London, 1939.

Aspects of Hebrew Genius (essays ed. by Leon Simon, London, 1910).

Babylonian Talmud, The (ed. by Rabbi I. Epstein, London, 1935).

Bacher, W. ("Le mot 'Minim' dans le Talmud", *Revue des Études Juives*, XXXVIII). *Die Agada der palästinensischer Amoräer*, 3 vols., Strassburg, 1892–99. *Die Agada der Tannaiten*, 2 vols., Strassburg, 1903.

Baeck, Leo, *Wege im Judentum, Aufsätze und Reden*, Berlin, 1933. *The Essence of Judaism*, Engl. by V. Grubwieser and L. Pearl, London, 1936.

Baldensprenger, *Die messianisch-apokalyptischen Hoffnungen des Judentums*, Strassburg, 1903.

Balleine, G. R., *A History of the Evangelical Party*, London, 1911.

Bardenhewer, O., *Patrologie*, 3rd ed., Freiburg/Br., 1910.

Baring-Gould, S., *The Lost and Hostile Gospels*, London, 1874.

Bartmann, Bernhard, *Der Glaubensgegensatz zwischen Judentum und Christentum*, Paderborn, 1938.

Ben-Chorin, Shalom, and George L. B. Sloan, *Das christliche Verständnis des Alten Testaments und der jüdische Einwand*, Jerusalem, 1941.

Bentwich, Norman (*Aspects of Hebrew Genius*, ed. by Leon Simon, London, 1910). *Solomon Schechter, A Biography*, Cambridge, 1938.

Bergmann, J., *Jüdische Apologetik im neutestamentlichen Zeitalter*, Berlin, 1908.

Bernstein, A., *Some Jewish Witnesses for Christ*, London, 1909.

Bert, Georg, *Aphrahat's des persischen Weisen Homilien, Texte und Untersuchungen*, Leipzig, 1888.

Bevan, Edwyn (*International Review of Missions*, XXII, 1933). (*Legacy of Israel.*)

Beveridge, W. (*Hastings Encycl. of Rel. and Ethics*, V).

Biesenthal, Joachim, *Auszüge aus dem Buche Sohar*, 1837.

Bloch, Joseph S., *Israel und die Völker*, Berlin-Wien, 1922.

Blötzer, Joseph (*The Catholic Encycl.*, VIII, 1910).

Bonsirven, Joseph, *On the Ruins of the Temple*, London, 1931.

425

Bousset, Wilhelm, *Die Religion des Judentums im neutestamentlichen Zeitalter*, Berlin, 1906. *Jesus der Herr*, Göttingen, 1916. *Kyrios Christos*, Göttingen, 1921. *Die Religion des Judentums im späthellenistischen Zeitalter*, Tübingen, 1926, 3rd ed.

Box, G. H. (*The Legacy of Israel*, Oxford, 1927). (*Expository Times*, xv, 1903-4.) (*Church and Synagogue Quarterly*, various articles on a Hebrew-Christian Church.)

Brandes, Georg, *Jesu-Sage*, Berlin, 1925.

Brandt, Wilhelm, *Elchasai*, Leipzig, 1912.

Branscomb, B. H., *Jesus and the Law of Moses*, London, 1930.

Brewster, Bertram (*Noble Families among the Sephardic Jews, by Isaac Da Costa, with some account of the Capadose Family, and an Excursus on their Jewish History, by Cecil Roth*), Oxford, 1936.

Buber, Martin, *Vom Geist des Judentums*, Leipzig, 1916. *Der heilige Weg*, Frankfurt/M., 1920. *Jewish Mysticism*, Engl. by Lucy Cohen, London, 1931. *Die Stunde und die Erkenntnis*, Berlin, 1936.

Büchler, A. (*Festschrift, Hermann Cohen*, Berlin, 1912).

Buhl, Frants, *Canon and Text of the Old Testament*, Engl. by John Macpherson, Edinburgh, 1892.

Burkitt, F. C., *Christian Beginnings*, London, 1924. (*Legacy of Israel*, Oxford, 1928.)

Cadoux, C. J. (*The London Quarterly and Holborn Review*, July, 1935).

Carlyle, Gavin, *A Memoir of Adolph Saphir*, London, 1893.

Chajes, H. P., *Markus-Studien*, Berlin, 1899.

Charue, André, *L'Incrédulité des Juifs dans le Nouveau Testament*, Gembloux, 1929.

Christian Approach to the Jews, The, being a report of conferences on the subject held at Budapest and Warsaw in April, 1927, London, 1927.

Christians and Jews, A report on the Conference on the Christian Approach to the Jews, Atlantic City, New Jersey, May 12-15, 1931, New York and London, 1931.

Church and Synagogue, A Quarterly Magazine and Statement of the Work of the Parochial and Foreign Missions to the Jews, ed. by Oesterley and Box, 12 vols., Oct. 1896–Apr. 1910.

Chwolson, D., *Das letzte Passamahl Christi und der Tag seines Todes*, St. Petersburgh, 1892.

Cohen, A., *Tractate Berakot*, Cambridge, 1921. *Everyman's Talmud*, London, 1932. *Midrash Rabbah, Ecclesiastes*, London, 1939.

Cohen, Hermann, *Die Religion der Vernunft aus den Quellen des Judentums*, Leipzig, 1919.

Cohen, Israel, *Jewish Life in Modern Times*, London, 1929.

Cohen, Philip, *The Hebrew-Christian and his National Continuity*, London (no date).

Cohon, S. S. (*International Review of Missions*, xxii, 1933).

Cook, S. A., *The Old Testament, A Reinterpretation*, 1936.

Cournos, John, *Hear, O Israel*, London, 1938.

Crafer, T. W., *The Apocriticus of Macarius Magnes*, London, 1919.

Curtis, W. A., *Jesus Christ the Teacher*, 1943.

Da Costa, Isaac, *Israel and the Gentiles*, Engl. Mary J. Kennedy, London, 1850; see also Brewster, Bertram.

Daiches, S., *Aspects of Judaism*, Selected essays, London, 1928.

Dalman, Gustaf H., *Christianity and Judaism*, an essay, Engl. by G. H. Box, London, 1901. *The Words of Jesus*, Engl. Edinburgh, 1902. *Jesus Christ in the Talmud, Midrash, Zohar and the Liturgy of the Synagogue*, Engl. by A. W. Streane, Cambridge, 1893.

Danby, Herbert, *The Jew and Christianity*, London, 1927. *The Mishnah*, London, 1933.

Danielou, Jean, *The Theology of Jewish Christianity*, Vol. I, 1964.

Danziger, Adolph, *Jewish Forerunners of Christianity*, London, 1904.

Davies, T. Witton (*Transactions of the Third International Congress for the history of Religions*, Oxford, 1908, II).

Dawidowicz, Lucy S., *The Golden Tradition*, 1967.

Delitzsch, Franz, *Ernste Fragen an die Gebildeten jüdischer Religion*, Leipzig, 1888. (*Saat auf Hoffnung, Zeitschrift für die Mission der Kirche an Israel* ed. by Franz D. and Pastor Becker, May, 1863, and subsequent numbers.)

Der Weg (Yiddish), bi-monthly magazine founded by J. I. Landsman in Warsaw, Poland, in connexion with the work of the Church Missions to Jews, Jan. 1927–Aug. 1939.

Deutsch, David, *Befestigung im Glauben*, ספר חזוק אמונה, Sohrau und Breslau, 1873.

Dienemann, Max, *Judentum und Christentum*, Frankfurt/M, 1919.

Dubnov, S. M., *History of the Jews in Russia and Poland*, Engl., Philadelphia, 1918.

Edersheim, A., *The Life and Times of Jesus the Messiah*, 2 vols., 1907.

Eisenmenger, Johann Andreas, *Entdecktes Judentum*, etc., Königsberg/Pr., 1711.

Eisler, Robert, *The Messiah Jesus and John the Baptist, according to Flavius Josephus' recently rediscovered "capture of Jerusalem" and other Jewish and Christian sources*, Engl. London, 1931.

Encyclopedia, The Catholic, 15 vols., New York, 1907–12. *The Jewish*, 12 vols., 1901–06. *Vallentine's Jewish*, London, 1938. *Of Missions*, 1904. *Britannica*, 11th edition.

Enelow, H. G., *A Jewish view of Jesus*, New York, 1920.

Epstein, I., *Judaism*, London, 1939.

Ewald, F. Ch., *Abodah Sarah*, Nürnberg, 1856.

Felsenthal, Emma, *Bernhard Felsenthal, Teacher in Israel*, New York, 1924.

Findlay, A. F., *Byways in early Christian Literature*, Edinburgh, 1923.

Finkelstein, Louis I., *The Pharisees*, 2 vols., Philadelphia, 1938.

Fishberg, Maurice, *The Jews: a Study in Race and Environment*, London, 1911.

Fleg (Flegenheimer), Edmond, *Jesus: told by the Wandering Jew*, London, 1934.

Fleury, L'Abbé M., *The Ecclesiastical History from A.D. 400 to A.D. 429*, Engl., Oxford, 1843.

Frank, Arnold, *Witnesses from Israel, Life-stories of Jewish Converts*, ed. by, Edinburgh and London, 1903. (*Zeugen aus Israel*, Hamburg.)

Frazer, Sir J. G., *Folk-Lore in the Old Testament*, 3 vols., London, 1919.

Frenkl, David, *She'elot u-Teshubot ha Ribash ha-Hadashot*, Munkács (Hebrew). (*The Responsa by Isaac ben Sheshet Barfat (Ribash)*.)

Friedländer, David, *Sendschreiben an den Oberconsistorialrath Teller zu Berlin von einigen Hausvätern jüdischer Religion*, Berlin, 1799.

Friedlander, Gerald, *The Jewish Sources of the Sermon on the Mount*, London, 1911. *Hellenism and Christianity*, London, 1912. *Rabbinic Philosophy and Ethics*, London, 1912. *Pirkê de Rabbi Eliezer*, London, 1916.

Friedländer, Moriz, *Die religiösen Bewegungen innerhalb des Judentums im Zeitalter Jesu*, Berlin, 1905.

Friedländer, M., *The Jewish Religion*, London, 1900.

Friedman, H., *Midrash Rabbah, Genesis*, London, 1939.

Fürst, A., *Christen und Juden*, Strassburg, 1892.

Geiger, Abraham, *Urschrift und Ubersetzungen der Bibel in ihrer Abhängigkeit von der inneren Entwickelung des Judentums*, Breslau, 1857. *Sadducäer und Pharisäer*, Breslau, 1863. *Das Judentum und seine Geschichte*, Breslau, 1864.

Gidney, W. T., *The History of the London Society for promoting Christianity amongst the Jews*, London, 1908.

Gillet, Lev (*International Review of Missions*, April, 1942.) *Communion in the Messiah*, London and Redhill, 1942. (*Theology*, ed. by Alec R. Vidler, XLVII, Oct., 1944.)

Ginzberg, L. (*Jewish Encyclopedia*, v.)

Goodman, Paul, *The Synagogue and the Church*, London, 1908.

Gorodetzky, N., *The Humiliated Christ in Modern Russian Thought*, London, 1938.

Gottheil, G. (*Judaism at the World's Parliament of Religions*, Cincinnati, 1894).

Graetz, H., *History of the Jews from the earliest times to the present day*, Engl., 5 vols., London, 1891-92.

Grayzell, Solomon (*Vallentine's Jewish Encyclopedia*).

Gressmann, H., *Der Messias*, Göttingen, 1929.

Grundmann, Walter (*Zeitschrift für die neutestamentliche Wissenschaft*, herausg. von H. Lietzmann and W. Eltester, Bd. XXXVIII, 1939).

Güdemann, M. (*Jewish Quarterly Review*, IV).

Guignebert, Ch., *The Jewish World in the time of Jesus*, Engl. by S. H. Hooke, 1939.

Harnack, A. von, *Abriss der Dogmengeschichte*, Freiburg in B. and Leipzig, 1893. *Die Mission und Ausbreitung des Christentums in den ersten drei Jahrhunderten*, Leipzig, 1902. *Sprüche und Reden Jesu*, Leipzig, 1907. *Die Apostelgeschichte*, Leipzig, 1908. *Untersuchungen zu den Schriften des Lukas*, Leipzig, 1908. *Judentum und Judenchristentum in Justins Dialog mit Trypho, Texte und Untersuchungen*, XXXIX, Leipzig, 1913.

Hastings Dictionary of the Bible, 5 vols., Edinburgh, 1898-1906.

Hastings Dictionary of Christ and the Gospels, 2 vols., 1906-8.

Hastings Encyclopedia of Religion and Ethics, 13 vols., 1908-26.

Hebrew Christian, The, The Quarterly organ of the International Hebrew Christian Alliance (various numbers).

Heman, F., *Geschichte des jüdischen Volkes seit der Zerstörung Jerusalems*, Stuttgart, 1908.

Hennecke, Edgar, *Handbuch zu den neutestamentlichen Apokryphen*, Tübingen, 1914.

Herford, Travers R., *Jesus Christ* (small pamphlet), London, 1901. *Christianity in Talmud and Midrash*, London, 1903. *Pharisaism, its Aim and its Method*,

London, 1912. *The Pharisees*, London, 1924. ("Christianity in Jewish Literature", *Hastings Dict. of Christ and the Gospels*, II.) (*Jewish Studies in Memory of Israel Abrahams*, New York, 1927.) (*Judaism and Christianity*, III: *Law and Religion*, London, 1938.) (*Essays presented to J. H. Hertz*, London, 1942.)

Hermann, E., *Eucken and Bergson, their significance for Christian thought*, London, 1912.

Hertz, J. H., *The Pentateuch and Haftorahs*, London, 1938. *Affirmations of Judaism*, London, 1927.

Hilgenfeld, A., *Die Ketzergeschichte des Urchristentums*, Leipzig, 1884.

Hirsch, S. A. (*J. Q. R.*, IV).

Hirschfeld, Hartwig, *Judah Hallevi's Kitab al Khazari*, transl. by, London, 1905.

Hoennicke, Gustav, *Das Judenchristentum im ersten u. zweiten Jahrhundert*, Berlin, 1908.

Hollmann, G., *The Jewish Religion in the Time of Jesus*, Engl. by E. W. Lummis, London, 1909.

Hooke, S. H. (*Judaism and Christianity*, 1).

Hort, F. J. A., *Judaistic Christianity*, London, 1898.

Hoskyns, E. C. ("Jesus the Messiah", *Mysterium Christi*, ed. by G. K. A. Bell and Adolf Deissmann, 1930).

Hosmer, J. K., *The Jews, ancient, medieval and modern*, London, 1917.

Husik, Isaac, *A history of Medieval Jewish Philosophy*, New York, 1916.

Hyamson, A. M. (*Vallentine's Jewish Encycl.*).

Imperial Dictionary of Universal Biography, 3 vols. (no date).

Innes, Taylor A., *The Trial of Jesus, a legal monograph*, Edinburgh, 1905.

In Spirit and in Truth, ed. by George A. Yates, London, 1934.

International Review of Missions (various numbers).

Isaac ben Sheshet Barfat, see Frenkl.

Isaac of Troki, ספר חזוק אמונה, ed. by David Deutsch, Sohrau and Breslau, 1873, 2nd ed.

Jackson, Foakes, F. J., *Josephus and the Jews*, London, 1930.

Jastrow, M., *Dictionary of the Targumim, etc.*, 1926.

Jehuda Halevi, ספר הכוזרי ed. by Dr. Zifrinowitsch, Warschau, 1926.

Jewish Chronicle, Organ of British Jewry, established Nov. 1841.

Jewish Quarterly Review, ed. by Israel Abrahams and C. G. Montefiore (Old Series, 1888–1909).

Jewish Studies in memory of Israel Abrahams, New York, 1927.

Jocz, J., *Is it Nothing to You?* London, 1941.

Joël, M., *Blicke in die Religionsgeschichte zu Anfang des zweiten christlichen Jahrhunderts*, I–II, Breslau, 1880.

Joseph, Morris, *Judaism in Creed and Life*, London, 1903.

Judaica. Festschrift zu Hermann Cohens siebzigsten Geburtstage, Berlin, 1912.

Judaica, edited by Robert Brunner, Walter Eichrodt and Gottlob Schrenk for the "Verein der Freunde Israels zu Basel," März, 1945 (appears quarterly).

Judaism at the World's Parliament of Religions, Cincinnati, 1894.

Judaism and Christianity, Essays presented to P. P. Levertoff, ed. by L. Gillet London, 1939.

Judaism and Christianity: I, *The Age of Transition,* ed. by W. O. E. Oesterley, London, 1937. II, *The Contact of Pharisaism with other Cultures,* ed. by H. Loewe, London, 1937. III, *Law and Religion,* ed. by Erwin I. J. Rosenthal, London, 1938.

Jung, Leo, *Yoma,* London, 1938.

Kaam, Adrian L. van, *A Light to the Gentiles:* the Life Story of the Venerable Francis Libermann, 1959.

Katz, Solomon, *The Jews in the Visigothic and Frankish Kingdoms of Spain and Gaul,* Cambridge, Mass., 1937.

Kayserling, Moritz (*Jewish Encycl.,* III).

Kellermann, B. (*Festschrift zu Hermann Cohens siebzigsten Geburtstage,* Berlin, 1912).

Kidder, Richard, *A demonstration of the Messiah in which the truth of the Christian Religion is proved especially against The Jews;* in two parts, London, 1684–99.

Kirk, K. E., *The Vision of God* (New impression), 1941.

Klausner, Joseph, *Die messianischen Vorstellungen des jüdischen Volkes im Zeitalter der Tannaiten,* Berlin, 1904. *Jesus of Nazareth, his life, times and teaching,* London, 1925. *From Jesus to Paul,* Engl. by W. F. Stinespring, New York, 1943.

Klostermann, E., *Das Markusevangelium,* Tübingen, 1926. *Das Matthäusevangelium,* Tübingen, 1927.

Knox, W. L. (*Judaism and Christianity,* II).

Kohler, Kaufmann (*Judaism at the World's Parliament of Religions,* Cincinnati, 1894). (*Jewish Encycl.,* 1901–6.) *Jewish Theology, systematically and historically considered,* New York, 1918. (*Grundriss einer systematischen Theologie des Judentums auf geschichtlicher Grundlage,* Leipzig, 1910.) *The Origins of the Synagogue and the Church,* ed. with a biographical essay by H. G. Enelow, New York, 1929.

Kohut, Adolph, *Berühmte israelitische Männer und Frauen in der Kulturgeschichte der Menschheit,* Leipzig (no date), 2 vols.

Kosmala, H. (*International Review of Missions,* July, 1941).

Kosmala, H., and R. Smith, *The Jew in the Christian World,* London, 1942.

Koven, Henry J., *The Spiritans,* 1958.

Kraemer, H., *The Christian Message in a Non-Christian World,* London, 1938.

Krauss, S. (*Jewish Quarterly Review,* v). *Das Leben Jesu nach jüdischen Quellen,* Berlin, 1902.

Laible, Heinrich, *Jesus Christus im Talmud,* Berlin, 1891; Engl. transl. by A. W. Streane, Cambridge, 1893.

Lake, Kirsopp (*Jewish Studies in Memory of I. Abrahams*).

Lawlor, Jackson H., and J. E. L. Oulton, *Eusebius,* 2 vols., London, 1927–28.

Lazarus, Josephine (*Judaism at the World's Parliament of Religions*).

Lazarus, O., *Liberal Judaism and its Standpoint,* London, 1937.

Legacy of Israel, The, ed. by Edwyn R. Bevan and Charles Singer, Oxford, 1928.

Lehrman, S. M. (Vallentine's *Jewish Encycl.*).

Lestschinski (*Encycl. Judaica,* II).

Leszynsky, Rudolf, *Die Sadduzäer,* Berlin, 1912.

Letters of St. Bernard, transl. by Bruno Scott James, 1953.

Levertoff, O. T., *The Wailing Wall,* London, 1937. (*Judaism and Christianity,* ed. by L. Gillet.)

Levertoff, P. P., *Love and the Messianic Age*, London, 1923. (*Liturgy and Worship*, ed. by W. K. Lowther Clarke, London, 1936.)

Lévi, Israel ("Le Mot 'Minim' ", *Revue des Études Juives*, xxxviii).

Levine, Ephraim (*The Parting of the Roads*).

Levy, M. J., *Hebrew Christianity and Jewish Nationalism*, 1931.

Lichtenstein, J., *Judaism and Christianity*, Engl. by Margaret M. Alison, Edinburgh, 1893. *Eine Bitte an die geehrten Leser*, Budapest (no date).

Lichtigfeld, Adolph, *Twenty Centuries of Jewish Thought*, London, 1937.

Lieberman, Saul, *Greek in Jewish Palestine; Studies in the Life and Manners of Jewish Palestine in the II–IV centuries C. E.*, New York, 1942.

Lightfoot, J. B., *The Apostolic Fathers*, London and New York, 1893. *Saint Paul's Epistle to the Galatians*, London, 1902.

Lindeskog, Gösta, *Die Jesusfrage im neuzeitlichen Judentum*, Uppsala, 1938.

Lipshytz, C. T., *Der Ebionitismus in der Judenmission, oder Christentum und national-jüdisches Bewusstsein*, Schriften des Institutum Judaicum in Berlin, No. 41.

Loewe, Herbert (*In Spirit and in Truth*). (*Judaism and Christianity*, i, ii.) (*Vallentine's Jewish Encycl.*) (*A Rabbinic Anthology*), see Montefiore.

Lublinski, Samuel, *Das Werdende Dogma vom Leben Jesu*, Jena, 1910.

Machen, J. Gresham, *The Origin of Paul's Religion*, London, 1921.

Macmurray, John, *The Clue to History*, London, 1938.

Maimonides, *Yad Hachazakah*, Engl. by H. H. Bernard, Cambridge, 1832. *Yad Hachazakah*, Engl. by Rabbi Simon Glazer, New York, 1927.

Manson, T. W. (*Judaism and Christianity*, iii). *The Teaching of Jesus*, Cambridge, 1935 (2nd ed.).

Manson, W., *Jesus the Messiah*, London, 1943.

Maritain, Jacques, *Antisemitism*, London, 1939. *Redeeming the Time*, London, 1943.

Marmorstein, A., *The Doctrine of Merits in Old Rabbinical Literature*, London, 1920. (*London Quarterly and Holborn Review*, July, 1935.)

Mattuck, Israel I., *What are the Jews?* London, 1939. (*In Spirit and in Truth.*)

McCaul, Alex., *The Old Paths, or a comparison of the principles and doctrines of Modern Judaism with the religion of Moses and the Prophets*, London, 1846.

Meelführer, M. R., *Talmude Sive Dissertatio Philologica*, Altdorf, 1699. *Consensus veterum Hebraeorum cum Ecclesia Christiana*, 1701. *Synagogae errantis*, 1702.

Meisl, Josef, *Haskalah*, Berlin, 1919.

Meyer, Arnold, *Die moderne Forschung über die Geschichte des Urchristentums*, Freiburg/B., 1898.

Mishcon, A., *Abodah Zarah*, London, 1935.

Moehlman, Conrad H., *The Christian Jewish Tragedy*, New York, 1933.

Moffatt, James, *The Approach to the New Testament*, Hibbert Lectures, 2nd Series, London, 1921.

Montefiore, C. G., *Lectures on the Origin and Growth of Religion as illustrated by the religion of the ancient Hebrews*, London, 1897. (*Jewish Quarterly Review*, Jan., 1901.) (*Hibbert Journal*, iii, 1904–5; xx, 1911–12; xxxiii, 1934–35.) *Truth in Religion, and other Sermons*, London, 1906. *The Synoptic Gospels*, London, 1909; 2nd ed. 1927. *Some elements of the Religious Teaching of Jesus*, London, 1910. *Outlines of Liberal Judaism*, London, 1912. *Liberal Judaism and Hellenism, and other essays*, London, 1918. *The Old Testament and After*, London, 1923. *Rabbinic Literature and Gospel Teachings*, London, 1930. (*In Spirit and in Truth.*)

Montefiore, C. G., and H. Loewe, *A Rabbinic Anthology*, London, 1938.
Moore, George Foot, *Judaism in the first centuries of the Christian era*, 3 vols., Cambridge, 1930.
Mozley, J. K., *The Heart of the Gospel*, London, 1925.
Muller, J. A. *Apostle of China: Samuel Isaac Joseph Schereschewsky: 1831-1906*, 1937.
"*Nathaniel*", a missionary magazine founded by Prof. H. L. Strack in 1883.
Nestle, Eberhard, *Introduction to the Textual Criticism of the Greek New Testament*, Engl. by W. Edie, ed. by A. Menzies, 1901.
Neubauer, A. (*The Expositor*, 3rd series, VII).
Newman, Louis I., *Jewish Influence on Christian Reform Movements*, New York, 1925. *Hasidic Anthology*, New York and London, 1934.
Niven, W. D., *The Conflicts of the Early Church*, London, 1930.

Oesterley, W. O. E. (*Judaism in the Days of Christ, The Parting of the Roads*, ed. by Foakes Jackson, London, 1912). ("The Jewish and the Christian Doctrine of Mediation", *Church and Synagogue Quart.*, X-XII.)
Oesterley and Box, *A Short Survey of the Literature of Rabbinical and Medieval Judaism*, London, 1920. *The Religion and Worship of the Synagogue*, London 1911.
Oldham, J. H., *Christianity and the Race Problem*, London, 1925.

Pallière, Aimé, *Le Sanctuaire Inconnu*, 1926; Engl. *The Unknown Sanctuary*. *Pilgrimage from Rome to Israel*, New York, 1928.
Palmer, H. P., *Joseph Wolff*, London, 1935.
Parkes, James, *The Conflict of the Church and the Synagogue*, London, 1934. *Jesus, Paul and the Jews*, London, 1936. (*Judaism and Christianity*, 11. *The Jew in the Medieval Community*, London, 1938. (*Theology*, ed. by Alec R. Vidler, XLVII, Oct. 1944.)
Parting of the Roads, The, Studies in the development of Judaism and Christ anity, ed. by F. J. Foakes Jackson, London, 1912.
Paul, Herbert, *Letters of Lord Acton to Mary, daughter of the Rt. Hon. W. B. Gladstone*, London, 1904.
Peake, A. S., *Paul and the Jewish Christians* (reprinted from *The Bulletin of the John Rylands Library*, XIII, Jan. 1929).
Pearlson, Gustav, *Twelve Centuries of Jewish Persecution*, Hull, 1927.
Peers, E. Allison, *Ramon Lull, A Biography*, London, 1929.
Perles, Felix (*Festschrift, Hermann Cohen*, Berlin, 1912).
Pfannmüller, Gustav, *Jesus im Urteil der Jahrhunderte. Die bedeutendsten Auffassungen Jesu in Theologie, Philosophie, Literatur und Kunst bis zur Gegen wart*, Berlin, 1939.
Philipson, David, *The Reform Movement in Judaism*, New York, 1907.
Platina, B., *The Lives of the Popes*, 2 vols., Engl. London (no date).
Poljak, Abram, *The Cross in the Star of David*, London, 1938.
Prelooker, Jaakoff, *Under the Czar and Queen Victoria*, London, 1895.
Preuschen, Erwin, *Die Apostelgeschichte*, Tübingen, 1912.

Rabbinowitz, J., *Mishnah Megillah*, London, 1931.
Reider, Joseph (*Vallentine's Jewish Encycl.*).
Reinach, Salomon, *Orpheus, A history of religions*, London, 1931.

Resch, Gotthold, *Das Aposteldekret nach seinem ausserkanonischen Textgestalt*, 1905.

Robertson, A. T., *The Pharisees and Jesus*, London, 1920.

Robinson, C. H., *History of Christian Missions*, 1915.

Roi, J. F. A. De le, *Die evangelische Christenheit und die Juden*, 3 vols., Berlin, 1884–92.

Rosadi, G., *The Trial of Jesus*, Engl. by Emil Reich, London, 1905.

Rosenthal, D. A., *Convertitenbilder aus dem neunzehnten Jahrhundert*, Schaffhausen, Weisenburg, 1866–70.

Rosenzweig, Franz, *Der Stern der Erlösung*, Frankfurt/M., 1921.

Roth, Cecil, *A short history of the Jewish people*, London, 1936. *A History of the Marranos*, Philadelphia, 1932. (*The Jews in the Middle Ages*, Cambridge *Medieval History*, Cambridge, 1932, VII.)

Sabatini, Raphael, *Torquemada and his Spanish Inquisition*, London, 1913.

Salvador, J., *Jésus-Christ et sa doctrine; histoire de la naissance de l'Eglise, de son organisation et de ses progrès pendant le premier siècle*, Tome I–II, Paris, 1838.

Samuels, M., *Memoirs of Moses Mendelssohn*, London, 1825. *Mendelssohn's Jerusalem*, Engl. I and II, London, 1838.

Scialetti, Moses, *A letter written to the Jews*, London, 1663.

Schachter, Jacob, *Sanhedrin*, London, 1935.

Schechter, S., *Studies in Judaism*, London, 1896; 2nd series, London, 1908. *Some Aspects of Rabbinic Theology*, London, 1909. *Documents of Jewish Sectaries*, 2 vols., Cambridge, 1910. (*J. Q. R.*, x.)

Schlatter, Adolf, *Die Tage Trajans und Hadrians*, Gütersloh, 1897. *Die Kirche Israels vom Jahre 70–130*, 1898. *Geschichte Israels von Alexander dem Grossen bis Hadrian*, Stuttgart, 1925.

Schleiden, M. I., *The Importance of the Jews for the Preservation and Revival of Learning during the Middle Ages*, Engl., London, 1911.

Schmidtke, Alfred, *Neue Fragmente und Untersuchungen zu den judenchristlichen Evangelien*, Leipzig, 1911. *Texte und Untersuchungen*, XXXVII.

Schoeps, H. J., *Jüdisch-christliches Religionsgespräch*, Berlin, 1937. *Theologie und Geschichte des Judenchristentums*, Tübingen, 1949. *Aus frühchristlicher Zeit*, Tübingen, 1950.

Schoettgen, J. Chr., *Horae Hebraicae et Talmudicæ in universum Novum Testamentum*, Leipzig, 1733.

Schofield, Guy, *In the Year 62: The Murder of the Brother of the Lord and Its Consequences*, 1962.

Schonfield, H. J., *According to the Hebrews*, London, 1937.

Schürer, E., *The history of the Jewish People at the time of Christ*, Engl., 6 vols., 1898–1900.

Schwaab, Emil, *Historische Einführung in das Achtzehngebet*. (*Beiträge zur Förderung christl. Theologie, herausg. A. Schlatter u. W. Lütgert*, Heft V, 1913.)

Schweitzer, A., *Geschichte der Leben-Jesu-Forschung*, Tübingen, 1921 (Engl., *The Quest of the historical Jesus*, 2nd ed., London, 1926).

Silver, A. H., *A History of Messianic Speculation in Israel, From the First through the Seventeenth Centuries*, New York, 1927.

Simkhovitch, V. G., *Toward the Understanding of Jesus*, New York, 1937.

Simon, Leon (*Aspects of Hebrew Genius*). *Studies in Jewish Nationalism*, London, 1920.

Simpson, W. W., *Jews and Christians to-day. A study in Jewish and Christian relationships*, London, 1940.

Singer, Charles and Dorothea (*The Legacy of Israel*).

Singer, J., *Sollen die Juden Christen werden?* Wien, 1884.

Singer, S., *Annotated edition of the authorized Daily Prayer Book*, ed. by Israel Abrahams, London, 1914.

Sloan, G. L. B., see Ben-Chorin.

Smith, R., see Kosmala.

Soden, Hermann von, *The History of early Christian Literature*, Engl., London and New York, 1906.

Sparrow-Simpson, W. J., *The Letters of St. Augustine*, London, 1919.

Spiegel, Shalom, *Hebrew Reborn*, London, 1931.

Spinoza, B., *Short Treatise on God, Man and his Well-being*, Engl. by A. Wolf, London, 1910.

Stanton, V. H., *The Jewish and the Christian Messiah*, Edinburgh, 1886.

Stokes, H. P., *A Short History of the Jews in England*, London, 1921.

Strack, H. L., *The Jew and Human Sacrifice*, Engl., 1909. *Jesus, die Häretiker und die Christen nach den ältesten jüdischen Angaben*, Leipzig, 1910. *Introduction to the Talmud and Midrash*, Engl., Philadelphia, 1931.

Strack and Billerbeck, *Kommentar zum Neuen Testament aus Talmud und Midrasch*, 4 vols., München, 1922–28.

Streane, A. W. (*Jesus Christ in the Talmud, Midrash, Zohar, and the Liturgy of the Synagogue*, Cambridge, 1893).

Streeter, B. H., *The Four Gospels, a Study of Origins*, London, 1924. *The Primitive Church*, London, 1929.

Teller, W. A., *An einige Hausväter jüdischer Religion, von einem Prediger in Berlin*, Berlin, 1799.

Tollinton, R. B., *Selections from the Commentaries and Homilies of Origen*, London, 1929.

Toy, C. H., *Judaism and Christianity*, London, 1890.

Trattner, E. R., *As a Jew sees Jesus*, New York and London, 1931.

Trilling, Wolfgang, *Das Wahre Israel*, 1958.

Volz, Paul, *Jüdische Eschatologie von Daniel bis Akiba*, Tübingen und Leipzig, 1903. *Der Prophet Jeremia*, Leipzig, 1928. *Jesaia II*, Leipzig, 1932.

Wagenmann, Julius, *Die Stellung des Apostels Paulus neben den Zwölf in den ersten zwei Jahrhunderten*, Giessen, 1926.

Wagenseilius, Ch., *Tela Ignea Satanæ*, etc., 1681.

Walker, Thomas, *Hebrew Religion between the Testaments*, London, 1937.

Weber, Ferdinand, *Die Lehre des Talmud*, Leipzig, 1880.

Weiss, Johannes, *Das Urchristentum*, Göttingen, 1917.

Weizsäcker, C. von, *The Apostolic Age of the Christian Church*, Engl., London and New York, 1894.

Werfel, Franz, *Barbara oder die Frömmigkeit*, Berlin-Wien, 1929.

Williams, A. Lukyn, *Missions to Jews: A historical Retrospect*, 1897. *A Manual of Christian Evidences for Jewish People*, I, London, 1911; II, London, 1919. *The Hebrew-Christian Messiah*, London, 1916. *Tractate Berakoth, Mishna and Tosephta*, London, 1921. *Adversus Judaeos*, Cambridge, 1935. *The Doctrines of Modern Judaism considered*, London, 1939.

Windisch, H., *Der Hebräerbrief*, Tübingen, 1913.

Wise, I. M., *The Martyrdom of Jesus of Nazareth*, Cincinnati, 1874. *Judaism and Christianity*, Cincinnati, 1883.
Wolf, J. Ch., *Bibliotheca Hebraea, Sive Notitia tum Auctorum Hebr., etc.*, 4 vols., Hamburg and Leipzig, 1715–1733.
Woolf, B. Lee, *The Authority of Jesus and its Foundation*, London, 1929.
World Dominion and the World to-day, An International Review of Christian Progress.
Wünsche, August, *Pesikta des Rab Kahana*, 1885.

York-Steiner, H., *Die Kunst als Jude zu leben (Minderheit verpflichtet)*, Leipzig, 1928.
Ysander, T., *Studien zum B'estschen Ḥasidismus*, Uppsala, 1933.

Zeitlin, Solomon, *Who Crucified Jesus?* 1942.
Ziegler, Ignaz, *Der Kampf zwischen Judentum und Christentum in den ersten drei christlichen Jahrhunderten*, Berlin, 1907.
Zöckler, *Aus Jechiel Lichtensteins hebräischem Kommentar zum Neuen Testament*, Leipzig, 1895.
Zuckermandel, M. S., *Tosephta*, ed. by, 2nd ed. Jerusalem, 1937.
Zukerman, William, *The Jew in Revolt*, London, 1937.

Note : Brackets indicate the writer's contribution to a composite work.

GLOSSARY

Hebrew words and phrases not explained in the text.

Amoraim (sing. *amora*)—"speakers"; teachers of the law of the post-*Mishnaic* period, i.e. from close of second to the fifth centuries.

Amidah—see *Shemoneh Esreh*.

Abinu malkenu—"Our Father, Our King"; the opening words of a penitential prayer.

atah beḥartanu—"Thou hast chosen us"; a phrase occurring in the liturgy; cf. Deut. 4. 37; 7. 6.

Birkat ha-minim—"blessing" of heretics (euphemism).

Baraita (pl. *Baraitot*)—"extraneous" (*i.e.* outside the *Mishnah*), but nevertheless belonging to *Tannaitic* tradition.

Bene Abraham—sons of Abraham.

Berakha (pl. *Berakot*)—blessing, benediction.

galut—dispersion, Diaspora.

ger ẓedek—righteous proselyte, *i.e.* full proselyte who has become a Jew from conviction.

gere-toshab—partial proselytes, *i.e.* such as have accepted Monotheism but not the implications of Rabbinic law; probably "resident aliens".

goi ẓaddik—righteous people.

Haggadah—Scriptural exegesis of a homiletical nature as distinct from *Halakah*.

ha-kol bide shamayim huẓ miyirat shᵓmayim—all is from Heaven (*i.e.* God) except the fear of Heaven (*i.e.* God).

Halakah—"to go, to follow", *i.e.* rules of observance formulated by the Rabbis and based on the Pentateuch.

ḥasid (pl. *ḥasidim*)—"pious"; adherent to a mystical revival which originated in Eastern Europe in the eighteenth century.

maamine yeshua nozri—believers in Jesus of Nazareth.

maaminim—believers.

Maḥzor—the liturgy for the various Festivals in the year.

massit um-maddiaḥ—inciter and leader astray (*sc.* to worship idols; cf. Deut. 13. 13.

Megillah—"scroll", particularly the Scroll of Esther.

meshiḥiim (sing. *meshiḥi*)—messiahists, followers of the Messiah.

Midrash—old Rabbinical Commentary.

minhag—*usus*, custom hallowed by tradition.

minim (sing. *min*)—"heretics".

minim shel posh'im—heretics and sinners.

minim we-shel resh'aim—the heretics and the godless.

minut—heresy.

mipne darke shalom—for the sake of peace.

Mishnah—"teaching", "repetition", the legal part of Rabbinic tradition, compiled by R. Judah at the end of the second century.

mizwot—meritorious deeds, Commandments.

mizwot bene Noah—the commandments which, according to Rabbinic tradition were given to Noah and his sons.

nabi ha-sheker—false prophet.

nozrim—Nazarenes.

'olam—world.

'olam ha-ba—the world to come.

perushin—Pharisees.

Shemoneh Esreh—"Eighteen" (*sc.* benedictions); the benedictions which form the basis of the liturgy for the Daily Service, often referred to as *Amida* (from *'amad*—to stand) or *Tephillah, i.e.* the Prayer *par excellence.*

sifre minim—books for heretics.

Talmud—"learning", "study"; the discussions on the text of the *Mishnah* by Palestinian and Babylonian Rabbis from the third to the fifth centuries.

tannaim (sing. *tanna*)—"teachers", "guardians of tradition"; a term applied to Rabbis of the *Mishnaic* period.

tehiyyat ha-metim—resurrection of the dead.

Tephillah, tephilla—see *Shemoneh Esreh*; or prayer in general.

teshubah—"turning", *i.e.* repentance.

tol'dot—genealogy, history, biography.

torah hadashah—new teaching, new law.

torah she-be'al peh—the teaching delivered by word of mouth, *i.e.* traditional law.

torah she-beketab—the written law, *i.e.* the Law of Moses.

Torat Mosheh—the Law of Moses, the Pentateuch.

torato shel mashiah—Messiah's *torah*.

we-ha-sheb ha-'abodah lidebir beteka—restore the (Temple) Service to the oracle of thy House.

yemot ha-mashiah—the days of the Messiah.

yezer ha-r'a—the evil inclination.

yezer tob—the good inclination.

INDEX OF SUBJECTS

439

INDEX OF NAMES